THE
OLD NORTHWEST
PIONEER PERIOD
1815-1840

Volume II

"I loved thee, when first down thy placid wave
And round the bend of hills, myself I gave
To the wide reaching West. . . ."

THE
OLD NORTHWEST
PIONEER PERIOD
1815-1840

BY

R. CARLYLE BULEY

VOLUME TWO

INDIANA UNIVERSITY PRESS • BLOOMINGTON

in association with the
INDIANA HISTORICAL SOCIETY

Initially published by the Indiana Historical Society as
part of its contribution to the observation of the
Sesquicentennial of Indiana Territory in 1950.

Winner of the Pulitzer Prize in history, 1950

Manufactured in the United States of America

Library of Congress Cataloging in Publication Data

Buley, R. Carlyle (Roscoe Carlyle), 1893-1968.
The old Northwest.

Includes bibliographical references and index.
1. Northwest, Old—History—1775-1865. I. Title.
F484.3.B94 1983   977   83-48117
ISBN 0-253-34168-X
4 5 6 7 8 87 86 85 84 83

CONTENTS

Volume II

Harrison—Campaign arguments—The election of 1836—
Ohio election of 1838—Indiana-Illinois politics 1838—
Michigan politics—Beginnings of parties in Wisconsin Territory—The campaign and election of 1840—The money
question—Party arguments—The Northwest for Harrison

Distribution of surplus revenue—Ohio canals—Indiana
internal improvements system—Illinois system of 1837—Internal improvements in Michigan and plans for their financing—Improvements in Wisconsin Territory—The depression comes—Discussion of the depression—Effects on prices
—Banking facilities in the Northwest—Ohio banks—
Effects of depression upon Ohio improvements—Indiana
improvements and the depression—State Bank of Indiana
—Illinois improvements and state finance—Abandonment
of the Illinois system—Progress on the Michigan improvements—Michigan banks; "Safety-Fund" banking law of
1837—Nature of the new banks—Breakdown of the banking system—Banking in Wisconsin Territory—Beginnings
of railroads in the Northwest: Problems of building—The
fur trade—Commerce of the Northwest; exports and
imports—Prospects of the Northwest

Attitude of the people toward education—Early private
schools—Female education—Academies—Indiana county
seminaries—Influence of academies—Lancasterian schools—
Criticism of new theories—Movement for public schools
in Ohio: The law of 1825, The school lands, The Western
Literary Institute and College of Teachers, Educational
periodicals, The law of 1838, Samuel Lewis—Legislation
for schools in Indiana—In Illinois—In Michigan: Work
of John D. Pierce, first state superintendent—Schools in
Wisconsin Territory—Country schools and teachers—
Teacher qualifications and salaries—Teaching methods—
Spellers, readers, and arithmetics—Other textbooks—"Ob-
jectives" and curriculum—Colleges: Ohio University;
Miami; Vincennes University; Indiana University; the
Catholepistemiad or University of Michigania of 1817; the
University of Michigan, 1837, and its branches; "The
Wisconsin University" of 1836; Western Reserve College;
Hanover College; Lane Seminary; Illinois College; Knox
College; Wabash; Oberlin; Shurtleff College; Frank-

Joseph 'Rodes Buchanan—Communitarian experiments: Rappite Harmony; The Owens and New Harmony— Life at New Harmony—New Harmony and culture— The abolition movement in the Northwest: Leaders and importance of—The Northwest contemplates its future

ILLUSTRATIONS

MAPS

Personal Politics and Republican Solidarity, 1815–1825

It is an equal you meet there; an equal in political rights; one to whom honors and office, even the highest, are as open as to yourself. . . . I have heard in many a backwoods cabin, lighted but by the blazing log heap, arguments on government, views of national policy, judgments of men and things, that, for sound sense and practical wisdom, would not disgrace any legislative body upon earth.
Robert Dale Owen, in the United States House
of Representatives, April 22, 1846

POLITICS in its broadest sense is that group of activities which deals with organization, regulation, and administration of the state; in its narrowest sense it is the art of getting into office—and staying there—or of controlling those who do. Neither politics nor "democracy" was invented on the Midwest frontier, but the inhabitants of that region had their ideas on, and made their contributions to, both. The study of politics in the Old Northwest in the pioneer period will reveal no truth more profound than that man is, at least in part, a political animal, full of contradictions and inconsistencies. Although throughout the period few citizens would contradict the fundamental principle that ours is a "government of measures, not of men," in practice few would be governed by it. Already the American had the dual heritage of Puritanism with its desire to regulate the other fellow's conduct and of Scotch-Irish frontier individualism, which made him on the one hand the "law passingest" person on earth, and, since he always reserved the sovereign right to overrule his own sovereignty, on the other hand, the "law violatin'est."

As the West settled, the organization of new counties and states created an abundance of political offices after which the politicians scrambled as avidly as the settlers and speculators did after the land. In fact, at times the anticipated jobs were often the real, if not the apparent, reason for creating them. It would be hard to prove that the average pioneer could extinguish a horsefly with tobacco juice at twenty feet; it would be equally hard to prove that he did not feel fully qualified to serve in any political capacity from assistant dog catcher or fence viewer to governor or even president. It was a period in which Americans were accustoming themselves to the idea that they were "free men," subject not to the beck and call of monarch or potentate. The idea was ever to the front; it was constantly discussed in church, newspaper, and court; it was shouted from the housetops by politicians. If the frontiersman swallowed large quantities of spellbinding oratory "loaded seven fingers"[1] and liked to be appealed to as a free man and patriot who held the destiny of the nation in the hollow of his hand, he also mixed in a liberal amount of solid food and whiskey and took it all with a grain of salt. He did a lot of plain living and serious political cogitation. He reserved the right to distrust anyone whose talents, manners, or "high-falutin' " ideas set him off too distinctly from the common run, yet was quick to recognize and reward outstanding merit, whether of character, mind, or physical and military prowess. In fact, it might well be argued that, on balance, he was far less gullible, had a more critical spirit, and was better able to pass sound judgment than the mass of citizens of our day.

Of course, issues and problems were simpler, and the voters' practical experience in daily life and local affairs was sufficient training. Government was not highly centralized, complicated, all-inclusive, and far away. Most voters had an obvious property stake in society; there was as yet no landless proletariat. Demagogues there were in plenty, but perhaps the technique of their art had not been sufficiently perfected nor technologically increased in range and power to render them dangerous. Also, perhaps the pioneer had not yet had his mother wit dimmed by a school system predicated largely on the idea that in those studies dealing with past human experience (history, government, economics, and the like) "the material of instruction *will be selected* and organized for the purpose of" creating the proper attitudes, rather than of furnishing the facts, pleasant or otherwise, and letting the individual act as his own juror.

---

[1] The distance the ramrod projected after the piece was heavily loaded. Presumably a fair drink, also.

Politically as well as geographically and economically the Old Northwest has occupied a strategic position in our history. As the West settled the new states became increasingly important in national councils. And of the West that part north of the Ohio River came to control the balance of power in many important questions. Ohio, Indiana, and Illinois were admitted into the Union under Jeffersonian Republican auspices. For two decades following the War of 1812 the political history of these states was characterized by personal politics and Republican solidarity. By the middle 1830's there had developed an opposition party, the Republicans had changed their label to Democrats, and for almost two more decades was waged a struggle for supremacy between Whigs and Democrats, a struggle complicated by the newer immigration, economic sectionalism, and the rapidly rising slavery question. Later Michigan and Wisconsin were also admitted under Democratic regimes, but eventually threw their weight into the balance with northern Ohio and Illinois, helped effect the alliance between the Northwest and the Northeast, and, after the death of the Whigs, to bring the section as a unit to the side of Lincoln and the Republicans in 1860.[2]

Ohio, since it was settled earlier than the other states of the Old Northwest, had a population of varied origins. As a result its political history became the most complex and in some respects the most interesting. New Englanders settled Marietta and Ohio Company lands, Cleveland, and the Western Reserve. Virginia settled and controlled the big south-central triangle to the west of the Ohio Company settlements. People from New Jersey and Kentucky prevailed in Symmes' Purchase around the Miami. From Pennsylvania came Scotch-Irish and Germans; from Virginia, Kentucky, South and North Carolina, Scotch-Irish and Quakers. Later into northern Ohio came York staters as well as Yankees. From all over came the Americans—already a hybrid people.

Territorial days (1787–1803) had witnessed conflicts between a Federalist governor from Pennsylvania and the Virginia Jef-

---

[2] To which party, on the whole, the Old Northwest has remained loyal since the Civil War. For a brief view of the political history of the region see R. Carlyle Buley, "The Political Balance in the Old Northwest, 1820–1860," in *Studies in American History* (Bloomington, Ind., 1926), 405–55.

fersonian Republicans. It was the Republicans who urged early admission to statehood, who controlled the most important committees of the constitutional convention, and it was southern and Middle States' votes in Congress which furnished the majority for the enabling act.[3] The Republicans, however, split roughly into two groups during the next ten years, and at times the Federalists practically controlled the political balance. Republican leaders from New England settlements, such as Samuel Huntington and Return Jonathan Meigs, were often more closely aligned with Federalists than with the Virginia group leaders such as Edward Tiffin, Thomas Worthington, and Nathaniel Massie. Political struggles were based on both principles and personal rivalries. Perhaps the main controversy centered around the question of judicial review.

When men such as Judges Calvin Pease, Samuel Huntington, and George Tod (all Connecticut men) began to propagate the doctrines of John Marshall and declare acts of the legislature unconstitutional, the ensuing fight carried over into the gubernatorial election. Although Huntington was elected governor over Worthington, the Assembly brought impeachment proceedings against Tod and Pease. With their acquittal the Jeffersonian Republicans of the Virginia following carried on the battle by attempting to limit the term of *ad interim* judicial appointments to the unexpired term. To the "true Jeffersonian" the New England brethren's stand on this question was rank Federalism. With the coming of Tammany societies politics grew even more heated.[4] Worthington, the "Idol of Tammany," was defeated by Meigs for governor in 1810, but the Tammany block in the legislature was strong enough to prevent the conservative Republicans from repealing the "sweeping resolution" of the 1809–10 session which had precipitated the battle over judicial

[3] William Henry Smith (ed.), *The St. Clair Papers* . . . (2 volumes. Cincinnati, 1882), II, 482 ff.; *Annals of Congress,* 7 Congress, 1 session, 1161–62. Ohio politics in the territorial period is covered in Beverley W. Bond, *The Civilization of the Old Northwest* . . . (New York, 1934), and Randolph C. Downes, *Frontier Ohio, 1788–1803* (*Ohio Historical Collections,* III, Columbus, 1935).
[4] The Chillicothe *Scioto Gazette,* which had been the organ of the Virginia element from the beginning, was by 1810 the leading Tammany paper. See files of the Cincinnati *Liberty Hall,* Hamilton *Miami Intelligencer,* the Chillicothe *Independent Republican,* Chillicothe and Circleville *Fredonian,* and Zanesville *Muskingum Messenger,* for the newspaper Tammany War, 1810–11.

terms. The election of 1811 went against the Tammanyites, however, and the conservatives won their point.[5]

The Tammany Republicans had supported President Madison, and although some conservative Republicans voted for De Witt Clinton in 1812, the Tammany order had the honor of casting the electoral vote of Ohio for Madison. The War of 1812 now became the important thing and the factional strife became less noticeable. The General Assembly of 1811–12 districted the state, for Ohio now had six representatives in Congress. In the election of 1812 five of the six elected were conservative or non-Tammany Republicans. In the legislative session of 1812–13 the New Englanders and Clinton supporters voted for Judge Calvin Pease for United States Senator as against Jeremiah Morrow but Morrow was elected. Although as Senator, Thomas Worthington had opposed the declaration of war in 1812, he was elected governor of Ohio in October, 1814, by a large majority.

Territorial days in Indiana, 1800–16, saw the voters divided by three issues, all of which were local and interrelated. Most important of these was slavery. There were possibly one hundred and fifty slaves in Indiana Territory in 1800, mostly in the Illinois towns and around Vincennes. Although relatively few inhabitants gave much thought to the slavery question, some who sought to retain control of a few household servants for a decade sent almost annual petitions to Congress. Failing to get sanction for slavery, they took refuge under the indenture laws which were in effect between 1803 and 1810.[6] At the time of the

[5] The most detailed study of Ohio political history in this period is William T. Utter, "Ohio Politics and Politicians, 1802–1815" (1929), Ph.D. thesis, University of Chicago Library; see also his "Judicial Review in Early Ohio," in *Mississippi Valley Historical Review*, XIV (1927–28), 3–24. A good summary of the subject may be found in *The Frontier State, 1803–1825* (Columbus, Ohio, 1942, being Volume II of the *History of the State of Ohio*, edited by Carl F. Wittke), by the same author.

[6] There is little or no evidence to substantiate the charge that William Henry Harrison, when he came to Vincennes as governor of Indiana Territory, became the leader of a proslavery party which sought to set aside the Ordinance of 1787 and open the Territory to slavery. He was closely associated with men of the proslavery group and as a result of his position as governor would naturally be looked upon as a leader. Dorothy Burne Goebel, in her biography of Harrison (pp. 74–78), follows Jacob Piatt Dunn in labeling him a proslavery man. Dunn, in his *Indiana, A Redemption from Slavery*, saw little else in the early history of Indiana besides the slavery issue. For a less one-sided study, see Logan Esarey, "Some Unsolved Questions of our Early History," in *Indiana History Bulletin*, extra number, February, 1924, pp. 56–58.
Harrison is accused of trying to get Article Six of the Ordinance of 1787 repealed

repeal of the indenture law in 1810 there were 237 slaves listed in Indiana Territory. Active slavery agitation then ceased in the Territory, though slavery remained a political bogey until long after statehood.

A second issue centered around the organization of the militia. Governor Harrison had organized the Indiana militia under the law of the Northwest Territory of 1789, which took in all the able-bodied men between eighteen and forty-five years except preachers. In 1810, with Indian wars threatening, the Quakers of the Whitewater Valley along the eastern side of the Territory sent delegates to protest. Although the Quakers were exempt, the Governor did not conceal his contempt. Thereafter the Quakers entered into politics against Harrison and his friends with an ardor somewhat greater than they had shown for military service.

Both the above questions were related to the third: the election of a delegate to Congress and the location of the territorial capital. Division of opinion between the eastern and western portions of the Territory, distinct in every meeting of the Assembly from 1809 (when Illinois Territory was set off) to 1816, was partly a matter of geography and partly of sentiment. Jonathan Jennings, who carefully cultivated the idea in the eastern section that Vincennes politicians were all aristocrats,[7] took advantage of these conditions and received the sturdy support of the antislavery, Quaker, and capital-moving votes, which made him the most successful politician of his day.

As noted in an earlier chapter,[8] there were no definite political

---

by Congress and, having failed, of introducing the territorial law of 1803—"The law concerning servants"—to achieve the same end. Considering conditions this notorious indenture plan was not so bad. The settlement on the Wabash had never experienced much government until the arrival of Harrison. Persons of color were best protected from kidnaping when owned by or attached to some respectable citizen able to protect them. By no means all of the slaveholders were believers in slavery. In many cases the Negroes had preferred coming along with their masters to being sold into slavery or even freed in slave territory. It is difficult to separate the bona fide antislavery criticism of Harrison from that which was made to cover up other aims. In breaking up the lawless Indian trade in the Territory Harrison had made enemies who at times even endangered his life.

There were indenture laws in 1803, 1805, and 1807. The act of 1810 repealed that of 1807.

[7] Federalism and Republicanism were not issues in Indiana Territory, but succeeding elections in Franklin, Clark, Jefferson, and Wayne counties on the east side of the state certainly showed more Federalistic tendencies than any in Knox.

[8] Chapter II.

issues or party alignments in the election of delegates to the Constitutional Convention of 1816. There was only one party. Indiana entered the Union at the beginning of the era of personal politics.

While the Illinois country was still a part of Indiana Territory, political factions developed around the slavery issue, sectionalism, and personal ambitions. Harrison had the support of Pierre Menard, Dr. George Fisher, of Kaskaskia, and the two Shadrach Bonds (uncle and nephew), of Cahokia. The opposition group, led by John Edgar and William and Robert Morrison, demanded not only the introduction of slavery, but the separation of Illinois from Indiana Territory. Matters were complicated by bitter struggles over land-fraud investigations which Governor Harrison was supporting. The eastern Indiana antislavery group combined with the Edgar-Morrison faction to get a majority in the territorial legislature in favor of division. Their candidate for delegate in Congress was Jesse B. Thomas, of Dearborn County. When elected, he helped steer through the act of separation of 1809.

The factional alignment between the Harrison and anti-Harrison groups—the "ins" and the "outs"—did not greatly concern the majority of the Illinois voters. Furthermore, its continuity was broken when Ninian Edwards, of Kentucky, was appointed governor of Illinois Territory upon its creation and Nathaniel Pope of the same state was made secretary.[9] Edwards confined his appointments to neither faction. Soon, however, the question of reform of the judiciary as well as patronage led to the development of an Edwards and an anti-Edwards party. Edwards, Pope, Daniel Pope Cook—nephew of Pope and later Edwards' son-in-law—Leonard White, and Thomas C. Browne were the main leaders of the Governor's party.[10] In the other camp were Thomas, Elias Kent Kane, of Kaskaskia—born in New York and a graduate of Yale—and John McLean, who came from Kentucky to Shawneetown in 1815. Shadrach Bond, Pierre Menard, Dr. George Fisher, and other prominent men apparently were not closely aligned with either group. "On the whole, it would appear that the political factions during the last

[9] Thomas got one of the judgeships.
[10] White was United States agent at the saline at Shawneetown of which Edwards was superintendent.

years of the Illinois territory may be characterized as combinations of men for the purpose of holding or seeking appointive offices, either local or territorial."[11] The majority of the voters voted for the man or on some local issue, and probably considered themselves members of neither group.[12]

From the end of the War of 1812 to 1824, while the Republican party under Monroe ruled unopposed in national politics, the voters of the Old Northwest were but little interested in national elections. Personal and local politics occupied most of their attention. In Ohio, despite the fact that now and then they were accused of lulling trusting citizens to sleep with talk of "good feelings" in order that they could continue their conspiring,[13] the Federalists were finished. They reasoned that since the Republicans had adopted "good old Washingtonian principles," there was no further reason for opposition. At times even newspapers refused to take a stand on candidates, but merely recommended men of natural understanding and moral integrity, "men fearing God and hating covetousness, and such as . . . [would] be a terror to evil doers and a praise to them that do well."[14]

In 1816 eight presidential electors were named by the "Chillicothe Caucus" in January, and as late as October apparently no other list was presented.[15] The names of James Dunlap, of Ross County, and Ethan Allen Brown were announced for governor against Worthington, but the latter was re-elected by a two-thirds majority. Two years later Brown defeated Dunlap by an even larger majority, and in 1820 he received almost three fourths of the votes, defeating Jeremiah Morrow.[16] In 1822 Allen Trimble won in a spirited personal race against Mor-

[11] Buck, *Illinois in 1818,* 203.
[12] Illinois territorial politics is best reviewed in Clarence W. Alvord, *The Illinois Country,* Chapter XIX; Buck, *Illinois in 1818*; and Theodore C. Pease (ed.), *Illinois Election Returns, 1818–1848 (Illinois Historical Collections,* XVIII, 1923), Introduction.
[13] *Western Herald and Steubenville Gazette,* May 30, 1818.
[14] Chillicothe *Weekly Recorder,* August 2, 1814.
[15] *Zanesville Express,* October 24, 1816; Hamilton *Miami Intelligencer,* January 26, February 2, 1816. The Chillicothe *Weekly Recorder* did not mention the presidential election and carried only two or three items on the state and Congressional elections.
[16] When Brown resigned during the middle of his second term to fill the unexpired term of Senator William Trimble, Allen Trimble, speaker of the Ohio Senate, became acting governor.

row,[17] but in the next election Morrow was elected by a narrow margin. In all of these contests the issues were personal and local; there were no noticeable differences among the candidates on such vital matters as the war against the Bank, canals, and a public school system. How completely the old party lines disappeared during this period is evidenced by the fact that Charles Hammond, one of the staunchest of Federalists in the war period and editor of the St. Clairsville *Ohio Federalist,* took the lead in upholding state rights in Ohio's war against the United States Bank.

The Bank struggle was by far the most exciting thing in Ohio politics in this period.[18] The tax measure proposed in the legislature of 1817–18 was discussed rather judiciously in the newspapers until the sudden contraction of loans by the Bank during the following summer. Some doubted the right of a state to tax an agency of the United States; some thought the agency of questionable constitutionality. James Wilson, editor of the *Western Herald and Steubenville Gazette,* had no qualms about the state's right to tax such an institution.[19] Governor Brown, who had studied law in the office of Alexander Hamilton, agreed.

The tax bill of February, 1819, was intended to drive the two branches of the second Bank of the United States out of the state. Chief Justice Marshall's decision in *McCulloch* v. *Maryland,* March 9, was published in full in the Ohio papers before the end of the month. Some editors received the decision with mild chagrin, but Wilson cried in bold type: "The United States Bank, Everything! The Sovereignty of the States, Nothing!!" and argued that the state might as well return to territorial status. Hammond, though not so furious, was not satisfied and hoped that the "freemen of Ohio feel enough of the spirit of independence to afford the Judges an opportunity of reviewing their opinion."[20]

Although Ohio's action in seizing the money for the tax from

[17] Two complete tickets for state offices and Congress were presented in this election, but there were no party divisions. The many letters published in the newspapers were on the merits and demerits of the candidates. *Liberty Hall and Cincinnati Gazette,* March 2, August 31, and September issues, 1822.

[18] For the main events in the fight against the Bank, see Chapter VIII, 587 ff.

[19] See issue of September 19, 1818.

[20] *Liberty Hall and Cincinnati Gazette,* April 6, 1819. For other comments see Chapter VIII.

the Chillicothe branch has been criticized by some historians as an act of defiance against the mandate of the Supreme Court,[21] the act was generally upheld by public opinion and the leading citizens of Ohio. The more judicious view is that "the people of Ohio had a very good case against the Bank, that they were convinced of the justice of their position, and that they proceeded to test their rights in constitutional, legal, and peaceful ways."[22] Ohio's struggle against the Bank was the result of prejudice against the Bank and conditions in Ohio banking at the time. It was not primarily a presentation of the theory of state rights but a matter of the state protecting what it thought were its economic interests. Most of the men who were leaders in the fight were lined up with the National Republicans when it came to Federal aid for internal improvements and support of the tariffs of 1816 and 1824.[23]

Somewhat overshadowed by the Bank war was the question of calling a constitutional convention to revise the Ohio Constitution. The Constitution of 1802 provided that any time after 1806 two thirds of the General Assembly might "recommend to the electors" a vote on a convention, for the purpose of revising or amending.[24] Several reasons for revision were advanced. The judiciary system, devised for a state of some 60,000 population, was finding it difficult to function for 500,000 or 600,000. The Supreme Court, which was required to ride circuit and hold court once each year in each county was having its troubles with fifty-two counties by 1822.[25] There were too many kinds of cases to be handled by the same tribunal. Some deprecated the lack of a provision against the appointment of legislators to positions created by the Assembly of which they were members. Lobbying for these jobs was not an uncommon practice. Also the constitution was charged with being poorly written and ambiguous. The terms "citizen" and "inhabitant" were used interchangeably; in two places it appeared that aliens could vote, in another

[21] Utter, *The Frontier State*, 305, citing McMaster, *History of the People of the United States*, IV, 498; James Schouler, *History of the United States of America under the Constitution* (7 volumes. New York, 1880–1913), III, 246; Sumner, *History of Banking in the United States*, I, 253.

[22] Ernest L. Bogart, "Taxation of the Second Bank of the United States by Ohio," in *American Historical Review*, XVII (1911–12), 323n.

[23] Utter, *The Frontier State*, 312.

[24] Article VII, Section 5.

[25] *Hamilton Intelligencer and Advertiser*, January 14, 1822.

not.[26] "We do not recollect ever to have seen a written document so replete with inaccuracies of language, ambiguities and contradiction as the constitution of this state; and yet this is the instrument that the people are afraid to trust themselves to revise," said the *Liberty Hall and Cincinnati Gazette*.[27]

The General Assembly of 1818–19 by joint resolution provided for a referendum on the calling of a convention.[28] "This . . . is one of those momentous epochs which mark at intervals, the progress of national improvement—a political climacteric, which calls for the most anxious attention of every lover of his country. It is a fearful crisis fraught with circumstances which must excite interest in every reflecting mind," said the *Columbus Gazette*.[29] Either the crisis was artificial or else there were not enough "reflecting minds," for in the October election, in a light vote, the proposal was defeated five to one. The subject continued to be agitated for some time, but nothing came of it.[30] No doubt the appearance of the slavery issue in the debates over Missouri's admission aroused fear in the minds of the voters that the question would arise in a constitutional convention.

There were no important state questions of general interest before the voters of Ohio in the early 1820's. The legislature of 1820–21 was regarded as a disappointment. The Circleville *Olive Branch* stated that of forty newspapers, only one (the *Steubenville Gazette*, whose editor was a member) could make an apology for it.[31] Some voters complained that the state's laws were becoming much too numerous and complicated, variable, notoriously partial, and too largely local in nature.[32] By 1824, however, the three big topics of statewide importance had come to the front—canals, schools, and tax-law reform.

The campaign for state offices was somewhat overshadowed by the presidential contest. Very little news relative to state tickets appeared prior to August. Many letters on schools and canals filled the columns of the newspapers, but since practically

[26] *Ibid.; Liberty Hall and Cincinnati Gazette*, October 7, 1820.
[27] October 7, 1820.
[28] The Constitution of 1802 had not been submitted to the people. *Western Herald and Steubenville Gazette*, January 16, 1819.
[29] April 15, 1819.
[30] See for instance the four-column legislative explanation to the people of Ohio, in *Liberty Hall and Cincinnati Gazette*, January 5, 1822.
[31] Cited in *Cleaveland Herald*, July 3, 1821.
[32] "Portage," in *ibid.*, April 9, 1822.

all candidates were in favor of these, there was no party division. Allen Trimble sought to retain the governorship but was defeated by Jeremiah Morrow. Despite the lack of spectacular differences between the candidates and the general agreement on program, the state election in October brought out far more voters than did the presidential election in November.

The legislature of 1824–25 was a busy one. Out of it came the laws for a statewide school tax, canals, and an *ad valorem* tax on land and other property.[33] Politically these three important measures were interrelated. Support was gained for the controversial tax measure from those who needed canal votes. Ephraim Cutler in the Senate kept the tax bill ahead of the canal bill on the legislative calendar, thus holding in line votes from the Scioto and Miami settlements.

The noise of battle between Federalists and Republicans never reached Indiana and Illinois. In the surge of nationalistic democracy which followed the War of 1812 Federalists were held in low repute, particularly in the West. The epithet was still hurled in political argument against Whigs a quarter of a century later. To call a man a Federalist was equivalent to a challenge to fight.[34]

Political affairs in the first decade of statehood in Indiana were run largely by three men, a sort of Hoosier triumvirate. These men were Jonathan Jennings, of Clark County, William Hendricks, of Jefferson, and James Noble, of Franklin. All were Republicans.[35] How closely they co-operated is not clear, but they never actively opposed each other.

[33] These laws are discussed in Chapters XIII, VII, and VIII, respectively.

[34] O. H. Smith, in *Early Indiana Trials and Sketches,* 120–22, states in 1857 that the Franklin County (Indiana) Circuit Court fined one John Allen $1,000 for calling Joshua Harlan a Federalist. Smith's memory was somewhat in error for the court records show the case as *Joshua Harlan* v. *Nathaniel Herndon.* Herndon was fined $10 plus costs, but he called for a new trial and later withdrew his motion when the plaintiff relinquished his claim to the $10. Record of Franklin County Court of Common Pleas, 1813–14.

[35] Jennings, a New Jersey Presbyterian, was one of the distinguished citizens of Charlestown. As a delegate in Congress from Indiana Territory, he had been in charge of the enabling act. He was a delegate to the Constitutional Convention of 1816, and as president of that body issued the call for the first election; he was the successful candidate for governor and put the constitution into operation. After serving the constitutional limit of two terms, he served in Congress until intemperance drove him from office.

Hendricks was a man of fair ability, a hard worker who attended to the interests of his constituents, and cultivated the newspapers and the soldiers. For a sketch of his career, see Nina K. Reid, "William Hendricks," in *Indiana Magazine of History,* IX (1913), 167–86.

In the first election for state offices there were no issues beyond a carry-over of jealousy between the eastern and western settlements of territorial days. In an election campaign marked by many letters by and about the candidates,[36] Jennings was elected governor over Thomas Posey, then territorial governor, and Hendricks was elected temporary representative in Congress. The General Assembly in its first session elected James Noble, Virginia-born Jennings' partisan, and Waller Taylor, anti-Jennings man, to the United States Senate. The three Supreme Court judgeships were parceled out to the three factions. Jennings, the most important of the triumvirate, was a professional politician who, though a poor speaker, was a prolific letter writer and constant attendant at all sorts of pioneer assemblies where he "dropped in" on his way somewhere else. He had been a businesslike territorial delegate in Congress and was a skillful manipulator of elections. Hendricks was the choice of the leaders for Congress in the 1817 election; Thomas Posey was his opponent. A lusty battle ensued in which the attack against Hendricks was led by the *Indiana Herald* of Corydon and the Vincennes *Western Sun*, but Hendricks won by a comfortable majority.[37] The following year in the regular Congressional election he defeated Reuben W. Nelson, editor of the *Herald*, and won an even more decisive victory over the same opponent in 1820.

In 1818 when Governor Jennings accepted an appointment to serve as an Indian treaty commissioner,[38] the opposition group accused him of violating that section of the Indiana constitution which prohibited "any person holding any office under the United States" from exercising the office of governor or lieutenant governor. When Jennings left the capital, the lieutenant governor, Christopher Harrison, took charge of the state seal in the office of the secretary of state, but when he, in turn,

Noble was never a candidate before the people after statehood. He was an eloquent jury lawyer and imposing in militia musters. He traveled to and from Washington on horseback. He served as Senator from Indiana 1816–31. Nina K. Reid, "James Noble," in *ibid.*, IX (1913), 1–13.

[36] There are ten columns of candidates' letters in the *Western Sun* of July 20, 1816.

[37] Hendricks defended himself in an open letter in the Madison *Indiana Republican*, September 16, 1817.

[38] Jennings, Lewis Cass, and Benjamin Parke negotiated the "New Purchase" treaty of 1818. See Chapter III.

left Corydon, Jennings returned and carried away the seal and refused to surrender it. Harrison had decided that Jennings, by accepting the other job, had virtually abdicated his office as governor.[39] The matter was taken to the legislature, and when that body failed to act against Jennings, Harrison resigned.[40]

Jennings' opponents were sniping against the day when he should run for re-election. One wrote: "The contemptible cabal of office-seeking adventurers who are busily engaged in writing slander and falsehood for Jennings' *Centinel* [Vincennes] yet go on, their reward, however, awaits them."[41] But Jennings thrived on opposition, and outside Knox County, the seat of the old William Henry Harrison following, he was popular. He defeated Jesse L. Holman, of Aurora, for the governorship in 1819 by better than four to one. Jennings played the slavery issue for all it was worth (probably more), and after serving his second term, was elected to Congress from the second district in 1822. Hendricks was elected governor in that year practically without opposition. Contests in the three Congressional districts to which Indiana became entitled by the census of 1820 were also conducted on personalities rather than issues.

In 1824 when Ratliff Boon, lieutenant governor, resigned to run for Congress, James B. Ray of Brookville was elected speaker *pro tempore* of the Senate. He was re-elected the following year, and when Hendricks resigned the governorship to go to the United States Senate, Ray became governor for the unexpired term. Ray's rise brought a new and striking figure into Indiana politics. A native of Kentucky, he was above medium height, had a high rather projecting forehead, and wore a long queue. He was noted for his powerful stump speeches and soon was to become famous for his ability to throw the English language around with great abandon. In 1825 he announced himself for governor:

I have lived in this Western country thirty years—am a native—a republican—the friend of civil and religious liberty—to the freedom of the Press, to law—have long been an open advocate for internal improvement

[39] Open letter from Harrison in Vincennes *Western Sun and General Advertiser,* November 14, 1818.
[40] Of this affair the *Liberty Hall and Cincinnati Gazette,* November 17, 1818, said: "For the honor of free government, we hope such a scene will not be again exhibited in this country. It demands the decided reprobation of the public sentiment."
[41] *Western Sun and General Advertiser,* September 26, 1818.

—for Domestic Industry—a friend to Education—to freedom and to peace —to equal privileges—to my country, her interests, inhabitants and glory. . . . With the land that flourishes, I flourish. In the country that withers, I die.[42]

Such frank seeking after office was shocking to one of the country's leading news gatherers: "A proceeding which we think can not be approved of, whatever the merits of the individual in other respects."[43]

Judge Isaac Blackford was the leading candidate in opposition. There was no discussion of principles or party in the election which Ray won.[44] Ray had refused to take sides in the party alignments which were developing and believed that national politics should not affect state elections.

The sessions of the General Assembly, which met annually, presented no issues of statewide importance during this period. There was little general legislation; most of the acts were local in nature and often decided by the logrolling process. Governor Jennings in his message of 1819 called attention to the need for legislation on taxation, banking, internal improvements, public education, and roads. Among these subjects were to be found differences of opinion, which, combined with national questions, would lead to the development of political parties in the state.[45]

Early state politics in Illinois continued the factional and personal strife of the territorial period. Aside from the slavery question, there were no important political issues not explainable on the basis of the Edwards and anti-Edwards factional alignments. The Edwards following, to a certain degree, was held together by common business interests—land, townsites, banks. Ninian Edwards had dominated the Illinois political scene since he had come from Kentucky to be governor of Illinois Territory in 1809. He has been well described:

Kindly, charitable, generous, and at the same time pompous, overbearing, and affected, he had many warm friends, many enemies too, and perhaps

---

[42] Indianapolis *Indiana Journal*, June 7, 1825.
[43] *Niles' Weekly Register*, XXVIII, 387 (Aug. 20, 1825).
[44] *Indiana Journal*, July 12, 1825.
[45] The best account of early politics in Indiana are Logan Esarey, "Pioneer Politics in Indiana," in *Indiana Magazine of History*, XIII (1917), 99–128; and Adam A. Leonard, "Personal Politics in Indiana 1816 to 1840," in *ibid.*, XIX (1923), 1–56, 132–68, 241–81.

many associates who humored his foibles so long as doing so would promote their own advantage. The quality of mental balance was almost completely lacking in Edwards. By turns he was bold and overcautious, headstrong and vacillating. . . . A mental shiftiness sometimes led him into equivocal positions which he could justify only by elaborate explanations. . . . His contemporaries, like students in these latter days, doubtless grew weary of reiterations and of elaborate proofs of his abilities and integrity.[46]

In 1818 the way in which the important leaders of both groups were settled into the various state and national offices would seem to indicate some sort of arrangement or at least a temporary truce. Shadrach Bond, who belonged to neither faction, had in August, 1818, withdrawn from the contest for delegate in Congress[47] and left that position certain for Pope in case statehood should not be achieved. Bond in turn had no opposition for governor of the new state. Pierre Menard was elected lieutenant governor. Elias Kent Kane was appointed secretary of state.

John McLean was elected by fourteen votes over Cook for representative in Congress and the legislature elected Cook attorney general. The legislature elected Edwards to one United States senatorship and Jesse B. Thomas of the anti-Edwards group to the other. Pope was taken care of with a Federal judgeship.

The Edwards-Thomas rivalry in the United States Senate had its repercussions in Illinois politics. Thomas favored William H. Crawford for the Presidency, while Edwards became involved in a series of charges against Crawford regarding the maladministration of public moneys which he could not prove and which practically ruined him politically.[48] The affair cost Edwards the ambassadorship to Mexico, which he had resigned from the Senate to accept, and hurt his personal finances severely.

Daniel Pope Cook was elected to Congress in 1819 over McLean in a contest in which Cook took an antislavery stand.

[46] Pease, *The Frontier State,* 93.

[47] His notice is in the Kaskaskia *Illinois Intelligencer,* August 19, 1818.

[48] This Edwards-Crawford affair was known as the "A. B. Plot," from the signature of the letters, supposedly written by Edwards, which made the charges in the Washington *Republican.* The affair was widely discussed in the newspapers. See, for instance, the column of editorials in *Liberty Hall and Cincinnati Gazette,* May 4, 1824, or the Vandalia *Illinois Intelligencer* of July 1 and 8, 1825, which printed ten columns of Edwards' letters. The best summary is in Pease, *The Frontier State,* 98–103.

The issue was not clear but the result showed the general feeling of those who were voting on principle; there was a tendency to cut across the factional lines with strong proslavery Edwards men leaving Cook's side and many antislavery men of the opposition coming to his support. Cook's personal popularity carried him through again in 1820 over Kane, in 1822 over McLean again, and in 1824 over Bond. Various charges against him, such as abuse of the franking privilege and associating with Federalists, seem to have had little effect. He emphasized local issues, a system of internal improvements, and, in the presidential scramble of 1824 promised, if the election went to the House of Representatives, to vote as the people of Illinois had voted.

The Missouri question, 1819–20, brought the slavery issue to the front in the three states and served for a time to connect local and national politics. Ohio was more aroused than either Indiana or Illinois. The *Cleaveland Herald* said that a question of "more interest and anxiety" had not been presented since the formation of the Federal Constitution and stated that if the opportunity were permitted to pass without giving a deadly blow to further extension of slavery "we may ever after give up the contest as unavailing and meekly yield to her horrible practice of trafficking in human flesh."[49] The state legislature requested the Ohio senators and representatives to "use their utmost exertions, to prevent the admission or introduction of slavery into any of the territories of the United States, or any new state, that may hereafter be admitted into the Union."[50] In Congress Senator Benjamin Ruggles said that the Ordinance of 1787 had "been to the people of the Northwestern territory a rule of action—a guide to direct their course—a 'cloud by day, and a pillar of fire by night.' "[51]

Indiana and Illinois papers did not take the Missouri question quite so seriously as did those of Ohio. The *Detroit Gazette*

[49] February 8, 1820.
[50] Ohio *Senate Journal*, 1819–20, p. 169.
[51] *Annals of Congress*, 16 Congress, 1 session, 281. Ruggles' speech was published in full, with editorial comment, in the *Western Herald and Steubenville Gazette*, March 11, 1820. This paper deprecated the talk of disunion, however, and said constituents would have different ideas on this matter from that of the debaters. March 4, 1820. The *Zanesville Express* (quoted in *Franklin Chronicle*, of Delaware, Ohio, on March 6) argued that Congress had the right to admit a state, hence to prescribe conditions.

pointed out, however, that though from a selfish viewpoint the people of Michigan should prefer slavery in Missouri in order that no more free and industrious emigrants would go there, from a moral and general-welfare viewpoint, they were hoping it would be prohibited.[52]

In the United States Senate when the Thomas amendment (Missouri to be admitted with slavery, but no more slave states north of 36° 30′) was submitted, the only senators from the Northwest who voted against it were Noble and Taylor of Indiana.[53] On the passage of the whole bill to engrossment and third reading, Thomas and Edwards, of Illinois, voted for, while Noble, Taylor, and the two Ohio senators, Ruggles and Trimble, voted against it. On the final vote in the House which inserted the Senate line of 36° 30′ and passed the bill, none of the representatives of the Northwest voted nay.[54]

On the adoption of the Compromise the *Western Herald* which had carried much antislavery discussion merely reported the question settled,[55] but the editor of the *Ohio Monitor*, then state printer, wrote:

Much to our grief and some to our astonishment, Missouri has been admitted into the Union with permission to hold slaves. . . . It is more to our desire, than our hope, that the period will never come, when this nation will have to take up her lamentation, and say of this foul deed, *"Let the day be darkness,* let no light shine upon it," in which the United States Senate forced the passage of this impious act.[56]

With the settlement of the Missouri question the slavery issue as an influence on political parties was replaced for a generation by economic problems. The attitude of the Northwest at this time was indicative of the drift from its connection with the Old South to a closer agreement with the East.[57] It remained for economic and cultural ties to consolidate the connection at a later period.

The presidential election of 1820 received but scant attention in the Northwest. Virginia and Pennsylvania had early named

[52] February 25, 1820.
[53] *Annals of Congress,* 16 Congress, 1 session, part I, 427.
[54] *Ibid.,* part II, 1587.
[55] *Western Herald and Steubenville Gazette,* March 18, 1820.
[56] Columbus *Ohio Monitor,* March 21, 1820.
[57] Homer C. Hockett, *Western Influence on Political Parties to 1825 (Ohio State University Contributions in History and Political Science,* No. 4 [Columbus], 1917), 129.

Monroe and Tompkins electors and no serious opposition was expected or resulted. "There appears no great excitement in any quarter, concerning the next presidential election. . . . In most of the States the elections occur with great quietness, too great, perhaps, for the general safety of the Republic," wrote the *Ohio Monitor* in April.[58] In midsummer the *Cleaveland Herald* thought it would "not be amiss to remind our fellow citizens, that an important election takes place in this State on the second Tuesday in October. . . . It is true the old division of parties are but little known in this quarter; but this ought not to abate the vigilance necessary to perpetuate our happy form of government. . . ."[59] Newspapers carried the state tickets regularly but only rarely did a list of electors appear. After the election the *Ohio Monitor* noted: "We have received from authority the following list of Electors of President and Vice President chosen by the people of the State."[60]

In Indiana the General Assembly selected the electors and after they had cast their votes for Monroe and Tompkins a notice to that effect appeared in a Corydon paper.[61] Not until 1824 did Indiana provide for the election of electors by popular vote. In Illinois Governor Bond by proclamation divided the state into three electoral districts and eleven men offered themselves for the three places. The day after the election the *Edwardsville Spectator* reported: "An election for electors of president and vice president of the United States was held in this State yesterday."[62] One Edwards man and two of the opposing faction were elected, their combined vote being 938 against 499 for the eight other candidates.[63]

The representation in Congress for the three states after the elections of 1820 consisted of six senators and eight representatives—all Republicans. Only in the first Congressional district in Ohio had there been any indication of any other party

---

[58] April 11, 1820.
[59] *Cleaveland Herald*, July 25, 1820. The results of the presidential election were not mentioned in the *Herald* until February 13, 1821, after the official counting of the vote. The *Liberty Hall* published the lists of electors at least once, but offered no comment on the campaign.
[60] November 18, 1820.
[61] Smith, *Early Indiana Trials and Sketches*, 85.
[62] November 7, 1820.
[63] *Edwardsville Spectator*, September 19, 1820; Pease, *Illinois Election Returns*, 7.

having ever existed. There Joseph Vance had been opposed by Philemon Beecher, a former Federalist. The editor of the *Monitor* wrote that in the days of amalgamation this fact was not to be emphasized, but entreated the voters to remember what had been their feelings in the late war.[64]

The biggest political excitement in the Northwest between Ohio's war on the Bank and the presidential election of 1824 came as a result of the proposal for a state constitutional convention in Illinois. In Indiana the slavery question, despite some slight division of sentiment on the subject, had been settled by the convention of 1816, but in Illinois it still remained open and the most important single influence on politics until 1824.

In 1821 a resolution in the Illinois legislature to ask Senators Edwards and Thomas to resign, since their votes against the restriction of slavery in Missouri did not represent the opinions of the people of the state, was defeated by a small majority.[65] At the same time the *Edwardsville Spectator* and the *Missouri Republican* were issuing warnings to the friends of freedom that efforts were going to be made to repeal the antislavery clause of the Illinois constitution.[66]

The first definite proposal for a slavery amendment apparently came from Henry Eddy who, in his campaign for the legislature in Gallatin County in 1820, announced for a convention. When elected he introduced resolutions to this end. The hard times of 1819–20—the slump in land values, the pinch in state finances —lent plausibility to the arguments that removal of slavery restrictions would attract well-to-do planters to the state and promote better times.

In the election of governor in 1822 the slavery issue was the most important. The four candidates were Edward Coles, Joseph B. Phillips, James B. Moore, and Thomas C. Browne. Coles, Virginia Jeffersonian, anti-Edwards, and opposed to slavery on

---

[64] Columbus *Ohio Monitor,* September 16, 1820.

[65] Illinois *House Journal,* 1820–21, p. 134.

[66] Charles Manfred Thompson, *The Illinois Whigs before 1846* (*University of Illinois Studies in the Social Sciences,* IV, no. 1, Urbana, 1915), 16; *Edwardsville Spectator,* July 4, 11, 25, August 1, 1820. The editor of the *Spectator,* Hooper Warren, was an Edwards man. In the issue of July 11, he stated that McLean was to purchase an interest in the *Illinois Gazette* (Shawneetown) and to influence the *Intelligencer* also. Kane was also attacked but struck back at Edwards and his twenty-two slaves.

consideration for the next president with claims "powerful if not irresistible."[75] By 1822 Calhoun, Crawford, Clinton, and Clay—"What a C of troubles"[76]—were all obvious candidates. A series of letters in the *Liberty Hall* in the autumn set forth the merits of Clay, Clinton, and even Adams.[77] A mass meeting in Cincinnati in December proclaimed for Clinton, whose interest in canals and the "domestic system" appealed to the north-eastern part of Ohio and to those in Cincinnati who did not like Clay's close association with the Bank. The Cincinnati *National Republican* advertised him as "decidedly the most popular Candidate in Ohio and we understand such is his standing in Indiana and Illinois."[78] Citizens' meetings at Steubenville and elsewhere in December resolved for Clinton for president and Jackson for vice-president.

Crawford, who as secretary of the treasury had built up a strong political machine among the banks, was not popular in Ohio but received a boost from the Vincennes *Western Sun* as "the able, firm and intelligent Secretary of the Treasury."[79] Calhoun had some support in Ohio in the early stages of the campaign,[80] but Adams and Clay were the strongest candidates. Adams was supposed to satisfy the New Englanders and Quakers on the slavery question. Clay, despite his connection with the Bank and lack of an antislavery record, was, on the basis of his "American System" and personal popularity, supported by James Wilson of the *Steubenville Herald* and Charles Hammond of the *Liberty Hall and Cincinnati Gazette.* The *Cleaveland Herald* pointed to Clay as the only real advocate of domestic industry. In January, 1823, the Ohio legislature took a poll of its members and nominated Clay by fifty votes to seven scattered

[75] "Cincinnatus" argued its case in a three-column communication to the Chillicothe *Scioto Gazette,* copied in *Liberty Hall and Cincinnati Gazette,* October 20, 1821. Population, geography, policy of cementing the Union, all demanded it. The United States could not follow Rome's policy of adding provinces which extended the empire but did not strengthen it.

[76] *Ohio Monitor,* August 24, 1822.

[77] *Liberty Hall and Cincinnati Gazette,* October 12, 19, November 23, 1822. Another series in April, 1823, which reviewed the history of political parties and the candidates made it appear that the next election was only a week or two distant.

[78] September 19, 1823.

[79] February 2, April 27, November 20, 1822.

[80] The *Liberty Hall and Cincinnati Gazette,* for instance, favored Calhoun in December, 1823.

among Clinton, Adams, and Calhoun.[81] Clay was also favored by the *Illinois Intelligencer* as a man of high distinction with valid claims to the Presidency, and by the Madison *Indiana Republican* which believed Clay was most attached to and interested in the prosperity of the West.[82]

Clinton's prospects waned when New York failed to give the voters the right to select the electors, and Crawford lost ground in the West after his caucus nomination and in Indiana as a result of the bank failures of 1821–22.[83]

Meanwhile Jackson's candidacy was rumbling in the background. There were reports of Jackson enthusiasm in Pittsburgh. In March, 1823, the *Liberty Hall* ran a long argument against him and in August was surprised that Jackson should still be considered. On merit, he was nothing but a general. To elect him would establish a bad precedent.[84] Since all candidates were Republicans, old party lines would play no part unless there were degrees of Republicanism sufficient to constitute reasons for preference.[85]

The Jackson candidacy began to gather impetus by the spring of 1824. With Clinton out the Cincinnati *National Republican* swung to Jackson and by May was in part responsible for the

[81] Cincinnati *National Republican*, January 14, 1823. The rising dislike for caucus methods in the West made itself known in severe criticism of this meeting as well as of Congressional caucus nomination advocated by eastern Republican papers.

The editor of the *National Republican* considered that the mischievous consequences of legislative caucusing had "rendered this mode of selecting candidates for elective offices universally odious and obnoxious to the people" and viewed its advocacy by eastern Republican papers "with mingled emotions of surprise and indignation." February 7, 24, 1823. Throughout the spring and summer he continued his attacks against "The Caucus Junto" both state and national, and stated that "a more anti-democratic and tyrannical doctrine cannot be imagined." On February 27, 1824, he spoke of the caucus as follows: "It is the last rattle in the tail of that political Dragon which stands before the capitol, ready to devour the first born of liberty in this great republic, and democracy of the nation."

A resolution was introduced in the Indiana House that "any attempt by congressional nominations, in caucus or otherwise, to exercise this invaluable privilege [to select a president] unless authorized by the constitution, should be regarded, by the American people, as a dangerous encroachment on their rights, tending to the ruin of the republic." It was postponed indefinitely, however, by a vote of 36 to 38. *Niles' Weekly Register*, XXV, 361 (Feb. 7, 1824).

[82] Vandalia *Illinois Intelligencer*, June 14, 1823; Madison *Indiana Republican*, November 4, 1824.

[83] Said the Cincinnati *National Republican*, February 27, 1824: Sixty-two aristocrats "principally apostates from the old Federalist Party have nominated William H. Crawford, a notorious *apostate Federalist,* as a candidate for the Presidency and Albert Gallatin, a foreigner by birth, for the Vice-Presidency."

[84] March 19, August 19, 1823.

[85] August 29, 1823.

building up of a strong Jackson organization in Cincinnati and neighboring counties. "Seventy Six" in a long argument convinced "Plowshare" that Andrew Jackson was a great hero and the only man.[86] The *Western Sun,* influential in Indiana, shifted from its Crawford stand of 1822, to Clay or Jackson in 1823, and all-out Jackson in 1824. The Indiana legislature in January gave the people the right to select the electors on a general ticket,[87] but since there was no precedent to follow, there was some doubt as to the exact method to use. Newspaper efforts to agree upon a ticket proved futile,[88] whereupon Elihu Stout, publisher of the *Western Sun,* proposed a convention of delegates. Several counties held meetings and finally on September 16, 1824, eighteen delegates representing fourteen counties met at Salem.[89] The selection of electors, a committee of correspondence, and the classical address to the people presented by Samuel Judah and others gave the Jackson men an impetus and organization never to be seriously challenged by that of any other candidate.[90]

In Ohio a Jackson meeting was held at Columbus on July 14, at which electors were chosen. Many county ratification meetings followed during the next two months.[91]

In Illinois, since Ninian Edwards had quarreled with Crawford over the authorship of the "A. B." letters and bank policy, it would have seemed logical for the anti-Edwards groups to

[86] *Western Herald and Steubenville Gazette,* May 1, 1824.

[87] *Laws of Indiana,* 1823–24, p. 174.

[88] In May, of 14 newspapers in the state, 7 were listed as for Adams, 4 for Clay, 1 for Clay and Adams, and 2 for Jackson. Among the Adams papers were the Corydon *Indiana Gazette, Lawrenceburg Oracle,* and the Richmond *Public Leger.* For Clay were the *Brookville Enquirer,* Madison *Indiana Republican, Vevay Register, Indianapolis Gazette,* and the *Indianapolis Censor.* The complete lineup is given in the Corydon *Indiana Gazette,* May 19, 1824.

[89] This was one of the first, if not the first, convention of delegates of representatives of the people for the nomination of candidates ever held in the United States. The New York convention, for which the claim has been made, represented factions opposed to a legislative caucus nomination for governor, and met September 21–22. *Niles' Weekly Register,* XXVII, 68 (Oct. 2, 1824).

[90] "In every age we have seen men endowed with a universality of genius, a combination of talent, capacitating them to uphold their country's honor amid the storms of war, or to preside in the consultations of statesmen, and to guide their fellows in the paths of peace to happiness and prosperity. . . . Virtue had ceased to exist at Athens, the brightness of her glory was stained—venality pervaded every department of the state, and every class of men—the meretricious charms of wealth had inspired every person, and luxury had enfeebled every mind before Philip triumphed at Chaeronea." Vincennes *Western Sun and General Advertiser,* October 16, 1824.

[91] Cincinnati *National Republican,* July—August, 1824.

support the Secretary of the Treasury. But neither Crawford nor Clay was thought to be sufficiently strong in the state to deserve much attention. The contest, complicated as it was by factional fights and the district system of choosing electors, seemed to lie between Jackson and Adams. In the end Jackson, Adams, Clay, and Crawford all had electors before the voters.[92]

Adams electors were selected "by a respectable number of members of both houses of the general assembly" in Ohio on February 15, and advertised as "The Free Electoral Ticket."[93] Although Adams occupied a favorable position on slavery in the minds of large numbers of Ohio people, some efforts were required to prove that he possessed democratic principles.[94] Copies of the Alien and Sedition Acts were sent to Adams supporters and their candidate was called an aristocratic infidel. The editor of the *Cincinnati Emporium* held aloof from the Adams candidacy until midsummer, but after examining the papers from various parts of the country he concluded that Adams was the people's candidate and his election so certain that nothing short of divine intervention could prevent it.[95]

All the candidates were Republicans, but their views on important questions differed. Although for a while the slavery question threatened to play an important part, especially in Ohio, in the main it was the tariff, internal improvements, distrust of an officeholding class, and the personality of Andrew Jackson which dominated the campaign. The Jacksonians had not yet accepted and developed the issues which began to be associated with their party a few years later. In 1824 it was Andrew Jackson, the Indian fighter, the hero of New Orleans, the champion of the frontiersmen, and the representative of uncontaminated and virile democracy, a man with "a character for honor, integrity, and purity of motive, sacred to Americans and

[92] September 24, 1824, the Vandalia *Illinois Intelligencer* reported a meeting of Republican and Democratic citizens at Edwardsville. In the resolutions, which were for Clay and Jackson, the term "Republican Democratic" party appeared. Two weeks later this paper printed four columns of Clay argument and a list of Clay electors, but carried a list of Adams electors as well.

[93] Columbus *Ohio Monitor*, April 24, 1824.

[94] *Ibid.*, March 6, 1824.

[95] *Cincinnati Emporium*, July 15, 1824. On October 28 appeared a three-column letter by "A Citizen" which contrasted Adams' fine character with Clay's proslavery leanings.

spotless in the halls of fame," who rose above principles and issues. Westerners were becoming resentful of what they regarded as the aristocratic influence in government with its caucus system and machine politics. Jackson, in their minds, typified all that was opposed to these things. Furthermore, he was regarded as standing right on the thing uppermost in their minds —internal improvements. What if he was somewhat uncertain on the tariff—favored a "judicious tariff"[96]—perhaps that was not so important after all. His partisans were aggressive and ever alert. "We believe it will not be questioned, if zeal and noise could effect such a result, that General Jackson would long since have been elected," wrote the *Liberty Hall* in September.

As the election neared, it appeared that in Indiana and Illinois it was Jackson against the field; in Ohio a tossup between Clay, Adams, and Jackson. In Ohio, though Adams men argued that their candidate's character, knowledge of the art of government, and training in foreign affairs far outweighed the qualities of the warrior or the gifts of eloquence, his silence on domestic questions weakened his chances. The fact that two western candidates were likely to divide the region led to various unsuccessful attempts at coalition, but the only outcome was a sort of general support of a Southerner for the vice-presidency with Jackson, and of a representative from the East on the Clay ticket. The Adams men even tried to nominate Jackson as vice-president on the Adams ticket.[97] Rumors of coalition were spread by the Jackson men as the election approached. They said Clay electors were to be kept in the running to prevent the election of Jackson by the people and to secure the election of Crawford.[98] The only remedy was for the plain people, denounced as "rowdies," "ignoble rabble," "the very dregs of the community," to stand forth in defense of their rights, sovereignty, and character, and by force of numbers to conquer

[96] Referring to the Coleman letter of April 26, 1824. The *Liberty Hall and Cincinnati Gazette,* May, 1824, gave the tariff quite a bit of space.

[97] John Quincy Adams, *Memoirs* . . . (12 volumes. Philadelphia, 1874–77), VI, 253.

[98] Cincinnati *National Republican,* September 21, 1824. William Henry Harrison denied this as "a base, unfounded and malicious falsehood." *Ibid.,* October 12, 1824.

under the motto, "No intrigue, no corruption, Andrew Jackson."[99]

In the November election the results in Ohio were as follows: Clay, 19,255; Jackson, 18,489; Adams, 12,280,[100] making a total vote of 50,024 as against 76,634 cast in the gubernatorial election in October. Jackson carried the group of counties in the southwestern part of the state next to Indiana and the Ohio, including the two most populous counties of Hamilton and Butler, and a group in eastern Ohio settled largely by Pennsylvanians. The Adams counties were chiefly in the Western Reserve and Washington, Meigs, and Athens on the Ohio—counties settled by New Englanders. Clay carried four counties in the Reserve, probably won by the internal improvements issue, and counties scattered over the state.[101] The Indiana vote stood: Jackson, 7,343; Clay, 5,315; Adams, 3,093.[102]

Illinois, voting for electors in three districts, returned an Adams elector in the first district and Jackson electors in the other two.[103] In the first district there were two Jackson men who split the vote for elector, in the second there were three, while three ran for Clay elector in the third. The split did not affect the results in either case. In the first district one elector ran under the designation "Jackson or Clay," but his 629 votes were listed at the time as Crawford votes. The total vote for the state was: Adams, 1,540; Jackson, 1,272; Clay, 1,046; Crawford, 219; and the 629 cast for the "Jackson or Clay" elector in the first district.[104] These last votes added to either Clay or Jackson would have given the recipient a plurality over Adams.

The popular vote for the three states stood: Jackson, 27,104;

[99] Cincinnati *National Republican,* October 26, 1824. This paper had been Jackson's most vociferous advocate since April when it abandoned Clinton. On the same day the *Edwardsville Spectator* was calmly announcing that "On Monday next, the citizens of this State will have an important duty to perform—to give their suffrages for electors of a Chief Magistrate of the Union. . . ."

[100] Ohio Secretary of State, *Ohio Statistics,* 1914 (Springfield, 1915), 255; Utter, *The Frontier State,* 333–34; *Liberty Hall and Cincinnati Gazette,* November 15; *National Republican,* November 19; *Cincinnati Emporium,* December 16, 1824. The campaign was reviewed in the *Liberty Hall and Cincinnati Gazette,* November 26, 1824.

[101] The Ohio returns are mapped in Utter, *The Frontier State,* 334; see also Eugene H. Roseboom, "Ohio in the Presidential Election of 1824," in *Ohio Archaeological and Historical Society Publications,* XXVI (1917), 214–18.

[102] Vincennes *Western Sun and General Advertiser,* December 4, 1824.

[103] Pease, *Illinois Election Returns,* 30–35.

[104] *Ibid.* The totals in Pease, *The Frontier State,* 107, and in *Election Returns,* 30–35, vary a couple of votes.

Clay, 25,616; Adams, 16,913; Crawford, 219; and 629 not counted in the Illinois first district. The sixteen electoral votes of Ohio were cast for Clay for president and for Nathan Sanford for vice-president; Indiana's five votes went for Jackson, and two in Illinois were for Jackson and one for Adams. Jacksonian papers, such as the Cincinnati *National Republican*, charged that Adams men had joined the Clay forces to defeat Jackson and held that the "Caucus Junto" was preparing another Burr intrigue in the House of Representatives.[105] Some hoped that the electoral votes would be cast for Jackson.[106]

In the election in the House of Representatives the influence of Clay, who believed that Adams was the second choice of the West, was decisive.[107] The Ohio delegation gave two votes for Jackson, two for Crawford, and ten for Adams. Thus Ohio's vote was cast for Adams though he had run third in the popular vote. The Indiana representatives agreed and Indiana's vote was cast for Jackson. The three Illinois electoral votes rested in the hands of Daniel Pope Cook, the state's sole representative, who had announced in the campaign that should such a tie-up occur he would vote according to the wish of the majority.[108] Since the Illinois electors were divided and no candidate had a majority of the popular vote, his position was difficult, but he decided that had only Adams and Jackson been running, the former

[105] *National Republican*, November 23, 1824.

[106] *Cincinnati Advertiser*, November 24, 1824. The *National Republican*, January 14, 1825, said that the people ought not complain that the electors threw away the vote of the state, for they were under an implied contract to vote for Clay, unless released by some special act of the Almighty. Clay was not to be withdrawn. Such fantastic tricks: "The Slaves of Europe would look with indifference on such scenes. Not so with the people of Ohio, when they lose their rights or their influence in the National government it is by fraud."

[107] For reasons for Clay's support of Adams, see Hockett, *Western Influence on Political Parties to 1825*, 139–40 and note. There seems to be no doubt that after Clay was eliminated Adams was the choice of Ohio. The protests of some of the Republican papers over the outcome were vigorous. Said the *National Republican*, February 22, 1825: "The members of the following States represent the voice of their constituents and have conferred lasting honor on themselves by voting for Andrew Jackson, the peoples candidate. . . . The votes of the following states were *obtained* for J. Q. Adams. . . . [Ohio, Illinois, etc.] May his administration be limited to the shortest constitutional term, and may he go out of office, as his father did, and without the privilege of appointing his successor." The editor of the *Newark Advocate*, February 17, 1825, dressed his paper in mourning and wrote: "Hung be the heavens in black!" The *Columbus Gazette*, however, was satisfied. "The elevation of Mr. Adams appears to be quite satisfactory to the friends of the other candidates, who reside in this vicinity."

[108] Washburne, *Edwards*, 261.

would have been the choice for Illinois, and cast the vote of Illinois for Adams.

In the Congressional election Ohio returned fourteen representatives. In the October election Jeremiah Morrow had been elected governor over Allen Trimble by 2,818 votes, in an election which polled some 26,000 more votes than the presidential election. Indiana had been gerrymandered into three Congressional districts in 1822; Governor Jennings went to Congress from the second, while Congressman Hendricks became governor. In 1824 Ratliff Boon, Jonathan Jennings, and John Test were elected to Congress. For Illinois Daniel Pope Cook still was the sole representative from the state. The delegation of the Northwest in Congress consisted of 18 representatives and 6 senators, all Republicans, but beginning to divide into Clay and Jackson camps.

The Ohio legislature of 1825, despite its busy session on canals and schools, found time in February to elect William Henry Harrison to the United State Senate. The state elections of that year aroused little interest; no organized parties had developed as yet and the vote was light. In 1826 a number of candidates offered for the governorship which Jeremiah Morrow was expected to vacate. Allen Trimble, well known in state politics, polled 72,434 votes to approximately four thousand for each of his three opponents.[109] Within the next year or two national affairs tended to develop an administration party and an opposition group.

As previously noted, James B. Ray had been elected governor of Indiana in the August election of 1825. He had supported Clay in the presidential election and his opponent, Isaac Blackford, had been an Adams elector. The Congressional campaign of 1826 was likewise free from the influence of the presidential contest.[110] Candidates announced themselves without reference to

[109] The official returns as given in the *Ohio State Journal,* October 26, 1826, were: Trimble, 72,434, Alexander Campbell, 4,939, John Bigger, 4,248, and Benjamin Tappan, 4,605.

[110] In the first district Ratliff Boon, a Jackson supporter, ran against Thomas H. Blake, who had supported Clay, and Dr. Lawrence S. Shuler. In the second Jonathan Jennings who had been a Clay advocate in 1824 but cast his vote in Congress for Jackson, though he would personally have preferred Adams, was without opposition. In the third district two Clay men, Judge John Test and Oliver H. Smith, were the candidates. Leonard, "Personal Politics in Indiana," in *Indiana Magazine of History,* XIX, 35–36.

party. The three successful representatives were Thomas H. Blake, Jonathan Jennings, and Oliver H. Smith, all Clay men. Another year and this result would have been improbable in Jackson-minded Indiana.

In Illinois the last round in the bout of purely personal and factional politics took place in 1826. Joseph Duncan, Jackson County farmer with a military record from the War of 1812, began to campaign against Daniel Pope Cook for Congress a year before the election of 1826. He was supported by the anti-Edwards faction. Ninian Edwards, with the Crawford controversy and his defeat in the legislature in 1824 for the Senate still in mind, sought vindication at the hands of the voters by running for governor. He carried on an arduous statewide campaign, attacked the financial mismanagement which had resulted in Illinois money being circulated at one third its face value,[111] denounced the legislature, and sailed into his enemies in general. His opponent was Thomas Sloo, not a very strong candidate. Considerable wind was taken out of Edwards' sail by George Forquer, former Edwards partisan, who under the name of "Tyro" went after Edwards. He reminded Edwards that the day had passed when the factional strife of the territorial groups could hold men in line:

The sycophants of territorial bondage have lost their influence and dwindled into contempt. The dazzling halo, with which the former exercise of lordly power, occasioned the ignorant to associate your name, is broken, and you now stand before them as an object of political charity—a naked, crumbling monument of a morbid ambition. A race of men, honorable in their views, pure in their feelings, with talents hereafter to be felt, are now in political embryo, who have not been tamed or degraded under the banners of either of the old parties that originated the territorial feuds, and which have ever since harassed the country with the most intolerant proscription.[112]

For a number of years Cook and Edwards had had to confront the charge that from personal motives they had voted against the reduction of the price of government land. A more serious embarrassment to their political fortunes was the charge that they and their friends and relatives constituted a ruling

[111] Chapter VIII.
[112] Published in the Vandalia *Illinois Intelligencer*, July 6, 1826. See also Pease, *The Frontier State*, 107–11.

family in Illinois. In addition Cook had to defend his vote for
Adams for president. The result was that Duncan defeated Cook
for Congress and Edwards barely won the governorship by a
plurality over the weak opposition of Sloo and Adolphus F.
Hubbard, who was regarded as little more than a joke in Illinois
politics.[113] The vote for Adams as a factor in Cook's defeat has
probably been overemphasized. Although Edwards became governor, the heyday of his influence was passed. A majority of the
voters had voted for second-rate men in protest against a ruling
clique, as they were shortly to do nationally.

Although the inhabitants of Michigan Territory did not participate in national elections in this period, they did not suffer
from a lack of political activity. The settled portion of Michigan
had remained a part of the Northwest Territory until 1803; its
existence as a part of Indiana Territory had been brief—February 19, 1803, to June 30, 1805—and the results negligible. The
population in 1800 was listed at 3,457 white persons, most of
whom were settled around Detroit, Frenchtown, and Mackinac.[114] They were separated from the Ohio-Wabash settlements
not only by distance but by numerous Indians. Petitions for separate territorial status were quickly recognized.

President Jefferson appointed William Hull, Yale graduate
and Massachusetts officer in the Revolution, governor, Stanley
Griswold secretary, and Augustus B. Woodward, Frederick
Bates, and John Griffin judges.[115] None of these men, excepting
Judge Bates, had lived in the West. They were confronted with
the dual task of rebuilding Detroit, which had been completely
destroyed by fire on June 11, 1805, and establishing the new
government.

A code of laws was prepared, the tangle of land claims taken
up,[116] and a bank chartered.[117] When the bank was voided by

---

[113] The vote was: Edwards, 6,280; Sloo, 5,833; Hubbard, 580. Pease, *The
Frontier State,* 111.
[114] The census of 1801 gave Wayne County 3,206 and listed Michilimackinac's
251 under Indiana Territory. The census takers apparently were working under
a misapprehension. See Madison's letter of transmission of the census to the President, December 8, 1801. There were also some settlers at the Sault Ste. Marie not
included in these figures. Carter, *Territorial Papers,* III, 199, VII, 25.
[115] Samuel Huntington and William Sprigg had declined appointments and
Griffin was appointed in 1806.
[116] See Chapter III.
[117] Chapter VIII.

Congress, dissension, recrimination, and chaos prevailed in the territorial government. The demise of the bank, Judge Woodward's pet project, was but one cause for contention between him and Governor Hull. The cantankerous and crafty Judge blamed the Governor for the "melancholy and alarming state in which we now stand" with "a great storm" threatening;[118] he succeeded in getting Griswold, who had been acting governor, recalled, and in 1810 in the absence of the third judge, wiped from the statute books all laws passed during the preceding three years. During these years of strife the Legislative Board had been airing its troubles before the public. The effects were neither edifying nor stabilizing.

The War of 1812 proved even more distracting than territorial politics. One result was the appointment of Gen. Lewis Cass as governor. William Woodbridge, of Ohio, became secretary. Cass was a firm believer in republican processes and at times found the action of the Judges somewhat trying, but his good sense enabled him to avoid the open controversies of the Hull administration.

By 1818 the increase in population made Michigan eligible for second-grade territorial status and representative government. There were the usual complaints against the indignity of arbitrary government expressed in long-winded letters by "Rousseau" and others to the *Detroit Gazette*.[119] Those in favor of the step argued that it would give the Territory a delegate in Congress, elevate the moral character of the population, increase immigration, and raise real estate values. The only argument against it was the added expense and this was overestimated.[120] It was sufficient, however, combined with the indifference of the French inhabitants to the supposed advantages of self-government to bring about the defeat of the proposal.[121]

Since the Territory had sufficient population as stipulated by the Ordinance of 1787, Congress disregarded the vote and in 1819 gave the Territory the right to elect a delegate to that body. William Woodbridge, secretary to the Territory, became the

---

[118] Judge Woodward to the Legislative Board in Moore (ed.), "The Beginnings of Territorial Government in Michigan," in *Michigan Pioneer and Historical Collections*, XXXI (1901), 566–68.

[119] November—December 1817. There were replies by "Anti-Demagog."

[120] *Detroit Gazette*, February 6, 13, 1818.

[121] *Ibid.*, February 20, 1818.

first delegate.[122] This being the only elective office in the Territory, the elections aroused considerable interest and controversy, but it was personal rather than partisan.

Although the people had voted down representative government, agitation against government in the hands of Governor and Judges continued. "Xenos," for instance, used a whole page of the *Gazette* demanding redress for grievances.[123] What the grievances were was not made clear. "Baliotarius" was somewhat more specific. He excepted Governor Cass and a few others, but complained of the appointment and actions of a number of the members of the "legislature" and the Supreme Court.[124] In 1822 when Congress was petitioned for second-degree territorial status and an elected legislature, a meeting held in Detroit opposed the step; the people had lived for seventeen years under the government of Governor and Judges and were satisfied with it.[125] The *Gazette*, however, favored an elected legislature and limiting the term of Supreme Court judges to four years.[126] When the New York *Commercial Advertiser* in an article on Michigan Territory quoted Judge Woodward as saying that the Territory resembled "an overgrown cow with a thousand exuberant teats," the *Gazette* replied that in view of the fact that Woodward practically constituted two members of the legislature and two of the Supreme Court, she resembled rather "a meagre sucking calf butting hard for that nourishment which its dam refuses to yield; and struggling hard for that growth which will enable it to shift for itself."[127]

Congress by law of March 3, 1823, reorganized the government of Michigan Territory. Legislative power was placed in the Governor and Council, the latter composed of nine men appointed by the President from a group of eighteen elected by the voters. The legislature was given the power to submit to the people at any time the question of establishing a general assembly under the provisions of the Ordinance of 1787. Terms of

---

[122] Woodbridge, who retained his secretaryship, soon resigned as delegate and in 1820 was succeeded by Solomon Sibley. In 1823 the Reverend Gabriel Richard, rector of St. Anne's Catholic Church, became delegate.

[123] *Detroit Gazette,* August 11, 1820.

[124] *Ibid.,* September 8, 1820.

[125] *Ibid.,* November 29, 1822.

[126] *Ibid.*

[127] *Ibid.,* December 27. 1822.

the Judges were limited to four years, and under the new arrangement which was to go into effect February 1, 1824, Judge Woodward, around whom so much trouble had centered, was not reappointed. On February 5, 1825, Congress authorized the Governor and Council to divide the Territory into townships and provide for the election of township officers—also all county officers with representative functions. This excluded sheriffs, clerks, and judges. Governor Cass, however, in his desire to encourage representative government, stated that he would appoint to these offices also, whomever the people might elect.

Although the presidential election of 1824–25 was followed by the Detroit press, it was the election of a territorial delegate in 1825 which generated more heat. The candidates were Major John Biddle, Father Gabriel Richard, and Austin E. Wing. All sorts of charges, including fraud, were hurled. Religion, the French question, and the citizenship of Father Richard all were involved. There was complaint and quibbling about the Judges, the treasurer, the "Juntocrats," and everything else. The *Gazette* believed that party strife was as rife in Michigan Territory as anywhere in the Union, and suggested it was the rather too imperious tone of the territorial government which had aroused the warm spirit of republicanism.[128]

Even though Major Biddle apparently received the most votes, the canvassing board, composed of the secretary, the treasurer, and attorney general (Woodbridge, Abbott, and Larned), certified Mr. Wing as duly elected.[129] The Council appointed a committee to investigate, but it accomplished nothing. The House of Representatives' committee on elections made no effort to

---

[128] *Ibid.,* October 4, 1825.

[129] One point at issue was the forty-nine votes cast for Biddle at Sault Ste. Marie, some of them by Indians, half-breeds, and discharged soldiers who were either not residents for a year or had not paid county or territorial taxes. These were rejected by the canvassing board, but thirty-eight of them were restored by the House of Representatives' committee on elections. Father Gabriel Richard had not claimed a plurality, but he would have had one except for the intimidation of Detroit voters by constables friendly to his opponents. The canvassing board listed the results as Wing 728, Richard 724, and Biddle 689. The committee on elections made the final count Wing 725, Richard 722, Biddle 714. Testimony may be found in *A Report of the Proceedings in relation to the Contested Election for Delegate to the Nineteenth Congress from the Territory of Michigan . . .* (Detroit, 1825). This report is reproduced in Carter (ed.), *Territorial Papers,* XI, 711–69. See also Report of Committee on Elections, February 13, 1826, in U. S. *House Reports,* 19 Congress, 1 session, No. 69. The election is summarized in Sister M. Rosalita, "A Page from Pioneer Politics," in *Michigan History Magazine,* XXIII (1939), 377–90.

examine the causes which "prevented a candidate from getting a sufficient number of votes to give him a seat" but did attempt to determine who had "the greatest number of legal votes actually given at the election." During the next two years the *Gazette* was strongly anti-Wing and anti-Woodbridge, while the Wing following seems to have had a connection with the *Herald* and the Monroe *Michigan Sentinel.* Just what relation the bitter personal feeling stirred up in this election had with the later development of political parties in Michigan is not clear. No party alignment was visible.

Political organization and election machinery in the period of personal politics were relatively simple. Candidates for state and national office were usually announced or "nominated" by friendly newspapers. This might be by way of editorials, communications of "Many Voters," or even the candidates' own communication. Candidates for local offices might announce at a logrolling, muster, or to a number of voters who might be standing around the county town on court day. Or a candidate's "friends" might call a "mass meeting"—sometimes a dozen or fewer attended—to launch the candidacy of their man.[130] The results of these meetings were always publicized in the nearest friendly newspaper. With the county conventions of 1824 and the "State Convention" in Indiana of that year, the convention system was well on its way in. Until the middle 1830's, however, most voters reserved the democratic right to run for any office, any time, regardless of whoever else might be running.

Important politicians found the friendship or control of one or more newspapers almost a necessity. Frequently factions within the same political group had their rival newspapers. Although the isolated settler probably made his first contacts with politics and got his first lessons in citizenship in a new community by way of the assessor, fence viewer, road commissioner, or militia captain who came to his cabin in the clearing, it was not long before he was attending court and reading, or hearing read, a newspaper. The Americans' addiction to newspaper reading as well as "seegars" and tobacco chewing was generally noted by European travelers. The fact that his papers were filled

---

[130] A "mass meeting" was held in Gallatin County, Illinois, in 1824 to select a candidate for presidential elector.

largely with politics and political news was owing partly, it is true, to other causes, but largely to the readers' demand for exactly that.[131]

Campaigning on the whole required energy, persistence, and a certain amount of egotism, or at least lack of modesty, rather than money. Professional office seekers were ever at it. Although the abstract rules of the game required that the call come from the people, adept politicians could detect the call at a distance. Seasoned campaigners, such as Jonathan Jennings, could participate in dozens of logrollings or cabin raisings in a season— by stopping to inquire the way to the next important town whither he was going on business. The real business lay on the way. Candidates had to be careful about their dress, speech, and methods of travel, lest they create the idea that they were "stuck-uppity."[132] Sometimes the following stratagem was resorted to: A candidate would ride to the top of a rise within distant view of a farmer, yell the name of his opponent by way of identification, state that it was pretty muddy down there in the bottom, but ask the good man to vote for him come election. Then he would disappear, hide his horse, and come wading in in person. After stripping a few tobacco leaves, shucking a few shocks, or taking a turn at the plow "just to keep his hand in," he would give his own name and ask the voter to help him out at the polls if he felt like it. Very often, considering the circumstances, the farmer did.

At country sales, on court days at county-seat towns, at militia musters, at protracted meetings even, the politician was much in evidence; once the business in hand was disposed of, the serious business of the day, politics, was taken up.

They [the people] came by dozens from all parts, and on every road, riding on their ponies, which they hitched up or tied to the fences, trees, and bushes. . . . The candidates came also, and addressed the people from wagons, benches, old logs, or stumps newly cut. . . . The stump speeches being over, then commenced the drinking of liquor, and long before night a large portion of the voters would be drunk and staggering about town, cursing, swearing, hallooing, yelling, huzzaing for their favorite candidates, throwing their arms up and around, threatening to fight, and fighting.[133]

[131] For newspapers see Chapter XV.
[132] See Chapter VI, 361–62.
[133] Ford, *History of Illinois*, 104–5.

Candidates frequently made available free liquor at the leading groceries for several weeks before the election; there was
no better advance poll than the respective emptiness of the strategically located whiskey barrels of the rival aspirants for office.
This system was not infallible, however, as there were some
voters so perverse as to prefer to weaken a political enemy by
drinking up all of his "likker." Even preachers, when they got
into politics, sometimes conformed to the rules of the game.

Mr. Kinney was one of the old sort of Baptist preachers; his morality was
not of that pinched up kind, which prevented him from using all the common arts of a candidate for office. It was said that he went forth electioneering with a Bible in one pocket and a bottle of whiskey in the other;
and thus armed with "the sword of the Lord and the spirit" he could preach
to one set of men and drink with another, and thus make himself agreeable
to all.[134]

Viewing the political stump meetings or barbecues of the West
with their attendant drinking and gambling, a visitor from the
land of steady habits said:

All this strikes a stranger, and especially one from New England, as not
only peculiar but full of all moral evil, and leads to the hasty conclusion
that the purity, not only of elections but of personal virtue, must be sadly
affected thereby. . . . There can be no doubt but that these political gatherings are productive of much evil in the gross, but it must be remembered
that that which strikes us as the most *prominent* evil attending them, is not
and cannot be considered as attached—part or parcel—to the political institutions of the west. Gamblers and blacklegs and bullies there are every
where, and they are ever on the alert for a gathering—no matter whether
it be a horse-race at the south, a barbecue at the west, or a militia-muster
or a camp meeting at the east. Gambling and dissipation are not the *results,*
they are but excrescences which attach themselves to any large body from
which they can most readily draw their nutriment: and they ought no
more to be called the legitimate offspring of a political caucus here, than
of a camp-meeting in New England. Each is the *occasion,* merely, of the
evil, and ought no more to be denounced therefor, than the establishment
of an extensive, commercial city for the licentiousness which it is the occasion of concentrating within its walls.[135]

The political meetings to which these "excrescences" attached
themselves were necessary in a region in which the citizen could
not keep informed on "his country's weal or woe" and had "no

[134] Ford, *History of Illinois,* 104.
[135] A. D. Jones, *Illinois and the West,* 79, 81–82.

mode of informing himself but by mounting his horse and riding ten, twenty, and even fifty miles to a post-office or a political gathering." The same writer continued:

It seems to me to be exceedingly proper that candidates for office should be permitted to speak for themselves. Assailed as they are sure to be on every hand with abuse, vilification and misrepresentation, there seems to be a fitness in appealing directly to the understandings and hearts of those whose interests are confided to their hands. Here they can meet their accusers face to face, and forever silence, by a frank avowal of their views and intended course ot conduct, the cabal which their opponents have raised. Be it remembered that these gatherings are composed of men of all political creeds, who, with their respective candidates have come up hither to try their strength in fair expository, argumentative combat. It does seem to me that the "dear people" would be far more likely to come at truth and think for themselves by thus hearing both sides of the question than, as with us, by poring exclusively over a print devoted to but one interest, and that there would be far less danger that men would prevail over principles. . . . And on the whole, I am led to think that the general principles involved in these political caucuses are sound and may be safely adopted in all parts of our country. They have already undergone essential changes, and the advanced state of refinement which is rapidly approaching will so modify them that most of what is objectionable will be removed. They will then become what now they profess to be, merely meetings for political purposes. And what better opportunity could be afforded for a fair discussion of any great national or sectional question? What better calculated to act as a moral check upon the licentiousness of a party press? What fairer chance for the people to arrive at the real political views of the men who claim their suffrages, and to ascertain the opinions and doings of those of opposite opinions?[136]

Although a successful politician stated that "stump speaking was just coming in fashion" in 1826,[137] political speeches, whether from a stump or elsewhere, were certainly not invented at this late date. The pioneer speaker's ability to engage in oratorical gouging contests was too well appreciated not to have been earlier cultivated. Sometimes he meant what he said; often it was merely a performance. Newspaper communications—the modern "voice-of-the-people" column—were frequently long, weighty, and serious. At times political treatises were serialized in this

[136] *Ibid.*, 84–85, 86–87.
[137] O. H. Smith, *Early Indiana Trials and Sketches,* 80. The Columbus *Ohio State Journal,* October 12, 1826, said: "We have always been free in Ohio from the husting speeches of England, or the *stump* speeches of Indiana and Kentucky, which are nothing more than a mass of egotism and empty declamation."

form and signed with a classic signature or just "Plain Citizen." Other letters were brief and to the point, "no holts barred" and devil take the hindmost. Political pamphlets and broadsides were run off by the local printer and circulated, but these were more numerous on national than local issues. They diminished in importance as newspapers began to run special campaign issues devoted almost exclusively to politics.

There was no regular procedure for raising money for electioneering purposes. Some candidates were capable of financing their own campaigns; others took contributions from friends, possibly with the understanding that if not successful, the "loans" would not be repaid. Or an editor might pay "in kind" and be rewarded with the public printing or other perquisites when his man was elected.

Women, of course, were denied the direct pleasures of politics as well as sports. No doubt they played their parts behind the scenes. Now and then one spoke her mind in print. In 1820 at Edwardsville, Illinois, when one Squire Eberman stated that his opponent, a Mr. M'Collum, intended to remove to Vandalia, the latter's wife took up the cudgels. She announced "To the Public": "I think it would be degrading my husband to put him on a par with a man that would paper fight a woman; as I think myself equal in intellect with Squire E. and far superior in soul for I would not make a false statement against him or any other person."[138]

Election days were days of excitement; until 1828 the local elections were more so than the national. The story was told of a Frenchman's reaction to western elections.

"Sare," said he, "I come to *Amerique* to see von *grande nation* enjoy de *liberté*. I look for find all broder, all vise. In my *imagination* I see von people dat work to make the whole happy, dat chose de vise men and de good men for ruler, and in de choice, act togeder like de friend. Mais, parbleu! I find de same fight of dose in de power, and dose out of de power. I find de bribe, de quarrel, de hard word. I go to de *hotel*, and *ma foi*, dey say, ha! you Jaqueson or Clay? I get in de stage, and dey say 'gain, you sare, you Jaqueson or Clay? Every-where dey vorry me to piece. Ah, Monsieur! you have von *grande countrie*, you have de people *avec beaucoup de force*, but vid all de liberti, I see much dat vould make me *miserable*. I shall go back to France, sare, dere we have von *revolution*, and all is

[138] *Edwardsville Spectator*, August 22, 1820.

still again; here, it seems to me, *revolution* all de time. I shall go back to France, sare, *tout a pres.*"[139]

Even before the Jackson-Clay battles Cincinnati's satiric poet-merchant, Thomas Peirce, had described election day:

> The smiling morning of the day of races
>   To sleepless candidates arrived at last;
> Abusive placards shone from public places,
>   And pamphlets, handbills, cards, were flying fast;
> Where'er you moved, a crowd with anxious faces
>   And rapid steps, ran o'er you as you past:
> All, all alike were busy—farmers, rogues,
>   Attornies, gamblers, bards, and demagogues.
>
> . . . .
>
> Sot, Swindler, office-hunter, villain, rogue,
>   Were words in general use among the rabble,
> And when applied to either demagogue
>   Named in the ticket, brought about a squabble;
> And this ere long became so much in vogue
>   Few could be found who in it did not dabble;
> And many a veteran, you may well suppose,
>   Came off with ebon eyes and crimson nose.
>
> From morn till evening—nay, throughout the night
>   Each grog-shop, tippling-house, contained a crowd
> Of patriots, full of whisky and of fight,
>   On themes politic ever warm and loud;
> And though unlike in sentiment, all right,
>   And of the liberty of drinking proud;
> For more than either speaking, writing, thinking,
>   They held the glorious privilege of drinking.[140]
>
> . . . .

This picture, while not exceptional, was of course not the whole picture. While the minority in any community made rough and loud demonstrations, thousands of citizens voted quietly and decently. This fact was neither news nor subject for caricature. Voters were reminded in prose and poetry of the responsibility of the franchise. "The Poor Voter's Song" illustrates the patriotic appeal:

[139] Quoted in William H. Venable, *Beginnings of Literary Culture in the Ohio Valley* . . . (Cincinnati, 1891), 239–40.
[140] "Billy Moody," Chapter XXIX, in Cincinnati *National Republican*, July 15, 1823.

They knew that I was poor,
  And they thought that I was base,
And would readily endure
  To be covered with disgrace;
They judged me of their tribe,
  Who on dirty mammon dote,
So they offered me a bribe
  For my vote, boys, vote!
    Oh shame upon my betters,
      Who would my conscience buy!
    But shall I wear their fetters?
      ˉNot I, indeed, not I!

My vote? It is not mine
  To do with as I will;
To cast, like pearls to swine,
  To these wallowers in ill.
It is my country's due,
  And I'll give it while I can
To the honest and the true,
  Like a man, boys, man!
    Oh shame, &c.

No, no, I'll hold my vote
  As a treasure and a trust;
My dishonor none shall quote
  When I'm mingling with the dust,
And my children, when I'm gone,
  Shall be strengthened by the thought,
That their father was not one
  To be bought, boys, bought!
    Oh shame, &c.[141]

[141] The *Marshall* (Mich.) *Statesman,* September 12, 1839.

X

The North Settles, 1825–1840
Michigan and Wisconsin Territory

It is the peculiar region for the young swarms of the northern hives
to take up their lodgements in; and from capital and industry which
they will bring along with them, it will indeed, be the land where
milk and honey shall abound.

Vandalia *Illinois Intelligencer,* October 7, 1825

THE hard times of 1819 to 1824 considerably slowed,
but did not stop, westward emigration. About five years
sufficed to write off or liquidate the bulk of the economic incidence of inflation and speculation. Belts had been tightened, debts
had been paid or forgotten, a little money had been saved. Soon
forgotten by most people were the disastrous results of the attempted magic of the "halcyon days." Confidence restored, it
became ebullient and rampant. The West, where fortunes were
to be made, was still there, its appeal never more certain. A bigger western boom was in the making; a bigger depression at
its end.

By 1825 "Emigration [was again] powerful to the West."[1]
Lake Erie boats were taxed to handle the three hundred persons
who sought to go West weekly, largely to Ohio and Michigan.
Emigration was booming, said the *Detroit Gazette*[2] which estimated that three thousand had landed from boats before the end
of June; how many by other means none could know. "Michigan
is settling rapidly," said the *Ohio State Journal.* "In a short time
her population will entitle her to a marriage portion."[3] In May,
1829, about eleven hundred landed at Detroit in eleven days, and
by the middle of May, 1831, two thousand had arrived.[4] Busi-

---

[1] A "Northern New York Paper," quoted in *Liberty Hall and Cincinnati Gazette,*
June 21, 1825.

[2] June 28, 1825. Only one steamboat was operating in 1825 but several were in
use in 1826. Many of the emigrants came on sailing vessels.

[3] September 7, 1826.

[4] *Detroit Gazette,* May 28, 1829, May 18, June 15, 1831. The Detroit *North-
Western Journal,* January 13, 1830, stated that five thousand persons had come in
the preceding year.

ness was bustling, houses in demand. By July observers gave up counting. Yet two years later, "The cry is, still—they come."[5] The newcomers, crowded and jostled, were eager to escape from the stacks of bedding, furniture, pots, tools, and even musical instruments amidst which they had slept as best they could; "eager to touch the soil, on which they intend to plant their future fortunes, with undoubting trust of quick and abundant returns. . . . One may almost imagine he sees the limbs of this young territory expand daily, nay hourly; its sinews acquiring new strength, and its hardihood, giving promise that it will, ere long, attain a giant stature."[6]

Nor was everyone going to the northern parts. Scores of movers passed through Vandalia in the autumn of 1825 headed for the Sangamon country and other "upper parts of the state."[7] "All that Illinois wants to make her one of the most desirable parts of the Union, is an enterprising, industrious population, to unfold and develop its latent resources. . . ." Still faster they came four years later.[8] A Charleston, Virginia, paper reported that during September, 1829, no less than eight thousand emigrants, mostly from lower Virginia and South Carolina, went through on their way to Indiana, Illinois, and Michigan.[9] And from Centerville, Indiana, came the report that the numbers passing through Wayne County would appear incredible if not actually seen. Many emigrants were equipped with wagons and livestock; others were poor. "We will occasionally see a mother, and some two or three half-naked children, with a bag of old plunder, mounted on a limping, lantern-ribbed pony, and the father, with five or six other little barefooted urchins walking alongside."[10]

Indianapolis, which in 1827 saw a number of families, largely from Kentucky, heading for the Wabash country, in 1830 reported that the "tide . . . is still flowing mightily on."[11] Some

[5] *Detroit Journal,* May 14, 1833.
[6] *Detroit Courier,* quoted in Cincinnati *Farmer's Reporter and United States Agriculturist,* August, 1831, p. 51.
[7] Vandalia *Illinois Intelligencer,* October 7, 28, 1825.
[8] *Ibid.,* October 31, 1829.
[9] *Detroit Gazette,* December 3, 1829.
[10] *Centerville Western Times* quoted in *Cincinnati Daily Gazette,* October 20, 1829.
[11] Indianapolis *Indiana Journal,* November 20, 1827 (quoting the *Saturday Evening Chronicle*), September 8, 1830; *Indianapolis Gazette,* October 30, 1827.

observers even surmised that the western states might eventually contain forty million people.[12]

Impressive as are the many such notices and the sheer statistics of population increase, they are relatively uninteresting in comparison to the manifestations of western exuberance over it all. Puffing the West was as unavoidable as the ague in Michigan. Everyone indulged: editors, speculators, squatters, even preachers. Local jealousies there were in plenty, but by and large it was the West against the whole wide world.[13]

Here the genial sun which warms the prolific earth, and occasions it to yield, by your industry, an abundant supply of all the substantials of life, will not be less kind to you and your companions. Its genial rays will strengthen and keep alive the ardor of your affections, and crown your labors with a comfortable old age, a numerous progeny to bless your memories, and be the solace of your declining years.[14]

Since the beginning of the present century, the tide of emigration has silently poured its thousands into the bosom of the wilderness. The forest has disappeared under the blows of the sturdy backwoodsman, and gay villages and tilled fields have arose on every side to break the long chain of savage life, and to establish in its place the social and peaceful habits of civilization.[15]

Caleb Atwater, writing of the Illinois country, thought that infinite wisdom and goodness had never on earth created so fine a country. No man worth the name could do other than believe that it would be used and improved by numberless millions of men. "No poor man in the Eastern states, who has feet and legs, and can use them has any excuse for remaining poor where he is, a day or even an hour."[16]

And a committee of the Indiana legislature, getting ready to welcome Lafayette, wrote:

[12] Columbus *Ohio State Journal*, August 17, 1827.

[13] When the *Detroit Gazette* and the Detroit *Michigan Herald* dilated on the advantages of Michigan—its salubrious climate, the clearness of the atmosphere, the beauty and fertility of the land, and referred incidentally to Cleveland's poor harbor and unhealthful situation, Ohio papers rose to the defense. The *Sandusky Clarion* (October 29, 1825) said thirteen inches of snow fell on the level along the St. Clair River. The *Cleaveland Herald* (November 11) hit back with a double-column broadside, yet said it felt no jealousy towards Michigan Territory.

[14] Vandalia *Illinois Intelligencer*, October 7, 1825.

[15] Columbus *Ohio State Journal*, August 17, 1827.

[16] Springfield *Sangamo Journal*, September 8, 1832, quoting Atwater's Journal covering his service as commissioner to treat with the Indians.

On the west of the Alleghany mountains, our illustrious guest, will behold extensive communities of freemen, which within the period of his own recollection, have been substituted for the trackless wilderness. Where, forty years ago, primeval barbarism held undisputed sway over man and nature; civilization, liberty and law, wield the mild sceptre of equal rights, it is here that our illustrious friend will find his name, his services, and we trust, his principles flourishing in perennial verdure. Here too, may he enjoy the exulting prospect of seeing them, in the language of a favorite son of the west, "transmitted with unabated vigor down the tide of time, to the countless millions of posterity!"[17]

Ohio in 1825 had a population of almost 800,000 people. It had gained approximately three quarters of a million in twenty-five years. Of its present eighty-eight counties, seventy-three were laid off, although seven of these in the northwestern corner of the state were not yet organized. There remained 7,630,000 acres of public land.[18] More than a half million acres of forfeited and relinquished lands had come back on the market. Particularly in the Ohio Company purchase, in the United States military district, around Zanesville, and in the Steubenville and Chillicothe land-office districts, were many parcels available.[19] Excepting for a few minor reservations the land within the state had been cleared of Indian title by 1818.[20] By 1825 only 2,350 Indians remained in the state, and they claimed title to only 409,000 acres of land.[21]

In the older settled portions of the state Marietta had declined from its earlier importance. Situated where the river made one of its noblest sweeps and the Muskingum came winding down "among the wood crowned hills to join the happy waters of the Ohio," its population showed "little energy and less property to add beauty or grandeur to the place." Steubenville was known for its woolen mills and was to become the center of carriage and stagecoach manufacturing. By 1830 Zanesville was an important manufacturing town; its population of three thousand made it second only to Cincinnati. Portsmouth at the southern

[17] Joint resolution relative to Major General Lafayette's intended visit to the West, in *Laws of Indiana*, 1824–25, p. 109.
[18] Columbus *Ohio State Journal*, August 14, 1827.
[19] *Western Herald and Steubenville Gazette*, January 24, 1824; *Ohio State Journal*, January 11, 1827.
[20] See Chapter III, and map, I, 111.
[21] Out of a total of 24,810,246 acres, of which in 1829, 4,984,000 acres still remained unsold. *Hamilton Intelligencer*, June 3, 1825; May 12, 1829.

end of the Ohio Canal was a village of "rising a thousand people." To the north lay the fertile valley of the Scioto and the towns of Chillicothe, Circleville, and Columbus. The last in the dozen years of its existence had attained a population of 1,500. High Street, with its broad, brick-paved sidewalks and two blocks of two- and three-story business buildings, wagons, horses, and stages, presented a busy appearance. Although it was the state capital, the public buildings were not particularly distinctive.

Cincinnati was outstanding, not only in the state but in the entire West. From a town of about 2,300 in 1810 it had grown to a bustling city of 16,230 in 1826. Of this increase 4,000 had come within the short period since 1824. The legislature in 1825 granted the city a new charter which gave liberal powers to the council.[22] Besides the numerous business houses, banks, hotels, and churches, Cincinnati had a university, museum, theater, athenaeum, bazaar, and hospital. The better private homes were two- and three-story brick or stone buildings. By 1826 some five hundred families were supplied with water from the city reservoir which was filled from the river by a steam-driven pump. The newspapers advertised the latest in fashions from London and New York, furs from the Pacific, sweetmeats from Havana, and oysters from Philadelphia. So striking was the contrast with any other city in the West that travelers were inclined to be very enthusiastic about Cincinnati.[23]

[22] Published in *Liberty Hall and Cincinnati Gazette,* January 31, 1826. The editor thought that the new charter was too liberal in spots: for example it did not confine common beggars and prostitutes to the streets but permitted them to pursue prospective patrons to their homes.

[23] Of Cincinnati in 1832 one wrote: "Cincinnati was never mentioned in America without the addition of such surnames as 'The Wonderful,' 'The Western Queen, &c. Flattering epithets of this kind are generally exaggerated; . . . but in this instance they were justified." Carl D. Arfwedson, *The United States and Canada, in 1832, 1833, and 1834* (2 volumes. London, 1834), II, 126. Corroborating this view was Ebenezer M. Chamberlain: "The city of Cincinnati, in its growth, the acquirements of wealth, eminence, and fame—political, commercial and literary, may doubtless, for an inland city, defy the world for a parallel. Its situation is handsome and salubrious; the surrounding country almost unsurpassed for fertility. From its canals and its turnpikes are poured treasures in upon her. The roads are thronged with teams from the interior of Ohio and Indiana. Her canal boats are laden with goods and produce, to and from the same regions, and the majestic Ohio swarms with steam-boats bringing the tributes from every region to this emporium of the west." "Journal of Ebenezer Mattoon Chamberlain 1832–5," edited by Louise Fogle, in *Indiana Magazine of History,* XV (1919), 239. Even Mrs. Basil Hall, who in almost nine thousand miles of travel in the United States, 1827–28, had seen practically nothing to admire, had to admit, "Cincinnati is certainly an astonishing place." *The Aristocratic Journey,* 285.

A few miles to the north was Hamilton with a population of several hundred and a good newspaper. Farther north on the Miami lay Dayton, a beautiful little town of some 1,500 people, which was already showing signs of industry.[24] East from the river, but soon to be on the main line of traffic of the National Road, was Springfield. Despite the fact that the town was surrounded by timbered lands, many of the houses were of brick, and on Sundays well-dressed people in the city rode to church in carts or on horseback.[25]

On the Western Reserve the village of Cleveland was beginning to grow. Forty new houses were begun in the early months of 1826, but it was not thought that it would ever be necessary to pave the streets or sidewalks.[26] By 1830 an increasing number of emigrants were landing on their way to the interior, but it was not until after the completion of the Ohio Canal in 1832 that Cleveland began to have city aspirations. In the middle 1830's it became a lively trading and shipping port, and by 1840 had more than six thousand inhabitants. Painesville, on the main road from Buffalo to Detroit, and Fairport Harbor, which offered a better landing for the lake boats than Cleveland, were towns of some importance. The towns in this region with their "commons," broad streets, and white-belfried churches presented an appearance which reminded the observer more of New England than of the West.[27] Off the beaten trails on the Reserve lay the dense timber which was just being penetrated by the settlers. To the west at the entrance of Sandusky Bay was Portland or Sandusky City,[28] with about five hundred inhabitants. Prior to the completion of the Ohio Canal in 1832 this port was often used by those going east by way of Lake Erie.

New towns were being prospected at various points in the state. Akron was located at the portage summit of the Ohio

[24] By 1828 Dayton had 5 taverns, 16 dry-goods stores, 3 millwrights, 3 tan yards, 2 breweries, 2 sickle factories, four hat factories, 9 shoeshops, 4 chairmakers, 5 blacksmiths, 4 watchmakers, 2 tobacco factories, and 1 gunsmith. *Cincinnati Daily Gazette,* January 26, 1829.

[25] Karl Bernhard, Duke of Saxe-Weimar-Eisenach, *Travels Through North America, During the Years 1825 and 1826* (2 volumes. Philadelphia, 1828), II 144.

[26] *Cleaveland Herald,* April 21, 1826.

[27] The advantages of the Reserve and the expected favorable effects of the Ohio Canal on settlement and commerce were well presented in the Ravenna *Western Courier,* May 28, 1825.

[28] Still known by the former name as late as the early 1830's. Sandusky lay within the Firelands rather than the Western Reserve proper.

Canal in the autumn of 1825; within ten years it was to become a local manufacturing center of about 1,500 population. The same year lots were advertised for the town of Hebron, to be located where the Ohio Canal was expected to intersect the National Road.[29] But it was the northwestern quarter of the state, cleared by the Indian treaty of 1818, which was receiving the most attention.[30] An attempt to found a town at the mouth of the Maumee in 1816 had proved abortive, but in 1832 Vistula was an incipient town in the shanty stage. Its rival, four miles upstream, was Port Lawrence.[31] Soon the name of Toledo took over, and the first issue of the *Toledo Gazette*, August 14, 1834, set forth the advantages of the location, cheapness of lots, and the prospects of a railroad.

In 1830 Ohio's population was 937,000. Except for the sparsely settled northwestern quarter, and some concentration in the Miami, Scioto, and Muskingum valleys, it was fairly evenly distributed.

In Indiana the crescent of settlements along the Whitewater, Ohio, and Wabash rivers, so distinct in 1820, was not only filling in but expanding northward into the New Purchase (acquired by treaty in 1818) and the Wabash country. The older river towns of Lawrenceburg, Madison, Jeffersonville, New Albany, Leavenworth, Rockport, Mount Vernon, and Vincennes were being augmented by others. The line of settlements stretched west and north from New Albany along the line of the Wea trail to Paoli, Bedford, and Bloomington, reached Greencastle in 1820, and by 1824 was penetrating the big flat woods as far as Sugar Creek. Here it merged with the push of settlers from the Nashville region which had advanced through Henderson, Kentucky, up the Evansville-Vincennes road, and along the old Piankashaw trail by way of Carlisle, Terre Haute, Rockville, Covington, and Attica. At this point in 1824 Crawfordsville was laid out.

Along the eastern side of the state the Whitewater Valley

[29] *Liberty Hall and Cincinnati Gazette,* November 25, 1825.

[30] For detailed description of the merits of this area see the two-column write-up by S. Y. Bayard and editorial comment in Columbus *Ohio State Journal,* May 21, 1829.

[31] Cincinnati speculators with sites on the opposite sides of the river had combined as the Port Lawrence Company, then lost their lands. When they recovered a part of them, it was the Toledo site.

settlements which had reached Richmond in 1816 were blending with the emigration which came by way of the National Road. In 1825 the tide of emigrants surpassed anything previously known. The main street of Richmond was crowded with movers headed west and north.[32] Trading posts and squatters stretched on to the Upper White River area. Land entries were made in this region in the early 1820's, and Delaware County with its seat at Munseytown was established in 1827. William Conner, who had established a trading post on White River in 1802, with Josiah F. Polk platted a town near by in 1823 and called it Noblesville.[33]

In 1821 the population of the whole New Purchase[34] was estimated at 1,300 people, whereas, by 1827 Indianapolis alone had a thousand inhabitants, with 25 brick, 60 frame, and 80 hewn-log houses, a courthouse, a jail, and Baptist, Methodist, and Presbyterian meetinghouses. By the latter date 21 counties had been organized in the Purchase and the population was 55,000.[35]

Along the trace from the Upper Whitewater Valley across to Andersontown, down the White River to Strawtown, thence across to the Wabash by the wilderness road came Sandford Cox and his family in 1824. The land office was moved from Terre Haute to Crawfordsville in 1823. "The land sales commenced here to-day, and the town is full of strangers. The eastern and southern portions of the State are strongly represented, as well as Ohio, Kentucky, Tennessee, and Pennsylvania. There is but little bidding against each other. The settlers, or 'squatters,' as they are called by speculators, have arranged matters among themselves to their general satisfaction," wrote Mr. Cox on December 24, 1824.[36] Soon the Crawfordsville Land Office took first rank for sales in the United States, a position formerly held by the Vincennes, Jeffersonville, and Brookville offices. Through Indianapolis from the east and Bloomington from the south, daily came throngs on their way to the Wabash country.[37]

[32] Richmond *Public Leger*, October 22, 1825.
[33] Charles N. Thompson, *Sons of the Wilderness. John and William Conner* (*Indiana Historical Society Publications*, XII, Indianapolis, 1937), 135.
[34] See map, I, 111.
[35] Indianapolis *Indiana Journal*, February 20, 1827; Vincennes *Western Sun and General Advertiser*, November 10, 1827.
[36] Cox, *Recollections of the Early Settlement of the Wabash Valley*, 17.
[37] Indianapolis *Indiana Journal*, October 11, 1825; Bloomington *Indiana Gazette*, October, 1825.

"For a week our town has scarce been clear of immigrant wagons," wrote the editor of the *Indiana Gazette*.[38] Centerville reported two hundred families passing through during September and October, 1827, for the Wabash country.

Early in 1826 the site of Lafayette was surveyed by an enterprising Crawfordsville citizen, and when Tippecanoe County was organized, the village was made the county seat. In spite of ample promotional publicity, the town did not grow with a great flourish (in 1829 it claimed 29 cabins and 30 frame houses and four years later 20 "places of business"),[39] and it was sometimes referred to by its jealous neighbors to the south as "Lay flat" or "Laugh at."

The small tract of land around Fort Wayne had been cleared of Indian title by the Treaty of Greenville in 1795, and surveyed in 1803. Land sales began at the Fort Wayne office in 1823. The post was already surrounded with traders and squatters. South Bend, which lay within the tract ceded at Chicago in 1821, was a mere trading-post annex to Fort Wayne. The narrow strip of land which lay north of the Wabash and east of the Tippecanoe was not ceded by the Potawatomi until 1826. Two years later John Tipton, one of the treaty commissioners, brought his Fort Wayne Indian agency to the mouth of Eel River, on the site of Logansport, which was platted that same year.

The "Wabash country" at this time included the whole region from the middle of the state north to Lake Michigan. Its southern reaches were timbered with hardwoods interspersed with prairies. Of the Wabash Valley proper a contemporary wrote:

The traveller who passes through this most productive valley, meets continually with much calculated to excite his admiration. For miles, his course frequently meanders along the borders of some gently rolling prairie, whose surface, as far as the eye can reach, seems gemmed with flowers of all varieties, the brilliancy of whose coloring baffles all description. Again, his path, more open than before, will lead him through these beautiful *parterres* of nature, and along the banks of many a sweet stream, that winds round and round in almost innumerable convolutions, as if flowing

[38] October 30, 1827.
[39] Centerville *Western Times* in *Hamilton* (Ohio) *Intelligencer*, March 17, 1829. The site was purchased by William Digby who laid off 140 lots, then, reserving ferry rights and twenty acres adjoining, he sold out to Samuel Sargeant. Sargeant soon sold forty lots to Crawfordsville businessmen.

with reluctance to pour out its treasures on the waters of the Wabash. Again, leaving this enchanting region, he journeys amid the deep solitudes of a western forest, whose silence is broken only at intervals by the bounding footstep of the deer, or the sharp crack of the rifle.[40]

But in this instance the praise of the land agent and speculator was modest in comparison with that of ordinary folks. Settlers "spoke in most enthusiastic terms of the Wea, Wild Cat, and Shawnee prairies and declared that 'the Wea plain was the prettiest place this side of heaven,' a fact which has never been disputed by anyone who ever saw it."[41] And the preacher wondered "why a merciful providence kept this country hid from civilized man, or why he did not create an especially gifted race for its occupation."[42] The nature of the land offered combinations of prairie and timber in single holdings, in any proportions desired. Those interested argued that it cost $12 per acre to clear timbered land and about half as much to put prairie land under cultivation. They did not emphasize the difficulty of plowing the prairie sod, but were right about its being able to grow grass without plowing. The land was particularly well adapted to stock raising. Hay was abundant and some thought the region as well adapted to the sugar beet as France. As for fencing, ditches and hedges were cheaper than rails.[43]

Farther north lay poorly drained lands and swamps. When E. P. Kendricks surveyed the northern Indiana boundary in 1827, he described the lake shore as a "continued chain of hills formed of beautiful white sand, in most places very high, and little or no vegetation. Back of these sand hills is generally swamp and marsh, therefore there are but few places that the Lake can be approached without difficulty. No harbors or islands to be seen."

Difficulty of access was the explanation of the relatively late discovery of the wonders of the Wabash country. The Upper Wabash furnished an uncertain thoroughfare, and roads from

[40] Ellsworth, *Valley of the Upper Wabash,* 1-2. In addition to the work of Ellsworth and Cox, Solon Robinson wrote from firsthand experience of the region. For description of the northwest corner of the state, see particularly his letters to the Madison *Republican and Banner,* January 15, and April 30, 1835, in *Solon Robinson, Pioneer and Agriculturist,* I, 51-64.

[41] Cox, *Recollections of the Early Settlement of the Wabash Valley,* 14.

[42] Rev. George Bush to corresponding secretary of the Home Missionary Society. in Bloomington *Indiana Gazette,* April 3, 1827.

[43] Ellsworth, *Valley of the Upper Wabash,* 34-35.

the Ohio were practically nonexistent.[44] The northern entry by way of the Maumee did not become important until after the opening of the Erie Canal, but even then few of those people who came west from Buffalo entered this region.[45] Nevertheless, settlers pushed up as close as possible from the south and east, and newspapers carried numerous notices of the sale of town lots: Andersontown, Knightstown, and Munseytown in 1827; Delphi, 1828; Marion, 1830; Lebanon, South Bend, and even La Porte in 1832.

The Illinois census of 1825, which recorded a population of 72,817, was a disappointment to speculators, politicians, and proud citizens. No doubt agitation of the slavery question and the convention struggle of 1824 had to some extent proved detrimental to settlement.[46]

Settlers had found the Sangamon country in 1819–20. Springfield, called Calhoun 1823–25, dates from 1821, and the crescent of settlements along the Wabash, Ohio, and Mississippi began to widen at its western end to include the areas east of the Lower Illinois. A group of new counties which included Sangamon, Greene, Morgan, and Madison showed the most rapid growth during the next five years.[47] At the same time settlers other than squatters were taking up homes in the Military Tract, the region between the Illinois and Mississippi rivers, which had been granted by the General Government to veterans of the War of

[44] *Ibid.*, 2.

[45] H. L. Ellsworth (father of H. W.) in a letter written in 1837 stated that of five thousand who left Buffalo in one day, not one was headed for the Wabash country. Springfield *Sangamo Journal,* August 5, 1837.

[46] The editor of the Vandalia *Illinois Intelligencer* also blamed the lack of a sound circulating medium in the eastern states which made it difficult for emigrants to sell out at fair prices. Why this should affect Illinois more than neighboring states he did not say. He did not mention chaotic money conditions in Illinois (see Chapter VIII) which, though placing outside speculators at an advantage with reference to state taxes, gave no help at the United States land office. *Ibid.,* December 22, 1825.

[47] *Ibid.* Sale of town lots (with promise of warehouse and ferry) in Naples on the Illinois was announced in 1824. *Ibid.,* January 9, 1824. A traveler in 1827 described the road east from Springfield: "It passes up the Sangamo River on the south side 30 miles, & then traverses a wilderness across the West & East Forks of the Kaskaskia, and two forks of the Embarrass, 70 miles; in which distance there is no trace of inhabitants, except a few deserted wigwams. . . . Should I dwell in this region three or four years, I anticipate seeing the water courses in this wilderness, where now not a single cabin is erected, lined with habitations." E. G. Howe, Paris, Illinois, April 7, 1827, to Absalom Peters. Papers of the American Home Missionary Society, in Charles G. Hammond Library of the Chicago Theological Seminary.

1812. Peoria, in the northeastern part, an old Indian town and later the site of Fort Clark, received its first settlers in 1819; the county was organized in 1825. Pike County near the southern end was set up in 1821, Fulton in 1823, and nine other counties were set off in the military district in 1825–26. Of these, Adams on the Mississippi, with Quincy as its county seat, was the most populous. By 1830 there were about 13,000 people in the district. In the lower counties emigrants from Virginia, Kentucky, Tennessee, and Pennsylvania intersettled with people from Ohio, Indiana, Missouri, and southern Illinois. Since the settlers followed the rivers the interior counties on the military lands were but thinly populated until after 1830.

Just off the tract on the other side of the Illinois was Naples, a small town, and farther up the river was the incipient Pekin, "a beautiful place for a village," wrote one traveler, "but there was not much of one there when we were there."[48] The proprietors were holding out for $100 to $200 for small building lots. Ottawa, platted in 1830—to be the seat of La Salle County—was largely a one-man town. "There was not a house in the town but one, and a little small grocery store that had Indian goods in it. . . . Dr. Walker was the man who constituted the whole town at that time. He was chief burgess, town council, justice, constable, physician, &c., &c. . . . The scenery was splendid; and it appeared that the Maker had designed it to be a place of some importance in time."[49]

Chicago, eighty miles away, according to one visitor, consisted of a hotel, "about a half dozen houses, and the rest Indian wigwams."[50] After the government trading factory had been closed in 1822 and the garrison of Fort Dearborn evacuated the next year, a few families of French-Canadian *voyageurs* and other traders constituted the settlement which by 1825–26 had fourteen taxpayers. Jean Baptiste Beaubien and John Kinzie, employees of the American Fur Company, were the leading citizens during this period. With the return of the soldiers in 1828 and the projection of the Illinois—Lake Michigan Canal the settle-

---

[48] In 1831. *Journal of Travel, Adventures, and Remarks, of Jerry Church* (Harrisburg, Pa., 1845), 22.

[49] *Ibid.*, 23.

[50] *Ibid.*, 25. Other accounts give slightly different inventories. See Andreas, *History of Chicago*, I, 111–14.

ment began to come to life; the town was platted in 1830, and Cook County established early the following year. Population of Chicago at the time was about fifty persons.[51]

Excepting the lead-mining region around the Fever (or Galena) River in the northwestern corner of the state (and reaching over into the Michigan Territory on the north and what was later to be Iowa Territory on the west), northern Illinois received little attention prior to 1830. The history of the lead-mining settlement is both extensive and interesting.[52]

Although the Indians apparently had not used lead, as they had copper, prior to contact with the French, the latter, ever on the lookout for minerals as well as furs, had heard of this rich lead-bearing region by the middle of the seventeeth century in the reports of Radisson and Groseilliers. Father Hennepin showed it on his maps of 1683, and possibly some smelting was conducted here prior to 1700. Le Sueur, Cadillac, de Renault—"director general of the mines of the Royal India Company of Illinois" in 1719—were other French names of importance connected with lead mining. Spasmodic frontier mining was conducted in the early 1720's and again in the 1740's. French miners continued to operate west of the Mississippi after Louisiana was ceded to Spain. Julien Dubuque, a half-breed, in the 1780's discovered lead in the bluffs near the town which bears his name and from lead and furs acquired wealth.

[51] Population table 1829-39 in Bessie Louise Pierce, *A History of Chicago . . .* (2 volumes. New York, 1937, 1940), I, 44.
[52] Among accounts which serve as an introduction to the early history of this region are: Col. Daniel M. Parkison, "Pioneer Life in Wisconsin," in *Wisconsin Historical Collections,* II (1855), 326-64; Meeker, "Early History of the Lead Region of Wisconsin," in *ibid.,* VI, 271-96; Reuben Gold Thwaites, "Notes on Early Lead Mining in the Fever (or Galena) River Region," in *ibid.,* XIII (1895), 271-92; E. B. Washburne, "Lead Region and Lead Trade of the Upper Mississippi," in *Hunt's Merchants' Magazine,* XVIII (1848), 285-93; "Galena and its Lead Mines," in *Harper's,* XXXII (1865-66), 681-96; *History of Jo Daviess County, Illinois* (Chicago, 1878); Willard Rouse Jillson, "Early Mineral Explorations in the Mississippi Valley (1540-1840)," in *Transactions of the Illinois State Historical Society,* 1924, pp. 41-57; William Vipond Pooley, *The Settlement of Illinois from 1830 to 1850* (Madison, Wis., 1908), 461-73; Joseph Schafer, *The Wisconsin Lead Region (Wisconsin Domesday Book, General Studies,* III, Madison, 1932). Among contemporary descriptions of the region probably the best are Caleb Atwater in his *Remarks Made on a Tour to Prairie du Chien; Thence to Washington City, in 1829* (Columbus, Ohio, 1831), also published among other places in the Detroit *North-Western Journal,* February 17, 1830; Major Thomas Forsyth, "Journal," in *Wisconsin Historical Collections,* VI (1869-72), 188-215; and Dr. Moses Meeker's article cited above. R. W. Chandler's map of the Fever River lead country, published in 1829, is reproduced in *Wisconsin Historical Collections,* XI (1888), 400.

The first United States citizen of record in the lead country was George E. Jackson, of Missouri, who in 1811 opened a lead furnace on an island in the Mississippi River. The treaty signed at St. Louis in 1816 gave the Indians (Ottawa, Potawatomi, and Chippewa) right to the land north of a line drawn through the southern tip of Lake Michigan, but reserved a tract not to exceed five leagues square on or near the Wisconsin and Mississippi rivers to include the lead mines. By 1819 several traders and miners were located in the Fever River district. Among them was Col. James Johnson, of Kentucky, brother of the better-known Richard M. Johnson who was later vice-president of the United States. In 1822 when the first government leases were granted in this area, Johnson, among others, secured one. He brought in slaves and soon had a fair-sized smelter operating where Galena was later located. Another lessee was Dr. Moses Meeker who in 1823 brought in some Cincinnati workers. The lessees were not protected in their rights and independent operators rushed in.

By the summer of 1825 about one hundred persons were mining the Fever River diggings, and a year later the number had grown to 453; total population was estimated at 1,000.[53] New mines were opened at Hardscrabble, Council Hill, Vinegar Hill, East Fork, New Diggings, Buncombe, Gratiot's Grove, Shullsburg, Stump Grove, Wiota, Sinsinawa Mound, Platteville, Mineral Point, and elsewhere. In 1827 more than five million pounds of lead were produced in the Fever River district; in 1829 more than thirteen million pounds. Some doubt seems to have existed in the beginning of the boom as to whether the Fever River diggings lay in Illinois or in Michigan Territory. In 1825 when thirty-five settlers were taxed by Michigan Territory, they sent a memorial to Governor Coles, of Illinois, who obtained a decision from the War Department that they were residents of Illinois.[54] Two years later the main settlement, about six miles from the mouth of the Fever River, took the name of Galena. Within another year it was estimated that there were 10,000 people in the lead-mining region.

[53] Report of Lieut. M. Thomas, U.S.A., to Congress, 1826. U. S. *House Executive Documents,* 19 Congress, 2 session, part II, 7. The *Illinois Intelligencer* (cited in *Ohio State Journal,* November 2, 1826) stated that between four and five hundred were at work and the prospects good.

[54] Vandalia *Illinois Intelligencer,* July 1, 1825.

Most of the early miners were native Americans. Those from near-by Illinois often went home for the winter to return in the spring, while others had to "dig in" and "stick it out." This is probably as good an explanation as any for the origin of "Suckers" and "Badgers." By 1830 farming was a more extensive pursuit in the lead region than either mining or smelting. It was estimated that between two and three thousand acres of "promising wheat" were growing;[55] there were at least a half-dozen mills. Caleb Atwater described the country as beautiful and rich, and Hoffman met many men of education and intelligence there.[56] Schoolcraft thought it as valuable for agriculture as for lead mining. In 1831, after a period of dullness, mining prospects were looking better; lead was selling at $14 to $15 a ton, freight to St. Louis was only 50 cents per hundred, and wages were $20 per month.[57]

§

Although the vast central part of Illinois had been cleared of Indian title by 1820 (mainly by the Kickapoo cession of 1819), over 5,000,000 acres of land were still claimed by various tribes in 1825.[58] Licensed Indian traders still operated at Sangamo and Danville. Illinois land sales had reached the depression low in 1822 of about 28,000 acres, but increased to 80,000 in 1826. The threat of impending war with the Winnebago Indians in 1827 not only discouraged further settlement in the northern part of the state but resulted in actual retreat of settlers to Galena and Prairie du Chien, where crowded conditions, cold, and shortage of food brought about considerable suffering.

The encroaching settlements irritated the Indians, especially the Winnebago, whose young warriors were eager to act. The abandonment of Fort Crawford at Prairie du Chien in October, 1821—the garrison was sent to Fort Snelling two hundred miles farther north—gave them encouragement.[59] In 1826 the family

---

[55] Ibid., May 21, October 7, 1831.
[56] Detroit North-Western Journal, February 17, 1830; Writings of Caleb Atwater (Columbus, 1833) 348–52; A Winter in the West, II, 46–47.
[57] Illinois Intelligencer, October 7, 1831.
[58] Mostly Menominee, Kaskaskia, Sac and Fox, Potawatomi, and Chippewa.
[59] Various protests appeared against this decision, which would result in settlers having to abandon their homes. The Detroit Gazette, August 7, 1827, called abandonment of frontier forts "military humbug."

of a French-Canadian settler was killed just above Prairie du Chien on the west side of the Mississippi, and in June of the following year the young chief, Red Bird, and two of his warriors killed a settler and an old soldier. The same day two keelboats of Capt. Allen Lindsey on their way down from St. Peters (Fort Snelling) were attacked. A number of the Indians "lashed their canoes to his boats; but he gave them a quietus in the act, and they bequeathed their canoes to him in return, and became bait for the fish of the Mississippi."[60] Four of Lindsey's men died as a result of this skirmish. When the boats reached Galena, the alarm was spread, miners rushed in for refuge, a committee of safety was appointed, and a company of mounted volunteers was organized with Henry Dodge, a newcomer to the region, as captain.[61]

Governor Ninian Edwards, of Illinois, called out a regiment of mounted volunteers, which under Col. Thomas M. Neale marched to the mining country. Meanwhile, Governor Lewis Cass of Michigan Territory, who had come to Butte des Morts, on the west side of Lake Winnebago, to treat further with the Chippewa and Winnebago, when he learned of the trouble, had hastened to Galena by way of Prairie du Chien, and then to Jefferson Barracks at St. Louis for army aid. He returned by the Illinois–Chicago–Lake Michigan route to Butte des Morts—having covered 1,600 miles in four weeks.

Gen. Henry Atkinson led five hundred regular soldiers from St. Louis to Fort Crawford (Prairie du Chien) which they reached July 29, 1827. Red Bird and his Winnebago warriors retired up the Wisconsin, followed by Atkinson's regulars and Dodge's mounted volunteers. Another force of regulars under Maj. William Whistler moved up the Fox River from Fort Howard (Green Bay) to the Wisconsin portage.[62] Red Bird,

---

[60] John Allen Wakefield, *History of the War Between the United States and the Sac and Fox Nations of Indians* . . . (Jacksonville, Ill., 1834, reprinted by the Caxton Club, Chicago, 1908), 27.

[61] Dodge's father, who had fought in the Revolution, had moved to Kaskaskia and thence to the lead-mining area around Ste. Genevieve in Missouri (then Louisiana). Henry Dodge achieved the rank of colonel in the War of 1812 and later was a member of the Missouri Constitutional Convention. In 1827 he took up lead mining east of Prairie du Chien (near the present Dodgeville, Iowa County, Wisconsin). Here he built a stockade and held forth in defiance of the law.

[62] Cass was reported to have said that they "cut the road through the portage of Ouisconsin not with axes but with guns." *Detroit Gazette*, August 28, 1827.

caught between the two forces, advanced under a white flag and surrendered himself for his crimes. He was a man of fine physique and bearing, who struck the fancy of his soldier contemporaries, as well as that of the modern poet.[63] Later two other murderers, as well as two attackers of the keelboats were turned over to General Atkinson. A peace proclamation was issued on September 22.

Pending further arrangements the settlers were allowed to remain on the mineral lands. At Prairie du Chien in July and August, 1829, Col. John McNeil, Pierre Menard, and Caleb Atwater acting for the United States met the Chippewa, Ottawa, Potawatomi, and Winnebago. The first three nations ceded their land between the Illinois and Wisconsin rivers and the Winnebago gave up the western part of their land south of the Wisconsin.[64] In September, 1832, at Fort Armstrong (Rock Island) the Winnebago, partly because of their assistance to Black Hawk, surrendered the remainder of their lands south and east of the Wisconsin-Fox rivers. In a few more years agitation developed for their complete removal west of the Mississippi.[65]

The "Winnebago War" had thrown a scare into the sparse population of northern Illinois and the adjacent part of Michigan Territory, but soon came events which not only spread panic in the locality but had far-reaching repercussions. Few events in the history of the Old Northwest have aroused more interest, or produced a more voluminous literature than Black Hawk's War; in fact, the emphasis on it has been entirely out of pro-

[63] "An extraordinary fellow, this Red Bird—sculptured as if by some ancient Greek artist out of the brown-red stone of these primeval bluffs . . . lithe, graceful, quietly triumphant as an Apollo Belvedere stained with walnut juice." William Ellery Leonard, *Red Bird* (New York, 1923), 105. Red Bird died in prison at Fort Crawford.

[64] Royce (comp.), *Indian Land Cessions*, 722–24; Kappler (ed.) *Indian Affairs, Laws and Treaties*, II, 297–303. The Chippewa, Ottawa, and Potawatomi, among other considerations, were to receive $16,000 annually "forever in specie" and be permitted to hunt on the lands ceded until they should be offered for government sale. The Winnebago were granted, among other things, an annuity of $18,000 for thirty years. The Indians' solemn grief and speeches are recorded in Caleb Atwater's *Remarks on a Tour to Prairie du Chien*.

[65] Kappler (ed.), *Indian Affairs, Laws and Treaties*, II, 345–46. Joseph Duncan, of Illinois, a member of the committee on public lands, spoke in Congress early in 1831 in favor of immediate government surveys following extinguishment of Indian title. He estimated 10,000 people in northern Illinois beyond the surveys and another 10,000 north of the state line. He said the only opposition came from land speculators. Putnam, "Life and Services of Joseph Duncan," in *Transactions of the Illinois State Historical Society*, 1919, p. 134.

portion to its importance as a war.[66] The reasons are fairly obvious. It was the last Indian war in the Old Northwest; as such it had to be cultivated and cherished in memory. Controversies which arose as the result of the scramble for a war record on the part of participating politicians-on-the-make, resulted in a welter of conflicting testimony which gave the historians something to work on. Since a number of men of some later importance were involved, these reached no mean proportions.[67] Also, this war, coming as it did when the Indian was no longer a major menace in the region, made more apparent than ever before the innate tragedy of a broken race. Last but not least were the results of the war, which were important.

At St. Louis in 1804 certain spokesmen of the Sac and Fox Indians, in return for an annuity of $1,000, had ceded to the General Government some fifty million acres of land. The portion east of the Mississippi was roughly bounded on the north by the Wisconsin, on the east by the Fox of Illinois, and on the south and east by the Illinois River. The Indians were not

[66] Among the older histories are Wakefield, *History of the War,* and Benjamin Drake, *The Life and Adventures of Black Hawk: With Sketches of Keokuk, the Sac and Fox Indians, and the Late Black Hawk War* (Cincinnati, 1838), and republished under the title *The Great Indian Chief of the West: or Life and Adventures of Black Hawk* (Cincinnati, Philadelphia, 1856). *The Life of Ma-Ka-Tai-Me-She-Kia-Kiak, or Black Hawk . . . Dictated by Himself,* was supposedly dictated to a government interpreter in 1833 and was published by J. B. Patterson, of Rock Island, at Cincinnati in 1833 and Boston in 1834, and republished, with an appendix on Black Hawk's death, at St. Louis in 1882. The definitive edition is by Milo M. Quaife (Chicago, 1916). Earlier historians were doubtful of this work, but later ones concede it some validity. A contemporary military account, "Narrative of the Expedition against the Sauk and Fox Indians . . . by an Officer who served in General Atkinson's Brigade," was published in the *Military and Naval Magazine of the United States* (August, 1833), and reprinted, New York, 1914. Brief contemporary accounts are given in Reynolds, *Pioneer History of Illinois,* and in his *My Own Times;* also in Ford, *History of Illinois.* Good sketches of Black Hawk and Keokuk may be found in Thomas L. McKenney and James Hall, *History of the Indian Tribes of North America . . .* (3 volumes. Philadelphia, 1836–44), II, 29–48 and 63–80. Many documents may be found in Frank E. Stevens, *The Black Hawk War . . .* (Chicago, 1903), various county histories, newspapers, and Volumes II, V, XV, etc., of the *Wisconsin Historical Collections.*
Ford, who had no sympathy whatever for the Indians, claimed that Black Hawk's autobiography was written by a printer for "catch penny publication." A recent study, somewhat superficial, is Cyrenus Cole, *I Am a Man—the Indian Black Hawk* (The state Historical Society of Iowa, Iowa City, 1938). The best brief accounts are Reuben Gold Thwaites, "The Story of the Black Hawk War," in *Wisconsin Historical Collections,* XII (1892), 215–65; Pease, *The Frontier State,* Chapter VIII; and Quaife, *Chicago and the Old Northwest,* Chapter XIV.
[67] Among the public men and generals known to later history were Lincoln, Zachary Taylor, Jefferson Davis, Winfield Scott, Henry Dodge, John Reynolds, Henry Atkinson, Albert Sydney Johnston, Joseph E. Johnston, John A. McClernand, and Robert Anderson.

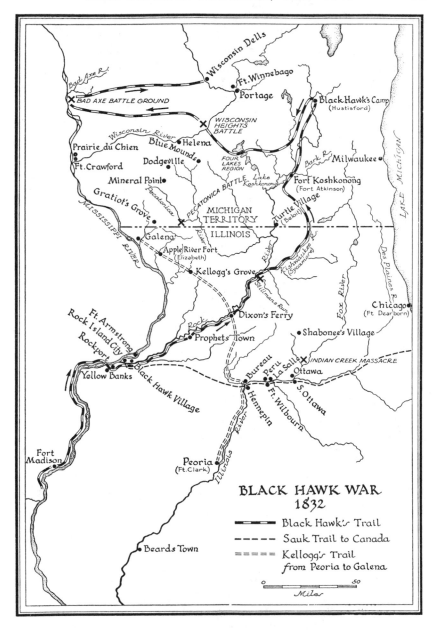

Wisconsin Dells

Ft. Winnebago

Portage

Black Hawk's Camp
(Hustisford)

Bad Axe R.

X BAD AXE BATTLE GROUND

X WISCONSIN
HEIGHTS
BATTLE

Wisconsin River

Blue Mounds · Helena

Prairie du Chien

Ft. Crawford

Dodgeville

Mineral Point

Gratiot's Grove

FOUR
LAKES
REGION

Bark R. · Milwaukee

Lake
Koshkonong

Fort Koshkonong
(Fort Atkinson)

Pecatonica

X PECATONICA BATTLE

Turtle Village
(Beloit)

MICHIGAN
TERRITORY

ILLINOIS

MISSISSIPPI RIVER

Galena

Apple River Fort
(Elizabeth)

Kellogg's Grove

Rock River

Kishwaukee
(Sycamore)

Stillman's Run

Fox River

Des Plaines R.

LAKE MICHIGAN

Chicago
(Ft. Dearborn)

Dixon's Ferry

Shabonee's Village

Ft. Armstrong
Rock Island City

Rockport

Yellow Banks

Rock R.

Prophets Town

Black Hawk Village

Bureau R.

Peru
La Salle

Hennepin

X INDIAN CREEK MASSACRE

Ottawa

S. Ottawa

Ft. Wilbourn

Fort
Madison

Peoria
(Ft. Clark)

Illinois River

Beards Town

BLACK HAWK WAR
1832

━━━━━ Black Hawk's Trail

╴╴╴╴╴ Sauk Trail to Canada

═════ Kellogg's Trail
from Peoria to Galena

0   50
Miles

pledged to remove at once, but retained the privilege of "living or hunting" upon the lands as long as they should be a part of the public domain. Whether the five chiefs who signed the treaty acted on their own or on instructions from the tribe is not clear, but owing to the very nature of Indian government, it was always difficult to make a tribe abide by agreements made by a few of its representatives. Although the treaty of 1804 was later confirmed in general terms,[68] Black Hawk denied the right of the chiefs to sell the tribal lands and advised against acceptance of the annuities when he understood their meaning; also he denied that he had understood the terms of the treaty when he confirmed it in 1816.[69]

Ma-ka-tai-me-she-kia-ki-ak, or Black Hawk, was neither an hereditary nor an elected chief, but something of a brave and headman in his native village on Rock River. Most of the Sac and Foxes fought under the British banner in the War of 1812, and after the war Black Hawk, as leader of the "British Band," maintained close relations with the British at Malden. He was restless and ambitious, preyed upon the prejudices of his people, was somewhat easily duped, yet had a high sense of honor and was a bold and sincere champion of his race. He was jealous of Keokuk, chief of the Sac, and never became entirely reconciled to the latter's pacific policy toward the whites.[70]

By 1823 squatters, passing by fifty or sixty miles of unsettled land, began locating on the fertile lands of Black Hawk's people near the mouth of Rock River, turned stock into the Indian cornfields, erected fences, beat squaws who climbed over them, plowed up Indian graves, and finally in 1827, when the natives were away on a hunting trip, set fire to the vacant lodges. Protests by the Indians to the white authorities were in vain.[71] Keokuk and the majority of the tribe, knowing that at best their

[68] At Portage des Sioux, 1815, at St. Louis in 1816 and 1822, and at Prairie du Chien in 1825. For text of these treaties, see Kappler (ed.), *Indian Affairs. Laws and Treaties,* II, 74–77, 120–22, 126–28, 250–55.
[69] Indian agent, Thomas Forsyth, in Kinzie, *Wau-Bun,* appendix; *Life of Black Hawk* (1834 ed.), 69. For cession see map, *ante,* I, 111.
[70] Keokuk was not only a distinguished warrior but a skilled negotiator. As an orator he was compared to John C. Calhoun. McKenney and Hall, *Indians of North America,* II, 79. His peaceful rule during the long years following the War of 1812 proved too monotonous to some of the more restless braves.
[71] In 1829 when James Hall visited Fort Armstrong on Rock Island, Black Hawk was asked why he did not represent these outrages to the President. He replied that the Great Father was too far away, that the Indians' letters, in conflict with those of the whites, would not be believed.

stay east of the Mississippi would be brief, prepared for peaceful removal to the other side of that river. Those who determined to remain continued passive; they made no preparation for war.

In the spring of 1830 Black Hawk's band returned from west of the Mississippi to find their homes devastated. Their leader went to Malden where he received some moral support from his "British Father" and then visited White Cloud, the half-Winnebago, half-Sac prophet, whose village was thirty-five miles up Rock River. The latter was a cold, reckless hater of the whites, and Black Hawk's "evil genius."[72] In the spring of 1831 after further aggression on the part of the settlers, some of whom had taken out pre-emption rights on most of the land which covered the Indian village, Black Hawk warned the intruders to remove from his people's lands or be forcibly evicted.[73] Rumors immediately spread that the hostile Sac were planning to unite with the Winnebago and the Potawatomi to wipe out the whites. Petitions from an aroused citizenry were presented to Governor John Reynolds, and finally a delegation of citizens waited on him in person. "The Old Ranger" caught the war spirit, issued a call for volunteers and spoke of the "state of actual invasion of the State."[74] He wrote Gen. William Clark, Indian superintendent

---

[72] Thwaites, "The Black Hawk War," in *Wisconsin Historical Collections,* XII, 224.

[73] He later denied that he meant bloodshed, and stated that he permitted one settler with a large family to remain to make his crop. *Life of Black Hawk* (1834 ed.), 101. Wakefield conveys the feeling of the times: "Here this terrible and warlike nation of Indians committed all kinds of outrage on the citizens near this place. The citizens had purchased the land they lived upon from the General Government, and had opened good farms, built houses, and had been living in peace and quietness for nearly three years, when these wretched monsters in human shape attempted to drive them from their homes, and take possession of them themselves; which in fact they did. But this was not all those savage monsters did. They turned their horses into their wheat fields, killed their stock, and laid waste whole farms." *History of the War* (1908 ed.), 29. He might have added that the Indians even destroyed a barrel of whiskey, or at least so Black Hawk said. *Life of Black Hawk* (1834 ed.), 89. See also John W. Spencer, *Reminiscences of Pioneer Life in the Mississippi Valley* . . . (Davenport, 1872), reprinted (Chicago, 1942) under the title *The Early Day of Rock Island and Davenport* . . . , Milo M. Quaife, editor.

[74] The petitions, depositions, and correspondence may be found in Wakefield, *History of the War* (1908 ed.), appendix, 159 ff., and Stevens, *The Black Hawk War,* 82 ff. The Vandalia *Illinois Intelligencer,* May 21, 1831, speaking of the Indians' depredations said that the Governor should teach them to respect solemn treaties.

Governor Reynolds later wrote: "It is astonishing, the war spirit the western people possess. As soon as I decided to march against the Indians at Rock Island, the whole country, throughout the northwest part of the state, resounded with the war clamor. Everything was in a bustle and uproar." *My Own Times,* 209.

at St. Louis, and the latter got in touch with Gen. Edmund P. Gaines, commander of the Western Division of the Army.

In June the volunteer army, of uncertain size,[75] assembled at Beardstown. None had brought food and many had failed to bring guns. Here the force was organized and supplied, and on June 15 began its march towards Rock Island. General Gaines, who had brought several companies of regulars to Fort Armstrong, now furnished a boatload of supplies and joined the volunteers at Rockport, about eight miles below the Indian village. Here the volunteers were sworn into the service of the United States. A plan of attack was discussed and the following day Gaines's steamboat and the regular contingent advanced up the Rock. The volunteers were to force the crossing and meet the regulars at the village. In the attempt to cross the river the troops got so mixed up that neither officers nor men could identify their companies or regiments, and Gaines's artillery was placed where it would, if fired, do most damage to his own troops. When the army finally got across the river in scows, it found Black Hawk's village abandoned. In spite of a torrential rain it fired the Indian shelters, then retired to Fort Armstrong. Altogether it was "a most abortive and humiliating campaign!"[76]

The Indians, having seen the overwhelming force, had retired across the Mississippi in the night of June 25. The volunteers encamped for several days on the east bank (Rock Island). It was a picturesque situation. Fort Armstrong, on a rocky cliff at the south end of the island, viewed the low river banks which reached back to the bluffs.

The river here is a beautiful sheet of clear, swift-running water, about three quarters of a mile wide, its banks on both sides were uninhabited, except by Indians from the lower rapids to the fort, and the voyage upstream after several days' solitary progress through a wilderness country on its borders came suddenly in sight of the white-washed walls and towers of the fort, perched upon a rock surrounded by the grandeur and beauty of nature, which at a distance gave it the appearance of one of those en-

[75] Wakefield says 1,500, Thwaites and Stevens 1,600, and Pease 600. The brigade was headed by Gen. Joseph Duncan; the regimental commanders were James D. Henry, of Sangamon County, and Daniel Lieb, of Morgan. There were two odd battalions.

[76] Stevens, *The Black Hawk War*, 95. Thomas Ford, later governor, who was a private on this expedition, was a leading critic of General Gaines's conduct of the campaign. *History of Illinois*, 114–15.

chanted castles in an uninhabited desert, so well described in the Arabian-Nights Entertainments.[77]

The volunteers left for home July 2.[78]

Here at Fort Armstrong on June 30, 1831, Governor Reynolds and General Gaines signed "Articles of Agreement and Capitulation" with the chiefs and braves of the "band of Sac Indians, usually called 'The British Band of Rock River' " and with their allies of the Potawatomi, Winnebago, and Kickapoo nations. The United States guaranteed to the united Sac and Fox Indians the integrity of their lands west of the Mississippi. None of the British Band was to recross the river to his former home without the express permission of the President of the United States or the Governor of Illinois.

But Black Hawk's people were soon short of food. When some of the young men recrossed the river to gather roasting ears from their former fields, the settlers protested vigorously. Then before the dawn of July 31 a war party of Sac and Foxes fell upon a band of Menominee assembled at the agency at Prairie du Chien. "Menominees loved whiskey and these Indians drank themselves socially full. . . ." It was their undoing, for not only were they *hors de combat,* but for obvious reasons the squaws had hidden their weapons. But few of the party of thirty or forty escaped either death or serious wounds. The Indian agent demanded the delivery of the murderers and a council was held at Fort Armstrong in September. The Sac chiefs explained that the young men did not remember the tragedy of Prairie du Chien; that they went on war parties while their elders were asleep. Even Keokuk explained that his people were merely balancing the scales. (Eight Sac and Fox chiefs had been killed the preceding year.)

Meanwhile Neapope,[79] second to Black Hawk in his band, had been on a visit to Malden. He returned in the autumn by way of White Cloud's village with optimistic promises of aid from the British, Winnebago, Ottawa, Chippewa, and Potawatomi. Black Hawk was to cross to the Prophet's Town the following spring,

---

[77] Ford, *History of Illinois,* 115–16.
[78] Edwardsville *Illinois Advocate,* July 8, 1831.
[79] Meaning "soup." Neapope was something of a curiosity (he used neither tobacco nor whiskey) as well as a medicine man. He was a close friend of White Cloud, the prophet.

raise a crop, then, with the aid of his allies, undertake the recovery of the Rock River lands in the autumn.

Black Hawk wintered near the mouth of the Des Moines, prepared his band and negotiated with the Winnebago and Potawatomi; no definite agreement was made. Keokuk advised against action, but most of the squaws agreed with Black Hawk because of desire to recover their cornfields.

On April 6, 1832, Black Hawk's band, numbering four or five hundred mounted warriors and their squaws and children, perhaps a thousand souls in all, crossed the Mississippi into Illinois at the Yellow Banks below the mouth of the Rock River "to make corn."[80] Two days earlier Gen. Henry Atkinson, in command at Jefferson Barracks, St. Louis, having finally received an order to demand the surrender of the principal murderers of the Menominee, had started six companies of regular soldiers (220 men) up the Mississippi in the steamboats *Enterprise* and *Chieftain*. At Fort Armstrong he learned from Keokuk that the culprits had joined Black Hawk's band and the demands were not pressed.

Black Hawk sent messengers to the Potawatomi, but their chief, Shabbona, refused to be influenced. When some of his tribe, under Big Foot, threatened to take the warpath, Shabbona spread the alarm to the settlers in northern Illinois. A number of settlers were scattered along Kellogg's Trail from Galena to Peoria and along the various Indian trails which traversed the region. On the Upper Illinois above Peoria were clusters of cabins at Peru, La Salle, South Ottawa, and other points. At Chicago between two and three hundred people were gathered around Fort Dearborn, while far to the north Solomon Juneau held forth at his post at the mouth of the Milwaukee and a garrison and officials resided at Fort Winnebago. Just across the Illinois line in Michigan Territory was Henry Gratiot's mining settlement, while a few miles farther north were the larger Mineral Point and Dodgeville diggings. Among the worthy pioneers

---

[80] The Springfield *Sangamo Journal* of March 8 had been slightly premature in its announcement, based on what "was deemed good authority," that five or six hundred Sac and Foxes had recrossed the Mississippi. It continued: "If this be true . . . we are inclined to believe that a more summary process will be employed to rid our territory of these Indians than was used on a former occasion."

were the usual numbers of ruffians, loafers, and adventurers. Many of the first retained memories of Indian violence or else inherited the Indian-hating tradition; many of the last were ready for excitement and easy government money. All held vague fears and were moved by the wild and uncertain rumors which spread by word of mouth. Even in faraway Michigan Territory east of the lake, where Black Hawk's name was not yet known, the belief spread that the Sac and Foxes, united with the Sioux, allied with the Winnebago and Chippewa, and picking up the Potawatomi and Ottawa, were in irresistible force to sweep with blood and carnage all the way to Detroit.[81]

The excitement at the state capital was not so intense. The *Sangamo Journal* of April 12 merely reported that "Travellers from Rock River state that Black Hawk and his companions do not at all relax in their determination of 'making corn on their old grounds.' These Indians must be taught to respect their treaties." It observed that since six companies of regulars were ordered to Fort Armstrong from Jefferson Barracks, the Indians might be induced to recross the river.

On April 14 Governor Reynolds issued his call to the militia of northwestern Illinois to assemble at Beardstown. He considered "the settlers on the frontiers to be in imminent danger." No citizen should remain inactive when his country was invaded. The *Journal*, April 19, 1832, was glad that the Governor appeared to be acting. "There can be no object in parleying any farther with him [Black Hawk] and his gang. Summary and spirited measures must be used, or our citizens will be subjected yearly to the incursions of this Indian banditti." A week later it admitted that the militia call came at a most unfortunate time—corn planting—and that drafts would have to be resorted to in part.

Three days later General Atkinson accepted delivery of three young men from Wapello and Keokuk, in appeasement for the Menominee raid.[82] He then sent Henry Gratiot, of Gratiot's

[81] Henry Little, "A History of the Black Hawk War of 1832," in *Michigan Pioneer and Historical Collections*, V (1882), 152–78, gives in retrospect a semihumorous account of the war and news of war in this section. See also the papers of Gen. John R. Williams, in *ibid.*, XXXI (1902), 313–471.

[82] The *St. Louis Times* had reported that since Keokuk was friendly and the murderers of the Menominee were not of his band, General Atkinson had not pressed the point of giving hostages. Springfield *Sangamo Journal,* April 26, 1832.

Grove,[83] to try to hold the Prophet in line. White Cloud protected his white friend and aided him to escape from menacing Sac warriors who threatened his life, but Gratiot failed in his appeal to Black Hawk. The latter, who had received a letter from General Atkinson, said that his heart was bad; that he and his companions were going on up the river, and if molested would fight.

The ultimate intentions of the Indian bands were not clear.[84] Their immediate object in crossing the Mississippi was to make a crop of corn with the Rock River Winnebago. With food assured and help forthcoming from other tribes, war could be decided upon by autumn.[85] But circumstances were to take the power of decision out of Black Hawk's hands.

The Illinois troops rallied at Beardstown where they were organized into regiments and two odd battalions under the command of Brig. Gen. Samuel Whiteside. Governor Reynolds rated as a major general. All but two companies of the 1,600 men were mounted. On April 30 Atkinson informed Reynolds that Black Hawk had started up the Rock River. Reynolds might have moved to head him off at Dixon's Ferry, but since the infantry battalion had been ordered to move by steamboat to the mouth of Henderson's River (just below Yellow Banks), and since supplies were being mobilized at Yellow Banks, the army was marched to Fort Armstrong. It arrived May 7 and on the following day was sworn into the United States service.

Two days later Whiteside's mounted force started up the east bank of the Rock in pursuit of the Indians. General Atkinson followed in boats with the 300 volunteer infantry, 400 regular army infantry, ordnance, supplies, and some baggage.[86] The

[83] Agent under John Kinzie to the Rock River band of Winnebago. For sketch of Gratiot and details of this mission, see *Wisconsin Historical Collections*, II (1855), 336 ff.; X (1888), 235–59, 493–95; Wakefield, *History of the War* (1908 ed.), 37 ff.

[84] "They were hampered with many women and children, and had no intention to make war." Mrs. J. H. Kinzie, *Wau Bun,* Appendix.

[85] Black Hawk stated that General Atkinson's threat to pursue and drive him back if he did not return peaceably, "roused the spirit of my band, and all were determined to remain with me and contest the ground with the war chief, should he come and attempt to drive us. We therefore directed the express to say to the war chief, 'If he wished to *fight* us, he might come on!' We were determined never to be driven, and equally so, *not to make the first attack,* our object being only to act on the defensive." *Life of Black Hawk* (1834 ed.), 114.

[86] Col. Zachary Taylor was in command of the regulars who had been assembled from Forts Crawford (Prairie du Chien) and Leavenworth.

Prophet's Town was found to be deserted. At Dixon's Ferry on May 12 the mounted troops found two independent battalions (341 men under Majors Isaiah Stillman and David Bailey), not a part of the regular levy, well supplied and eager to do something dashing. With Whiteside's permission they advanced as scouts and on the 14th took up a good defensive position in a small open grove of scrub oak surrounded by prairie near the mouth of Sycamore Creek.

Black Hawk, having found the Winnebago noncommittal, moved his main band to the Kishwaukee River, where they were joined by about one hundred Potawatomi whom Shabbona was unable to hold. With some forty of his men he met the Potawatomi chiefs at the mouth of Sycamore Creek several miles to the south. Unable to get help from them, he was, on May 14, preparing to give a dog feast, when information came that armed whites were encamping three miles down the Rock. Anticipating another summons from General Atkinson to return west of the Mississippi, he sent three men under a white flag to arrange for a parley,[87] and five others to stay at a distance and observe.

But this was not Atkinson's force; it was Stillman's, camping helter-skelter, undisciplined and disorderly. The envoys were hustled into camp with threats and yelling. When the five observers were discovered, they were pursued by a group of the mounted militia and two of them were killed. When the others returned to Black Hawk and reported that the flag bearers had also been killed,[88] the leader, angered by this perfidy, tore up a white flag he was preparing, and led his forty warriors to the field of action.

The disorganized white soldiers rushed out to meet them, but when the handful of Sac took their stand behind a pile of brush, the ardor of the attackers suddenly cooled; the futility of trying to overcome the eight hundred warriors whom they thought they saw there was overwhelming. Black Hawk seized the opportunity and ordered what he thought was a suicidal charge. The Indian war whoop mingled with cries of "Injuns! Injuns!" Noise, darkness, and danger were upon Stillman's men. Without firing a vol-

[87] He later stated that he intended to tell his people to go back across the Mississippi. *Life of Black Hawk* (1834 ed.), 117–18.

[88] Only one of the flag bearers was shot in Stillman's camp; the two others escaped.

ley they began to retreat. The retreat became a stampede; no officer was able to stop it. Only a handful of brave men stood their ground; most of them were killed. Fear chased the fleeing men right through their camp and on to Dixon's Ferry twenty-five miles away. Some did not stop even there, but galloped all the way home. Such was Stillman's defeat—300 or more brave-talking soldiers routed by 30 or 40 Indians.[89] Stillman's casualties were 11 killed; the Indians lost only the 3 killed in advance of the battle. The ample supplies captured by the Sac were much needed. Not among the least surprised by the result was Black Hawk. But mixed with the elation of victory was the realization that war was now at hand. An accident had made it unavoidable.[90]

While scouts kept in touch with Whiteside's army, Black Hawk, guided by friendly Winnebago, removed the women and children to the swampy wilderness of Lake Koshkonong around the headwaters of the Rock River in Michigan Territory (southern Wisconsin). The Sac warriors, joined by some of the Potawatomi and Winnebago bands, proceeded then to harass the border settlements. Again Shabbona spread the warning and the settlers forted up, but many, overconfident or too slow, were caught.[91] Possibly two hundred lost their lives; the Indians also suffered casualties.

[89] An account of Stillman's defeat, along with Governor Reynolds' call of May 15 for 2,000 new volunteers, appeared in the Springfield *Sangamo Journal*, May 24, 1832. A personal account followed in the issue of June 14. It was later told that, as a roll call of Stillman's company revealed many absentees, "a brave (?) man congratulated those who had escaped the foe, from a stump in the following strain;—'Sirs, Bonaparte—Wellington never commanded such disciplined forces. The most imposing scene of all was their outflanking us. They out-flanked us in the majesty of their greatness, and their muskets glistened in the moonbeams.'" Josiah B. Grinnell, *Sketches of the West, or the Home of the Badgers* (2d ed., Milwaukee, 1847), 8.

[90] "I had resolved upon giving up the war—and sent a *flag of peace* to the American war chief—expecting, as a matter of right, reason and justice, that our *flag would be respected* . . . that we might explain our grievances . . . thereby giving up all idea of going to war against the whites.

"Yet, instead . . . I was *forced* into WAR, with about *five hundred* warriors, to contend against *three* or *four thousand!*

"The *supplies* that Ne-a-pope and the prophet told us about, and the reinforcements we were to have, were never heard of; (and it is but justice to our British father to say, *were never promised—his chief having sent word in lieu of the lies that were brought to me,* 'FOR US TO REMAIN AT PEACE, AS WE COULD ACCOMPLISH NOTHING BUT OUR OWN RUIN, BY GOING TO WAR!'" *Life of Black Hawk* (1834 ed.), 123–24.

[91] "The alarm and distress on the frontier cannot be described. . . . It was heart-rending to see the women and children in an agony of fear, fleeing their homes." Letter from a soldier in *Beardstown Chronicle*, extra of May 26, cited in Springfield *Sangamo Journal*, May 31, 1832.

The day after Stillman's rout, Atkinson's and Whiteside's forces buried the dead and on May 19 proceeded up the Rock River. When Stillman's remnant, left at Dixon's Ferry to guard the supplies, went home instead, Atkinson returned with the regulars. Whiteside's men were now tired of war and protested against following Black Hawk across the state line. Some of them had plundered peaceful Indian villages. Governor Reynolds held a conference and the army was marched southward to Ottawa. Not even the sight of fifteen corpses—men, women, and children—on Indian Creek could stimulate interest. "The utter disregard of the troops for discipline; their contempt for superiors; contempt for their period of enlistment, not one-half expired, and almost open insubordination, cannot be appreciated by the present generation. . . ."[92] The men were mustered out of the service May 27. About three hundred rangers (six companies) volunteered for a twenty-day emergency service to protect the settlements while a new army was being raised.[93] General Atkinson, whose headquarters had been moved to the mouth of the Fox, had asked for a thousand men. The north country, particularly the mining region, was in a bad way.[94]

Governor Reynolds had issued his call on May 15 for "at least 2,000" additional mounted volunteers, to assemble at Henne-

"Nothing can be more deplorable than the dreadful situation to which the failure of the crops last year, and the present Indian war have reduced our fellow citizens in the northern part of this state," wrote Ninian Edwards. *Ibid.*, June 21, 1832.

One settler who had heard the cry of wolf too often said that he did not intend to seek refuge until he saw a man running towards him with a bullet hole in him and the blood running out of it and strange voices in pursuit.

Some comedy was mixed with the tragedy. One father had carried his children one at a time across the high waters of the Iroquois River. When the family started to move on, one more youngster was heard to cry from the other side. The father, well-nigh exhausted, was starting back for the four-year-old when his wife protested, "Never mind Susan; we have succeeded in getting ten over, which is more than we expected at first—and we can better spare Susan than you, my dear." Susan, the eleventh, was later rescued by hunters. See Wakefield, *History of the War* (1908 ed.), Chapter V, for episodes of this period.

[92] Stevens, *The Black Hawk War*, 163.

[93] Henry Frye, colonel, James D. Henry, lieutenant colonel. General Whiteside enlisted as a private, and Abraham Lincoln became a captain.

[94] "The situation of this whole country . . . in the state and territory . . . about 400 miles long and 60 or 70 broad, is at this time in a condition of distress, unparalleled in the history of our country.

"Travel east, west, north or south, we see nothing but waste, destruction and dilapidation. Fields half plowed for sowing and planting; some just planted; gardens partly made; hogs, cattle, fowls etc. running wild; houses vacated, and left with all the furniture within them, and not an inhabitant within sixty miles, presents an aspect too gloomy for reflection." *The Galenian*, June 6, quoted in Springfield *Sangamo Journal*, June 28, 1832. Galena had been placed under martial law by order of Colonel Strode, and plans for its defense undertaken. *Sangamo Journal*, June 7, 1832.

pin on June 10. General Atkinson's headquarters were then at Fort Wilbourn (Peru) and here, when the men arrived May 15, the 3,200 new troops were organized into three brigades.[95] Including Colonel Frye's rangers and Col. Henry Dodge's Michigan Territory rangers, the army mustered about 4,000 men.[96] The United States ordered more regulars to the seat of the war, and late in June Gen. Winfield Scott left Fortress Monroe, Virginia, with nine companies.

The three brigades left Fort Wilbourn for Dixon's Ferry on June 21 and 22.[97] Major Dement's spy battalion of Posey's brigade was sent ahead. On the 24th a party of 150 under Black Hawk had run into heroic resistance on the part of the settlers, including women, at a blockhouse on Apple River.[98] The Indians then moved east to Kellogg's Grove where the next day they ran into Dement's men. The latter, absolutely disregarding orders, rushed a few of the enemy and were almost ambushed by the main party. When penned up in the log buildings, they held their own until Posey's brigade, on its way to join Dodge at Fort Hamilton, sent reinforcements and the Indians departed.[99] Numerous other skirmishes followed.

To anticipate possible retirement of the Indians across the Mississippi, Alexander's brigade was ordered to Plum River. When it was learned, however, that the main Indian camp was still near Lake Koshkonong, General Atkinson left Dixon's on the 27th with the other brigade and the regulars, to begin the march up Rock River. Three days later this force crossed the Illinois line near the present Beloit and followed Black Hawk's

[95] Commanders: first, Brig. Gen. Alexander Posey; second, Brig. Gen. M. K. Alexander; third, Brig. Gen. James D. Henry. Governor Reynolds decided that all officers above the rank of captain should be elected by the men. Some Indiana volunteers also presented themselves, but were not used.

[96] Henry Dodge was head of the Michigan territorial militia west of Lake Michigan. When the Sac crossed the Mississippi, he rallied twenty-seven rangers and went to Dixon's Ferry. When news of Stillman's defeat came, he returned home, consulted with the Winnebago in the Four Lakes region, then raised two hundred rangers for the war. They were active around the mining regions for a while.

[97] Stevens says Posey's brigade left on the 20th. *The Black Hawk War*, 193.

[98] For details, see Captain Flack's letter in Wakefield, *History of the War* (1908 ed.), 66-69.

[99] Dement's men had been rather thoroughly dressed down by Col. Zachary Taylor of the regulars at Dixon's Ferry a few days earlier. They resented it, but Dement knew they needed it. Taylor's distrust of "citizen soldiers" was to crop up again in the war with Mexico.

trail to the Koshkonong region, which it reached July 2. General
Alexander returned from his wild goose chase July 4.

Posey's brigade had reached Fort Hamilton on the Pecatonica,
June 28. There he gave Colonel Dodge his orders to join his
command and proceed to the main army at Koshkonong.[100] The
brigade moved east by way of the Four Lakes, led by some Winnebago who were pretending to lead it to Black Hawk's camp.
Dodge, though angered when orders came to join at once the
main army on Bark River on the east side of Lake Koshkonong,
was probably thereby saved from a trap.

When the army was formed for advance against Black Hawk's
well-situated camp on the east bank of the upper Rock, Dodge
objected to his location in the left wing next to Posey's men, and
General Atkinson ordered Alexander to change places with
Posey. The regulars under Taylor, and Henry's third brigade
constituted the right wing. Discouraged by several days of floundering in the swampy country, lack of provisions, and the apparent hopelessness of catching Black Hawk, Governor Reynolds
and his staff left for home July 10.[101] Many of the men apparently did likewise, for by the middle of July the volunteers had
diminished by half.[102] The war had ceased to be a frolic; it was
lasting too long.

Food being even more necessary than Indians, Henry's and
Alexander's brigades, together with Dodge's rangers, were sent
to Fort Winnebago at the portage eighty miles away to get sup-
plies. One regiment of Posey's brigade was returned to Dixon's
Ferry with a wounded officer, while the remainder were sent to
Fort Hamilton to protect the mining country. Atkinson and the
regulars retired to Lake Koshkonong and built a small fort on
Bark River.

At Fort Winnebago supposedly friendly Winnebago offered to
guide the troops to Black Hawk's camp.[103] Dodge and Henry

[100] Dodge's forces had been swelled to about three hundred by a Galena company, a few Menominee, and a handful of white and half-breed scouts under the
command of Col. William S. Hamilton (son of Alexander Hamilton), a pioneer
lead miner.

[101] "This condition of affairs forced on all reflecting men much mortification, and
regret that this campaign also would do nothing." Reynolds, *My Own Times,* 251.

[102] Ford, *History of Illinois,* 134.

[103] On July 12 at Fort Winnebago several hundred horses stampeded, rushed
through the camp, injured men, and finally ran thirty miles. Many were never
recovered or were useless when found.

decided to return by a circuit to the east (Hustisford Rapids of the Rock) to find Black Hawk. Alexander's troops refused to go and even Henry had trouble with some of his officers.[104] Additional recruits from Dodge's battalion arrived from Galena, but Henry's brigade was now reduced to about 450 effectives. With Winnebago as guides, the command began their march July 15 through the underbrush and swamps. No Indians were found at the rapids but as the Winnebago insisted they had gone north to Cranberry Lake, Henry determined to pursue. He dispatched two messengers to Atkinson to keep the latter posted. When about twenty miles on their way, the messengers, guided by the Winnebago chief, Little Thunder, ran into the unmistakable trail of Black Hawk.[105] Little Thunder dashed back to camp to warn his people that further trickery was useless.

On the morning of the 19th Henry's forces hit the trail. Discarded camp equipment indicated the haste with which the Indians were endeavoring to reach the Mississippi.[106] The men were eager now and pressed on hard. Baggage was dumped and equipment piled in the wilderness. Two days of hard rain failed to stop them; they ate raw meat and flour-and-water dough. The trail led northwest through the later towns of Lake Mills and Cottage Grove toward the Four Lakes. On the evening of the 20th the army camped just north of Third Lake (Monona). Of this country one of the men wrote:

I think they are the most beautiful bodies of water I ever saw. The first one that we came to, was about ten miles in circumference, and the water

[104] When a remonstrance, signed by Lt. Col. Jeremiah Smith and other officers of Col. Jacob Fry's regiment, was presented to General Henry, he ordered the signers arrested and sent to Atkinson for trial. The officers apologized, stating that they did not realize the import of their action. General Henry was a quiet, modest yet resolute man; he was not a candidate for any office, and was one of the few leaders who knew how to handle the militia.

Major Peter Parkison, Jr., in a letter to the Madison *Argus and Democrat*, written September 10, 1854, stated that there was no attempted meeting on the part of Henry's officers and men. "Strictures upon Gov. Ford's History of the Black Hawk War," in *Wisconsin Historical Collections*, II (1855), 393-401. Yet in an editor's note Lyman C. Draper called attention to the fact that the evidence did point to "something that squinted towards mutiny" among a portion of Henry's troops. Parkison remembered a lot of things as the exact opposite of other accounts, and gave Dodge greater credit throughout.

[105] Stevens says eight miles. The site was about halfway between the present Watertown and Jefferson.

[106] "The Indians Escaped," abandoned the Four Lakes stronghold, and headed north to the Chippewa country, reported the Springfield *Sangamo Journal*, July 19, 1832.

clear as crystal. The earth sloped back in a gradual rise; the bottom of the lake appeared to be entirely covered with white pebbles, and no appearance of its being the least swampy. The second one that we came to, appeared to be much larger. It must have been twenty miles in circumference. The ground rose very high all around;—and the heaviest kind of timber grew close to the water's edge. If those lakes were anywhere else, except in the country they are, they would be considered among the wonders of the world. But the country they are situated in is not fit for any civilized nation of people to inhabit. It appears that the Almighty intended it for the children of the forest.[107]

The next day the men crossed the neck of land between Third and Fourth lakes, followed around the southern shore of the latter (through what is now the campus of the University of Wisconsin) and northwest toward the Wisconsin. Many horses gave out. When the Indians reached timber and made a stand, every tenth man was detailed to care for the horses, and the rest advanced on foot. With gunfire and finally bayonets, they pushed the enemy into the Wisconsin River bottoms, then camped on their arms. Black Hawk had been directing the battle for the Indians. Their losses at the battle of Wisconsin Heights were variously reported at from 6 to 68 plus 25 who died of wounds.[108] Henry had lost 1 killed and had 8 wounded.[109]

During the night (July 21–22) the men heard a strange voice speaking from the hill from which Black Hawk had commanded. At first it was thought to be the leader ordering a charge, but nothing came of it. It was learned later that it was Ne-a-pope

[107] Wakefield, *History of the War* (1908 ed.), 109. Such was the impression of the site of the later capital of Wisconsin.

[108] *Life of Black Hawk* (1834 ed.), 132; Kinzie, *Wau-Bun;* and Wakefield, *History of the War* (1908 ed.), 113. During the night a number of women, children, and old men were started down the river on a raft and in canoes. It was expected that the garrison at Fort Crawford at the mouth of the Wisconsin would allow them to cross the Mississippi. Instead they were interrupted by a detachment of regulars, fifteen men were killed, and three dozen women, children, and old men captured. About as many were drowned. Of a group that took to the woods, all but a handful starved or were cut down by Monominee from the Green Bay region under the command of Col. S. C. Stambaugh. The news of this victory was put out by the Springfield *Sangamo Journal* in a handbill several days before the account in the regular issue of August 3. General Henry's letter to General Atkinson reporting the victory was published with the account.

[109] Dodge's letter to Captain Loomis, the commander at Prairie du Chien, July 22, in Stevens, *The Black Hawk War,* 219–20. In this letter, later published in the *Missouri Republican* and *Niles' Weekly Register,* Dodge told what he intended to do and asked for co-operation. Ford, *History of Illinois,* 147 ff., thought that Dodge was working with Dr. Addison Philleo, editor of *The Galenian,* to take credit for the victory. Henry was hardly mentioned in the news. Although considerable letter writing and rejoining followed, Henry and Dodge maintained good relationships.

suing for peace in Winnebago. He had expected the Winnebago guides of Henry's army to interpret, but they had left for Fort Winnebago earlier, and there was none to understand.[110] A second time ill fate had prevented Black Hawk's saving his people.

On the 22d Henry found the Indians had crossed the Wisconsin. Lacking supplies, he fell back to Blue Mounds, where on the 24th he was joined by General Atkinson with Alexander's and Posey's brigades. A certain amount of jealousy was shown by the rest of the troops toward Henry's command and its success at Wisconsin Heights. When the army began its united pursuit on the 25th, the regulars were up in front, followed by Posey and Alexander. Henry's brigade, in charge of baggage, brought up the rear. The Wisconsin was crossed by the 28th and the Indian trail followed into rough country not well known even to the Winnebago. The bodies of starved and wounded Indians marked the line of flight. On the evening of August 1, Atkinson gave orders to move at 2:00 A.M. for the banks of the Mississippi.

Black Hawk and his miserable band that day had reached the Mississippi just below the mouth of the Bad Axe. But few canoes were available for a crossing. A large raft loaded with squaws and children was sent down river, but it capsized, and most of the occupants were drowned. During the afternoon the *Warrior*, an army transport steamboat, arrived on its way north.[111] Black Hawk hailed it with a white flag and, speaking in Winnebago, offered to surrender. When a Winnebago on the boat relayed the message, Captain Throckmorton ordered Black Hawk to come aboard in a canoe. This was impossible, since the canoes were out of reach. Suspecting an ambush, the captain, after allowing fifteen minutes for the squaws to get out of the way, threw canister and musket balls into the Indians. Twenty-three Indians were killed and the *Warrior* returned to Prairie du Chien for fuel. A few Indians succeeded in getting across the river under cover of darkness.

The army resumed its advance before dawn of August 2. Black Hawk had ordered a small party of men to meet Atkinson's

[110] This episode is not mentioned by Black Hawk, but it is by Reynolds, Ford, and Wakefield. Ne-a-pope had said that the Sac had their women and children along, had been forced into war, and that if permitted to cross the Mississippi would cause no more trouble.

[111] Captain Throckmorton, with 15 regulars and 6 volunteers aboard.

forces, and gradually give way to the north, so as to lead the troops several miles upstream from the crossing. The regulars under Taylor, Dodge's battalion, and the brigades of Alexander and Posey advanced to the attack. Henry, still in charge of the baggage, arrived just in time to receive orders to send Frye's regiment to Atkinson. As the Indian decoys gave ground, Atkinson's forces followed. But Henry, who had received no battle orders (probably an intentional affront), sized up the situation, discovered the Indian trail to the river, dismounted his men and attacked. Although the Indians outnumbered his weakened brigade, they were driven back by gunfire, and finally a bayonet charge. Atkinson's forces, warned by a messenger from Henry, as well as the sound of battle, arrived in time to get in on the kill. The Indians, though weak from hunger, fought bravely. Many were killed. A few who escaped to an island were met with canister from the returned *Warrior*. Gunfire was followed by a bayonet charge by Dodge's and Henry's men. The Indians attempting to swim to the far shore were picked off by riflemen—women as well as men. The pandemonium and slaughter continued for three hours. As Governor Reynolds said, "the conflict resembled more a carnage than a regular battle."[112] Even Wakefield, who seldom wasted any sympathy on the Indians, said, "It was a horrid sight to witness little children, wounded and suffering the most excruciating pain, although they were of the savage enemy, and the common enemy of the country. It was enough to make the heart of the most hardened being on earth to ache."[113] It was estimated that about 150 Indians were killed in the battle and as many more drowned.[114] Atkinson lost fewer than a dozen killed and about the same number wounded.[115]

[112] *My Own Times*, 265

[113] *History of the War* (1908 ed.), 133. "But the Ruler of the Universe, He who takes vengeance on the guilty, did not design those guilty wretches to escape this vengeance for the horrid deeds they had done, which were of the most appalling nature." *Ibid.*, 132.

[114] *Ibid.*

[115] Stevens, *The Black Hawk War*, 224, gives totals: regulars—5 killed, 4 wounded; Dodge—6 wounded; Posey—1 wounded; Alexander—1 wounded; Henry —7 killed and wounded. Three of the wounded died the next day. Wakefield, *History of the War*, 133, says 27 killed and wounded. Reynolds, *My Own Times*, 265, reported 17 killed and 12 wounded. The Springfield *Sangamo Journal*, August 18, 1832, reported U. S. "losses" at 27. The *Journal's* one-and-a-half column account was taken from a *Galenian* extra, and the letter of Captain Loomis of Fort Crawford of August 2. It mentioned the accidental killing of many women and children.

The following day a party of 150 men crossed the river and beat the bottom for the Indians, probably about the same number, who had escaped. They found none, but a party of Sioux were more successful, for they captured Ne-a-pope and killed about half of the helpless remnant. Of the band of near a thousand Sac which had crossed the Mississippi in April, probably not more than a hundred and fifty survived.

Black Hawk had not been in the battle. Having made plans for it, he seemed to realize during the night that hope was futile; with the Prophet, a small party of warriors, and thirty-five squaws and children, he had started for a refuge in the rocky dells of the Wisconsin. The next day, conscience bothering apparently, he returned to witness the end of the battle from the bluff of the Mississippi. When it ended, he again turned toward the dells. There in the rocky canyons he was captured by two Winnebago who, desirous of cultivating the whites, delivered him to the agent, Joseph M. Street, at Prairie du Chien on August 25.

Black Hawk fared somewhat better than his unfortunate band. On September 21, when the treaty was signed with the Sac at Fort Armstrong, he, his son—whom facetious editors called Tommy Hawk—the Prophet, Ne-a-pope, and others were kept as hostages. They wintered at Jefferson Barracks where Black Hawk and Lt. Jefferson Davis became friends. In the spring they were taken to Washington and to Fortress Monroe. When released, the party was conducted, under army auspices, on a tour of eastern cities. They were invited to theaters, taken to museums, and in New York saw a balloon ascension. Everywhere Black Hawk was the center of attention. After two months the Indians were taken back to their people. Much talk ensued, but they were received into the fold by Keokuk. "To-day we shook hands with our brothers. . . . They traveled a long road and found the Americans like grass. . . . Those who listened to bad counsels, and followed our brothers, have said that their ears are closed. They will live in peace." In 1837 Black Hawk accompanied the old chief on his visit to Washington, not as a delegate, but as a friend. He died at his village on the Des Moines the following year.

In part a victim of circumstances,[116] and in turn a cause of his people's tragic suffering, this noted Indian achieved a fame and

[116] Stevens, *The Black Hawk War*, 267.

glamour greater than that of Keokuk and other better men of his tribe. He was romantic, rash, and gullible.[117] Yet he was honest, generally more honorable than his opponents, and above all a patriot. The year before his death he said: "Rock River is a beautiful country. I loved my towns, my cornfields, and the home of my people. I fought for it. It is now yours. Keep it as we did."

General Scott, who had been delayed by the cholera epidemic which hit his troops while coming up the lakes,[118] arrived at Prairie du Chien on August 7 and took command of the army. The volunteers were mustered out the following day; the regulars returned to Jefferson Barracks on the 17th.

The cholera had also reached the Indians. The treaty with the Winnebago was delayed until the 15th[119] and not until September 21 did General Scott and Governor Reynolds meet with the chiefs and warriors of the Sac and Fox. Since "under certain lawless and desperate leaders, a formidable band . . . commenced an unprovoked war upon unsuspecting and defenceless citizens of the United States, sparing neither age nor sex," the tribe was forced to cede all lands to which they had title or claim (roughly the eastern fifth of the present state of Iowa), excepting a tract of four hundred square miles.[120] In return, the United States promised an annuity of $20,000 for thirty years, plus a blacksmith shop, forty kegs of tobacco, and forty of salt.

The war had cost the settlers about 250 lives, all told, and the government almost $2,000,000. Arguments over who should pay the costs and who deserved credit for winning the war continued for some time.[121] The influence of the war on settlement was im-

---

[117] Thwaites, "The Black Hawk War," in *Wisconsin Historical Collections*, XII, 263. "Black Hawk was small in stature, and his figure was not striking; nor did his features indicate a high grade of intelligence. The strongest evidence of his good sense is found in an assertion contained in his autobiography, that he never had but one wife." McKenney and Hall, *History of the Indian Tribes*, II, 48.

[118] See Chapter V, 251, for the cholera. Scott had reached Fort Dearborn, Chicago, on July 10.

[119] *Ante*, 59.

[120] For text of the treaty see Kappler (ed.), *Indian Affairs. Laws and Treaties*, II, 349–51. Soon the settlers were discovering this reserve. The "Far West" was now moving into the Dubuque region, which was filling rapidly. *The Galenian*, August 16, 1833. A glowing description by "A Kentuckian" appeared in the Springfield *Sangamo Journal*, July 9, 1836: "How greatly the Universal Architect favored this country."

[121] Ex-Governor Ninian Edwards figured that the militia, whose pay in United States service was $6.66 per month, had lost $129,270 of labor and $300,000 of state pay ($50 cash for being drafted), or a total of $429,270, "all this fighting battles of the United States on account of a direct insult offered to them outside the limits of this state." *Sangamo Journal*, June 21, 28, 1832.

When the *Military and Naval Journal* published an article written by one of

portant though largely indirect. Black Hawk's band had occupied but a small area; it was not even familiar with the region in which the main actions were fought. The war scare delayed settlements in northern Indiana, Illinois, and Michigan Territory for a year. It ruined the Michigan Road land sales at South Bend in June.[122] Renewed anti-Indian feeling led to increased demands for removal of the Potawatomi from Indiana and the Winnebago from Michigan Territory. As in the case of earlier Indian wars, the attendant publicity and advertising of the region far outbalanced the adverse effects. During and after the war eastern newspapers gave much space to descriptions of the Rock River and Four Lakes country. Pamphlets and books appeared in abundance. Though these accounts were frequently somewhat on the "ultra" side, this was a region whose beauty and productivity were hard to exaggerate. The soldiers did not have to rely upon hearsay; they had seen for themselves. Many had spotted good land, and some returned to it.

§ §

While the left wing of settlement was advancing into the country between the Illinois and Wisconsin rivers, the right was also swinging forward. Michigan Territory in 1825 was still virtually beyond the bounds of civilization. Once beyond the strip which bordered the lakes on the east, the settler was confronted with a land of wolves, bears, mosquitoes, Indians, and rattlesnakes.[123] In 1824 there were but six organized counties.[124] Be-

General Atkinson's officers which did not flatter the volunteers, it was called "a tissue of misrepresentations and absurdities" by the editor of the *Sangamo Journal* and answered by "a volunteer" to the extent of several columns. September 7, 1833. When Wakefield's *History* appeared, arguments ensued regarding whether certain regiments had been in reserve or in the main charge at the battle of Wisconsin Heights. *Sangamo Journal*, July 12, 1834. Such little matters were always of great importance.

[122] Ella Lonn, "Ripples of the Black Hawk War in Northern Indiana," in *Indiana Magazine of History*, XX (1924), 307.

[123] Osband, "My Recollections of Pioneers and Pioneer Life in Nankin," in *Michigan Pioneer and Historical Collections*, XIV, 432–33. For settlements, 1815 to 1825, see Chapter I.

[124] Wayne, Monroe, Macomb, Oakland, Mackinaw, and St. Clair. Washtenaw and Lenawee were organized in 1825. Small settlements were at Monroe, Frenchtown, Brownstown, Truax's, St. Clair, Tecumseh, Pontiac, and Saginaw. Orange Risdon published a map of Michigan Territory in 1825 which showed the government surveys. These were confined largely to the counties named. See reproduction in Louis C. Karpinski, *Historical Atlas of the Great Lakes and Michigan* (Lansing, 1931), 91.

sides Detroit, there were a dozen hamlets. There were land offices at Detroit (1804) and Monroe (1823), but only 61,919 acres of land had been sold. The only access to Detroit by land from the older settled regions was by way of the trail which led from the falls of the Maumee around the west end of Lake Erie. Other trails led from Detroit to Ann Arbor,[125] to Pontiac and Saginaw, and west (the Great Sac Trail), south and west toward Chicago.[126]

Although Detroit had received a city charter in 1824, it was still essentially an old French town. The three streets which paralleled the river were intersected by six cross streets; in all the mud was axle deep in season. There were no sidewalks north of Jefferson. Many of the houses were of the French-Canadian type, whitewashed and with picket fences. There were but few carriages and these were used mostly in summer. Women shopped and went to church in two-wheeled French carts; gentlemen called in them, children used them for going to school, and wedding parties assembled in them. French *voyageurs* as well as Indians, both in picturesque dress, were still much in evidence. Among the city's businesses were some 30 stores, 6 taverns, 5 wharves, a gristmill, a carding machine, a tin factory, a soap and candle factory, and a brewery-distillery. There were also the land office, capitol, jail, council house, the magazine (for the garrison), market house, public storehouse, a Roman Catholic chapel, two Protestant churches, and a reading room which received between sixty and seventy newspapers from divers places. Among other assets were a half-dozen physicians, about as many teachers, and fourteen attorneys.[127]

The water supply depended upon buckets and barrels until 1827 when a Mr. Wells began pumping it through a log pipeline into a reservoir near the council house. The line ran along Jefferson Street as far as the market and had branches to a number of

[125] Named by two settlers for their wives in 1824 when they erected a temporary shelter arbor for their protection.

[126] This Great Sac Trail was not completely surveyed until 1832.

[127] *Detroit Gazette*, January 2, 1824. The population was listed at 1,325 plus the garrison; buildings at 366, of which 155 were dwellings. Thomas L. McKenney stated that in 1826 Jefferson Street was fairly well filled, but that buildings were scattered back of Jefferson. *Sketches of a Tour to the Lakes* . . . (Baltimore, 1827), 141. These descriptions of 1824–26 might be contrasted with the detailed descriptions of 1815–16 in *Detroit Journal and Michigan Advertiser*, August 1, 1834, and of 1820 in Schoolcraft, *Narrative Journal*, 51.

buildings.[128] As the streets along the shore filled in with buildings, older citizens, remembering the fire of 1805, thought of the fire danger. Fire fighting with bucket brigades was quite informal. Every man and boy was a director while scores who never took their hands from their pockets served as advisers. Salvaged goods were passed around promiscuously and sometimes never found their way back to the owner.[129] A committee of the common council in 1827 looked into the problems of sewage disposal, fire protection, and paving.[130]

Next to Detroit in importance was Monroe, about three miles up the Raisin River on the south bank. Frenchtown, across the river, was the older settlement, but when Monroe County was established in 1817, the new settlement was made the county seat. Its growth was slow, but population increased one third in 1825.[131] By 1830 there were still fewer than five hundred inhabitants. Most of the earlier settlers in Monroe County landed at Detroit and then backtracked by way of the bad roads. Beyond Detroit on the Clinton River was another promising village, Mt. Clemens, which had been platted in 1818. Beginnings of settlement in the interior counties—Oakland, Washtenaw, Lenawee— had also been made during the period between 1817 and 1825.

The important development of Michigan dated from the opening of the Erie Canal and the improvement of steam navigation on the Great Lakes. Land sales at the Detroit office, which for several years had hardly covered salaries of the agents, suddenly stepped up to one ninth of the United States total.[132] Sales, of course, did not represent settlement, since many purchases were for speculative account. Detroit businessmen as well as outsiders were buying lands as surveys were completed and sales opened.

In the preroad period nearness to Detroit and the lake shore determined the order of survey and settlement. Oakland, Washtenaw, and Lenawee counties began to fill first.[133] St. Clair and

---

[128] *Detroit Gazette*, July 31, 1827.
[129] Detroit *North-Western Journal*, April 28, 1830.
[130] George Newman Fuller, *Economic and Social Beginnings of Michigan . . .* (Lansing, 1916), 135–36.
[131] Detroit *Michigan Herald*, April 26, 1826; *Detroit Gazette*, December 13, 1825.
[132] *Detroit Gazette*, February 7, 1826.
[133] Although Pontiac was founded in 1818, Oakland County had a population of only 330 in 1820 (in 1825 there were 282 houses; in June, 1826, 341), but by 1830 it had reached 4,911. For detailed study of the settlements of Michigan, Fuller, *Economic and Social Beginnings of Michigan* is indispensable. See also the scores of articles in the *Michigan Pioneer and Historical Collections*.

Macomb, though lake-shore counties, settled more slowly. While soil, timber, availability of damsites, the nature of the land, type of scenery even, were all-important factors in determining settlers' locations, most important was the lack of roads. Not until the early 1830's did this handicap begin to diminish in importance.

The earliest inland road, from Detroit to Saginaw Bay, though just a trail, was improved somewhat in the early 1830's, and intersecting roads gave some access to the land on either side.[134] The Chicago Road, authorized in 1825, ran west to Ypsilanti, turned southwest to Tecumseh (the survey cut across north of Tecumseh), thence west to Coldwater and White Pigeon, crossed the St. Joseph River about three miles south of Niles, then the Indiana line, and ran on towards Chicago.[135] Although stages were running twice a week on this road, at least as far as Ypsilanti, in 1830, service was not dependable until improvements began a year or two later. The Black Hawk War scare suspended traffic for a while in 1832, but by 1835 daily stages were running.

The Territorial Road (St. Joseph Road), authorized in 1829, forked from the Chicago Road just east of Ypsilanti, continued west through Ann Arbor to the Kalamazoo River which it followed until the stream made its big bend to the north (Kalamazoo), then swung southwest across Van Buren County to the mouth of the St. Joseph.[136] Although the road was not "surveyed and opened"[137] until 1836, it was passable and used in part five or six years earlier. Since the main traffic, including stages,[138] cut directly from Kalamazoo southwest to Niles, this road was in

---

[134] *Detroit Journal and Michigan Advertiser*, May 18, 1831. Stages had run from Detroit to Pontiac as early as 1826.

[135] The Chicago Road is frequently referred to as passing through Niles. Maps sometimes so show it. The confusion no doubt results from the fact that when stage service was carried through to Chicago, the stages detoured through Niles. *Tourists Pocket Map* (Philadelphia, 1835) reproduced in Fuller, *Economic and Social Beginnings of Michigan*, lxv; Orville W. Coolidge, *Twentieth Century History of Berrien County* (Chicago, 1906), 38. The road is correctly mapped in Quaife, *Chicago's Highways*, 220.

[136] Apparently the mail from Kalamazoo to St. Joseph in 1836 did not follow the survey, for John Allen who had the contract ran the route through Keeler in the southwest corner of Van Buren County and about twenty miles due east of St. Joseph. Oran W. Rowland, *A History of Van Buren County, Michigan* (Chicago, 1912), 553. See also *History of Berrien and Van Buren Counties* (D. W. Ensign & Co., Philadelphia, 1880), 477.

[137] Coolidge, *Twentieth Century History of Berrien County*, 38.

[138] *Tourists Pocket Map*, in Fuller, *Economic and Social Beginnings of Michigan*, lxv.

the mid 1830's more important than the western section of the Territorial Road.

To the north of the Territorial Road developed the Grand River Road, authorized in 1832, and in use, at least as far as Ionia, the following year. It ran northwest from Pontiac, crossed the Shiawassee at Byron (the statute said "Sciawasee"), then followed the north side of the Looking Glass and Grand rivers to the lake.

As the New York–New England arrivals moved west out of Detroit, some took the Chicago Road, others the Territorial. The former settled the first or southern tier of counties, the latter the second tier. Somewhat later the Grand River Road served as settlement axis for the fourth.

Early in 1825–26 Detroit papers were calling attention to the progress of the land surveys and the excellent lands on the St. Joseph River, a region just on the verge of rediscovery.[139] Jolliet had featured the river on his map,[140] La Salle had built a fort at its mouth, and later a trading post and mission were established near the site of the future Niles.[141] Though abandoned by the French in 1696, the fort was afterwards re-established and garrisoned until 1763. An unknown French *voyageur* had described the country in 1718 as "the best adapted of any to be seen for purposes of living as regards the soil. There are pheasants . . . quail . . . the finest vines in the world. . . . It is the richest district in all that country."[142] In midcentury perhaps fifty families lived at the St. Joseph post, but by the end of the American Revolution there were only eight. After the war new traders had come in, among them John Kinzie, formerly of Detroit and later of Chicago fame.

When Governor Lewis Cass visited the country east of Lake Michigan in 1820, it was still almost a trackless wilderness, inhabited only by Indians and a few French traders. After the Chicago Treaty of 1821,[143] desiring to cultivate a friendly feeling, Cass encouraged the Rev. Isaac McCoy, Baptist missionary at

[139] *Detroit Gazette*, March 18, 1825; *Michigan Herald*, February 14, 1826.
[140] Reuben Gold Thwaites (ed.), *The Jesuit Relations and Allied Documents* (73 volumes. Cleveland, Ohio, 1897–1901), LIX, 86.
[141] George Paré, "The St. Joseph Mission," in *Mississippi Valley Historical Review*, XVII (1930–31), 26.
[142] O'Callaghan (ed.), *New-York Colonial Documents*, IX, 890.
[143] See Chapter III.

Fort Wayne, to establish the Carey Indian Mission on the St. Joseph (just west of the business section of the present Niles). About fifty persons braved the rough trail from the head of the Maumee, built six mission houses, and cleared about fifty acres.[144] Outside the St. Joseph settlement there were in 1825 only nine white families west of Tecumseh.[145] Although McCoy did not encourage settlement,[146] the mission and reports of the fertile prairie openings fringed with forests attracted settlers. A Hoosier squatted near the mission and began selling liquor to the Indians; several families settled on Pokagon Prairie, a few miles to the north; several others settled at Edwardsburg on Beardsley's Prairie, a few miles southeast; and by 1827 still others (from Ohio and Indiana) located on the White Pigeon, a tributary of the St. Joseph, some forty miles to the east. Within two years three families from Wayne County, Indiana, platted the village of Niles near the mission, others from the same place settled at Portage Prairie, North Carolinians located at Berrien Springs, and New Englanders and New Yorkers founded St. Joseph (at first called Newburyport) at the mouth of the river. In 1828 the country west of the principal meridian was divided into counties and Cass and St. Joseph were organized. A year later post offices were established at the new settlements of Edwardsburg and Niles. At this time there were fewer than two thousand people in the region.

Consequently, as the eastern emigrants began to penetrate the St. Joseph country, they found themselves preceded by the settlers from the South. No novices, these folk, at squatting; seldom did they fail to select the best lands, usually tracts which combined prairie and woods. With them they brought the hog-corn-bread system and supplemented it in the early years with the abundant fish, venison, turkeys, and wild fruits of the region. "Drinks at meals were wheat, corn, evans root, and sassafras tea and coffee; otherwise, whiskey generally for callers, and nearly

[144] Isaac McCoy, *History of Baptist Indian Missions* . . . (New York, 1840), 172 ff.

[145] A. P. Copley, "Early Settlement of Southwestern Michigan," in *Michigan Pioneer and Historical Collections,* V (1882), 149, citing Howard S. Rogers, *History of Cass County* (Cassopolis, Mich., 1875).

[146] "Our location was so remote from the settlements of white people . . . that we hoped, at that time, to be able to push forward the work of civilization to a state not much liable to injury by the proximity of white population, before we should be crowded by it." McCoy, *Baptist Indian Missions,* 264.

always at raisings, log rollings, harvest and hog killing times."[147]
Though traditionally not supposed to be so well equipped to
stand up at a bargain as Brother Jonathan, these Southerners got
there first. They sold some produce to the Yankee arrivals and in
1829 when St. Joseph County land went on sale, though the
squatters feared they would have to pay $8.00 to $10 per acre,
the speculators, understanding the situation, behaved very nicely
and bid on no occupied lots.[148] In 1831 a land office was opened
at White Pigeon, where first sales were held in June. Cassopolis,
Jonesville, and Branch were also laid out this year, and Coldwater was platted in 1832.

In 1830 Henry Whiting, army officer and Detroit poet, in *The
Age of Steam* described the answer to the traveler's inquiry concerning the Michigan country:

> Asks he how thrives the country back?
> Let him just ride to Pontiac;
> Or take the stage to Washtenaw,
> The finest land he ever saw,
> Except St. Joseph's, which, 'tis said,
> Is where the Paradise was laid.
> St. Joseph's now is a disease,
> Which emigration seems to seize,
> And carries off, at sundry times,
> Whole families—to distant climes,
> Where fertile counties proudly claim
> Old Hickory's and Van Buren's name.

Following the Washtenaw Trail west from Ann Arbor and
the Kalamazoo River, the early settlers of the prairie counties
of Kalamazoo and Calhoun were attracted by the rich lands of
the river valley even before the Territorial Road materialized.[149]

[147] Copley, "The Early Settlement of Southwestern Michigan," in *Michigan
Pioneer and Historical Collections*, V, 150. A little farther north (in Calhoun
County) in 1833 Charles Fenno Hoffman thought that even city folks "might
manage with the aid of cranberry sauce to rough it on venison and wild honey,
backed by the finest potatoes and best wheat bread in the world." *A Winter in
the West*, I, 184. Hoffman reported that in the Prairie Ronde region the settlers
from the South and West outnumbered those from New York. *Ibid.*, I, 216. Other
accounts of settlement of this region are in *Michigan Pioneer and Historical Collections*, III (1879–80), XVIII (1891).
[148] *Detroit Gazette*, June 25, 1829. Health and crops were good, and many new
arrivals from Indiana, Illinois, and elsewhere, came in, reported the *Buffalo
Journal*. Cited in *Piqua Gazette*, August 15, 1829.
[149] A. D. P. Van Buren, "Pioneer Annals of Calhoun County," in *Michigan
Pioneer and Historical Collections*, V (1882), 246–47. The Kalamazoo Valley—
Territorial Road counties were organized as follows: Kalamazoo, 1830; Jackson,
1832; Calhoun, 1833; Allegan, 1835; Van Buren, 1837.

View of the Great Indian Treaty at Prairie du Chien, 1825. *J. O. Lewis*

Fort Crawford at Prairie du Chien. *Henry Lewis*

Fort Winnebago at the Portage. *Mrs. John H. Kinzie*

Grand Kaukauna of the Fox. *Samuel M. Brooks* and
Thomas H. Stevenson, 1856

Green Bay. *Samuel M. Brooks* and *Thomas H. Stevenson*, 1856

Battle of Bad Axe. *Henry Lewis*

View of Southport (Kenosha) in 1842. From *Garland of the West*

CINCINNATI IN 1841.
FOR THE FAMILY MAGAZINE.

Whig Print, 1837

"Col. Johnson's mounted men charging a party of British Artillerists and Indians at the Battle fought near Moravian Town October 5, 1813, when the whole of the British force commanded by Gen. Proctor surrendered to the Army under Gen. Harrison and his Gallant followers."

"This Log Cabin was the first building erected on the North Bend of the beautiful Ohio River with the barrel of Cider outside and the door always open to the traveller. The wounded Soldier is one of Gen. Harrison's comrades, meeting him after his celebrated Victory at Tippecanoe and not only does the brave old Hero give his comrade a hearty welcome but his dog recognizes him as an old acquaintance, and repeats the welcome by a cordial and significant shake of his tail! If the looker-on will only watch close enough he can see the tail absolutely shake in the picture, particularly in a clear day, and if it is held due East and West, so as to feel the power of the magnetic attraction from the Great West."

Democratic Print, 1840

THE SCHOOLMASTER.

THE PEDDLER.

Darley Drawings, from McConnel's *Western Characters*

Camp Ground

Yours Truly
James Hall

Great Inland Sea Serpent. *George Winter*, 1838

The Lower Wabash. *Charles Bodmer,* 1832

New Harmony. *David Dale Owen*, 1830

New Harmony—All Owin' and No Payin'. *George Cruikshank*

The larger prairies were settling in 1829–30, but the burr- and white-oak openings were not neglected. These parklike woods were so open that a cabriolet could have been driven through them for miles; a traveler compared them to pear orchards. "What a country this is. Into land like this, which is comparatively undervalued by those seeking to settle in the prairie, a man can run his plough without felling a tree; and, planting a hundred acres, where he would clear but ten in the unsettled districts of New-York, raise his twenty-five bushels of wheat to the acre in the very first season."[150]

Saugatuck (originally called Kalamazoo) at the mouth of the river, Kalamazoo (originally called Bronson), Battle Creek, and Marshall, as well as Jackson, one county to the east, were first settled in 1830–31. Allegan, though off to a late start (1835), was booming by 1836.[151]

The Black Hawk War and the cholera epidemic of 1832 slowed settlement somewhat in southwestern Michigan, but immigration picked up noticeably in the years following. Although the Territorial Road was far from being a dependable affair,[152] people did get through. Marshall and Kalamazoo became thriving towns. The latter, with its "sweet white houses, scattered over the plain, among the Burr oak trees" was a beautiful village. Marshall was "not so pleasant . . . but with more natural advantages." The land office was removed to Kalamazoo from White Pigeon in 1834, and with it came the newspaper; a branch of the bank of Michigan was opened the same year.[153] Marshall, with a store, a hotel, a sawmill, and a gristmill, was debating

---

[150] Hoffman, *A Winter in the West*, I, 183.

[151] This village was the project of a stock company of Boston—New York men which in 1833–34 purchased 20,000 acres on the Lower Kalamazoo and started workmen clearing a site. Water power, lumber, a mill, and good navigation were emphasized. *Detroit Daily Free Press*, February 8, 1836; *Detroit Daily Advertiser*, November 29, 1836.

[152] The statement that "covered wagons literally whitened its entire length from 1832 to 1837" (O. C. Comstock, "History of Calhoun County," in *Michigan Pioneer and Historical Collections*, II [1877], 194) should not convey the idea that it was a turnpike. A. D. P. Van Buren, "Pioneer Annals . . . ," in *ibid.*, V (1882), 237 ff, describes this rugged road as of 1836 in considerable detail.

[153] By the territorial census of 1834 the population of Kalamazoo County was almost equal to the combined population of its neighbors, Calhoun and Jackson. Land sales at "Bronson" in 1835 were $931,875, or one tenth of the total of all sixty land offices of the United States. Kalamazoo *Michigan Statesman* copied in *Chicago Democrat*, January 27, 1836. Total sales in the Kalamazoo district (Calhoun, Branch, Kalamazoo, Cass, Berrien, Barry, and Allegan counties) to January, 1838, were 3,086,138 acres or $3,869,135. *Detroit Daily Advertiser*, May 2, 1838.

the possibility of a railroad through the valley and was well on its way to becoming "one of the most flourishing villages of the peninsula." Jackson, though at the intersection of eight Indian trails, developed slowly in its early years, but made rapid strides in the late 1830's. In 1836 a Presbyterian missionary said "Jacksonburgh is the New Orleans in health and morals of our county seats west. But two or three women there and one man promised me that they would lay the foundation of something better."[154] As immigration along the Territorial Road increased between 1834 and 1837, the balance in numbers turned in favor of the Easterners.[155]

Although the "Sciawassa Company" may have reached the Grand River country in 1821,[156] the region attracted no important attention until the early 1830's. Joseph La Framboise, an employee of John Jacob Astor, had established a trading post about fifty miles from the mouth of the Grand River in 1806. His widow sold out to Rix Robinson in 1821 and the latter moved the post some ten miles south to the mouth of the Thornapple. Robinson, who was perhaps the real founder of the Grand River settlement, had been educated in New York for the law, but after dodging the draft in the War of 1812 moved west and worked for Astor at various places. (He later became a lumberman, banker, and state senator.) In 1825 Isaac McCoy sent a missionary to the Rapids of the Grand to work among the Ottawa and the following year Louis Campau moved over from Saginaw where he had had a trading post since 1815. Soon other members of the family arrived from Detroit and the nucleus of Grand Rapids was established. First land entries were made in 1831 at which time a farmer reported that the land along the Grand, all things considered, was the finest in the Territory.[157] A post office was opened the following year, and lots which sold for $25 in 1833 were selling for more than $500 two years later. The new village was estimated to have a population of 1,000 in 1837 and, with its water power and industrial prospects, was

---

[154] William Page, Ann Arbor, March 2, 1836, to secretary. Papers of American Home Missionary Society.
[155] And Jackson County moved ahead of Kalamazoo in population.
[156] See Chapter I. United States surveyors briefly described the lands about the rapids in 1826. *Michigan Herald*, April 26, 1826.
[157] *Detroit Journal and Michigan Advertiser*, November 9, 1831.

being referred to as "The Rochester of Michigan."[158] Kent County, organized in 1831, included the old Framboise place, the Robinson settlement, and Grand Rapids. Access to this region was possible by way of Lake Michigan and the river, by the Territorial Road—taking the Indian trails north from Jackson, Marshall, Battle Creek, and Kalamazoo—and by the Grand River Road which ran north and west from Pontiac. Sometimes the settlers cut across the open country.

Settlers from New York located at Ionia some miles farther up the Grand River in 1833, and after the treaty of 1836[159] by which the Ottawa and Chippewa ceded the land north of the river, a new land office was opened here. Land sales flourished, many of them for speculative account.

Rix Robinson, manager of numerous American Fur Company trading posts, was operating a post at the mouth of the river in the 1820's, but Grand Haven was not laid out until 1835.[160] Soon the village had four hundred people and became the county seat in 1838. New York and Philadelphia speculators projected a magnificent paper city of 124 blocks on the lake shore just south of Grand Haven in 1836–37, and spent thousands of dollars for dwellings, mills, a luxurious hotel, and a lighthouse, but "Port Sheldon" died aborning. "Here once stood the proud city of Port Sheldon, a victim of high jinx, high wines, and high finance."[161] Bellevue, Charlotte, and Vermontville on the Indian trail between Marshall and Ionia (all in Eaton County) date from the mid 1830's; by 1837 the county had about 2,000 population.

Barry County just to the west was hardly discovered by settlers until the height of the "Michigan Fever" in 1836. Hastings, later to be the county-seat town, as yet had no inhabitants.

[158] Grand Rapids Grand River Times, April 18, 1837, quoted in Fuller, Economic and Social Beginnings of Michigan, 425.

[159] See map, ante, I, 111. Also Z. G. Winsor, "Early Settlement of Ottawa County," in Michigan Pioneer and Historical Collections, IX (1886), 234–37.

[160] Robinson had operated trading posts near the head of Lake Michigan in 1817, on the Lower Illinois in 1819, and around Milwaukee in 1820, before he built the cabin on the Grand River at the junction with the Thornapple in 1821. For years the departure of his trading fleet from the Grand River was an event. Mrs. Mary F. Robinson, "Rix Robinson, Fur Trader," in Michigan History Magazine, VI (1922), 277–87.

[161] Ralph C. Meima, "A Forgotten City," in Michigan History Magazine, V (1921), 409.

A far more likely prospect at this time was Yankee Springs on the Indian trail which ran from the St. Joseph Valley to the Grand River Rapids. Here William Lewis, of New York, who had given a look at Indiana and Illinois, in 1836 located his famous tavern miles from the nearest settlement. He put in a four-acre garden, began clearing 320 acres, brought in supplies, traded with the Indians for berries and maple sugar, and added outbuildings. "Yankee Lewis," full of anecdote, discriminating charity, and knowledge of people, was reputed never to have forgotten a face. Though the combination of his wife's culinary prowess with his own genial disposition and good management made his hostelry one of the most famous in the West, and took Lewis to the state legislature, Yankee Springs never developed into a city.[162]

Farther up the Grand Valley speculators in 1836 planned a city to take advantage of the water power and timber.[163] But what was destined to be the future capital of the state did not get off to a strong start. The paper city was sold for taxes and did not get in on the predepression boom. Ingham County had a population of 822 in 1837 and Clinton, its neighbor on the north, only 529.

A hundred miles north and west of Detroit lay the Saginaw country, a rolling terrain of hardwood and pine forests, oak openings, "wet prairies" or swamps, and rich river bottoms. Early tales of the miserable nature of this country[164] were soon disproved, but its reputation for "unhealthiness" and the abandonment of Saginaw as a garrison post in 1823 did not encourage rapid settlement in the 1820's;[165] neither did the fur traders of the region, nor the speculators and promoters of lands nearer Detroit. The lack of local newspapers to puff the country was a further handicap.[166] Nevertheless, favorable but sane notices began to appear which emphasized navigability of the river, rich

---

[162] George H. White, "Yankee Lewis' Famous Hostelry in the Wilderness," in *Michigan Pioneer and Historical Collections*, XXVI (1894–95), 302–7.

[163] *Detroit Daily Free Press*, May 11, 1836.

[164] See Chapter I, 20.

[165] Dr. Zina Pitcher, post surgeon, had reported that "nothing but Indians, muskrats and bullfrogs could exist" there. *History of Saginaw County* (1881), cited in Fuller, *Economic and Social Beginnings of Michigan*, 368.

[166] *The Saginaw Journal*, 1836–38, was the only paper prior to 1839.

prairie lands, fish, timber, salt, and building stone.[167] Improvements of the Indian trail north to Saginaw were begun by an army detail in 1822, but by 1835 they extended only a few miles beyond Flint, and the road, until completed by the state in 1841, was barely passable for wagons.

Agents of the American Fur Company were well acquainted with the Saginaw country prior to 1820; several of their trading posts became the sites of later towns. Louis Campau, of Detroit, the first important pioneer of the Saginaw Valley, planned the town of "Sagana" in 1822, but when the United States garrison was removed, the project languished until 1832 when "Saginaw City" was platted and a number of settlers came in. In the optimistic days of 1837 Detroit capital was ventured and a city of 400 blocks was envisaged. Actually the village at that time had about 50 houses, 4 stores, 2 steam sawmills, a church, and a hotel in the process of being erected; the population of 900 shrank by half during the depression following. Saginaw in the early period, like most frontier towns, faced life with gusto. The appearance of a new settler, the visit of a friend, a good business deal, served to start one of the famous "Saginaw trains," in which champagne as well as more potent drinks flowed freely.[168]

Around the crossing of the Flint (Grand Traverse), Jacob Smith, married to a Chippewa wife, got a reservation of 5,760 acres by the Treaty of Saginaw in 1819. His successor set up a ferry and a tavern at the ford in 1825, which marked the beginning of the village of Flint, first platted in 1835. The next year the land office for the Saginaw district was opened there, but the village did not become important for several years.

Two fur traders from Oakland County—Boston natives by way of Detroit—in 1831 drove across country, founded a post and cultivated land at the place later known as "Shiawassee town." Five years later settlers from Huron County, Ohio, moved in and soon the village had two dozen houses, two mills, and the "Exchange Bank of Shiawassee." But hard times caught

---

[167] *Detroit Gazette*, May 9, 1826; *North-Western Journal*, April 21, May 26, 1830. These notices were copied in eastern papers and brought inquiries to Detroit editors.

[168] Judge Albert Miller, "Convivial Habits of the Pioneers of Saginaw," in *Michigan Pioneer and Historical Collections*, IX (1886), 137–39; "The Saginaw Valley," in *ibid.*, VII (1884), 228–77; and "Incidents in the Early History of the Saginaw Valley," in *ibid.*, XIII (1888), 351–83.

this incipient city and it was advertised to be sold at auction.[169]
Byron, on the Grand River Trail, appeared on Orange Risdon's
map of 1825 and was a county-seat project for Shiawassee
County. When creation of Genesee County left Byron in the
corner of Shiawassee, the village of Corunna was made the
county seat in 1836, but a year later, when platted, this "town"
had only a log house or two in it. Livingston County, at the south
edge of the Saginaw country, began to settle in 1835. Howell
("Livingston Center"), Brighton, and Livingston were early
villages.

Although by late 1838, 25,636 of the 56,541 square miles of
Michigan Territory had been surveyed, and a fifth, sixth, and
part of a seventh tier of counties had appeared on the maps—
making a total of 39—these new counties were mere legislative
creations; beyond Saginaw County there were no settlements
in the interior, and the region to the north was still called the
"Siberia of Michigan."

When in 1831 Tocqueville and a companion inquired of the
tavern keeper at Pontiac, "which, in twenty years perhaps, will
be a town," regarding the route to Saginaw, his host was astonished that two rational and well-brought-up strangers should
wish to go to Saginaw Bay. "Do you not know that Saginaw is
the last inhabited point this side of the Pacific Ocean; that from
here to Saginaw one finds only wilderness and unbroken solitude."[170] Allowing for some confusion in direction, the good citizen of Pontiac seemed to have forgotten the Sault. Here, on the
American side just below the Indian village, was a medley of
lodges, bark cabins, log buildings, and a few well-built frame
houses; there were between 150 and 200 inhabitants. Fort Brady
was variously described as a white barracks surrounded by green
grass which gave a feeling of neatness and comfort, with troops
who maneuvered with celerity and precision, and as a fortress
of cedar posts with an unmilitary-looking garrison.[171] A Baptist
mission and school had been set up in the late 1820's and

[169] Bela Hubbard, *Memorials of a Half-Century* (New York and London, 1887),
71.
[170] *Oeuvres et Correspondance Inédite* (2 volumes. Paris, 1861), I, 203.
[171] *Cleveland Herald and Gazette*, July 31, 1839 (series of three articles reporting on an excursion to the Sault and Mackinac); McKenney, *Tour to the Lakes*,
176; Anna Jameson, *Winter Studies and Summer Rambles*, cited in Grace Lee Nute,
Lake Superior (Indianapolis, 1944), 221.

Methodist and Catholic missionaries arrived a few years later. Here lived the numerous family of John Johnston and his Chippewa wife, and, until 1833, Henry R. Schoolcraft, Indian agent, traveler and author who had married Jane Johnston;[172] also Gabriel Franchere, one of the old hands of the American Fur Company. White fish, maple sugar, and some furs were leading staples of trade; the villagers also raised potatoes and other vegetables. Canoes in summer, snowshoes and dog trains in winter were the means of local transportation.

About fifty miles to the south, guarding the straits to Lake Michigan, was the bold and rugged island of Mackinac, a historic and romantic spot, richer in scenery than population, with its Giant's Arch, Skull Rock, and the ruins of Fort Holmes. The Presbyterian mission school housed more than a hundred children, ages four to eighteen—Indians, half- and quarter-breeds, and offspring of the villagers. The village homes, except the buildings of the American Fur Company, were small log affairs. Thomas McKenney of the Indian Department, well acquainted with the lakes scenery, described it in 1826:

Mackinac is really worth seeing. . . . It is not possible to give . . . even the slightest conception of the grandeur of the view from this vast elevation! The lake, Huron, spreads out before you in the east as far as the eye can see; its islands, green and ornamental, varying and beautifying the scene—Round Island—Bois Blanc, and others; and then the main to the west and north-west—the Rabbits' Back, and the opening into Lake Michigan, with the scenery of Michillimackinac itself, with its fort and beautifully varied surface, make altogether the most commanding display which the lake makes anywhere of its vastness, and variety, and grandeur.[173]

Thirteen years later a steamboat excursionist tried his pen:

We were lying in a tiny, crescent shaped bay—around which, buried in repose, the village clustered, and close in the rear rose the picturesque cliffs of the island, crowned with a snow white fortress from which lights were gleaming like stars set in mid air. The moon hung over the bay—tapering masts rose from the water and the spire of the missionary church from

[172] See McKenney, *Tour to the Lakes*, 181–90, for interesting description of the Johnston family; also C. H. Chapman, "The Historic Johnston Family of the 'Soo,'" in *Michigan Pioneer and Historical Collections*, XXXII (1902), 305–53.

[173] McKenney, *Tour to the Lakes*, 394, 397. McKenney thought that, if the steamboats came, Mackinac might become a place of fashionable summer resort where "temperate people may, with something like certainty, if not organically diseased, spin out life's thread to its utmost tenuity."

the land, clearly and distinctly defined in the sky. Stillness held dominion, and a delicious serenity seemed interfused in the night air.[174]

No other state in the Old Northwest has such an abundant amount of descriptive material available for its early years as Michigan. This is partly accounted for by its relatively late settlement, perhaps partly by the greater articulateness, at least in writing, of the New York–New England settlers, but most of all by the early activity of the Pioneer and Historical Society, which in 1874 began to collect and shortly to publish the stories and reminiscences of the pioneers. One lasting impression to be had from a reading of hundreds of accounts in the thirty-nine volumes of the *Collections* is that of the reaction of the new-comers to the beauty of the country.[175]

Headlining their memories were the oak openings, where the Indian fires had kept out the underbrush, and through which one could see, walk, ride, or drive a wagon. The traveler rode out of the dense forest into

clumps of the noblest oaks, with not a twig of underwood, extending over a gently undulating grassy surface as far as the eye can reach; here clustered together in a grove of tall stems supporting one broad canopy of interlacing branches, and there rearing their gigantic trunks in solitary grandeur from the plain. The feeling of solitude I had while in the deep woods deserted me the moment I came upon this beautiful scene, and I rode on for hours, unable without an effort to divest myself of the idea that I was in a cultivated country.[176]

Of oaks there were a dozen kinds, including the burr oak with edible acorns. In the woods were whitewood or *bois blanc,*[177] maple, beech, ash, black walnut, butternut (white walnut), and cherry; also hazel, reaching and tenuous grapevines, and black-berries. The openings as well as the prairies were often covered with a blue-jointed native grass, four or five feet high (one person testified twenty), a natural hay crop almost as nutritious as timothy. Soil which produced this grass—whether eighteen inches of gravelly loam or four feet or more of such as would

---

[174] *Cleveland Herald and Gazette,* July 31, 1839.
[175] Memories which the years would be less likely to distort than memories of specific facts.
[176] Hoffman, *Winter in the West,* I, 143.
[177] The "poplar" (*Liriodendron tulipifera*) to the settlers from the South. The differences between the "white poplar" and "yellow poplar" are slight, but the latter was much preferred for its wood.

"grease your fingers"—would when properly plowed produce thirty-five to forty bushels of wheat per acre or twice as much corn. In spring the prairies were literally a bed of flowers, but flowers grew in the marshes and woods, and in the summer and autumn, too: wild roses, crimson daisies, purple foxgloves, red columbine, snowy lilies of the valley, mauve adder's tongue, cardinal flowers, the brilliant fireweed, and dozens more.[178] Then there were the "limpid lakes," large and small—"so beautifully transparent . . . that the canoe suspended on their bosom seems to float in mid air"—pebbly bottomed brooks, and grass-banked creeks and rivers. "From time to time a small lake (this region is full of them) appears like a sheet of silver under the forest foliage. It is difficult to imagine the charm which surrounds these beautiful places where man has not yet made his abode, and where a profound peace and uninterrupted silence still prevail."[179]

Deer grazed leisurely, like sheep, in the openings. Gophers, chipmunks, and fox squirrels were often pests, while the madcap and piratical blue jay was something of a nuisance. In the early years there were no crows to steal the corn, nor house flies or house mice. Absent, too, were robins, wrens, and swallows, but the mocking bird furnished a complete repertory of music (and noises), while the whippoorwill, "bird of night . . . sad and wild," performed its monotonous and doleful ditty. Tocqueville, comparing the solitudes with those in the Alps, wrote:

Here the solitude is not less profound, but it does not create the same impressions. The only feelings which one has on travelling through these

[178] Interpreting not the language of flowers, but of the country itself: "Here she told of vast fortunes to be made in the lumber trade; but heavy blows and hard labor to be given ere the emigrant could get to farming. In her oak openings she said: 'here are lands, almost fitted for the plow; build a house of the wood here, fence into fields, thin out the timber, if in the way, keep the heaviest for woodland, and go to farming.' In her prairies she said—'here are your farm lands; build your house, fence off into lots and drive your team a-field.' In her marshes she said—'here is your meadow, all ready for the scythe; fence it off to keep the cattle from spoiling it, and mow in the proper season.' In her streams she babbled of mill privileges; of grinding wheat and corn; of turning machinery for shops, and of the manufacturing power to build up villages and cities. In her lakes she said—'here you have the useful and the beautiful; find me out.' And she said in more general terms—'I have vast stores of wealth concealed in the earth, find them and they are yours.'" Van Buren, "Pioneer Annals," in *Michigan Pioneer and Historical Collections*, V, 249–50. See also Cutcheon, "Log Cabin Times and Log Cabin People," in *ibid.*, XXIX, 615. Early catalogues of Michigan plants are in Douglass Houghton (first state geologist of Michigan), Report of 1839, reprinted in *Geological Reports of Douglass Houghton* . . . , edited by George N. Fuller (Lansing, 1928), 226 ff., and in Schoolcraft's *Summary Narrative* (1855).

[179] Tocqueville, *Oeuvres et Correspondance Inédite*, I, 206.

flowering wildernesses, where, as in Milton's *Paradise Lost*, all is prepared to receive man, are a quiet admiration, a gentle and sad emotion, a vague loathing of civilized life, a sort of primitive instinct which makes one reflect with sorrow that soon this delightful solitude will have ceased to exist. Already, in fact, the white race is advancing through the forests which surround it, and in a few years the Europeans will have cut the trees which reflect in the limpid waters of the lake, and will have forced the animals which populate its banks to retreat toward new wilds.[180]

Pioneer life in Michigan Territory east of the lake differed from that in the Ohio Valley in many details—in names of things, methods of cooking, plowing, in customs and manners—but the processes were the same.[181] Though the winters were longer and colder,[182] the later date of settlement compensated for this in improved travel facilities, better equipment, and the general friendliness of the Indians. Though in the rush of settlement there was at times a food shortage, so that farmers dug up and ate the potatoes they had planted, ordinarily food was adequate if not abundant. Venison and wild honey could be had from the Indians in exchange for salt. With the abundance of arable land, plenty of sunshine and rain, pure streams and excellent water supply, wild game and singing birds, the industrious farmer and his worthy wife could feel with the poet:

> These are the pleasures that give to his heart
> More than ambition or pompt could impart.
> Thus sang the emigrated man,
> Now fix'd at last in Michigan;
> No more a Pilgrim of the road,
> Roaming in quest of new abode,
> Uncertain where his course to bend,
> And where his pilgrimage would end.[183]

Approximately two thirds of the settlers derived from western New York, particularly the counties in and around the "Genesee country," and from New England—Massachusetts, Connecticut, and Vermont. Many of the New Yorkers were natives of New England. A fair portion of the emigrants came from Ireland,

[180] Tocqueville, *Oeuvres et Correspondance Inedité,* I, 207.
[181] See Chapter IV.
[182] Yet there were winters in the early 1820's when land was broken in December, January, and February. *Michigan Pioneer and Historical Collections,* VIII (1885), 238. The winters of 1839–40, 1840–41, 1841–42 were also mild; boys played ball at times in January and February. *Ibid.,* XXXI (1902), 211.
[183] Henry Whiting, *The Emigrant.*

England, and Germany.[184] Like most pioneers they were preponderantly young, hopeful, confident, and individualistic to a degree, but true to their heritage and nativities, they had a strong sense of social responsibility, and in many ways were more conservative in their outlook in religion, politics, and customs than their neighbors from the South.[185] There were fewer of the half-hunter, half-farmer type among them, and by and large they came with more money or material possessions than the Upland-South folk of southern Indiana and Illinois. Hoffman found himself "among the most intelligent population of the middle class (the bone and sinew of a community) I ever mixed with; and every one seems so contented, may even say delighted, with his adopted home, that I am catching a little of the spirit of those around me. . . ."[186]

The hospitality of the frontier prevailed at all times excepting during the inundations of land speculators. "These people were considered as public enemies. No personal violence was offered them . . . but every obstacle, in the shape of extravagant charges, erroneous information, and rude refusal, was thrown in their way."[187]

While the interest in settlement of the interior counties was rapidly approaching the mad speculative boom of the middle 1830's, Detroit was becoming a city. Growth was slow until 1830 (1,500 to 2,200), but four years later the population was almost 5,000, and by 1838 twice that number.[188] Boats frequently arrived with 600 passengers; hotels were filled. Many four-story buildings "were erecting" and mechanics were much in demand. Some of the French owners of the long narrow farms which

[184] For analysis of sample counties, see Fuller, *Economic and Social Beginnings of Michigan*, Chapter IX.

[185] As Mrs. Kirkland, in spite of a faint air of artificiality and superciliousness, was keen enough to see: "The customs of the West are such as might naturally be expected to grow up among a most heterogeneous population, contriving to live under the pressure of extreme difficulties, and living not in the present but in the future. This is the condition of shifts and turns—'expedients and inventions multiform;' encroachments, substitutes, borrowings; public spirit and individual selfishness; a feeling of common interest, conflicting strangely with an entire readiness to flirt with the first offer of 'a trade'; neighbourly kindness struggling against the necessity of looking out sharply for number one." *Western Clearings*, Preface, vii.

[186] *A Winter in the West*, I, 152.

[187] Mrs. Kirkland, *Western Clearings*, 2. For stories of tricks played on these gentlemen, see pp. 4-14.

[188] By 1834 census, 801 of the 4,973 persons were listed as French. *Detroit Journal and Michigan Advertiser* (semiweekly), April 8, 1834.

crossed the main street at the upper end of town were holding out for high prices on eager lot purchasers. Sales of lots in "Cass Front" in 1836 totaled about $190,000; water-front lots brought $146 to $220 per foot, rear lots $60 to $235.[189] Although one block of cobblestone paving had been laid the preceding year, wagons still got stuck in the mud on Woodward Avenue. The fire department was having growing pains: engines, hose, and ladders arrived separately at fires; wardens and engineers would not wear their insignia. Still it was active and efficient and put out seemingly impossible fires.[190]

The crude frontier trading post of the postwar period had come a long way. In 1817 receipts in the public treasury had totaled $254 (including $17 for use of the hay scales) for the fiscal year preceding.[191] In 1831 the city "budget" was $8,800, and the corporation had borrowed $1,500 and issued corporation money for $1,282;[192] in 1838–39 it was approximately $65,000 for salaries, waterworks, fire protection, streets, and markets.[193] In local politics discussion of taxes was so prominent that the *Free Press* accused the *Advertiser* of scaring emigrants away.

"Detroit," said a visitor in 1838, "is, in all its peculiar characteristics, an eastern city. It was peopled and built up by eastern men, in eastern style, and the habits of the east prevail above those of the west. It is a growing place, and destined to become one of the largest of western cities."[194] By 1840 the city was discussing the need for public improvements—shade trees and better architecture—and becoming conscious of its history and the possibilities of its literary and cultural institutions,[195] as was befitting a city with three bookstores, four printing offices, three daily newspapers, four weeklies, and one triweekly. Yet elections in this period were reported as barbaric,[196] and within a few years people were agitating—even holding prayer meetings—for re-

[189] *Detroit Daily Advertiser*, October 22, 1836.
[190] *Ibid.*, May 28, 1839.
[191] *Detroit Gazette*, May 21, 1817. Expenditures, including unpaid orders in the treasury, for two years were $583 over receipts. There were $180 of unpaid fines in the form of individual notes, etc.
[192] *Detroit Journal and Michigan Advertiser*, April 27, 1831.
[193] *Detroit Daily Advertiser*, April 17, 1839.
[194] A. D. Jones, *Illinois and the West*, 239.
[195] *Detroit Daily Advertiser*, April—May, 1838, ran a series of articles by O-ta-nung on these topics.
[196] Thomas W. Palmer, "Detroit Sixty Years Ago," in *Michigan Pioneer and Historical Collections*, XXXI (1902), 504, 507.

moval of the capital elsewhere. Whether this was because of fear that the "gross indecency and immorality" of the legislators were contaminating the city, or the frivolities of the city were affecting the manners and morals of the legislators may never be settled.[197]

By 1834 the population of Michigan Territory was 87,278, and the question of statehood was uppermost in the thoughts of all politically minded citizens.[198] In 1836, 1,475,725 acres of land were sold, more than one third of the total sold to that date. "This whole Territory is growing like the gourd of Jonah."[199]

§ § §

The years following the Black Hawk War marked the latter part of a prosperity cycle and another peak in the tide of westward emigration. Indian removals, canals and road improvements, steam lines on the Great Lakes, the great plenty of paper money, and, above all, the spirit of the times contributed to the surge. And not even a depression could stop it. Between new notices of the lapping of the waves, editors stopped to exclaim on the gathering momentum of the tide. Ohio, though settling steadily, was not spectacular, northern Indiana was filling to the boundary, and Michigan was qualifying for statehood; but the big play in publicity was for northern Illinois and the Wisconsin country.

From Kentucky late in 1833 came the report that the number of emigrants passing through to Illinois was immense.[200] The following summer the Jacksonville *Illinois Patriot* said: "The emigration to this state the present season is without parallel."[201] A contributor to the *Sangamo Journal* believed that the child was then alive who would live to see two million population in Illinois, and that by 2000 A. D. there would be 3,000,000.[202]

---

[197] *Ibid.* See also Mrs. Sarah E. Dart, "Early Lansing," in *ibid.*, XXVIII (1900), 174; Hoyt, "The Founding of Yankee Springs," in *ibid.*, XXX, 289–302.

[198] For the statehood battle and the Ohio-Michigan "War," see Chapter XI.

[199] William Page, Ann Arbor, March 2, 1836, to secretary. Papers of the American Home Missionary Society.

[200] Hopkinsville (Ky.) *Green River Advocate* cited in *Chicago American*, November 26, 1833.

[201] Copied in *Chicago Democrat*, July 2, 1834.

[202] April 13, 1833.

(By the census of 1835 there were 269,974.) The *Paoli* (Ind.) *Patriot*[203] estimated 150 wagons of movers had passed through in two weeks; many of these were headed on West. Indianapolis witnessed an earlier-than-usual autumn movement.[204] Streets were a moving mass of men, women, and children; of carriages, wagons, cattle, horses, hogs, and sheep, "all joyously wending their way to their new habitations."

Here decisions, if not already in mind, had to be made. Local advice might favor the near-by valleys of East and West forks of White River, and many heeded it. Some favored the timbered country stretching from the Upper Wabash on east to the Ohio line, of which Samuel Medary, editor of the *Ohio Farmer,* wrote that in "no portion of the Union that it has been our pleasure or our fortune to visit have we observed so many requisites for a dense agricultural population as in this."[205] Many did not agree with the idea that the prairies of northern Indiana, like those of Illinois, would not (for want of timber for fencing) be settled for years to come—and headed for them or similar land in Illinois.

Cleveland reported the westward movement "beyond any former example."[206] Each season saw the numbers increase. In the spring of 1835 fifty-six boats left Buffalo for the West in one week. Six to eight boats with 1,000 to 1,500 passengers passed Erie daily. At this rate the season's total by the lake route would be 200,000.[207] The next year was the same. In October, when Buffalo reported nine boats with 4,000 people having left for the West, they were welcomed with, "There is yet room, and all things are ready."[208]

By the Ohio and Mississippi, too, they came. At St. Louis in two days in November, twenty-seven steamboats arrived with nearly 1,800 passengers for the new country. Such traffic had never before been seen.[209]

[203] October 9, 1834.
[204] *Indiana Journal,* September 19, 1834.
[205] *Ohio Farmer and Western Horticulturist* (Columbus), September 1, 1835.
[206] *Cleveland Herald,* June 1, 1833; *Hamilton* (Ohio) *Intelligencer,* July 15, 1833.
[207] *Erie Observer,* May 16, 1835; Ravenna *Western Courier,* May 28, 1835.
[208] *Buffalo Commercial Advertiser,* October 24, 1836; *Chicago American,* November 12, 1836. So great was the demand for transportation that steamboats were estimated to "clear 50 per cent" and schooners 80 to 100 per cent.
[209] St. Louis *Commercial Bulletin,* November 24, 1836; *Milwaukee Advertiser,* December 1, 1836.

Hundreds of items of this sort were copied by the papers and commented upon. The western fever was contagious. In 1837 the "pressure of the times" was expected to swell the torrents as eastern cities would continue to throw thousands into the lap of the fast-growing West.[210] There (in the East) the want of employment affected not only the mechanic, but the speculator, merchant, and broker were "gathering up their little remaining fragments, preparatory to commencing their system of domestic economy in the West, where they may enjoy the comforts and necessaries of life far from the ostentation and extravagance of the Atlantic cities, to support which requires such a wear and tear of mental and physical abilities. . . . All the gentlemen emigrants are turning squatters."[211]

Where would it all end? If the rage for land did not subside, there soon would be none left.[212] If the plethora of town making did not cease, it would be necessary to petition Congress to reserve one or two sections in each township for agricultural purposes.[213] Where was the West? It was no longer Buffalo, nor even Chicago! A few years earlier Ohio was the West; now it was merely the starting point for the West. Whereas in 1833— in keeping with the idea of "the Great American Desert" of the Far West—some people believed that the effective limits of permanent Anglo-Saxon settlement for a century to come would be Missouri, Arkansas, and Wisconsin territories,[214] there were others who more accurately measured the bounds to which the spirit at large in the land would carry settlement. To contemplate, to dwell upon the fond anticipation of the future, constituted the supreme moment in the life of man:

What a field of enterprise . . . does the great West afford! . . . Situated in a country where the earth is pregnant with fortunes for those that seek, we are enabled to observe the zeal with which they prosecute their undertakings, and judge the spirit which buoys them up—whilst the clouds of gloom that o'erhang the head of the timid, drive them to pursuits of surer gain. 'Tis here that that spirit which carries men through undertaking of uncertain character, prevails to an extent approaching to unanimity. . . .

[210] *Cleveland Herald and Gazette* (weekly), May 6, 1837.
[211] *New York Star*, quoted in *Milwaukee Advertiser*, May 20, 1837.
[212] "An Illinois Farmer," in Springfield *Illinois State Register and Advocate*, April 29, 1836.
[213] *Miners' Free Press*, September 1, 1837.
[214] Springfield *Sangamo Journal*, April 13, 1833. (Although Wisconsin Territory had not yet been organized, it was often spoken of in anticipation.)

The fact that the country has sprung from its wild to its present condition, within a few years—that the buffalo has given place to the ploughman's herd—the wigwam to the mansion—the canoe to the magestic steamboat —tell[s] us that there is a spirit in the land that will not slumber til the settlements shall extend an unmeasured distance towards the Rocky Mountains.[215]

Then the waves would shortly be breaking over the Rocky Mountains "and the quiet vales of the Columbia" would team with a people whose progenitors dwelt in New England and looked upon the Appalachians as the impassable boundary of the western world.[216] "The vast tide of emigration cannot be stopped until the Pacific opposes a barrier."[217]

And the people—what were they like? An outsider, observing them, was reminded "of the invading hosts of barbarians under Ghengis Khan and Attila."

The multitude is in every sense of the word an invading army, ruled as armies are; where individuals count for nothing, and the mass is every thing. Wo betide the man, who, in his onward career, stumbles; he is inevitably crushed and trampled under foot. Wo betide the man, who finds a yawning precipice interpose between him and the goal of his wishes; the impatient multitude behind thrust him rudely forward, till he falls into the abyss beneath his feet. He is hardly missed, and soon forgotten, without one sigh even by the way of regret. Each man for himself. Help yourself, sir. The life of a true American, is like that of a soldier; here to-day, to-morrow fifty miles off. He must ever be on the alert, ever in a state of excitement. As is the case in camps, so in the west, quarrels are decided on the spot, with swords or rifles, as it may be. Theirs is a life of strangely blended success and reverses. To-day in abject poverty; to-morrow rolling in wealth; the day after, as poor as ever; according to the success or failure of their speculations; but still, as a nation, their prosperity is gradually, but most certainly increasing. As a soldier, the motto of a western man is "to conquer or die;" but conquering with him, means to make money; to build up a fortune from nothing, to buy lots at Chicago, Cleveland, or at St. Louis, and to sell them the next year at the rate of a thousand *per cent*.[218]

A New Englander observing from Wisconsin a few years later saw "the world in miniature":

[215] *Belmont* (Wis.) *Gazette,* November 30, 1836.
[216] Springfield (Ill.) *Morning Courier,* in *Cincinnati Daily Gazette,* November 10, 1840.
[217] *New York Spectator* quoted in *Du Buque Visitor,* November 9, 1836.
[218] M. Chevalier, "Letters on America," in *Western Monthly Magazine,* IV, 413–14.

The five races of both continents are present. . . . The Yankee is in his own latitude, and retains in full his unique identity. Men with European tongues gather in here like the dispersed of the tribes of Israel. All say welcome to each other. The Frenchman shortens his mustaches, and becomes American. The Irishman you recognize by his hardy form and native brogue. . . . Jews and Germans are here. . . . I see . . . a respectable representation of the people of color, and one small band of natives—real red men, but wearing paints of different colors on their cheecks.[219]

English, Canadians, Welsh, Scandinavians, and others might have been noticed also. Whatever their origin, the general attitude of the West toward the new emigrants was, "We welcome them. Our country is now the asylum for the oppressed of all nations."[220] At least this was the attitude of politicians, speculators, and others interested in mere numbers.

There were Westerners, however, who, taking the longer view of the interests of the West as well as those of the emigrants, spoke a word of caution and advice. All comers would receive a hearty welcome but some would meet with disappointment.[221] Even eastern papers, though advising laborers who were out of work to go West, told them to be prepared to throw off their coats, fare rudely, and work heartily.[222] Too many were inclined to come to the towns—speculators, merchants, even mechanics—whereas it was farmers and honest, industrious laborers who were needed.

We wish to see men come here, and women too—for we are sadly in want of wives—but we wish that every one would seek, before he starts, to know what he is coming to. They that come here and turn back again, disappointed, and they that make the worst of a bad bargain, and go into speculations that must in the end prove ruinous, alike wrong both themselves and us. If they cannot win a certain and safe livelihood in trade, at home or elsewhere, they had better strip off their coat, and take to the plough. To the capitalist, small or great; to the mechanic; to the farmer; to the household servant (for servants here are a luxury); to any one that is prepared to supply the true demands of the true population, the west affords a grand field. But the speculator upon unreal demands, . . . and he that attempts to cultivate a quicksand, must expect in the west, as

---

[219] Grinnell, *Home of the Badgers*, 17.
[220] Springfield *Sangamo Journal*, September 1, 1838.
[221] *Cleveland Herald and Gazette* (weekly), May 6, 1837.
[222] *New Yorker*, in *ibid.*

elsewhere in the world, to fail in his plans; to be considered foolish, if not knavish; and to be at last worse off than when he began.[223]

Besides emigrants who became disappointed and disgruntled because they found the West not a paradise but made up of the same earth and air, inhabited by beings of the same race as themselves, there was another kind of questionable value, people who emigrated and sought to settle in groups.[224] Whether these settlers were from foreign parts or New England, on occasion the established pioneers of the West, particularly those in Indiana and southern Illinois, distrusted their motives. When the *Boston Patriot* in 1834 carried a notice of the plans for an "Association" to emigrate to Illinois, the *Illinois Advocate and State Register* wished them success, but advised the settlers to come as families or individuals and hoped that they would get rid of certain Yankee notions.[225] No man ought to leave home for new parts if he were "so strongly imbued with the peculiar manners, notions, and ways of thought of that home, as to be unable to shake them off and adopt those of his adopted country. . . . For one to come here determined to hold on to his own tastes and habits, come what will, would be as unwise as for the stork to join a French *table d'hote* and hope to dine plentifully

[223] "R." on "Emigration," in *Western Monthly Magazine*, I (1833), 94.

[224] There was at least one society (the Old Colonial Brotherhood) in New England, organized with the purpose of promoting emigration to Illinois. *Chicago Democrat*, November 12, 1834. Nicholas Hesse, himself a recent immigrant, wrote: "Nothing is more foolish and nothing furnishes more telling proof of the absolute ignorance regarding conditions in the United States, than when German Emigration Societies unite and strive to realize here the chimerical plan of establishing settlements of communal interest." He predicted failure and gave reasons. *Das Westliche Nord-Amerika* . . . (Paderborn, 1838), *passim*.

[225] October 29, 1834. Two years earlier the *Sangamo Journal* had published James Hall's article from the *Illinois Monthly Magazine* in full.

New England editors were not adverse to poking fun at all this seriousness. Apropos the shortage of wives in the West—the *Nantucket Inquirer* proposed an embargo on female emigration to those parts: "What, send our fair daughters into the woods to become partners with the 'rougher half of humanity'; yea, the half horse, half alligator, snapping turtle breed; the 'Prairie Dogs,' the 'Hooshiers,' the 'Woolverines,' &c. Why they spend three-fourths of their time in the chase, and the other fourth, 'shanted out.' What do they want wives for, unless it be to skin wild cats, make moccasins, barbecue bears, parch corn and mark the place where the squatter has taken formal possession? 'Teach Music,' forsooth! Do not young wild cats mew, and young bears growl by instinct? And doth the young raven require a teacher to modulate her voice for the utterance of 'caw,' at the approach of an enemy?—'Tell them not that you want them for wives.' Deception, ha! That wont go. Our girls are not such fools. . . ." Whereupon the *Chicago American* said that the writer of this had probably not yet made his choice and wanted a glut on the local market. Quoted in Mineral Point *Miners' Free Press*, September 22, 1837. It was promised that "all who emigrate West will not be subject to a long and tedious courtship, as we do such things here by steam." *Chicago Democrat*, October 19, 1836.

on *soupe maigre*."[226] And George Flower, who had learned some things after more than twenty years in Illinois wrote: "The idea of forming exclusive settlements of Germans, English, or Irish is very erroneous and highly prejudicial to the interests of the settlers themselves."[227]

James Hall, by this time not only historian of the West but its custodian as well, had pointedly expressed the idea in 1832 when he pointed out that emigrants, whether from Europe, New England, or Virginia, "and settling *as such* [would] be less welcome, and less prosperous, than the same number of persons, coming separately, and dropping all local distinctions." Partisanship, dissension, grew out of differences of opinion on small things rather than important matters. Too much of the spirit of reform, of egotism, of arrogance would no more be appreciated in the West than would be a colony of backwoodsmen trying to force their manners and mode of life upon the people of Massachusetts. "But the fact is that persons who emigrate to the west, have to learn from our people here, a vast deal more than they can possibly teach them." As for the idea that group settlements mitigated the hardships while multiplying the pleasures and chances of success, it was a delusion.

An individual knows how to make calculations for himself, and his own household; he knows what they can do and suffer; but he ventures into

[226] *Western Monthly Magazine*, I (1833), 93. Hoffman, studying the emigrants and their plunder on a Great Lakes steamboat, noted the Yankee with a Dearborn wagon, a featherbed, some harness, and a few useful gadgets; the Englishman who attempted to bring "even the fast-anchored isle itself" along with him; and the Swiss and Germans with heavy and impractical museum pieces which cost five times as much in freight charges as they were worth. "What an indignity it is to overwhelm the triumphal chariot [a wagon] with the beds and ploughs, shovels, saddles, and sideboards, chairs, clocks, and carpets that fill its interior, and to hang those rusty pots and kettles, bakepans, fryingpans, and saucepans, iron candlesticks, old horse-shoes, and broken tobacco-pipes, like trophies of conquest over Time, along its racked and wheezing sides." The owner of all this looked as if he had come from another planet, and probably had only the vaguest of ideas as to the kind of country he was headed for. Yet "visit him on his thriving farm ten years hence, and, except in the single point of language, you will find him (unless he has settled among a nest of his countrymen) at home among his neighbours, and happily conforming to their usages; while that clean-looking Englishman next to him will still be a stranger in the land." *A Winter in the West*, I, 106–8.
A New Englander advised emigrants from his section to remember that things in the West were conducted on a larger scale. Haggling over cents or even picayunes would astonish a western man, and appear to be mean. Small change made small men. "A mean, niggardly—or as it is here emphatically called, a '*picayune*' disposition, 'damns its possessor to everlasting fame.' Nothing is lost by adopting the enlarged spirit of the west, and in the end everything gained." A. D. Jones, *Illinois and the West*, 157–58.
[227] *The Errors of Emigrants*, 56.

the regions of conjecture, and brings many contingencies to bear on his fate, when he unites it with the uncertain fortunes of others. Men were not made for such confederacies; they are too narrow for patriotic feeling and christian benevolence, too wide for domestic security and comfort. They are built on a wrong basis. A man has one set of affections and responsibilities for his own fireside, another for his country and human nature. These are natural, and whatever is attempted to be compounded out of them, and aside from them, is artificial. The ordinary ties of kindred, country, neighborhood, and benevolence, are strong enough, without forming those artificial confederacies which sooner or later always crumble into their original elements. The industrious member of such a society gets tired of helping his lazy neighbor, the peaceable man grows sick of the quarrels of his litigious friend, and the whole society feels degraded if one of its members happens to fall into the hands of the sheriff for an unlucky felony. After all every one is the best manager of his own business, and the best judge of what is good for his own family; and he who emigrates will consult his own happiness and interest, by trusting to Providence, to his own exertions, and to the hospitality of those among whom his lot may be cast.[228]

Allowing for an increment of envy on the part of the more carefree Southerners of the thrift, industry, and success of Germans and Yankees, the latter "a shrewd, selfish, enterprising, cow-milking set of men,"[229] these words of Judge Hall (by birth

[228] *Illinois Monthly Magazine,* I (1831), 423. "R. B." in his *View of the Valley of the Mississippi,* 233–34, gave Easterners simple and candid advice: "The eastern emigrant will find warm-hearted friends in every neighbourhood in this state. The people of the West have much plain and blunt, but sincere hospitality. And any emigrant who comes among them with a disposition to be pleased with the country and its inhabitants,—to partake of their hospitality cheerfully,—to make no invidious comparisons,—to assume no airs of distinction,—and in a word, to feel at home in this region, where, of course every thing is very different from what he has been accustomed to, will be truly welcome. Fastidious and reserved manners, a disposition to be forever unfavourably contrasting the West with the East,—and to find fault with every thing around him,—will speedily render any emigrant an object of dislike and neglect."

[229] *Chicago American,* February 2, 1837, quoting a correspondent of the *National Intelligencer.* "An old Tennessee woman, who had a terrific opinion of the Yankee, said: 'I am getting skeery about them ere Yankees; there is such a power of them coming in that they and the Injuns will squatch out all the white folks.'" Tillson, *Reminiscences of Early Life in Illinois,* 15.

Noting the objections expressed by the natives to the Yankees, a British traveler said: ". . . the western people generally seem, I think unfairly, prejudiced against their eastern countrymen, who generally are decidedly the most enterprising farmers in the West. They may be a little too 'slick' for the Illinois *suckers.*" Oliver, *Eight Months in Illinois,* 178. Most New Englanders agreed with John Quincy Adams: "I consider them [Yankees] as an excellent race of people, and as far as I am able to judge, I believe that their moral and political character far from degenerating improves by emigration. I have always felt on that account a sort of predilection for those rising western states. . . . There is not upon this globe of earth a spectacle exhibited by man so interesting to my mind or so consolatory to my heart as this metamorphosis of howling deserts into cultivated fields and populous villages which is yearly, daily, hourly, going on by the hands chiefly of New England men in our western states and territories." John Quincy Adams to Benjamin Waterhouse, October 24, 1813, in Worthington C. Ford (ed.), *Writings of John Quincy Adams* (7 volumes. New York, 1913–17), IV, 526.

a Pennsylvanian) expressed as well as any the Midwesterner's idea of his chosen way of life for a century to come.

But back to the settlements, to the valleys of the Illinois and the Wisconsin, in the minds of their advocates "beyond all comparison the garden spots of America."[230]

By 1833 settlements had passed the pioneer stage in the Sangamon country. Between Springfield and Jacksonville, "What a country!" exclaimed an Easterner. In Springfield picket fences and shade trees were appearing on the public square. Although there was a shortage of common labor and the town needed a flour mill,[231] it entered the contest for location of the permanent state capital with no handicap of false modesty.[232] A new line of four-horse stages was beginning semiweekly service to St. Louis (two routes), Vandalia, and Beardstown, and weekly to Terre Haute. Also from Peoria to Galena by way of Dixon's Ferry, Peoria to Ottawa, and Ottawa to Chicago.[233]

Jacksonville, "a very pretty and flourishing place" of more than 1,000 population, had nineteen stores, numerous craftsmen's shops, several small manufactories, and a college.[234] Alton, with its nine shops and stores, steam mill, and thirty-one new houses was "fast improving."

Other towns in the central part of the state were growing,[235] but it was in the Illinois Valley, on the Military Tract, and in the northeastern part of the state that development was most rapid. Despite the fact that many of the military warrants had passed into speculative hands (some forfeited for nonpayment of taxes), much land was still available from the government.[236] Estab-

---

[230] *Milwaukee Advertiser*, May 20, 1837. The best brief account of the settlement of northern Illinois is Pease, *The Frontier State*, Chapter IX; for more detailed treatment, see Pooley, *The Settlement of Illinois*, 220.

[231] Springfield *Sangamo Journal*, May 18, July 6, October 19, 1833.

[232] The law of 1833 provided for a vote. Chief contenders were Vandalia, Springfield, Alton, and Peoria. Many long-winded articles appeared on this subject (for example, *Chicago Democrat*, April 1, *Sangamo Journal*, June 21, 1834), but when, after a struggle of about three years, Springfield was selected, the *Journal* announced the fact in three inches of type so small it was hardly legible (*Sangamo Journal*, March 4, 1836).

[233] For distances, time, and fares, see Chapter VII, 464 ff.

[234] Jacksonville *Illinois Patriot* in *Sangamo Journal*, May 17, 1832.

[235] Danville, for instance, begun in 1827, now had eighty-one houses, "a usual number of out houses," a courthouse, jail, land office, seven stores, two taverns, etc. Description and prospects in first number of *Danville Enquirer*, August 5, 1833; reprint in *Journal of the Illinois State Historical Society*, IV (1911–12), 351–53.

[236] A new law, which provided that sale of tax-delinquent lands take place in the county seats of the counties where they were located, was regarded as beneficial in advertising the country, since speculators and strangers would be brought to see it. Springfield *Sangamo Journal*, June 8, 1833.

lished towns were competing with the new ones being founded almost weekly. Beardstown, barely five years old and not yet a county seat, with its down-river pork business, three steam mills, a distillery, and numerous stores was claiming to be transacting more business than any other town in the state.[237] Lots at Carthage, now assured a post office, were selling in 1833 at from $6.00 to $105; 200 lots were offered at Joliet (called Juliet in its early years). Even little Meredosia, a dozen miles down river from Beardstown, a year old and containing twenty-two families, was offering the suggestion that, should the state capital be removed, no more eligible site for its location could be found.

The counties along the middle stretches of the Illinois were the borderland in settlement between the southern and eastern emigrants. Kentuckians, Tennesseeans, people from southern Indiana and Illinois usually occupied the timbered sections; as New Englanders, Middle States men, and Germans came in, they entered first the smaller edging prairies, then the larger. The half-hunter half-farmer and the serious farmer lived side by side.

"The spring of 1833, may be marked as a new era in the history of Chicago, and in fact of the northern part of the state of Illinois. . . ."[238] When Jeremiah Church returned in that year, he "found a large town built up in three [two] years." Within a few months population had increased from 150 to almost 1,000; buildings from 30 to 180. The village was described as "one chaos of mud, rubbish, and confusion . . . in many instances families were living in their covered wagons while arrangements were made for putting up shelter for them." Among the people, besides officers and commissioners, storekeepers, hotel keepers, doctors, and settlers there were

. . . the birds of passage . . . and emigrants and land-speculators as numerous as the sand. You will find horsedealers, and horse-stealers,—rogues of every description, white, black, brown, and red—half-breeds, quarter breeds, and men of no breed at all;—dealers in pigs, poultry, and potatoes; —men pursuing Indian claims, some for tracts of land, others, like our friend Snipe, for pigs which the wolves had eaten;—creditors of the tribes,

---

The history of the Military Bounty Lands and Illinois settlement was well presented in a five-column article, copied from the *Bounty Land Register*, in Springfield *Illinois Advocate and State Register*, July 8, 1835.

[237] *Beardstown Chronicle* in *Chicago Democrat*, March 25, 1834.

[238] *Chicago Democrat*, January 28, 1834. In 1832 many had fled from the cholera and the war.

or of particular Indians, who know that they have no chance of getting their money, if they do not get it from the Government agents;—sharpers of every degree; pedlars, grog-sellers; Indian agents and Indian traders of every description, and Contractors to supply the Pottawattomies with food. The little village was in an uproar from morning to night, and from night to morning; for, during the hours of darkness, when the housed portion of the population of Chicago strove to obtain repose in the crowded plank edifices of the village, the Indians howled, sang, wept, yelled, and whooped in their various encampments. With all this, the whites seemed to me to be more pagan than the red men.[239]

Civic consciousness was manifested by ordinances which forbade pigs running at large without rings in their noses, running of horses, or indecent exhibition of stallions in the streets. Laborers attacked the bar at the mouth of the river so that boats might enter it. A steamer ran intermittently from Buffalo to Chicago until the end of the summer of 1834; in addition there was weekly service to St. Joseph by the *Pioneer*. The stage came twice a week from Niles and four or five schooners plied constantly across the lake for passenger service. People were so busy they seemed indifferent, even to the mails. The food shortage became noticeable; potatoes became scarce in the spring of 1834 and by June of the following year the Chicago market was bare of all kinds of provisions. Flour was selling at from $12 to $20 per barrel, mess pork at $20, and whitefish at $8.00.[240] The unusually cold summer of 1835, with frost each month, had cut down the supply of local vegetables. The *Chicago Democrat* asked its friends on the Wabash and downstate to bring in foodstuffs.[241]

In the spring of 1834 lots outside the business center sold for $250, an increase of 500 per cent in four years; lots along the river sold for as much as $3,500. A year later some lots sold for as high as $155 per front foot.[242] Eastern papers reported even higher prices and of the "extravagant delusion" wrote:

[239] Charles J. Latrobe, *The Rambler in North America* (2 volumes. New York, 1835), II, 152–53. When Charles Fenno Hoffman arrived at the end of the year he noted the crowded conditions but was agreeably surprised at being entertained at a lively New Year's ball and a wolf hunt on horseback. *Winter in the West*, I, 236–37, 247.

[240] *Chicago Democrat*, April 30, 1834, June 3, 1835; *Chicago American*, June 20, 1835.

[241] John T. Kingston, "Early Western Days," in *Wisconsin Historical Collections*, VII (1873–76), 338; *Chicago Democrat*, June 3, 1835.

[242] *Chicago American*, August 15, 1835.

"We can hardly conceive of a more lamentable spirit of infatuation than seems to prevail at Chicago." Chicago denied any "delusions" except on the part of outsiders and pointed to sound growth based on situation, promised opening of the Michigan Canal, and general growth of business.

"The flood gates of enterprise seem to be let loose upon us . . . and still they come. . . . The cloud of emigrants which we then saw rising, now darkens the Eastern sky, and seems still to be thickening upon us."[243] "Speculators are arriving in regiments, and a heavier business is doing in lands than in any other town in the Union."[244] In 1835 it began to appear that there was some truth to the charge of lot mania. Lands along the canal route had been sold to the extent of $354,000 in June, but the passage of the canal bill early in 1836 led to sales of more than $2,500,000 of canal lots in June of that year.[245] Maps were followed as eagerly as stock ticker tape a century later. "Each map had its eager and interested groups of inquirers. . . . Eastern speculators had fallen upon a wonderful and prosperous country. Rivulets were magnified into noble rivers—canoes appeared as steamboats. . . . Near each map was always to be found some *honest* and *disinterested* individual, ready to explain the surrounding and unseen advantages, as well as the ultimate greatness of the city before them. Literally it was 'diamond cut diamond.' "[246]

Lands were bought on time, and changed hands often. The

[243] *Chicago American,* June 13, 1835.
[244] Letter from Chicago, June 20, to New York *Commercial Advertiser,* quoted in *Daily Cleveland Herald,* August 20, 1835.
[245] *Chicago American,* July 18, October 10, 1835; June 25, July 2, 1836.
[246] Kingston, "Early Western Days," in *Wisconsin Historical Collections,* VII, 340, speaking of the 1835 sale. Miss Martineau witnessed the scene: "Chicago looks raw and bare. . . . I never saw a busier place. . . . The streets were crowded with land speculators, hurrying from one sale to another. A negro, dressed up in scarlet, bearing a scarlet flag, and riding a white horse with housings of scarlet, announced the times of sale. At every street-corner where he stopped, the crowd flocked round him; and it seemed as if some prevalent mania infected the whole people. . . . As the gentlemen of our party walked the streets, store-keepers hailed them from their doors, with offers of farms, and all manner of land-lots, advising them to speculate before the price of land rose higher. A young lawyer . . . had realised five hundred dollars per day, the five preceding days, by merely making out titles to land. . . . Of course, this rapid money-making is merely temporary evil. A bursting of the bubble must come soon. The absurdity of the speculation is so striking. . . . wild land on the banks of a canal, not yet even marked out was selling at Chicago for more than rich land, well improved, in the finest part of the valley of the Mohawk, on the banks of a canal which is already the medium of an almost inestimable amount of traffic." *Society in America,* I, 259–61.

speculative flurry in government lots, the talk of canals and rail-roads affected other Chicago real estate as well, and prices advanced generally; the boom then spread out over the map.

Meanwhile, the streets presented a disgraceful appearance; sinkholes, sloughs, and frog ponds gave off nauseous odors and miasmic fumes. The main streets were being macadamized, ditched, and drained, but others were marked merely by stakes and tracks.[247] Buildings were erecting as rapidly as labor and materials could be had. Ogden and Newberry advertised for a million brick and 200,000 feet of pine lumber for the next season (1836). Brick went from $6.00 to $10 per thousand. Wages were "most enormously high." Carpenters and masons were in demand at $2.00 to $3.00 per day, common labor at $1.50 to $2.00. Good board could be had at $4.00 per week. Domestic or "female help" was practically nonexistent at $2.00 to $4.00 a week. Though the number of frame buildings, many three-stories high, created a fire hazard, the town apparently did not have even a volunteer bucket brigade until a fire scared the town trustees in the autumn of 1835 into passing an ordinance providing for wardens and fire companies, and ordering a fire engine and equipment from the East.[248]

The following summer the Chicago Hydraulic Company was incorporated by the legislature to furnish water. Population by the autumn of 1835 was about 3,300; it was to double in the next three years. A hundred merchants, some of whom were taking full-column advertisements in the newspapers, were competing for the numerous four-story brick buildings which were beginning to rise. Soon four hotels—the Sauganash, the City Hotel, the New Tremont House, and the Lake House, which stabled a hundred horses—were offering accommodations. The citizens adopted a charter early in 1837 and held municipal elections in the spring. The *American* vociferously resented an article by a correspondent of the New York *Commercial Advertiser* who thought that the site at the mouth of the Maumee (Toledo)

---

[247] *Chicago American,* June 20, 1835, July 9, 1836; *Chicago Democrat,* October 7, 1835.

[248] *Chicago American,* October 10, November 7, 1835. Chicago's first major fire ("Awful Conflagration ! ! Nineteen Buildings Burnt") came in November, 1839, when the business block bounded by Lake, Clark, South Water, and Dearborn streets was practically wiped out. Springfield *Illinois State Register,* November 2, 1839.

was destined to be the big development in the West.[249] More to the liking of Chicagoans were the words of another eastern visitor who wrote: "Chicago is, without doubt, the greatest wonder in this wonderful country. . . . The wand of the magician or the spell of a talisman ne'er effected changes like these; nay, even Aladdin's lamp, in all its glory, never performed greater wonders."[250]

By 1839 Chicago had a daily newspaper (*Daily Chicago American*) and a debt of $12,000, the scrip for which was rapidly depreciating. Truly Chicago was becoming a city, but "sudden wealth and paper profits obscured the depth of the mud; a scanty population in the back country and an absence of any export staple, to act as a substitute for the trade in town lots, gloriously failed to cast shadows before the bewitched inhabitants."[251]

Simultaneous with Chicago's rapid growth came the increased tempo in the settlement of central and northern Illinois. John Mason Peck's *A Guide for Emigrants* of 1831 was followed by his *Gazetteer of Illinois* in 1834, *A New Guide for Emigrants* in 1836, and a new and revised *Gazetteer* in 1837. Not so widely circulated, but also giving Illinois a good write-up, was R. B., author of *View of the Valley of the Mississippi* (1832 and 1834).[252] *Illinois in 1837* (published by S. Augustus Mitchell,

[249] October 17, 1835.
[250] "Letters from a Rambler in the West" (a correspondent of the *Pennsylvania Inquirer and Daily Courier*) reprinted in S. Augustus Mitchell (comp.), *Illinois in 1837* . . . (Philadelphia, 1837), 135.
[251] Pierce, *A History of Chicago*, I, 66. Miss Martineau predicted: "When the present intoxication of prosperity passes away, some of the inhabitants will go back to the eastward; there will be an accession of settlers from the mechanic classes; good houses will have been built for the richer families, and the singularity of the place will subside. It will be like all the other new and thriving lake and river ports of America." *Society in America*, I, 261.
More noncommittal was a nineteen-year-old visitor's estimate made in 1843: "There are men here, sensible reflecting men who affect to believe that in a few years it will be one of the great cities of the Union. They are men who have an abiding faith in the growth & prosperity of what they call the 'Great Northwest.' You never heard much about it nor I either until now, and they regard Chicago as the Great Commercial Center of the Great West—perhaps they are right. We shall see." Letters of George B. Smith, in *Wisconsin Magazine of History*, V (1921–22), 406.
[252] Peck said: "In no part of the United States can uncultivated land be made into farms with less labor than in Illinois." Though cautioning that no one got rich suddenly, that the secret of success was the *"gradual rise of property, by the advantageous application of manual labour,"* he stated that in general, the "rise in property" the preceding ten years had been 25 to 30 per cent per annum; in some of the towns 1,000 per cent in three years. "It being by far the richest State

Philadelphia, 1837), was based largely on Peck's *Gazetteer*, but contained Henry L. Ellsworth's letter on cultivation of the prairies and the six descriptive "Letters from a Rambler." Works such as these were widely quoted, often used as the basis for feature articles in the newspapers.[253] Illinois developments were reported in eastern papers by local correspondents and even special correspondents came west to view the scene.

One of the latter from a Philadelphia paper in 1837 wrote:

This whole region (particularly the states of Illinois, Michigan, and Wisconsin Territory,) is filling up with great and unexampled rapidity. Assuming this fact as granted [that every one must be the architect of his own fortune] I would refer to the superiority of the western portion of our continent over the eastern, as regards the *acquisition of wealth—professional eminence—political distinction,* and the opportunity offered of *exercising influence on society* and *the destinies of our common country.*[254]

And he proceeded to show why.

The power of the printed word might inspire the Easterner either to emigrate, buy land "sight unseen," or write a poem:

There came a voice from the far off West!—'twas not the savage yell,
That once arose in that fair vale, sad deeds of blood to tell;

---

in soil in the Union, of course it holds out the greatest prospect of advantage to farmers. . . . Indeed, Illinois may with propriety be called the 'Canaan' of America!" *A Gazetteer of Illinois* . . . (Philadelphia, 1837), 88–89, 328.

R. B.'s description of Illinois was more brief, but similar. He added: "In no part of our country is it possible to convert an uncultivated piece of land into a good farm, sooner than in this state . . . this state is one of great fertility of soil, and capable of sustaining a vast population. It has the finest situation of all the western states. . . . This is a country of vast and beautiful plains, with noble streams." *View of the Valley of the Mississippi,* 230, 233.

The Vandalia *Illinois Advocate and State Register,* December 3, 1834, said of Peck's *Gazetteer*: "—we now and then find a 'notion' smacking strongly of the 'Northern Hive.' "

[253] For instance, a series of articles, based largely on Peck, in *Chicago American,* February—March, 1836. The *Sangamo Journal,* 1836–37, ran numerous write-ups on Illinois towns. Abner Dumont Jones, a New Englander who wrote a firsthand and judicious account in his *Illinois and the West,* said that Mitchell's *Illinois in 1837* was "full of exaggerated statements, and high-wrought and false-colored descriptions, and cannot safely be relied on as a text book or gazetteer. . . . I do not set up myself as censor, or as being better able to judge, than the compilers of this book; but only as more impartial and unprejudiced, and as being far more likely to give an uninfluenced opinion, than one having large interests in western lands." 148–49.

[254] "Letters from a Rambler," in Mitchell, *Illinois in 1837,* 140. Jones, in *Illinois and the West,* 147, exposed the danger of false notions regarding rapid advancement and wealth, and gave sound advice regarding who should emigrate and what to expect. "The truth is . . . the 'west' and particular portions of it in particular have been 'cracked up' beyond what it ever was, and most false impressions given of Illinois, especially in New England." Aside from certain warnings and precautions, Jones was strong and sincere in his praise of the country.

'Twas not the growl of angry beasts, that roam abroad for prey—
Oh no, far different are the sounds that greet my ear to-day.

. . . .

There came a voice! it spake of cots where once the gaunt wolf prowled
And cities, where but late the fierce and vengeful panther howled;
Of villages, that grace the shores, and vessels on the stream,
Till now unknown;—say, is it not a romance or a dream?

There came a voice! it spake of fields, scarce needing lab'rer's toil,
Where genial suns, and gentle rains, and redolence of soil,
Give plenty to contented souls, who dwell in simple cot
Where earth is all a garden, and life a blissful lot.[255]

. . . .

It is to be hoped that this effusion was more effective advertising than it was good poetry; at least it was no more imaginative than the serious broadsides of land promoters.

In 1833 the Springfield land office had taken the lead in sales among the Illinois offices, held it again in 1835, but in 1836 surrendered first place to Quincy.[256] The state census showed a population of 269,974 in 1835, and the prospect for "the speedy settlement of Illinois" was excellent, said the *Sangamo Journal*, noting the activities of several large outside land associations. In one issue of the *Journal* were lot advertisements for Beardstown, Chicago, Cicero, Huron, Newcastle, Pittsfield, Princeton, Springfield, Tremont, and Waynesville.[257] Towns were springing up in great numbers on every available spot; the whole West was literally in commotion. Aladdin's lamp could not cause greater astonishment.[258]

Settlements spread up the Illinois and Fox River valleys. Of the Upper Illinois Valley the New England traveler wrote:

. . . nature seems to have been exceedingly lavish of her provisions for the comfort of man on this portion of the world. Certainly the original curse seems to have fallen here more lightly than upon any other portion of our earth I have seen or read of. There is here, in unequalled proportions, the richest variety of local inducements to the busy and restless spirit of man to plant himself and be at home. No richer soil, no blander climate, no greater

[255] "Cora," in *Western Monthly Magazine*, I (1833), 10
[256] During this period the older offices at Shawneetown, Kaskaskia, Vandalia, etc., had fallen far behind. A convenient tabulation of sales at the ten Illinois land offices between 1820 and 1839 is in Pease, *The Frontier State*, 176–77.
[257] April 9, 1836.
[258] *Chicago American*, July 2, 1836.

variety of beautiful landscape, no more exhaustless mines of wealth and comfort beneath the soil, does any section of the same extent in the wide world afford. But all this has not struck me more than the provision and foresight of nature in respect to this, the *El Dorado* of her demesnes.[259]

Havana, merely a landing point in the early 1830's, a few years later received, among others, Canadian and German arrivals. Pekin had a dozen stores by 1836 and was the landing for Tremont, nine miles back from the river. The 100-foot-wide streets, 10-acre public square, and white-painted buildings of the latter village proclaimed its New England sponsorship. "There are besides a very intelligent class of citizens from New York, Kentucky, and other places in the Union, whose sectional feelings merged in the general interest."

At Ottawa began a new country, mostly Yankee. It was estimated that there were not more than one hundred people in the Fox Valley in 1834, but that four years later there were ten times that number.[260] Ottawa, at the mouth of the Fox, had seventy-five or eighty families, but was expected to boom with the coming of the canal, and Peru, a few miles down river at the head of navigation on the Illinois, though boasting but one humble dwelling at the time, was expected to "become one of the greatest inland towns in the West, and second only to Chicago." Lots were said to be "commanding from $1000 to $2500 apiece."[261] Joliet (still called Juliet in 1838) on the Des Plaines River at the height of land between the lake and the Illinois, was a town of five or six hundred with more than a dozen stores and three taverns. Local limestone quarries provided material for canal locks as well as business buildings and residences. Although lands were not open for entry in the Indian cession of 1833[262] (Lake and McHenry counties) until three years later, some settlers had jumped the gun.

In the southern counties of the Military Tract the Southerners dominated, but by 1836 the northern counties were filling rapidly. In Knox County in 1836 appeared forty New York settlers to found a center of anticipated moral and intellectual importance which they named Log City (Galesburg), while about the

[259] A. D. Jones, *Illinois and the West*, 65–66.
[260] *Sangamo Journal*, April 7, 1838.
[261] "Letters from a Rambler in the West," in Mitchell, *Illinois in 1837*, 135.
[262] *Post*, 124.

same time a committee purchased 20,000 acres in Henry County for a more extensive project of New York settlers. Peoria and Quincy were thriving towns of more than 1,000 population each. The former was advertising seven steam packets as plying between that point and St. Louis, and one direct to Pittsburgh. Lots sold as high as $100 per front foot, neighboring farm land at $1.25 to $30 per acre. For several miles above the town the river widened into a lake from one to three miles wide, with a sluggish current. On either side were densely timbered heavy bottoms, occupied in only a few spots by settlers.

No other Mississippi River town was improving more rapidly than Quincy, where lots sold as high as $78 a front foot. The rich lands of the inland counties had been discovered by the middle 1830's and settlers, among them a number from Ohio and Indiana, moved in. Health conditions were not entirely good, but not so bad as they had been described. Spring high waters were followed by summer heat, and illness came, but part of the illness was due to natural hardships of new settlements, to lack of acclimation, and to carelessness.[263]

In the Rock River Valley the rich rolling grove-spotted prairies developed rapidly.

Rock River is the present attraction. Thither are flocking such hosts of immigrants, as must soon densely people the wild and beautiful tracts. . . . The country bordering on this stream, is allowed, on all hands, to be one of the finest and most fertile in the whole west, as well as possessing the most salubrious climate. It is principally open, high, undulating prairie, abounding with fine springs of the purest water, although rather sparcely wooded. The river is liberally fed with large rushing tributaries. . . . The current is very rapid and the waters clear as chrystal. It is a sight to make one leap with delight, as he gazes for the first time on this beautiful stream. Its wild rush of waters, tumbling, foaming, sparkling, as it passes over its rocky bed, its clear, bright waves reflecting the minutest object that lies upon its bottom, and ploughed by countless shoals of pike, catfish, redhorse or perch, each weighing from three to ten pounds, not to speak of lesser fry,—all this is a sight to gladden the eye, and give a most vivid idea of health and comfort.[264]

[263] A judicious survey of health conditions in Illinois was published in the *Illinois Champion and Peoria Herald* in May, 1835, copied in *Ohio Farmer, and Western Horticulturist* (Batavia), May 15, 1835. A strong defense of Illinois climate and healthfulness was published by the Quincy *Illinois Bounty Land Register,* copied in *Sangamo Journal,* April 30, 1836.

[264] Jones, *Illinois and the West,* 165–68. A good description of the prairie and Rock River country written for the *New York Daily Express* was published in the

A cluster of counties was organized between 1835 and 1837.[265] Rock Island City, the site of Black Hawk's old home, was being surveyed and lots advertised in 1836.[266] East Rockford and West Rockford were separate villages (not combined until 1839); Dixon and Freeport were frontier villages of importance by 1837. A band of horse-thieving, counterfeiting "Prairie Pirates" infested the Rock River country in the late 1830's, but were finally handled by direct action on the part of the more law-abiding settlers. In 1840 the traveling missionary wrote that the country bordering the Pecatonic was the finest for farming in the region and was fast filling up "with an interesting population."[267]

The prairie region of eastern Illinois was not filling rapidly in the middle 1830's. Still prairie shy, the settlers edged along the streams and timber strips.[268] Decatur, Paris, Bloomington,[269]

Sangamo Journal, May 13, 1837. Jones, speaking of the Illinois country, in general, wrote: "And I believe it utterly beyond any one's power to give any description of the face of the country, which shall convey anything like an adequate idea. . . . It is perfectly unique. . . . Its prairies, in particular, have been represented as exceedingly flat and even. . . . But the country is all unequal—not precipitous—and the prairies present a continual change of tables and sloughs, while the 'timbers' are broken by high knolls and deep ravines. . . . The timber on the 'bottoms,' is dense and heavy, and tangled with the most luxuriant growth of vines, shrubs, briars, and rank grass. These bottoms are on all the rivers and creeks, skirting the prairies and making beautiful belts running in every direction through the country. Besides these, there are the 'barrens,' or 'oak openings,' as they are called, which are composed of large trees of the various kinds of oak, hickory, maple, elm, etc. These trees are quite sparsely scattered around, making a most beautiful park, entirely free from underbrush, and the ground is covered with a luxuriant growth of grass and flowers. The openings are all on unequal—nay, broken ground—high abrupt hills and gentle swells, alternated by deep precipitous ravines or most picturesque valleys of perfectly easy access even with a carriage. Nothing can exceed the beauty of these unique forests—no art or man's device could have accomplished on so grand a scale a work so perfectly splendid and enchanting." *Illinois and the West,* 88–90.

[265] Rock Island, Boone, Whiteside, Ogle, Winnebago, Stephenson, and De Kalb.

[266] *Northwestern Gazette and Galena Advertiser,* July 9, 1836.

[267] William M. Adams, Pecatonic, Illinois, August 16, 1840, to Milton Badger. Papers of American Home Missionary Society.

[268] There was seldom any doubt in the minds of the emigrants from the South regarding the respective merits of timber and prairie, but differences of opinion often existed among Easterners. A Vermonter who settled in Illinois tried to persuade his brother who had settled in Michigan to join him, but the latter asked what would one do for timber. "Buy it," was the reply. "You will spend the best part of your life chopping down and burning timber in order to raise crops, while we go to work at once and raise crops to buy all the timber we need." *Michigan Pioneer and Historical Collections,* XXXI (1901), 181. It was not that simple, however, until the new plows made prairie farming practicable. See Chapter IV.

[269] Paris and Bloomington lot sales announced these new towns in 1837. *Northwestern Gazette and Galena Advertiser,* April 15, 1837.

Urbana, and Danville ranged from hamlets to fair-sized towns. Potawatomi and Kickapoo still resided in Iroquois County until 1838 and, though friendly, somewhat retarded settlement. A colony of Pennsylvanians, however, settled at Milford in 1835 and a group of Norwegians on Beaver Creek the same year. The latter, discouraged by the unhealthfulness of the site, moved on to Wisconsin two years later. A town at the "head of navigation on the Iroquois . . . one of the handsomest locations for a city in the world" was projected by the Plato Company, but it turned out to be merely another paper town which, like many others, possessed all the elements of an active, thriving city, except people, buildings, and business.

The lead-mining area had developed rapidly after the Black Hawk War. Galena which by 1835 had a population of perhaps 1,500[270] was the center of a scattered settlement which was prospecting and digging all over the "whole earth, north, east, and south." The upper street, on which were located the two principal public houses, was hung on the face of a high steep hill. On the business street, which ran along the Fever River, "the stir and bustle of business, the influx of market and farm wagons, the ponderous ox teams drawing the lead to its place of shipment, the rattling of carts, drays, hackney coaches and carriages . . . announce the present and growing importance of Galena."[271] The town with its mixed and often transient population remained rough and dirty, though by the time it was incorporated in 1839 it boasted not only a fire department and a branch of the State Bank of Illinois, but also a temperance society, two triweekly newspapers,[272] a library association with a library of more than eight hundred volumes, three new brick and stone churches, and a theater. Main Street was being macadamized and sidewalks paved; new daily stagecoaches were scheduled to make the forty miles to Mineral Point in eight hours, and to depart for Madison

---

[270] Variously estimated in 1832 at 669, 1,000 to 1,500 and 5,000 to 7,000.

[271] W. R. Smith, *Observations on the Wisconsin Territory*, 107.

[272] The *Miners' Journal*, established in 1826, became the *Galenian* in 1832 and four years later changed its name to the *Democrat*. The *Advertiser* had a short life (1829–30). The *Northwestern Gazette and Galena Advertiser* dated from 1834.

Hoffman, in 1834, had said: "This, for a frontier-town, built indifferently of frame and log-houses, thrown confusedly together on the side of a hill, is certainly doing very well." "The town, for its size, is one of the busiest places in the Union." *A Winter in the West*, II, 40–41.

and Milwaukee semiweekly.[273] A year later the population was 3,000 and many thought Galena was destined to become the largest and most flourishing city of the West north of St. Louis.[274]

Outside the town the miners' homes and shacks, some well built, others so frail that it appeared that they should be tied to a post when the wind blew, were scattered over the ochre-colored countryside, often located in the ravines. Society was rough and democratic; drinking, quarreling, and fighting were not unusual, and carrying concealed weapons was not frowned upon as in more Yankeelike communities. Yet there were eastern aristocrats as well as southern gentlemen among the inhabitants. Col. William S. Hamilton, West Pointer, lawyer, soldier, drover, and miner (and son of Alexander Hamilton) was introduced to Charles Fenno Hoffman as follows: "Colonel H. is at present disguised in a suit of broadcloth; to have him in character, sir, you should see him in his leather shirt and drawers, driving his ox-team with a load of lead into town." When Hamilton spoke to a crowd of miners in dignified words, Hoffman explained that there were many educated persons among them.[275]

Game was still abundant in the mining region and the miners furnished a good local market for those farmers in the vicinity who had a surplus.[276] Pork at times sold for $40 the barrel, plus $4.00 for hauling. The bulk of the lead was shipped down the Mississippi in steamboats, but some went overland to Chicago,

[273] *Northwestern Gazette and Galena Advertiser*, October 27, 1838; *Wisconsin Enquirer*, September 14, 1839; *Quincy Whig*, June 29, 1839. A Methodist circuit rider, who was probably slightly prejudiced, described conditions in the lead country: "infidelity tryumphed, & religion had but a nominal existance. Add to this, the spirit of money making seemed to absorb the whole community. Money was made with the greatest facility, & spent with the greatest profusion; & as a matter of course, gambling, drunkeness, &c., were the common order of the day, with the majority. This population contained a good share of inteligence & more than ordinary share of enterprise. . . ." Brunson, "A Methodist Circuit Rider's Tour," in *Wisconsin Historical Collections*, XV, 287.

[274] *Madison Express*, February 1, 1840.

[275] Hoffman, *A Winter in the West*, II, 44.

[276] Prairie chickens, partridges, quail, ducks, geese, and deer abounded; within forty miles of Galena the wolves and rattlesnakes were annoying. Theodore Rodolf, "Pioneering in the Wisconsin Lead Region," in *Wisconsin Historical Collections*, XV (1900), 353.

It was said that the wolves could be handled by throwing "assafoetida" on an open fire. ". . . the wolves . . . howl . . . in the most mournful manner; and such is the remarkable fascination under which they seem to labor, that they will often suffer themselves to be shot down rather than leave the spot." A. D. Jones, *Illinois and the West*, 218. The rattlesnakes were not so easily taken care of.

or (from the Wisconsin diggings) by way of the Wisconsin-Fox rivers and out at Green Bay. Alton, rather than St. Louis, merchants handled much of the down-river lead.[277]

The land problem in the mining region was still unsettled. Since 1821, when administration of mineral lands was transferred from the Treasury Department to the War Department, there had been confusion, uncertainty, and probably favoritism in the leasing and tenure. The lands were leased on shares and collection was difficult, particularly since the idea had been advanced that the government could not constitutionally lease its lands.[278] Much of the reserved land contained no minerals, but was rich agricultural land; unscrupulous persons, by taking advantage of the mining-lease system, could enter upon the enclosures of settlers (squatters) and start digging. Both the Commissioner of the General Land Office and the Illinois legislature recommended the sale of mineral lands to individuals, but not until 1845 was this made possible by law.[279]

Not even the depression, the full effects of which were not felt in the West until 1839, appreciably slowed the emigration to Illinois. The canal and railroad building brought in Irish and other laborers; Norwegians were beginning to arrive; in 1839 several thousand Mormons took over Commerce and vicinity. A big year—perhaps 40,000 new arrivals—was expected.[280] The

[277] There was some complaint against the freight rates, "but owners had no alternative except to yield to the demands of the steamboats or keep the lead over the winter." *Niles' Weekly Register*, LIX, 144 (Oct. 31, 1840). The *Galena Gazette* reported 20 million pounds exported from Galena in 1840. *Niles' Weekly Register*, LIX, 400 (Feb. 20, 1841) ; *Wisconsin Enquirer*, December 22, 1838.

[278] *Galena Advertiser*, July 20, August 3, September 14, November 9, 1829; *Miners' Journal*, July 22, September 20, 1828.

[279] The collection of rents was abandoned in 1835 but restored in 1841. In March, 1838, the *Northwestern Gazette and Galena Advertiser* was asking when were "our" lands going to be surveyed and put on the market; since lands to the north had been surveyed, the people of the Galena section had reason to complain of neglect. Yet a year later complaints and petitions came from the citizens of the mining country protesting that the Mineral Point Land Office had illegally sold mining lands reserved by the President's proclamation of July 4, 1834. *Wisconsin Enquirer*, April 6, 1839.

[280] Springfield *Sangamo Journal*, April 12, 1839; *Ohio State Journal*, April 30, 1839. "The next year (1839) will probably exhibit such an immigration as no one year before has ever exhibited. Why should it not? There are tens of thousands in the thickly peopled portions of the United States, who, although they may be able to gain a bare subsistence, must do it with much toil and sacrifice, and be perpetually harassed with the reflection that should sickness overtake them, or, at last, when old age must, they and theirs, for whom they live alone, must suffer and come for support upon the cold charity of the world, or the hard pittance of the pauper. Immigration is, to him, what it was to the Israelitish brickmakers in Egypt—a certain good for an uncertain one, a competence for subsistence, a prospect of plenty for a penurious old age." A. D. Jones, *Illinois and the West*, 248.

state was growing rapidly, people were becoming acclimated, prospects were fine; all that remained was to cultivate them. "Illinois is destined to be a great state—great in her political and moral influence, as well as in her physical resources. It is to be made thus through foreign influence—the influence of immigration."[281]

The history, present condition, and future prospects of the State of Illinois, furnish a theme for contemplation which would have thrilled the bosom of an ancient historian with delight. Especially the progress of settlement, the establishment of churches, schools, printing offices and other engines of improvement of civilization, in this Illinois River region;—and the multiplication of towns, farms, orchards and all the machinery of wealth and comfort, has been so unprecedentedly rapid and exhuberant, that an Herodotus, a Tacitus, or a Gibbon would be astounded at the recital.[282]

§ § § §

In 1822, so remote was the Wisconsin country that the United States government, on the recommendation of Dr. Jedediah Morse, Congregational clergyman and famous geographer, considered seriously the policy of reserving the whole region as an Indian habitat.[283] And Secretary of War Calhoun in 1825 thought that the Indians of Ohio, Michigan, and Illinois should not be removed west of the Mississippi, but to the region west of Lake Michigan.[284] Even in 1830, when a bill was introduced in Congress to create the Territory of Huron, with its capital at Menominee Village (or Shantytown, a part of the Green Bay settlement), it was said that so much of the present state of Wisconsin was still in the possession of the Indians that the new territory, so far as settlement was concerned, would have been limited to an area of six miles square.[285] True, in addition to the

[281] A. D. Jones, *Illinois and the West*, 250.

[282] *Peoria Register and Northwestern Gazetteer*, May 4, quoted in *Cincinnati Daily Gazette*, May 15, 1839. A good firsthand description of Illinois in 1839 is in a series of articles by the editor of the *Daily Chicago American*, July, 1839.

[283] *A Report to Secretary of War . . . on Indian Affairs . . .* (New Haven, 1822). Morse had been sent by the War Department in 1820 to investigate the condition of the northwestern tribes.

[284] See *American State Papers, Indian Affairs*, II, 541-42, on the condition of the Wisconsin country in 1831.

[285] "Report on the Quality and Condition of Wisconsin Territory, 1831," Samuel Stambaugh, Indian agent at Green Bay, to the Secretary of War, November 8, 1831, in *Wisconsin Historical Collections*, XV (1900), 429. The bills for the creation of a territory of Chippewau, Wiskonsin, or Huron had been promoted between 1824 and 1830 by Judge James Duane Doty. Reuben Gold Thwaites, "The Boundaries of Wisconsin," in *ibid.*, XI (1888), 463-65.

cession by the treaties of Prairie du Chien of 1829[286] in the southwest corner of the present state, there were the Menominee cessions on either side of the Fox River (ceded by the treaty made in Washington, February 8, 1831), but much of this land was claimed by the New York Indians.

The story of the New York Indians is long and complicated.[287] Prior to the War for American Independence William Occom, an Indian, and Samuel Kirkland had been teaching and doing missionary work among the Oneida, as a result of which some 250 of these Indians under Skenandoah served on the American side in the war. Some years later the Oneida offered shelter and deeded land to scattered New England and Long Island tribes under Occom's influence.[288] The New York "Brothertown" of these remnants was organized in 1785. There, also, at the invitation of the Oneida, came the friendly Stockbridge from New England. But tribal and factional dissensions, the encroaching advance of the whites, and the westward-moving spirit of the times led these Christian Indians to consider another move.

The Delawares ("Grandfathers" of the Stockbridge) who had earlier accepted an invitation to settle among the Miami in the West, in turn invited the Stockbridge-Brothertown remnants to join them.[289] Title to a parcel of land on White River, Indiana Territory, was attested by President Jefferson in December, 1808. But when, ten years later, a company of Stockbridge emigrants under the leadership of the Moravian-educated John Metoxen got as far west as Ohio, they found that the Miami and Delawares had ceded their lands.

Government policy, the influence of the American Board of Foreign Missions, and the efforts of the Ogden Land Company

[286] Chippewa, Ottawa, Potawatomi, and Winnebago. *Ante,* 59.

[287] Summarized in John Nelson Davidson, "The Coming of the New York Indians to Wisconsin," in *Wisconsin State Historical Society Proceedings,* 1899, pp. 155-85. See also Albert G. Ellis, "Some Account of the Advent of the New York Indians into Wisconsin," in *Wisconsin Historical Collections,* II (1855), 415-49, and his "Recollections of Rev. Eleazar Williams," in *ibid.,* VIII (1877-79), 322-52, for defeat of Williams' plans for an Indian empire west of Lake Michigan. The *Wisconsin Enquirer,* June 15, 1839 published a two-and-a-half-column account of the history of the Brothertown Indians.

[288] Including Narragansetts, Pequots, and Mohegans.

[289] The formal invitation was extended at a council held by the Delawares, *et al.,* at White River, July 3, 1809.

of New York[290] to get all the Iroquois out of the state, combined to promote finding a new home for the New York Indians. At this time Eleazar Williams, opportunist, self-appointed lobbyist, missionary, and delegate at large for the Oneida, visioned a grand confederacy or Indian empire in the West with one supreme head.[291] Delegates representing the Oneida and Stockbridge went to Green Bay in 1821 with the consent of the War Department and, in spite of the settlers' suspicion of Williams, secured a narrow strip of land which lay on both sides of the Fox River. Although the Oneida refused to be interested, the promoters tried again, and in September, 1822, got from the Menominee "all the right, title, interest, and claim" in a large tract, but the Menominee were to retain the right of joint occupation. President Monroe, however, in approving the treaty, limited the rights of the Oneida, Tuscarora, St. Regis, and Munsee tribes to an area roughly bounded by Sturgeon Bay, Green Bay, the Fox River, and Lake Michigan.

The wandering band of Stockbridge under Metoxen made its way up to the Grand Kakalin of the Fox in the autumn of 1822, where they were joined by other tribesmen from New York the following year, and still larger groups in 1825, when New York purchased their lands in that state. Brothertowns settled near by in 1823. Only a few of the Oneidas had been persuaded by Williams' schemes to emigrate. Possibly 150 came in 1823–24; in 1825 a small group settled near Green Bay. In the Treaty of Butte des Morts in 1827, by which the Menominee ceded the land around the southern end of Green Bay, the claims of the New York Indians were referred to the President for settlement. By 1830 the Menominee, supported by the Winnebago and Green Bay whites, were eager to throw over their agreement with the New York Indians. A President's commission failed to straighten out the conflicting claims, but by the Treaty of Washington in 1831 the Menominee, though protesting any claims

[290] Successor of the Holland Land Company which had bought the Gorham-Phelps pre-emption rights to about six million acres in western New York claimed by Massachusetts.

[291] Williams was descended from the daughter of the Rev. John Williams, of Deerfield, Massachusetts, and belonged to the St. Regis or Catholic branch of the Mohawks which had settled on the St. Lawrence. Backed by prominent white families and educated by the aid of missionary societies, Williams was working among the Oneida in 1817 when the first Stockbridge group came West.

of the New York Indians against themselves, nevertheless agreed to allow the President to set aside lands out of their cession for the newcomers. Accordingly the Oneidas were given the tract north and west of the Fox River, the Stockbridge-Munsees two townships (46,080 acres), and the Brothertown one township on the east shore of Lake Winnebago.[292]

Following shortly after the Winnebago cession at Fort Armstrong in 1832 came the gathering of the tribes—southern Chippewa, Ottawa, and Potawatomi—at Chicago in September, 1833. It was said that between 5,000 and 8,000 Indians were fed at the expense of the government and drank at their own. Dogs, ponies, squaws, and papooses littered the prairie. Everywhere were "warriors mounted, on foot, squaws, and horses."[293] Races, quarrels, wild singing, sobbing, and wailing added variety to the solemn conclave. Since the Indians were to be paid $186,-000 in goods and cash under the terms of earlier treaties, traders, venders, horse dealers, grog peddlers, speculators, and gamblers gathered round.[294]

In return for the land along the west shore of Lake Michigan between the Rock and Milwaukee rivers, the tribes were given "not less than 5,000,000 acres" west of the Mississippi, $100,000 to certain individuals in lieu of reservations, $150,000 to satisfy claims against the Indians, $100,000 in goods and provisions, $280,000 for annuities, $150,000 for mills, houses, agricultural implements, stock, and so forth, $70,000 for education and domestic arts, and sundry other stipends. The total was about $1,000,000.[295] The scene at the distribution of goods following the signing of the treaty was a wild one. Unscrupulous traders used whiskey freely.

Such scenes as have been acted out during this payment I never saw before and never wish to see again. . . . They [the Indians] will give anything they have for whiskey and as soon as they are drunk they are stripped to the skin by the whites. Such infernal villainy would make the Devil blush. . . . I have seen females give a dram of whiskey to an Indian and take his

[292] Maj. Samuel Stambaugh was one of the commissioners who represented the United States at this negotiation. Williams later claimed to be the lost Dauphin, son of Louis XVI and Marie Antoinette of France.

[293] Latrobe, *The Rambler* (1835 ed.), II, 155.

[294] Shirreff, *A Tour Through North America*, 227 ff., and Latrobe, *The Rambler*, II, 154 ff.

[295] Kappler (ed.), *Indian Affairs, Laws and Treaties*, II, 297–307.

blanket. Last night many have been robbed of their money, and where they attempt to trade with the whites the greatest extortion is used, a pint of whiskey is often sold for a dollar.[296]

Meanwhile in 1832 at Tippecanoe the Potawatomi had surrendered the remaining lands (about 4,000,000 acres) in Indiana north of the Wabash, and remnants in Michigan Territory, and the Ottawa the tract around Toledo. At the end of 1833 the Secretary of War could congratulate the nation that "the country north of the Ohio, east of the Mississippi, including the states of Ohio, Indiana, Illinois, and the Territory of Michigan as far as the Fox and Wisconsin rivers" had been practically "cleared of the embarrassments of Indian relations."

Although the estimated 5,000 Indians remaining in the Northwest still ranged over large areas, the policy of government removals was culminating rapidly. In 1834 the Miami and Potawatomi in separate treaties parted with scattered tracts (some of them reservations from former treaties) in Indiana. Two years later the Ottawa and Chippewa were persuaded by Henry R. Schoolcraft and others to part with the vast tract in Michigan stretching from the Grand River north to Lake Superior. The same year the Menominee surrendered two tracts in central Wisconsin and the area immediately north of Green Bay. In 1837 the Winnebago ceded their lands north of the Wisconsin, and the Sioux gave up their lands adjoining on the northwest, thus clearing title to the west-central side of the present state. The same year the Chippewa surrendered their lands—the remainder or northwest one fourth of the present state, excepting a strip forty to sixty miles wide across the northern border and running into the western part of northern Michigan.[297] This strip, ceded in 1842, was the only area of any size still owned by the Indians in the Northwest in 1840.[298]

Keeping track of the Indian treaties and land cessions, with their overlappings, duplications, and amendments is difficult

[296] Dr. Henry Van Der Borgart, quoted in Pierce, *History of Chicago*, I, 41.
[297] On the conclusion of this treaty Governor Henry Dodge of Wisconsin Territory congratulated the whole Upper Mississippi Valley on the acquisition of the soil, pineries, and mineral resources of so important a region.
[298] For accurate delineation of the various Indian cessions it is necessary to consult the maps in Royce, *Indian Land Cessions*. The treaties are summarized in Harmon, *Sixty Years of Indian Affairs*; presented in full in Kappler (ed.), *Indian Affairs. Laws and Treaties*.

enough; to give an adequate idea of the conflicting forces, influences, and attitudes which brought about the removal of the Indians from the Northwest is almost impossible. The literature of bewailing and lament over a cruel Indian policy—mostly written well after the event—is sizeable. Suffice it to say that, though the expression "the only good Indian is a dead Indian" never truly represented the attitude of a majority of the pioneers over any length of time, nevertheless, between 1825 and 1830 the people of the region became convinced that the Indian should go—the farther the better. It was no longer, after 1832 at least, fear of the Indian; nor was it merely a desire for his lands. It was the belief in the final inability of the Indian to make the grade of the higher white civilization (or so the white man regarded it) and to live in adjustment within or alongside it. Though the "Indian hater," not an uncommon type in the earlier period of border wars, was becoming rare in the Middle West, he had left a heritage of a double standard of behavior in the minds of many—two consciences as it were, one for the white and another for the red man. Writing from "Ouisconsin Territory" in 1834 Charles Fenno Hoffman said:

You smile incredulously at such an anomaly in morals; but however paradoxical it may appear upon paper, it is a fact as notorious as the open day, that there have been and are men on the frontiers whose dealings with civilized society, whose general humanity, whose exact attendance even to their religious duties, are such as to ensure them respect, if not to give them weight, in any well-ordered community,—and that with these very men the rights and privileges, the property, the life of an Indian, do not weigh a feather.[299]

As the pioneer penetrated beyond the Indian boundaries, he counted upon the General Government catching up with him in its treaties. At times, as in Michigan Territory east of the lake, settlers and Indians lived side by side in friendly relations. Here, when sober, the Indians (largely Potawatomi) were kind, mild mannered, and honest.[300] They traded fish, venison, cranberries, maple syrup, and honey for flour, bread, pork, and potatoes. The

[299] *A Winter in the West*, II, 29–30.
[300] Henry R. Schoolcraft told of a distinguished Potawatomi warrior who presented himself to the Indian agent at Chicago, told what a good Indian and friend of the white people he was, and asked for a dram of whiskey. The agent

syrup or honey, having been strained through a dirty Indian blanket, was often unacceptable to finicky housewives, yet the intent was good. Aside from the somewhat disconcerting habit of looking in the window of the settler's house before announcing his arrival, and his weakness for the smell of baking bread, he was not a bad fellow. Boys and young men jumped, ran, wrestled, shot bows and rifles in competition with him. The Indians generally excelled at only hunting, fishing, and lacrosse. West of the lake the Potawatomi and the Menominee were likewise a fairly dirty, lazy, and harmless lot, but the settlers felt differently towards the Winnebago.

Sooner or later, however, the Indians' land became valuable enough to be coveted by the settlers. Governor Cass, of Michigan Territory, aided by Henry R. Schoolcraft, was among the more successful administrators of Indian affairs. He believed that the Indian, if treated with tact and fairness, could be persuaded to surrender his lands for a reasonable price and move west. But even after the cession the Indian, set down probably among strange and hostile tribes, again confronted by the skirmish line of distrustful pioneers, perhaps separated from a market for his wild meat and hides, was likely either to take to shooting the settlers' hogs, running into debt at a trading post, or sneaking back to live a furtive life on the lands of his ancestors. "The isolated condition of the Indian is, alas! too well known."

Although the Westerner was aware of the problem, he wasted little sentiment on it. In the autumn of 1832 when a detachment of Shawnee and Ottawa from Ohio passed through Edwardsville on their way West, the *Illinois Advocate* noted that it *was* possible to get the Indians out. "We hope that our own State will be relieved of its aboriginal inhabitants, in the course of one or two years at the furthest."[301] In commenting on the deplorable condition of the Potawatomi along the northern borders—unable to raise crops, begging, and stealing—the *Sangamo Journal* said that, since they were willing to sell their lands and remove,

---

explained that he never gave whiskey to good Indians, because they did not drink it or ask for it. "Then," said the Indian, "me damn rascal." Mrs. Anna Jameson, "Detroit to Mackinac Island, 1837," in *Michigan History Magazine*, VIII (1924), 165–66.
[301] November 5, 1832.

the Government should act.[302] When the Chicago Treaty of 1833 was announced, at least two papers wrote: "The citizens of this State, in common with those of Michigan and Indiana, may well congratulate themselves that there is now a certain prospect, that within three years they will be rid of a useless and, perhaps, dangerous population."[303]

But when some of the Indians dispossessed by this treaty and not inclined to go west of the Mississippi, passed through Green Bay on their way to the Lake Superior region, the *Green-Bay Intelligencer* discoursed on the Indian problem in philosophical, even sentimental vein.

There is something connected with the emigration of these miserable, misguided creatures, from their old hunting grounds which we cannot bear to contemplate. When a white man leaves his home, it is usually upon mature calculation of the propriety of the change. His health, social connection, or pecuniary advantage, any, or all of these considerations may induce him to bid adieu to everything endeared to him, by previous habit and feelings, for he has deliberately reflected, and acts promptly upon conviction of what he owes to himself or to his family. But Indians are governed by their passions; they are incapable of those efforts of the understanding, which, in the most difficult and trying situations, direct and control our conduct; giving dignity to misfortune, and elevating us in the hope of better days. Their fate is a hard one, and they do everything to aggravate it, and seem bent upon the annihilation of their race.[304]

Though approving the removal policy of "our venerable President," the writer called attention to the fact that it did not work too well. Bad advice or something prevented the Indians from accepting kindness "at our hands." Every means, short of physical force, should be used to make them go to the territory assigned; either that, or whole nations would be pushed out of life. He continued:

Talk of our intercourse laws! They avail *nothing,* and cannot be enforced while the tribes are scattered along the whole line of our frontier. And can any man who has a knowledge of their habits, suppose that those tribes who are surrounded by a white population, will be protected from the vices and rapacity of the *unprincipled*? A cordon of armed men around their settlements will not effect it.

---

[302] December 29, 1832.
[303] *Sangamo Journal*, October 26, 1833; Jacksonville *Illinois Patriot*, November 2, 1833.
[304] May 30, 1835.

Those of us who have lived for some years at this place, and have seen the gradual decay of the tribes in our neighborhood, can feel the effects of the preceding remarks. It is awful to reflect upon the ravages of a few years! Many persons yet alive, distinctly remember when the shores of Fox River, were populous with its villages, and its waters covered with canoes. Where are they now? The subject is too affective to be pursued further: but it is instructive, it teaches us that curses and witherings are sometimes made the lot of nations as well as of individuals, and that our present conduct should be ordered with direct reference to the happiness of future existence.[305]

As Tocqueville noted, few Americans of the period saw anything to wonder about in this process; it was a part of the usual march of events in this world, of the immutable order of nature.[306]

The Winnebago treaty of 1837 had been negotiated under questionable practices. The chiefs had been kept in Washington all winter, high-pressured into signing, and been told that they might remain on their lands eight years when the government really meant eight months. The following summer when Simon Cameron and James Murray came to divide and pay out $100,-000 to the half-breeds and a like amount in claims of traders against the Indians, they gave most of it to the American Fur Company. So flagrant was the dereliction of the commissioners that their action was not recognized by the War Department.[307] Then the practice of paying the various treaty annuities in goods rather than specie as promised displeased not only the Indians but merchants and traders as well. The *Detroit Daily Advertiser,* for instance, took up the case of the Saginaw Indians, "Another Chapter of Wrongs."[308] And the *Wisconsin Democrat,* calling attention to delays, changes in place of payment, and the like, stated that treaty stipulations, as far as binding the government was concerned, were a mere dead letter, "but woe to the

[305] *Green-Bay Intelligencer,* May 30, 1835. Something of the same attitude was expressed by the *Milwaukee Advertiser,* October 27, 1836, when, speaking of the treaty Governor Dodge helped negotiate with the Sac and Fox, it noted that the government was beginning to pay some attention to the "melancholy condition of the savages" and give them something approximating the value of their lands.

[306] *Oeuvres et Correspondance Inédite,* I, 174.

[307] The inquiry into the conduct of the commissioners is published in U. S. *House Documents,* 25 Congress, 3 session, VI, No. 229. See also note by Lyman C. Draper in *Wisconsin Historical Collections,* VII (1873–76), 396n.

[308] May 3, 1838.

poor Indian, if in one jot or tittle, *he* breaks what he is taught to believe is a solemn convenant with his Great Father."[309]

Regardless of government derelictions the people of Wisconsin Territory were determined that the Winnebago should go. Although there were still some fine-looking men among them, whiskey and intercourse with the whites had robbed the tribe of whatever former character it had possessed as a nation.

"The young brave feels no longer the dignity of man as his once proud step falters; and the maiden, once coy and modest, now recklessly throws herself away to vice and criminal indulgence. But with all this they are yet *Indians*, with all the Indian peculiarity and singular characteristics." One soon lost all idea of romance when brought into contact with them, hooting around, waiting for their annuities. "Yet there is much to interest—their keen penetration and sagacity never deserts them—nothing escapes their attention, and he who attempts to treat them, even when drunk, as *fools*, soon finds himself uselessly endeavoring to 'catch a weasel asleep.' "[310] There was an element of truth in the statement: "The Indian the white men despise is the Indian the white men have made."

In January, 1839, Governor Henry Dodge in his message to

[309] October 6, 1838. Yet when Captain Marryat in his diary criticized the government for taking the lands from the Indian at a little over a cent per acre and selling them at $1.25, the *Wisconsin Enquirer*, September 7, 1839, pointed out the error of the captain's ways in no uncertain words. Others have made similar errors of oversimplification. Harmon, in *Sixty Years of Indian Affairs* (1941), 297, calculated that by some fifty treaties between 1830 and 1838, $137,349,946 worth of Indian land was acquired at a total cost of $70,059,505. "Uncle Sam was developing into a good business man; in eight years he had cleared $67,290,441 in his business transactions with the red men." Such items as cost of Indian wars and surveys seem to have been overlooked.

The whole business of sale prices, claims against the Indians, and individual allotment of annuities was, considering that many Indians did not know the difference between one figure and another, more or less impossible to administer. The administration of Indian affairs under Commissioner Carey A. Harris in the middle 1830's was particularly vulnerable to criticism. Schoolcraft accused Harris of being "overreached by a noted commercial house" who sold him Indian goods on credit, but promptly cashed the drafts for specie at western land offices. *Personal Memoirs of a Residence of Thirty Years with the Indian Tribes . . .* (Philadelphia, 1851), 597n. As Caleb Atwater said regarding the temptations to fraud in the distribution of large sums of money: "The poor Indian's voice is too feeble to be heard by the government, and all the white people who could complain loud enough to be heard are interested in keeping their own secrets." *Writings*, 325.

[310] Unsigned letter from Prairie du Chien, in *Ohio Farmer and Western Horticulturist* (Columbus), December 1, 1839. For description of a pay-day orgy of the Menominee, usually much less obnoxious than the Winnebago, see the article by Gustave de Neveu, in *Wisconsin State Historical Society Proceedings*, 1910, pp. 153–64.

the territorial legislature stated that if the government did not remove the Winnebago by early spring, he would assume the responsibility of raising a corps of mounted volunteer riflemen, head them in person, and attend to the matter; the legislature memorialized Congress for immediate removal. Secretary of War Joel R. Poinsett replied that apparently the Governor was not aware of the government's plans; that it was exploring a site for the Winnebago and trusted that Dodge would co-operate. Soon the *Wisconsin Enquirer* protested the people having to await the tardy movements of the Secretary of War, meanwhile submitting to the insults of the Indians. "Will the settler of Wisconsin submit to these things? . . . We think not. If they remain among us, *they will steal as usual,* and the settlers will *shoot,* and the consequences are, an Indian War. . . . They check emigration and destroy that security which is so necessary to our peace. We say then, let us remove them *peaceably* if we can, but *forcibly* if we must—and upon us, citizens of Wisconsin, be the responsibility."[311]

The Wisconsin territorial legislature, which had resolved that papers in the War Department relating to the Winnebago be laid before it, was put in its place by Secretary Poinsett when he informed it that the War Department had no documents which it considered proper to publish at the time, and that the Department would have to be the judge of the expediency of removal. The situation finally worked itself out. By May most of the Winnebago had gone west of the Wisconsin for corn planting, and it was expected that the Governor could keep them from returning. The following spring peaceable removal to new homes across the Mississippi took place.

The settlement of Wisconsin in the 1830's developed from two opposite corners. Stretching a half-dozen miles up the Fox from Green Bay, and half as far back on either side of the river, were (in 1833) about four hundred houses, French-rustic in type, with low ceilings, small windows, often whitewashed, and furnished with Indian mats in lieu of carpets. The inhabitants were largely retired *voyageurs,* half-breeds, and Menominee. The town of Navarino, laid out in 1819, and the American Fur Company post of Astor adjoining it on the south later united

[311] March 30, April 6, 1839.

as Green Bay. The land, title to which had been awarded by
Congress in the preceding decade,[312] was cleared only half a
mile back from the river; the long narrow farms, laid out in
French fashion, each had a few hundred feet of water frontage;
2,500 acres were under cultivation, the rest was wilderness. One
lone gristmill, its nearest competitor being several hundred
miles away, tried to take care of the local needs. Cattle and ponies
ran at large on the meadows; there were few wagons and carts
but numerous trains and carioles for winter use. On low land on
the west bank of the river about a mile back from the bay stood
Fort Howard, built in 1816, and until 1827 when most of the
garrison was removed to Jefferson Barracks, the center of military and social life.[313] Deer, wild fowl, and fish attracted not
only the Indians but garrison officers and citizens as well.

With Eleazar Williams in 1821 had come Albert G. Ellis to
help teach the Oneida, but after conducting semisubscription and
garrison schools for a few years, he became a surveyor;[314] in
1833, with a partner, he founded and edited the *Green-Bay Intelligencer*, Wisconsin's pioneer newspaper.[315] After Williams
lost out with the church board, a Protestant Episcopal mission
and boarding school for the Indian children was set up by the
Rev. Richard F. Cadle at Shantytown.[316] Among the prominent
early citizens of the settlement were the five Grignon brothers,[317]
John Lawe, public-minded and charitable fur trader, and James
Duane Doty, judge of the United States Circuit Court.

The land office was opened in 1835 and Green Bay, "The
Jumping off Place, the End of the West" ("Green Bay or Botany
Bay—it was all the same"), suddenly came to life.[318] "Terra

---

[312] By laws in 1820, 1823, and 1828.

[313] From 1820 to 1822 the garrison was posted at "Camp Smith," about three
miles upstream on the east side. The small settlement built on the abandoned
camp came to be known as Shantytown.

[314] In 1838 surveyor general for the Wisconsin-Iowa district.

[315] General Ellis' "Recollections" are in *Wisconsin Historical Collections*, VII
(1873–76), 210–68.

[316] For account of the Cadle mission, see *Wisconsin Historical Collections*,
XIV (1898), 394–515.

[317] Descended from Charles de Langlade. Pierre A. Grignon, "head of the family,"
had died in 1823. Louis, with John Lawe, sponsored the early schools. Augustin,
noted for his princely hospitality, spent most of his life in the Indian trade. Ellis'
"Recollections" portray the early settlers in some detail.

[318] In the winter of 1833–34 the settlement had even been cut off from direct
mail service to Chicago. Mail came by way of Dixon's Ferry and Mineral Point.
Mail from Galena, two hundred miles away, took three weeks. Buffalo papers
of mid-October got through by January. *Green-Bay Intelligencer*, January 8, 22,
February 4, 1834.

Mania" had at last reached the outposts. The talk was "land, land, town plots and speculations." How long the boom would continue or how far it would go, no one could determine.[319] In August two tracts, one about 25 by 75 miles around the Four Lakes–Wisconsin Portage region, the other 30 by 50 miles in the Lake Winnebago–Fox River–Lake Michigan area, were put on sale. All told there were nearly one hundred townships of more than two million acres. Buyers from Chicago, Detroit, and elsewhere were in attendance, and, since there were few pre-emptions, sales were brisk; land around the head of Lake Winnebago went readily at $5.00 to $20 per acre.[320] Sales did not stop with the closing of navigation. By March, 1836, Milwaukee was an old place, and Sac Creek, "Sheboyagan," Sleeping River, and Manitowoc were the rage. Lands at Manitowoc advanced from $20 to $250 an acre in a week. Damsites, as ever, were in demand. Birmingham (Portsmouth or Depere), six miles up the Fox, and "Sheboyagan" were thought to have hydraulic possibilities. No vacant land remained along the Rock from the Illinois line to Lake Koshkonong. There was much talk of early construction of a canal at the Fox-Wisconsin portage.

Green Bay naturally had become a busy place. A bank was opened, and the ladies of Christ Church made $2,000 at a fair (including $1,100 profit on four lots). Lack of a harbor was a handicap to lake boats, but private citizens set up seven buoys to mark the winding channel.[321] The Green Bay–Mississippi Road was completed (creeks bridged and hills graded) to within thirty miles of Green Bay by the autumn of 1835.[322] Building materials and mechanics were in demand; prices of foodstuff were high—pork $20 to $30, and flour $15 to $25 the barrel. When in 1837 the *Milwaukee Advertiser* facetiously wanted to know (to the extent of one column) where was "Green Bay" and what right it had to the name, the Green Bay *Wisconsin Democrat* rose to the bait and explained that Navarino and Astor *were* Green Bay and that the population at or near the mouth of the river was 2,300.[323] The population of the town proper was nearer 1,000. There were numerous stores, two churches,

---

[319] *Ibid.*, July 20, August 22, 1835.
[320] *Chicago American*, December 12, 1835.
[321] *Green-Bay Intelligencer*, May 19, 1835.
[322] *Ibid.*, October 31, 1835.
[323] March 17, 1837.

and three hotels. The town, like others, felt the impact of the depression of the late 1830's; in 1839 hundreds of lots were advertised for sale for delinquent taxes.[324]

At the other end of the Military Road on the Mississippi, just above the mouth of the Wisconsin, was the old French village of Prairie du Chien. Across a slough of the river a mile or two to the south stood Fort Crawford, around the northern environs of which grew up the new town. Thirty miles to the south, on a narrow bottom, stood Cassville. Here were a few dozen houses, a tavern, and a storehouse where the subagent kept the government's share of lead. Some sixty miles up the Wisconsin on the south bank the village of Helena appeared in the late 1820's; it became a shipping point for lead and the seat of a shot tower which produced shot from the Black Hawk War to the Civil War.[325] Mineral Point, Dodgeville, Belmont,[326] and other towns had developed in connection with the lead-mining boom of the 1820's. Henry Dodge and William S. Hamilton, prominent among the early leaders, had arrived in 1827. As in the Galena district most of the settlers were from Illinois, Kentucky, and Tennessee. While mining was the all-important interest, the connections of this region were largely with the country to the south.

Government surveys of the mineral area were speeded up[327] and by the end of 1833 most of the land as far east as the Rock River was ready for sale. With the opening of the Wisconsin Land District in 1834, with its headquarters at Mineral Point, serious agricultural settlement began.[328] "Fancy must fail in imagining a more lovely country: the agriculturist in vain might seek for a richer or more productive soil," said the land looker.[329]

[324] One full page in the *Wisconsin Democrat* of October 29, 1839.

[325] Orin Grant Libby, "Chronicle of the Helena Shot Tower," in *Wisconsin Historical Collections*, XIII (1895), 335–74.

[326] The meeting place of the first territorial assembly in 1836.

[327] Based on the northern Illinois boundary as base line and the fourth principal meridian which intercepted this line at its western end. The township and section lines of 180 townships in Wisconsin were run in little more than a year. *Green-Bay Intelligencer*, April 9, 1835.

[328] Only 14,336 acres were sold the first year but four years later the three Wisconsin offices (Milwaukee having been added) sold about twice as many acres as those of Illinois, and about five times as many as those of Michigan.

[329] W. R. Smith, *Observations on the Wisconsin Territory*, 3. Schafer, *The Wisconsin Lead Region*, is the definitive study of the soil, land, and settlement of this part of Wisconsin.

Schoolcraft on his way from Galena to Fort Winnebago in 1831 was pleased to

Roads . . . are sometimes for the distance of half a mile cut through clusters of half-grown trees, in which are found abundance of blackberries, May-apples, crabapples, gooseberries, wild plums, and other indigenous fruit. Passing through here in June, I enumerated the game I saw, and what I heard. Two deer were bounding in the distance. I saw the grey squirrel,—rabbits darting into the bushes,—and heard the prairie hen calling together her brood, and the music of the birds that sang in the oaks. The thrush and the sweetest prairie singers gave voluntaries, and I thought of the poet's true answer to the question, "What does the bird say?"[330]

The region of southwestern Wisconsin was a tilted upland. From the Military Ridge (roughly the line of the Military Road) the longer gentler slope led south across the Illinois line; the shorter steeper slopes ended in the 300- to 500-foot bluffs of the Wisconsin and Mississippi. Excepting for the narrow thin-soiled ridges the country—prairies and broad wood ridges—was good farm land. Glaciers had not scooped and gouged here, nor left their boulders and gravel deposits. The soil, largely weathered limestone, was seven to ten feet deep. Although timber was scarce in spots, and the winters severe, spring wheat, potatoes in quantity, and even corn and winter wheat could be raised. The rolling prairie country was broken noticeably by the Platte and Blue mounds, about fifty miles apart, visible for many miles. From the top of the former the traveler with an eye for beauty, viewed the scene in the summer of 1837:

Below us, on the plain, is the little village of Belmont, with its bright painted dwellings; the brown lines in the broad green carpet indicate the

note that the people were finding the region "as valuable for the purposes of agriculture as for those of mining, and as sylvan in its appearance as if it were not fringed, as it were, with rocks, and lying at a great elevation above the water. . . . The surface of the country is not, however, broken but may be compared to the heavy and lazy-rolling waves of the sea after a tempest. These wave-like plains are often destitute of trees, except a few scattering ones, but present to the eye an almost boundless field of native herbage. Groves of oak sometimes diversify those native meadows, or cover the ridges which bound them. . . . Numerous brooks of limpid water traverse the plains, and find their way either into the Wisconsin, Rock River, or the Mississippi. The common deer is still in possession of its favorite haunts; and the traveller is very often startled by flocks of the prairie-hen rising up in his path. The surface soil is a rich black alluvion; it yields abundant crops of corn and, so far as they have been tried, all the cereal gramina. I have never, either in the West or out of the West, seen a richer soil, or more stately fields of corn and oats, than upon one of the plateaux of the Blue Mounds." *Summary Narrative of an Exploratory Expedition to the Sources of the Mississippi River in 1820: Resumed and Completed by the Discovery of Its Origin in Itasca Lake, in 1832* (Philadelphia, 1855), Appendix, 561.
[330] Grinnell, *Home of the Badgers* (2d ed.), 29.

roads and tracks over the prairie; the grazing cattle are scattered over the wide surface looking like sheep or dogs in size; whilst in the distance are seen travelling wagons of emigrants, and ox-teams hauling lead, merchandise, and lumber; the horseman and foot-traveller are passing and repassing; pleasure and travelling carriages are whirling rapidly over the sward, as if the country had been improved for a century past, instead of having been only five years reclaimed from the savages. This picture is not exaggerated; it fails of the original beauty, in the attempt to describe that scene which is worth a journey of a thousand miles to contemplate in the calm sunset of a summer day, as I have viewed it from the top of the Platte mounds.[331]

Mineral Point, with its irregular streets, had 1,500 inhabitants by 1837 and was the seat of the executive offices of the Territory. There were four public houses, seven dry-goods stores, and a brewery. Town lots were selling at from $100 to $800; wages and prices were high. Lead had been found on some of the lands not reserved as mineral, which made the purchases worth several thousand dollars.

In the twenty-two miles from the Blue Mounds to the Four Lakes the country became more wooded and irregular.

In whatever direction your eyes turn . . . that which imparts an indescribable charm to the whole scene . . . is the inimitable grace with which the forests and clumps of trees are disposed. . . . Every part within range of the horizon is alike, in that each, turn where you will, concurs to cherish and render more indelible the new and pleasing impression, whilst the parts separately, having each a softness of character contrasted occasionally with the noble escarpments that peer out from the bluffs at the very moment when you are ready to say that Nature has exceeded the finest style of English park scenery, tell you in terms that must be listened to,

[331] W. R. Smith, *Observations on the Wisconsin Territory*, 94. Smith believed no gentleman should visit Europe until he had made the grand western tour and seen such sights as this. Here, as in Michigan, Illinois, and elsewhere, the prairie flowers impressed the newcomer. Among them were the "mineral" plant with a bluish-purple flower, which was supposed by the miners to indicate the presence of lead, and the turpentine weed or "compass" plant, the leaves of which were said invariably to point north and south. See also Atwater, *Writings*, 340.

Atwater's party in 1829, having ascended the hills on the south side of the Wisconsin, paused: "We stood in breathless silence several minutes. . . . Not an animated being beside ourselves was to be seen, nor a sound heard. An awful silence reigned, as to us, throughout creation. Before us lay spread out in all directions, except towards the deep and gloomy basin of the Wisconsin behind us, a boundless prairie, or bounded only by the horizon. Above us was a flaming sun at noon day, and the pale blue heavens; the sky looked as pure as the Spirit who made it, and not even one breath of air was in motion, nor a spear of grass, nor a dry leaf rustled in the plain or among the trees, nor did even one grasshopper, by his heart cheering song, break the awful silence which reigned over this vast plain." *Ibid.*, 340.

that you have never seen any thing so beautiful, so really attractive, before, and that it is a pure American scene, the elements of which no magic could enable all Europe to bring together. . . . Who would have thought that brokers, speculators, and sharpers could already have done so much to stigmatize the character of one of the finest domains that Nature ever offered to man.[332]

Wakefield's report on the Four Lakes as the "most beautiful bodies of water I ever saw"[333] was corroborated by others[334] but time very quickly proved the falsity of the prophecy that "the country is not fit for any civilized nation of people to inhabit."

Government surveyors mapped the region in 1834, and in the autumn of 1835 James Duane Doty, long familiar with the site, entered one hundred acres between the third and fourth lakes, at the Green Bay Land Office. Later with Stevens T. Mason he organized a land-holding company and entered 1,200 additional acres. Lucius Lyon, surveyor, also had purchased surrounding land. Doty's efforts were important in influencing the first territorial assembly, which convened in December, 1836, to locate the capital at the site of Madison, as yet a nonexistent city.[335] In April, 1837, a log tavern was begun for the proprietor of a tavern at Blue Mound mine, and on the last day of May, forty workmen and six yoke of oxen left Milwaukee to start work on the capitol building. Lot proprietors were promoting "East Madi-

---

[332] Letter of G. W. Featherstonhaugh, Esq., to *National Intelligencer*, July, 1837, quoted in W. R. Smith, *Observations on the Wisconsin Territory*, 65–67.

[333] *Ante*, 74–75.

[334] "This lovely shore is studded and adorned with spots of wood and thick groves, giving the idea of the park scenery in England, or the rich views of Italy; and more beautiful than either, in its natural state." Smith, *Observations on the Wisconsin Territory*, 57–58.

[335] Jealousy over location of the capital, business, political, and personal rivalries, led to a lively spat over Doty's honesty and ethics. In 1839 when Doty ran against Byron Kilbourn for territorial delegate, he was accused of bad faith, fraud, and collusion. The Mineral Point *Miners' Free Press* and the *Milwaukee Advertiser*, Kilbourn's paper, led the attack; the *Milwaukee Sentinel* and the *Wisconsin Enquirer* stood the defense. In the Green Bay *Wisconsin Democrat*, July 16, 1839, Mason was accused of keeping Doty at home under pretense of coming to see him, then going to Madison, claiming all the land, and denying Doty's power of attorney. Doty's letter is published in this issue. Not only were titles to town lots in question, but title to the capitol site as well. In his long report regarding the latter, Moses M. Strong, United States attorney for the Territory, stated that Doty had sold his one-half interest in the lands to Mason, but that the latter had appeared to convey part of the same to Doty as trustee of the Four Lakes Company. *Wisconsin Enquirer*, January 26, 1839. Strong decided Mason had title to the capitol site, which he deeded to the Territory of Wisconsin in January, 1839. See also the *Enquirer*, April 20, *Sentinel*, July 9, *Democrat*, July 30, 1839, *Advertiser*, January 11, 1840.

son," "North Madison," the "City of Four Lakes," and "Mandamus." What six months earlier had been in a state of nature now had a population of more than a hundred active mechanics; there were about thirty houses "in a state of forwardness," and the contemplated city was looking forward not only to "boats in great numbers" which would ascend the Rock River and navigate the Four Lakes, but a canal connection with the Milwaukee River and Lake Michigan. Within two years Madison was a village of more than two hundred people, and boasted three hotels. When on one Sunday in midsummer, 1839, four stages left for four different places—Chicago and Milwaukee by way of Janesville, Milwaukee by way of Jefferson, Galena by way of Mineral Point, and Green Bay by way of Fort Winnebago and Fox Lake—the *Enquirer* remarked that soon travelers would be able to get about in "our territory."[336]

In the autumn of 1838 a few families settled at Prairie du Sac on the Wisconsin River about thirty miles northwest of Madison. A little farther directly north at the portage, where Fort Winnebago had been established in 1828, workers who were rafting out timbers for the government buildings constituted the nucleus of a settlement (Portage). The Fond du Lac Company, Doty president, recorded a town plat and sold lots in the summer of 1836; three years later settlers near the entrance of the Fox into Lake Winnebago met and named their village Oshkosh.

The "Milwauky Country" came to the front suddenly in 1834.[337] Morgan Lewis Martin, of Green Bay, had seen the possibility of a townsite in 1833, mapped the bay, and made an agreement with Solomon Juneau to pre-empt the site and to develop it jointly. The next year Byron Kilbourn, assigned to Green Bay as surveyor, and his partners began developing the

---

[336] August 3, 1839.

[337] *Green-Bay Intelligencer*, April 16, 1834. French traders had resided at the mouth of the Milwaukee River in the 1760's and 1770's; one of them, Jacques Le Garder, Sieur de St. Pierre, was still there in 1779. Jacques Vieau, who came in 1795, has been honored by the Milwaukee Old Settlers Club as being the first "permanent" settler. Solomon Juneau, married to Vieau's daughter, arrived in 1818, bought out his father-in-law's post, and was soon joined by his brother Peter. See Edwin S. Mack, "The Founding of Milwaukee," in *Wisconsin State Historical Society Proceedings*, 1906, pp. 194–207, for sketch of Milwaukee beginnings. Also Quaife, *Lake Michigan*, 200–1.

A good description of the Milwaukee region appeared in a letter to the *Lexington Intelligencer*, reported in *Milwaukee Advertiser*, November 17, 1836.

tract south and west of the river.[338] Squatters swarmed in and
trouble was anticipated between them and the speculators at
Green Bay in August, 1835, when four fractional townships were
put on sale, but all went off harmoniously.[339] "The Milwauky"
became all the rage; the *Green-Bay Intelligencer* apologized for
recurring to the subject, but "what all the world is in a fever
about, must certainly be interesting to many."[340] Although there
were only between fifty and a hundred settlers, promoters talked
of having the town already laid out, of lots selling at $500 to
$600, and of there being a hundred buildings by autumn. Soon
the town would rival Chicago. The proprietors (Juneau on the
east, Kilbourn on the west side of the river) spent thousands
of dollars grading streets and bridging the Menominee River.[341]
"Juneau's Side" and "Kilbourntown" were rival promotions and
from 1837 to 1839 were organized as separate towns.[342] In
August, 1836, the sheriff's census showed the population at 1,206
for the settlement and 2,893 for the newly organized county
which comprised the southeast corner of the Territory.[343]

Lot sales were brisk and prices advanced 100 per cent in thirty
days;[344] some lots were reported to have sold at $1,000 to
$5,000.[345] The speculative spirit and newness of the settlement
made commodity prices extremely high. Flour and wheat were
$15 the barrel, mess pork $35, apples $10 to $12, hay $10 to
$15 per ton, corn $2.00 to $2.50 per bushel, salt $7.00 to $8.00,
lard 25 cents, butter 45 to 50 cents, New Orleans sugar 14 to 17
cents, whiskey 50 to 55 cents, and fourth-proof brandy $2.50.
People were petitioning the legislature to authorize construction
of a railroad to the Mississippi, passing ordinances against
gambling, and organizing an agricultural society. In the season of

[338] Kilbourn in a letter to his constituents, January 29, 1836, stated that in 1834
he had found only a fur trader and one other settler on the scene. *Milwaukee
Advertiser*, July 14, 1836.
[339] *Green-Bay Intelligencer*, September 5, 1835.
[340] July 17, August 6, 1835.
[341] *Milwaukee Advertiser*, July 28, August 25, 1836.
[342] "Town of Milwaukee on the East Side of the River" and "The Town of
Milwaukee on the West Side of the River."
[343] *Milwaukee Advertiser*, August 11, 25, 1836. For map of the six counties of
1836, see Schafer, *Agriculture in Wisconsin*, or William Francis Raney, *Wisconsin;
A Story of Progress* (New York, 1940), 97. The legislature of 1836 created fifteen
new counties in what is now Wisconsin.
[344] Letter in *Green-Bay Intelligencer*, May 11, 1836.
[345] *Ibid.*, March 2, 1836.

1838 there were 244 arrivals and departures of steamboats and 268 of sail. There was much talk of the Milwaukee and Rock River Canal. Two hundred and fifty European immigrants, mostly Prussians, arrived.[346] Semiweekly stage mails were begun to Madison, the fare was reduced to $6.00; service to Mineral Point and Galena was improved.

Settlers had been following the commissioners up the Chicago –Green Bay Road as it was laid out. Racine and Kenosha to the south, Upper Milwaukee, Sheboygan, and Manitowoc to the north, were the seats of sawmills, prospective townsites or actual settlements by 1836. Proprietors at Racine had obtained title to the town plat by floating claims. Sheboygan proprietors had purchased land in 1836 and with active promotion, which included talk of a canal to Lake Winnebago, disposed of some of their lots at $2,000 per acre.[347] Kewaunee, Mahnawauk, Van Buren, Centerville, and Dunkirk Falls were other townsites in the development stage.[348] After several postponements, sales for the Milwaukee land district opened in November, 1838, but the first important sales were in February and March, 1839, when some $600,000 worth of land was sold.[349]

The country of southeastern Wisconsin, a rolling terrain of glacial terminal moraine, was a mixture of prairie, oak openings, forests, and lakes. Oak, beech, and maple prevailed on the high land, marsh conifers on the low. [350] The soil was generally rich.

The country [near Whitewater] . . . is one of continued and increasing beauty and interest. Such wheat fields I have never seen, nor can they be found elsewhere, I am sure, than in this Elysium of the West. The Oak openings, with their winding circuitous roads, or no roads at all (for you can ride through them as your fancy dictates), with the flowers peeping from behind the trees, the startled gopher, hieing him to his home, the ravishing notes of the feathery tribe, and the untutored swine, running hither and yon, all form rather a wild and picturesque scene.

[346] *Milwaukee Sentinel*, October 8, 1839.
[347] *Milwaukee Advertiser*, June 28, 1836.
[348] *Ibid.*, August 25, November 10, 1836; March—April, 1837.
[349] *Ibid.*, March 16, 1839.
[350] See maps in Joseph Schafer, *Four Wisconsin Counties (Wisconsin Domesday Book, General Studies*, II, Madison, 1927). This work is a unique study of the terrain, soil, settlement, and agriculture of a region in the Old Northwest. For contemporary description, see Col. Samuel Stambaugh's report to Secretary of War on the land ceded by the Treaty of 1833, published in full in *Green-Bay Intelligencer*, August 22, 1835.

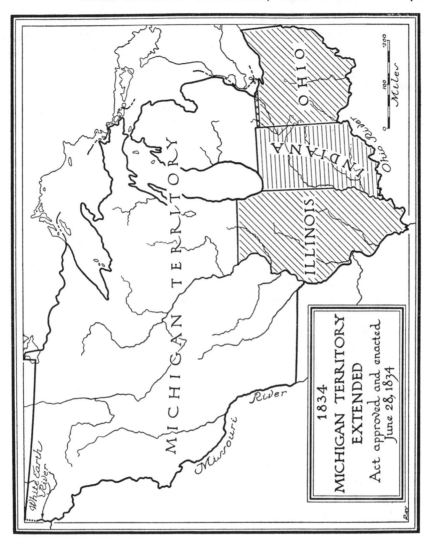

OHIO

INDIANA

ILLINOIS

MICHIGAN TERRITORY

Ohio River

Missouri River

White Earth River

0 100 200
Miles

1834
MICHIGAN TERRITORY
EXTENDED
Act approved and enacted
June 28, 1834

Ray

Thus wrote a traveler in 1846.[351] And of the land around Racine:
"If homesick men will defame the character of Wisconsin, they
dare not speak of this lake scenery."[352]

As in northern Illinois, the ideal location for the newcomer
would be largely prairie upland with some woods. Since most
roads were as yet unlocated, the settler tried to avoid cutting
himself off from port or stream by intervening swamps. The
settlers with means could afford to develop prairie farms; the
poorer, as in Indiana and Illinois, took to the woods. Wheat was
the main crop in the minds of most, supplemented by hay, oats,
and some corn. The Yankees who came in at the lake ports were
good judges of land and frequently picked the best at first glance,
but successful settling, like other things, was a matter of personal
rather than national or regional ability. The dividing line in
Wisconsin between the people from the South and the New
York-New England (later the German) settlers was not, as in
Illinois, and to a certain extent in Indiana, an east-west line; it
was a north-south line located somewhat east of Madison.

Wisconsin, achieving separate identity as it did during the
expansive years of the early 1830's, had a good press. Naturally,
the early territorial newspapers dilated on the advantages of the
region,[353] and eastern papers copied widely. The reports of Col.
Samuel Stambaugh, the writings of Schoolcraft, the English geologist Featherstonhaugh, and others who described the country
as the finest part of America, were quoted directly and at
length.[354] News incident to the Indian treaties, opening of new
land offices, and the birth of a new territory was also good
advertising.

For a number of years it had been apparent that a separate
territory would be organized west of the lake. In 1829 Caleb
Atwater had written: "Nature seems to have intended this
country should form a State by itself; but man has determined

[351] Grinnell, *Home of the Badgers* (2d ed.), 36.
[352] *Ibid.*, 20.
[353] The traveler, inclined to discount the stories of the *Green-Bay Intelligencer*
as mere puffs, admitted after seeing the country that "the half was not told me."
Intelligencer, May 30, 1835.
[354] For example, see the long letter to New York *Commercial Advertiser* reprinted
in *Milwaukee Advertiser*, April 29, 1837; a three-column discussion from the
Kinderhook Sentinel in *ibid.*, April 21, 1838; one column from the *Washington
Globe*, in *ibid.*, May 5, 1838.

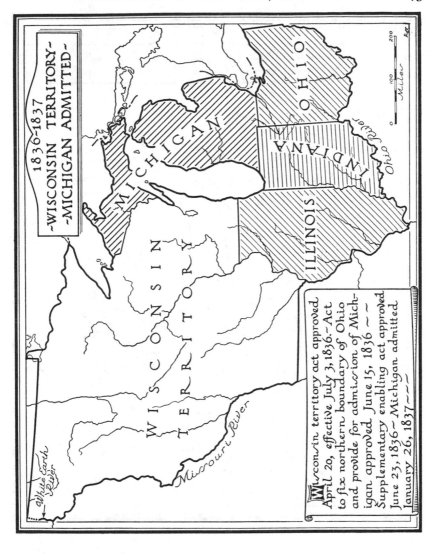

1836–1837
– WISCONSIN TERRITORY–
– MICHIGAN ADMITTED –

Wisconsin territory act approved
April 20, effective July 3, 1836.– Act
to fix northern boundary of Ohio
and provide for admission of Mich-
igan approved June 15, 1836 –
Supplementary enabling act approved
June 23, 1836– Michigan admitted
January 26, 1837 –

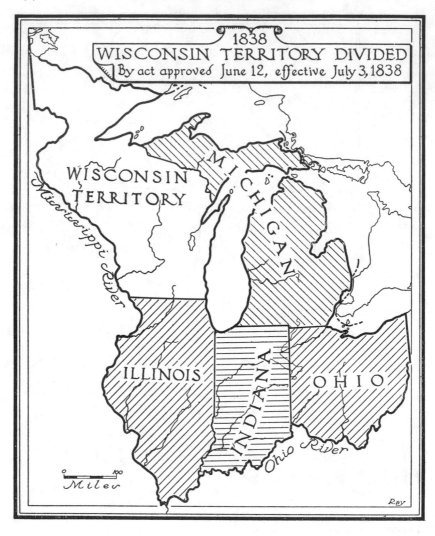

1838
WISCONSIN TERRITORY DIVIDED
By act approved June 12, effective July 3, 1838

otherwise."[355] Man finally ratified Nature's intent, for by law approved April 20, 1836, to be effective "from and after the third day of July next," the Territory of Wisconsin was established. The Illinois and Michigan boundaries were essentially as now, but on the west the country north of Missouri and east of the Missouri and White Earth rivers (Iowa, Minnesota, a third of South Dakota, two thirds of North Dakota) was included.[356] Though obviously temporary, this arrangement had the effect of giving the people on the west side of the Mississippi a deciding voice in early territorial affairs. Des Moines and Dubuque counties, by the census of 1836 had 10,531 population as compared to the 11,683 in the four counties[357] of Wisconsin proper.

Land-speculation possibilities, as well as the $20,000 General Government appropriation for public buildings, made the selection of a territorial capital an important matter. Most active contenders were Dubuque, Cassville, Mineral Point, Platteville, and Belmont; Green Bay had hopes, but few chances.[358] Governor Henry Dodge, having taken a census and apportioned the 13 councilors and 26 representatives, selected the hamlet of Belmont, practically a paper town in the southwest corner of the mineral region, as the meeting place for the first territorial assembly.[359] But from here on Judge Doty, who has been described as "a consummate political manipulator, a master of chicane, and a lobbyist of unusual charm and impressiveness,"[360] took over. His land holdings were not limited to the Four Lakes

---

[355] *Writings*, 357.

[356] This land, the part of Missouri Territory not to be included in the "Indian Country," was mentioned in the Territory-of-Huron bill of 1830, and had in 1834 been annexed to Michigan Territory "for administrative purposes." In 1838, by the organization of Iowa Territory, Wisconsin Territory was limited to the land east of the Mississippi and a line drawn due north from its headwaters. See map, 144.

[357] Brown, 2,706; Iowa, 5,234; Crawford, 850; Milwaukee, 2,893.

[358] Mineral Point citizens had petitioned Congress in behalf of their town in 1833, but Green Bay had said that any point on the Mississippi River would be a "flagrant injustice to the northern counties." *Green-Bay Intelligencer,* December 25, 1833.

Michigan having set up a "state government" in 1835, the acting governor of the Territory had called an election in the region west of the lake for October. Of the members of the Council then elected, nine assembled at Green Bay in January, 1836. This "Rump Council," which in the absence of the acting territorial governor had no powers, had favored Cassville for the capital of the new Territory.

[359] The name of Belmont was in 1867 removed to a new town three miles to the southeast. The original Belmont was near the modern town of Leslie.

[360] Schafer, *The Wisconsin Lead Region*, 63.

region. By playing Dubuque, which even started a newspaper to promote her cause, against Mineral Point (supported by Green Bay and Milwaukee), and promoting Fond du Lac as the favorite (where sale of Doty lots was encouraged), and perhaps by judicious distribution of lots on favorable terms, he finally brought in Madison as the permanent seat of government.[361] Burlington was made the temporary capital,[362] fifteen new counties were created, several roads were "authorized," and a railroad chartered.

Since the inhabitants were no longer "Wolverines" there was some public discussion of the proper nickname. "Wisconsians" was awkward and "Wisconsinners" did not appeal to many; some suggested "Hawkeyes," only to be reminded that they had long possessed the honorable cognomen of "Badgers."[363] Doty, who became governor in 1841, insisted on "Wiskonsan" as the proper spelling, but was not so successful in this as in locating the capital.[364]

So generous was the treatment of the new Territory at the hands of the General Government—public buildings, lighthouses, roads, and the like—it was sometimes called its pet.[365] After the excitement of the hard-pressing days of 1835–36 had subsided, actual settlement slowly but steadily increased. Though pretentious internal improvements, including railroads, were being made the order of the day,[366] so unsettled was the country northwest of the Wisconsin-Fox boundary, that when a charter for a railroad from Milwaukee to Superior was applied for, the editor of the *Advertiser* did not know where Superior was.[367] By 1841 the population of the territory was 30,000.

[361] Governor Dodge wrote a year later that Doty believed that men "have all their prices, and if they will not receive a bribe directly they can be interested in speculations which will oblige them to cooperate with him in such a manner as will enable him to react on them as may suit his views." *Annals of Iowa*, 3 series, III (1897-99), 395. The records indicate that, soon after the assembly selected Madison, Doty transferred Madison property to at least fifteen of the thirty-nine assemblymen, to clerks of the two houses, to the governor's son, and to others. Schafer, *Wisconsin Lead Region*, 73 and note.

[362] Burlington, on the west side of the Mississippi about half way between St. Louis and Galena, although only three years old, had about 1,200 population by 1837. There were about twenty stores, two hotels, and a newspaper. *Wisconsin Territorial Gazette* in Mineral Point *Miners' Free Press*, July 21, 1837.

[363] *Milwaukee Advertiser*, July 21, 1836.

[364] The territorial legislature by joint resolution in 1845 made the present spelling official. *Laws of Wisconsin Territory*, 1845, p. 121.

[365] *Belmont Gazette*, April 12, 1837.

[366] See below, Chapter XII.

[367] *Milwaukee Advertiser*, September 15, 1836.

§ § § § §

The land boom, which swept the United States between 1830 and 1836, was the biggest experienced up to that time. Receipts from sales of public lands rose from fewer than two and a half million dollars to more than twenty-five million. From the forests of Maine to the swamps of Mississippi and the cotton lands of the Red River, professionals and amateurs whooped up their holdings and promoted their schemes. Money and credit were plentiful, prices of commodities had advanced rapidly—from 25 to 50 per cent. As Webster had pointed out, only the price of government land remained chained by statute to the minimum of $1.25 per acre. And the people of the country were land minded.

In no region was land speculation more active, nor on the whole based on more solid ultimate value, than in the region north of the Ohio. There it was not wild lands as in Maine, where parcels were sold which did not even exist, but mostly agricultural land and townsites.[368] Of the $25,000,000 receipts for land in 1836, one fifth was for lands in Michigan.

Town jobbing was more attractive in many ways than large-scale land speculation. The turnover, if any, was relatively quick and profitable; since little capital was required almost anyone could try his hand at it. Fortunately, only a small portion of the paper towns materialized. It was estimated that almost all of northeastern Illinois was platted and promoted as townsites at one time or another. At the other end of the state elegant colored maps portrayed the thriving metropolis of Cairo, situated at the junction of the Ohio and Mississippi rivers, shortly to be busier and more prosperous than New Orleans and Cincinnati combined. Lots were platted for miles up the banks of both rivers. A flood left only a shanty and a few domestic animals. The town finally materialized, but not as portrayed in the speculative optimism of 1836. "Each town has its day and each day has its town."[369] And along the Ohio town promoters would "advertise and trumpet forth the qualifications of a town in the moon, if there was a chance of selling any of the lots. . . . No

[368] The general background is presented in A. M. Sakolski, *The Great American Land Bubble* (New York, 1932), Chapter XI; and in Robbins, *Our Landed Heritage*, Chapter IV.
[369] *Chicago Democrat*, July 1, 1835.

doubt, every earthly thing must have a beginning, but some of these towns are evidently 'the beginning of the end.' "[370] Success in exploiting townsites was as unpredictable as the outcome of the throw of the dice. Promotion played a part but so did luck. Some locations which possessed every advantage of geography died aborning; others with no apparent qualifications caught on and developed into prosperous towns.

In the business of buying land and selling at a profit, as in other affairs, there were "tricks to the trade." Speculators, sometimes representing organized money, more often not, might agree to make no bids on a given section. Then one of them would acquire the section at minimum price and prorate it among the group. Or they might "swap sections," that is, agree in advance not to bid on each other's sections. A more reprehensible form of collusion was for one of a group to bid up a tract to a price high enough to scare off competition, then after the sales crowd had dispersed, forfeit on his purchase. The land then became subject to entry in the usual manner, "and this being known only to a few privileged individuals, of course, they can enter the land at the minimum price."[371]

Then there was the use of "floats" by speculators. Since early in the century, squatters or "actual settlers" had constituted a strong political group,[372] and either by "usage of the country" or legislation of Congress, efforts had been made to protect their "rights." Thomas Hart Benton and other prominent western politicians had made "pre-emption" an important vote-getting issue. By the pre-emption law of 1830 (renewed in 1832 and 1834), the actual settler or squatter who had cultivated public land in 1829 was given the right to purchase 160 acres at the minimum price.[373] If two settlers occupied the same quarter sec-

[370] Oliver, *Eight Months in Illinois,* 41.
[371] *American State Papers, Public Lands,* VII, 524.
[372] See Chapter III.
[373] The pre-emption act of May 29, 1830, which gave squatters as of 1829 rights to 160 acres at $1.25 per acre, was to extend for one year. By an act of January 23, 1832, all persons who had purchased land under the pre-emption act of 1830 were given permission to assign and transfer their certificates of purchase. By the act of July 14, 1832, persons who were entitled to a pre-emption under the provisions of the act of 1830 but who, because the public surveys had not been made or for other reasons, had not been able to take advantage of it, were authorized to enter their lands on the same conditions provided they did so within a year after the surveys were made. Since the purpose of this law was to take care of these

tion, each was given pre-emption right to eighty acres and a floating claim to eighty acres, good anywhere in the surveyed portion of the land district. Further, each "independent cultivator" in the family was entitled to such a "float." So man and wife, brothers, cousins, and children from age one to twenty-one claimed and got them. And not all were bona fide squatters; many were cultivating pre-emption privileges rather than the soil. It was an unenterprising speculator who, with one hundred dollars in hand, could not raise six to a dozen of these claims in a single squatter family.[374] Then, fortified with a pocket full of "floats," he could purchase, against no competitive bidding, hundreds of acres of land worth $30 or $40 per acre, at $1.25. Often townsites were entered by this method.

Yet many bona fide settlers who had staked their all on carving out homesteads on the public domain did not fall strictly within the requirements and protection of the law of 1830 and its extensions. Speaking of the "lameness" of that law, the *Green-Bay Intelligencer,* just before the August, 1835, sales, hoped that the human instinct of bidders to recognize their own rights would take care of the situation.[375] When at the July sales in Chicago, general respect was paid to the claims of settlers despite lack of the protection of a pre-emption law, the *Chicago Democrat* said that after all "Lynch's Law is the best of preemption laws."[376]

Large-scale speculation by absentee capital played a far more important part in the disposal of the public lands in the middle 1830's than in the earlier periods. Hence northern Indiana and Illinois, Michigan, and Wisconsin were more affected than the southern areas settled previously.

Charles Butler, William B. Ogden, and eastern associates of the American Land Company bought heavily, under contract sales, of lots in Chicago and Toledo, and served as general land-jobbing agents. Paper profits loomed large prior to the crash of 1837. Thomas Ludwell Lee Brent, of Virgina, was reputed to have purchased 70,000 acres in Genesee and Saginaw counties,

special cases, it carried no time limit on its provisions. The pre-emption law of 1834 was a renewal of the act of 1830 and applied to those who had got on the public domain after 1830. It carried a time limit of two years.

[374] See speech of Senator Thomas Ewing, of Ohio, March 15 and 16, 1836, in *Congressional Globe,* 24 Congress, 1 session, part III, 233–34, 237.

[375] August 10, 1835.

[376] July 1, 1835.

Michigan, in 1836. Henry L. Ellsworth, of Connecticut, an early advocate of prairie farming, set up an investment-management service and purchased 18,000 acres at the Fort Wayne, Crawfordsville, and Danville offices in 1835.[377] Heaviest holdings were in Benton and Tippecanoe counties, Indiana, and Vermillion and Iroquois counties, Illinois. Among Ellsworth's numerous clients was Noah Webster. Solomon Sturges, farmer and businessman of Zanesville, Ohio, also started buying Indiana and Illinois prairie lands in 1836. Even Daniel Webster, associated with Thomas H. Perkins, of Boston, bought heavily in northern Indiana, Illinois, and Wisconsin.[378]

Reactions to activities of speculators and large-scale investors in western lands were varied. The advent of "big money" into a region was often welcomed and boasted of by newspapers and settlers as corroborating evidence of the desirability of their location. On the other hand, the viewpoint of the "actual settlers" was strongly presented in petitions, editorials, and letters. Speculation was viewed with alarm as an impediment to agriculture. With much land standing idle within the sight of villages, "honest farmers" despaired of even the beginnings of a system of cultivation until all the lands were sold. Land speculation, they said, was a species of gambling in which men rely upon uncertain events, rather than honest labor.[379] Lands held by absentees, being exempt from taxes for five years after purchase from the government,[380] enhanced the local tax burden, yet western states had considered this a good bargain, and some of them, notably Illinois and Michigan, had encouraged speculation by their rag-money bank systems.

[377] Ellsworth's holdings later totaled many times this amount. For these, as well as other large-scale speculators, see Paul Wallace Gates, "Land Policy and Tenancy in Indiana," in *Indiana Magazine of History,* XXXV (1939), 1–26. Ellsworth was commissioner of patents at the time. *The Valley of the Upper Wabash with Hints on its Agricultural Advantages* appeared under the name of his son Henry William Ellsworth. This work, though partly promotional in purpose, was on the whole a fair description and contained valuable information on agriculture, especially for large-scale farmers.

[378] Webster planned a thousand-acre estate for his son near Peru, Illinois. After the expenditure of considerable sums between 1836 and 1840 for improvements and cattle, the project was abandoned. Webster correspondence cited in Gates, "Land Policy and Tenancy," in *Indiana Magazine of History,* XXXV, 8, note 19.

[379] Kalamazoo *Michigan Statesman* in *Du Buque Visitor,* November 9, 1836; *Belmont* (Wis.) *Gazette* in *Chicago Democrat,* December 3, 1836.

[380] In the enabling acts of Ohio, Indiana, and Illinois (but not of Michigan), granted in return for the 5 per cent of the proceeds from sale for internal improvements.

It is easy to exaggerate the pernicious effects of large-scale land speculation in preventing the acquisition of farms by individuals and in the development of tenancy.[381] The speculations and peculations of a few dozen large-scale operators are easily spotted; the same activities on the part of the ten thousand and one pass unnoticed. The difference was mainly in size, not in the nature of the operations. "Actual settlers" tried to hog desirable areas, the timberland, and acquire more land than they could use.[382] Had the government given away lands, there still would have been tenants. The fact seems to be that, either because of inertia, fear of accepting responsibility, "getting tied down," or just plain constitutional inability to work as well for themselves as for someone else, a certain percentage of mankind is destined to work for others.

Nor were the commonality of settlers, had they a mind to use them, without effective means short of "Lynch's Law" for countering the schemes of speculators. "Public opinion is stronger than law, and we trust that a stranger who comes among us, and especially our own citizens, will not attempt to commit so gross

---

[381] Robert J. Walker, chairman of the Senate Committee on Public Lands, spoke of "this worse than feudal vassalage" and a condition "which, whilst it drains the east of millions of capital, condemns to a period of long sterility vast portions of the beautiful valley of the west, containing a soil inexhaustibly fertile, but remaining in the hands of speculators barren and unproductive." *Congressional Globe,* 24 Congress, 2 session, part IV, Appendix, 169. His bill to limit sales to two sections each to actual settlers was defeated in the House in March, 1837.

Gates ("Land Policy and Tenancy in Indiana," 19) says: "It is remarkable that Ellsworth was criticized neither by the press of Indiana, including the farm journals, nor by politicians for proposing to introduce into pioneer Indiana an institution which all agreed was un-American." The "un-American alien-institution" label to a practice that had prevailed from earliest colonial times was largely politicians' window dressing. Despite his talk of everybody being just as good as everybody else and his distrust of "big bugs," the pioneer, by and large, admired success, was tolerant of the other fellow's "racket," and hoped possibly to do likewise. If he wanted land, it was hard to prevent him getting it; if he did not, it was impossible to make him take it. Though he recognized misfortune as a factor in success and knew about "orneryness," he had never heard of the doctrine of the "underprivileged." At least one young ex-soldier walked out on a quarter-section of fine Wabash Valley prairie land to return to the thin-soiled hills; not even the United States Government could make a freeholder out of him in a region where the houn' dogs didn't sing right. Much depends on the viewpoint. Like the city-bred land seeker who approached a native of one of the poorer sections pretending to want stock; in the bargaining he acquired not only four calves but, what he regarded as much more important, one hundred acres of land. As he departed, the native observed: "Guess that will hold him for a while; wanted the calves so bad he let me throw in that danged sassafras."

[382] Letter "Pro Bono Publico," in *Chicago Democrat,* April 16, 1834. They also took millions of feet of timber from both the public domain and lands of absentee owners without fear of conviction from juries of their peers. See Richard L. Lillard, *The Great Forest* (New York, 1948).

an act of injustice as to interfere with the purchase of the quarter sections on which the settler has made improvements."[383] The rights of the settlers on the public lands should be respected, held sacred even; this was the prevailing attitude.[384] If they were not, bona fide settlers and others took matters in their own hands. The practice of not bidding against each other at the auctions, and combining to make it obviously "unhealthy" for any outsiders who did so, was an old one.[385] It was but a step to the organization of formal land-claims associations. These varied from brief informal agreements to substantial organizations with written rules, "registers," and "arbitrators." Settlers in Lake and Porter counties, Indiana, so organized in 1836.[386]

In March, 1837, about a thousand settlers on the public lands in Milwaukee, Jefferson, Washington, and Dodge counties met at Milwaukee,[387] and formulated resolutions and rules which filled two and a half columns of newspaper. They resolved that, whereas Congress had by repeated pre-emption laws led them to believe that they would have the protection of these laws, but that since the region was so recently settled, the provision reported in the late session of Congress would not affect them, therefore, any person who had prior to the meeting claimed and made improvements to the amount of $50 on not to exceed one section of land, should have the right to retain it upon complying with the rules. Among the sixteen rules were the following provisions: if a person claimed a quarter section, he was to cultivate three acres within six months of entry and finish a house within a year; if two quarter sections, cultivate ten acres, etc.; if the land was woodland he was to clear timber under ten inches and fence it. All claims were to be entered with the "register" of the association and no person should make a claim on any other person's entry. All bids at the sale were to be made by the appointed agent of the association and none was to bid against him.

---

[383] *Chicago Democrat*, June 3, 1835.

[384] Writer from Wisconsin to *New York Star*, in *Wisconsin Democrat*, March 16, 1839.

[385] An Illinois squatter who was reported to have said "if any *speculator* bids for my land I'll shoot him," was practicing this art of suggestion. *Cincinnati Daily Gazette*, December 15, 1835.

[386] The constitution of this association is in *Solon Robinson, Pioneer and Agriculturist*, I, 69–76. Notices of settlers' meetings were frequent during 1836–37. See for instance articles and notices in the *Chicago American*.

[387] *Milwaukee Advertiser*, March 18, 1837; *Wisconsin Democrat*, March 31, 1837.

All affairs were to be handled by an executive committee of fifteen and a judicial committee for each district. The latter was to adjust disputes between claimants, but appeal might be made to the executive committee which constituted a board of trial. The litigant was required to give notice in writing to the opposite party six days before either committee would conduct a hearing. When a decision was rendered, certificates to claims were to be awarded the successful disputant. Various "orders" and decisions of the association were published from time to time in the newspapers.

Although local opinion generally approved these associations, occasionally there were outspoken protests. The *Belmont* (Wis.) *Gazette,* for instance, spoke of these actions as "directly at variance with the spirit of our laws . . . nullification."[388] The *Advertiser* defended them as necessary in the absence of United States and territorial laws to cover the situation; they avoided much bad feeling, bloodshed even. It assured those inclined to sneer at the regulations of *squatters* "that there is no mistake here; the people of this county are fully competent to carry into effect any and all of the resolutions put forth at the meeting."[389] And the *Sentinel,* after reprimanding the settlers for their indifference in getting organized, reported that land sales and settlers' claims were going smoothly. The settlers, having adjusted their disputes, encountered no competition. Capitalists found it more profitable to lend money than bid for land.[390] So strong was the influence of the settlers that, in 1839, when they petitioned to have the sale of the even or government sections of Wisconsin canal lands postponed (since many had not yet qualified by residence), the sale was postponed.[391] The squatters were "well pleased."[392]

[388] In *Milwaukee Advertiser,* May 6, 1837.

[389] May 6, March 18, 1837. The *Advertiser,* September 15, 1836, explained that the Specie Circular did not take the place of a pre-emption act (the law of 1834 having expired in 1836); that Congress' refusal to pass such was not due to hostility towards the actual settler but to the frauds via floating claims practiced under the former laws. These had prevented thousands from emigrating for fear of losing the lands they might settle on.

[390] *Milwaukee Sentinel,* November 6, 1838, February 23, March 5, 1839.

[391] The commissioners, by a liberal interpretation, had ruled that settlers with improvements on the even or government retained sections might be compensated by a like amount of land on the odd or territorial sections. When the President's proclamation of sale of the even sections appeared, a meeting was held August 5 and resolutions passed against it. The *Advertiser* said sale was favored by the Doty-*Sentinel* crowd who hoped to profit thereby. *Milwaukee Advertiser,* August 3, 10, 1839.

[392] *Wisconsin Enquirer,* October 5, 1839.

Harder to deal with than the speculators were the conniving, corrupt, and often absentee land-office agents, some of whom had connections which reached to the General Land Office, even to Congress. Since these men were the appointees of the elected officials of the "sovereign people," the latter had little recourse. As the result of laziness or ignorance of the agents, many of the land certificates were defective.[393] Worse, many engaged in speculation in scrip,[394] and in note shaving. Instances of collusion between the receivers and local merchants or bankers—in at least one case the agent was the president of the bank—were common.[395]

The Specie Circular, intended to stop speculation and help the small buyer, not only dealt him a crushing blow but provided a field day for corrupt land agents and bankers, the latter frequently members of the Whig party.

The scramble for land which reached its height in 1836–37 was probably not again duplicated in our history, except for mining rushes, until the Florida boom of the 1920's. In the words of one who lived through it:

The years 1835 and 1836 will long be remembered by the Western settler —and perhaps by some few people at the East, too—as the period when the madness of speculation in lands had reached a point to which no historian of the time will ever be able to do justice. A faithful picture of those wild days would subject the most veracious chronicler to the charge of exaggeration; and our great-grand-children can hope to obtain an adequate idea of the infatuation which led away their forefathers, only by the study of such detached facts as may be noted down by those in whose minds the feeling recollection of the delusion is still fresh. . . .

[393] An investigation of the land offices in some of the states was begun in 1833. The inspector reported that a high percentage of those issued in Indiana were defective, in some places as many as one fifth.

[394] Due bills given for cash paid in by land purchaser before forfeitures, and good for payments on later purchases. (See Chapter III.) Receivers bought up scrip at heavy discount and turned it into cash; eastern speculators bought it up and cashed it with dishonest receivers.

[395] At Indianapolis in 1833 the agent, working with a local merchant, had accumulated $98,000 of scrip which was turned into the land office at face value. The merchant had used the money to "shave" bank notes (convert notes not acceptable for land purchases into acceptable notes at a discount). Then the receiver was in partnership with a broker who entered lands for others and took a lien at 50 per cent. Except for use of public moneys to "transact a large business" the receiver's "character stands fair." Investigator's report, *American State Papers, Public Lands*, VII, 202. At Crawfordsville the agent used the land-office money to set himself and bondsmen up in the mercantile business and to buy 3,200 acres of good land at minimum price. The investigator's reports, fraud affidavits, etc., on the offices in Ohio and Indiana fill more than one hundred pages in the volume cited.

"Seeing is believing," certainly, in most cases; but in the days of the land-fever, we, who were in the midst of the infected district, scarcely found it so. The whirl, the fervour, the flutter, the rapidity of step, the sparkling of eyes, the beating of hearts, the striking of hands, the utter *abandon* of the hour, were incredible, inconceivable. The "man of one idea" was every where: no man had two. He who had no money, begged, borrowed, or stole it; he who had, thought he made a generous sacrifice, if he lent it at cent per cent. The tradesman forsook his shop; the farmer his plough; the merchant his counter; the lawyer his office; nay, the minister his desk, to join the general chase. Even the schoolmaster, in his longing to be "abroad" with the rest, laid down his birch, or in the flurry of his hopes, plied it with diminished unction.

> "Tramp! tramp! along the land they rode,
> Splash! splash! along the sea!"

The man with one leg, or he that had none, could at least get on board a steamer, and make for Chicago or Milwaukie; the strong, the able, but above all, the "enterprising," set out with his pocket-map and his pocket-compass, to thread the dim woods, and see with his own eyes. Who would waste time in planting, in building, in hammering iron, in making shoes, when the path to wealth lay wide and flowery before him?

Ditch diggers and other laborers could make more "standing round," watching for bargains than working.

This favourite occupation of all classes was followed by its legitimate consequences. Farmers were as fond of "standing round" as any body; and when harvest time came, it was discovered that many had quite forgotten that the best land requires sowing; and grain, and of course other articles of general necessity, rose to an unprecedented price. The hordes of travellers flying through the country in all directions were often cited as the cause of the distressing scarcity; but the true source must be sought in the diversion, or rather suspension, of the industry of the entire population.[396]

Even at the time there were those who realized that the speculation was not something to boast of; that it retarded solid effort and sound development.[397] After the fever collapsed, sober-minded observers hoped that the days of speculative humbug and panic were over; everyone now admitted that the old-fashioned method—labor—was best.[398] Actual settlement and sound foundations for progress could now proceed.[399]

During the decade in which the advantages and prospects of

[396] Mrs. Kirkland, *Western Clearings,* 4–5.
[397] *Milwaukee Advertiser,* July 28, 1836.
[398] *Wisconsin Democrat,* December 30, 1837; *Wisconsin Enquirer,* May 18, 1839.
[399] For the depression of 1837 and its results, see Chapter XII.

Illinois, Michigan, and Wisconsin had been the big news, the steady but not so spectacular growth of Ohio and Indiana was taken for granted. Cincinnati with 46,338 people by 1840 was far ahead of Cleveland, Dayton, and Columbus with slightly more than 6,000 each.[400]

The canals and additional roads had made all Ohio more accessible than many parts of the eastern states. The north-western corner, still most sparsely settled, was filling up. To the mixed population of Virginians, Middle States men and New Englanders were added many Germans and Irish. Negroes came in numbers, particularly to the areas nearest the Ohio River. A few hundred Indians remained but their days were numbered.[401] Although Ohio's population in 1840 was 1,519,467, making it the third state in the Union, the state was noticing the emigration from its borders, particularly to Iowa Territory. The tables had turned; Ohio now advanced some of the arguments against emigration that New England had used a quarter of a century earlier against going to Ohio.[402]

In Indiana the settlers had edged to the borders of Lake Michigan, retreated for a spell with the war scare of 1832, then returned in greater numbers. La Porte, South Bend, Michigan City[403] became towns. Internal improvements and the sale of canal lands attracted speculators and settlers; Wabash Valley towns such as Lagro, Peru, Miamisport, Logansport, Lockport, Lafayette, Williamsport, Attica, and Covington began to grow up. The Ohio River towns of New Albany (4,226) and Madison (3,798) were still the largest; Indianapolis (2,692) was a poor third. The population of the state had doubled during the decade —from 343,031 to 685,866.

The Indians were doomed after 1832; by one means or another agents began removing small bands within a year. Chief

---

[400] A Cincinnati directory of 1839, which listed some 10,000 names, listed places of birth as follows: Germany, 1,578; Pennsylvania, 1,098; Ohio, 916; Ireland, 717; New Jersey, 717; New England, 679; New York, 607; Virginia, 521; Maryland, 487.

[401] By treaty in 1842 the Wyandots, at Upper Sandusky, gave up their remaining lands and were removed the next year.

[402] *Ohio State Bulletin* in *Cleveland Herald and Gazette* (weekly), June 5, 1839. Ohio's population in 1830 had been 937,906.

[403] "The whole city looks just as if the houses had been built somewhere else & moved here—& indeed this is true of many of them." (Moved from another near-by settlement which "didn't take.") Letters of George B. Smith, in *Wisconsin Magazine of History*, V, 404.

of the remaining Indians were the Potawatomi who had reservations in Marshall and adjoining counties. Treaties of 1836 acquired title, but the occupants were given two years time to remove.[404] Squatters rushed in to establish pre-emption rights. When violence followed in 1838, Governor David Wallace ordered John Tipton, of Logansport, to embody the militia of Cass and Miami counties. Arrived at Twin Lakes Tipton proceeded to round up some seven hundred Indians and start them on the long march of forcible removal which later became known as "the Trail of Death."[405]

By 1840 in Ohio only slightly more than one tenth of the public land remained for sale; in Indiana, about one fifth. In Illinois almost one half was yet available, in Michigan, two thirds. Wisconsin Territory still had the great bulk of its lands unsold, most of them unsurveyed.[406] Illinois, in 1820, was a

[404] For these cessions see Indiana (Detail) Map, Plate CXXVII, in Royce (comp.), *Indian Land Cessions.*

[405] Irving McKee, *The Trail of Death: Letters of Benjamin Marie Petit* (*Indiana Historical Society Publications,* XIV, no. 1, Indianapolis, 1941). Few persons at the time, however, thought of the removal by this title.

[406] The statistics as of March 31, 1841 (Report from the Secretary of the Treasury, June 10, 1841, in *Senate Documents,* 27 Congress, 1 session, No. 62), convey the general picture:

	Estimated quantity of land to which Indian title extinguished, or lands ceded to United States	Estimated quantity of unsurveyed land to which Indian title not extinguished	Quantity unsurveyed to which Indian title extinguished
Ohio	16,555,952	107,816	
Indiana	20,592,761	456,400	
Illinois	32,073,427		2,794,720
Michigan	31,118,392	11,056,640	7,618,915
Wisconsin	29,863,925	17,377,675	20,704,107

	Quantity sold	Granted—aggregate, exclusive of the 16th section	Offered at public sale now subject to private entry	Estimated quantity surveyed and unsurveyed not offered at public sale
Ohio	14,173,986	1,143,087	859,035	
Indiana	14,108,810	854,889	4,782,853	311,365
Illinois	11,848,547	650,269	14,358,832	3,848,066
Michigan	9,189,431	105,360	11,864,397	8,550,942
Wisconsin	1,935,694	217,280	6,436,894	20,892,076

	Quantity unsurveyed in each district	Estimated quantity reserved from public sale	Quantity ceded, but not attached to any district
Ohio }			
Indiana }	19,239,771		335,178
Michigan }			5,597,680
Illinois		42,240	
Wisconsin	38,081,782	101,120	

western frontier state; in 1840 it was being spoken of as in the center of the United States, and anticipating soon being thought of as in the eastern division of the western states. Population had trebled—157,445 to 476,183—during the last ten years.

Although thousands of persons from the Old Northwest would shortly follow the paths of empire to a new Northwest—and to Kansas and California—many reasoned that there were no greener pastures beyond, that they had reached the land of promise. Though written a few years later, the words of the New Englander who had recently discovered the Upper Mississippi Valley well convey the idea:

What a people we are! What a country is this of ours! How wide in extent—how rich in productions—how various in beauty! I have asked in my travels, for the West, in the streets of the Queen of the West—a fairy City, which but as yesterday was a wilderness. They smiled at my inquiry, and told me it was among the "Hoosiers" of Indiana, the "Suckers" of Illinois, or the "Badgers" of Wisconsin. Then I passed along, crossing great rivers and broad Prairies, and again I asked for the West. They said it was in Iowa. I arrived at the Capitol. They complained that *they* were "too far down East." "But go," they said, "if you wish to see the West, days and days, and hundreds and hundreds of miles up the Missouri —farther than from us to New England, and beyond the Rocky Mountains, and among the Snake Indians of Oregon, and you may find it." It was the work of months to find the West, and I turned about in despair—and here I am, in this Empire City of Wisconsin—which but as yesterday was a wilderness. . . . I have found no bounds to my country. I have searched for them for months, in almost every clime—under the torrid sun of Louisiana, the land of the orange and the olive, and beneath the cold sky of Maine. I have seen the rice-planter gathering rich treasures from a bountiful soil, and the fisherman anchoring his little bark on the rocky island, dropping his hook as carefully as if the ocean were full of pearls, and not of—mackerel.

I have seen the mill-man, sawing wood on the fartherest soil of New England; and I have beheld the same wood floating down the Alabama, or the beautiful Savannah in a great variety of forms; it may be, in a clock, regularly ticking off the time, or in a pail—perchance, in a button; and for aught I know, in a tasteless ham, or in an infamous nutmeg! I have never been off the soil of my own country; and yet I have seen the sun go down a ball of fire, without a moment's notice—twilight, flinging over rich, alluvial lands—blooming with magnolias and orange trees—a robe of gold; and again I have stood upon the bare rocks of colder climes, and when the trees were pinched by early frosts, I have marked the same sunshiny

rays reflected from the leaves, as if a thousand birds of paradise were resting in their branches; then I have fancied that I was indeed in a fairy land.

I have been over the Table lands of Mexico and Northern Texas—
Dog Star rages, scattering pestilence in its train; where the long moss
hangs from the trees. There pale faces and sad countenances give admoni-
tions—that this is the regions of death. I have travelled the great prairies,
and beheld the green billows rise and fall, and the undulations, checkered
with sun-light and shadow, closing, one after the other, over the wide
expanse.

And I have gone amid the storms of winter, over the high hills, upon
the loud cracking crust, amid the music of the merry sleigh-bells—and
again I say to you, here I am—in this great Mississippi valley; which is
unequalled for richness of soil—which has more feet of rich vegetable
mould than New England can boast of inches—possessing natural advantages over any foreign country, and in view of all this I can but exclaim
in the language of a very graphic writer—"Oh, my Country, my Country!
If our destiny be always linked as one of the same flag, with its glorious
stripes, the flag of our Union—never unfurled or defended but by Freemen
—then poetry and prophecy, stretching to their utmost, cannot pre-announce
that destiny."[407]

[407] Grinnell, *Home of the Badgers* (2d ed.), 40-41.

XI

Political History, 1825–1840

FREEMEN! A Tremendous Conflict is close at Hand! On its
results depends the Preservation of our LIBERTIES and sacred
RIGHTS—Freemen to the Rescue! . . .

> March to the battlefield,—
> The foe is now before us
> Each heart is freedom's shield
> And Heaven's banner's o'er us.
> *Sangamo Journal*, October 23, 1840

THE election of John Quincy Adams to the Presidency
by the House of Representatives in 1825 led to the formation of the Jacksonian party in the Northwest and created
party alignments which lasted for many years. The "Old Hero"
had been robbed of his rights, a minority candidate had been
elected, the will of the majority disregarded and defied; not only
had the people of the West been misrepresented but the spirit of
the Constitution had been violated.[1] Jackson men turned against
Clay, and the story of the "black coalition" was told and retold.
The campaign of vindication began even before the nomination
of Jackson by the Tennessee legislature in the autumn of 1825.[2]
Aside from a rather general and deep-seated distrust of an

---

[1] Vincennes *Western Sun and General Advertiser,* April 2, 1825.

[2] When General Jackson resigned from the Senate, his letter received wide notice.
Typical of the sentiment of the Democratic press was the editorial from the Cincinnati *National Republican and Ohio Political Register,* November 8, 1825: "The
time has now arrived when every friend to the purity and stability of our free government, must be convinced of the strong and absolute necessity of such amendments
in our Federal Constitution, as will place the election of President *exclusively in
the hands of the People*; and of such restrictions upon Executive patronage as will
exclude members of Congress from any office within its gift. The corrupt bargains
and shameful management which brought John Q. Adams into the presidency,
against the express voice of the People, should rouse the nation to the most determined exertions, not only to prevent a repetition of such disgraceful transactions,
but also to put it beyond the power of artful and designing men ever to cheat the
citizens of their constitutional rights in the choice of the first officer of the government. Whatever may be the result of the next Presidential election, the political
principles of *Andrew Jackson,* like his public conduct, 'will be found to stand un-
shaken by the test of human scrutiny, of talents and of time.'"

A six-column article by "Warren," unfavorable to General Jackson, was published in the Columbus *Ohio State Journal* and copied in the *Liberty Hall and Cincinnati Gazette,* December 9, 1825.

"officeholding class," "government by aristocrats," there was no issue beyond the wrong to Jackson, the man of the people; and the rugged Westerner, to exonerate his hero, organized a personal prejudice into a political force that was positive, warlike, and powerful.

Sharp as this political warfare was, national and state politics were still largely separate affairs. This was illustrated not only by the election of James B. Ray, a Clay man, to the Indiana governorship in August, 1825, but also in the Congressional elections of the following year.[3]

In Illinois the Jackson issue added another element to the shifting factional political alignments. Daniel Pope Cook's vote for Adams in the House received the general approval of the northern or anticonvention party, while the conventionists or Thomas-Kane-McLean group were thus naturally led to the Jackson camp. The majority of the old Edwards following also seems to have supported Jackson after 1825.[4] Three parties were distinguishable in the state as a result of the convention struggle and the Adams-Jackson contest: the "whole hog" Jackson party, the "milk and cider" men, also for Jackson, and the anti-Jackson group of the northern antislavery elements. The first and last represented in embryonic form the later Democratic and National Republican-Whig parties, while the "milk and cider" men divided both ways.[5] In 1826 Ninian Edwards was elected governor by a plurality vote, but Cook in his sixth race for Congress was defeated, his vote for Adams having caused him a general loss of votes throughout the state. In the next two years radical factional changes took place in state politics.[6] The Crawford men went over to Jackson as did a majority of the Clay and Calhoun leaders. The Adams following was divided, some supporting and others opposing Edwards; included among them were many of the later Jackson leaders.[7] In December, 1826, a resolution which declared Adams elected by a bargain and which endorsed Jackson was introduced into the Illinois legislature; finally, on

[3] *Ante*, 14–15, 30–31.
[4] Thompson, *The Illinois Whigs*, 30; Ford, *History of Illinois*, 75.
[5] Thompson, *The Illinois Whigs*, 31.
[6] For the shifting allegiance of the leaders, see *ibid.*, 33.
[7] *Ibid.*, 34, citing G. Forquer to H. Eddy, December 15, 1827, in Eddy MSS.

the last day of the session, with five Adams men absent, a resolution declaring for Jackson was passed.

Generally speaking, the Jackson men in the Northwest gained
a distinct advantage over their opponents in the business of organization. They began at the bottom and in every instance
possible got control of township, county, and militia offices; the
administration might control the bank and land offices, but the
local offices outnumbered these. The party of "the common
man," which emphasized the individual's right to run for and
serve in any office, was first to subordinate that right to party
success in the practice of local convention nominations. In Indiana, for instance, an organization was perfected which began
with the township assessors and culminated in a State Committee
of General Superintendence, which directed the listing of voters,
assigned stump speakers, and mapped personal solicitation campaigns.[8] A state convention (Indiana's second) was held at
Indianapolis on January 8, 1828, and delegates representing
twenty counties selected the Jackson electors. It was organization
such as this which made it possible for the Jackson party to carry
most of the presidential elections in Indiana, regardless of the
fact that the state, on national issues, was opposed to its aims.

The administration party could not boast such a well-developed
organization; they depended largely upon the eloquence of their
speakers, the support of strong newspapers, and the appeal of
their platform to the "better classes." Some Adams men advised
taking a leaf from their opponents' book—better organization
and unified action.[9] Ohio supporters of Adams held a meeting
at Columbus on December 28, 1827, in which, despite the condition of the roads, sixty-six of seventy-three counties were represented. It selected electors, passed resolutions in support of
the administration, condemned the "coalition" charges, and
issued a long address to the voters.[10]

The interest of the Northwest in internal improvements and

[8] Indianapolis *Indiana Journal*, January 9, 1828.
[9] Columbus *Ohio State Journal*, October 18, 1827.
[10] More than four columns in the *Ohio State Journal*, December 29, 1827.
Yet earlier in the year the *Liberty Hall and Cincinnati Gazette* (April 27) had
said: "We had rather see the most ambitious and dangerous man in the Union,
elevated to the presidential chair by the free voice of the people, than the best and
wisest elected by the efforts of a disciplined party like the one Mr. Van Buren leads
in the State of New York."

the tariff was so great that discussion of these issues carried into the state legislatures. The Indiana legislature instructed Governor Ray to write a letter to Jackson to get the latter's views on Federal appropriations for roads and canals, the tariff, and other issues.[11] In reply Jackson referred the Governor to the Coleman letter of 1824 and his advocacy of a "judicious tariff." On these questions the Adams men had believed that they had the advantage, and that their reiterated cry of "measures, not men" had carried some weight. But now the Jacksonians could add to the personality of their candidate the plank of a "judicious tariff," and Adams men in numbers, including three of the Adams state committee in Indiana, satisfied with this term, whatever it meant, came over to Jackson.[12]

The attack on Jackson centered around his rough character, the fact that he was a "military chieftain," and the charge that he had permitted the execution of six militiamen for desertion after their terms had expired.[13] He was called a rowdy, a cockfighter, a gambler, and a duelist; he was said to possess no qualifications for office and a violent temper. Resenting the charge of being Federalists at heart, the Adams men hurled it back and accused Jackson of being a Federalist in disguise and having voted for a property qualification while in the Tennessee legislature and of padding his expense accounts.[14]

The question of Jackson's Burrism (his connection with the Burr affair in 1805) was exploited in the Adams press,[15] and the marital status and character of Mrs. Jackson were questioned by innuendo and loud whispers.[16] Even Thomas Jefferson was called upon to testify vicariously that the popular furor for the military hero had caused him to doubt the future of republican

[11] Indiana *Senate Journal,* 1827–28, pp. 57, 63.

[12] Vincennes *Western Sun and General Advertiser,* April 26, 1828; Leonard, "Personal Politics in Indiana," in *Indiana Magazine of History,* XIX, 47–51.

[13] *Ibid.,* XIX, 53–54; Vincennes *Western Sun and General Advertiser,* March 8, 1828; *Liberty Hall and Cincinnati Gazette,* June 12, 1827.

[14] Shawneetown *Illinois Gazette,* June 7, 1828; Vandalia *Illinois Intelligencer,* August 4, October 13, November 17, 1827, April 5, May 24, 1828; *Liberty Hall and Cincinnati Gazette,* April 17, 1827.

[15] See, for instance, articles in *Cincinnati Daily Gazette,* August, 1828, especially August 25.

[16] Charles Hammond of the *Cincinnati Gazette* even published a paper, *Truth's Advocate,* in order to blaze abroad this question more fully. When reminded by a Jackson editor that he had spoken in the Ohio Senate in 1815 against criticisms of the character of women, Hammond replied that the current Republican code was to inquire into the character of no woman, chaste or not. *Gazette,* April 15, 16, 1828.

institutions more than anything which had occurred since the American Revolution.[17] Besides the attacks on Jackson, the Adams party kept the American System well to the front. They emphasized particularly the value of the tariff and internal improvements—at Federal expense—to the economy and prosperity of the West. Friends of the Old Hero struck back with interest. "Adams the Aristocrat," "Adams the Federalist," "Adams the Unitarian" (the latter in the West equivalent to atheist or heathen), as well as the "Corrupt Bargain" headings ("pimp of the coalition—pimp of the palace") spotted the editorial columns and news articles, and were dilated upon by stump speakers. That Adams was born "with a silver spoon in his mouth" was bad enough—but that he had no control over; that a billiard table had been added to other White House trappings (presumably at public expense) was too much in the minds of righteous voters.[18]

State politics began to be affected seriously by the presidential contest in 1828. Members of the Ohio Jackson convention of January 8, which nominated electors, after adjournment nominated John W. Campbell for governor to run against Allen Trimble, administration candidate. The northern counties polled heavily for Trimble, and he was elected by 53,971 to 51,951 votes in the October election.[19]

For the second time in Indiana the state and national elections came in the same year. Governor James B. Ray, who had carried the state in 1825 on his internal improvements platform, was a candidate for re-election, but he believed national and state politics should be separate affairs and refused to run as either a Jackson or administration man.[20] Party lines were more closely drawn than in 1825 and both administration and Jackson

[17] Governor Edward Coles of Illinois, former secretary to James Madison, in Vandalia *Illinois Intelligencer*, December 1, 1827, reporting on Jefferson's views of the candidates in 1825.

[18] It was the luxury and expense of the thing rather than a question of morality. "When I saw the billiard table charge in Mr. Adams' account, I told . . . before I knew the sentiment of a human being, that it would make thousands of Jacksonians. . . . That charge has made tens of thousands." Elisha Whittlesey, prominent Ohio politician, to Daniel Webster, June 23, 1831, cited in Francis P. Weisenburger, *The Passing of the Frontier* (*History of the State of Ohio*, III, Columbus, 1941), 229.

[19] Ohio Secretary of State, *Ohio Statistics*, 1914 (Columbus, 1915), 255; *Cincinnati Daily Gazette*, November 24, 1828.

[20] *Western Sun and General Advertiser*, April 26, 1828.

parties brought out their own candidates, the former nominating Harbin H. Moore and the Jacksonian press informally nominating Israel T. Canby. Governor Ray in his attempt to ride two horses muddled things badly. He informed the Jackson men that Jackson's reply to his letter had convinced him that the General's stand on internal improvements and the tariff was sound, and promised them to come out openly for Jackson after the election.[21] At Brookville, among Adams men, Ray maintained his attitude of studied indecision, but the editor of the *Repository* in an interview got the Governor to declare that the opposition to the administration was an outrageous and violent faction which it was the duty of all good men from the Governor down to oppose. When this was reported to the Jackson state chairman, he called a meeting of the state committee; Governor Ray was promptly disowned and Canby formally nominated. The newspaper ridicule put the Governor in an impossible situation, but the election was so near that knowledge of his double-dealing did not become general.[22] The returns stood Ray, 15,141; Canby, 12,315; Moore, 10,904.[23] Governor Ray was the last Indiana governor who tried to maintain a position independent of national politics.

As the November election approached, the appeals of the Jackson press were broadcast; warnings of fraudulent tickets and forthcoming rumors of Jackson's death too late to deny before election were sent out. But the tide had definitely turned. The vote totaled: Ohio, Jackson 67,597, Adams 63,396;[24] Indiana, Jackson 22,237, Adams 17,052; Illinois, Jackson 9,600, Adams 4,687.[25] Adams' strength in the Western Reserve counties of Ohio could not hold even that state against the Jackson swing.

Conservative Ohioans were shocked by the outcome. Hammond of the *Gazette* wrote before the event:

[21] Indianapolis *Indiana Journal*, April 3, 1828, contains the legislature's resolutions, Ray's long letter to Jackson, Jackson's reply, and the Coleman letter of 1824.
[22] *Ibid.*, July 10 and 17, 1828; *Western Sun and General Advertiser*, July 19, 1828; Lawrenceburg *Indiana Palladium*, July 19, 1828.
[23] *Indiana Palladium*, December 13, 1828; Indiana *House Journal*, 1828–29, pp. 29–30, and Appendix A.
[24] *Ohio Statistics*, 255. *Niles' Weekly Register*, XXXIX, 212 (Nov. 20, 1830), gives 67,596 to 63,456, as does the *Cincinnati Daily Gazette* of November 24, 1828.
[25] Indianapolis *Indiana Journal*, November 27, 1828; Pease, *Illinois Election Returns*, 57.

I had thought in political affairs I could be surprised at nothing. But the events of the last four months have filled me with both surprise and sorrow. The combination which has been formed against the administration, the parties that compose it, its principles of action, and the men who seem prepared to unite with it, taken all together, present an extraordinary spectacle. And one well calculated to excite alarm for our future destiny as a people.[26]

After the election the editor of the *Ohio State Journal* showed both his pique and astonishment:

For an event as mortifying as it was unexpected, it would, perhaps, be impossible to account satisfactorily, otherwise than by attributing it to the momentary influence of one of those fits of political delirium, of which the history of the human race affords too many examples. . . . Where the Jackson votes came from is, in sober truth, a perfect mystery.[27]

Congressman Elisha Whittlesey explained it thus: "Office seekers and the discontents of every party united on him [Jackson]. It is a remarkable fact, that so soon as a man became soured towards his neighbor, or towards his family, or towards his brethren in the church, he was sure to support General Jackson, the better to satisfy his revenge."[28] And Clay consoled Hammond as follows: "You infidels in the virtue and intelligence of the people require too much. You require that the people should never err, but be always right. I require them only to be *generally* right. The late election I look upon as the exception . . . you make it the rule."[29]

Indiana had in 1826 three congressmen, all Clay or Adams men; in 1828, despite the prevailing Jackson sentiment, the August election returned only one Jackson man, Ratliff Boon, from the first district. His majority was ninety-one. Jonathan

[26] Hammond to Clay, March 28, 1827, Clay MSS., cited in Weisenburger, *Passing of the Frontier*, 226.

[27] November 13, 1828.

[28] Letter to Clay, September, 1829, in Clay MSS., cited in Weisenburger, *Passing of the Frontier*, 235–36. Whittlesey agreed with George D. Prentice in his estimate of the Adams administration: "When the spirit of faction shall have spent its strength and died—when the flood of calumny, which, like the stream from the mouth of the Apocalyptick Dragon, has overspread the land with its pestilential tide, shall have passed off into the Dead Sea of common oblivion, the virtue of the last administration will be remembered, and will glow, undimmed over the waste of after corruption, like 'night's diamond star' above the dark outline of a sky of storm." Of Adams Prentice said: "The tranquil majesty of his mind was like that of the ocean, when its Controller has laid the finger of his silence upon every wave." *Biography of Henry Clay* (Hartford, Conn., 1831), 241, 255.

[29] From Ashland, May 27, 1829. Clay MSS. in Indiana University Library.

Jennings, on his personal popularity, was re-elected by an over-whelming majority, as was Judge John Test, another adminis-tration man in the third.[30] In Illinois Congressman Joseph Dun-can ran for re-election, but the Edwards forces supported George Forquer, an administration man. Efforts to keep the presidential question out of the campaign failed, and Duncan was re-elected 10,447 to 6,158 votes.[31]

Party lines were reaching into the state legislatures as well, and from the election of 1828 remained established. The Ohio legislature elected in October, 1827, was listed as 66 Adams and 41 Jackson men, with 2 "on the fence"; the legislature elected in 1828 retained enough Clay-Adams men to elect Judge Jacob Burnet, anti-Jacksonian, to the United States Senate to succeed William Henry Harrison who had resigned.[32] The Indiana mem-bers had tried to ignore national issues, but the new legislature still contained enough Adams men to elect the speaker.[33] The "whole hog" Jackson men predominated in the General Assem-bly of Illinois, but a number of Adams men were elected from the northern counties. These men, however, seemed to work with Edwards, and at his request aided in securing the senatorship for McLean by a unanimous vote.

The spirit which led to the triumph of Jackson in 1828 con-tained in itself the makings of a political party, but the policies which came with his election made possible the birth of an organ-ized opposition. The widespread removals and filling of offices with friends began early in the new administration. No office was too small to be overlooked.[34] General sentiment against such a system gave the Clay and Adams men a means of attack. Also the tariff and internal improvements which had been so promi-nently displayed in the campaign were found suddenly to have become forgotten by the new administration after the election. Interest in these questions had existed side by side with interest in Jackson in 1828, and Jackson's strength had varied inversely

[30] *Niles' Weekly Register*, XXXV, 98 (Oct. 11, 1828).

[31] Pease, *Illinois Election Returns*, 54.

[32] *Niles' Weekly Register*, XXXIII, 374 (Feb. 2, 1828). Regarding the phrase used to describe the independents, Niles said, "A very significant term, but one we have met with for the first time, we believe." *Ibid.*, XXXV, 259 (Dec. 20, 1828) ; *Cleave-land Herald*, December 18, 1828.

[33] *Niles' Weekly Register*, XXXV, 259 (Dec. 20, 1828).

[34] The *Cincinnati Daily Gazette*, March—April, 1829, carried a cut of a double-ended broom at its masthead with the motto, "Sweep, Ho! Sweep!"

with the importance attached to them. Ohio, most concerned because most populous, nearer to the eastern markets, and further
advanced economically, gave the smallest percentage of majority,
and Illinois, least populous and most frontierlike, the highest.
For Illinois the policies on public lands and Indians far outweighed either tariff or internal improvements at this time. The
cohesion resulting from the spirit of enthusiasm for Jackson the
man, combined with the change in policies on the part of Jackson
as political leader, brought about a rearrangement of party lines.
After 1828 the inherent strict constructionism of Jackson came
prominently into play. From the "judicious tariff" and internal
improvements stand of 1824, he came around to the Maysville
Road veto and war on the Bank.

The Jackson or "whole hog" press tried hard to defend the
Maysville Road veto, but it was not easy in the Northwest,
where Federal aid to internal improvements was a matter of
vital interest.[35] The Cincinnati *Western Tiller,* ostensibly an agricultural paper, said: "The change in policy . . . is so opposed to
what were generally considered the sentiments of the President
. . . that it has surprised and bewildered us more than any circumstance of equal importance that has ever occurred in the history of our country."[36] Opposition papers bore down heavily on
the veto, which they maintained met with universal disapproba-
tion in the West. In view of the fact that Indian removals might
require twenty-five million dollars, they saw no hope for internal
improvements for years to come. Clay's American System was
emphasized as being the program for the West.

The West is vitally concerned in the work of Internal Improvement.
We have no other public expenditures, and the payment on our lands has
constantly drawn from this section of country, a great portion of its resources. On the sea-board there are fortifications, light-houses, break-waters,
navy-yards, and a hundred other sources of expenditure, which cause the

[35] All the Ohio congressmen of both parties, except one, had voted to override the
veto. Jackson in his veto of the bill to provide Federal funds for a road lying
within the state of Kentucky had said that appropriations for a local project would
lead to "the subversion of the federal system."
[36] Quoted in Indianapolis *Indiana Journal,* July 14, 1830. The *Liberty Hall and
Cincinnati Gazette,* December 30, 1830, published two columns of criticism of Jackson's attitude on internal improvements. It said that the same arguments Jackson
used against internal improvements would apply to all expenditures made by Congress. It further noted that Van Buren voted against internal improvements on
every occasion and that this fact demanded the serious attention of the nation.

public money to be disbursed; in the West we have no navy-yards, no fortifications, no break-waters, no light-houses. We have nothing but Internal Improvements, which can enable the Federal Government to return to us, a part of our monies which it annually withdraws. If this is to be cut off, we shall be poor indeed.[37]

The Maysville veto disconcerted many Jacksonians and further muddled the pond of personal politics, particularly in Illinois. Most of the Crawford following in the Northwest, that is, in Illinois, took with them into the Jackson party the Jeffersonian ideals of 1798 and, led by Elias Kent Kane, William C. Kinney, Theophilus W. Smith, Shadrach Bond, and John McLean, were recognized by the administration as regular Jackson men. Edwards had been wavering between Jackson and the opposition, but was strongly urged by his brother-in-law, Duff Green, to prove to Jackson that his support was sincere.[38] The Jackson spirit would tolerate no halfway position; the new Crawford adherents fitted in better than the "milk and cider" men and became more insistent on party regularity than the original Jackson men. In the state election of 1830 Kinney, a Baptist minister, was the candidate for governor of the "whole hog" party, and John Reynolds, who had said he was a "milk and cider" Jackson man but who sought support from the anti-Jackson party, was supported by Edwards. Reynolds succeeded in getting many votes from the Adams counties without losing too many Jackson votes, and by thus "playing to all the pockets" won the governorship.[39] The "whole hog" party won the legislature by a large majority, however, and took their dig at Edwards by electing Kane and J. M. Robinson, two of his enemies, to the United States Senate. In the last election in which the whole state formed the Congressional district, held in August, 1831, Joseph Duncan de-

[37] *Cincinnati Commercial Advertiser,* quoted in Indianapolis *Indiana Journal,* June 23, 1830.

[38] E. B. Washburne (ed.), *The Edwards Papers* . . . (*Chicago Historical Society's Collection,* III, Chicago, 1884), 447.

[39] For the personality of the men, conduct of the campaign, and newspaper line-up, see Pease, *The Frontier State,* 129 ff.; Ford, *History of Illinois,* 104 ff. Reynolds had said, "I must stir or git beat. The people is with me," and promised internal improvements and lighter taxation. One opponent suggested he promise also to have the Mississippi reverse its flow every six months for the advantage of traffic. Both candidates were short on education but shrewd fighters. The pamphlet and newspaper gouging in this contest offers one of the best examples of pioneer politics in this chaotic period. See files of Vandalia *Illinois Intelligencer,* edited by James Hall, Shawneetown *Illinois Gazette, Galena Advertiser,* etc.

feated Sydney Breese, Edward Coles, and two other candidates by a clear majority.[40]

The Ohio state elections of 1830 indicated that the hold of the Jackson party on the state was not too secure. The candidates for governor were Duncan McArthur, of New York Scottish descent, former scout, surveyor, and soldier, and Robert Lucas, Virginia Democrat, who also possessed a military record.[41] At the October polling the anti-Jackson men gained throughout the state. Hamilton County, which had given Jackson a majority of 2,201 in 1828, gave Lucas a majority of only 406.[42] The total vote was: McArthur 49,668, Lucas 49,186, with 226 scattered.[43] Three more congressmen were lost by the Jackson party, which left them only five of fourteen representatives.[44] In the new legislature the anti-Jackson men had a majority of nine to fourteen on joint ballot.[45]

In Indiana Governor Ray had attempted to maintain his independent position, but the legislature, with its disposition to draw party lines, soon found cause for controversy over appointments to internal improvement jobs and the courts, and the Governor's work in codifying the laws.[46] The struggle between the partisan legislature and the proud and not too tactful Governor lasted

[40] Thompson, in *The Illinois Whigs,* calls this "the same election" as the gubernatorial which took place in 1830.

[41] Lucas had served in the legislature since 1816. In 1832 he was chairman of the National Democratic Convention at Baltimore. He later became governor of Iowa Territory and superintendent of Indian affairs.

[42] *Niles' Weekly Register,* XXXIX, 212 (Nov. 20, 1830). The Western Reserve and lake counties gave big majorities to McArthur as they had to Adams in 1828; Meigs and Preble also gave large majorities to McArthur.

[43] *Ohio Statistics,* 255.

[44] In *Ohio Statesmen and Annals of Progress,* edited by William A. Taylor (2 volumes. Columbus, 1899), I, 149, James Shields, Jackson man, is wrongly listed as elected in the second district when he was defeated by Thomas Corwin. See *Hamilton Intelligencer,* November 2, 1830; Elliot Howard Gilkey (ed.), *The Ohio Hundred Year Book* . . . (Columbus, 1901), 581; *Congressional Directory,* 22 Congress, 1 session, 28. William Stanbery in the eighth district, not approving of the Maysville Road veto, was endorsed by the anti-Jackson men and re-elected. Somewhat similar was the re-election of William Kennon in the tenth district.

[45] In the Senate—18 Jackson men, 18 Clay men; in the House—29 Jackson men, 38 Clay men, and 5 elected in opposition to the Jackson caucus ticket. *Niles' Weekly Register,* XXXIX, 171 (Nov. 6, 1830).

In the House of 72 members, 42 were natives of Pennsylvania and Virginia and only one of Ohio. *Ibid.,* XL, 141 (Apr. 23, 1831).

The *Scioto Gazette* of November 8, 1830, confirmed the "truly gratifying intelligence" that Indiana had elected a Clay legislature. Ohio too should do her duty and make a solid western front "against the anarchy and misrule which for eighteen months past has scattered desolation and ruin over the finest portion of our country and brought contempt and derision on our republican institutions."

[46] Indiana *Senate Journal,* 1830-31, pp. 59, 63-64.

three years; it not only cut short Ray's political career but ended the period of personal politics with reference to the higher state offices in Indiana. By 1831 the newspapers and party organizations tried to maintain strict party division.[47] The candidates for governor were judged largely on their stand on national issues, but the party alignment did not yet extend sufficiently far down among the voters to make the national issue the determining one, nor did the candidates run strictly and avowedly on party tickets.[48]

Gen. Noah Noble, one of the best-known and most popular men in the state, the gubernatorial candidate of the anti-Jackson forces in 1831, was favored by the anti-Ray faction as well. When James G. Read announced himself as a candidate, he made no mention of national issues, but later decidedly approved of the general policy of the administration, of Jackson's message on the tariff and internal improvements, and declared himself against the doctrines of southern nullifiers.[49] State questions he touched upon only in a general way. The pleas of the party press were unavailing, and though Indiana was safely Jacksonian on national issues, the personality of Noble drew heavily; he was elected by a vote of 17,959 to 15,168.[50] Milton Stapp, an independent candidate, received only 4,424 votes. The vote indicated little beyond the fact that Noble was the more popular with the

[47] The Lawrenceburg *Indiana Palladium* made a strong appeal for party voting: "In the first place they try to make it impossible for any man to come out on the question as they call it. What do they do next? Whenever a Jackson man is a candidate for any office they immediately raise the cry that he had 'come out on the question,' and how often they have defeated the election of known and tried Republicans? . . . Do you know a Clay man in all your acquaintance who ever voted for a Jackson man for the legislature? In the eyes of the Clay men the Jackson man never has merit. They invariably find merit on the Clay side. . . . I ask this sincerely, do Jackson men support the administration when they elect men who support different measures?" Quoted in Vincennes *Western Sun and General Advertiser,* May 28, 1831.

The *Madison Herald* was working toward the same end. "What is it that prompts the Clay party in this state to oppose every friend of General Jackson who aspires to office? What is it that induces them to cry 'question! question!' the moment a Jackson man appears in the field? They will tell you they are opposed to the principles and measures of his administration, and they want to put them down— that they cannot conscientiously support a man who favours the policy of the President." Quoted in *Western Sun and General Advertiser,* June 11, 1831. Commented the editor of the *Sun,* "Avowing this they have the effrontery to ask the Jackson men to support them."

[48] Leonard, "Personal Politics in Indiana," in *Indiana Magazine of History,* XIX, 257.

[49] Vincennes *Western Sun and General Advertiser,* May 14, June 4, 1831; Madison *Indiana Republican,* June 16, 1831.

[50] Indiana *House Journal,* 1831–32, p. 29.

voters, for both candidates had supported Jackson and were internal improvements men.

The legislature elected in 1830 had been anti-Jackson by a majority of about twenty; it re-elected William Hendricks, a Clay man, to the Senate over Ratliff Boon, a Jackson candidate. The new legislature also had an anti-Jackson majority, but in a nonpartisan election sent Gen. John Tipton to the United States Senate to succeed James Noble who died in February, 1831.[51]

By the law of 1829 the time of holding Congressional elections was changed to the odd years, and thereafter vigorous Congressional campaigns paralleled the state campaigns.[52] As a result of a superior organization and greater harmony within the ranks, the Jackson party succeeded in electing all three of its Congressional representatives in 1831, though the party polled much fewer than half the votes cast.[53]

§

On January 3, 1831, President Jackson was nominated for re-election by the General Assembly of Illinois by a large majority.[54] Later in the same month fifty-two members of the Ohio legislature wrote him, "your course as the chief magistrate of the nation, observant of those principles [correct constitutional principles], and firm in adherence to them, we assure you is approved by a majority of the people of Ohio, although accident has given a different appearance," and assured him that no meas-

[51] "It is a remarkable fact that with a large majority of the State in favor of Jackson there has at all times been a majority of Clay and Adams men in the legislature." Vincennes *Western Sun and General Advertiser*, August 20, 1831. Estimates as to the majority varied. See *Niles' Weekly Register*, XLI, 1, 17 (Sep. 3, 10, 1831).

[52] *Laws of Indiana*, 1828–29, p. 28.

[53] In the second district there were four independent candidates including ex-Governor Ray, Jonathan Jennings, a Clay man on national issues, John H. Thompson, and Isaac Howk. William W. Wick, a well-known and popular campaigner, was the anti-Jackson candidate, though he became a Jackson man in 1835. Gen. John Carr was the Jacksonian candidate. These two fought it out on national issues while the others adhered largely to local issues. The vote was Carr 4,855, Wick 4,610, Ray 1,732, Jennings 1,681, Thompson 1,486, Howk 454. *Niles' Weekly Register*, XLI, 36 (Sep. 17, 1831).

In the third district the opposition was divided between O. H. Smith and John Test, while the Jackson party gave its vote to Jonathan McCarty, who received 6,243 votes to 5,289 for Smith and 3,107 for Test. *Ibid.;* Madison *Indiana Republican*, October 13, 1831.

[54] Illinois *Senate Journal*, 1830–31, p. 170.

ure was more important than his re-election.[55] Jackson in his reply on February 9, stated that he had hoped a constitutional amendment for direct election of president and one-term tenure, as recommended in his first message, would release him from further service, yet, considering the numerous declarations of friends, another term might be necessary to bring to completion measures already begun.[56]

Concerted opposition to the National Democrats, as the Jackson men were now calling themselves, began in 1831 when on November 7 and 8 a convention of Clay men, now calling themselves National Republicans and claiming to be the party of Jefferson, met in state convention at Indianapolis.[57] The spoils appointments, Indian policy, attacks on the Bank, and failure of retrenchment of the administration were condemned. To preserve the vital interests of domestic industry and internal improvements as well as to remedy the evils of Jacksonianism, the delegates recommended the elevation of Henry Clay to the Presidency. Resolutions for a protective tariff and encouragement of internal improvements were passed, a state committee of correspondence was appointed, and three delegates selected for the convention of National Republicans to be held at Baltimore in December. In Indiana, party lines were drawn about the two western leaders, Jackson and Clay.

The Ohio opposition talked up the Young Men's National Republican Convention to be held at Washington in May and urged that each county send delegates.[58] A general meeting at Columbus in February appointed a state central committee, and the latter issued its letter to the "Free and Independent Electors of the State" in July. The proposed direct-election amendment was attacked as contrary to the spirit of the Constitution, the spoils system and tampering with the courts were condemned, and the early retirement of Jackson recommended as a "consummation devoutly to be wished."[59] Charles Hammond, of the *Cincinnati Gazette,* temporarily disgruntled at Clay's lack of recognition of his services, had flirted with the idea of promoting

[55] *Niles' Weekly Register,* XL, 127 (Apr. 16, 1831).

[56] *Ibid.*

[57] Indianapolis *Indiana Democrat,* November 23, 1831; Indianapolis *Indiana Journal,* November 12, December 14, 1831.

[58] Chillicothe *Scioto Gazette,* February 15, 1832.

[59] *Ibid.,* July 18, 1832.

Judge John McLean for the Presidency. Circumstances did not break, however, and the McLean boom did not get very far at this time.

The Democrats in the Northwest did not enter into the campaign of 1832 with overconfidence. Since 1828 the opposition had elected the governors of both Ohio and Indiana and the legislatures of these states were in their control, while the contest in Illinois between the adherents of Martin Van Buren and Richard M. Johnson for the vice-presidency, which was carried into the national convention, threatened to split the party.[60] The effects of the removals from office, the influence of the Bank of the United States with its great wealth, and the efficacy of the newly established organization of the National Republicans could not be foreseen with certainty. Moreover, the race would have to be made against Henry Clay, also a western man, a most skillful politician and campaigner with a personal following second only to that of Jackson.

The Bank issue had been precipitated into the campaign by Jackson's veto of the charter, which took even the Democrats more or less by surprise. About the only preparation for such a decisive move had been provided late in 1831 when western papers began copying anti-Bank articles from the *Albany Argus*.[61] Some were inclined to place the blame upon Van Buren, who was never very popular in the West, but the party avoided the worst consequences by soft-pedaling the Bank and centering the attack on "Nick Biddle" and all the evils popularly associated with his name. With the President's statement that the people were to decide whether they would "have General Jackson and no Bank

[60] Many extreme Jackson men, such as A. P. Field, John Dement, Zadoc Casey, and Joseph Duncan, were for Johnson, while W. L. D. Ewing, Samuel McRoberts, and other "whole hog" Jacksonians were for Van Buren. At a Jackson meeting at Vandalia on January 2 and 3, 1832, McRoberts and Ewing withdrew with their followers, leaving the Johnson men in control. The latter, supported by Edwards and Reynolds, declared against instructed delegates for the Baltimore convention. Warning from the *Illinois Advocate* that endorsement of Johnson would give Clay the state, went unheeded, and a Johnson convention met at Vandalia to select Jackson and Johnson electors. In the national convention the vote of the Illinois delegation was divided. After Van Buren's nomination the majority of Johnson supporters came over to the regular ticket, but the differences were not forgotten and threatened serious consequences in 1836. Some of the members of the Johnson convention became Whigs. See Thompson, *The Illinois Whigs*, 38; Vandalia *Illinois Intelligencer*, January 21, 1832; Washburne (ed.), *Edwards Papers*, 579-80.
[61] Vincennes *Western Sun and General Advertiser*, October 1, 1831.

or the Bank and no General Jackson," the issue was made clear. This stand was generally acceptable to the Jackson men in Ohio and most attractive to the voters of Indiana, whose earlier approval of the Bank under Crawford had turned to hatred and distrust. The *Hamilton Intelligencer,* however, argued that unless the people rose and put down this "high-handed, domineering, egregious folly of the President, the Western country is ruined."[62]

The *Illinois Advocate* spoke for Democrats of that state: "We hazard nothing in saying that three-fourths, perhaps many more, of the people of Illinois, hail the rejection of this chartered *monopoly* as the salvation of our country."[63]

The National Republicans rallied to support the Bank and exposed the consequences of Jackson's antagonistic and destructive policies. In December preceding, a resolution was introduced into the Indiana legislature petitioning Congress for the extension of the charter.[64] Refusal to recharter would leave the country without a circulating medium.[65] Memorials from mass meetings were sent to the congressmen, and Jackson's opposition to the Bank was denounced as a political grudge.[66] When news of the veto came, friends of the Bank called it an act of despotism, "defeating the legislation of Congress and the expressed will of the great majority of the American people. . . . The Bank of the United States is to be prostrated to gratify the malignity of Isaac Hill, Amos Kendall and Co. . . . Will the people of this country submit to this wide-spread ruin which is thus wantonly inflicted upon their country?"[67] It was stated that withdrawal of nineteen millions of capital from the western country would bring distress and sacrifices unparalleled in its history. A "dark and endless train of disasters" would befall farmers, mechanics, merchants, and property holders; the depressing effects would come home to the fireside of every one except the capitalists who

[62] July 28, 1832.
[63] September 4, 1832. The Clay party was referred to as the "Nationals." *Ibid.* October 9, 1832.
[64] *Indiana Journal,* December 14, 1831.
[65] *Ibid.,* January 14, 1832.
[66] *Ibid.,* June 23, 1832.
[67] Chillicothe *Scioto Gazette,* July 18, 1832. The Columbus *Ohio State Journal,* July 28, printed a two-column editorial as well as a letter of the same length which it claimed was written by a "Jackson Man."

possessed means to take advantage of the distress of the less fortunate.[68] Major Jack Downing's "Proclamation" was copied as a shrewd interpretation of the goings on. "The rich folks have pretty much all the money, but as we can out vote 'em they ought to shell out—and that's pretty much Mr. Van Buren's notion too. . . . We want money, and must have it. Some of our folks who have been workin' hard for us haint got any, and we have no more offices to give 'em."[69] Mass meetings were held at Indianapolis by Democrats as well as by friends of the Bank. Much of the blame for the act was placed upon Martin Van Buren, but Richard M. Johnson in his western stumping tour condemned the Bank for its political work and strongly supported the veto.

In Illinois prior to 1832 the national issues had not so seriously influenced the political alignment, but in 1832 the Clay men drew together in attack against Jackson's tariff, internal improvements, and Bank policies, and Jackson men were no longer satisfied if their candidates expressed only a personal loyalty to the President. But it was not easy for the Jackson forces to stand solid on a platform, for there were many diverging views on leading questions. A Jackson meeting at Vandalia, December, 1831, had taken no definite stand on the tariff but emphasized rather the President's service in ousting vested interests and the Indians.[70] The Democratic press did likewise. The National Republican Convention in October issued a long address to the voters which, while not questioning Jackson's patriotism or bravery, directly questioned his capacity for statesmanship.[71]

[68] Springfield *Sangamo Journal,* July 26, August 3, 18, 1832.
[69] Jacksonville *Illinois Patriot,* November 2, 1833. The original Major Jack Downing was the pseudonym for Seba Smith, whose contributions appeared in the *Portland* (Me.) *Courier,* 1830–33.
[70] Springfield *Sangamo Journal,* December 8, 15, 22, 1831; January 5, August 2, September 22, October 27, 1832; Vandalia *Illinois Intelligencer,* February 18, 1832.
[71] *Sangamo Journal,* October 20, 1832.
A young man from New Salem, in announcing for the legislature in March, ignored party lines completely:
"Every man is said to have his peculiar ambition. Whether it be true or not, I can say for one that I have no other so great as that of being truly esteemed of my fellow men, by rendering myself worthy of that esteem. How far I shall succeed in gratifying this ambition, is yet to be developed. I am young and unknown to many of you. I was born and have ever remained in the most humble walks of life. I have no wealthy or popular relations to recommend me. My case is thrown exclusively upon the independent voters of this county, and if elected they will have conferred a favor upon me, for which I shall be unremitting in my labors to compensate. But if the good people in their wisdom shall see fit to keep me in the

The Anti-Masons appeared as a third party in 1831. They selected electors in Ohio and Illinois and a committee in Indiana to sound out the candidates on their views. They nominated William Wirt for president and Amos Ellmaker for vice-president. The committee wrote to Clay in September to find out whether he was a Mason.[72] Clay evaded the direct question by stating that the question of Masonry was not a constitutional one, and that he would not express his personal opinion regarding it until he saw how the subject was one that the government should meet.[73] Soon afterwards the Indianapolis *Indiana Journal* said that the Anti-Masons had decided to support Clay, and shortly before election it dropped Wirt and Ellmaker from its list of candidates.[74] After Governor McArthur, renominated by the National Republicans of Ohio, withdrew his name and entered the race for Congress in the seventh district, the National Republicans united with the Anti-Masons in support of Darius Lyman against Robert Lucas, the Democratic candidate; the Anti-Masons withdrew their ticket and adopted that of the National Republicans.[75] In the October election Lucas received 71,251 votes to 63,185 for Lyman.[76] The Anti-Masonic state committee in a public address to the citizens stated that "of late the face of things had changed," that they had mistaken the character of the National Republican electoral ticket, that it was in reality unpledged, contained no Masons, and recommended that it be supported. A letter was sent to each Clay elector stating that he was understood to be unpledged and could vote for Wirt and Ellmaker if in his judgment it seemed for the best interests of the country.[77]

---

background, I have been too familiar with disappointments to be very much chagrined.

                              "A. Lincoln
                                   "New Salem, March 9, 1832."

Published in *Sangamo Journal*, March 15, 1832.

[72] *Western Sun and General Advertiser*, December 3, 1831.

[73] Indianapolis *Indiana Journal*, December 3, 1831.

[74] *Ibid.*, October 6, 1832.

[75] *Niles' Weekly Register*, XLIII, 118–19 (Oct. 20, 1832). The National Republicans had been much concerned, for the Anti-Masonic movement had attracted most support in the counties which they counted heavily upon. The nomination for governor was offered to Calvin Pease and Alfred Kelley by the Anti-Masonic State convention in June, before it was accepted by Lyman. The inept and futile attempts on the part of the National Republicans to get Lyman's name withdrawn in favor of a mutually acceptable candidate did not strengthen the anti-Jackson party.

[76] *Ohio Statesmen and Annals of Progress*, I, 157; *Ohio Statistics*, 255.

[77] *Niles' Weekly Register*, XLIII, 138 (Oct. 27, 1832).

The anti-Jackson papers featured the President's vetoes of internal improvements, his "broken promises" regarding the Bank, and his defiance of the Supreme Court. The policy of the administration was held to be so clear that he who runs may read: "It is hostile to Internal Improvements—to the National Bank,—and to the manufacturing industry of the United States. We are sincerely of the opinion that on the success of the principles thus denounced by the present administration, depend the growth, the wealth, and the happiness of the Western Country."[78] Since Van Buren was more vulnerable than Jackson, editors emphasized the developing "oppugnation" in the West to the Democratic vice-presidential candidate. They pretended that great numbers of voters were renouncing their allegiance to Caesar and pledging themselves to support the welfare of Rome; they were now going to "go for their country." The Democratic organization, however, proved more effective in vote getting than the appeal of the platform, strong leaders, and important newspapers of the National Republicans. The Democrats held most of the Federal offices and hence had all the advantages of easy access to the voters, while their opponents had to carry on their electioneering at a greater sacrifice of time and effort. Besides, there were many who voted merely for Andrew Jackson, a great personality. As Charles Hammond of the *Cincinnati Gazette* had said in 1829: "Men of honour and integrity" belonged to either the party which advocated a tariff and internal improvements, or to the opposite; but there was a third party of "Swiss politicians" who followed a mere personality.[79]

The November presidential election showed a solid Democratic Northwest. In Ohio the vote stood, Jackson 81,246, Clay 76,539, and Wirt 509;[80] in Indiana 31,552 to 25,472;[81] and in Illinois 14,617 to 6,754, with 97 for Wirt.[82] As in 1828 the percentage of Democratic majority increased from east to west. In Ohio in addition to the Western Reserve counties, Clay practically doubled the vote of Jackson in Champaign, Clark, Logan,

[78] Springfield *Sangamo Journal,* October 27, 1832.
[79] *Cincinnati Gazette,* September 17, 1829.
[80] Columbus *Ohio State Journal,* November 17, 1832; *Ohio Statistics,* 255.
[81] Lawrenceburg *Indiana Palladium,* December 8, 1832; *Vevay Weekly Messenger,* December 15, 1832.
[82] Pease, *Illinois Election Returns,* 80–81.

Medina, Meigs, Miami, Portage, and Ross.[83] Clay found it impossible to take his own defeat as philosophically as he had taken that of Adams four years earlier. Shortly after the election he wrote to his friend Hammond, though the latter had been seeking a new hero in Webster: "The dark cloud which has been so long suspended over our devoted country, instead of being dispelled, as we had fondly hoped it would be, has become more dense, more menacing, more alarming. Whether we shall ever see light, and law and liberty again is very questionable."[84]

Clay carried nineteen of the sixty-six counties of Indiana. The vote was uniformly Jacksonian except in the third and sixth Congressional districts in the eastern and southeastern parts of the state which, with the Wabash Valley, constituted the commercial sections. The heaviest Clay vote and the largest majority in any county was in Wayne County in the Whitewater Valley, later to be a center of Quaker antislavery sentiment. The influence of Jackson's veto of the Wabash improvement bill in the early autumn was felt in the vote of the river counties of Cass, Fountain, Tippecanoe, Vigo, and Knox.[85] Jackson received his strongest support from the triangle south of Indianapolis and based upon Madison and Evansville, a district that consistently remained faithful to the Jacksonian Democracy for a hundred years. Of the fifty-three counties in Illinois, Clay carried eight, and five of these were newly created northern counties with a total vote of only 529 for all candidates.[86] The returns showed

[83] The vote in the strong Clay counties was:

	Jackson	Clay
Ashtabula	489	2032
Champaign	782	1468
Clark	714	1693
Cuyahoga	691	1587
Geauga	782	2403
Huron	1035	1646
Medina	497	1137
Meigs	385	717
Miami	957	1441
Portage	1406	2327
Ross	1778	2367

From Indianapolis *Indiana Journal*, December 1, 1832.

[84] From Ashland, November 17, 1832. Clay MSS. in Indiana University Library.

[85] This veto did not seriously affect the state vote in 1832 but was of considerable importance in determining the result in 1836.

[86] Cook, Hancock, La Salle, Putnam, and Warren. The other Clay counties were Pike, Tazewell, and Wabash. Pease, *Illinois Election Returns*, 80–81.

the state thoroughly Jacksonian, with just a faint trace of the location of some of the later strongholds of opposition.

The Congressional elections of 1832 in Ohio and Illinois took place under new apportionments; Ohio's nineteen districts had been outlined by a special session of the legislature in June, and Illinois had become entitled to three congressmen under the census of 1830. The anti-Jackson forces were able to carry only eight of the nineteen Ohio districts, although they lost one by only two votes, and had a total vote of 66,956 to 61,588 for the Democrats.[87] The discrepancy between the vote and the results was hardly the product of any gerrymander, or at least not a successful one, for at the time of the redistricting of the state the legislature and governor were both anti-Jackson. It was caused rather by the exceedingly large majorities given the Clay men in the third, sixth, tenth, fifteenth, and sixteenth districts. In three of these districts there were two candidates against the Jackson men, and their total majorities over the Democratic candidate ran from 1,200 to 3,300 votes.[88] The Clay districts almost encircled the state: in the Reserve territory were the fifteenth and sixteenth, the eleventh and the long Ohio River sixth carried almost over to the fourth, tenth, and third, which ran up the western side. Only the thirteenth projected into central Ohio; all the rest of the state, including the fringe of counties next to the Ohio River and Indiana boundaries from Scioto to Darke, was included in Democratic districts.

The Illinois Congressional campaign of 1832 was merely another scramble among the Jackson adherents. From three to five candidates were on the ballots in each district, and Charles Slade in the first and Zadoc Casey in the second were both elected on pluralities. Joseph Duncan, still a Jackson adherent, was elected in the third with more than three fourths of the total vote.[89]

The Indiana reapportionment increased the Congressional districts from three to seven, and the campaign, coming as it did

---

[87] In the seventh Allen defeated ex-Governor McArthur by two votes. *Niles' Weekly Register*, XLIII, 135 (Oct. 27, 1832), copied from the Columbus *Ohio State Journal* of October 20.

[88] In the third the majority of the two anti-Jackson candidates was 1,126; in the fifteenth 2,292; in the sixteenth 3,298. In the sixth Vinton's majority was 1,496, and in the tenth Vance's majority was 2,988. *Niles' Weekly Register*, XLIII, 135 (Oct. 27, 1832).

[89] Pease, *Illinois Election Returns*, 74-79.

after the excitement of the election of 1832, saw some relaxation in the strict party alignment. The opposition tried particularly to break down party ties and emphasize the merits of the candidates. They could not get away from the two national questions of the Bank and the public lands, however, and six of the seven congressmen elected were "dyed-in-the-wool" Jacksonians.[90] John Ewing was elected in the second district by a majority of two votes. National Republican organization was again lacking; in the first district there were four candidates and an Anti-Mason against the Democrat. The Democratic hold on the Congressional delegation of the Northwest was still secure, twenty of twenty-nine representatives being Jacksonians, and four of the six senators.[91]

§ §

The second election of Jackson in 1832 marked the high tide of Jacksonian Democracy in the Northwest. The Old Hero had been completely vindicated. The struggle against the Bank of the United States, failure in the expected support of internal improvements, removals, backstairs' cabinet influences, and the attempt to will Van Buren upon an unwilling West brought issues to the fore which served to dampen the enthusiasm of part of the President's following. In the years ahead, the personal popularity of the candidate and mere party organization would not suffice. The old leaders in the Northwest were dropping out, and with the passing of the politicians of the pioneer period in Ohio, Indiana, and Illinois came new men, new emphasis on local issues, and new party divisions and alliances. With the growth in population of the northern territories, the expulsion of the Indians from northern Indiana and Illinois, and the flow of new settlers, largely from New England and New York, to these sections, came a corresponding shifting of the center of population. Development of surer and quicker transportation, a common school system, colleges, churches, and the press brought changed political ideas and different methods. Economic and social life

[90] *Vincennes Gazette,* September 7, 1833.
[91] Morris of Ohio, Tipton of Indiana, Robinson and Kane of Illinois, Hendricks of Indiana, and Ewing of Ohio were Clay men.

were in transition and politics in a more or less disturbed condition. From this period of milling around of issues and factions emerged an organized Democratic party and a more or less organized opposition, which confronted each other in national and local politics for the next two decades.

The nullification controversy, which came to a head late in 1832 with Jackson's blasting proclamation to the people of South Carolina, though closely followed was not argued on a partisan basis.[92] Although the Democratic party leaned heavily on the state-rights belief, both Democratic and National Republican papers generally said "amen" to Jackson's firm stand for the Constitution and the Union.

The internal improvements movement which swept Ohio and Indiana in the 1820's reached Illinois in force in the 1830's.[93] Despite the fact that they twice voted for Andrew Jackson, the voters of Ohio and Indiana "went for" a protective tariff, a United States Bank, and internal improvements (at Federal expense). In Ohio after 1824 and in Indiana after 1828 the "Internal Improvements Party" controlled state politics by overwhelming majorities. During the period the messages of the governors, journals of the legislatures, reports of the auditors, and the newspapers were filled with plans and discussions of "systems." Internal improvements advocates were to be found in both parties. In Indiana two of the most active were Samuel Judah, who wrote the Jackson platforms of 1824 and 1828, and Noah Noble, elected governor in 1831 and 1834, both Jackson men, though Noble later became a Whig and Judah stumped for Harrison.

The Bank veto and the order for removal of the government deposits brought the currency question solidly before the people, and it took its place alongside internal improvements in importance. The movement for state banking began as soon as the election of 1832 killed all hopes of recharter for the second Bank of the United States. Governor McArthur of Ohio in his unsuccessful campaign for Congress had advocated a state bank and the possibility was mentioned in his message in December. Governor-elect Robert Lucas was reported to favor the idea. All

[92] See for instance articles in *Liberty Hall and Cincinnati Gazette,* August 31, 1831, January—February, 1833.
[93] See Chapters VII and XII.

told three different plans for a state bank were submitted to the legislature of 1832–33 but none was adopted. Instead the capital stock of the Commercial Bank of Cincinnati was doubled and a charter granted to the Franklin Bank of Cincinnati. The Indiana legislature of 1832–33 was confronted with a bill for chartering a state bank and five plans were set forth for securing a circulating medium.[94] After prolonged discussion action was postponed. Party division was almost absent in this assembly, for Jackson men as well as Clay men favored the idea, and thirty Clay men voted for Tipton for United States Senator. Failure to act on the bank bill resulted in an assembly composed largely of new members in 1833.

In Indiana the voters were coming out from under the spell of Andrew Jackson's name and turning their attention more to state affairs. In 1834 Governor Noah Noble and James G. Read again contested the Indiana governorship. Read was nominated by a convention in which about twenty-five counties were unrepresented, and which the Whigs called a "Caucus."[95] Noble was supposed to be a Jacksonian Democrat, at least he was so labeled by the Whig *Indiana Journal,* but in his advocacy of internal improvements and a state bank he leaned toward Whig policies and sought support from the voters of both parties. Most of the Clay papers supported him.[96] Read also claimed to be a non-partisan. Since both men were well known and had stumped the state three years previously, they signed a pledge not to make an active canvass.[97] Read received 27,302 votes to 36,925 for Noble, and carried only 16 of 70 counties, 14 of these being in the Jacksonian triangle.[98] The legislature elected in 1834 was of

[94] Indianapolis *Indiana Journal,* January 2, 1833. See Chapter VIII, 614–15.

[95] *Ibid.,* January 11, 1834. The *Journal* began using the word "Whig" in May.

[96] Indianapolis *Indiana Democrat,* June 27, 1834. The *Democrat* said: "We have learned . . . that Noble's friends are deserting him like leaves in wintry weather, and rallying under the Democratic standard." Quoted in Indianapolis *Indiana Journal,* August 9, 1834.

[97] Indianapolis *Indiana Journal,* April 26, 1834.

[98] *Logansport Canal Telegraph,* September 6, 1834. The official returns given in the Indiana *House Journal,* 1834–35, p. 25, were 27,676 for Noble and 19,994 for Read.

"Beyond the election of Andrew Jackson vs. John Quincy Adams and Henry Clay the people of the State have never been drilled to wear the collar of party. Our state legislature has never been thus constituted and it has elected senators in Congress from Clay districts and vice versa. This is in the main as it should be." Vincennes *Western Sun and General Advertiser,* September 13, 1834.

uncertain political complexion, but probably would have had an anti-Jackson majority on a joint ballot.[99] Though in this election many Democratic leaders became inactive or else opposed the party in state affairs, the Whigs failed to take advantage of the opportunity to consolidate their organization as was shown by the result of the Congressional election the following year.

The Indiana Congressional election of 1835 was devoid of party enthusiasm and comparatively free from national issues. All seven representatives elected were Jackson men. In the legislature party division was again lacking. The keen enthusiasm and high party feeling of the past ten years were subsiding somewhat. With Jackson vindicated, no big issue in sight, and hard times in the offing, there came a halt in the Democratic advance, to be followed by a period of defensive warfare after the break in 1836 and the reaction following the panic.

Ohio, never so thoroughly Jacksonian as Indiana and Illinois, was also feeling the conflict of forces which was to swing the balance to the opposition. National Republicans, Anti-Masons, and some Democrats had worked together against Robert Lucas with fair success in 1832. The Whig party in Ohio may be said to date from this time, and it drew votes from Democrats, particularly in the commercial centers, who opposed Jackson's banking policies.

The legislature of 1832–33 selected Thomas Morris, a Bank-hating Democrat, for United States Senator to take the seat of Benjamin Ruggles, National Republican;[100] the legislature of 1833–34, in which the Democrats had a majority of twenty-six, adopted a joint resolution of instruction and request to senators and representatives in Congress, which endorsed Jackson's removal of the deposits, opposed a recharter of the Bank, com-

---

". . . Indiana is Democratic to the core . . . That circumstances wholly unconnected with general politics, may have occasionally presented a state of things here, which would perhaps lead those who are unacquainted with our local affairs to a different conclusion is no doubt true. That our gubernatorial election. That our election for members to Congress, and to the state Legislature may have resulted in a choice *sometimes* of those who differed from the great body of the Democratic party in their views of men and measures, so far as the general government is concerned, is also no doubt true." "The gubernatorial question then I repeat, had nothing to do with general politics, or with the succession to the Presidency." Vincennes *Western Sun and General Advertiser*, December 20, 1834.

[99] Leonard, "Personal Politics in Indiana," in *Indiana Magazine of History*, XIX, 270.

[100] *Ohio Statesmen and Annals of Progress*, I, 159.

mended his veto, and condemned the Clay land bill.[101] This legislature chartered ten new banks and revived two others. The election of 1834 brought a political reversal and the Whigs had a majority of fourteen on joint ballot in the legislature of 1834–35.[102] The resolutions were rescinded on January 12, 1835, in the House of Representatives, by vote of 40 to 28, but it was stated that such action was not to be taken as an expression of opinion favorable to recharter of the Bank of the United States.[103]

Gen. James Findlay, former mayor of Cincinnati and member of Congress, was selected to run against Governor Robert Lucas, who was renominated by the Democrats. The name of Joseph Vance had been inserted in many papers, but he withdrew and threw his support to Findlay. Findlay had formerly been a Jackson man but had switched his support some time previously; his candidacy was closely hooked up with the attempt of Whigs and anti-Jackson Democrats to promote the presidential boom of John McLean.[104] Findlay, a man of excellent character, was advertised as being unfriendly toward land speculators. Although his interest in internal improvements and the tariff was supposed to gain votes from National Republicans, some remembered his former Democratic affiliations and preferred Governor Lucas to an untried man. The *Ohio State Journal,* a leading Whig paper, gave Findlay but lukewarm support while admitting the general popularity of Lucas and his administration.[105] The Democratic charge that Findlay was being used by the Bank no doubt held in line many votes in that party. The Anti-Masonic agitation was still active; in some parts of the state Findlay was rumored to be a bigoted Roman Catholic, and in others represented as a staunch anti-Catholic. In the election Governor Lucas was the winner by a vote of 70,738 to 67,414, a margin of victory less than half that of 1832.[106] In the Congressional election of 1834 the Whigs made a gain of two since they carried the first, seventh, and

---

[101] *Ibid.,* I, 162; *Niles' Weekly Register,* XLV, 371 (Jan. 25, 1834). In Congress twelve Ohio representatives voted against restoring the deposits, seven in favor.

[102] *Niles' Weekly Register,* XLVII, 138 (Nov. 1, 1834).

[103] *Ibid.,* XLVII, 355 (Jan. 24, 1835).

[104] Weisenburger, *Passing of the Frontier,* 289. See also Francis P. Weisenburger, *The Life of John McLean (Ohio University Contributions in History and Political Science,* No. 15, Columbus, 1937), 81 ff.

[105] October 25, 1834.

[106] Columbus *Ohio State Journal,* December 6, 1834.

twelfth districts and all of those they had won in 1832 except the eleventh, which gave them ten of the nineteen representatives.[107]

The convention system and right of instruction, by now incorporated into the Democratic belief, occasionally were taken too seriously, as when Representative Robert T. Lytle, after being defeated in the first district, resigned and stood in a special election November 8 so as to be able conscientiously to finish his term.[108] Although Ohio was having its own bank problem in 1835,[109] the election of the state legislature was on the whole a listless affair. The outcome again reversed the political complexion of the legislature by giving the Democrats about the

[107] Typical Democratic doctrine was laid down in the short catechism submitted by the Cheviot convention to each candidate put in nomination for the legislature and for Congress in the first (Cincinnati) district:

"1. Do you firmly adhere to the principle of instruction from constituents to representatives, and if elected will you obey such instructions or resign your seat? (Yea)

"2. Do you believe the act of congress incorporating the bank of the United States to be constitutional? (Nay)

"3. Are you opposed to a recharter of the bank of the United States with or without modifications or restrictions? (Yea)

"4. Are you opposed to the creation of any new national bank by congress? (Yea)

"5. Do you approve of the veto, proclamation and protest of President Jackson and of the measures of his administration generally? (Yea)

"6. Will you sustain the democratic party by giving preference to the firm and constant members thereof, in all appointments to office that shall be made by the legislative body of which you may be a member? (Yea)

"7. Will you support the ticket nominated by the convention, and publicly decline being a candidate for any office at the approaching election, unless nominated by the convention? (Yea)"

Niles' Weekly Register, XLVII, 12 (Sep. 6, 1834).

Whig fighting points were illustrated by the resolution of the Young Men's Meeting at Chillicothe, August 30: A crisis existed in our history; the chief magistrate had forfeited the confidence of the people; the existing political system was a gross perversion of powers; the government seizure of public money was without parallel in history; Jackson's vetoes were unconstitutional; a National Bank was indispensable; and the bankruptcy of the Post Office Department was the result of a system of "bribery and corruption."

"Ours is a contest for principles—for the principles of liberty as regulated by the Constitution. These principles we trust will be as lasting as the sun; and ever form as they now do, the cheering hope of liberty throughout the world." Chillicothe *Scioto Gazette,* September 3, 1834.

[108] This district had given Jackson about 2,200 majority in 1828 and 1,370 in 1832. In 1834 Lytle, defeated by Bellamy Storer by 96 votes, resigned. In Congress he had refused to heed a petition signed by several hundred friends of the Bank, and pointed to the will of the people as expressed in the last election. In the campaign Lytle had come round to a stand in favor of the Bank with modifications. In the special election he was returned to finish his term. *Niles' Weekly Register,* XLVII, 178–79 (Nov. 22, 1834).

[109] The Ohio Life Insurance and Trust Company of Cincinnati chartered by the Democratic legislature in 1834, capitalized at $2,000,000, had grown into what some Democrats regarded as a monopoly almost as bad as the Bank of the United States.

same size majority that the Whigs had the preceding year. Of fifteen senators elected, the administration party secured eight with total district majorities of 1,577, while the Whigs got only seven, although their majorities totaled 7,806.[110] As usual this was the result of the overwhelming majorities given the Whig candidates in certain anti-Democratic strongholds.[111] The bold front put up by Governor Lucas in the Michigan boundary dispute may have had some influence on the election. By a definite party vote the new legislature imposed a 20 per cent tax on bank dividends, and approved Benton's crusade in the United States Senate to expunge the censure of Jackson for removing the deposits.[112]

Illinois politics between 1830 and 1835 were in chaos. No longer was it possible to explain things on the basis of the two-faction division of the 1820's. Instead numerous cliques existed, most of whose leaders professed allegiance to Jackson, but who felt in no way bound to support his measures. Only when ideas of party regularity appeared did there develop from this confusion two real political parties. When Jackson began to take a decided stand on various questions and demanded that his followers support his measures as well as his name, the "milk and cider" or moderate Jackson group in Illinois found itself in an anomalous position. It could maintain itself as an independent organization only by alliance with anti-Jackson men. State problems were increasing in importance; old leaders were dead or retired from active politics.[113] The influence of the growing population of the northern counties was beginning to be felt, and anti-Jackson sentiment crystallized. The "milk and cider" party furnished recruits to both sides; many became National Republicans, and later Whigs, while the remainder, definitely drawn into the Democratic party, served to tone down the views of the ultra-Jackson, or "whole hog" group.

The Whig party was at first nothing more than a collection of

[110] *Niles' Weekly Register*, XLIX, 214 (Nov. 28, 1835).

[111] The Whig majority in the Ashtabula senatorial district was 3,689, and in the Athens-Hocking district it was 1,843; average majorities were from 200 to 500 votes. See *ibid.*, XLIX, 214 (Nov. 28, 1835), for the returns.

[112] See Chapter VIII, 611–12.

[113] By 1834 Ninian Edwards, Shadrach Bond, Daniel Pope Cook, and John McLean were dead. Jesse B. Thomas, Joseph Phillips, and Thomas Sloo had left the state; Thomas C. Browne, Nathaniel Pope, and T. W. Smith were on the bench. Thompson, *The Illinois Whigs*, 40.

various antiadministration elements, and included some Democrats who were friends of the Bank of the United States and unsuccessful office seekers, as well as followers of Henry Clay. General agreement was not possible on the Bank, tariff, Federal aid to internal improvements, or a national leader; the only sentiment common to all elements was opposition to Van Buren. For this reason the Whig party was slower to become an organized political force than was its rival, and during the formative years it was hard to judge with any accuracy the strength of either party. "It is difficult to catch the hang of parties here for although there is considerable party feeling there is very little party organization."[114]

The defection of individuals and groups from one party to another is illustrated by the elections of 1834. Gen. James D. Henry, the state hero of the Black Hawk War and an independent in politics, was nominated for governor by county meetings. His candidacy was strongly supported by the *Sangamo Journal,* but he died early in the year. The field finally narrowed down to four, William Kinney, Robert K. McLaughlin, Joseph Duncan, and James Adams. Kinney was nominated by a convention at Belleville, and McLaughlin by the Vandalia convention. Both were "whole hog" Jackson men. Adams was a strong anti-Jackson man.[115] Joseph Duncan's political position was in doubt. In 1827 he had been a staunch Jackson man at Washington and a "whole hog" man at home, but after 1831 he thought that Jackson had changed his policies, for which he blamed Van Buren and the President's unofficial advisers. He voted to override the Maysville Road veto, and in June, 1834, argued that unless the Bank was continued the resulting currency chaos would hit the West a body blow.[116] By 1833 the opposition in Illinois was pre-

[114] Dr. Finley to Joseph Duncan, May 27, 1834. Cited in Putnam, "Life and Services of Joseph Duncan," in *Transactions of the Illinois State Historical Society,* 1919, p. 144.

[115] *Chicago Democrat,* July 23, 1834.

[116] Putnam, "Life and Services of Joseph Duncan," in *Transactions of the Illinois State Historical Society,* 1919, p. 142. Jacksonville and Springfield papers during the late months of 1833 and the early months of 1834 gave much space to discussion of Duncan and the Bank. Duncan filled two and a half colums of the *Sangamo Journal,* January 25, 1834, in stating his attitude.

The Jacksonville *Illinois Patriot* of November 2, 1833, recalled Duncan's pretension of friendship for the Bank but stated that prior to his recent departure for Congress he had declared himself hostile to it. This had led to criticism of Duncan for circulating a large number of bank notes of the Patriotic Bank of the City of

pared to give him its backing. The *Vandalia Whig* had announced his candidacy early in 1833, and the Whig papers gave their support. It is probable, however, that a considerable portion of the ultra-Jackson men knew and approved of Duncan's stand against Jackson's policies.[117] His position was attacked and defended, but he made no renunciation of Jackson during the campaign. The result of the election was Duncan 17,330, Kinney 10,224, McLaughlin 4,315, Adams 887.[118]

The Duncan vote was composed of anti-Jackson votes as well as those of "milk and cider" remnants and ultra-Jackson men.[119] Duncan's civil and military record had been good and some voters no doubt either did not know or care about his opposition to Jackson. Contained within his vote was a majority from all counties north and east of the mouth of the Illinois River except Macoupin, Sangamon, Montgomery, Coles, and Shelby. Kinney's vote was confined to southern Illinois but was less sectional than that given Adams or Duncan.[120] Some of the Democratic papers pretended to celebrate the victory, but the majority took it for granted that Duncan was no longer of their party.[121] In the Congressional campaign in the second and third districts the Jackson and anti-Jackson division was not clear-cut, but in the first, Reyn-

---

Washington. The president of this bank was a big Illinois landholder and Duncan, who was his sales agent, had stated that these notes would soon be acceptable at the land office. "If the Bank of the United States is to be superceded by such means, it is proper that the people should know it. We believe that its most inveterate opposers are endeavoring to effect its downfall, for the purpose of enriching themselves. . . . Every discerning man can see that much mischief will ensue by encouraging the circulation of bills introduced under such circumstances." The *Patriot* called upon Duncan to repudiate the charges, which he did. See *Sangamo Journal*, November 16, 23, 1833.

[117] Thompson, *The Illinois Whigs*, 45, bases this view on the attitude of the *Vandalia Whig and Illinois Intelligencer*, April 3, 1834; Springfield *Sangamo Journal*, October 4, December 6, 1834; Columbus (Ohio) *Western Hemisphere*, August 27, October 1, 1834; *Alton Spectator*, May 8, 1834; *Chicago American*, July 23, 1834; and letters of A. F. Grant to J. Dement, June 26, 1833; and J. Reynolds to A. F. Grant, February 17, 1834 (in Eddy MSS.).

[118] Pease, *Illinois Election Returns*, 86–87.

[119] Thompson, *The Illinois Whigs*, 46. The explanation of this mixed support is based upon study of election returns by counties and a wide range of newspaper opinion of the state.

[120] From the vote and Duncan's actions, it is fairly evident that he was a Whig at this time. See *ibid.*, 47; Pease, *The Frontier State*, 146.

[121] When the *Chicago Democrat*, June 24, July 1, 1835, attacked Duncan as an aristocrat, speculator, and friend of bankers, the editor of the *Jacksonville Sentinel* replied to "the imported hypocrite who edits the 'by authority print,' or mud machine at Chicago . . ." as follows: "While this puny white-livered slanderer was warming himself in nurse's arms, Governor Duncan was facing the cold blasts of Canada," etc.

olds, who was emerging from his period of hesitancy to land on
the Jackson–Van Buren side, played for the votes of the opposition men who had helped him before and were now supporting
Duncan for governor. His opponent was A. W. Snyder, a pro-
Bank Jackson man. The Jackson–Van Buren candidates were
successful in all three districts. The election of a lieutenant governor and a large majority of the members of the General Assembly by the Democrats clearly indicated the loyalty of the state
to Jackson.

It was almost impossible to determine the party affiliations of
the members, but the introduction of national questions into the
session of the legislature of 1834–35 made more rapid the formation of parties. The anti-Jackson men, who numbered 28 out of
81, were usually a unit in favoring a continuation of the Bank of
the United States but failed to unite on a candidate for the Senate. They tried to prevent the Van Buren party from denying
them the use of the name "Democracy," and protested against
the resolution which proclaimed the use of "Whig" an arrogant
and false act.

§ § §

The political history of the Northwest in the middle 1830's
was enlivened somewhat by Michigan's struggle for statehood,
complicated as it was by the Ohio boundary dispute and the fact
that 1836 was presidential election year. The so-called "Toledo
War," in proportion to the forces involved and the casualties
suffered, was one of the wordiest wars in history.[122] If at times it
seemed to degenerate into farce activated largely by personal

[122] The best brief accounts are: Weisenburger, *Passing of the Frontier*, 297–307;
Quaife, *Lake Michigan*, 208–16; and Carl Wittke, "The Ohio-Michigan Boundary
Dispute Re-examined," in *Ohio Archaeological and Historical Society Publications*,
XLV (1936), 299–319. Arthur Schlesinger, "The Basis of the Ohio-Michigan
Boundary Dispute," in *Final Report of the Ohio Co-operative Topographic Survey*,
I (Mansfield, 1916), 59–70, contains the reports of the boundary commissioners,
surveyors, and maps of the final line of 1915. The articles by Annah May Soule,
"The Michigan-Indiana Boundary" and "The Southern and Western Boundaries
of Michigan," in *Michigan Pioneer and Historical Collections*, XXVII (1896),
341–45, 346–90, carry numerous references as well as maps; also Claude S. Lar-
zelere, "The Boundaries of Michigan," in *ibid.*, XXX (1906), 1–27; Personal Recollections, "How They Fought . . . ," appear in *ibid.*, VII (1884). Other
articles are in *Ohio Archaeological and Historical Society Publications*, II (1888),
340–44, IV (1895), 199–230; *Magazine of Western History*, III (Nov., 1885—Apr.,
1886), 457–80; *American Historical Record*, I (1872), 154–58. George J. Miller,
"The Establishment of Michigan's Boundaries: A Study in Historical Geography,"
in *Bulletin of the American Geographical Society*, XLIII, No. 5 (May, 1911),

ambitions and petty politics, it must not be overlooked that beneath lay questions not only of state pride but valuable territory, law, and justice. The question was, would Toledo and the Maumee Bay belong to Ohio or to Michigan.

The framers of the Ordinance of 1787 fixed the boundaries of the three states which became Ohio, Indiana, and Illinois, but anticipating the possible expediency of creating two more states, provided that the latter should lie "north of an east and west line drawn through the southerly bend or extreme of Lake Michigan." Equitable distribution of lake frontage for the future states, had it appeared important at the time, would have been impossible in view of the indefinite geographical knowledge as expressed on the maps of the day.[123] John Mitchell's map of 1755—or one making the similar error of placing the southern end of Lake Michigan too far north—was apparently used by the boundary makers.[124] By it the "east and west line" would intersect Lake Erie above the mouth of the Detroit River.

The enabling act of 1802 for Ohio followed the line of the

339–51, emphasizes the geography as well as the history. W. V. Way, *The Facts and Historical Events of the Toledo War of 1835* . . . (Toledo, 1869) is a detailed account of the "War" with accounts of participants. Documents may be found in Carter (ed.), *Territorial Papers*, X, XI, and XII; Ohio legislative documents; and the documents and debates of the 20th, 23d, 24th, and 25th Congresses, particularly U. S. *Senate Documents*, 23 Congress, 1 session, IV, No. 354, and 24 Congress, 1 session, III, No. 211, and U. S. *House Reports*, 24 Congress, 1 session, II, No. 380. The main collection of manuscript letters of participants—many of which are cited in Wittke—is in the Ohio Archaeological and Historical Society Library, Columbus. Ohio and Michigan newspapers constitute the main source for public opinion in the controversy.

[123] Considering the southern extreme of Lake Michigan in relation to Lake Erie in some of the better-known maps of the period: De Vaugondy (Paris, 1753) showed the tip of Lake Michigan even with the south Erie shore, but his maps of 1749 and 1755 showed it on a level with the north shore of Erie; Evans (Philadelphia, 1755) showed it level with the north Erie shore (western end), as did Mitchell (London, 1755); Huske (London, 1755) showed the tip completely south of Lake Erie as did the Homann-D'Anville map (Nuremberg, 1756) and Delamarche (Paris, 1785); Palairet (London, 1755) and Gibson (London, 1763) placed the tip north of the main body of Lake Erie; Popple (London, 1733), Bellin (Paris, 1743–45), and Fitch (Philadelphia, 1785) on a level with the middle of Lake Erie. D'Anville (Paris, 1746) had the tip completely south of Erie, but his map of 1755 showed it in the same latitude as the north shore (western end); Jeffreys (London, 1761) on one map placed the tip north of the north shore of Erie (west end) and on another completely south of that Lake—both maps in his *Natural and Civil History of the French Dominions*. The De Vaugondy 1753 map was perhaps the most nearly correct, though both the south shores are about 40 minutes too far north. For quick comparisons, see Karpinski, *Historical Atlas of the Great Lakes and Michigan*.

[124] John Mitchell, Virginia physician and botanist, had prepared his *Map of the British and French Dominions in North America* for the Lords of Trade and Plantations. It was used in establishing the Proclamation Line of 1763 and the boundaries of the United States in 1782. The Senate Committee on the Judiciary in 1836 stated that this was the map used in 1787.

Ordinance. But while the Ohio Constitutional Convention was in session, an old hunter, practical geographer rather than student of cartography, reported that the southern end of Lake Michigan lay much farther south than Mitchell's map indicated.[125] The precaution, therefore, was taken of inserting in the Ohio constitution the provision that if the line of the northern boundary by the act of 1802 should be found to intersect Lake Erie east of the mouth of the Maumee River, then, Congress consenting, the northern boundary should be based on a straight line drawn from the southern extreme of Lake Michigan to the most northerly cape of Maumee Bay. Congress refused to consider the special boundary proviso, but admitted Ohio under the constitution which contained it.

Michigan Territory was established in 1805 on the line of the Ordinance. Ohio was eager for a survey and settlement according to its constitution, but a United States law of 1812 provided for the survey according to the enabling act provisions. The War of 1812 postponed the survey and when Edward Tiffin, of Ohio, surveyor-general of the United States, ordered William Harris to run the line in 1817, the latter was instructed to follow the provisions of the Ohio Constitution rather than of the enabling act. Although Harris questioned his instructions, he carried them out.[126] Governor Cass, of Michigan Territory, protested, but Tiffin supported the legality of the Harris line and added, "Let the proper authorities say which shall govern." When Michigan brought pressure to bear upon Congress, President Monroe ordered another survey under the provisions of the act of 1812; this "east and west line" was run by John A. Fulton in 1818. Between the two lines lay the "Toledo Strip" of some 468 square miles. Governor Brown, of Ohio, and the legislature stood on the

---

The statement by Wittke and Weisenburger that Mitchell's error was "apparently challenged only once [Fitch, 1785] before 1830 in a map" is hardly true. Wittke, "The Ohio-Michigan Boundary Re-examined," in *Ohio Archaeological and Historical Society Publications*, XLV, 300; Weisenburger, *Passing of the Frontier,* 298. From the Coronelli map (Venice, 1695) to Carey and Lee (Philadelphia, 1822) a dozen or more maps besides Fitch's showed that a line east from the southern tip would run south of Maumee Bay. The Amos Bradley, Jr., map (Philadelphia, 1804–5) even drew the line (southern boundary of Michigan Territory).

[125] Jacob Burnet, *Notes on the Early Settlement of the North-Western Territory* (Cincinnati, 1847), 360.

[126] Harris to Tiffin, January 11, 1817. Ohio-Michigan Boundary MSS., cited in Wittke, "The Ohio-Michigan Boundary Dispute Re-examined," in *Ohio Archaeological and Historical Society Publications,* XLV, 304.

OHIO ~ MICHIGAN BOUNDARY DISPUTE

- ⌣ Lake Michigan in relation to Erie, according to Mitchell Map, 1755
- ·········· Boundary according to Mitchell Map
- ----- Harris Line, 1817
- ——— Fulton Line, 1818 ~ Ordinance Line
- ///////// Disputed Territory
- ○○○○○○○○ Indiana Boundary, 1816
- +++++++ Illinois Boundary, 1818

Scale of Miles

Harris line as the legal survey; Secretary Woodbridge, of Michigan, protested to Brown and to John Quincy Adams, secretary of state, against the validity of Ohio's claim; Congress refused to establish either line as the true boundary. Also, since Indiana by its enabling act had edged ten miles into Michigan Territory (about 1,100 square miles), the Governor and Judges of the latter had recorded their opposition to this precedent; the people seemed unaware of the loss.[127]

So for some years, during which there were minor moves on both sides, matters rested.[128] The sparsely settled area in dispute was governed by Michigan, although Ohio made a pretense at exercising duplicate jurisdiction. But in the early 1830's, with the anticipated extension of the Miami Canal and rising statehood aspirations in Michigan Territory, the question became one of more than theoretical interest.[129]

Two different attempts were made to get a Michigan enabling act in 1834. Shortly after he became acting governor of Michigan Territory, twenty-two-year-old Stevens T. Mason advised the special session of the territorial Council to "abstain from legislating on a question which ought to be left to the adjustment of the two sovereign States" and, population proving sufficient, to declare their intention of claiming admission into the Union.[130] A census was ordered and a population of 85,856 reported; Mason then, in November, reminded the Council of the words of the Ordinance of 1787 and emphasized the "shall."[131] Accordingly, the Council called a convention to "form for them-

[127] See Chapter II.

[128] Congress failed to act on a boundary bill in 1829. In 1831 the Michigan territorial Council offered Ohio the land east of the Maumee in return for an equivalent cession in the west; Ohio refused. Governor Cass and the Ohio legislature both memorialized Congress the next year. In 1832 Congress provided for another survey which, when completed in 1834, confirmed the Fulton line. Soule, "The Southern and Western Boundaries of Michigan," in *Michigan Pioneer and Historical Collections*, XXVII, 354–55.

[129] In an election in 1832 on the desirability of statehood the vote had been 1,817 for, 1,190 against, but sentiment became more favorable in the next two years.

[130] Mason had been appointed secretary of Michigan Territory by President Jackson, July 25, 1831, at the age of nineteen. On the sudden death of Governor George B. Porter in July, 1834, he became acting governor. The Council met in September to consider the boundary dispute.

[131] "And, whenever any of the said States shall have sixty thousand free inhabitants therein, such State shall be admitted, by its delegates, into the Congress of the United States, on an equal footing with the original States in all respects whatever; and shall be at liberty to form a permanent Constitution and State Government. . . ."

selves a constitution and a State government." The convention met at Detroit May 11, 1835, framed a constitution, and drew up an appeal to the people of the United States which set forth the rightfulness of Michigan's cause in the boundary dispute.[132]

A bill to establish the Harris line as the boundary passed the United States Senate but failed to get by John Quincy Adams' committee in the House.[133] Michigan had warned against "all efforts to rob her of her soil and trample upon her rights," but offered, with Mason's approval, to negotiate with Indiana and Ohio. Governor Robert Lucas, of Ohio, in a special message to the state legislature said that the matter was one to be settled between the state of Ohio and the United States, and recommended legislative action to extend Ohio's jurisdiction up to the Harris line. Michigan countered (February 12, 1835) with a law providing a maximum penalty of $1,000 or five years imprisonment for any one except territorial officers who would accept office or exercise official functions in the area. The Ohio legislature (February 23, 1835) created two new townships in the disputed strip and provided for taking over control by April 1. Mason instructed Gen. Joseph W. Brown of the Michigan militia to prevent, peaceably if possible, Ohio's occupation; and Governor Lucas put Maj. Gen. John Bell in charge of Ohio's army.[134] The respective forces, accompanied by the governors, advanced to the scene of action. "Boy Governor" confronted "Old Governor"; even President Jackson, on the eve of a delicate national election, "was stumped."[135] Nor did he get any comfort

[132] For personnel and work of the convention, see *post,* 204–5.

[133] Indiana and Illinois were by this time lined up with Ohio. Senator John Tipton, of Indiana, who earlier had defended Michigan's stand, reversed himself completely after a resolution of instruction from the Indiana legislature. Adams was aware of the danger of antagonizing three states and twenty-nine representatives by standing by the unpopular side. In his diary he said: "Never in my life have I known a controversy of which all the right was so clear on one side and all the power so overwhelmingly on the other; never, a case where the temptation was so intense to take the strongest side and the duty of taking the weakest was so thankless."

[134] Sebried Dodge, engineer on the line of the Wabash and Erie Canal, wrote from Maumee on April 10 that the Governor of Ohio would not be able to run the line without a strong militia force, since Michigan had 300 men under arms at Monroe, 600 soon to come, and 1,500 stands of arms from the United States arsenal at White Pigeon. Indianapolis *Indiana Journal,* May 1, 1835.

[135] Ohio had twenty-one electoral votes, Indiana and Illinois fourteen more, and Michigan Territory none; yet it was important to get both Michigan and Arkansas, which were paired, into the Union before 1836, because both were supposed to vote for Van Buren electors.

from the opinion of his attorney general which, though evasive, asserted that the disputed zone legally belonged to Michigan. So the President dispatched two commissioners to the scene of trouble.[136]

Early in April these men tried to persuade Mason to leave the matter to Congress; when he refused, they hinted at possible removal by the President. He failed to be impressed by threats of "executive usurpation," and Michigan officials issued writs for arrest of the Ohio officials. A few days later the commissioners presented compromise terms based largely upon joint occupation, and submitted them to the belligerent governors.[137] Lucas and Ohio, having nothing to lose, were willing to accept, but Mason considered the terms "disreputable and dishonorable." The Council was willing to permit the marking of the Harris line, but not to accept concurrent jurisdiction.

The Ohio commissioners appointed to remark the Harris line were to have started work April 1, the day that local elections returned duplicate sets of officials. As the surveyors progressed eastward, General Brown's scouts kept track of them; when they reached Lenawee County (about halfway) April 25, a sheriff's posse went after them. The commissioners escaped, but the posse arrested a few armed citizens and some members of the surveying party.[138] Governor Lucas protested to President Jackson; Ohio papers, particularly the Democratic, backed the Governor, who called a special session of the legislature.[139] His resentment

[136] Benjamin C. Howard, of Maryland, and Richard Rush, of Pennsylvania. Elisha Whittlesey, of Ohio, went along as a volunteer pacificator.

[137] Michigan was to call off any prosecutions under the territorial act of February 12, Ohio was to be permitted to remark the Harris line, the people were to obey either Ohio or Michigan local officials and laws.

[138] By the sheriff's report the commissioners had "made good time on foot through the cotton wood swamp," suffering only the loss of their hats. By their own report they had been fired upon by forces under General Brown and barely escaped with their lives.

[139] The *Cincinnati Daily Gazette* (Whig), March 4, 1835, referred to Lucas' military preparations as a good April Fool's Day stunt. The *Hamilton Intelligencer*, May 7, thought hostile movements justified only by the puerile acts of the boyish acting governor. The Piqua *Western Courier*, March 21, said that Michigan could not be driven from its position unless overpowered by numbers at the point of the bayonet. The Columbus *Western Hemisphere* upheld Lucas; the *Toledo Gazette* yelled to high heaven against Michigan, etc.

"Wisconsin," with an ultimate stake in the outcome, followed the dispute with interest. The *Green-Bay Intelligencer*, April 28, 1835, spoke of the headstrong Governor of Ohio at the head of his "millions of freemen!" "But Michigan, though weak, perhaps in point of numbers, is strong in her *good and just cause*! she will have the sympathy and good wishes of all true republicans throughout the Union. . . ."

against the "murderous attack" was tempered in part by Jackson's lack of enthusiasm for strong-arm methods. The legislature, willing to accept the terms of the President's commissioners but doubting Michigan's intent to do so, in June appropriated $300,-000 (and authorized the Governor to borrow a like amount) to enforce Ohio's jurisdiction up to the Harris line. It created Lucas County, made Toledo the temporary seat of justice, and provided that the Court of Common Pleas of the Second Judicial Circuit hold a meeting there the first Monday in September. It further fixed a penalty of three to seven years imprisonment for anyone found guilty of "abducting" Ohio citizens. It was at this time (June) that the Michigan Constitutional Convention paused in its labor to declare that no other authority except that of the United States might be exercised in the disputed zone, and to issue its "Appeal." The territorial Council backed Mason with $315,000 to meet any emergency.

The next few weeks witnessed a war of writs, words, fists, and some gunfire, the latter apparently very inaccurate. One "Major" B. F. Stickney (who had named his sons One Stickney and Two Stickney) was arrested and subjected to the indignity of being tied onto his horse and forced to ride thus into Monroe. Two Stickney resisted arrest with a penknife and the sheriff was said by Governor Mason "to have been mortally wounded." Mason offered $500 for Two's capture but Lucas refused extradition.[140] Outrages were reported by both sides: houses broken open, citizens abducted, newspaper presses demolished.[141] Even an Ohio flag was torn down and, according to Ohioans, tied to horses' tails at General Brown's orders.

Governor Lucas, on July 29, ordered the surveyors to continue their line and informed them that sufficient rifles and muskets

[140] Major Stickney wrote a doleful letter to Lucas from "behind the grates of a loathesome prison" in Monroe. Two Stickney, evidently in hiding near Lower Sandusky, wrote the Governor to name the time when he should be permitted to "share with your excelence the glorious legacy, 'Death rather than dishonor.'" Cited in Wittke, "The Ohio-Michigan Boundary Dispute Re-examined," in *Ohio Archaeological and Historical Society Publications*, XLV, 309–10n.

[141] The *Toledo Gazette* of July 20, 1835, said it had hardly enough type saved from the outrages to lay the facts before the public. Nevertheless, it got off a two-column account of the activities of the "armed mob" under the sheriff of Monroe County, which was said to have had orders to burn the town if there was any resistance. This was "worse than Algerine robbery or Turkish persecution." Quoted in Ravenna *Western Courier*, August 8, 1835; also Indianapolis *Indiana Journal*, July 31, 1835.

had been forwarded in charge of the court for the sheriff's use in protecting them. Then, on August 3, he felt impelled to call for a muster of volunteer cavalry and riflemen to be ready to march, on a moment's notice, to defend the honor of the state.[142] The adjutant general promised three thousand cavalry and ten thousand riflemen.[143] Ten thousand or a million, Michigan promised them "hospitable graves." The Ohio Governor, though putting up a bold front, was apparently playing safe: he not only had earlier assurance from the President that he would veto a Michigan statehood bill if passed before the boundary dispute was settled, and Jackson's letter of July 4 advising him "to avoid forcible hostile collision," but through his personal representatives in Washington understood that, if bad came to worse, the President would remove Mason.[144]

In August, while Governor Lucas was mobilizing his new army, the Michigan Council had turned down the Rush-Howard compromises. The same month a Democratic convention met at Ann Arbor and (though the constitution had not yet been submitted) nominated Mason for governor of the new state and Isaac E. Crary for Congress. This body, dominated by the officeholders, was called a "caucus" by the Whig *Detroit Journal and Courier*, August 26, 1835. About a week later Secretary of State John Forsyth informed Mason that his zeal for Michigan's cause was not in keeping with the spirit of moderation and forbearance necessary for the preservation of the public peace. A copy of this letter was forwarded to Lucas and served as a hint to him. A face-saving operation would now be in order; to hold court in Lucas County in defiance of Michigan and without the sanction of the United States would be "exercising jurisdiction." Though the judges were juberous, preparations were made. General Bell and Adjutant General S. C. Andrews posted themselves as private citizens at a Toledo hotel; though the latter thought that a regiment of a thousand men would be needed, only about

---

[142] This was in addition to the call some months earlier for five hundred militia.
[143] The response was not so overwhelming. Adams County, with 21 volunteers, "caused the tree of Liberty to blush." The *Cincinnati Daily Gazette*, September 4, said there were "two proffers," presumably from Cincinnati. The Governor received much advice and many offers by letters, many with strings attached. See Wittke, "The Ohio-Michigan Boundary Dispute Re-examined," in *Ohio Archaeological and Historical Society Publications*, XLV, 311–12, for examples cited from the Ohio-Michigan Boundary MSS.
[144] Though trusting the President, Lucas was not so trustful of John Forsyth, secretary of state, B. F. Butler, attorney general, or Lewis Cass, secretary of war.

one hundred men and the sheriffs were supplied to furnish protection for the court which was to advance from Miami (Maumee).

All was ready when, on the evening of September 6, scouts reported that General Brown and 1,200 armed Michigan militia had just entered Toledo.[145] Contemplating the respective merits of discretion and valor, the judges were confronted by Col. Mathias Van Fleet of the Ohio militia, who was in charge of a bodyguard of twenty picked men: "If you are women, go home; if you are men, do your duty as judges of the court; I will do mine." Under cover of darkness they crept boldly into town and about one A. M. formally held court in a schoolhouse. A clerk and county commissioners were appointed and, no other business presenting, the court adjourned without day. The members proceeded to a tavern, registered their names, and had a drink all around, but were precipitated into flight by rumor of a large force of the enemy at hand. At the top of a hill safe in Ohio territory it was discovered that the record of the meeting (about a dozen lines), which had been deposited in the clerk's hat, had been lost in the retreat. This important proof of "jurisdiction" was finally recovered by the clerk, Van Fleet ordered two salutes fired in triumph, and the party returned to Maumee. Ohio had scored; Mason and Brown returned to Monroe and disbanded their army a few days later. Ohio made no further attempts at occupation. The military part of the war was over; total casualties, not counting hogs and fowl, two noble horses—one on each side.[146]

A Michigan bard in 1835 recorded the war in questionable meter:

"Come, all ye Michiganians, and lend a hearing ear;
Remember, for Toledo we once took up sword and spear,
And now, to give that struggle o'er and trade away that land,
I think it's not becoming of valiant-hearted men.

In eighteen-hundred thirty-five there was a dreadful strife,
Betwixt Ohio and this State; they talked of taking life.

[145] Only about one hundred men were in Toledo on the 6th. The main force arrived the next day.
[146] The "onpleasantness" had resulted in "a fearful war, and the destruction of many lives of chickens and honey bees, and occasionally a turkey." "Reminiscences of Rev. R. C. Crawford," in *Michigan Pioneer and Historical Collections,* IV (1881), 45.

Ohio claimed Toledo, and so did Michigan;
They both declared they'd have it, with its adjoining land.

. . . .

Mark the republic spirit that they have now displayed;
At first they'd have Toledo or lose their lives in aid;
But now the song they sing to us is: "Trade away that land
For that poor, frozen country beyond Lake Michigan."

They say that we must surely trade, or we shall be cast out;
That we shall lose our five per cent as sure as we do not;
That we can't be admitted into the bold Union,
But that we must, like the fifth calf, stand back and just look on."[147]

. . . .

John S. Horner of Virginia, appointed to Mason's place as secretary of Michigan Territory, though receiving no welcome from the citizens, carried out his orders.[148] He kept Governor Lucas informed, called off the Michigan prosecutions, but got no help from Michigan officials at Detroit, Monroe, or Ypsilanti, most of whom had hopes for state offices under the new constitution. The constitution was ratified on October 5; on the same date the voters elected Mason governor, Edward Mundy lieutenant governor, and Isaac E. Crary representative in Congress. The new state government organized November 2, and on the 10th the legislature elected Lucius Lyon and John Norvell to the United States Senate. The people generally still recognized the territorial judges, otherwise only the new state government.[149]

[147] From "Toledo War Song," in *Michigan Pioneer and Historical Collections,* VI (1883), 60–61. The author was probably R. C. Crawford, author of the above cited reminiscences. It was originally published in the *Lansing Republican,* September 5, 1873.

[148] He was said by the Columbus *Western Hemisphere,* November 11, 1835, to have been burned in effigy, publicly insulted, and had the windows of his hotel stoned.

[149] Not all agreed that this was the proper procedure. The *Detroit Journal and Advertiser,* November 28, December 3, 1835, arguing with the *Free Press,* Mason, Norvell, etc. (who, according to the *Journal,* thought they were the people of Michigan), said it was eager for statehood, "but we can never assent to her coming into the Union with the stigma of rebellion and incipient TREASON on her forehead. Let that abominable stain be washed out, and the men who tried to fix it there, repentant and humbled before the desecrated shrine of the laws, learn once more to respect the Constitution of their country. . . . If nullification in Michigan differs from nullification in South Carolina, in any thing, it is in being more eminently parricidal." The paper held the whole proceeding unconstitutional, even by the Michigan constitution, for persons not in the Territory more than three days had been permitted to vote. The constitution specified six months.

Most of the Ohio papers considered the Michigan action as "illegal and void." "There is a collection of individuals sitting, as the Legislature of the State of Michigan, somewhere in Michigan Territory. Master Mason deals with them as a

When the Twenty-fourth Congress convened in December, 1835, it was confronted with this foundling, two senators and a representative waiting for admission and ticklish questions of constitutional law.[150] Jackson conveyed the news to Congress, and Congress in an atmosphere, as John Quincy Adams said, "perfumed with . . . electoral votes" went to work. The two senators and representative were admitted to the respective houses as spectators. In March a Senate committee headed by Thomas Hart Benton presented the proposal that the Harris line be made the southern boundary but Michigan be compensated with territory in the Upper Peninsula.[151] When Wisconsin Territory was created in April, 1836, it was with a northeastern boundary as described in the Benton proposal. After long debate, the Arkansas-Michigan bills were passed in June. But Michigan was not a state. The "Act to establish the boundary-line of the State of Ohio, and to provide for the admission of the State of Michigan into the Union upon the conditions therein expressed" fixed the Ohio-Michigan boundary at the Harris line and required the assent of a special convention of Michigan delegates to be elected for that purpose.[152]

The "Convention of Assent" (called by the state legislature) met at Ann Arbor on September 26, and after four days turned

State Legislature—they recognize him as Governor. They talk of assuming all the functions of government, and superseding President Jackson and his Governor Horner. These are nice times.—Wickedness and silliness salute each other." And of the territorial Council west of Lake Michigan: "A body of men are collected at Green Bay, who denominate themselves as Legislative Council. This, like the Legislature of the State of Michigan, is a body unknown to the laws of the United States. Those laws seem to be *expunged* in the United States' Territories north of Ohio, Indiana, and Illinois." *Cincinnati Daily Gazette,* March 2, 1836.

[150] Could a state be organized without an enabling act; was its constitution "republican" in form; could there be a "state" within the United States, not yet a member of the Union; was such a state entitled to admission as a matter of right, having complied with the requirements of the Ordinance?

[151] That is, from the meridian of Mackinac west to the Montreal and Menominee rivers. Norvell, Crary, and most of the people of Michigan opposed this, but Lyon, probably acting on the knowledge of Cass and Schoolcraft, thought the proposition might eventually be of value to Michigan.

[152] The *Detroit Daily Advertiser,* July—August, contained many columns of editorials, letters, resolutions, etc. The paper, in general, was against what it called the Norvell submission party.

A supplementary act for the admission of Michigan, approved June 23, 1836, offered Michigan the customary grants: section 16 in each township for use of schools, 2 townships for a university, 5 sections for a capital, salt springs not to exceed 12, and 5 per cent of the proceeds of the sale of public lands lying within the state.

down the proposition.[153] But the decision left Michigan nowhere, and circumstances were commanding. Ohio had the territory by law of Congress. Besides there were Federal appointments awaiting statehood, and the threatened loss of the state's share of the treasury surplus—estimated at $400,000—if Michigan was not admitted by January 1, 1837; also the state was missing the 5 per cent of proceeds from the sale of public lands. Governor Mason did not see his way clear to call another convention, but believed that the people, "in their original capacity," had the right to reverse the acts of their agents "if found prejudicial to their interests." Petitions were demanding action. A self-appointed "Committee of the People" (the Democratic office-holding faction) called a second "Convention of Assent." This "Frost-bitten Convention" met at Ann Arbor on December 14, consented to the boundaries, and adjourned the following day.[154] Congress debated the propriety of the methods used but finally decided that the people "in their primary capacity" had the right. The admission act, though not approved until January 26, 1837, specified that Michigan share in the distribution of treasury surplus.

The war was over. From one point of view both Ohio and Michigan had acquired "lands that neither *had* any legal right to, after having exhibited their prowess in war without bloodshed."[155] Toledo had celebrated Ohio's victory in June, 1836; Detroit had a grand illumination February 9, 1837. Attempts to decide the "constitutionality" or justice of the outcome are futile; the points pro and con divided about evenly. Ballots no more than bullets make right, but they do make decisions. If at

[153] A minority were agreeable, thinking that if Michigan became a state she could take the matter before the Supreme Court. The majority believed that the "State" legislature had no right to call the convention and that Congress had no right to alter the boundaries of a state without its consent. Conservative Democrats and Whigs, supported by the *Detroit Daily Advertiser,* called the assenters the "Ohio Party"; the *Detroit Free Press* was the organ of the officeholding Democrats or assenters.

At a nonpartisan meeting at Berrien, September 2, strong sentiment was expressed against bartering away the rights of Michigan as guaranteed by the Ordinance of 1787. We "regard with feelings of abhorrence the efforts of a few bribed hirelings to stigmatize, as apostates from democracy, every man, who will not subscribe his own, and his country's death warrant, to subserve their base schemes of unhallowed ambition." *Niles Gazette,* September 7, 1836.

[154] "Michigan is coming to her senses," said the *Belmont* (Wis.) *Gazette,* December 28, 1836, and this seemed to be the general sentiment.

[155] Way, *The Toledo War of 1835,* 48.

times the proceedings took on an ominous aspect, it must be remembered that a spirit of levity and appreciation of the ludicrous overcast it all. Since Mason, Lucas, and Jackson were all Democrats, it was impossible even to get a party war lined up. Whigs sniped at all sides and, from across the disputed line, at each other. They agreed, however, that "President Jackson is an alchymist that turns everything to the profit of his parasites and to the advantage of his party."[156]

Michigan accepted the outcome, but Wisconsin Territory continued the fight for the Ordinance line for some years. In 1835 the *Green-Bay Intelligencer* pointed out that the region west of the lake was regarding the events "with intense interest, as a struggle for rights and principles which will furnish a precedent for a case at home at some future day."[157] The Wisconsin Council began memorializing Congress in 1837.[158]

§ § § §

In the decade preceding statehood the national party names had penetrated into Michigan politics but had less meaning perhaps than sectional and factional divisions. Generally the politicians from New England, eastern New York, and Virginia headed the conservative groups; those from frontier western New York were inclined to the less conservative opposition.[159] After 1829 territorial politics was dominated by the Jacksonian officeholders. Kentucky-born John Norvell, Detroit postmaster with the instincts of a natural boss, built up an organized Democratic following composed of lawyers, small farmers, laborers, the foreign voters, and politicians. Isaac E. Crary also belonged to this faction, commonly known as "the officeholders." Opposed to this group were such political figures as Lucius Lyon, of Kalamazoo, Elon Farnsworth, of Detroit, and others who rep-

[156] *Cincinnati Daily Gazette,* April 14, 1835.
[157] May 7, 1835.
[158] Madison *Wisconsin Democrat,* December 8, 1838. "Solon" in the *Green-Bay Intelligencer,* November 16, 1836, frankly admitted that the mining area in northern Illinois was a prize worth fighting for. The demand for the annexation of northern Illinois continued many years after 1840.
[159] Floyd B. Streeter, "The Factional Character of Early Michigan Politics," in *Michigan History Magazine,* II (1918), 166.

resented the better-to-do lawyers, merchants, and landowners.
The Whigs played a minor role.

By 1834 Detroit papers were giving much attention to national
as well as local politics. The *Journal and Advertiser* registered
its protest against the intensity of politics, which with its tendency to become a distinct profession was proving ruinous to
patriotism and morals.

It also has been reduced to an art or a science; not however belonging
exclusively to the province of the statesman; whose duty it is to sustain by
prudence, forecast from knowledge of human nature the peculiar interests
of his own country, when brought into collision with those of other
countries; but it has become the stepping stone, the hobby by which the
ambitious, the necessitous, the proud and the vain are enabled to ride into
power, supported by the follies and weaknesses of their fellow-men.[160]

To the Constitutional Convention of 1835 the Democrats
elected approximately 74 of the 84 delegates, though the president, John Biddle (brother of Nicholas Biddle), was a Whig.[161]
The convention produced a brief and simple frame of government which served Michigan for fifteen years. It provided for
the usual three departments of government, annual elections of
the legislature, and biennial elections of governor and lieutenant
governor. The governor, with consent of the Senate, was empowered to appoint the secretary of state, auditor general,
attorney general, and county prosecutors; with the consent of the
legislature in joint vote to appoint a state superintendent of public instruction. The state treasurer was to be "appointed" by a
joint vote of the legislature. The governor's veto could be overridden by two-thirds vote in each house. Nothing was specified
regarding county and township organization (beyond providing
that no existing county could be reduced by law to less than four
hundred square miles), though biennial election of county sheriffs,
coroners, treasurers, and registers of deeds was provided for;
also the election of county court judges and up to four justices
of the peace in each township, for four-year terms. Slavery was

---

[160] September 17, 1835.

[161] The *Detroit Journal and Advertiser*, April 10, 1835, stated that the Catholic
clergy had controlled the French vote which was "Tory," that is, Democratic; that
1,433 votes had been polled in Detroit where there were only 450 legal voters for
municipal elections. It also struck out at James D. Doty and eight other members
of the territorial Council who had voted to permit aliens to vote for convention
delegates as "infamous usurpers."

prohibited and the legislature mandated to provide a system of common schools, with one school in each district "at least three months in every year." As soon as the circumstances of the state would permit, a library was to be established in each township, and the land and funds granted for the support of a university were to be protected.

The bill of rights contained the statement, "No man or set of men are entitled to exclusive or separate privileges." A miscellaneous article provided that a two-thirds vote of each house would be necessary to pass an act of incorporation. In the debates on suffrage John Norvell, chairman of the committee on elective franchise, sought to give the vote to all males aged twenty-one who had resided in the United States two years, in the state six months, and had declared their citizenship intent; also to all white males who were resident in the Territory on the day of election of delegates to the constitutional convention. The conservative Democrats and the few Whigs held out for stricter qualifications. The compromise provision in the constitution gave the suffrage to white male citizens of twenty-one years with six-months residence in the state and to "every white male inhabitant" of twenty-one a resident at the time of the signing of the constitution. Otherwise the constitution showed few of the characteristics of the new trends favored by "Jacksonian democracy"; certainly not in the short list of elective state officers—two in the constitution of 1835 as compared with eight in the constitution of 1850.

The "officeholders" faction controlled the Democratic state convention of August, 1835, which nominated Mason for governor, Edward Mundy for lieutenant governor, and Crary for Congress.

The delegates accused the Whigs of trying to create a spirit of jealousy and distrust between the native-born citizens and foreigners; efforts to use bigotry and prejudice to bring odium upon naturalized fellow citizens, especially the Catholics, were contrary to the genius of republican institutions. "The federal Whig leaders, with their usual charity to all the measures of democracy, have waged war upon the constitution formed and adopted by the late convention." Further, they planned to run the national election into the House again and, following in the steps of their leaders who had tried to elect Burr instead of Jefferson, divide the votes and by bribing try for success.[162]

Mason received 7,508 votes to 814 for Biddle, his Whig opponent, in the October 5 election at which the constitution was also ratified. The new legislature had a Senate composed entirely of Democrats, about half "officeholders" and half conservatives; 45 of the 48 representatives were Democrats. All united on Lucius Lyon for the four-year United States Senate term, but a contest resulted between Norvell and Biddle for the other senatorship; Norvell finally won on a joint ballot.[163]

As previously noted, the conservative Democrats united with Whigs in acceptance of Congress' terms of admission and even went so far as to organize a coalition "States' Rights Party," not only to uphold Michigan rights but to break the strangle hold of the "junto" or "officeholders." The confused political terminology in the period is illustrated by the *Monroe Times'* classification of the membership of Michigan's second legislature. It divided the Democrats into Assenters, Dissenters, States' Rights Advocates, Regular Nominationists, Independent Electors, Party Electors, etc. The Federalists (Whigs) were also divided.[164]

§ § § § §

The first political campaign between Whigs and Democrats in the Northwest began in 1834 and continued with hardly a break until the apparent victory of the newly organized opposition in 1840. The Whigs possessed neither a formidable organization, a coherent platform, nor an outstanding available candidate, but the attempt to bring Van Buren into the Presidency presented the opening for attack and, after a period of unsuccessful experimenting with candidates, they found a man whose appeal in the West hit familiar chords and beat the Democrats at their own game as played in 1828.

Some papers, the *Hamilton Intelligencer,* for instance, were featuring "the next Presidency" in the spring of 1833, three years

---

[162] "Address to the Electors," in *Niles Gazette,* October 3, 1835.
[163] First vote in the Senate was 8 to 8, the second 10 to 6 in favor of Biddle. In the House Norvell was nominated 27 to 20. In joint session Norvell was elected.
[164] In *Detroit Daily Advertiser,* December 5, 1830.

before the next national election. A year later this paper was using the party labels of Whig and Tory (Democrats) though it often referred to the latter as "Muzzlecrats."[165] The Whig papers were hot on the trail of the "Kitchen Cabinet," Van Buren, and other Jackson liabilities.[166] A Cleveland meeting early in 1834 resolved that the removal of the deposits was a violation of the rights of the Bank and a breach of public faith; that the result was pecuniary distress throughout the country; that the Ohio senators and representatives should vote to have the deposits restored; and that the sentiments of the Ohio legislature were not those of the people. Other meetings were taking similar action.

Among the first in the field as a possible presidential candidate for the new party was Judge John McLean, of Ohio, who had been a Democrat for many years and was then serving on the Supreme Court by Jackson's appointment. McLean certainly lacked the appeal and personality of a Jackson or a Clay, but he was energetic, knew many people and politicians and, in the words of his biographer, possessed "a masterful countenance which gave an impression of extraordinary capacity."[167] He had taken a middle-of-the-road stand, cultivated men of both parties, but had failed to receive serious consideration in 1832 because no compromise candidate was wanted by either party. The next year friends obtained control of the *Columbus Sentinel*, which was edited in his interest; the *Hamilton Intelligencer*, the Cincinnati *Commercial Advertiser,* and to a lesser extent the *Cincinnati Gazette* backed him. Meetings were held 1833–34 at Lebanon, St. Clairsville, Mansfield, Eaton, Hamilton, Jefferson, and Cincinnati. He was "nominated" early in January, 1835, by the "Democratic-Republican" members of the legislature of his state, and "many respectable citizens" who were at Columbus during the session of the circuit court.[168] McLean's friends were encour-

---

[165] March 15, 1834.

[166] The *Hamilton Intelligencer*, November 20, 1834, quoted an article from the London *St. James Chronicle* to the effect that Van Buren would bring the Democrats around to a national system of *"Monarchal Obedience."*—Would we accept a Monarch? "NO NEVER!" protested the *Intelligencer*.

[167] Weisenburger, *Passing of the Frontier*, 253.

[168] Chillicothe *Scioto Gazette*, January 7, 1835. The citizens at the meeting availed themselves of the occasion to address their fellow citizens of the Union. They believed that no government should be permitted to transfer its power and influence to those it prefers, and that this could best be prevented by a "Union" of all those who concurred in this opinion. They presented the name of John McLean to "be put in nomination as the candidate of those with whom there is a community of

aged by endorsements from Baltimore, New York, and Tennessee, but his candidacy was handicapped by his having been tied up with the candidacy of the defeated governor (Findlay in 1834), by his having been too closely identified with Jackson, and by the suspicions of Clay's dyed-in-the-wool friends, who had resented the Hammond-for-McLean move in 1829.[169]

Outside of Ohio the McLean boom attracted little attention in the Northwest. The *Indiana Journal* thought that others had better claims and that the issues as well as the number of candidates excluded him from the eligible list. It agreed with the *Ohio State Journal* that personal preference must be yielded and that the "great object of all those who are desirous of seeing our government administered in its purity, must be *union*, UNION—UNION."[170]

William Henry Harrison, around whose name the Whigs and anti-Van Buren Democrats rallied and ultimately marched to victory, was the first son of the Northwest to have important presidential possibilities. Friends and success-hungry politicians saw in him a possible second Jackson, a man whose name and background might appeal to the people at large without reference to old party distinctions.[171] Jackson had the "corrupt bargain" and the "stolen election" of 1824 to arouse the spirit of justice in the West; so Harrison was deemed the possessor of a glorious

---

sentiment on the one great purpose of preventing an Executive from actually appointing his successor." The *Gazette* did not believe McLean to be the first choice and favorite of many in Ohio, but signified willingness to support him in a spirit of conciliation.

[169] The McLean candidacy is best followed in Weisenburger, *Passing of the Frontier,* Chapter X, and in his *Life of John McLean.*

[170] October 2, June 23, 1835.

[171] William Henry Harrison, son of Benjamin Harrison, a signer of the Declaration of Independence, was born in Virginia in 1773. After studying medicine for about a year, he entered the army in 1791. He was Anthony Wayne's aide-de-camp in his Indian campaign of 1794, became secretary to the Governor and Judges of the Northwest Territory in 1798, and delegate to Congress from the Territory the following year. In Congress he sponsored the land act of 1800 which has commonly been known by his name. He became governor of Indiana Territory in May, 1800, and served until 1813. He held a commission as major general in the Kentucky militia, and in 1813 was made a brigadier general in the regular army and given command of the Army of the Northwest. In 1814 he resigned from the army and retired to his home at North Bend near Cincinnati. He served in Congress, in the Ohio legislature, in the United States Senate, and for a brief time as minister to Colombia. Harrison's most noteworthy public service prior to 1836 was as governor of Indiana Territory, which task he performed with better than average success. For previous mentions of Harrison see Chapters II and IX.

military record, obscured and belittled by too ambitious politicians.

Questions of "who won the war" were always matters of importance in pioneer politics; they were cultivated and debated to satisfy local pride and political ambition. The arguments were similar to those used in a later day to establish the superiority of a state or region on the basis of the prowess of its football or baseball team; the decisions were often about as conclusive. Reminiscences, letters, and discussions of the western campaigns of the War of 1812 had appeared intermittently in the papers for two decades, but in 1833–34, with two prominent participants sparring for a political opening, the number and intensity increased, to reach a crescendo of fire and backfire in 1840.

Col. Richard M. Johnson, who had commanded the mounted Kentuckians at the Battle of the Thames, was very popular in the West and not at all averse to succeeding President Jackson. His military glory had expanded with each retelling through the years, until from colonel of the mounted Kentuckians who fought in the battle he had risen to be Gen. Richard M. Johnson, who had won the Battle of the Thames. By the time that a committee of Indianapolis citizens invited Harrison to be present for the celebration of the anniversary of the battle, October 4, 1834, resentment had so accumulated that General Harrison struck back with warlike vigor.[172] Since Johnson had also been invited, Harrison refused with a curt reply. He had seen reference in the *Indiana Democrat* to the celebration of the great victory won "by the American forces under General Harrison and Colonel Johnson." He recalled the Kentucky epic poem which had made Governor Isaac Shelby the Agamemnon and Johnson the Ajax Telemon, and had not mentioned the commander; also the Tammany celebration in New York in 1833 "in honor of the victory achieved by Colonel Johnson at the river Thames." Whoever heard of the Battle of New Orleans being won by General Jackson and one of his colonels, or that at Niagara by General Brown and Colonel Miller? The victory had been won by the army and Harrison was its commander, and to the army the glory should go. "Miserable indeed must be the situation of a commanding

---

[172] *Niles' Weekly Register*, XLVII, 173–75 (Nov. 15, 1834), gives the note and Harrison's reply of September 27.

general, if the pretensions of Colonel Johnson's friends are admitted."

Harrison's letter was widely copied throughout the West and the able defense of Governor Shelby and himself aroused not only his partisans and Whigs, but men of all parties. When during the same autumn a Pennsylvania newspaper mentioned Harrison for the Presidency, the General, whose financial situation was not too happy, heartily approved of the idea.[173] In January, 1835, a meeting of citizens at Harrisburg named Harrison and issued a long "address."[174] The same month two meetings were held in Hamilton County, Ohio. John W. Bailhache, influential publisher of the *Ohio State Journal* at Columbus, was still hoping for Clay but was not unfavorable to the Harrison movement. Some months later it began to appear to Ohio and Indiana Whigs that Harrison might be agreed upon as the candidate of the anti-Van Buren party, and if so the name of the Old General would receive the response of the West in one universal shout of assent.[175]

During the summer the General made a trip down the Ohio to Madison, New Albany, Louisville, and Vincennes, where it was said he was hailed and feted by all except a few Jackson politicians. The reception at Cincinnati upon his return was described as the largest and most enthusiastic since Lafayette's visit.[176] Soon the *Ohio State Journal* wrote: "Looking to our own State,

[173] Goebel, *Harrison,* 307.

[174] "In the history of every free government there are periods when a recurrence to primary principles is the only security for liberty. The tendency of every party organization, no matter upon what pure principles at first based, to degenerate into a combination hostile to the spirit of representative institutions and liable to become an engine, in the hands of selfish and interested men, to oppress the people, is the experience of all republics.

"A National convention, composed of delegates chosen by the recipients or expectants of public patronage, in packed, drilled, venal, and irresponsible assemblages, in which not one in a thousand of the people participate is now in contemplation, to dictate to a free people whom they shall choose for their ruler. The uncorrupted democracy of this Union never has and never will sanction such a measure," allied as it was with power, patronage, moneyed corporations, aristocratical principles, etc. Then followed a long review of the candidate's record and resolutions. Chillicothe *Scioto Gazette,* February 4, 1835.

In December the Pennsylvania Anti-Masonic convention nominated Harrison and the Whig convention concurred in the choice.

[175] A Whig meeting at Columbus, July 18, 1835, issued a long attack upon Jackson, Van Buren, New York machine politics, and executive usurpation; also a call for a Whig state nominating convention for February, 1836. The *Ohio State Journal* suggested many meetings, canvassing of preferences at each, then sending the returns to the *Journal* so that a legislative caucus could decide upon united action. *Scioto Gazette,* August 5, 1835.

[176] *Cincinnati Daily Gazette,* August 11, 1835, quoted in Indianapolis *Indiana Journal,* September 4, 1835.

the 'signs of the times' for these last few weeks plainly indicate that the star of Gen. Harrison is rising to the ascendant. As wave follows wave, meetings for his nomination are following meetings in various sections in succession." In November the Tippecanoe Battleground barbecue meeting nominated the old soldier; when the Indiana state Whig convention met at Indianapolis in December, it was merely to select Harrison electors.[177] Someone did mention Colonel Johnson as a vice-presidential possibility, but apologized to the Tippecanoe heroes for the insult.

The Harrison movement was represented as coming entirely from the people without respect to former political preferences. "The ostensible as well as real object of the Whig party is to check, if possible, the present rapid concentration of all power in the person of the President, and restore in reality, as well as in name, the government to its original purity and simplicity in management." In the earlier meetings party names were scarcely used nor were pointedly partisan subjects brought up by the speakers. The support of the church people of the Northwest, which had never been given to Clay, was thrown to Harrison. He was heralded as the man least obnoxious to sectional and party prejudices, as the man who had spent his life in the service of the people and was now the candidate of the people.[178]

> Rejoice! Columbia's sons, rejoice!
> To Tyrants never bend the knee;
> But join with heart, and soul, and voice,
> For Harrison and "Liberty."[179]

The Ohio Whig convention of more than a thousand delegates met at Columbus on February 22, passed resolutions favoring Harrison and Francis Granger of New York for vice-president, and in its "Address" referred to its candidate as "the gallant defender of his country in the hour of danger . . . a statesman and a patriot . . . who [would] make the offices . . . agencies for the benefit of the people, and not bribes with which to purchase votes."

The Harrison candidacy did not unite the opposition in Illinois

---

[177] The electors, except two, were old National Republicans. Chillicothe *Scioto Gazette,* January 6, 1836.

[178] Whig Harrison meeting at Chillicothe, Ohio, September 26, 1835. *Ibid.,* September 30, 1835.

[179] Columbus *Ohio State Journal,* September 25, 1835.

as it did in Ohio and Indiana, for there were many Democrats who were opposed to Van Buren yet who could not definitely decide to leave the old party. Hugh L. White, of Tennessee, who was read out of the party by the Democratic press for opposing Jackson's choice of Van Buren, was the favorite of many of these voters. The Illinois Senate, though Democratic by almost two to one, endorsed White for the Presidency by a vote of 13 to 12, and at the same time condemned the Van Buren party.[180] After the legislature adjourned, anti-Van Buren men gathered at Springfield, formally nominated White, and prepared an address to the voters. Although the five White electors, all anti-Van Buren Democrats, were subsequently carried in a number of the Whig papers, many of the White following insisted they were still as good members of the Democratic party as were the Van Burenites. Until late in 1836 the fight in Illinois was between Van Buren forces and a coalition of Whigs and White Democrats.[181] Whig leaders saw no particular reason for supporting a regular Whig candidate, but sought rather to take advantage of the split within the Democratic ranks. Many of the Whigs, however, especially in the northwestern counties, did not understand or else grew impatient with the coalition tactics, and Harrison sentiment developed; a meeting at Alton in August resolved for Harrison, and from that time the Democratic papers began to pay more attention to him. At a meeting in Edwardsville in September White electors were nominated, but it was understood that they were to cast their votes for Harrison should he receive more votes than White in the other states.[182] Three of the White electors agreed to this proposition and the ticket was called the "Union anti-Van Buren Electoral Ticket."[183] The Jacksonville *Illinois Patriot*, Governor Duncan's paper, suggested that the voters in-

[180] Illinois *Senate Journal*, 1835-36, pp. 75 ff.; Thompson, *The Illinois Whigs*, 51-52.

[181] The Democratic papers called this opposition the "piebald party"; the Vandalia *Illinois State Register and People's Advocate*, leading Van Buren paper, centered its fire upon this group rather than upon the Whigs. The *Sangamo Journal*, the paper of the Sangamon County Whig Junto, had not considered the Harrison movement seriously. On May 1 it wrote: "The attempt to cover up the political deformities of Van Buren with the cloak of General Jackson, is done with the sole and only purpose of taking advantage of the feelings of the old friends of General Jackson, who do not discover the trick played off on them. The contest is between Martin Van Buren, the northern candidate, and Hugh L. White, the Western candidate."

[182] Vandalia *Illinois State Register and People's Advocate*, September 2, 15, 1836.

[183] *Ibid.*, October 7, 1836; *Sangamo Journal*, October 1, 15, 1836.

dicate their choice of Harrison or White in order that the electors, if elected, could cast their votes for the majority.[184]

The abundance of Whig candidates formed an impressive numerical opposition which made the Democrats fear the possibility of the election being thrown into the House of Representatives. At the same time sensible Whig leaders realized that with three or four candidates in the field it would be possible for the "Humbugs" to overwhelm them in detail. But organization was not one of the Whigs' fortes; they brought up a phalanx of candidates and prepared the way with a barrage of print and oratory against "locofocos" in general and Van Buren, the weak spot in the Democratic line, in particular. Few knew for sure what a "locofoco" was but it sounded bad; Democrats were never able to find a label for their opponents which carried equal opprobrium—not even "Federalist."[185]

As the numerous local meetings were held, "addresses" were formulated, printed, copied, and recopied in the papers, broadcast as handbills, and hurled forth from stump and platform. The argument ran thus: "A flame of political delusion has passed over the land and Martin Van Buren is decreed to be the Phoenix that is to rise out of it. The mountain of Jacksonism has been in labor and this cunning mouse is brought forth."[186] The fundamental principle of Van Burenism was that the government of the people should be carried on by a party organization and the benefits of that government accrue not to the people but to the party. "The party" was the "officeholders"; they and not the people had named the New York manipulator at the Baltimore convention (May, 1835). Had Jackson not picked him, the "Little Magician" would never have been thought of. "Take Martin Van Buren from Jackson, and Jackson remains—take Jackson from

---

[184] *Illinois State Register and People's Advocate,* September 15, 1836.

[185] The term originated in New York City in 1835. A faction of the Democrats calling themselves the Equal Rights men opposed the Tammany organization. When the latter left the meeting hall, they extinguished the lights on their opponents. The Equal Rights men, however, provided themselves with candles which they lighted with the new "locofoco" matches. By 1836–37 use of the term had become general in the Whig press. The general connotation which the users sought to convey was that of a simple person, an irresponsible half-wit. Governor Thomas Ford, writing ten years later, said that the name had "no effect whatever on elections" and that no squeamish man ran away from or became disgusted with a party "having this uncouth name." *History of Illinois,* 201.

[186] Address of Ross County (Ohio) Whigs, in *Scioto Gazette,* September 9, 1835.

Martin Van Buren and zero remains."[187] Let this precedent of
the President dictating his successor to the party become established and it would not be necessary to bother about elections in
the future. Van Buren was also listed as a Catholic and a friend
of the free Negroes.[188] Harrison was a soldier, a statesman, and
a hero; Van Buren was a "mere political grimalkin."[189]

Criticism such as this did not react in Van Buren's favor as
similar attack had in Jackson's case, but on the whole added to
his unpopularity in the West. The administration papers were
handicapped in their counterattack by the lack of editors as strong
penned as their opponents, and the fact that the opinions of those
they had were somewhat discounted as being dictated from
above.[190] So strict was the Jackson discipline that some of the
papers not held in line by Federal patronage deserted Van Buren
for Harrison. These were known as the "dug out" Whigs.

To the Van Buren papers Whigs were a mere conglomeration
of contradictory opinions and dissimilar interests, "a loose com-
pound of Hartford Convention Federalism and Royal-arch
Masonry."[191] The minute one of these immaculate self-con-
stituted busybodies became a candidate for office he began exclaiming against officeholders and trying to create an unjust prejudice
against the best and purest men in the country, just as if they were
not also citizens of it and entitled to all the rights and immunities
of free men. Treachery was their favorite weapon, their nature,
and their vocation; the only tie which held them together was
hatred of purer principles than they themselves had.

While the Whigs invoked invective, the Democrats looked to
their organization. To the party machinery built up in Ohio and
Indiana between 1828 and 1835 were added improvements; at the
same time established methods were extended to Illinois. When

[187] Richmond *Indiana Palladium,* quoted in Chillicothe *Scioto Gazette,* June 22,
1836.

[188] To be a Catholic was an unquestionable right, said the *Hamilton Intelligencer,*
August 18, 1836, "but merely to make pretensions, for no other than electioneering
purposes, is as unhallowed as it is dishonorable." An Ohio inquiry regarding Van
Buren's Catholic leanings received the reply that such rumors were "without the
slightest foundation in truth." Columbus *Western Hemisphere,* September 7, 1836,
and citations from Van Buren MSS. cited in Weisenburger, *Passing of the Frontier,*
324 n.

[189] Covington (Ind.) *Western Constellation,* October 23, 1836

[190] The Whigs called them the "collar press." The term probably originated with
editor John Douglass, of the Indianapolis *Indiana Journal,* who spoke of the papers
wearing the "chain and collar" of their master.

[191] Vincennes *Western Sun and General Advertiser,* October 24, 1835.

in 1835 the Ohio Democratic papers recommended a state convention, the state central committee took action. County meetings were held during the autumn; candidates were recommended. The Hamilton County convention resolved that no candidate should receive consideration who would not agree to abide by the decision of the convention.[192] When the state convention met at Columbus on January 8, 1836, almost eight hundred delegates were present. The delegates from each Congressional district selected the elector for that district, and a committee of delegates, one from each district, selected the two electors for the state. County committees of correspondence were chosen and the state committee made more effective by the appointment of five members who lived in or near Columbus.[193]

The Indiana convention which met at Indianapolis on the same day was organized by a committee of five from each Congressional district and the electors chosen as in Ohio. A committee of three from each district prepared a report on organization of the party in the state, which was adopted. At the top was set up the central committee of sixteen, a majority of whom were to live in or near the capital; in each Congressional district were set up committees of five; and in each county, committees of six. The county committees appointed the vigilance committees in each township; when these township committees had completed the roster of Democratic voters, the county committees were to apportion delegates and call county conventions.[194] The "Address to the People" was twelve columns in length and dull. The Whigs and their libels were condemned, Van Buren and Johnson praised.

Although Illinois had been under Democratic control since the beginning, the party organization had never been so well developed as in Indiana and Ohio. It was particularly weak at the bottom, for the township, which formed the base work in the two other states, was nonexistent as an important unit until after the Jacksonian period. Nor was the convention system so well accepted, even by the Democrats. It was regarded as "a fraud upon the people . . . a mere fungus growth engrafted upon the constitution . . . got up and packed by cunning, active, intriguing

---

[192] Columbus *Western Hemisphere,* September 16, 1835.
[193] *Ibid.,* January 9, 13, 1836.
[194] Indianapolis *Indiana Democrat,* November 21, 1835.

politicians, to suit the wishes of a few."[195] The Illinois Senate, December, 1835, had resolved that "every person eligible to the office of president had a right to come forward as a candidate for it without the intervention of caucuses and conventions"; it expressed disapproval of any convention system being forced upon the American people by the Van Buren party, the same being destructive of the freedom of the elective franchise, opposed to republican institutions, and dangerous to the liberties of the people. It deprived individuals by their own mere motion of the privilege of becoming candidates, and deprived each man of the right to vote for a candidate of his own selection and choice.[196] Illinois Whigs, who often by concentrating on one candidate had been able to defeat the more numerous Democrats in local elections, suddenly became aware that the convention system was a very bad thing—for the Democrats. The *Sangamo Journal* ridiculed such a system in a republic. The *Chicago American* said the people had the choice between being free, independent, and masters of their own suffrage, or of wearing the bonds and shackles of party and being "dictated to by a pack of demagogues, whose every move is self-aggrandizement!—office—!!—power!!! Will the people submit?"[197]

The Ohio Whig convention met February 22; no building could accommodate the 1,034 delegates, and sessions were held on the State House square. Electors were chosen for Harrison and Granger; Thomas Ewing was its choice for senator and Joseph Vance for governor.[198] A resolution to print 50,000 copies of the proceedings, 10,000 of them in German, was passed. The Whig papers pointed to the convention as a great movement of the people.[199]

Ohio Whigs were given an additional argument against officeholders by the legislative reapportionment of March, 1836. The Democrats, having an eye on the seat of Senator Thomas Ewing

---

[195] Ford, *History of Illinois*, 205.
[196] *Ibid.*, 206.
[197] *Chicago American*, August 1, 1835. See also *Chicago Democrat*, July 15, 29, 1835; Springfield *Sangamo Journal*, early months of 1836.
[198] Francis Granger, of New York, although charged by some with being an abolitionist, was recommended by Ewing in preference to John Tyler and his state rights views.
[199] Columbus *Ohio State Journal*, February 24, 1836; *Cincinnati Daily Gazette*, March 2, 1836. Extracts on the convention from the leading Ohio Whig papers were copied in the *Journal*, March 11, 1836.

whose term was to expire in 1837, carved the state to make their success more certain. The Whig papers analyzed the gerrymander and revealed that five strong Whig counties with a population of 28,818 were given five representatives, or one to each 5,763 males over twenty-one, while five Jackson counties with 18,468 population were given nine representatives, or one to each 2,057. Muskingum County with 6,316 voters was assigned one representative; Perry County with 3,062 was given two.[200] Ninety-two thousand voters of various sections of the state were given thirty-seven representatives while 142,000 were given only thirty-five.

Although the wild enthusiasm generated by hero-worship and hatred for "officeholders" did not reach a climax in the election of 1836, still a fair head of steam was raised. Democratic editors improved their "mud slinging" technique as the campaign progressed. When a young man at Columbus was reported to have related that the women of Chillicothe had voted Harrison a petticoat as the most fitting memento of his military prowess, the story with embellishments was widely copied. Harrison became "the Petticoat Hero," "the Hero of the Rear Guard," "the Old Woman" candidate. Harrison was the real aristocrat, a feeder at the public trough, a Federalist of the Old School who not only believed in the Alien and Sedition laws but who had even voted to sell common folks into slavery.[201]

Whig editors stigmatized the perpetrators of such tales as "liars and scoundrels," hell hounds of a rotten and sinking party who had dug up stale slander from the graves of bygone years. On the other hand who could doubt that Martin Van Buren had favored extending the ballot to free Negroes and mulattoes, or that he was so great a lover of the people that he had, in the New York convention of 1821, tried to save them the trouble of voting for sheriffs and justices of the peace. Or that Richard M. Johnson

[200] *Zanesville Republican* in Chillicothe *Scioto Gazette,* March 23, 1836. For table of apportionment see the *Gazette* for March 30, 1836.

[201] When in the Ohio Senate, 1820–21, Harrison had voted for a law to bind out paupers—a common practice at the time. The Warren (Ohio) *Trumbull Democrat* related the story of a visitor to Warren in 1825 who, hearing loud wailing, was drawn to the spot where the court was selling an old man. The victim, an old soldier, had used his crutch upon a young profligate, son of a banker, who had seduced his daughter; unable to pay his fine, he was being "sold" to someone who would. Whereupon friends of the true offender took up a collection and purchased the old man's freedom. The description of this sad scene and sale was heart-rending and tear provoking—good politics. Ravenna *Western Courier,* November 3, 1836.

was the father of a lot of mulattoes. "Gen. Harrison, in peace and in War, had supported his country. Mr. Van Buren, in peace and in war, had been *supported by his country*."[202] Serious political discussion centered around Jackson's Bank veto, Specie Circular, and the distribution law. To the Whigs the Specie Circular was but "another experiment made upon the credulity of the public by this wonder working administration," something devised to distress the common man rather than the banks and land speculators.[203] Ohio Whigs in particular were interested in the distribution of the Treasury surplus to the state, for Ohio's share was figured at $2,187,500. Although nominally a loan, it was not thought the distribution, once made, would ever be recalled.[204] This sum, applied to roads, canals, and public schools, would be an important aid. Since Van Buren, however, in reply to the questionnaire of a Kentucky congressman had declared against distribution to the states, the Democrats pretended to be disgusted with this disgraceful scramble for the public revenues. Equally costly to Van Buren was the belief held by many Westerners that he was hostile to the interests of their section. His voting record on internal improvements at Federal expense gave weight to this view.

The Ohio state election came October 11. "If ever was a time since the organization of the government, that every man who enjoys the inestimable right of suffrage should exercise it

---

[202] *Logansport Telegraph* in *Indiana Journal,* July 9, 1836.

[203] Whig papers attacked this "most alarming assumption of executive power" with all the vehemence at their command. The Springfield *Sangamo Journal,* for instance, ran seven long, solid articles on it during September and October. Even some Democratic papers, such as the *Detroit Free Press,* admitted the unpopularity of the Treasury order.

Elisha Whittlesey wrote in the autumn of 1836: "Such a mass of corrupt imbecility, and brute ignorance, as is now in the H. of Repts. I never saw together in Congress; and the fear of the people alone, can be made to operate on such an inert mass, destitute alike of moral feeling and shame." The principal cause was the unsound and dangerous deposit banks which paid no interest, and were incapable of regulating currency and business. "As to the *Chief,* he is as a King on his death bed, all look to his successor. No one cares what Jackson thinks now." Document edited by Abraham H. Venit, in *American Historical Review,* LI (1945–46), 685–88.

[204] A public meeting at Chillicothe on Saturday, June 4, resolved that since Ohio had paid about $16,000,000 into the public treasury, distribution of the surplus should be carried out. Control of such vast accumulating funds tended to corrupt the purity of our institutions and endanger the liberties of the people. Congressman William Bond was instructed to use his influence to help carry out Jackson's idea of 1830 to deposit this money in the pockets of the people. Chillicothe *Scioto Gazette,* June 18, 1836.

... now is the time," said the *Cleveland Herald* in its last appeal to the freemen of Cuyahoga County. Forty thousand freemen had been disenfranchised (the legislative gerrymander); in another year the state government might be destroyed.[205] In similar vein the *Scioto Gazette* proclaimed: "In the general government we have presented us the most bare-faced corruption and abuse of trust." Public agents hold offices only on condition of using their influence to support the powers that be. Money of the people is used to bribe and purchase votes. The whole fabric of government is converted into a tremendous electioneering machine. The whole state of Ohio is governed by a little knot of politicians at Columbus assisted by equally corrupt agents over the state who are but echoes of their masters at Washington. The bond of union is the spoils. "Under the spacious name of democracy they concocted and passed the Apportionment Bill of the last session, the most aristocratic measure ever attempted to be palmed off on the people."[206]

These attacks upon the Democrats were not in vain: Governor Joseph Vance received 92,204 votes to 86,158 for Eli Baldwin. Notwithstanding this majority of 6,046 for the Whigs in the state election and of 8,720 in the November election, the Democrats, by aid of their apportionment bill, succeeded in winning a majority in the legislature.[207]

The Ohio victory was jubilantly headlined by the Whig papers of the Northwest which urged renewed efforts for the big victory in November. Reams of paper and barrels of ink brought forth a final crescendo of warnings, appeals, and blasts. "To arms, TO ARMS, Whigs of the Union, we cry again TO ARMS. Victory is ours. Ohio speaks, and *Harrison can be our next President.*"[208] Came the cry: Wolves! Wolves! Wolves! . . . Snakes! Snakes! Snakes! Whigs look to your tickets! Democrats are heading tickets with two or three Harrison electors and filling in the rest with Democrats.[209] It is Now or Never! "*Freemen, to the Polls*—march fearlessly to the rescue of your Liberties, before it is FOREVER TOO LATE—Let no man's business keep

---

[205] *Daily Cleveland Herald*, October 7, 1836.
[206] October 6, 1836.
[207] *Huron Reflector* in Chillicothe *Scioto Gazette*, November 30, 1836.
[208] *Daily Cleveland Herald*, October 29, 1836.
[209] Not an uncommon practice when the party printed and gave out the ballots.

him from the polls. What is the small pittance which any man could make on tomorrow, compared to his *Liberties*, and the *free* institutions of his country."[210] There followed eleven arguments against Van Buren and twelve for Harrison.

The presidential election was held in Ohio November 4 and in Indiana and Illinois on November 7. The vote in Ohio was: Harrison 104,958, Van Buren 96,238.[211] Van Buren carried the regularly Democratic counties of the southwestern part (Butler, Hamilton, Clermont, Brown, Adams), most of the counties in the east-central region where Pennsylvania influence was strong, five counties in the south between the Muskingum and Scioto rivers, and seven counties in the north and west. Harrison gained a number of counties which had previously voted for Jackson. The Western Reserve counties gave him a majority of more than 7,000 votes. Noting this last fact the *Cleveland Advertiser* confessed that it was "somewhat grieved at the success, in this quarter, of the imbecile old man, in the soldier's coat, who is the Whig candidate for president."[212]

The voters of Indiana, hero worshipers before they were partisans, gave the General 41,283 to 32,772 for Van Buren.[213] The change from a Democratic victory of almost two to one in 1832 to the Whig victory was remarkable but not hard to explain. The spell of the name of one hero had been broken and that of another had taken its place. The Democrats without Jackson were put on the defensive, in which position they remained in general for two generations.

Illinois was the only state in the Northwest to give Van Buren a majority—18,459 votes to 15,240 for Harrison.[214] It is difficult to determine the Harrison vote for there were both Harrison and Tyler and White and Tyler tickets, as well as a variety of ways of voting. Sometimes the county clerks indicated the intentions of the voters, more often not. Though Harrison had got off to a late start in Illinois, just before the election he was considered the leading candidate against Van Buren. The deter-

[210] *Hamilton Intelligencer*, November 3, 1836. Three weeks later this editor said he understood that Van Buren had been elected: "Well we shall not 'tear our shirts' on the strength of it. We done all in our power, God knows."
[211] *Ohio State Journal* (semiweekly), January 27, 1837; *Ohio Statistics*, 255.
[212] *Cleveland Advertiser* (weekly), November 10, 1836.
[213] *Niles' Weekly Register*, LI, 258 (Dec. 24, 1836).
[214] Pease, *Illinois Election Returns*, 104.

mination to make him the official candidate probably cost the votes of some of the White followers; had the Whigs supported White and got all the anti-Van Buren votes, the outcome might have been similar to that in Ohio and Indiana. As it was, the Whigs depended upon lack of enthusiasm and harmony in the Democratic ranks rather than upon a vigorous campaign.

In Michigan the statehood struggle had almost entirely obscured the presidential election. Although the Whigs tried to show that the Van Burenites were taking Michigan Territory and giving it to Ohio in order to get the latter's electoral vote, the Democrats, organized and operating under New York methods, had the situation well in hand. The Democratic electors received about 7,350 votes (average) to 4,075 for the "Whig or unpledged" electors. If one considers the lack of organization of Michigan Whigs, it appears probable that many voters were unaware of the "Whig ticket"; in nine of twenty-two counties it appears the Whigs cast no votes. The *Advertiser* claimed the ticket was really selected by the Van Buren party.[215] Michigan, admitted almost three months after the election, was permitted to cast her three electoral votes for the record. A fourth state from the Northwest had entered under the Democratic aegis.

The total Whig vote in the Northwest in 1836 was 165,556 compared to 154,819 for the Democrats, and by the electors 30 to 8. The vote of Ohio and Indiana represented in part personal sentiment for Harrison, but this does not explain the majority of Whig votes in state and Congressional elections. The two frontier states of Illinois and Michigan did not possess as yet enough of the class of people who constituted the backbone of the Whig party, and the more popular doctrines and better organization of the Van Buren party still controlled.

The growing political importance of the West did not pass unnoticed. Apropos the fact that Ohio alone cast 82,000 more votes than all New England, the *Cleveland Herald* wrote:

What a subject does this present for the contemplation of the politician. The weight and political influence which the *west* is destined to exert in the Councils of this Country, will shortly be *felt* and *acknowledged*. The

[215] *Detroit Daily Advertiser*, December 1, 1836. *Niles' Weekly Register*, LI, 228 (Dec. 10, 1836), copying *Detroit Free Press* of November 26, gives 7,400 to 4,080.

preponderating influence, as heretofore, will no longer be with the east, the north or the south, but with the great west. Her voice will be heard; and her influence and vote will ere long direct the destinies of this great Republic.[216]

Although Van Buren was elected president, the Northwest had indicated the trend.[217]

Congressmen were elected in Ohio and Illinois. In Ohio the Whigs elected 11 of the 19 representatives.[218] All three of the Democratic candidates were returned in Illinois. In the first district there were two Democrats against one Whig, and their combined vote was 8,993 to 2,370. In the Indiana election held in 1837 clear party distinction in all districts was made for the first time. The Democratic party, which had slipped badly in 1836, now met with disaster. From a unanimous delegation of seven congressmen in the Twenty-fourth Congress, the Democrats were able to return but one.[219] With the representative from Michigan the Democrats of the Northwest had thirteen representatives in the Twenty-fifth Congress to seventeen for the Whigs.

The Ohio legislature on the thirteenth ballot selected William Allen, unsuccessful Democratic candidate for Congress in the seventh district, to fill Thomas Ewing's place in the Senate. The Democrats had in caucus selected Allen over Reuben Wood, Robert Lucas, John M. Goodenow, and Benjamin Tappan. The Whig members of the House, to prevent a two-thirds quorum in joint session, absented themselves from December 8, 1836, to January 18, 1837, when the election finally took place. The furor aroused among Democratic editors over this action had been considerable, and when Allen's election was announced, the *Ohio State Journal* claimed that Ohio, having voted Whig, was not to be represented in the Senate. "Locofocoism," in its most

---

[216] *Daily Cleveland Herald*, November 28, 1836.

[217] The *New York Times* noted that, with queens reigning in England, Spain, and Portugal, it was "truly the era of female rule!" The *Troy Budget* remarked that the coincidence would have been still more singular had Harrison been elected President of the United States. Mineral Point (Wis.) *Miners' Free Press*, September 1, 1837.

[218] *Niles' Weekly Register*, LI, 132 (Oct. 29, 1836).

[219] Ratliff Boon in the second district. "Indiana now commences a new era in Congress. Her delegation will find themselves natural allies of the destructive nullifiers of the South and Bare Bone's puritans of the North." Columbus *Ohio Statesman*, August 29, 1837.

hideous and loathsome shape, had usurped the right to speak. "Will they resign!"[220]

Both sides claimed a majority on joint ballot of the newly elected Indiana legislature but, in the senatorial contest in which Senator Hendricks, Governor Noble, Ratliff Boon, and Oliver H. Smith were all aspirants, Smith was elected. When the Jackson members found it impossible to elect Hendricks or Boon, they threw their votes to Smith in preference to Noble; he was elected on the ninth ballot, the only Whig senator from the Northwest.[221]

§ § § § § §

The Whigs of the Northwest took consolation in the fact that Harrison had made a better showing than had Jackson in his first campaign, and that Van Buren's popularity was only borrowed. The star of hope was above the horizon, and it remained only for the party to persevere in unflinching opposition to the abuses of the administration and to unite upon one candidate in order to achieve success. Almost immediately after the election the *Indiana Journal* posted Harrison's name at the masthead as the people's choice for president in 1840. Before the middle of the summer of 1837 a New York meeting had nominated Webster, the *Lexington Intelligencer* and *Pittsburg Advocate* had nominated Clay, the Ohio Whig convention had shown almost unanimous preference for Harrison,[222] and Van Buren had been renominated by the administration press. So within five months of the inauguration of the new president there were four candidates in the field for the election of 1840.[223]

[220] Columbus *Ohio State Journal* (daily), September 27, 1837.

[221] Democrats: Morris and Allen, of Ohio; Tipton, of Indiana; Robinson and Young, of Illinois; Norvell and Lyon, of Michigan.

[222] Chillicothe *Scioto Gazette*, July 13, 1837; *Cincinnati Chronicle*, July 9, 15, 1837. The Whig State Convention met at Columbus in June with Governor Trimble presiding. General Harrison's name was presented, but it was agreed to abide by the decision of a national convention.

[223] "The great *good of the people* is the leading motive with all these lovers of their country. If she survive the *political doctors*, she may hope to be cured of all other diseases." *Cincinnati Chronicle*, July 15, 1837. The *Circleville Herald*, March 4, 1837, philosophically rejoiced that Van Buren was president; when things were at their worst, any change would be for the better. And the Piqua *Courier and Enquirer*, August 19, 1837, said that as between Martin Van Buren and Andrew Jackson it was a matter of Tweedledum and Tweedledee: Tweedledum was Martin Van Buren carrying out the measures of Andrew Jackson; Tweedledee was the measures of Andrew Jackson carrying out Martin Van Buren.

The panic of 1837 brought the administration around to the subtreasury plan, and the one big topic of discussion was the subject of banking. The issue had been found on which Whigs and Democrats could draw the line. Except in Illinois the Democrats of the Northwest accepted Van Buren and his policies, and even in that state they were forced into line.[224] To the Democrats the question resolved itself into this: Shall we have a BANK GOVERNMENT, or a GOVERNMENT OF THE PEOPLE?[225] In their minds the state of financial embarrassment of the country was not the result of acts of the General Government but of over-trading and speculation. The doctrine of a National Bank to regulate the currency was the height of absurdity. The only safe means of regulating the currency was by a divorcement of Bank and State. Gold and silver were the natural currency of the world and all other must be based upon them.[226] "The power and vengeance of mercenary monopolies are upon you—the iron grasp of pandulent and irresponsible shavers must be broken."[227]

[224] Senators Young and Robinson favored the subtreasury. The three congressmen, Casey, May, and Snyder, were among the twelve Jackson Democrats in the House who voted to table the bill. *Illinois State Register and People's Advocate*, November 4, 1837. The *Register* said it was up to the people to inform and instruct their representatives before their return to Congress. See also *ibid.*, November 10.

[225] "Where is the Constitutional currency?" asked the Whig. "Locked up in the Whig banks," replied the Democrat. The poor man gives a personal note for bed or cow, is unable to pay, and is visited with all the rigor of the law. Bankers with millions of gold and silver point sneeringly to legislative enactment and laugh to scorn all efforts to compel payment. Is this Equality?—think of these things—. The *Bank* aristocracy are in the field resolved to triumph over you if money and deception can effect it. Remember, too, that power is always stealing from the many to the few, and that the *moneyed aristocracy* of the country are making bold efforts to obtain a controlling influence in this nation. "Freemen of Ohio: You are now called upon by every tie that binds you to your country—by your love for your families—your homes and our altars, and LIBERTY itself, to rally regardless of former political differences in opposition to the RAG BARONS of the nation who are forging chains to fetter your now free and manly limbs. Rouse ye, rouse ye." Letter in the Columbus *Ohio Statesman*, September 20, 1837.

[226] The Democrats could hardly find words to express their indignation at the conduct of the banks in refusing to pay specie to the holders of notes. They regarded the suspension of specie payment as a fraud on the community which should be punishable by law, and said that the banding of capitalists together with corporate and exclusive privileges was enabling the few to live on the industry of the many. "We believe that the great struggle of the bank party to procure the charter of a national bank is to secure to them political power, and sap the foundation of our liberties, and to secure to them the privileges of chartered monopolists, which are not warranted by the constitution." From Resolution of Democratic meeting at Bellefontaine, Ohio, September 2, 1837. Columbus *Ohio Statesman*, September 20, 1837.

[227] *Ibid.*, October 4, 1837. The columns of the *Cleveland Weekly Advertiser* were filled with antibank material: "Monopolies against the People," "Shin Plasters," "Beggars and Bankers," "The Bank Party," etc. See also Chapter XII.

In spite of such arguments the voters of Ohio returned a Whig majority to the legislature in the election of 1837.[228] Governor Vance said to the legislature, "That the people are ready to abandon the credit system by prostrating the banks and establishing what has been called a hard moneyed government, I do not believe. Such a revolution in the business of the country would be too oppressive on all classes of society. . . ."[229] As for internal improvements, the immediate expenditure of any large amounts should not be made until the works built began to yield something like interest on the investment.

Governor Duncan stated the views of the Whigs in his message to the extra session of the Illinois legislature in July when he said,

At the time the President of the United States assumed the responsibility of ordering the public money to be removed from their legal deposit in the Bank of the United States . . . there never was a sounder currency, or a more healthy state of things in any government in the world. . . . Before the public were aware of the ruin which this wild scheme portended, the Executive and a portion of his party seeing their error it would seem, endeavored to escape the consequence by amusing the people with the absurd and impractical project of an exclusive hard money currency. . . . There must be change, there must be reform.[230]

The Ohio Democrats nominated Wilson Shannon for governor on January 8, 1838, approved the doctrines contained in the Virginia Resolutions of 1798, and denied the charges of their opponents that they wished to destroy the established institutions of the state; they insisted only that the late suspension of specie payment by the banks was equivalent to a forfeiture of their charters. Shannon's party was not so dispirited as the Democracy in Indiana, and under the leadership of Samuel Medary, the very able editor of the Columbus *Ohio Statesman*, kept up a running

[228] Among the toasts at a Whig banquet in Cleveland were: The Constitution—the Sovereign People are interpreting it as they understand it; Henry Clay—his name is a guarantee of energy, wisdom and patriotism; Daniel Webster—one country, one constitution, one destiny; William Henry Harrison—the accomplished scholar, the able soldier, the honest man; Ohio—as fruitful in Whig principles as she is exhaustless in natural resources; the Bank of the United States—when wise legislators devise something better the people will accept it; Martin Van Buren—last in war, last in peace, and last in the hearts of his countrymen; the Treasury humbug—corn for the rich and cobs for the poor. *Cleveland Herald* in Columbus *Ohio State Journal*, November 22, 1837.
[229] *Ohio Statesman*, December 30, 1837.
[230] Quoted in Thompson, *The Illinois Whigs*, 58.

fire of attack upon the Whigs. When some of the Whig papers suggested that they should form an *American* party, he said it was a hopeful sign surely, for the Whig party had always been British heretofore; British in the Revolution, blue-light Federalist in 1814, and for Biddle's British Bank.[231] Of the Whig legislature nothing fair could be said. "If there ever was such a tyrannical federal crew as now disgrace the halls of legislation in the State of Ohio, we know nothing of the history of federalism."[232] By strict party vote the legislature defeated a resolution for an investigation of whether the banks had violated their charters; also an amendment to the *quo warranto* bill which provided that the property of stockholders be held liable when judgment was rendered against a bank.[233] On the other hand the Democrats played to the German vote by seeking to eliminate the "in the English language" clause from the common school bill. When the legislature adjourned on March 19, the *Statesman* said in summary, "The whole journals . . . are speckled with 'Yankee notions' which were crudely concocted and advocated without any apparent honest or settled principle. . . ." and proudly pointed to the fact that this Whig legislature had passed only 391 bills while its Democratic predecessor had passed 482. The *Statesman*, which carried at its masthead the motto, "a light and simple government," saw no irony in this logic.

Governor Joseph Vance was renominated by the Whigs and by summer a very lively state campaign was on. Vance said the banks were solvent; Shannon questioned it. "No executive has so debased himself, his State, and his country in acting the mere lick spittle for Bank frauds as Governor Vance. His whole soul is wrapped up in an irredeemable fraudulent shinplaster currency."[234] The sole question was, shall we have a government

---

[231] Columbus *Ohio Statesman*, July 5, 1837.

[232] *Elyria Republican* in *Ohio Statesman*, February 20, 1838.

[233] The vote on the first resolution was 37 Whigs to 31 Democrats. *Ohio Statesman*, February 20, 1838. On the second it was 35 Whigs to 32 Democrats. *Ibid.* The Democratic papers ran the names of the Whigs who so voted in little black-bordered boxes for some time afterward.

[234] *Ohio Statesman*, May 23, 1838. Medary could mix serious criticism with "horse play" very effectively. He claimed no Democrat could do business on the canals but at the risk of peace and fortune. Charles Hammond, Governor Vance, and "Solitude" Ewing, *et al.*, besides speculating, made it dangerous. When a party of Democrats started to the Newark convention, they had the water let out on them and were delayed fifteen hours. "This displays the true and dastardly spirit of federal bluelightism. Democrats of Ohio! brave and noble freemen as you are, will you rest one moment idle, and at your homes, and suffer such daring,

of the banks or of the people, a moneyed aristocracy or a free constitution. The Whig state committee circular which assigned county quotas for campaign funds was played up as a vast monument of corruption, bribery, and unparalleled effrontery.[235]

The Whigs refused to accept the title of Federalists or aristocrats.[236] If anyone deserved the title it was the Vanocracy, such men as Buchanan, of Pennsylvania, who "thanked his God that there wasn't a drop of Democratic blood in his veins," or Ingersoll who wrote that if he had lived in the time of the Revolution he would have been a Tory. The great majority of the Whig party were workingmen who did not own or borrow from banks, yet believed in banks properly conducted.[237] They believed that the prosperity of the country depended upon a sound currency and had no faith in a party which in the past ten years had created fifty millions of state-bank capital, twenty millions of treasury notes, and flooded the country with paper money.[238] They wore neither ruffled shirt, silk gloves, nor silk stockings.

Besides attacks upon Van Buren, "The Great Overrated," and the "Van-Jack press," the Whigs sought to transfer the

---

contemptible and infamous despotism to be established over you! No, we know you will not be caught idle before, or at home on the day of election. In Captain Lindsey [captain of the canal boat] the federal despots find a foeman worthy of his sires. Sons of liberty in Ohio, shall they not find equal bone and sinew in you on the day of trial? *yes!* YES!! *YES!!!* will respond from every part of the State." Copied in *Cincinnati Daily Gazette,* September 21, 1838.

[235] *Ohio Statesman,* August 21, 1838. The chief points of the negative Democratic platform were:
No fifty million monster of a Federal bank.
No oppressing the poor to give privileges to the rich.
No combination of Bank and State.
No lending of our taxes to banks and their dependent speculation.
No emptying the pockets of the sunburned farmer to fill the vaults of the shade-covered banker.
"It has been specie for the Banks and rags for the people about long enough. If we mistake not the signs of the times, it will be specie for the people and rags for the Banks before another year." *Ibid.,* April 4, August 29, 1838.

[236] Except Hammond of the *Gazette,* who said he was and was proud of it. *Cincinnati Daily Gazette,* November 29, 1837. The Xenia (Ohio) *Greene County Torch-light,* December 13, 1838, said that the old Federalist party had advocated enlargement of the powers of the executive, which is just what the so-called Democrats stand for; the independent treasury plan which they were pushing would do more to bring the nation into subjection to British money than any other ever before attempted.

[237] *Greene County Torch-light,* September 14, 1838.

[238] From Resolutions of Young Men's Whig Convention, Mount Vernon, September 20, 1838. *Ibid.,* September 29, 1838. "The office holders shout 'Reform the Banks.' The people shout back 'Reform the Office holders.'" The Whigs will help reform them out of their present state. How could the Irish and Germans vote for the "Loco Foco Ticket" when the Locos say any number of Irish votes could be bought for a quart of whiskey. *Ohio State Journal,* July 31, September 28, 1838.

petticoat charge (which had circulated on Harrison) to Senator "Petticoat Bill Allen." They hinted that Allen had received so many petticoats as presents that, had he been the Grand Turk with a harem of five hundred, he could still supply the whole establishment with "unthinkables" without the cost of a dollar.[239] When the Democrats sought to line up the German vote against their enemies, "The Whigs and Native Americans," the *Gazette* said that if the Germans did not know who their friends were, they would be like the frozen snake which, taken in the house and warmed out, rewarded the good deed by biting the children. And farmers working hard in their fields should remember that, while they were drinking out of the old oaken bucket, Democratic officeholders were lying in the shade and drinking *iced* champagne—paid for out of the treasury and the farmers' hard toil.[240]

The October election gave Shannon 107,884 votes to 102,146 for Vance.[241] Eleven Democrats and eight Whigs were returned to Congress.[242] The Democrats elected 13 of 19 new state senators and 38 representatives to 34 for the Whigs, which gave the former a majority of 6 on joint ballot.[243] In December the legislature elected Judge Benjamin Tappan to take the seat of Thomas Morris in the United States Senate; Morris' abolition leanings were not acceptable to his party.

The Whigs saw no other way of accounting for the defeat but by accusing the abolition and state-rights men of throwing them over, and blaming the withdrawal of Harrison's name for losing the votes of Jackson men, who could not support Clay or

[239] *Louisville Journal* in *Cincinnati Daily Gazette*, September 21, 1838. (The *Gazette*, November 10, 1837, in a complete history of the petticoat yarn, had exonerated Allen from inventing it.)

[240] *Hamilton Intelligencer*, July 26, 1838. Already at this early date the *Intelligencer* carried at its masthead the names of Harrison and Vance for president and vice-president in 1840. It argued for an early start.

Among the other Whig papers which took an active part in the campaign of 1838 were the *Circleville Herald, Cincinnati Whig, Cleveland Intelligencer, Dayton Journal, Scioto Gazette, Springfield Pioneer,* and *Wooster Journal.*

[241] *Ohio Statistics*, 255. Official vote by counties in *Ohio Statesman*, December 11, 1838, gives Vance 102,156.

[242] Democrats in first, second, fifth, ninth, eleventh, twelfth, thirteenth, fourteenth, seventeenth, eighteenth, and nineteenth. For Congressional returns by counties see *Ohio Statesman*, December 18, 1838. Among the counties polling the heaviest Whig vote were Ashtabula, Champaign, Clark, Cuyahoga, Franklin, Muskingum, Ross, and Warren.

[243] *Ohio Statesman*, October 31, 1838.

Webster.[244] The more optimistic thought the effect would be salutary in that it would destroy overconfidence and influence the nomination for the Presidency. The Democrats were satisfied that the result would be good if both Whigs and Abolitionists were convinced that the two would not work together in politics. When, as a result of the election for the legislature in 1839, Whigs were outnumbered two to one in both houses, a state of gloom permeated the Whig press.[245]

The Democracy of Indiana was so dispirited by the loss of the state in 1836 that they found it impossible to get a candidate for the governorship the following year; after trying three different prospects and receiving refusals in each instance, they finally gave up. When the Whig Lieutenant Governor David Wallace, one of the most popular leaders in the state, announced his candidacy on a platform of extensive internal improvements, his only opponent was John Dumont, also a Whig. Dumont stood for classification—building the most-needed works first—while Wallace was for simultaneous construction of the whole works. Wallace was elected by 45,240 to 36,197 votes.[246] Six of the seven congressmen elected were Whigs and the legislature was decidedly Whig.[247]

The Whig state convention of 1838 nominated delegates to the national convention and instructed them to vote for Harrison but pledged support to Clay if he were nominated.[248] The Van Buren convention discussed the bank question, denounced the Whigs as Federalists, and praised Jackson and Van Buren. The next year the Democrats elected three congressmen to four for the Whigs.[249] So violent had the newspaper discussion become that W. W. Wick, the successful Democratic candidate in the

[244] Xenia Green County Torchlight, October 20, 1838; Ohio Statesman, October 30, 1838.

[245] Ohio State Journal, October 22, 1839. The Cleveland Herald and Gazette (weekly), August 28, had stated that the Whigs were altogether too independent as a party to be successful with their present mode of warfare against such an enemy as they had to contend with. Stronger organization, a strong boss, were needed.

[246] Indiana House Journal, 1837–38, pp. 28–29.

[247] Senate: Whigs, 29, Democrats, 18; House: Whigs, 60, Democrats, 36, others, 4. Logansport Telegraph, September 1, 1838.

[248] See Indianapolis Indiana Journal, January 23, 26, 1838, for the proceedings.

[249] Returns by counties are in the Logansport Telegraph, September 14, 1839.

The first Congressional district convention in Indiana was held at Bloomfield in the second district, March 18, 1839; delegates were present from each county. Leonard, "Personal Politics in Indiana," in Indiana Magazine of History, XIX, 275.

seventh district, requested that no newspaper support his candidacy.[250] Little attention was paid to the candidates' views on
slavery; all candidates denied any connection with abolitionism.
The legislature elected in 1839 had a Whig majority of one in the
Senate but the Democrats controlled the House. It was one
of the most helpless and useless assemblies ever convened in the
state. Aside from accumulating a mass of reports on internal
improvements and disrupted state finances, it accomplished nothing. Petitions were presented for a speedy adjournment; when it
finally came the *Indiana Journal* wrote: "This body after a
stormy, protracted session of eighty-five days has at last adjourned, and may heaven for all time save us from such another."[251] The worst stage of the depression did not strike the
state until after the elections of 1839, but when it came the legislature was as helpless as the people to cope with the situation.

The Illinois Whigs had not yet consolidated into a coherent
party by 1838, nor had they achieved real party organization or
come round to the convention system.[252] Clear-cut principles were
still lacking, but in general they believed that the legislative
power was above the executive, "went for" a United States bank
and tariff, and were somewhat prejudiced against the foreigners
and Roman Catholics, many of whom were working on the
canals and affiliating with the Democratic party.[253]

Illinois Democrats were divided on the financial policies of the

[250] *Logansport Telegraph*, June 8, 1839. The *Hickory Club*, a Democratic campaign paper published at New Albany, charged that George H. Proffit, Whig
candidate in the first district, had kicked the Bible out of his house and administered the Lord's Supper with buttermilk. Proffit was also under the shadow for
bedecking himself in finery unbecoming a "sarvint of the people." He was elected,
however.

[251] Indianapolis *Indiana Journal*, February 26, 1840.

[252] The Springfield *Sangamo Journal*, which in 1836 had derided "caucuses,"
conventions, and "chains," was asked by the *Chicago American* for its opinion
regarding a Whig state convention for 1838. The *Journal* hedged somewhat by
stating that it favored "meetings of the people," not knots of politicians, but was
lukewarm toward the idea. December 9, 1837.

[253] "We are satisfied that Loco Focoism cannot succeed in our State. The liberal
and intelligent portion of the Van Buren party can never sustain its doctrines. We
could point, if we chose, to a vast number of Van Buren men, who, while they
regret the course Mr. Van Buren has taken, cannot, will not, further follow
him in sustaining principles which they believe to be hostile to the best interests
of the country. . . . Mr. Van Buren has lost the confidence of a great portion of
the party. They know that every promise which has been made to them has been
broken. They yielded their opinion in the war against the U. S. Bank, because
they had confidence that the administration would furnish them with a 'better
currency.' And although they were apprehensive that the hundreds of new banks
which were established to carry out the views of the administration, and by its
recommendation, they still were disposed to give the administration experiment
a fair trial. It has had its trial; and it HAS FAILED. All the pledges—all the

Jackson–Van Buren administrations as well as upon factional lines. Although the "locofocos" controlled most of the Democratic papers, it was impossible for them to read out of the party such "conservatives" as Zadoc Casey and William L. May, who had opposed some of the administration measures. The Whigs, however, were unable to take advantage of the dissension in the ranks of their opponents, for with the convention system, even in the face of an embarrassing situation, the Democrats were able to maintain a front and pull through.

In 1838 the Democrats nominated James W. Stephenson, of Jo Daviess County, in the extreme northwestern part of the state. (The Whigs maintained that the convention had to pass up the party's best men—John Reynolds, William C. Kinney, Zadoc Casey, and A. W. Snyder—because of fear regarding their orthodoxy.) When it was discovered that Stephenson was a defaulter to the United States government in the amount of $40,000 to $74,000, the people decided he would be too heavy a burden to bear. A hastily summoned skeleton convention nominated Thomas Carlin, an honest but ignorant man, to take his place.[254] The Whig candidate was Cyrus Edwards, a brother of Governor Ninian Edwards. The Democrats tried to show that the Whigs were opposed to internal improvements.[255] Edwards

---

promises of the government have passed away like the morning dew, and instead of having a currency, such as existed eight years ago, and which was as good as desired, and the best in the world,—we have now a miserable shin plaster currency—from the paper of the Treasury down to the cent notes of corporations." Springfield *Sangamo Journal*, January 27, 1838.

[254] May's *Backwoodsman* (published at Grafton) led the attack against Stephenson. Some of the Democratic papers defended their candidate but, as it became an impossible task, they dropped his name one by one. The Whig papers enjoyed the situation immensely. The *Quincy Whig*, May 12, 1838, advertised: "Wanted Immediately, in the State of Illinois, a candidate for the office of Governor . . ."; qualifications specified were: must be well recommended as a Van Buren, Locofoco, Sub-Treasury Man.

The second Democratic convention in its resolutions proclaimed that the party principles were founded on truth and justice, and were the only ones to promote human happiness, the cause of intelligence and morality, to extend moral culture, and remove all inequalities in human conditions. *Alton Spectator*, June 14, 1838.

[255] This issue further confused the political scene in Illinois where the incidence of the state internal improvements program seemed to catch up with the voters sooner than in Indiana. The Democratic Vandalia *Illinois State Register and People's Advocate*, March 6, 25, 1837, sought to show that the Whigs had opposed the bill; the *Sangamo Journal* argued otherwise. February 9, 1838, the *Register* was backtracking from its claims. The Democratic Springfield *Illinois Republican* was for the system in August, 1838, against it by May, 1839. By early 1839 Democratic papers were alternately blowing hot and cold on internal improvements. The *Chicago Democrat*, July 15, asked whether Illinois was going to follow up the insane program. When Democratic papers tried to hand the foundling to the Whigs, the latter ducked.

had the support of Whigs and White Democrats, but because of his activity in the Lovejoy disturbances failed to get the votes of those inclined toward abolitionism. The Democrats elected Carlin by 30,648 to 29,722 votes, two of three members of Congress, and the majority of the General Assembly.[256] The votes of those working on the state public-works contracts were probably enough to account for Carlin's victory.[257] From this point on the Illinois Whigs, although still uncertain of a name, were a political party rather than a group of factions in opposition.[258]

Early Michigan state politics were almost as badly confused as were Illinois politics. In addition to the existing Democratic factions—the "officeholders" and the conservatives (or the "central junto" and the "malcontents")—a western group, and by 1838, an offshoot of the Norvell following which was opposed to chartered banks, monopolies, and slavery, were becoming distinguishable. The Whig leaders were also dividing into factions, one led by Detroit politicians (called by their opponents the "Canandaigua Clique") and the other, not so active politically, led largely by well-to-do landowners and businessmen. The Whigs, almost a hopeless minority in 1836, made important gains in the next three years. They were aided in part by the big internal improvements program launched by the Democratic legislature of 1837, which included three railroads, three canals, and three rivers. The Whigs, steadied by the influence of the better-to-do businessmen, thought completion of the central railroad only sufficient at the time.[259]

In 1837 the "officeholders" supported Mason and Mundy for

[256] Pease, *Illinois Election Returns*, 107 ff.; Thompson, *The Illinois Whigs*, 60.

[257] "It is humiliating to reflect, that the political destiny of this large State, are controlled by a transient population of about 3,000 voters. But such is the fact." *Quincy Whig*, September 1, 1838.

The *Sangamo Journal*, September 15, 1838, classified the legislators as Republicans (Whigs), Van Buren men, and Conservatives; it claimed a majority for the first. Some support is given this estimate by the fact that when the legislature met, Lincoln, Baker, and other Whig leaders maneuvered through both houses resolutions which condemned the Independent Treasury—metallic currency system. This action was condemned by Democratic papers, which called the Democrats who so voted base hypocrites.

[258] In December, 1839, when the state convention published its seven-column "Address of the Democratic-Republican Convention to the People of Illinois," the Democratic *State Register*, December 18, wrote: "Our opponents have alternately ranged themselves under the names of 'Federalists,' 'Federal Republicans,' 'Peace Party,' 'National-Republicans,' 'Anti-Masons,' 'Democratic Whigs,' 'Whigs,' and 'Conservatives.' If they cannot change things, they can easily change names."

[259] *Detroit Daily Advertiser*, February 4, 20, March 20, 1837.

governor and lieutenant governor, while the "malcontents" backed E. D. Ellis and John Biddle. Both factions were pro-Van Buren. On August 2, the Whig convention at Ann Arbor nominated Charles C. Trowbridge for governor and resolved in favor of the restoration of a sound currency. The *Detroit Daily Advertiser* conducted a vigorous campaign against the Democrats whom it referred to as "Tories." "Banks, Office-Holders, Tories, Frauds" were the explanation for Michigan's "rotten politics"; the Tories chartered the banks, they ran them. Yet despite the *Advertiser's* emphasis on the fact that the French inhabitants, though voted by the Democrats, were "unnaturalized foreigners," at the same time it proclaimed that "the Tories are against Catholics."[260] It said that the "Junto," though it had taxed the state $30,000 for the Toledo War and $4,000 for an illegal convention, had nevertheless treacherously surrendered Michigan land; furthermore, it had allowed Mason $500 for rent and $58 for "stationary" at groggeries.[261]

In the November election Mason was elected by a few hundred votes,[262] but Trowbridge's 14,800 (or 14,546) votes stood in marked contrast to the 814 cast for Biddle two years earlier.[263] The period of financial uncertainty had brought many of the more prosperous Democrats over into the Whig ranks, and others already with Whig inclinations began to take a more active part in elections.

In the Detroit city election in the spring of 1838 the Whigs won by a slight margin. "Detroit is herself! Locofocoism is gone," said the *Advertiser*.[264] During the summer and autumn Detroit papers printed politics almost to the exclusion of all other news. In the Congressional election Crary defeated Hezekiah G. Wells, his Whig opponent, by 261 votes.

[260] July 21, August 22, October 25, 1837.
[261] *Ibid.*, October 31, 1837.
[262] *Ibid.*, December 14, 1837, listed the "official returns" at 14,800 to 15,415, a difference of 615, but five days later amended the difference to 259. The *Michigan Official Directory and Legislative Manual*, 1913, p. 422, lists the difference as 768 votes.
[263] The Democrats carried most of the southern tier of counties and the Grand River Valley, while the Whigs were strongest in the central tier and the Saginaw Valley, where there were strong commercial interests, and Wayne County, which the Democrats said was the seat of aristocracy and vested interests. *Detroit Free Press*, November 14, 1837. The vote is mapped by counties in Floyd B. Streeter, *Political Parties in Michigan, 1837–1860* (Michigan Historical Commission, Lansing, 1918), 11.
[264] April 4, 1838.

In 1839 the Whigs went to work in earnest. Their candidate for governor was Judge William Woodbridge, while the Democrats after a factional fight had nominated the conservative Elon Farnsworth. Woodbridge polled 18,195 votes to 17,037 for his opponent[265] and a Whig legislature was chosen.[266] When the Detroit Whigs held a big "flare up" in celebration, their opponents considered it a bank celebration and said all were happy because they would have to pay no debts of their own contracting.[267] Some thought the Democratic defeat was the price paid for the creation of so many state banks in the preceding legislature, and too much Democratic speculation, but the demand for the general banking law had not been partisan, and it had passed with only three dissenting votes.[268]

Although Wisconsin Territory would play no part in the presidential election of 1840, political parties were forming in anticipation of statehood. As usual, what agitation there was for early statehood came largely from the politicians who looked forward to the additional offices. The *Milwaukee Advertiser* had complained bitterly of the state of territorial vassalage and stated that, unless Congress awakened to the needs of the Territory, immediate statehood would be demanded.[269] Others, however, pointed out how well off the Territory was, with the United States paying all the expenses, and only the politicians complaining.[270] National politics received relatively little attention in the newspapers; the lengthy discussions were confined to territorial and local affairs. Some leaders were apparently afraid to indicate their political sentiments for fear of being on the wrong side when statehood came; consequently, party names were seldom used. Since the New England migration had not set in heavily yet, the majority of the people and politicians—especially in the southwestern part of the Territory—were Jacksonian Democrats. Besides the usual personal followings, the main political maneuvering was between the James Duane Doty-

---

[265] *Michigan Official Directory and Legislative Manual*, 1913, p. 422; the *Niles Intelligencer*, January 15, 1840, gives the official vote as 19,030 to 17,782.
[266] Senate: Whigs 10, Democrats 7; House: Whigs 34, Democrats 18. *Niles Intelligencer*, November 20, 1839.
[267] *Ibid.*, December 4, 1839.
[268] *Chicago Democrat* in *ibid.*, December 18, 1839. "It is better to see the Whigs carrying out their own sentiments than to see Democrats carrying them out."
[269] Quoted in *Detroit Daily Advertiser*, May 11, 1838.
[270] "Caution," in *Wisconsin Democrat*, March 24, 1840; *Wisconsin Enquirer*, May 27, 1840.

Milwaukee Sentinel crowd and the Byron Kilbourn–*Milwaukee Advertiser*–canal group; there was also a Dodge following.

The *Wisconsin Enquirer*, though "good Democrats," did not see the use of emphasizing party divisions;[271] the *Milwaukee Advertiser* in general agreed. The *Miners' Free Press* on the other hand favored organizing. In the endeavor of politicians to get parties lined up, two "conventions" met at Madison June 18–19 to nominate a candidate for territorial delegate. One group nominated James D. Doty, and accused the other group, which declared itself the "Democratic" convention, of being a "ridiculous assemblage of Whigs and administration men . . . calculated to excite the highest disgust and contempt of every party man."[272] The latter group nominated Byron Kilbourn; a third candidate, Thomas P. Burnett, also entered the contest. The Madison-Doty-*Enquirer-Sentinel* faction accused the enemies of Judge Doty of plotting to divide the vote by naming Kilbourn, "whose politics at best . . . [were] extremely doubtful." The same words, in view of the sectional and personal crosscurrents, would well have applied to all groups. In the election Doty received 2,125 votes to 1,158 for Kilbourn and 861 for Burnett.[273] Not until two years later did Whigs and Democrats establish party lines and organizations.

With an even chance for victory in Ohio, Indiana, and Michigan, the Whigs of the Northwest eagerly awaited the presidential campaign of 1840. Their papers had nailed the colors of General Harrison to the mast and under the motto, "Uncompromising Hostility to the Reelection of Martin Van Buren," got ready for action.[274] In December, 1839, influenced largely by the voice of the Northwest, the Whig National Convention at Harrisburg again nominated Harrison as the choice of the party.[275] No platform was adopted and press and stump oratory were unrestricted by written promises.

---

[271] May 11, 1839.

[272] *Wisconsin Democrat*, June 25, 1839.

[273] *Wisconsin Enquirer*, September 21; *Wisconsin Democrat*, October 1, 1839.

[274] Motto of the *Richmond* (Ind.) *Palladium*, 1836–40.

[275] "The Blue-light-federal-high tariff-nullification-states rights-abolition-proslavery-consolidation-national-republican-national bank-native-citizen-Irishmen's friend-internal improvement-paper-currency-general credit system-anti-Masonic-Whig National Convention nominated William Harrison of Ohio as their candidate for president and John Tyler of Virginia for vice president. We are very much pleased with the nomination. Our only fear was that the noble and heroic Scott would be brought forward by the opposition, in which case the reelection of Martin Van Buren would have been closely contested, and not as it will be now, a mere matter of

The campaign of 1840 was probably one of the most colorful, as well as one of the bitterest, political battles ever staged in the Northwest. It began as a movement against Van Burenism but developed into a frenzy of hero worship, social jollification, and idealization of the virtues of pioneer days. Newspapers had never been so prolific of interesting political articles, stump orators never quite so entrancing, nor had audiences possessed quite so much endurance. Most newspapers practically gave over all space usually devoted to commerce, settlements, and foreign and domestic events to solid pages of political harangue. Headlines startled the unaccustomed eyes of readers; woodcut cartoons broke the solid type. For the first time special campaign newspapers were printed in numbers;[276] handbills were scattered in profusion, and the talents of the poet and songmaster were recruited for all occasions. Tippecanoe clubs with the log-cabin raisings and free service, barbecues, torchlight processions, floats, transparencies, orgies of protracted spellbinding, and the inevitable barrel of cider and proudly displayed coonskin ceased almost to be a means and became an end in themselves.[277] Well might the Democrats regard their opponents as madmen.

The campaign was fought along the usual lines, but more

---

form. But 'whom the Gods would destroy, they first make mad.'" In the last canvass Harrison had been called "Old Woman," "the petticoat candidate," "the granny of Ohio," and the opinion was confirmed by a very respectable majority. If the wisdom and patriotism and talents of which the Harrisburg convention boasted could bring forth nothing better than a petticoat, "they might have given us a young petticoat, not an old greasy flannel garment. With a fine, fresh, tall, beautiful, engaging, ripe young woman as a candidate for President, we could have raised the very devil with Van Buren at the polls, and no doubt elected by acclamation, such a fair young Presidentess for this glorious land. But what on earth can we do with an 'old woman,' but supply her with snuff and see her buried decently? Mrs. Harrison of Ohio is undoubtedly a very excellent matron in her line, but if we must take a woman for next president, let's have youth and beauty, and not age and imbecility." *Niles Intelligencer,* December 25, 1839.

[276] Among the several dozen campaign sheets were the Newark (Ohio) *Democratic Rasp*; Canton (Ohio) *Hickory Club*; the *Plow Boy* (issued by the *Cadiz Sentinel*); *Straight Out Harrisonian* (from the *Ohio State Journal* press); *Expurger* and the *Constitution* (Van Buren) of Indianapolis; Jeffersonville (Ind.) *Ball of '40*; the *Kinderhook Dutchman*; the *Little Magician*; the *Spirit of '76* from the *Indiana Journal* press (Whig); *Old Hickory* (Springfield, Ill.); *Old Soldier* (Springfield, Ill.). These campaign papers, published for three to six months, were extra-subscription getters for established papers; new campaign papers, if their party won, might become regular papers.

[277] In Detroit, April 21, a 40-by-50-foot cabin was dedicated. The ladies provided hoecakes, pumpkin pie, parched corn, venison, bear's meat, apple sauce, etc., in quantities. Hundreds visited it, a procession was held, banners carried, and the cry was "Harrison, Tyler and the Constitution." *Detroit Daily Advertiser,* April 24, 1840.

intensely. There was the usual appeal to the "common man" against the "artistocrats"; to the prejudices against "office-holders"; to group, sectional, and personal prejudices; to the frontiersman's admiration of the honest, substantial virtues of the military hero as contrasted to the wily arts of the politician. But behind the externals of "hoopla" and "humbuggery" ran a constant and serious discussion of government policy on money and banking so often overlooked; in few elections in our history have monetary affairs received a more thorough treatment and probably in none did voters in general ever have a better understanding of the basic facts and conditions.

Whatever the reasons which influenced the National Whig Convention against a definite declaration of policy, there was no lack of platforms among the Whigs of the Northwest. The Illinois state convention of October 7–9, 1839, which seems to have included representatives of all the elements in opposition to Van Buren, bitterly denounced the subtreasury system, attacked Van Buren as "an artful politician and a selfish experimenter," reaffirmed the Whig doctrines of Webster and Clay, and repudiated the state banking system then in existence.[278] The Michigan convention resolved that the treasury bill was unconstitutional, warned against the reduction of wages that would result, and against removal of protection. The Ohio Whig convention declared against the executive usurpation of powers, the mercenary, corrupt, and despotic spoils system, the appointment of congressmen to presidential offices, and the retention of known defaulters in Federal jobs.[279] The Whig papers declared that their candidate stood publicly committed before the nation on the question of public lands, Indian policy, the tariff, the Bank of the United States, distribution of land proceeds, internal improvements, veto power, one-term presidential tenure, extent of executive powers, removals, abolitionism, nullification, and the subtreasury.[280] The party merely desired that the popular will should reign supreme in the legislation of the country and to preserve the dignity and integrity of the chief executive by limiting him to one term; that honest and capable men should be appointed to office and the veto limited to cases of constitutional doubt; that the

[278] Springfield *Sangamo Journal*, October 9, 1839.
[279] Xenia *Greene County Torch-light*, March 5, 1840.
[280] From the *Cincinnati Republican* in *Detroit Daily Advertiser*, July 17, 1840.

powers of the executive should be restrained, government expenses reduced, and the proceeds of the public land sales be appropriated to education and internal improvement; that the purity of the elective franchise be maintained at all costs and a sound currency restored.

In the minds of the Democrats there certainly was no lack of definiteness about Whig principles: Whigs were Federalists, the same gang as John Adams, Fisher Ames and company—condemned out of their own mouths: "Free suffrage is a curse to any people"; "It is a fundamental mistake that the people may be governed, or will govern themselves by Reason"; "Let the government take care of the rich and the rich will take care of the poor"; "The representative should not be trammeled by the will of his constituents"; "Our Federal Republic was obviously founded on a mistake; on the supposed existence of sufficient political virtue in the people, and on the permanency and authority of the public morals"; "Democracy is an illuminated Hell."

They said that the Whigs were opposed to universal suffrage and in favor of property and tax qualifications; that they opposed the naturalization of foreigners and the doctrine of instruction to representatives; that they favored legislating for property and not for men; that they were opposed to gold and silver as a currency and were afraid to avow their real principles, that is, legalizing the suspension of all broken banks and the perpetuation of an irredeemable currency. When Whigs were asked what were General Harrison's views on a Bank of the United States, the reply would be, "Great Harrison, he is the man to lead the sons of freedom on"; a question regarding his views on a protective tariff would bring forth: "While the little Mat the spoils is grabbin, the hero lives in his log cabin." Admittedly music and hard cider had a wonderful influence on the passions and actions of the human species, but such things only interested the illiterate and ignorant, obscured the issues and deceived the people.[281]

[281] "Come on up then, all ye Brutes of Creation and drink a little hard cider. Buzzards and coons, owls and asses, must all be charmed into the support of Old Tip." Columbus *Ohio Statesman* (semiweekly), June 23, 1840. "But democracy comes not eating and drinking. It asks no escorts nor serenades. It moves with the power and majesty of the people. The whigs are strong in money and the democrats strong in votes. In magnificent parades the democrats can no more compete with the whigs than the whigs can them at the polls." *Chicago Democrat*, May 20, 1840.

The "bank aristocracy," treasonably allied with the bankers of Europe, furnished funds for great doings but, if necessity arose to defend the honor of the country in time of war, they would fade away. Since the people were not fit to govern themselves, power must be taken from them; force, cannon, bloodshed, imprisonment, and death were to be used to shut the mouths of freemen in a land of liberty yet warm with the blood of revolution. Such, according to the Democrats, was the Whig or "Tory" doctrine.

On the other hand, in striking contrast to "Blue-Light Federalism" and political tomfoolery, stood the time-tested doctrines of Thomas Jefferson: equality of men; acquiescence in the decision of the majority; no special favors to banks or merchants; banks to be founded on substance and not on shadow; bank and state to be separated; economy in government; diffusion of information and freedom of religion; all associations under the name of Native Americanism are repugnant to the spirit of democracy.[282]

The money question in 1840 presented the not infrequent occurrence of a boomerang issue. Suspicious of eastern capital and doubtful of the "credit system," Andrew Jackson had utilized western desires for cheap money and more credit to put an end to the second Bank of the United States and the only currency, except the totally inadequate specie, generally acceptable at face value throughout the country. The Specie Circular hit hardest the noncapitalist "common man" upon whom Jackson relied largely in the West; the demise of the Bank led to the spawning of many banks, most of them worse than the slain "Monster." Bank notes there were in abundance but, after general suspension of specie payment, the average man had no idea of what they were worth. After 1837 the "Bank Note Table"—about a column in length

---

[282] Vincennes *Western Sun*, May 9, 1840. Address of Ohio State Democratic Convention to the people, in Columbus *Ohio Statesman* (weekly), January 8, 1840.

Not even Samuel Medary of the *Ohio Statesman* presented the old-line Democratic doctrine more persistently and sincerely than George A. Chapman of the Terre Haute *Wabash Enquirer*. The defeat of Van Buren merely stimulated him to stronger effort. Early in 1841 with his brother Jacob P. Chapman, of the Evansville *Southwestern Sentinel*, he bought the Indianapolis *Indiana Democrat* and renamed it the *Indiana State Sentinel*. The Rooster and legend, "Crow, Chapman, Crow," were then given a larger following. Chapman, in season and out, emphasized a simple and frugal government, no public debt either for state or General Government except for urgent necessity, constitutional barriers against improvident loans, no national bank to swindle the laborer, no special privileges to corporations by charters, no proscription for honest opinions.

—became a fixture in the newspapers, but only merchants, speculators, and bank-note shavers could keep posted.[283] Democratic "pet banks," land-office agents, defaulters, note shavers, the sub-treasury, and Whig bankers all got involved in the financial melee.[284]

To make matters more complicated the depression brought home to roost some of the financial chickens hatched by the states —by Democrats in Michigan and Illinois, by Whigs in Indiana. Democrats had referred to Whigs as the "Bank Party," "The Bank Bought Party," "Rag Barons," "Rag Currency Mongers," "Worshipers of Mammon," "Devotees of Shinplasters." Whigs replied, "Tote your own plunder";[285] that Democrats ("against all banks") had created the banks of Mississippi, Arkansas, Illinois, and the Fanny Wright litter of wildcats in Michigan; in fact, 490 new banks during Jackson's first six years.[286] Why try to pin the "credit system" upon the Whigs when the Democratic land-office agents redeposited the proceeds of sales (if any were left after the agents got through "swartwouting") with the bank from which the purchaser borrowed the money, so they could in turn be lent again to another or even the same speculator?[287] Who could get hold of "Constitutional currency," said by the

[283] During the next twenty-five years some eight thousand different bank-note issues—varying in value from zero to face—circulated in the United States, plus some four thousand kinds of counterfeits. Aside from the limited specie—only about nine million dollars of gold half eagles were minted between 1804 and 1834—there had been no other uniformly acceptable currency besides the notes of the Bank.

[284] See Chapters IX and XII. Whig papers copied widely lists of defaulting government officials, usually headed by Samuel Swartwout ($1,225,705) and ending up with some small fry ($593). Prominent in these lists were the land agents at the offices in the Middle West. See for instance lists in *Cleveland Herald and Gazette*, September 25, 1839; *Cincinnati Daily Gazette*, August 1, 1840.

Note shavers frequently advertised in the newspapers in 1836–37: "To Land Purchasers. Land office money exchanged at reasonable terms," etc.

[285] Columbus *Ohio State Journal*, May 24, 1839.

[286] *Quincy Whig*, September 28, 1839. The figure was a little high.

"The Anti-Bank-hard money-Benton-mint drop-Loco foco Legislature of Michigan is about establishing a State Bank with a capital of three millions of dollars— only! So we go. Van Buren, the great anti-rag-money President, has issued about a steam boat load of Treasury *shin plasters*, which are peddled in the streets of New York at a discount, and the gildibus legislatures of the different states are preparing to flood the country with 'greasy promises to pay.'" *Hamilton Intelligencer*, January 25, 1838.

[287] The Madison *Indiana Republican and Banner* noted a toast at a Van Buren jollification in Clermont County, Ohio: "Richard M. Johnson—a firm spoke in the wheel of liberty. Martin Van Buren—the hub of democracy—and Andrew Jackson, the axle-tree of the United States." To complete the sentiment it added: "Samuel Swartwout and William M. Price—the *running gears* of the Sub-Treasury." Indianapolis *Indiana Journal*, February 2, 1839.

Democrats to be locked up in Whig banks? "Officeholders," said the Whigs; a congressman paid in specie could discount paper (bank notes) before he left town for 10 per cent gain and discount that paper back home for another 20 per cent. "Gold and silver for the officeholders—Shin Plasters for the People." While wages of laborers had depreciated 50 per cent, officeholders' wages had in effect increased in the same ratio.[288]

When the Democrats said that the bankers were hoarding specie to force prices down so that they could buy up the poor man's property for a song,[289] Whigs replied that if all bank notes were called in and all specie put out, there would be only one third as much money in circulation and times would be still harder.[290] "The question is not what kind of money shall be circulated, but whether the people are to enjoy the beneficial use of any, good, bad, or indifferent."[291] One thing was obvious: In a commercial society metallic currency was not enough; paper money, established on a basis of precious metals, was indispensable.[292] "Promissory notes, bills and bankers' paper will be used notwithstanding all laws of the government that are designed to expel everything but specie."[293] "Wild cat legislation and wild cat banking will elbow each down to posterity as one of the magnificent humbugs of the great and glorious reign of Andrew the tyrant and Martin, his illustrious successor and imitator."[294] When the *Ohio Statesman* spoke of the Whigs' mania for a $50,000,000 Bank of the

---

[288] Columbus *Ohio State Journal*, March 7, October 5, 1840.

[289] "Farmer" in Springfield (Ill.) *Old Hickory*, May 4, 1840.

[290] *Hamilton Intelligencer*, October 31, 1839.

[291] *Cleveland Herald and Gazette* (weekly), December 13, 1837.

[292] Columbus *Ohio State Journal*, August 7, 1839. As George Flower said in *Errors of Emigrants*, 39, the hard-money countries were the backward and tyrannous countries. "Countries the most potent and free, are those that have banks and a paper circulation. . . . There is a quality in paper money which sets in motion the industry and ingenuity of man, and a facility that it offers to commerce, that hard money can never possess. . . . The amount of paper issued, appears never to be injurious when limited by that of new capital produced, by the labors which its agency calls forth."

James Hall in an article on "Finance," in *Western Monthly Magazine*, II (1834), 410–23, discussed the subject: "Where, then, have we to look for an efficient cause for the tremendous effects before us, if not to that total prostration of public confidence in individual credit, everywhere exhibited to us. This is the true seat of the disease, and if it be not constitutional, it is chronic in our country. Our conservative heads, have never considered the necessity, of supplying a national currency, in aid of industry and trade; individual credit has been forced, and left to grope its feeble way, unsupported and unprotected, by the nation, and the inevitable tendency of such an abandonment, has overtaken it."

[293] *Cleveland Herald and Gazette* (weekly), February 12, 1839.

[294] *Detroit Daily Advertiser*, April 20, 1838.

United States, it displayed six hands pointing to the eagle, upside down.[295] "Farewell bird of liberty. You are dead when an independent power is established over those who have placed their hopes for universal liberty under your wings." The Whig press replied that Van Buren was that "Independent Power." The *Cleveland Herald and Gazette* said, "Look on this!" and pictured a coin; "Then on this!" and pictured a sizeable cut of a $50 "United States Shinplaster" (treasury note).[296] It asked how the latter differed from a nonspecie-paying bank note.[297] Lincoln said, "The Savior of the world chose twelve disciples, and even one of that small number, selected by superhuman wisdom, turned out a traitor and a devil. And, it may not be improper here to add, that Judas carried the bag—was the Sub Treasurer of the Savior and His disciples."[298]

While some of the almost endless discussion of banks was merely the stuff of which politics is made, much of it was serious and sincere. Few questions so closely concerned everyone; few were more difficult to understand. Many men could reason or vote calmly on tariff or internal improvements who immediately got "all het up" on banks. Even an editor such as the widely quoted Dr. E. W. H. Ellis, of the *Goshen* (Ind.) *Democrat*, who, unlike Chapman with his blatant and often vulgar personalities, usually discussed acts and measures on a high plane, had one rigid inflexible cast-iron measuring stick for a man: if he was but a faithful Democrat, all other sins might be overlooked; but if he said one extenuating thing in favor of a bank, he was a liar and a scoundrel. Few were able to contemplate the problem of national bankruptcy "unparalleled in the financial history of the whole world" as impartially as the editor of the Mineral Point (Wis.) *Miners' Free Press* who said that it was not a party problem and that everyone would have to get to work on it. "The present peculiar crisis may never return again."[299] Nor as sensibly as the editor of the *Sangamo Journal* when he wrote: "The grand

---

[295] July 2, 1839.

[296] September 23, 1840.

[297] In the early autumn of 1838, when Ohio banks were paying specie, the *Cincinnati Daily Gazette*, August 14, pointed out that the United States Treasury had $8,000,000 of notes in circulation "not payed in anything"; just receivable in payment of debts.

[298] First published in Springfield *Sangamo Journal*, March 6, 20, etc., and widely copied in Whig papers.

[299] June 23, 1837.

error into which a large majority of mankind fall, in regards to money, proceeds from the notion . . . that to make money twice as plenty is to make the world twice as rich. . . . If changes in the quantity of money did not disorder the imaginations of men, and if there were no such thing as debts and credits existing at the time those changes take place, then no mischief would proceed from them."[300]

In the mass of conflicting statements the voter realized one thing: though the country's wealth had not diminished—there was the same soil, the same sun, the same labor and ingenuity—money was hard to "come by," and when one did lay hands on it, he was not certain what it was worth. The problem was stated definitely and clearly many times: The electors are to determine "whether the country shall have a good currency or a very bad one; a currency of specie and paper convertible into specie, or government and individual shinplasters, together with wildcat rags; whether we are to go back to the system under which the country became so prosperous, or try another experiment."[301] Though the voter may have understood little of the theory of money and banking, he did realize the condition which confronted him—depression. Disregarding the causes and ever reluctant to blame himself, he was inclined to blame the party in power.[302]

[300] The editorial column on this subject by Editor Simeon Francis in the *Sangamo Journal*, May 20, 1837, was a good example of sane exposition on the whole monetary situation and the psychological factors involved.

[301] *Cleveland Herald and Gazette*, September 13, 1838.

[302] The *Bloomington* (Ill.) *Observer* in 1838 abandoned its neutral stand in politics on this question: "When the measures of our National Executive become subversive of the constitutional end and purpose of Executive power, patriotism demands and justifies opposition. We regard the sub-treasury system as a measure of that character; as a measure insidiously devised to place our national treasure under executive control. No less do we dislike the late experiments on the currency, the war upon banks and credit, and the whole tissue of schemes and experiments, which have reduced our citizens to poverty, and our nation to bankruptcy." Copied in Springfield *Sangamo Journal*, February 10, 1838. Along the same line ran the editorial in the *Journal*, July 24, 1840: "Never since the days of this republic, have our blood-bought liberties been in more imminent danger than at the present moment; and never has there been a time when there was so much necessity for the energies of an untiring, and watchful vigilance—among the friends of free government. The party now in power, remarkable only for its profligacy and corruption, its venal abuses, and daring usurpations, has given us too many indications of its designs to permit a single doubt to remain—that nothing short of the destruction of the last and only asylum of human liberty, is meditated.

"One grand measure towards the consummation of this design has already been accomplished, in the passage of that 'bill of abominations' denominated by its friends the 'Independent Treasury,' and if the executive shall be equally successful in his proposition to create a standing army, the object of his wishes will then have been fully attained; and further resistance to his sovereign will,

The money question tied in closely with the appeal to class prejudices. Despite the distinct superiority of the Whig press in general, the Democrats had since 1828 held the advantage in appeal to the "common man." When the Whigs by means of the log-cabin, rugged-old-hero technique began to cut in on their following, Democratic speakers and editors came back with all weapons. If businessmen had a meeting, it was reported as "a bold attempt to rule and control the farmers of the country by a few federal merchants of the town."[303] "The game which these desperate men are playing is fairly revealed . . . the whole power of the moneyed aristocracy of England and the United States . . . will be brought to aid the accomplishment of this design [a Bank of the United States], and to put down the 'democracy of numbers.' "[304] "Lies . . . forgeries . . . humbugs . . . villainous schemes . . . sedition laws . . . reign of terror . . . spies . . . bullies . . . frauds . . . mares' nests."[305] "Look at the excesses to which they go . . . and ask yourself if the signs of the times do not forebode impending ruin—is not the storm gathering that will burst upon this devoted country destroying in its disolating progress that liberty and equality which is the pride and hope of our land?"[306] Federalists even bowed down to the graven image of their candidate in their wild parades.[307] The fact that thousands of them had time to gallop around to political meetings, carry big drums, and lavish liquor on all comers indicated that they were either loafers or well-to-do; none but speculators, "rag barons," and merchants could afford it. Why Harrison himself, the "poor man," drew $8,000 per year for doing nothing.[308]

---

must be but feeble and ineffectual. With full power to reward his friends and punish his enemies,—with the purse of the nation in one hand, and its sword in the other; what reflecting man can believe that effectual resistance on the part of the people can be made to such a fearful array of power? Already are the friends of the Executive in extacies at their partial triumph over struggling liberty. From the seat of Government the shout of triumph is raised, and the sound is echoed back from the Shores of the Mississippi."

[303] Indianapolis *Indiana Democrat* in Vincennes *Western Sun*, March 8, 1840.
[304] Vandalia *Illinois State Register and People's Advocate*, June 2, 1837.
[305] Springfield *Illinois State Register*, 1840, *passim*.
[306] *Hickory Club* in *Western Sun*, July 18, 1840.
[307] Springfield *Illinois State Register*, June 26, 1840.
[308] As clerk of Hamilton County, with deputies. Springfield (Ill.) *Old Hickory*, March 2, 1840.

The latest and most convincing argument for General Mum is that he intends to sleep on a bundle of straw in the White House. When Foreign Ministers and his cabinet council visit him, he will turn up a half bushel or peck measure and an old barn bucket for them to sit upon. To sleep on a pile of straw with a stable door for covering, would be the prettiest thing imaginable. . . . Oh for a Whig president and an "east room" of cider barrels and coon skins, and owls, and bank rags. . . . We democrats do these things out of necessity. . . . But when the "shade covered" lawyers and bankers do it to catch our votes, surely their sufferings are sufficiently intolerable to tap our tearful sympathies, as a Tippecanoe committeeman would tap a fresh cider cask.[309]

In striking contrast to the "Blue-Light Federalism" and political tomfoolery of the Whigs, the Democrats again pointed to the time-tested doctrines of Thomas Jefferson: equality of men; acquiescence in the decision of the majority; no special favors to banks or merchants; banks to be founded on substance, not on shadow; bank and state to be separated; economy in government; diffusion of information; and freedom of wages.

Naturally the Whigs resented such arguments when made by their opponents. "Among the many vicious and execrable practices resorted to by the past and present administrations to acquire and maintain power, there is none more deserving of abhorrence than the attempt to divide society, and to array one class of citizens against another." Other practices might plead heedlessness and excitement in extenuation but "this can spring only from a dark, deep and deliberate depravity which dares the justice of the Almighty, and defies the reproaches of man."[310]

While the votes of the Irish and Germans were not as important as they were to be later, they were sought by both sides. Here again, though they had not yet developed their "land-of-the-free, haven-of-refuge, come-one, come-all" slogans as thoroughly as they were to be in the next two decades, the Democrats held the advantage. Their contention that the Whigs were "anti-foreign" contained enough truth to worry the latter; in general the Whigs did oppose noncitizen voting. A German Whig paper,

[309] Columbus *Ohio Statesman* (semiweekly), July 17, 1840.

[310] *Detroit Daily Advertiser*, June 17, 1837. "The political pettifoggers attempt to humbug the common sense of the nation by arguing that our laborers are too well paid for their toil—that the farmer gets too much money for his produce—that the mechanic receives exorbitant wages for his work, and that a sub treasury screw is necessary to bring all down to the true 'Democratic' bearings." *Ibid.*, July 14, 1840.

the *Ohio Staats-Zeitung*, was started at Columbus, Ohio, in 1839. Some Whig papers in German communities, such as the *Quincy Whig*, worked hard to overcome the Democratic arguments.[311] In Illinois a test case, which Governor Thomas Ford declared was got up by Whigs, was decided in the circuit court at Galena in 1839 against the right of unnaturalized inhabitants to vote. When it was appealed to the state supreme court, decision was withheld until after the election.

Should any of the Irish be tempted to stray because of Whig propensities for building canals, they would well remember that for citizens of Irish birth to be found rallying under the "Federal, Anti-Masonic, and patchwork flag of all hues" would indicate an alliance with the "fiendish Orange Party of Ireland" and rob the Irishman of his last chance for happiness and a home.[312]

In Illinois both parties so assiduously cultivated the Mormon votes that the colony was assured of a charter which practically created a state within a state. Here, however, the Whigs had the edge.[313]

For the first time the abolition movement played a part in the national election in the Northwest. In April, 1840, James G. Birney, a converted Alabama slaveholder, had been nominated for the Presidency by the politically minded abolitionists; Thomas Earle, of Pennsylvania, was his running mate. Though the new party had no official name, it soon came to be spoken of as the Liberty party. Neither of the major parties wished to be associated with the idea of abolitionism. Ohio, with its New England Western Reserve, was most affected by the movement, and it was in that state that the Democratic attacks against Whig abolitionists were most common. When the Whig state convention at Columbus in February nominated Thomas Corwin for governor,[314] the *Ohio Statesman,* official organ for the Democratic party, said that Benjamin F. Wade, of Ashtabula, Thomas Morris, of Clinton, and Leicester King, president of the Ohio Anti-slavery Society, had put him across in this assemblage of

[311] July—August, 1840. This paper even went so far as to print some paragraphs in boldfaced German type.

[312] *Rushville* (Ind.) *Hoosier* in Vincennes *Western Sun*, June 20, 1840.

[313] The Mormons voted for all Whig electors except Lincoln, for whom they substituted a Democrat. Thompson, *The Illinois Whigs*, 78.

[314] Nominated on the twenty-second ballot after the abolitionists refused to have Elisha Whittlesey.

bankers, swindlers, gentlemen of leisure, and officeholders. "Whiggery and abolition are wedded in bonds indissoluble. . . . As far as the Whig Party in Ohio is concerned the Abolitionists have the complete ascendancy."[315] Some of the letters to Birney's *Philanthropist* argued for abolitionist control of the old parties rather than a separate organization, and reasoned that the nomination of Harrison was a great victory. When in early autumn Ohio abolitionists selected an electoral ticket, the *Hamilton Intelligencer* referred to them as a small group of obstinate men, said the idea did not make sense, and credited it to friends of the Van Buren administration.[316]

To weaken Harrison's chances with the abolitionists, the Democrats charged him with being proslavery and quoted his Cheviot and Vincennes speeches of 1833 and 1835. On the former occasion he was quoted as having said that "an incarnate devil only could look on the schemes of the abolitionists with approbation."[317] In defense Harrison stated in a letter "To the Public" that he had joined an abolition society at the age of eighteen and had a certificate to prove it. For this the *Ohio Statesman* called him "a Downright Prevaricating, Double dealing Imposter."[318] He finally conceded that the word "humane" and not "abolitionist" described the society more accurately.[319] On the other hand the *Illinois State Register* asked the people of Illinois how they could support a man selected "avowedly" because he could get the support of the abolitionists.[320] The Whigs were represented as entertaining Negroes at their meetings, and otherwise co-operating with the abolitionists.[321]

In addition to attacks on their political views, the candidates

---

[315] Columbus *Ohio Statesman*, February 25, April 3, 1840. Birney's Cincinnati *Philanthropist*, March 31, said: "The present administration, it is generally conceded, is essentially Southern in its principles and policy."

[316] September 11, 1840.

[317] *Cleveland Advertiser* quoted in Columbus *Ohio Statesman* (semiweekly), May 5, 1840.

[318] July 3, 1840.

[319] See correspondence between Harrison and James Lyons in *Philanthropist*, June—July, 1840, particularly the letter of June 1.

[320] January 22, February 28 ff., 1840. The *Register* printed many columns on Harrison, abolitionism, "The Black Flag," etc.

[321] "Whose blood does not rise with indignation when the federalists are seen hissing their negro followers to riot and assault on democrats. Fearful indeed are the times." Columbus *Ohio Statesman* (semiweekly), June 2, 1840. ". . . it was truly a beautiful spectacle—large Negroes with Whig badges on their hats." Fremont (Ohio) *Sandusky County Democrat* in *ibid.*, June 23, 1840.

in 1840 were submitted to a liberal portion of personal abuse. Harrison was said to believe in property qualification for voters; in selling poor white men into slavery;[322] imprisonment for debt; and to favor placing foreigners on a level with Negroes and mulattoes. He was a defaulter,[323] a seducer,[324] and a Black Cockade Federalist in favor of alien and sedition laws and a standing army. While Wellington lost 60,000 to become the hero of Waterloo, Napoleon a million to gain his title, and General Jackson 2,000 to win lasting fame, General Harrison had killed 000,038 of the enemy in a skirmish and lost twice as many of his own men. Since he didn't have sense enough to answer his own correspondence or make speeches, he had to be closely guarded by a committee of conscience keepers. When the caged hero or "General Mum" got loose, he always let some kind of cat out of the bag. "There is not a man in the nation, forty years of age, who does not know that General Harrison is now, and always has been, a weak and imbecile man. . . . a man of weak character and feeble intellect."[325] "Ask no questions and we'll tell no lies" was his motto. He had drawn $200,000 from the public treasury and been elected to fewer offices than any public man; he held a $6,000 sinecure obtained by influence, lived in a white mansion on a thousand-acre farm and called it a log cabin.[326]

As for Van Buren, he was also a "Blue-Light Federalist" in 1812, an enemy of Jackson in 1824, an abolitionist, supporter of Negro suffrage, unfriendly to the West and to free labor, opposed to internal improvements, and, worst of all, a pampered, snobbish aristocrat who lived like a king and spent lavishly the money of the people whom he despised for curtains, foreign mirrors, roses, lamps, footstools, silk cord, gilt, satin chairs,

---

[322] The Springfield *Sangamo Journal*, June 5, 1840, used about thirty different type faces in explaining that Harrison had voted to make criminals and felons work rather than rot in jail.

[323] His son John Cleves Symmes Harrison had been removed from the Vincennes Land Office and General Harrison, his security, had never made good the deficit, according to the Democrats.

[324] The story of an affair with a Miss Bower of Cincinnati was printed, with letters, in the *Cincinnati Republican* and *Ohio Statesman*. The *Ohio State Journal*, July 10, 1840, replied hotly to the revival of this "exploded slander" of 1825.

[325] Springfield (Ill.) *Old Hickory*, May 25, 1840.

[326] Columbus *Ohio Statesman* (triweekly), May 13, July 5, 7, 10, 22, 28, 1840; Springfield *Illinois State Register*, October 30, 1840; Vincennes *Western Sun*, July 11, 25, August 1, September 19, 1840; *Madison* (Ind.) *Courier*, July 25, 1840.

and gold spoons. While Adams' yearly expenditures had averaged twelve millions and Jackson's eighteen millions, Van Buren and his defaulters had averaged thirty-seven millions.[327]

It was a year of conventions and meetings. There were county conventions, district conventions, and state conventions; first voters' conventions, young men's conventions, and, more spectacular still, the great barbecue assemblies. Among the more important of these were the Whig state convention at Columbus, February 22, when "more than 20,000 met in holy friendship around the altar of American Liberty;[328] the Fort Meigs meeting June 10, where 20,000 welcomed Harrison;[329] the Detroit meeting September 30, where a mighty gathering of 15,000 people advanced, hour by hour, in the rain;[330] the Springfield, Illinois, convention in June, where 15,000 attended and "not a man was intoxicated and no spirits were used either in the tents or at the barbecue";[331] and the great Dayton meeting of September 10 when the whole Miami Valley came to Dayton and "100,000 freemen were in council."[332]

The great granddaddy of these political gatherings was the Tippecanoe rally at the Old Battleground, May 29. For days in advance the delegations converged on selected rendezvous and then advanced to the battleground. Weeks had been spent preparing banners, floats, food, and speeches. Delegations from Illinois, Michigan, Kentucky, Tennessee, and Indiana vied with each other for noise, music, outfits, and enthusiasm. It had rained for days and the roads were deplorable, but it made no difference. By boat and by stage, ox team, horseback, and on foot through the mud over corduroy roads they came. The people of Tippecanoe County opened their houses and their barns, their hay-

---

[327] Xenia (Ohio) *Greene County Torch-light,* April 16, 1840.

[328] *Ibid.,* March 5, 1840. The estimates are all Whig.

[329] The Michigan delegation took five steamboats, and with banners, bands, and lots of hilarity advanced up the Maumee from Toledo to Fort Meigs. *Detroit Daily Advertiser,* June 13, 1840.

[330] "The big Van Buren meeting on Monday—a fair day—had 591 present." *Ibid.,* October 2, 1840.

[331] *Ibid.,* June 17, 1840.

[332] *Cincinnati Daily Gazette,* September 12; Columbus *Ohio State Journal,* September 15, 1840. General Harrison spoke for an hour. Three measurements of the mass of the crowd were made and allowing four persons to the square yard the estimates were 75,000, 77,000, and 80,000, with 20,000 on the outside.
The *Ohio Statesman* estimate on the Columbus meeting was 2,722 as follows: 538 bank directors and officers, 743 officeholders, 346 lawyers and doctors, 1,095 merchants and speculators. In *Illinois State Register,* March 20, 1840.

stacks and their corncribs. The old soldiers pitched their tents and cooked army fare—and reminiscing, pointed to the place where comrades had fallen. In the morning they rose by reveille and had a salute of twenty-six guns. On the big day the procession led off with the brig *Constitution* pulled by six white horses, banners floating on the breeze.[333] Followed canoes, log cabins, 'coons, cider barrels, corn bread, bands, traps, music, speeches, and feasting. Over all was the spirit of hero worship and feeling of "democracy losing its chains."

Who shall describe the Battle-Ground Gathering? Aye, who *can* describe the thrilling spectacle presented by the assemblage of Thirty Thousand Freemen, not in obedience to the nod of a monarch—not in the blind devotion which leads the deluded pilgrim to the shrine—not in compliance with the mandates of any power,—but moved by one generous impulse,—nerved by the intelligent views of their rights, actuated by one motive,—the common good of their common country? Here was the pioneer beneath whose axe, the sturdy forest of the West had trembled—here the farmer who had left his plow in the field and the mechanic whose hammer rested in silence upon the anvil. The merchant had abandoned his counter—the professional man his books—and men engaged in the various pursuits in life were "as of one accord in one place." Here might be seen the grey-haired man, the buoyancy of youth—the vigor of manhood. Here the veteran who battled for that liberty which he would hand down to the son who stood by his side to direct his feeble steps. Here were the representatives of those primitive dwellings of our country—the log cabins of the West, the rude tenements, taunted and jeered at by an aristocratic party—yet still, the citadels of our young Republic—the low but mighty towers of our Nation —the home of free unfettered souls. And who shall say that one sordid, selfish motive found its abode in the hearts of such men? Who will not

[333] Among the mottoes on transparencies were: "Union of the Whigs for the sake of the Union"; "The Hoosier boys are always ready to do their own voting as well as their own fighting"; "Log cabin freedom is better than White House Slavery"; "Indiana will cherish in her manhood the defender of her infancy"; "Rags are better than nakedness"; "You can't come it over the Suckers."
Cartoons were displayed on banners and floats. One represented a dugout laden with "cabinet furniture for sale" on its way to salt river. Another pictured a barrel of hard cider rolling down a hill from a log cabin, in its path stood Van Buren yelling "stop that barrel." At the bottom of the hill in the mud was a subtreasury turtle. One showed the commander-in-chief of the Florida bloodhounds, surrounded by his troops and seeking peace with the Seminole chief, who is addressed thus: "We must abandon this fatal war. My troops are in a deplorable condition and my friends are leaving me. I beg you to give up your prisoners and cease hostilities." The chief points to a bloodhound in the coils of a snake and replies, "Me no got prisoners. Snake eatum up. Me no treaty, me fight." Ponto, of the bloodhound army, in despair howls, "We have met the enemy and we are theirs."

say that such an assemblange was demanded by that crisis to which our beloved country has arrived?[334]

The picturesque military record of General Harrison made him an ideal newspaper and stump-orator candidate, and the appeal, both to the gregarious instinct and hero-worship propensities of the frontiersman, was too much for the Democrats. It also presented a vulnerable spot which the opposition was quick to take advantage of. Harrison had been criticized at the time of his military campaigns between 1811 and 1814, but the War of 1812 as refought in the election of 1840 was more bitter, if not more bloody, than the original. Harrison supporters not only had to cry down Richard M. Johnson, of Kentucky, Van Buren's running mate, who had served under Harrison at the Thames, but establish for their hero a record equal to or better than that of Andrew Jackson. The controversy centered around the battles of Tippecanoe, the River Raisin, Fort Meigs, Fort Stephenson, and the Thames. The newspapers and speakers threshed it out in barrels of ink and miles of type.[335] To some Harrison was established in mind as at least equal to Jackson in military prowess; to others he remained the "old granny . . . the petticoat candidate," in war as in politics.

In their efforts to belittle the outrageous hard-cider tactics of their opponents the Democrats almost hit upon the temperance issue. For several years the churches had been active in agitation for moral reforms, and especially among the evangelical churches had the liquor question aroused interest. Widespread organization under the name of the Washingtonians had been effected, and the connection between taverns, rum, and politics was discussed.[336] In their competition for the rough and simple life the Whigs had gained the jump, so Democratic campaign orators

[334] Indianapolis *Spirit of '76*, June 6, 1840.

[335] The subject is best discussed in Mary Louise Ford, "The Repercussions of the War of 1812 in the Political Campaign of 1840" (1940), MS. M.A. thesis, Indiana University. The controversy can be well followed in the *Cincinnati Daily Gazette*. In a speech at Lafayette, Indiana, October 17, 1840, Colonel Johnson had said, "I planned the battle and asked Gen. Harrison's leave to bring on the attack. General Harrison was not in the fight but was where I always thought he ought to have been, with the main army ready to lead on the battle in case I fell, and I think it is a great deal more credit to Gen. Harrison to be placed where I place him than where his friends wish to place him." Indianapolis *Indiana Journal*, November 14, 1840.

[336] See report of Marion County (Indianapolis) grand jury on "Groceries and Grog Shops," in *Indiana Journal*, May 18, 1839.

and papers found good arguments by which they sought the temperance vote. The Federal brawls and corruption of the youth of the land were denounced and ministers of the gospel appealed to.[337] The wild hilarity, gourds, cider, canoes, crying babes, coonskins, and fighting of the Whig meetings were contrasted with the peaceful and thoughtful decorum of the Democratic meetings, but all to no avail.

When denunciation of Whig tactics and appeals to the former glory of the Democratic party did not bring results, the Democrats organized Hickory Clubs and in Indiana a "Democratic Association."[338] The Whigs had extended the hand of fellow-

---

[337] "I have great fear of evil from the genius of that party's action when in power, which to gain success, will sell the virtue and morals of the people to obtain it." Rev. J. N. T. Tucker of New York, quoted in Columbus *Ohio Statesman*, July 22, 1840. Peter Cartwright, of Illinois, was reported as having said that had he ever been a Whig he would have returned a Van Buren man after seeing the Baltimore convention. *Ibid.*, July 14, 1840.

"Come up, then, all ye 'brutes of creation' and drink a little hard cider. Buzzards and coons, owls and asses, must all be charmed into the support of Old Tip by these musical choristers.—Drunken debauchery.—Drunken Federalists.—The old granny let loose to amuse the children with spook stories and recount the wonderful adventures of his life.—Bacchanalian row.—Doggerel rhymes and vulgar pictures.—Negro-loving, song-singing, cider-sucking hypocrites." *Ibid.*, July 7, 1840. The Whigs were even accused of singing on Sunday mornings on their return from political meetings.

The *Indiana Democrat*, August 21, 1840, carried a parody of a Whig Tippecanoe song:

> Come all ye brother Fed'ralists,
>   We'll all together go,
> And we'll so lay our gulling schemes
>   That Chapman cannot crow.
> . . . .
>
> Of defalcations let us speak,
>   Which drain'd the Treasury low;
> And thousands will believe the tale,
>   And Chapman cannot crow.
>
> Log cabins, too, we'll build around,
>   They'll please the rabble so
> That on the election 'twill be found
>   That Chapman cannot crow.
>
> And ev'ry stale humbugging tale
>   Throughout the land we'll blow;
> We'll send our lies forth like a gale,
>   And Chapman cannot crow.

[Here the Whigs were interrupted by an impudent Loco-foco responding from the lobby—]

> "But stop! November's tale will tell
> "Your hopes are all laid low,
> "Your party will be blown to h-ll,
> "AND CHAPMAN THEN WILL CROW."

[338] Vincennes *Western Sun*, August 29, 1840.

ship to the erring brethren of the Democratic faith and did not abuse Jackson but lamented the maladministration of Van Buren and the officeholders.[339] In Illinois the Jackson influence was still strong and the Whigs pointed to Harrison as being more Jacksonian than Van Buren.

The struggle for votes was more complicated than in any previous election. The Whigs were striving to hold in line the various elements which constituted their following, and for the first time the abolition vote, the temperance vote, and the foreign vote were important enough to affect results. The Whigs had the closest hold on the abolition vote, not because their principles were more favorable, but because a majority of the abolitionists had been Whigs. The temperance and foreign votes were largely Democratic, for the Democratic party was first to see the moral and social questions as great nonsectional issues, and had always stood for quick citizenship and an easy franchise.

The August state elections in Indiana and Illinois were followed with great interest throughout the Northwest. Indiana Whigs had nominated Samuel Bigger, a distinguished Rush County judge, for governor; he ran on an internal-improvements program. His Democratic opponent was Gen. Tilghman A. Howard, who had previously stood for "classification," but at this time, although straddling somewhat, in general favored letting up on construction until the financial condition of the state improved. The internal improvements idea proved stronger than the fear of state bankruptcy; also the outcome was influenced by the presidential campaign. Bigger received 62,678 votes to Howard's 54,083.[340] The new legislature also indicated the popular attitude toward the internal improvements program; the Whigs elected better than a two to one majority. A by-election in the seventh congressional district returned Henry S. Lane, a Whig. The Democrats explained the defeat as being the result of the united efforts of bank officers, stockholders and depend-

---

[339] Samuel Judah, who wrote the Indiana Jackson platforms of 1824 and 1828, stumped the state for Harrison.

[340] Indiana *House Journal*, 1839–40, p. 30. Howard polled about three thousand more votes than Van Buren received in November. The total vote in both elections was practically the same. "Tell Chapman to Crow," taunted the *Cleveland Herald and Gazette* (weekly), August 12, 1840. George A. Chapman of the Democratic Terre Haute *Wabash Courier* had originated the Rooster, later to be famous for its crowing over Democratic victories as it stood at the masthead of the *Indiana Sentinel*.

ents, merchants and clerks, landlords, speculators, and note shavers, all of whom joined in one shout for "Harrison, Hard Cider and Log Cabin," and who thought that, since Van Buren was responsible for the hard times, any change was better than none.

Partisanship in Indiana, in state as well as in national politics, dates from this election; independent voting on the former scale became a thing of the past.

When the Illinois Democrats elected fifty-one members of the lower house of the legislature to forty Whigs, the *State Register* proclaimed that the prairies were on fire and that hard cider could not prevent "Federalism" being consumed in the flames.[341] But this result signified little for the November election, as the northern counties, which were Whig, had been growing rapidly since the apportionment of 1836.

The Ohio state and Congressional election, which was held on October 13, was a Whig triumph. Thomas Corwin defeated Wilson Shannon by 16,000 votes, whereas Shannon had carried the state in 1838 by 5,727 votes and Harrison in 1836 by 8,457.[342] The total vote showed the surprising increase of 22,000 in two years. By virtue of the holdovers the Democrats retained a majority in the Senate but the Whigs elected forty-nine representatives out of seventy-two. Twelve of the nineteen congressmen elected were Whigs.[343] The first reaction from the Democratic press was one of stoical acceptance. "Not being used to defeat, we know nothing of excuses or apologies in such cases."[344] But after the first shock, the papers came back with cries of fraud—deep, dark, and audacious—and tried as far as possible

[341] August 7, 1840. The *Chicago Democrat,* August 13, declared that the "High Comb Cock" was on his legs again and issued a one-hundred-gun salute for Illinois.

[342] The vote for governor was 145,442 to 129,312. *Ohio Statistics,* 255 ff. Democratic counties of more than 1,000 majority were: Butler, Fairfield, Monroe, and Richland. Whig majorities of more than 1,000 were polled in Ashtabula (2,700), Clark, Cuyahoga, Greene, Geauga, Lake, Muskingum, and Warren. The *Ohio Statesman* (semiweekly), October 30, 1840, gives the vote for governor as 144,054 to 127,962 but the returns were evidently incomplete.

[343] Ohio was reapportioned by the legislature in March, 1840, and three new counties created, but the number of representatives in the house and senate was not changed. The official vote by districts is given in *Ohio Statesman,* December 22, 1840. The total Whig vote given here was 145,397 to 128,284 for the Democrats.

The *Quincy* (Ill.) *Whig* in its happiness over this news ran a four-line headline one inch high and four columns wide: "O. K.—Illinois to the Rescue—William Henry Harrison—John Tyler."

[344] Columbus *Ohio Statesman* (semiweekly), October 20, 1840.

to minimize the anticipated adverse majority in the November election.

The last month before the election was one of feverish activity on both sides. Barbecues, hard cider, songs, and log cabins became magnificent obsessions; Hickory Clubs marched with renewed energies. The heavy artillery among the orators were sent out for the last-minute efforts; even presidential electors campaigned as if they were after remunerative jobs. Newspapers brought forth even bigger log cabins and headlines: "You can't stop that Ball" (the expected Whig landslide). Almost every paper had its version of the caption carried at the head of this chapter. Typical of the solemn last-round warnings to the sovereign people were those of the two leading partisan papers in Illinois. Editor Simeon Francis wrote: "We caution the citizens . . . against *forged letters—forged extracts from Newspapers—lying hand bills—exploded calumnies—refuted slanders—and all the tricks* which desperate and depraved party leaders may invent to defeat the Whigs at the coming election."[345] Messrs. William Walters and George R. Weber responded with headlines "Fraud! Fraud! Fraud! . . . Irishmen beware . . . Everybody beware."[346] Democratic editors were quick to take advantage of foolish and loud talk on the part of some Whigs to the effect that if they were not successful at the polls, they would be ready to resort to arms.

Ohio, "the great battlefield of interest," voted for president on October 30; the three other states on November 3. On the latter date, when the Whig victory in Ohio was assured, the *Ohio State Journal* wrote: "The figures which record the triumph of a Free People over the willing slaves of a corrupt power, speak a language more eloquent than words." The Ohio results were not generally known to the voters in the other states by election day.

The Northwest proved loyal to the old General; only in Illinois was the Democratic tradition strong enough to stave off defeat. Ohio gave Harrison 148,157, Van Buren 124,782, and

[345] Springfield *Sangamo Journal*, August 2, 1840.
[346] *Illinois State Register*, October 30, 1840. "A base attempt by FEDERALISTS to use the name of the son of Thomas Addis Emmet, to excite you to turn against MARTIN VAN BUREN your uncompromising friend that your necks may be crushed between the wheels of oppression."

Birney, the Liberty party candidate, 892 votes.[347] The vote in Indiana was 65,276 to 51,695,[348] and in Michigan 22,911 to 21,106, with 294 for Birney.[349] Van Buren carried Illinois by 1,867 votes in a total vote of 93,179. The vote was Van Buren 47,443, Harrison 45,576, and Birney 160.[350] The thirty-three electoral votes of Ohio, Indiana, and Michigan were cast for Harrison, and Illinois' five votes for Van Buren.

In Ohio the Whigs carried all but twenty-six of seventy-eight counties voting. The heavy Harrison majorities of the Western Reserve and such Whig counties as Muskingum, Gallia, Lawrence, and Franklin did not account for the 23,375-vote majority over Van Buren. Substantial Whig majorities were general. The twenty-six Democratic counties fell conspicuously in three groups. First there were five counties of the old Pennsylvania-Virginia territory in the southeastern part of the state. Then there were the four counties of Clermont, Brown, Adams, and Butler of Virginia-Maryland origins which had been the center of Jacksonian strength.[351] The third group stretched entirely across the state just south of the Western Reserve from boundary to boundary; it was composed of counties settled largely by western Pennsylvanians, Virginians, and Marylanders, or by people from parts of Ohio settled by them. This district remained rather consistently Democratic throughout the period.[352]

The eleven Democratic counties of Michigan were scattered but included Wayne and the city of Detroit. In Indiana Harrison drew heavily from the old Jacksonian following, as well as from the commercial centers, and only a part of the strong Demo-

[347] Columbus *Ohio Statesman* (semiweekly), November 13, 1840; *Ohio Statistics*, 255. The official returns in the Columbus *Ohio State Journal*, November 13, varied slightly from these figures.

[348] *Richmond* (Ind.) *Palladium*, November 28, 1840. The Liberty party received 3 votes in Jefferson County, 8 in Jennings, 3 in Dearborn, and 16 in Morgan, for a total of 30.

[349] *Niles Intelligencer*, December 2, 1840. The heaviest Whig majorities were in Washtenaw and Jackson counties; the heaviest Democratic in Wayne and Macomb. In proportion to the vote cast the Liberty Party received twice as many votes in Michigan as in any other state in the Northwest, and more than in any other state in the Union. Theodore Clarke Smith, *The Liberty and Free Soil Parties in the Northwest* . . . (New York, 1897), 46. The Whigs also elected the congressman and a majority in the legislature. The latter, early in 1841, elected William Woodbridge to succeed John Norvell in the Senate.

[350] Pease, *Illinois Election Returns*, 117 ff.

[351] Hamilton, with Cincinnati, went Whig.

[352] See George M. Gadsby, "Political Influence of Ohio Pioneers," in *Ohio Archaeological and Historical Society Publications*, XVII (1908), 193-96.

cratic territory of the south center was left intact. Such Democratic counties as Floyd, Knox, Vanderburgh, and Dubois went
Whig.

In Illinois the vote was more strictly sectional. Excepting the
river counties along the Wabash and in the old American Bottom,
the southern half of the state returned Van Buren majorities; in
eleven of the counties the Whig vote was one third or less of the
total. As a result of the unpopularity of Van Buren and for
other reasons there was considerable defection from the Democratic following of earlier days, but this loss was more than balanced by the vote of the foreigners, especially along the line
of the Illinois and Michigan canal. Cook County, for example,
gave almost two thirds of its vote to Van Buren. The Mormons,
as noted previously, supported Harrison, but substituted James
H. Ralston for Abraham Lincoln for elector.

The political controversy over the ousting of Alexander Pope
Field, Whig, from the office of secretary of state had handicapped the Whigs in the election. Field had held the office since
his appointment by Edwards. Meanwhile he had become a strong
Whig. Governor Carlin had appointed two members of his own
party to the office, only to have them turned down by the Senate.
After adjournment of the legislature, he appointed John A.
McClernand *ad interim,* but Field held on to his job and was
sustained by the supreme court. Field supported his stand by
pointing out that the constitution did not specify a term for
which the secretary of state was chosen. Later the nomination
of Stephen A. Douglas was turned down and the supreme court
reconstituted by the Democrats.[353] The Whig contention that an
appointive officer held office at his own pleasure and the new
executive had no right to fill the place where no vacancy existed
proved unpopular, and probably cost the Whigs enough votes
to bring about the defeat of Harrison. There were many charges
of fraud after the election but, as they were mostly against the
Whigs who were defeated, they were not pushed.

A week or two after the election when the news of the Harrison victory was certain, Whig jubilation was hard to hold.
Real headlines—among the first used in western papers—announced that the "Earthquake Voice of the American People"

[353] Pease, *The Frontier State,* 278–81; Thompson, *The Illinois Whigs,* 80–87.

had spoken; a standing army and the subtreasury had been condemned; the flag still flew and the "Union was O.K."; "Little Van was a used up man"; the country was safe. Houses were illuminated, the rest of the cider consumed.

The Democratic party, so long dominant in the Northwest, found it difficult to take defeat. The Indianapolis *Indiana Democrat,* though admitting,

> "We flap'd our wings and tried to crow,
> Alas! Alas!! It was no go—
> Chapman and we are now K. O."

still explained that "all the factions of the nation combined in their wrath to take vengeance on the Democratic party by whom they had so often been defeated"—the old Federalist party through its forty changes of name, the abolitionists, the Anti-Masons, Quakers, Nullifiers, tariff men, and antitariff men.[354] Democrats tried to make believe their party had been assailed with unusual virulence; that bankers' gold, perjury, slander, falsehood, moral debasement, corruption, and the newfangled paraphernalia of coonskins, cider, and "pipe-laying" attacks had proved too much for an honest party fighting for its dearly bought principles with argument and reason. It was not the defeat so much as the degradation and violation of the people by the Whigs that hurt. It was ridiculous to suppose that the people preferred the principles of Federalism to those of Democracy. They had merely been cheated out of their rights and misled.[355] They had passed upon no great measure or issue, but were stimulated by promises of a golden harvest and desire for a change. The charm of novelty and fancy of the imagination had eclipsed the understanding and overwhelmed reason and judgment. The moneyed monopolies had prevailed and, if the Democrats had in the past skirmished against the Bank, it would now be war to the knife and the knife to the hilt. It remained only to organize for a long fight and the final prostration of the infernal system would be achieved. "In the meantime let us sit as quietly under the national disgrace of an old granny president as possible. Sad and sickening as is the fact, that an

[354] November 14, 1840.
[355] Columbus *Ohio Statesman,* November 10, 1840; *Niles Intelligencer,* November 18, 1840.

old dotard, a man almost drivelling with age, and besotted with vanity, has by the most foul and disgraceful means attained to the elevated office of President of this republic, let us bear it patiently." The election of Harrison was merely another of those scourges of Providence occasionally sent to chastise and purify a people.[356]

The Whig victory of 1840 in the Northwest did not represent, as is sometimes indicated, the mere triumph of ballyhoo and sentiment over issues. The pageantry and noise were in part vote-getting technique, in part a tribute to a military candidate associated in the minds of the voters with the period and spirit of conquest in the West. Further, they commemorated the passing of the frontier period and the hardships and sacrifices which went with it; they romanticized and idealized the "good pioneer virtues" and hopefully heralded their return to politics. Underneath the superficialities of the prolonged campaign lay solid and serious consideration of basic issues in politics and economics. The election marked the overthrow of the party of Jefferson and Jackson in the West; for when another son of the West sought to carry Jacksonian democracy to the next logical advance, the slavery issue cast its shadow over all, split his party, and cut short his career.

The country was fulfilling the prophecy written a decade earlier by one of the leading historians of the Old Northwest:

To all human appearance, the census of 1840 will place the national government in the hands of the people in the valley of the Mississippi. To resist this event, would involve the necessity of preventing the revolution of the earth around the sun and upon its axis, and the whole course of nature. To mourn over it, involves the extreme folly, of repining at the happy lot of a majority of the nation, and of our posterity, forever. From the growth of this nation, the lover of liberty has nothing to fear, because our people, from their cradles, are taught to be republicans. They are such, as if by instinct; and all those principles which tend to make them MEN, are taught them from the first moment they see the light, breathe American air, and taste their mother's milk.[357]

[356] *Cleveland Advertiser* in *Ohio Statesman* (semiweekly), November 17, 1840.
[357] *The Writings of Caleb Atwater*, 358.

CHAPTER XII

Economic History, 1836–1840

It requires no stretch of fancy, nor can it be said to be a visionary speculation, to look forward to the no distant period when the ports of Oswego, Lewiston, Buffalo, Cleveland, Detroit, and Chicago, will be studded with the canvass of the ships of foreign nations laden with the rich productions of Asia and Europe.

Report of the U. S. House Committee on Roads and Canals,
January 25, 1838

THE latter part of the year 1836 witnessed the crest of the great wave of prosperity which was sweeping over the West. Land sales had reached unprecedented heights, money in the form of bank notes was plentiful, trade was brisk, and neither the Specie Circular nor a presidential election could entirely dampen the ardent spirits of the people. In June, President Jackson had signed the law for the distribution of the surplus treasury funds among the states in proportion to their populations. These funds, to be paid in four quarterly installments starting January 1, 1837, though technically a loan without security or interest, were generally understood to constitute a gift.[1] At last it appeared that the West was going to get something back from the General Government. It was estimated that Ohio would receive about $2,676,000, Indiana $1,147,000, Illinois $640,000, and Michigan $382,000. These fair prospects added substance to the hopes for big things.

In Ohio various proposals for using the surplus were discussed by newspapers, politicians, and at meetings of the voters. Governor Vance said a word for schools; legislative committees recommended investment in bank stock; the *Cincinnati Gazette* favored using the money for internal improvements, which would benefit all, and the idea received strong support from the Western Reserve.[2]

[1] The amount distributed, about $28,000,000, is still carried on the Treasury books as due from the states.

[2] The argument for investment in bank stock was that the yield of 10 per cent would give a continuing fund for school aid and interest on internal improvement loans. The legislature, March, 1837, provided for distribution to the counties in

The state, having started its canal building a decade earlier, had no comprehensive system of internal improvements to inaugurate.[3] Under a new Board of Public Works, work continued on the Miami Canal, behind schedule because of lack of laborers. It was hoped soon to have it open to Troy. Twenty-three miles of the Walhonding and Mohican Canal out of Roscoe were under contract, as were some sixteen miles of the Hocking Valley Canal. The Whitewater Canal was the big project still in the promotion stage. State finances were considered adequate: the anticipated two and a half million Federal surplus quota, plus sales of canal lands, should meet all immediate needs.[4]

In Indiana the building of the Wabash and Erie Canal effectively overcame what opposition remained to a state internal improvements program. The discussion had been general, the arguments convincing; the people had made up their minds. Party politics were largely overlooked in the legislature of 1834–35, which was organized by the internal improvements men who controlled all but seven counties.[5] The strongest groups centered around the counties of the Whitewater Valley, the Wabash, and the southwestern part of the state. Key to the whole logrolling process was the Whitewater Canal,[6] which was to serve about ten counties and an area of 3,150 square miles, reduce freight rates almost two thirds, and furnish power for 318 pairs of millstones. No plan was agreed upon until the General Assembly of 1835–36 yielded to the lobby of the counties which were determined to have a macadam road from New Albany to Vincennes. On January 27, 1836, Governor Noah Noble signed the bill which provided for a state system of internal improvements at an es-

proportion to the number of voters, county commissioners to lend to canal, road, or railroad companies, to the state, and to individuals. Annual proceeds were to be used for common schools. All loans were to be liquidated by 1850 when the principal might be applied to the state canal debt if the legislature saw fit. Ohio received, in the three distributions made, $2,007,260.

[3] See Chapter VII.

[4] *Cincinnati Daily Gazette,* February 6, 1837.

[5] Switzerland, Harrison, Crawford, Perry, Spencer, Posey—all on the Ohio—and Hendricks.

[6] Surveyed and reported on in 1834, to run seventy-six miles from near Cambridge City in Wayne County, close to the National Road, down the west bank of the Whitewater, crossing it at Somerset, recrossing at Brookville, and on to the Ohio. Seven dams and fifty-five locks were planned to take care of 491 feet of descent; cost was estimated at $1,142,126. *House Journal,* 1834–35, pp. 255–64.

timated cost of $13,000,000, or one sixth the wealth of the state.[7]

By this law an Internal Improvements Board of six members was created to work with the existing canal board. Main parts of the system with appropriations were: (1) the Whitewater Canal, $1,400,000; (2) a canal (or railroad) to connect the Whitewater with the Central, $1,400,000; (3) the Central Canal from a point on the Wabash between Fort Wayne and Logansport, through Munseytown, Indianapolis, down West Fork of White River to its junction with East Fork, and thence to Evansville on the Ohio, $3,500,000; (4) extension of the Wabash and Erie Canal from the Tippecanoe to Terre Haute and via Eel River to the Central Canal, $1,300,000; (5) a railroad from Madison via Columbus and Indianapolis to Lafayette, $1,300,-000; (6) a macadamized road from New Albany via Paoli and Washington to Vincennes, $1,150,000; and (7) a resurvey, for a railroad (or turnpike) from New Albany via Salem, Bloomington, and Greencastle to Crawfordsville, $1,300,000.[8] The fund commissioners were authorized to borrow up to $10,000,000 at 6 per cent for 25 years; the canals, roads, railroads, tolls, profits, and faith of the state were pledged to payment of interest and principal.

Passage of the law was celebrated from one end of the state to the other; other states hailed the enterprise and spirit of Indiana. Enthusiastic advocates of the "System" had promised that not only would no additional taxes be necessary, but that soon the tolls and receipts would provide the state with revenue for all purposes. Few people seemed to note that the young state had voted itself a program far beyond its means.

Illinois' prolific plans for roads, canals, and railroads crystallized into action simultaneously. The act of 1835 which provided for the Illinois and Michigan Canal had been largely the work of the northern counties; now the rest of the state wanted its share. The legislature of 1835–36 granted a dozen or more charters for railroads; neither the charters nor the

[7] Laws of Indiana, 1835–36 (general), Chapter 2. "Taken in all its aspects, its consequences immediate and remote, it was the most important measure ever signed by an Indiana governor." Esarey, History of Indiana, I, 412.
[8] Also $50,000 for improving the Wabash River and a survey of a canal (or railroad) from the Wabash and Erie Canal near Fort Wayne via Goshen, South Bend, and La Porte, to Michigan City.

prospective railroads conformed to any logical system. Canal lot sales boomed in Chicago in the summer of 1836, and a little dirt was made to fly out of the proposed ditch, which was to be big enough to accommodate steamboats. In the next legislative session, 1836–37, Stephen A. Douglas reported a resolution for a canal-railroad system, as did Ninian W. Edwards. The House Committee in January, noting that the people had spoken, submitted a plan. Though not specific as to total cost, railroads were estimated at not to exceed $8,000 per mile.

On February 27 was passed "An Act to establish and maintain a General system of Internal Improvement."[9] A Board of Fund Commissioners (three members, elected by the General Assembly) was authorized to negotiate all loans "to be effected by the legislature," let contracts and construct "within a reasonable length of time" the following items for which appropriations were made: improvements in the Wabash, Illinois, and Rock rivers, $100,000 each and in the Little Wabash and Kaskaskia rivers, $50,000 each; improvements on the Great Western mail route (Vincennes to St. Louis), $250,000; a railroad (the Central) from Cairo to the southern end of the Illinois and Michigan Canal, $3,500,000; a "Southern Cross" railroad from Alton to Mt. Carmel, and a branch from this line at Edwardsville southeast to Equality in Gallatin County, $1,600,000; a "Northern Cross" railroad from Quincy on the Mississippi to Danville and the Indiana line, $1,850,000; a branch of the Central Railroad from some point where a direct line from Hillsboro to Shelbyville would intersect the same, on towards the general direction of Terre Haute, $650,000; a railroad from Peoria to Warsaw on the Mississippi, $700,000; a railroad from Lower Alton via Hillsboro to the Central Railroad, $600,000; a railroad from Belleville via Lebanon to intersect the Alton and Mt. Carmel, $150,000; a railroad from Bloomington to Mackinaw with forks to the Illinois at Peoria and to Pekin, $350,000. Consolation money, amounting to $200,000, was divided among the counties which were missed. A Board of Public Works of seven members was to have charge of the projects.

Thus was appropriated more than $10,000,000 to come from a

---

[9] *Laws of Illinois*, 1836–37, pp. 121 ff.; Vandalia *Illinois State Register and People's Advocate*, March 6, 1837.

fund to be constituted from the proceeds of sales of state stocks or bonds, appropriations from the state's revenue from land taxes, and from tolls, rents, and profits on land purchased by the state. The state's interest (equity) in all the works as well as the faith of the state were "irrevocably pledged" to payment of interest and principal on the loans. The law provided for simultaneous construction on all projects.

As in Ohio in the 1820's the arguments in favor of such pretentious works appeared overwhelming, and there were few James Wilsons to ask, "Where is the money coming from?" The cost could be estimated accurately enough, more settlers would roll in, land values appreciate, tax receipts increase, water-power rentals and tolls on each section as completed would take care of interest and sinking funds, the state stock issued would command a premium which could be used for the same purpose, and skilled financiers who would be appointed as fund commissioners would administer the finances without burden to the people. Governor Duncan favored the Illinois and Michigan Canal but thought the remainder of the improvements should be left to private initiative. Thomas Ford, arguing that Governor Duncan would have vetoed the measure had the Illinois governor possessed a veto, and saved the state much embarrassment, wrote: "I am aware that demagogues and flatterers of the people, have so far imitated the supple parasites in the courts of Monarchs, whose maxim is that the 'king can do no wrong,' as to steal the compliment and apply it to the people. They are contending everywhere that the people never err. Without disputing the infallibility of the people, we know that their representatives can and have erred; and do err most grievously."[10] And he might have added that, when they do err, they never admit it, soon forget it, and learn nothing from the experience.

The *Northwestern Gazette*, in summarizing the program, said that though it appeared gigantic and extravagant, the advantages were so great that everyone should get behind it and see that it was completed. "We go strong for internal improvements and for the present bill in particular."[11] The *Illinois State Register*, doubting not that the passage of the act had doubled the value

[10] *History of Illinois*, 190. Ford was Democratic governor during the early 1840's when the wreckage of the system was being cleaned up.
[11] *Northwestern Gazette and Galena Advertiser*, March 14, 1837.

of Illinois land, thanked the legislature and the Van Buren party for the good deed.[12]

Michigan lost little time in attempting to follow the mandate in her constitution to ascertain "the proper objects of improvement" "as soon as may be."[13] Governor Mason had said that the time had come, and the legislature agreed. In March, 1836, a law provided for a board of commissioners to "lay out and establish" some sixty-odd roads named in the act; the same session of the legislature chartered a dozen railroads.[14]

A year later, March 20, 1837, an act was passed "to provide for the construction of certain works of internal improvement, and for other purposes."[15] It appropriated $550,000 for the survey "and making" of three railroads: (1) from near Monroe to New Buffalo in Berrien County (the Southern Railroad); (2) from Detroit to the mouth of the St. Joseph River (the Central Railroad); (3) from Palmer or near the mouth of the Black River in St. Clair County to the navigable waters of the Grand River in Kent County, or on Lake Michigan in Ottawa County (the Northern Railroad). The Board of Internal Improvements was authorized to "purchase out" the rights and surveys of any chartered company which might duplicate or interfere with the above-mentioned plans. Appropriations were also made for surveys for a canal (or canal and railroad) from Mt. Clemens to the mouth of the Kalamazoo River; a canal to unite the Saginaw River with the Grand River; and $40,000 and $15,000 were appropriated for construction of these two works, respectively, if the board should so decide. The board was also directed to purchase the charter rights of the Havre Branch Railroad. A separate act appropriated $25,000 to survey a canal route around the falls of the St. Marys River and gave the commissioners power to commence the work.[16] The following day a loan of $5,000,000 was authorized; tolls, proceeds, dividends of state-

[12] *Illinois State Register and People's Advocate,* March 6, 1837. When repeal of the system was voted down in the special session of 1837, the *Register* expressed the hope that this marked the end of opposition. July 15, 1837.

[13] Article XII, Section 3, read in part: "And it shall be the duty of the legislature, as soon as may be, to make provision by law for ascertaining the proper objects of improvement in relation to roads, canals and navigable waters . . ."

[14] *Laws of Michigan,* 1835–36, pp. 90–103, 267–378.

[15] *Ibid.,* 1837, pp. 130–33.

[16] *Ibid.,* 1837, pp. 144–45.

owned bank stock, and the faith of the state were pledged.[17] Michigan's share of the distribution of the surplus was also allotted to the internal improvement fund.[18]

The House committee had reasoned that the $5,000,000 was not an expenditure, but an investment, equally divided among the people of the state. Assuming an income of 10 per cent from this investment, "we have a clear income over and above interest upon the capital of five per centum" or $250,000 per year. Allowing five years to complete the system, and omitting the fact that earlier completed portions would be paying interest upon their cost,

we shall have for the sixth year an income of two hundred and fifty thousand dollars, which at interest for nineteen years at seven per centum, is five hundred and eighty-two thousand five hundred; for the seventh year with a like interest for eighteen years, five hundred and sixty-five thousand; and this calculation carried out, or which is the same if we take the whole amount of the receipts for twenty years, with interest on the half of it for nineteen years, or interest on the whole for half the time, we have:

Receipts for twenty years, $250,000 per year	$5,000,000
Interest at seven per cent, $5,000,000, 9½ years	3,325,000
Amount	$8,325,000
Deduct amount of loan	5,000,000
	$3,325,000

A sum of $10,000 annually for managing this fund and a like amount to cover occasional losses would subtract $400,000 in twenty years and leave $2,925,000, plus possession of the works. "The principal being paid the income is doubled and the fund may be allowed to increase or the rates of toll be reduced to correspond with the wants of the state. Besides filling the public coffers it will add millions to the value of our soil and to the amount of productive industry."[19]

Although the figuring is a little hard to follow, it sounded good at the time; lack of population and income was no handicap to well-developed mathematical imaginations.[20] As Governor

[17] *Laws of Michigan*, 1837, pp. 152–53. The loan was redeemable after 25 years; interest was not to exceed 5½ per cent.

[18] *Ibid.*, 1837, p. 269. But later all but $26,751 was transferred to the general fund.

[19] Michigan *House Journal*, 1837, pp. 122 ff.

[20] The state treasurer's report to the legislature (for the preceding year) was as follows: Receipts from loans $100,000; from taxes $5,611; total $117,544. Expenditures: for interest and ordinary expenses of government, $50,301; extraordi-

Alpheus Felch later said, "There is abundant evidence . . . that the members took no narrow or unworthy view of the work they were chosen to perform."[21]

When in the autumn of 1837 ground on the Mt. Clemens— Kalamazoo Canal was broken near Mt. Clemens, Governor Mason and staff and a large concourse of citizens celebrated with food, refreshment, and oratory. It was a day of great expectations.

Wisconsin Territory, though in no position to embark upon a state internal improvements program, was none the less determined to have the improvements. When the Territory was hardly a month old, the *Milwaukee Advertiser* was writing up the Territory's needs and prospects; numerous roads, canals, and railroads were projected.[22] The Green Bay *Wisconsin Democrat* discussed ways and means as well as needs. Roads were the most pressing, but the Milwaukee and Rock River Canal was much emphasized. In 1836 the territorial legislature authorized several roads and chartered the La Fontaine Railroad Company to build from La Fontaine on Fox River to Lake Winnebago. The Milwaukee and Rock River Canal Company was chartered by the territorial legislature in January, 1838 (capital stock $100,000 which could be expanded to $1,000,000) to build a canal from Milwaukee to Rock River and a branch to connect with the Fox River. The future state was to have the right to purchase. The company, Byron Kilbourn, president, was successful in getting a land grant from Congress to the Territory,[23] and territorial

---

nary expenses $33,631; locating county sites $1,481; total $90,414. The *Detroit Daily Advertiser*, February 4, 1837, had argued that the projects should be undertaken in order of need and promise of early returns, but each section of the state held out for its own interests; the Detroit and St. Joseph Railroad could not be approved without the two others.

[21] *Proceedings of First Legislative Reunion*, 1886, p. 21, cited in Hannah E. Keith, "An Historical Sketch of Internal Improvements in Michigan, 1836–1846," in *Publications of the Michigan Political Science Association*, IV, 8 (July, 1900).

[22] *Milwaukee Advertiser*, August 11, 18, October 20, 1836, May 20, 1837, and following issues.

[23] Alternate sections five miles on either side of the proposed canal. The United States government sections were to sell at $2.50 an acre and not be subject to preemption. Petition for the grant had estimated cost at $798,000. Kilbourn, Juneau, and associates were heavy promoters. *Milwaukee Advertiser*, April 21, July 28, 1838; February 23, 1839; Green Bay *Wisconsin Democrat*, August 27, 1839. There was some criticism of the territorial law of February 26, 1839, which forbade any director, commissioner, stockholder, or engineer of the company purchasing or being interested in any of the canal lands. Many of the stock subscribers were settlers on the land ceded by Congress to the Territory. The law tended to place stock ownership outside the Territory. Memorial in *Milwaukee Advertiser*, February 1, 1840.

legislation which authorized a $50,000 loan. Since the bonds could not be sold, the loan was not effected.[24] Canal land sales were opened in June, 1839; buyers were to pay 10 per cent down, the remainder in four installments beginning in 1844. "Hang out our banner on the outer wall," announced the *Advertiser*. On July 4 Milwaukee celebrated the beginning of the canal with speeches and a parade.

Meanwhile, a year earlier, the Fox River Hydraulic Company, having sold $75,000 worth of its stock in the East, had let contracts for a canal at the portage.[25] The United States topographical engineer recommended that Congress act to complete the Green Bay–Chicago Road, the roads from Fond du Lac to the Wisconsin, Milwaukee via Madison to the Mississippi, Racine via Janesville to Sinipec, and the Military Road (Fort Howard to Fort Crawford).[26] The appropriations were meager, however; only about $78,000 for improvements came to the Territory up to 1840.

Contemplating the system of great works planned by the states to connect the Great Lakes–Mississippi routes, a contemporary reviewer wrote: "The cause is glorious, and worthy the foresight and energy of the vigorous young communities that have embarked in it—and that will, with the blessing of God, in a few short years, carry it forward to a triumphant completion."[27]

§

While the extensive internal improvements plans of 1836–37 were in progress, came notices and talk of "the money pressure" and "the deranged currency." With the presidential election out of the way, it had been hoped that the worst effects of the withdrawal of the deposits, the demise of the Bank, and the Specie Circular were past; that good times would continue and develop apace. But this was not to be. Hard money began to disappear, credit to tighten. Shortly after the election the *Chicago American* noted that the pressure in the money market "con-

[24] *Milwaukee Advertiser*, October 12, 1839.
[25] *Wisconsin Democrat*, August 4, 1838.
[26] Letter from Thomas J. Cramm to Governor Henry Dodge, in *Wisconsin Democrat*, January 14, 1840.
[27] J. W. S., "Internal Trade," in *The Hesperian*, I, 119.

tinued" with unabated severity. "It forms a singular circumstance in the present position of affairs, that people should be suffering for money, our enterprising business men breaking for the necessary accommodation of means, when our treasury is running over, and the revenue of the country accumulating in an increasing ratio. . . . We are waiting anxiously for better times."[28]

In March the *Cincinnati Daily Gazette*, commenting on the situation, asked why bankers could not discern the cause; more demand, more banks, then still more demand; "a gluttony never palled by plethora, but made keener by indulgence until suddenly extinguished by apoplexy."[29] In April the *Cleveland Herald and Gazette* thought that what the local money market needed for circulation and to use in settling debts was about $50,000 of something that would "not run away."[30] Business at Cincinnati and Louisville was "dull," "heavy," "no demand"; reports of tight money markets in eastern cities and business failures in New Orleans were widespread. There were rumors that eastern merchants had, through their spies, compiled a *Black Book* or list of unsafe-credit-risk western merchants. Many towns in the West were interested in "ferreting out the author of this vile stigma on our character."[31]

The currency was so deranged that some papers ceased publishing their bank-note tables. Despite soothing advice that everyone should exercise mutual forbearance, kindness, and confidence, pay his own bills and refrain from repeating and spreading the widespread gloom—"Do as you would be done by"—and pretense that there was no depression,[32] the thing was too evident to overlook. "The pressure is now the prevailing and absorbing theme of attention and remark, from the grave and didactic newspaper essay on cause and effect, to the familiar conversation of the multitude." Ruin was not confined to the large class of enterprising dealers denounced by the late tyrant who ruled with

[28] *Chicago American*, November 19, 1836.

[29] March 22, 1837.

[30] April 20, 1837 (weekly). "Where is Monsieur Benton's gold currency in this time of need? We have in this section Upper Canada paper of the unchartered Banks, and now and then a Mormon bill, with a small sprinkling of the thousand and one banks of Michigan . . . but the gold and silver which has been so long promised, still lags behind." *Cleveland Herald and Gazette*, April 29, 1837.

[31] *Chicago American* quoted in *Western Courier and Piqua Enquirer*, May 6, 1837.

[32] The *Cleveland Weekly Advertiser* in the early months of 1837 took the attitude that it was only a few eastern failures of ordinary course.

a rod of iron, but reached all classes. The Specie Circular, the Pandora box of present distresses, was cursed by both parties.[33] "These are sad times, truly; and such as to make the stones of Rome to rise in mutiny. Doubt, doom and despair seem to have taken possession of all classes—men of all parties are becoming alarmed at the state of things—one project after another is suggested to relieve the distress of the mercantile community; but without avail. The notaries and lawyers are the only persons benefitted by the universal loss. If the present is a foretaste of the promised *golden age*, God help our country."[34]

On May 10 the New York banks suspended specie payments and others followed. The news was not long reaching the West; all doubts were now removed. "Bankruptcy and ruin are covering our country as with a pall. A pestilence, sweeping off thousands, who had hoped to escape the blight, is upon us."[35] It had been foretold but none believed that "the money grippe," "the *Experiment*" would spread its devastations far and wide.[36]

Fearful *catastrophe* indeed it is, that we are witnessing around us— sweeping over the whole land, like the rolling progress of a general earth- quake, till it shall reach its farthest extremities—and strewing its fair surface with the shattered fragments of a great nation's prosperity and pride! The whole financial system of the country has fallen to the ground. Magnificent in its dimensions, and glittering in golden gorgeousness, as the stupendous fabric showed to the eye, its rotten and disproportionate foundations have yielded beneath its weight, and the whole edifice now lies prostrate, an unsightly chaos of splendid ruins. . . . The nation is bankrupt; most disastrously, most disgracefully bankrupt!

[33] *Chicago American*, May 13, 1837.
[34] *Western Courier and Piqua Enquirer*, May 6, 1837.
[35] *Louisville City Gazette* cited in *Cincinnati Daily Gazette*, May 19, 1837. Calvin Fletcher of Indianapolis wrote to Senator John Tipton, August 27: ". . . you have given your support to an administration before which the best interests of your country have vanished like the morning dew—you have witnessed the distruction of our tariff—the abolishing of a system of internal improvements & lastly the utter ruin & confusion of our currency—you now see the eyes of a whole nation turned towards that body for relief of which you are a member—& such is the fear & alarm of the best interests of our common country & so long have they witnessed one distruction & one mischif after another that the government has become such a despot such a tyrant that on the least rumor as to its future course stocks grain & every commercial commodity rise & fall as irregular as the wind that blows. The acts of the government have kept the whole community in fear, dread & agitation for years past—Every patriot every good citizen is called on to put an end to such a course—If things continue as they are, the aiders & abet- tors of this mischif will receive the execrations of an indignant people within the next 4 years—I shall look to you to take a firm open stand against all further experiments." *The John Tipton Papers*, III, 429.
[36] *Cincinnati Daily Gazette*, May 19, 1837.

Though the real wealth of the country had not been destroyed, "the vast system through which all the commercial and financial action of the country used to work has stopped, broken and disjointed by its own too rapid operation. . . ."[37]

In the discussion of causes and remedies views were determined in large part by political partisanship—or vice versa—but not entirely. Many realized that money, prices, honesty, and confidence were matters not entirely controllable by political formula. The *Detroit Daily Advertiser*, staunch Whig in outlook, apropos the speculation and high land prices pointed out that such a condition could not continue; there was bound to be a reaction. As the dollar became scarcer and dearer it would buy more. Business would be curtailed, but this alone would not affect the prosperity of the country; it would, however, have "a temporary embarrassing effect" while the process of contraction was going on.[38] It was not the Specie Circular, but millions tied up in land speculation and internal improvements that was causing the trouble.[39] Similar to the effects of alcohol and opium upon the human system were those of over banking,[40] and for over banking everybody was to blame.

More dogmatic were the arguments of the Democratic papers which blamed "the money power," the "rag barons," Nick Biddle, and the "Bank Aristocracy"; and of the Whig papers which blamed the currency tinkering of the General Government for the devastating ruin.

The leading Democratic paper in Illinois in its first mention of the money pressure wrote: "The Panic, which the Bank of England and its Branch, the Bank of the United States, has

[37] Mineral Point (Wis.) *Miners' Free Press*, June 23, 1837.
David T. Snellbaker in a lengthy review of the hard times, 1837–40, in the *Cincinnati Daily Gazette*, February 12, 1840, wrote: "Men absolutely became dizzy at the height to which they were elevated—nor paused to reflect—but each urged the other on by example, when suddenly, in 1837, the storm that had been gathering for years, burst with the fury of an avalanche over the whole country; when numbers who had been crowding too much sail, found themselves among the breakers on a lee shore, and were speedily wrecked; others of much more prudence and discernment weathered the storm, but strained at every nerve, have been compelled to hold back until the troubled sea has sunk down into a dead calm; the great sinews of the body politic have become completely paralyzed; thousands of honest, industrious men are anxious to work, but none need their assistance." He said the nation had run head and ears into debt and John Bull wanted the cash.
[38] April 6, May 8, 1837.
[39] *Milwaukee Advertiser*, April 22, 1837.
[40] *Cleveland Weekly Advertiser*, July 20, 1837.

created in this country, has not . . . reached the Western States." Though hundreds of business houses in the East had stopped payment, there had been only one failure in the West, thanks to Jackson's Specie Circular which had kept specie distributed. But look out, "Biddle and his bribery banks are trying to drain specie from the West and make a panic. No use to try this game on the Suckers, old boy."[41]

At the same time the rival Whig paper was writing, "Where are we now? With our Country at peace with all the world—blessed with all those advantages which unite to make a prosperous and happy people—without public debt—with a population remarkable for their industry and enterprise—with twenty millions of dollars nominally in our National Treasury—with these and other untold advantages—we present the singular and novel spectacle of a people reduced to insolvency and ruin—the Government sunk into a state of bankruptcy—and all the result of the wickedness, blunders and ignorance of our rulers." Nothing remained for the people to do "but to commence the harvesting of the crop of glory which they have been sowing, and plowing in, for the last eight years." The people had been listening to demagogues instead of to honest men.[42] These told them the Bank of the United States was an aristocratic institution and must be destroyed. "He spoke and it was done."[43] When politicians incited the "poor against the rich," all suffered.[44] The Presbyterian Church even deplored this development. "One of the most formidable evils of the present crisis, is the wide spread and ever restless spirit of *Radicalism*, manifest both in church and state."[45]

It was questioned whether retrenchment and strict economy on the part of the wealthier and middle classes was the remedy; when these classes quit spending, the laborer suffered. Perhaps "the pressure" was not an unmitigated evil; it made the poor man more content with his lot because he saw the wealthy getting poorer too. A great bold and moral revolution was really neces-

[41] Vandalia *Illinois State Register and People's Advocate*, May 13, 1837.
[42] Springfield *Sangamo Journal*, April 29, June 3, 1837; also *Cincinnati Daily Gazette*, June 15, 24, 1837.
[43] *Sangamo Journal*, May 20, 1837.
[44] Columbus *Ohio State Journal*, September 12, 1837.
[45] Circular Epistle of General Assembly in *Cincinnati Daily Gazette*, July 28, 1837.

sary to prove to the world and future generations that "our glorious system of government stands on the principles of freedom."[46] Some maintained that there was no use arguing about either causes or remedies; the more the talk the worse things got. The "Sand Boat" rhymester must have been a convert to this idea:

> In these our latter days of troubles,
> Of bursting boilers, banks and bubbles,
> And other 'ship and shore' disasters
> Such as long faces and 'shinplasters,'
> Lank bodies, and yet purses lanker
> Humbugs and protests of the banker—
> In imitation of the times
> I jingle out my "Sand Boat" rhymes.[47]

Commodity prices were at first not so drastically affected by the pressure; excepting at Chicago and Milwaukee, where the land boom and transportation were important factors, they had not advanced to such heights as land prices.[48] Even so the decline was noticeable. By August flour at Cincinnati had declined about 30 per cent, wheat 40 per cent, and other commodities, excepting pork which held its price, in proportion. By early autumn with specie at 7½ per cent premium and scarce, the market reported "a calm deathlike calm pervades us."[49] Prices continued to fall, business failures increased, the currency became more disordered. The winter of 1837–38 was a hard one, particularly so for the new settlers (and speculators) in Michigan and Wisconsin Territory. Potatoes and salt were the chief diet

[46] *Cincinnati Daily Gazette,* July 8, 1837.

[47] *Northwestern Gazette and Galena Advertiser,* July 15, 1837.

[48] For comparison in the winter of 1836–37:

	Milwaukee	Chicago	Cincinnati	Detroit	
flour	$14.00–$16.00 bbl.	$12	$7.75	$5.50	
wheat	—	—	$1.25	—	
corn	$ 2.00– 2.50 bu.	—	.37	.62½	
beef	.14– .16 lb.	.84	—	$12.00–$13.00	bbl.
mess pork	$33.00–$35.00 bbl.	$25–$28	$16.00–$18.00	$25.00	
butter	.45– .50 lb.	.38–.50	—	.20	
lard	.22– .25 lb.	.15–.20	.10	—	
salt	$ 7.00–$ 8.00 bu.	—	—	—	
potatoes	—	.75 bu.	—	.40	

The prices which the farmer received at the general store or from the local buyer were usually considerably below these market prices.

[49] *Cincinnati Daily Gazette,* October 4, 1837. For further information on Cincinnati prices, see Thomas Senior Berry, *Western Prices before 1861; A Study of the Cincinnati Market* (Harvard University Press, 1943).

for those caught; town lots in Milwaukee valued at $500 to
$1,000 a short year before, were swapped for a barrel of flour.[50]
By late winter it became obvious that the West was in for a
period of "hard times"; no ray of light penetrated the horizon
and it appeared that the worst was yet to come. "The prospect
before us is gloomy enough to satisfy Diogenes himself, or any
other cynic that ever lived. Three, six or even nine months
ago, the darkness brooding over the land was that of midnight,
but now it is Egyptian—a darkness that may be felt."[51]

The states of the Northwest were variously equipped with
banking facilities for carrying business and state finances through
a depression.[52] The note circulation of the chartered Ohio banks
had fallen from the 1836 high of $9,675,644 to $8,326,974 in
January, 1837; specie on hand was $3,153,334; deposits were
$3,463,450.[53] By May the figures were, circulation $7,697,261,
specie $2,311,614. Nevertheless, Ohio banks stopped paying
specie about a week after the eastern banks. At a meeting in
Columbus on June 5, a majority of the Ohio banks agreed to
protect their specie, receive in payment for debts notes on the
other banks represented, to limit the issue of notes, and to keep
each other posted regarding conditions. Antibank Democrats
insisted the banks had forfeited their charters by suspension, but
since proof had to be established by judicial process, the matter
was not pushed.

The law against the issue of bank notes smaller than $5.00,
finally to take effect July 4, 1837,[54] made small business transactions difficult. Two banks were excepted from the provisions,[55]
and the Miami Exporting Company, the Urbana Banking Company, and the Bank of Circleville refused to comply. It was feared
that the issue of 25- and 50-cent notes, once begun, would become general; that business houses would issue the small "shin-

---

[50] Amherst W. Kellogg, "Recollections of Life in Early Wisconsin," in *Wisconsin Magazine of History*, VII (1923–24), 484.
[51] *Cleveland Herald and Gazette* (weekly), February 8, 1838.
[52] For state banking to 1836, see Chapter VIII.
[53] State auditor's report in *Cincinnati Daily Gazette*, March 16, 1837. Regarding chartered banks as versus a state bank, the *Cincinnati Daily Advertiser*, March 10, 1837, said the legislature had its choice. In addition to the 32 in existence, charters for 39 new banks were introduced. "The *iron* age has gone—the *golden* age will not come, and paper money or *rag* currency (as it has been styled by some) is to pervade the land. May it be averted."
[54] See Chapter VIII, 612.
[55] The Commercial Bank and the Franklin Bank of Cincinnati.

plasters," and small coins would be driven out altogether. Such "shinplasters" were issued in a number of towns but did not become general.[56]

Early in September in his message to the special session of Congress President Van Buren faced the depression; he wrote of "a concurrence of circumstances . . . redundancy of credit," and noted that banking had become "a political topic of the highest interest"; no government could prevent abuses of credit and excesses of speculation, but every government should refrain from stimulating them. The government of the United States was not created to render "specific aid to the citizen to relieve embarrassments . . . or to create systems of agriculture, manufactures, or trade. . . . To avoid every unnecessary interference with the pursuits of the citizen will result in more benefit than to adopt measures which could only assist limited interests, and are eagerly, but perhaps naturally, sought for under the pressure of temporary circumstances." He registered his opposition to re-establishment of the Bank of the United States, defended the Specie Circular, advocated the Treasury handling government funds, and recommended that the October, 1837, installment of surplus distribution to the states be withheld.

Although this was good Democratic doctrine it did not carry quite as much authority, coming from the pen of Van Buren, as it had from that of Andrew Jackson. Some of the party papers in the West were willing to "clear our skirts" of locofocoism and live and let live as far as banks were concerned.[57]

Ohio, with its nine pet banks, was worried lest the Treasury would demand return of the government deposits within a few months. Governor Vance in his message in December, 1837, pointed out that the state, though paying heavily for roads and

<hr />

[56] Circleville, Chillicothe, Lancaster, Somerset, Thornville, and Marietta. When the *New York Times* taunted Cincinnati with having worn its one quarter dollar of change down to a pistareen borrowing it for postal purposes, the *Gazette,* October 5, 1837, replied that while Cincinnati, by resisting shinplaster change had got along pretty well, New York was understood "to be literally overrun with all manner of creeping things." Cleveland, by city ordinance, February 1, 1838, provided for issuance of $80,000 of $1.00, $2.00, and $3.00 notes (bearing 6 per cent interest and payable in one year) on the city's credit. *Cleveland Herald and Gazette* (weekly), February 8, 1838.

The Kirtland Safety Society had an estimated $40,000 of "Mormon money" in circulation. Since this phantom money was not cashable, it circulated little outside the community. *Cleveland Weekly Gazette,* February 1, 1837.

[57] *Cincinnati Republican,* quoted in *Cincinnati Daily Gazette,* October 6, 1837.

schools was getting its money's worth, but at the same time, as a result of the war on the Bank, it was paying high interest rates on money, and taking heavy losses through depreciation of bank notes, with no return. He commended the sound condition of Ohio's banks whose note circulations were but slightly more than twice the specie on hand and advocated repeal of the Specie Circular.[58] The Whig legislature refused to investigate the banks and repealed the law against issue of small notes, but specified that Ohio banks should resume specie payments July 4, if the eastern banks did.[59]

Although in April the *Ohio State Journal* had written that "Public confidence in bank and individual credit is paralyzed, and unless speedily strengthened and relieved, will become utterly prostrate,"[60] things looked better as spring advanced. Early in June came news of the repeal of the Specie Circular; it was thought that resumption of specie payment by banks and a stimulating effect on business would follow.[61] Ohio banks were not helped, however, since notes of banks which issued denominations smaller than $5.00 were not acceptable by the Treasury.[62] Ohio banks at a meeting in Columbus, June 5–6, decided to resume specie payment when eastern banks did. The date agreed upon by the latter was August 13. Indiana and Illinois banks also resumed on this date.[63] Resumption, though pleasant news, caused little sensation. There was no rush for specie. "Those who have been most noisy against the banks are principally such as handle so little of either bank notes or specie, that they have no operations to make, when clamor ceases to be of any account."[64] "The Crisis Past . . . Cincinnati Erect," announced the *Cincinnati Chronicle.*[65] Yet two months later two full pages of the *Cleveland*

---

[58] *Ohio State Journal,* December 2, 1837. The auditor's report showed $1.00 in specie to each $2.23 of notes in circulation.

[59] The *Ohio State Journal, Hillsborough News,* and other papers had advocated the repeal of the small note law.

[60] April 18, 1838.

[61] *Cleveland Herald and Gazette* (weekly), June 14, 1838.

[62] *Ohio State Journal,* June 5, 1838.

[63] Suspension, said the *Journal,* was caused fifteen months earlier by the "Van Jackson Party"; many legislatures had legalized suspension, but not one Whig legislature. August 7, 1838. Detroit banks had begun some specie payment in May.

[64] *Cincinnati Daily Gazette,* August 27, 1838. The *Cleveland Herald and Gazette* had issued an extra Saturday, July 29, to announce the date of resumption, decided upon by a Philadelphia meeting July 23; news reached Cleveland by the Pittsburgh mail.

[65] August 25, 1838.

Herald and Gazette were required to list the tax delinquent properties.[66]

The Democratic victory in the state election in 1838 brought about no basic changes in Ohio banking. Governor Wilson Shannon was not of the Benton-Jackson hard-money belief; he denied that Ohio Democrats desired the wiping out of bank currency, but did recommend limiting note issues and stricter control of charters by the legislature. The legislature passed a law to prohibit corporations other than banks issuing notes for circulation, and another, the Bank Commissioner Act, to limit notes of banks to three times the amount of specie possessed, not counting deposits. Directors and stockholders were made liable for any excess issue. Banks which suspended specie payment for more than thirty days in one year were to be closed. Three bank commissioners, selected by the legislature, were to examine the banks and report regularly.

The apparent business revival of 1838–39 proved a false dawn. By autumn, 1839, eastern banks again suspended specie payment. Ohio banks suspended intermittently, but managed to pay some specie before thirty days elapsed, so as to save their charters. Some banks issued noninterest-bearing post notes (payable at some future date) for making loans and paying depositors, a practice which was condemned in the first annual report of the bank commissioners.

The Democrats had a two-thirds majority in the legislature which met in December, 1839. Governor Shannon called attention to the great state of financial embarrassment in the country and credited it largely to excess of imports over exports and the resulting flow of coin abroad. He noted that Ohio banks had reduced their discounts from $19,000,000 to $8,237,000 between May, 1837, and September, 1838, and that note circulation had been decreased $1,800,000. Although he mentioned the possibility of a state bank, or a general banking system, he recommended continuance of the existing chartered banks. He pointed out that the state's liabilities were in excess of $12,000,-000. The message was less acceptable to some of the hard-money Democratic papers than to the Whigs. The legislature passed another law against banks issuing notes under $5.00 and pro-

[66] November 1, 1838.

hibited issue of certain kinds of post notes. This law made it difficult to transact small business and pay taxes. In December, 1840, Governor Shannon spoke bravely of the choice being "between reformation and destruction," with reference to the banks, but a new Whig state administration was at hand and his words carried little weight.

The financial uncertainty of the times naturally affected Ohio's internal improvements program. Upon the suspension of specie payments in 1837 the Canal Fund Commission ordered work on construction of several of the canals suspended, but after the state made a loan on favorable terms, work was resumed. By law of March, 1837, the legislature authorized the state to make loans to, and subscribe to the stock of canal, railroad, and turnpike companies. Under this law, later sometimes referred to as the "Plunder Law,"[67] loans or stock subscriptions were made to the Little Miami and to the Lake Erie and Mad River railroads; to two dozen turnpike companies; and to the Pennsylvania and Ohio, and Whitewater and Cincinnati Canal companies. Of the $900,000 subscribed by the state in 1837 about half was to the Pennsylvania and Ohio Canal. The Whitewater and Cincinnati Canal, to which the state pledged $150,000, was begun in the spring of 1838, but construction was suspended in the autumn of the following year because of inability to collect the stock subscriptions.[68]

After Governor Vance's emphasis upon the importance of the improvements to the people, the legislature of 1837–38 made heavy appropriations for continuing the Ohio works. To help satisfy claims of counties not already provided for in the improvements, six new works were authorized at an estimated cost of $8,577,300.[69] In 1838 a loan of $2,010,000 was placed (6 per

[67] Bogart, *Internal Improvements and State Debt in Ohio,* 53. Under this law the state had no choice. When certain conditions were met, the state was to subscribe to the extent of one half of the stock of turnpike companies, one third the stock of canal companies, and to lend to railroad companies an amount equal to one third of their capital. All told the state put up $2,973,000 and received $31,362 in dividends. The loans and stock subscriptions totaled 65 per cent of the total state debt at the time of passage of the law.

[68] The city of Cincinnati had subscribed $200,000, the state $150,000, and individuals $100,000. By late 1840 the company, after spending $599,123, had $149,123 of notes in circulation, $75,000 still due from the state, and $127,856 due from individuals. *Cincinnati Daily Gazette,* December 4, 1840.

[69] Extension of the Miami Canal to Lake Erie, the Wabash and Erie Canal, the Walhonding Canal, the Hocking Valley Canal, Muskingum River Improvement, and the Western Reserve and Maumee Road. The estimated cost was equal to about one-and-a-half times the state debt as of December, 1837.

cent), one million of which was taken by the Ohio Life and Trust Company of Cincinnati.[70] The next year a loan of $2,416,123 was floated. For a while it appeared that the arguments of the canal advocates would prove out: the Miami Canal, for instance, which had cost $727,864 plus $162,499 for repairs, had returned between 1828 and 1837 $402,214 in tolls—about 5 per cent, after maintenance, on the total investment.[71] A year later, after the legislature of 1838–39 had appropriated $1,790,000 additional,[72] a clearer picture was to be had. The total expended and appropriated by 1839 on the "collateral works" was $4,387,614,[73] plus an estimated $1,000,000 in loans of the state's credit to various other projects.[74] For the Ohio Canal and the Miami Canal, and its extension, almost $7,000,000 had been spent and appropriated, making a total of about $12,000,000.

Although the Ohio Canal had taken in some $382,000 in receipts, upkeep and repairs had absorbed about $200,000 of this amount. "It is now certain that the Public Works do not maintain themselves; but are, every year, to some extent, a charge upon the State revenue. Should we not begin to think about calling a halt in making appropriations for new works?"[75] The

---

[70] *Cincinnati Daily Gazette,* August 21, 23, 1838.
[71] Engineer's report in *ibid.,* May 9, 1838.
[72] Wabash and Erie Canal $700,000
Muskingum Improvement 430,000
Hocking Canal 300,000
Walhonding Canal 150,000
Western Reserve and Maumee Road 100,000
Warren Canal Company 60,000
Zanesville Work 50,000
Ohio State Journal, June 11, 1839.
[73] Wabash and Erie Canal previously expended $697,767
Balance of 1838 appropriated from land sales 297,303
1839 appropriation 700,000 $1,695,070
Muskingum Improvement previously expended........... 785,215
1839 appropriation 430,000   1,215,215
Hocking Canal previously expended.................... 350,000
1839 appropriation 300,000   650,000
Walhonding Canal previously expended 287,885
1839 appropriation 150,000   437,885
Warren Canal Company previously expended........... 139,444
1839 appropriation 60,000   199,444
Zanesville Work   50,000
Western Reserve and Maumee Road previously expended 40,000
1839 appropriation 100,000   140,000
                                                    _____
                                                    $4,387,614
[74] These included the Little Miami and the Lake Erie and Mad River railroads; the Batavia-Miami Bridge; the Ohio, Dayton and Springfield, and Cincinnati-Montgomery turnpikes; and the Whitewater and Cincinnati Canal.
[75] *Ohio State Journal,* June 11, 1839.

state auditor estimated annual interest on the state's debt at $660,000 in 1839, more than a third of which could only be paid by further borrowing. Governor Shannon told the legislature that the time had come "when we are forced by the dictates of prudence to pause and consider what can be done to arrest the accumulation of our state debt." The "Loan Law" of 1837 was repealed early in 1840, but commitments already made weighed heavily. The Governor went to New York where he obtained another loan ($400,000) but before the end of the year the auditor was being called upon to advance $200,000 from the general revenue to meet interest charges. By 1841 the credit of the state was so impaired that it was impossible to market additional bonds in either Europe or the United States.

Regardless of the increasing financial burden, the opening of canals was still a thrilling event. On April 3, 1840, when a boat cleared the summit of the Pennsylvania and Ohio Canal, the way was open from Cleveland to Pittsburgh. The hundred-mile ditch from Beaver by way of Newcastle, the Mahoning, to Warren, Ravenna, and Akron had been built (with some $400,000 aid from Ohio) by a company chartered jointly by the two states in 1827. Normally free of ice almost a month ahead of the Erie Canal, its completion was regarded by Cleveland interests as the greatest event since the last war.[76]

Indiana started its big improvements program with a rush. Governor Noble appointed the six members of the Board of Internal Improvements, which at its first meeting, March, 1836, requested the fund commissioners to float a loan of $2,000,000. Work to be undertaken was parceled out among the members of the board for supervision. Since each member was assigned the district closest to his home, the scramble for funds was lively. In addition to the resident engineers for each work, engineers-in-chief were appointed for canals and railroads and a full corps of surveyors employed for each project. These superfluous workers, who cost thousands of dollars annually, came to be known as the "Eating Brigade." Regardless of strong sentiment in the legislature for "classification" or building one project at a time on the priority of need and revenue possibility, contracts were let simultaneously for miscellaneous sections of the various

[76] *Cleveland Herald and Gazette* (weekly), April 8, 1840.

projects nearest the homes of the sponsoring board members.[77]

Trouble and bitter criticism began at once. Labor was scarce, contractors bid against each other as well as against those in neighboring states, and the question of road or railroad for the New Albany–Crawfordsville, Madison–Lafayette, and New Albany–Vincennes projects was unsettled.

Governor Noble, ex-Governor Ray, and David Wallace were the leading orators at the big Brookville celebration, September 13, 1836, which marked the beginning of the Whitewater Canal. Almost a thousand men were engaged in its construction; by the end of 1838, the ditch was completed almost to Brookville, to which place boats ran the following June. Costs ran considerably ahead of both estimates and appropriations; tolls the first six months were $670.

Surveys and construction of the Central Canal progressed intermittently during 1836–37; unconnected sections were finished; when the Pigeon Creek section was finished, the creek, which was to furnish the water, was dry. The New Albany–Vincennes road was constructed as far as Paoli, 41 miles, and an additional 27 miles were graded. Outside engineers were consulted regarding making a railroad of the New Albany–Crawfordsville route, but when the cost was estimated at $7,000,000, the legislature in 1838 ordered the board to build a macadamized road. Almost $400,000 was spent grading two unconnected sections of this road. After $445,000 had been spent surveying and building the Madison–Indianapolis–Lafayette Railroad, the state engineer, January, 1838, advised a turnpike instead for the northern end. During the next year and a half, at the cost of $1,493,000 some 28 miles of railroad were so constructed, and about 25 miles additional were graded. Expenditure of $156,000 on the "canal or railroad" line from Fort Wayne to Michigan City resulted in nothing more than a wagonload of surveyors' notes.

The Board of Fund Commissioners, created in 1831 to borrow

[77] Whitewater Canal from Lawrenceburg to Brookville; 22 miles of Madison Railroad out of Madison; Wabash and Erie Canal west to Lafayette; Cross-Cut Canal from Terre Haute to Eel River; Central Canal along Pigeon Creek to Evansville; bridges and grading on the Vincennes–New Albany road; Central Canal from feeder above Indianapolis to Port Royal bluffs; and 20 miles of the Jeffersonville–Lafayette road. For relationship between the board members and work started, see Esarey, *Internal Improvements in Early Indiana*, 104–5.

money for the Wabash and Erie Canal,[78] was continued by the law of 1836. It had violated the law in making loans, kept no books, and rendered unreliable reports. Bonds were apparently delivered to different members to sell on whatever basis they could arrange; notices of individuals placing loans appear in the newspapers of the day. Within a year after passage of the mammoth internal improvements bill $3,827,000 was spent. Since the legislature had made no provision for interest (the politicians had said the system would be self-sustaining), this amount also had to be paid from loans. In 1837 $1,600,000 more was spent. When the legislature in December asked for an estimate of interest required, it was told that the "System" would cost $23,000,000, hence interest (at 5 per cent) would be $1,150,000 annually. Since revenues of the state from taxation were about $45,000 per year, this was a sizeable sum to face. In 1838 the outlay was nearly $2,000,000. By the end of the year Governor Wallace, who, a year earlier had painted a rosy picture of the situation, noting that interest due was $193,350, said: "If this condition does not startle us, it should at least awaken us." The solution, he thought, was for the state to borrow more money, invest it in bank stock, and use the proceeds on its debts.[79]

The advocates of classification, previously overridden, now began to receive a hearing.[80] The legislature in February, 1839, reduced the Board of Internal Improvements to three members and ordered it to classify and build one project at a time. At the same time it placed the affairs of the old Board of Fund Commissioners in the hands of two men, each to be bonded at $100,000.[81] But action came too late; "the state was bankrupt beyond the power of any remedial law."[82] On August 18, 1839,

[78] See Chapter VII.

[79] Message, December 4, 1838.

[80] John Dillon, Whig editor of the Logansport *Canal Telegraph,* was one of the first to point out, in 1837, that construction of upwards of one thousand miles of canals and railroads at an unknown cost, was too much for the slender resources of the state.

[81] *Laws of Indiana,* 1838–39, Chapters I and XVI. Ex-Governor Noah Noble was placed on the Internal Improvements Board whose expenditures were limited to $1,500,000 per year. Milton Stapp and Lucius H. Scott were made the new fund commissioners.

[82] Esarey, *Internal Improvements in Early Indiana,* 109. In 1836 the fund commissioners received only $202,000 on a $500,000 bond sale to the Cohens of Baltimore, before the firm suspended business. The next year the commissioners accepted, in settlement of the balance due, a lot of railroad bonds, deeds to several hundred New York and Brooklyn city lots, a decaying sperm and candle factory

Noah Noble announced that the fund commissioners were unable to borrow more money and that it would be necessary for the state to stop payment on its contracts.

Stoppage on the work was a jolt to business in general. Hundreds of contractors found themselves broken, thousands of laborers without their wages. Although the fund commissioners announced that money would soon be forthcoming, the people of the state began to realize the seriousness of the situation. Hopes that the General Government would help out the states, as advocated by some of the Whigs, failed when Congress declined the proposal.[83] By autumn the Rothschilds and other creditors were demanding interest on their bonds, and contractors, to whom more than $1,000,000 was due for work already done, were petitioning for relief.

The legislature of 1839–40 was quite incapable of understanding or handling the financial mess; its talents were no match for those of the politicians and manipulators who were pilfering the state's treasury and destroying its credit. Seventeen reports were submitted to the House, eighteen to the Senate; the members listened, played politics, and did little. Citizens of Cass County, believing that the Assembly had no capacity other than for spending money, petitioned for its adjournment. Aside from the legislative inquest on the defunct "System," only one thing

---

in Brooklyn, later often referred to in the newspapers, and other odds and ends. All told, from January, 1837, to January, 1839, the fund commissioners had marketed a total of $5,627,000 of bonds. When the new commissioners in 1840 tried to straighten things out with the Morris Canal and Banking Company, which owed the state $854,364, they received $36,566 in cash, $266,000 in the company's certificates of deposit, and $280,000 in its notes, leaving an unsecured balance of $271,998. On a debt of $240,000 due from the Bank of Western New York and Georgia Lumber Company, Indiana finally got some 300,000 acres of land in Georgia, which it later (1849) sold for $1,000. Many of the securities accepted in lieu of cash proved worthless, or nearly so. When it is remembered that the state had pledged its faith for every cent, principal and interest, on its bonds, it can be partly realized what a wild and loose game of high finance the fund commissioners had been playing. For details of further losses to the state, see report of House Investigating Committee in Indiana *Documentary Journal*, 1841–42, part II, no. 12, pp. 215–468.

[83] Various proposals for getting out from under the depression were advanced as early as 1837. One called for creation of United States stock at 3 per cent, irredeemable for fifty years, to be exchanged for stocks and bonds of the states, with the condition that, when $50,000,000 was out, holders of the United States stock be permitted, by adding $25,000,000, to establish a Bank of the United States. Another called for an issue of $300,000,000 of United States stock to exchange for state stocks, with proceeds from land sales to go to a sinking fund. *Hamilton* (Ohio) *Intelligencer*, December 5, 1837. Senator O. H. Smith, of Indiana, suggested that the United States assume the state debts at least to the extent of land sales made within the states. Governor Bigger in his inaugural speech in 1840 advocated the same plan.

was accomplished: in January, 1840, a law was passed which provided for an issue of $1,200,000 in treasury notes with which to pay the contractors.[84]

The people were both disgusted and aroused at the turn of events. A state debt of more than $13,000,000[85] was bad enough, but when it became apparent that some $3,000,000 of state bonds had been "sold" for which the state had received nothing, that fund commissioners could not account for sales and receipts, the reaction was positive. Noah Noble tried hard to straighten out the affairs of the Internal Improvements Board, but the finances of the fund commissioners were beyond his powers. The report of a legislative committee in 1841 on the work of Commissioner Stapp might well have applied to that of other commissioners as well:

Not what he has done wrong, but what is there in his whole business correctly done? His complicated negotiations with Sherwood, Danforth, Dodge, Robinson [irresponsible bankers of New York and Ohio], and others, his loans of state property to sustain tottering swindling shops, his antedated letters and receipts, his negligence and confusion in business, his improper connection with brokers, shavers, and swindlers, are facts too glaring to be denied, too grossly wrong to admit of palliation, and too palpably indefensible to invite attack.[86]

The legislature of 1840–41, in an endeavor to salvage something of the system, finally got around to a classification bill, but this lies beyond the scope of this chapter.

Whereas in 1836 practically all the newspapers of the state, except those of Vevay and Corydon had been blatant advocates of the "System," three years later they were singing a different tune. Although both parties were equally responsible for the situation—"improvements" had outweighed party division in the voters' minds—each now blamed the other. Wrote the *Indiana Democrat*: "The Whigs have ruled and ruined the State. It is time that a change should take place . . . but while the system is under Whig managers, let them manage. They have got the

---

[84] The next legislature issued more scrip.

[85] Esarey, *Internal Improvements in Early Indiana*, 121.

[86] *Documentary Journal*, 1841–42, part I, no. 6, p. 177. Dr. Isaac Coe, one of the first commissioners, had been a stockholder in the Morris Canal and Banking Company, which owed the state $2,536,611. M. B. Sherwood, a crooked wildcat banker, obtained one way or another $1,300,000 of Indiana bonds, and worked with the Morris Canal Company to split commissions thereon. Almost $2,000,000 of bonds were out and unaccounted for. For tabulation and itemized list of Indiana's bonded debt in 1841, see Esarey, *Internal Improvements in Early Indiana*, 125, 128–29.

state into a scrape, let them get it out. We intend to urge nothing, propose nothing, to do nothing until *every Whig* who has had any management of the system is turned out of office."[87]

Few editors had the courage or the honesty to face the situation. The Lawrenceburg *Political Beacon* spoke truly when it said:

Now that the system is becoming a little unpopular it is not fair, it is not generous, that one party should attempt to sneak out of it, and throw all the blame on the other, when both are equally responsible for the good or evil effects resulting from its adoption. Better would it be for all of us to come up to the work like men, like patriots, frankly acknowledge our error and strive to ward off the approaching evil. If the measure was a bad one, let us do the best we can with it.

Though the second State Bank of Indiana was closely connected with the internal improvements program, it came through the depression in much better shape than the fiscal affairs of the state. Men such as Samuel Merrill, its president, J. F. D. Lanier, president of the Madison branch, and Hugh McCulloch, of the Fort Wayne branch, were of a different caliber from those who were trusted with handling the funds of the state. Not even the mismanagement and derelictions of the fund commissioners could drag down the State Bank. In 1836 when the legislature authorized the state to buy an additional $1,000,000 of stock of the bank, Dr. Isaac Coe, secretary of the fund commissioners, placed the bonds with a firm of New York brokers with which he had connections; all but $20,000 of the issue was lost to the state. The bank had counted (and discounted) heavily on the additional capital, and coming as it did with the depression and breakdown of the state's finances, this bad luck weighed heavily upon it. Further, the fund commissioners kept their funds in the bank and frequently overdrew; in 1839 when the state stopped paying the contractors, there was an overdraft of $650,000 at the bank.[88]

In 1836 the United States Treasury had $2,267,489 on deposit in the State Bank of Indiana, but in 1837 this was reduced to

[87] The *Goshen Democrat* suggested that the Whigs start a soap factory, "gather in all the ashes and soap grease of the Union—kindle the fire—set the pot boiling —make 100,000 pounds of soap, sell it for one dollar per pound—start the public works again, and then sing anthems to the praise of David Wallace and his Whig allies."

[88] Esarey, *State Banking in Indiana*, 258. In 1840 the state issued $722,640 of bank scrip to enable the bank to pay the overdraft.

$576,277.[89] The Specie Circular had also hit the bank a hard blow. In May, 1837, when news of specie suspension in the East reached Indianapolis, the bank board, despite the charter provision, decided upon immediate suspension for the bank and all branches.[90] Since at this time the United States had $1,500,000 specie on deposit, the situation was serious. Lanier went East with $80,000 in gold to negotiate with Secretary of the Treasury Woodbury. Since the Bank of Indiana was the only one which offered, or paid, any specie, the Treasury made no special demands and drew upon its deposits only as needed.

The bank board explained matters to the people of the state :[91] suspension was not forced but deliberate; the bank would continue to receive its notes at par; if the people would preserve their confidence, the bank would preserve their money. The action of the board, though a subject of much bitter discussion in the press and a considerable jolt to business, proved generally acceptable to the people and to the legislative committee which investigated its conduct. When it became certain that the bank would pull through, confidence became general.[92] In the long bank-note quotation lists which became a fixture in the papers of the period, notes of the State Bank of Indiana were always quoted at par, though east of the mountains they frequently took a 5 per cent discount during the suspension periods. The bank resumed specie payment with the others on August 13, 1838, and likewise suspended again on November 19, 1839, not to resume until June 15, 1842, after being ordered to do so by the legislature.[93]

[89] Esarey, *State Banking in Indiana*, 258. The condition of the bank as of November, 1836, was: Liabilities: public deposits $2,276,357; individual deposits $431,703; notes in circulation $1,927,050; capital stock $1,585,481. Assets: specie, not reported but about $1,000,000; discounts $3,176,613; currency $1,204,737.

[90] *Indiana Journal*, May 20, 1837.

[91] Among other things, that the bank had $1,000,000 of its notes on deposit in eastern banks, which could be used to drain the state of specie.

"Indiana in 1837, had the largest amount of circulation and of specie, in proportion to its capital, of any state in the Union." Tucker, *Theory of Money and Banks*, 374.

[92] The Logansport *Canal Telegraph*, November 25, 1837, listed 108 broken and defunct banks scattered over 21 states and Canada. The only Indiana bank on the list was the Farmers' and Mechanics' Bank of Madison, then in process of liquidation.

[93] Prior to November 19 the bank had apparently been in a state of "partial suspension," that is it had redeemed its notes in specie for individuals but not for other banks and brokers. *Centreville Chronicle* cited in Springfield *Illinois State Register*, November 16, 1839.

Though the fact that the bank's notes were at a small discount in the East worked a hardship on Indiana merchants, it did not interfere with the bank's profits, an important part of which came from the purchase and sale of exchange.[94] Since the bank took advantage of being "off specie" and expanded its note circulation 30 to 40 per cent, its profits ran 10 to 15 per cent during these years; the state's profit on its stock up to 1839 was $391,334.[95] Governor Wallace's idea of the state purchasing more stock had not been as flighty as it might have seemed.

The failure of the state to procure the extra capital led to sharp curtailment of the loans of the bank. In 1839 at President Merrill's suggestion it began to reduce its loans to merchants and increase those to exporters; also to weed out directors whose main interest was to be eligible for loans.[96] Considering that the bank was carrying a debt due from the state of over a million, and three-quarters of a million of its loans were tied up by protests and suits, it did very well.[97] Its record stands out in contrast with most of the flimsy banks of the day.

The Illinois Board of Public Works, pursuant to the law of 1837, began construction on the different projects simultaneously. At the board's first meeting the state was divided into three districts with a chief engineer for each. Contracts were soon let for 105 miles on the Northern Cross Railroad, 69½ on the Illinois Central, 24 on the Peoria and Warsaw, 15 on the Alton and Shawneetown, 38 on the Alton and Mt. Carmel, 33 on the Alton

[94] It was customary for the bank to buy bills on New Orleans from shippers during the autumn and winter, then Lanier would go to New Orleans, cash them in the spring and buy exchange on eastern cities. Eastern exchange bills would then be sold to Indiana merchants; thus the bank turned over its money three times per year. Discounts on these bills, as a result of the depreciated currency, would run from 8 to 15 per cent.

[95] *Sketch of the Life of J. F. D. Lanier* (New York, 1871), 17; President Merrill's report, in Indiana *Documentary Journal*, 1839–40, part II, no. 6, p. 90.

[96] The 1840 report showed loans to merchants of $1,032,136; to farmers $600,310; to manufacturers $610,754; to exporters $723,842. A year later loans to merchants were $982,602, to exporters $1,111,747. Of loans in 1840, $1,338,599 were to directors and stockholders; to all others $2,399,819. *Documentary Journal*, 1840–41, part II, no. 7, p. 94; 1841–42, part II, no. 9, p. 109.

Though Indiana was better fixed for money than most western states, the deflation nevertheless caused hardship. "Money matters here are in a bad state. There is no money in circulation and no collections can be made. Our legislature is Locofoco and will give no relief . . . ," wrote a Hoosier to a friend in Illinois. *Northwestern Gazette and Galena Advertiser*, February 2, 1840.

[97] The legislature of 1841 appointed a special examiner to make an investigation of the bank. His detailed report was, on the whole, favorable. It also makes clear the impact of the depression upon the business of the state. *Documentary Journal*, 1842–43, part I, no. 6.

and Shelbyville, and 9¼ on the Bloomington and Pekin.[98] Each section of the state, of course, wanted its portion of the system built first, even though the result might resemble a sort of jointed snake "which had been whipped into so many pieces that some of them would be decayed and rendered useless before they could crawl to each other's relief."[99]

In addition to the state system, various private improvement projects were being planned or in progress. There were the Beardstown and Sangamon Canal to which it was hoped the state would subscribe one third of the capital stock, the Bloomington and Rock Island Railroad, and others.

In 1835 when the financing of the Illinois and Lake Michigan Canal was being discussed, a prominent newspaper had written that, since the legislature's sad experience over the notorious Wiggins loan of 1831, "it is hardly to be expected that a loan will be resorted to."[100] This was certainly a wild guess, for within a week of the passage of the internal improvements law an act was approved which empowered the fund commissioners to negotiate a loan not to exceed $3,000,000 of "Illinois Bank and Internal Improvement Stock" (at a rate not to exceed 6 per cent).[101] The same law increased the capital stock of the State Bank by $2,000,000 (from $2,500,000 to $4,500,000), the entire amount of which was to be subscribed by the state. The stock of the Bank of Illinois at Shawneetown was increased by $1,400,000, one million of which was to be subscribed by the state.[102] By the end of 1838 the fund commissioners had bor-

---

[98] Pease, *The Frontier State,* 216. The map, documents and reports through 1837 are in U. S. *Senate Documents,* 25 Congress, 2 session, III, 259.

[99] Governor William C. Kinney to citizens of Peoria, quoted in Pease, *The Frontier State,* 217.

[100] *Northwestern Gazette and Galena Advertiser,* January 1, 1835. For the Wiggins loan, see Chapter VIII.

[101] *Laws of Illinois,* 1836–37, pp. 18–22. Five additional directors, elected by the legislature, were added to the Bank of the State of Illinois and nine to the Bank of Illinois at Shawneetown.

[102] See Dowrie, *Banking in Illinois,* 79 ff., for a general account of Illinois banking in this period. The $1,000,000 additional shares (beyond $1,500,000 original capital stock as provided for by the charter) of the Illinois State Bank had been issued, but few had ever been "paid in." Hence the total capital liability was really not much more than $3,500,000.

The state had already borrowed $335,592 from the school fund; when the United States paid Illinois $477,919 as its share of the surplus distribution, the above amount was returned to the school fund and reborrowed to make a payment on the state's purchase of stock of the two banks. *Senate Journal,* 1842–43, p. 36. All profits on the bank stock were, "after liquidating the interest on loans contracted

rowed $2,204,000 against which the Board of Public Works had drawn for expenditures of $1,142,027.[103]

During the eighteen months of its existence prior to the time its fortunes were inextricably tied up with the internal improvements system, the State Bank had earned dividends of 9 per cent on its paid-up capital; the Bank of Illinois had done equally well.[104]

When, during the last week in May, the bank, along with others in the country, suspended specie payment, a problem was presented: not only did it violate its charter by so doing, but it tied up $800,000 of state funds.[105] To the special session of the legislature, called for July, Governor Duncan recommended that the state not subscribe to the three million of bank stock.[106] The special session suspended the charter provision regarding for-

---

for the purchase of such bank or other stock," to be applied to interest on the internal improvements loans.

The *Sangamo Journal,* November 11, 1837, said that it was well understood that $3,000,000 of bonds for the bank stock and $1,400,000 for the improvements and canal had been marketed, supposedly with the Bank of the United States. Surely the Van Buren party would not take the money while cursing the bank.

[103] Besides the river improvements of almost $16,000, main items were: Great Western Mail Route $94,932; Alton and Mt. Carmel and Alton and Shawneetown Railroad $126,516; Central Railroad $200,127; Northern Cross $521,420; branch of Central $56,789; Peoria and Warsaw $83,370; Bloomington and Mackinaw $43,075; the "unfortunate counties" $144,700. Unexpended balance was $1,019,604. Report of fund commissioners, 1838; *Sangamo Journal,* January 12, 1839.

When the fund commissioners went to New York with the "Bank and Internal Improvement" bonds, no bids were submitted. Forbidden by law to sell at below par the commissioners returned and disposed of $1,765,000 of them to the State Bank of Illinois; the Bank of Illinois agreed to take $900,000. This was high finance as daring, if not as successful, as Hamilton's in creating the Bank of the United States: the state borrowed the money from the Bank to subscribe to its shares of additional capital so the Bank could lend money for the improvements. The Bank of Illinois later succeeded in disposing of its shares, but the State Bank carried its portion as a financial albatross around its neck to the end of its existence.

[104] The legislature of 1836–37, regardless of Mr. Lincoln's opposition, voted an investigation of the bank. The joint committee of five gave it a very good bill of health and recommended its shares as a good investment for the state. *Senate Journal,* 1836–37, p. 244.

[105] *Sangamo Journal,* June 12, 1837.

[106] To the regular session of 1836–37 he had recommended that the state subscribe only the $100,000 worth of stock reserved for it by charter. On the July message the *Illinois State Register and People's Advocate* published two columns of criticism. "We have never read a paper, from an official source, which contained more perversions of facts and established republican doctrine." July 15, 1837. Even the *Sangamo Journal* disagreed with Governor Duncan regarding his idea that internal improvements should be built and owned by private corporations. The credit of the state was good, and the plan to get 10 per cent on the state's $3,000,000 of bank stock, while borrowing at 5 per cent, was an admirable one. July 15, 1837.

feiture until the end of the next session of the legislature;[107] it also authorized the state to sell its bank stock to individuals if necessary to meet interest on the improvements loan, but it refused to curtail the program.

The inevitable restriction of credit by the bank led to prolific criticism at the hands of the Democratic papers.[108] Stephen A. Douglas was leading the war on all banks; he said they took debtors' notes and gave out their own instead, making debtors pay interest while they paid none, and the debtors paid in specie while the banks paid in paper.[109]

Even William Ewing, one of the sponsors of the State Bank, turned against banks. Pressure of criticism was eased slightly when the Illinois banks resumed specie payment August 13, 1838.

Governor Duncan in his farewell message in December commended the banks for their voluntary resumption and once again suggested the repeal of the state's internal improvement system. Governor Carlin, an antibank Democrat, criticized the Illinois banking system,[110] but though he doubted the wisdom of such an extensive system of public works, he saw no way of turning back at this time. The legislature passed a law which

[107] *Illinois State Register and People's Advocate,* September 1, 1837. The charter was to be forfeited if the bank suspended longer than sixty days. Certain conditions were laid down: the bank was to pay no dividends during suspension; no specie was to be paid out except in amounts of $5.00 or less; note issue was not to exceed actual capital paid in; debtors were to be allowed to pay their notes in installments. *Laws of Illinois,* 1837 (special session), 6–7.

[108] *The Illinois State Register and People's Advocate,* June 3, 1837, had demanded that banks collect their debts, draw in their resources, lend no more money, and issue no more notes until notes equalled specie. "*This is their duty.* Justice *demands it.*" The *Register's* ideas regarding the effects this policy would have on business, agriculture, etc. were rather naive.

[109] The *Quincy Whig,* June 30, 1838, said that since William Gouge (antibank author of *A Short History of Paper Money and Banking* [1833], and editor of the *Journal of Banking,* Philadelphia, 1841–42), no one had so much right to the palm as "Mr. Douglass." It explained that all these banking transactions were voluntary; people could not be made to borrow money. Further, if the notes of the individual and of the bank were of equal value, why did the individual want the bank's notes? The *Sangamo Journal,* January 27, 1838, pointed out the inconsistency of the "Locofoco Press" howling and snapping at all banks and yet going all out for the internal improvement system. "Our internal improvement system is a part and parcel of the credit system. . . ." See also item from Shawneetown *Western Voice and Internal Improvement Journal* quoted in *ibid.* The latter paper reported the speech of William Gatewood [secretary to fund commissioners] to the effect that internal improvements would not require taxes but would increase the state's revenue. In a long statistical resumé Gatewood counted heavily on big profits from the state-owned shares of the bank. Reprinted in *Illinois State Register and People's Advocate,* February 9, 1838.

[110] For providing no means of enforcing the charters; for permitting meddling in politics; for loans to speculators, etc.

prohibited individuals and institutions from issuing notes or scrip,[111] and authorized about a million dollars worth of new improvements. Also, since the state was finding London, in a glutted market, more favorable to the state bonds backed by direct taxation, it enacted a revenue law which provided that the state receive 20 cents on each $100 of property on a full-value assessment. Counties and cities could levy up to 50 cents each. When the voters realized what they were going to have to pay, considerable agitation for repeal of this law developed.[112]

In May 1834, William Gatewood, secretary to the fund commissioners, in a letter to Editor Simeon Francis of the *Sangamo Journal* reported that he had sold $300,000 of canal bonds to John Delafield of the New York Banking Company and a million to "a wealthy house in Philadelphia" (Nicholas Biddle and the Bank of the United States); almost half a million had been sold in Ohio.[113] By midsummer the internal improvement funds were exhausted and the commissioners went to London, where they turned over $1,500,000 of bonds to John Wright and Company to sell, and got an advance thereon. The canal commissioners working independently also disposed of $1,000,000 of canal bonds.[114] The idea of Governor Carlin, who thought the very acme of all evil was British noblemen holding stock in the

[111] The city of Alton had in 1837 issued $10,000 of 6 per cent scrip, payable in one year, acceptable for taxes. *Alton Spectator,* October 5, 1837.

[112] The *State Register* called this the poor man's law since it made the rich speculator carry his share, and said that the tax was not necessitated by the improvements system but should have been enacted years ago. March 29, 1839. The *Sangamo Journal* said that this law should enable the state, which had borrowed 7 to 8 hundred thousand dollars from school funds for ordinary running expenses to return this amount where it belonged. The *Daily Chicago American,* May 4, 1839, adding the state levy of 20 cents, a county and city levy of 50 cents each, figured that $120 on the thousand was a trifle high. It would have been.

Meetings, held in Bond and Edgar counties and elsewhere, protested the law as calculated to impoverish the state, load the people with uncalled for, unwise, and injudicious taxes. They called for repeal and classification of the improvements. *Illinois State Register and People's Advocate,* April 19, June 21, 1839.

[113] *Sangamo Journal,* May 24, 1839. Delafield was to pay in installments starting the following December.

[114] Ohio stocks (bonds) maturing in 1856 and 1860 were quoted in London at 93–4, Indiana stocks at 92–3, and Illinois stocks of 1870 at 91–2. *Ibid.,* July 19, 1839. The *Journal,* October 4, had reported that General Rawlings and Colonel Oakley had sold a $4,000,000 loan in Europe.

Gatewood's letter describing the financial operations in England was published in the *Illinois State Register,* December 18, 1839. The Wright transaction was referred to as a "conditional contract," to be completed when the Board of Public Works had made requisitions for $2,500,000. When Wright and Company got $1,500,000 in bonds, the board could then draw on the company for £50,000, 9,500 tons of iron at £9 per ton, etc.

late Bank of the United States, peddling Illinois stock to the British, and trying to mortgage the state of Illinois, struck Editor Francis as humorous.[115]

It was obvious that the Illinois system was running low on power. There had been much argument and disagreement as to what to do: whether there should be another special session, to classify or not to classify, or to abandon. During the spring the Whig papers were generally in favor of a special session and classification; by early autumn they were not so sure regarding the special session.[116] Some Democratic papers which a year earlier had claimed the system as their own began to hedge and reverse themselves.[117]

In August the Board of Public Works voted to suspend all work on roads not on a continuous line from rivers, and all contracts let during 1839.[118]

On October 21, following news of eastern banks again suspending,[119] the Illinois State Bank did likewise. The Bank of Illinois held on for two weeks, then it too suspended.[120] The

[115] *Illinois State Register*, July 19, 1839.

[116] "A change came over the spirit of the dream," said the *Daily Chicago American*, May 29, 1839. It came out for classification. "Classify!" said the *Quincy Whig*, before the terrific tax burden discourages emigration to Illinois. April 20, July 6, August 10, 1839. By October 5 the same paper advocated paying the contractors, suspending the work, and leaving the decision to the legislature. The *Quincy Argus* took the opposite stand. A year earlier, during the autumn of 1838, the *Peoria Register* had published a series of articles on politics and the internal improvements system. It claimed that the spoils system had rendered the engineering department "rotten from the core to the surface." The author questioned the need for the various projects, pointed out that they could never pay for themselves, and called upon the people to call a halt. August 25, September 8, 22, 29, October 27, November 2, 1838; *Sangamo Journal*, September 15, 1838.

[117] The Springfield *Illinois Republican*, for instance, was strong for the system in August, 1838, against it the following May. When the *Chicago Democrat*, July 15, 1839, asked whether Illinois was going to follow up the insane system, the *Sangamo Journal*, July 28, reminded that the Democrats had claimed the system as their own and now were not so sure. The *Quincy Argus* said that Mr. Gatewood, the father of the system, was a notorious Federalist. The *Journal* (September 6) said three fourths of the legislature of 1836–37 was *Locofoco*, that if that party wanted to throw its bantlings at the Whigs, it would perish. The *Register*, September 14, quoted the *Journal* of February, 1839, as claiming the internal improvements system was not a party measure. Now the *Journal* called it a "Van Buren" measure and the *Register* called it a "Federalist" measure.

[118] The *Sangamo Journal*, September 6, 1839, contains the proceedings of the meeting.

[119] The *State Register* said that this was altogether for political purposes—to stop the Democratic ball from rolling on to victory.

[120] Prior to the second suspension, shares of the Illinois State Bank had been quoted at 75½ in New York. The Bank of Illinois had advanced the state $80,000 on the new state capitol, $200,000 to the Board of Public Works to pay contractors, and $40,000 in dividends on the state-held stock before they were due. *Illinois State Register*, December 25, 1839.

"tightness" and "the pressure" were again overwhelming. The state's credit had been stretched to $11,107,919—on which annual interests charges were $637,800; to complete the authorized work would require almost eleven millions more.[121] "It is difficult to conceive a worse condition of things than is now in prospect for the State of Illinois," said the *vox populi*.[122] Clearly something had to be done.

Democratic leaders were not too eager for a special session. After all, the system had been the creation largely of the southern half of the state; there would be a lot of explaining to do. The *Chicago Democrat* was critical of the idea, but the *State Register* finally admitted that the people were dissatisfied with things as they stood; what was not too large a project in 1837 was proving to be too extensive for the times of 1839. Governor Carlin knew what the people wanted and things could safely be left in his hands.[123]

Governor Carlin in his message to the special session on December 10 made a brief summary of the state of affairs. He listed the state's liabilities, including bank stock subscriptions, at $13,096,444; if the works were completed as planned, the debt would be $21,846,444. He explained the system as "the natural offspring of an inflated paper circulating medium," and recommended completion of only one or two of the most important works. Local sacrifices would have to be made for the common good. He took the State Bank over the coals for again suspending specie payment, disregarding the interests of the state and furthering those of speculation, and recommended a stringent investigation.[124] The Bank of Illinois got off with a request for an explanation regarding suspension. The legislature perforce

---

[121] *Reports of General Assembly* (Senate), 1839–40, p. 46. The *Illinois State Register*, December 18, 1839, by some optimistic figuring, deducted $2,400,000 of canal stock, $3,000,000 of bank stock, $800,000 of state bonds, and $477,999 of the state's surplus revenue share and arrived at a debt of only $4,330,000 in which interest charges would be $300,000. Since the United States Government could not be counted on and it was unfair to tax the people, the *Register* said the interest charges should be carried by dividends on the bank stock. This was an interesting suggestion from a paper which was continuously fighting banks, and a few weeks earlier (October 26) had criticized the Illinois State Bank for holding on to state bonds (the $2,000,000 state stock purchase) instead of selling them. In stating that the Bank had no more capital than it had before, the *Register* was impugning the state's credit.

[122] *Illinois State Register*, December 25, 1839.

[123] November 9, 1839.

[124] *Ibid.*, December 14, 1839.

suspended work on the internal improvements system which, as it happened, practically amounted to abandonment.

The Illinois State Bank was in a vulnerable position, nor was it entirely the result of its being tied up with the tottering state finances. It had made some loans to out-of-state residents, had carried Samuel Wiggins, of Cincinnati, on the books when he had failed to pay for his bank stock, and had aided Godfrey, Gilman, and Company, Alton lead merchants, to amass fortunes in diverting as much of the lead trade from St. Louis as easy accommodations would make possible. If it did not speculate in lead and pork on its own account, the fact was hardly clear from the evidence.[125] Special favors had been shown members of the legislature and heavy loans had been made to directors and firms in which they were interested.[126] It had carried questionable assets on its books at face value instead of market value, even suspended debts as assets.

Even the *Illinois State Register* had become worried at the pass to which things had come:[127]

It is difficult to conceive of a worse condition of things than is now in prospect for the State of Illinois. The vast debt already contracted will require an ad valorem tax of from one or two per cent for the interest merely, if no other means be provided for payment. The State has a large capital invested in the Banks, which will, of course, be wholly unproductive, in the event of this capital being withdrawn from those institutions, because the charter of the Bank requires, that upon the winding up, the note holders and depositors shall be paid first, and stockholders, including the State may be postponed probably for years. It is also understood that by a sale of bonds in New York the commissioners have contracted to receive Illinois Bank notes, in periodical installments, running through a period of three or four years.—If the currency of these banks becomes depreciated from any cause whatever, the New York capitalists will find it greatly to their interest to purchase these funds, and our State must become the loser in receiving them.

[125] The *Chicago Democrat*, May 1, 1839, said the bank had made a profit of $40,000 in the sale of pork to the canal commissioners from which the state got only $2,400 as its share (interest on $80,000). This paper also charged land speculations to the bank. The *Galena Democrat* revealed at length the operations of a Mr. Roberts, a brother-in-law of the president of the Galena Branch, in lead speculation. *Illinois State Register and People's Advocate*, July 5, 1839. Similar charges were made by the *Quincy Argus*. The *Daily Chicago American*, June 6, 1839, had said the bank could not extend accommodations to merchants because it had to protect itself against the "ultra Democrats" who were warring against it.
[126] The facts are summarized in Dowrie, *Banking in Illinois*, 89 ff.; the committee's findings are in *Reports of General Assembly* (Senate), 1839–40.
[127] Copied in *Sangamo Journal*, January 3, 1840.

It pointed out that if the State Bank should fall, the Bank of Illinois must fall also since a large amount of the notes of the latter would be received by the State Bank from its debtors, not to be paid out again, but to be presented for specie at the bank of their origin. Hence the Bank of Illinois could not resume specie payments while the process of winding up the affairs of the State Bank was going on. Further, the notes of the Illinois banks were extensively circulated in Missouri where the St. Louis brokers and banks would always be able to make heavy drafts of specie when it was to their interest to do so.

Take these considerations in connection with the general embarrassments to all branches of trade and industry, which would be the inevitable consequence of winding up the Banks, and it is sufficient to startle the apprehensions of the boldest and wisest. . . . What can the State Bank do? If the vaults are opened, who will profit thereby?—The capital of the state will be suddenly drained off to St. Louis. Our own resources will be exhausted—our business utterly prostrated.—*The question is not now an original one of Bank or no Bank, but it presents itself in a different aspect—interwoven with all our financial concerns and intimately connected with the value of every man's property and industry—it is not whether we are opposed to the present banking system but whether for the sake of theory we will desolate the country with ruin.* I admit that this position of things is a natural incident of the banking system—the legi[ti]mate offspring of a dangerous and false policy. But we must cure, not kill—reform not Destroy. The situation of the Bank has been brought about partly by the sinking credit of the State itself, and partly by the vicissitudes of fortune and circumstances throughout the land generally, and partly by mismanagement.

The joint committee of the legislature for investigating the bank agreed that it had forfeited its charter, but rendered three different reports on other charges and practices. Not even the Democratic majority—many of them hostile to banks—dared let the bank go overboard. A law was approved on January 31, 1840, which set aside the charter forfeiture and again permitted suspension of specie to the end of the next session of the legislature.[128] This did not help much, however. The notes of the State Bank, which had been quoted at a nominal par

[128] The Bank was not to dispose of any of its specie or bullion, lend or hypothecate any of its stock, put new notes in circulation beyond its paid-in capital, or lend more than $1,000 to any one person or firm. It was required to receive its own bills in payment of bank debts and to permit its debtors to pay in installments until it resumed specie.

or at worst a 3 per cent discount, were shortly quoted at 90. It was estimated that the people of the state were losing $160,000 a year by having to pay higher prices for eastern goods.[129] The bank continued to be attacked bitterly by the Democratic press which referred to its notes as "rags." The *Chicago Democrat*, for instance, said it did not wish unduly to alarm the people, but cautioned them against hoarding its notes or depositing money in it. The *Democrat* said the bank could not fail, since it was already suspended, but reiterated its "firm conviction of the truth of all the statements we have made respecting its iniquity, rottenness and insolvency. . . ." It agreed with the *New York Herald* that the Bank was "involved with cliques of brokers in Wall Street, who while professing to aid the state, have been undermining its credit, sinking its stock in the market, and silently but surely, leading it to the verge of bankruptcy."[130]

The special session of 1839–40 had questioned the validity of the deal in state bonds with Wright and Company of London; also the sale of the canal bonds.[131] Governor Carlin was undecided, but he finally confirmed the sale of the million dollars worth of canal bonds. Contractors took pay in bonds, some of which were later sold at a discount of 25 per cent to another English firm. In November, 1840, overloaded with American state bonds and beset with other troubles, Wright and Company went bankrupt. Complications followed regarding the Delafield and United States Bank contracts; a lawsuit was launched (*State of Illinois* v. *John Delafield*); fund commissioners worked against each other.[132] In August the fund commissioners reported a total state debt of $13,140,548; subtracting bank stock, railroad iron, and other items which would probably be paid to a sum of

[129] Speech of Representative John T. Stuart in Congress, quoted in *Vandalia Free Press*, June 26, 1840.

[130] *Chicago Democrat*, September 14, 1840. The state debt, its relation to the bank, etc., were here analyzed at some length.

[131] Whether the fund commissioners were ignorant and overreached, or understood what they were doing is not clear. They had agreed that a bond with a face value of £225 should yield only $1,000 in the United States; in paying interest and principal Illinois would have to pay far more than the par value translated into Illinois currency. Had the Illinois bonds been sold at par as the law had provided? In the Senate committee report were these words, " 'the shark is there, and the shark's prey—the spend thrift and the leech that sucks him.' " *Reports of General Assembly*, 1839–40 (special session), 140.

[132] See *Sangamo Journal*, September 17, 1840, for a summary; also Pease, *The Frontier State*, 227–29.

$3,828,000 left a debt of $9,312,548 above the state's visible means to pay.

Since by autumn the state was finding it difficult to pay interest, Governor Carlin was forced to call another special session of the legislature, to meet two weeks before the regular session. Some members thought that if the state would purchase another $3,000,000 of bank shares, the dividends on the state's holdings ($6,100,000) would solve all financial difficulties.[133] Finance of this type was too modern for Governor Carlin, who distrusted banks anyway. "Such schemes of producing wealth as the multiplication of banks and paper money all end in disaster. . . . Paper money multiplied, foreign debts created, visionary schemes of internal improvement commenced and abandoned—prodigality abounding in every department; until we find ourselves burdened with a debt of thirteen millions. The payment of this stock at the present rate of our bonds would involve borrowing four million to pay three." Governor Carlin may not have been a great statesman or an expert in finance, but he did understand arithmetic and the condition of the Bank.

The legislature did not help much. The Democrats adjourned the special session *sine die* on December 5—the regular session began on the seventh—and thereby trapped the bank on its permission to suspend until the end of the next session of the legislature.[134] Forced to resume at once, the bank ceased making loans, curbed its note issues, stopped making advances to the state, and even refused to cash salary warrants of state officials.[135] The legislature, now faced with insurmountable debt problems, even provided for a tax levy of 10 cents on the hundred dollars to be applied to payment of interest on bonds. Also, it authorized issuance of bonds in anticipation of this revenue, which might

[133] See letter of Dr. R. F. Barrett, fund commissioner, for summary of bond transactions and avoidance of taxes, in *Sangamo Journal*, September 25, 1840.

[134] Whig members planned to prevent a quorum and prevent adjournment by leaving the room, but they found the doors and windows guarded. Whig papers called this whole proceeding a Locofoco trick. *Quincy Whig*, December 12, 19, 1840.

[135] The legislature changed its mind early in 1841, set aside the forfeiture provision, permitted the bank to issue small notes, and imposed certain conditions. In 1843 President John Marshall and other reliable officers were ousted and the bank's policy "was soon changed to one of getting all that was possible out of a doomed enterprise before it should go to pieces." Relations between the state and bank were dissolved in 1843 and the liquidation of the bank was dragged out for sixteen years—until 1859—by which time the $1,500,000 invested in its capital stock was a total loss.

be hypothecated for whatever they would bring on the market.[136] The fund commissioners pledged internal improvement bonds for the January interest, but so low had the credit of the state fallen that it had to hypothecate $804,000 of the interest bonds with Macalister and Stebbings of Philadelphia for a loan of $321,600 of which the state received only $261,500.[137] This grasping-at-a-straw solution was opposed not so much on the grounds of its unsoundness but rather because many objected to the state, facing insolvency, paying interest at all, especially on bonds for which it had received less than par, or even nothing. It was bitter medicine to have to pay interest on more money than the state had actually received, but after all the bona fide bond purchaser could not be expected to suffer for derelictions of the state's agents.[138] And, as pointed out by the *Quincy Whig* (December 26, 1840), the finances of the state had been in the custody of those "whose ignorance would be a disgrace to a novice." Like children playing with straws, they had been willing to burden the state with even more than compound interest. "We can see but one of two courses before us: either a bold attempt to relieve the state by additional taxation or else the open avowal of our insolvency." Tax if necessary; it would be hard but the credit of the state would be maintained.

It must be sickening to the heart of an honest man to review the financial history of this State for a few years past. The People by the agency of their Representatives, adopted the Internal Improvement System. However much that system may be denounced now, when it was first adopted, we have no doubt but two-thirds of the People were in its favor.—But, unfortunately, from the first step towards carrying it out, it was made a political matter. . . . And what has been the result of this policy? Desperate adventurers have become rich—rioting in princely fortunes—while the State is without credit, and has not a dollar in her Treasury to pay the salaries of public officers.

[136] "This was a desperate remedy, and showed the zeal of the legislature in sustaining the public honor. It proposed a plan of raising money, which, if pursued as the settled policy of the state, must end in utter ruin." Ford, *History of Illinois*, 209.

[137] *Ibid.*, 210–11.

[138] "It seems to be a principle of law, as well as of equity, that if the State selects bad men, or those who are incompetent to act as its agents, the State thus abusing its power, and not individuals who had no hand in their appointment, ought to suffer the consequences of its folly, or want of devotion to its own interests. This doctrine, if established, will be a lesson to the people, and teach them to be considerate and careful in electing their public servants." *Ibid.*, 210. Ford was slightly optimistic about the efficacious results of such a policy.

And what is a most singular feature of this whole affair, it is impossible to ascertain the acts of public officers. . . . In the meantime rumor and reports, adverse to the honesty of public officers are rife in the land, and every door seems to be closed against scrutiny. The Board of Public Works are repealed out of office before they can be called upon for reports of the acts and doings of their predecessors; and if it is not the design of individuals to hush all enquiry, and mystify all proceedings in relation to themselves, their apparent course leads us into error.

We yet hope that all the truth will come out: and especially do we hope that all the transactions, in regard to the contracts with Wright & Co. will be made to see the day. Let the Representatives of the People do their duty—fearlessly and honestly. If prominent politicians have aided in defrauding the People—no matter of what party they are—let the facts come out! Let us know who of our public officers have been true to their duties, and who not.—The times and the People demand this exposure.[139]

The great Illinois "system" was through, abandoned before the state attained any advantages or income therefrom; it remained only to pick up the pieces of wreckage. With it went the state's credit which required years to rehabilitate.

§ §

Contracts on the Michigan works had been let in 1837. The Mt. Clemens–Kalamazoo Canal, despite the send-off of the opening celebration, never went into use beyond the first 16 miles of its 216 miles of proposed length. Costs ran at $18,000 per mile, exclusive of right of way.[140]

The Central Railroad, chartered in 1832 as the Detroit and St. Joseph, was already under construction between Detroit and Ypsilanti when taken over by the state in 1837.[141] On February 3, 1838, the *Detroit Daily Advertiser* announced the opening of a new era in the business relations of the city—the cars were leaving for Ypsilanti. Pulled by *The Governor Mason*, Governor Mason and party rode in the sixty-passenger car, equipped with cushions and a stove, to Ypsilanti; on the way back the Governor's namesake let them down, but horses got them back to

[139] *Sangamo Journal*, December 18, 1840.

[140] In 1845 the one boat in service on the portion of the canal east of Utica returned $90.32 in tolls; expenditures had been about $400,000.

[141] Michigan's first railroad charter was to the Detroit and Pontiac in 1830. The Detroit and St. Joseph Company had spent $116,902 on construction and the estimate for the 153 miles remaining was $1,381,040 when the state assumed all contracts.

Detroit. Freight charges were 30 cents per hundred pounds; net receipts the first year were $37,283. The section to Ann Arbor was opened in the autumn of 1839; the contracts for the section between Ann Arbor and Jackson, having exceeded appropriations, were continued on faith, and the road opened to Dexter, July 4, 1841.

The Southern Railroad progressed under difficulties; survey locations were changed, workmen were laid up with summer fevers, appropriations ran short. After an expenditure of $550,000, the first division, between Monroe and Adrian, was opened for use in November, 1840. This road, handicapped as it was at first by not reaching the lake at Monroe and by competition with the Erie and Kalamazoo at its west end, returned gross receipts of only $200 the first year.[142]

The Northern Railroad from Palmer (St. Clair) by way of Lapeer, Flint, Corunna to Grand Rapids was surveyed on to Lake Michigan, but beyond grubbing and grading on the section east of Lapeer, no work was finished. Likewise the Saginaw Canal, supposed to save 450 miles of dangerous lake navigation, failed to develop, though several sections were grubbed and some excavating was done. Eight thousand dollars was spent on surveys for the St. Marys Canal but when complications arose concerning the right of the state to build this work, it was postponed to future years. The $60,000 spent on river improvement brought a more immediate benefit.

The sobering impact of the depression led many people to question such a large program of state improvements. As a result the legislature first restricted the amount of funds which could be advanced to an acting commissioner, then in April, 1839, reduced the board of commissioners to three members. In the state election of that year the Whigs criticized the system and its management; consequently Governor Woodbridge in his message recommended the repeal of all laws for internal improvements except those necessary to administer the works already completed; also an investigation of the management to date. In March, 1840, the legislature placed the state treasurer and secre-

---

[142] To reach the lake the state bought the two-mile River Raisin and Erie Railroad, but since the connecting curve was too sharp for locomotives, only horsecars could be used. For the Erie and Kalamazoo, see below, 312–13.

tary of state on the board of commissioners; the other member was to be appointed by the governor.

Biddle's Bank of the United States took the $5,000,000 loan authorized by the legislature in 1837, at a slight premium.[143] Of the approximate $1,500,000 which the state had received by 1839, $500,000 was tied up in the broken Michigan State Bank. In March, 1839, the legislature gave the auditor authority to anticipate certain installments on the $5,000,000 loan, but early the next year the Morris Canal Company and the United States Bank defaulted on the installments. The state then issued scrip in anticipation of the installments (which were not paid); the scrip depreciated but passed at face value for payment of taxes and state obligations.[144]

As in the neighboring states, overoptimism, sectional jealousy, political bickering, plain mismanagement, and some dishonesty marked the affairs of Michigan's improvement plans. Though the House committee in 1840–41 in its long report made no accusation of major dishonesties, the evidence of minor derelictions and incompetency is there.

Long before the works were completed the people realized they had undertaken too sizeable a task; running the works after they were built would be a bigger job still. As a Senate committee reported a few years later: "The control of such a complicated mass of business as would arise from directing the transportation of freight and passengers, . . . and superintending all the financial concerns of this vast system, would indeed form a nucleus around which would gather a horde of greedy, half-starved political hacks, whose soul aim would be self-aggrandizement—in whose midst corruption, intrigue, and deception would riot in unlimited freedom."[145] The state, despite land-grant aid from the General Government, soon decided to get out from under the burden of threatened taxation by selling the roads. Michigan's

---

[143] The Whig *Detroit Daily Advertiser* asked whether it was true that the "old Monster Nick Biddle" had come to the aid of Michigan, and if it was so, why did not Governor Mason admit it, since there was no election in the offing. May—June, 1838, *passim*.

[144] In 1842 the Governor called upon the holders of $2,657,039.76 of the state bonds (the amount of loss sustained by failure of the contracting parties) to turn them in; or to turn in the whole $5,000,000 and get new bonds for the balance of $2,342,960.24.

[145] *Senate Documents*, 1846, No. 8, p. 20.

financial troubles were further enhanced by her own peculiar banking and currency situation.

By 1837 Michigan had, including the Bank of Michigan,[146] fourteen chartered banks, three with the privilege of branches, with a total capitalization of $7,100,000.[147] But this adequate banking equipment did not satisfy the young state, Jacksonian as it was and imbued with the feeling that chartered monopolies were hostile to free institutions. So the state decided to go into banking in a truly democratic way. By the law approved March 17, 1837,[148] any persons who wished to form banking "associations" might do so. When 30 per cent of the capital (minimum capital stock $50,000) should be paid in in "legal money of the United States" (elsewhere the statute said "specie"), the bank might open. Remainder of the capital stock was to be paid in, 10 per cent each six months. Note issues were not to exceed two and a half times capital stock paid in and actually possessed; no notes of less than $1.00 were to be issued. Debts were limited to three times capital stock paid in and possessed. For any excesses directors were entirely liable, and stockholders to the extent of their shares. Interest on loans was limited to 7 per cent; loans to directors (or to those whose notes were endorsed by directors) were limited to one sixth of all loans. The banks were to pay one half of one per cent of paid-in capital to the state each year. Semiannual reports were to be rendered to the state banking commissioner. Charters were to run for twenty years. Nothing was said about redeeming notes in specie.

This liberal law provided Michigan with adequate banks, if not banking facilities. Under it, in a little more than a year, 49 banking associations were organized, a litter frequently described as being the product of the "Fanny Wright" system.[149] Aggregate capital (nominal) totaled $4,000,000, which, added to that of the chartered banks, gave Michigan's approximately 200,000 people

---

[146] See Chapter VIII.

[147] Report of banking commissioner in *Detroit Daily Advertiser*, January 27, 1837. This report lists seventeen, but two are labeled "not in operation" and one as "broken." H. M. Utley, "The Wild Cat Banking System of Michigan," in *Michigan Pioneer and Historical Collections*, V (1882), 210, lists fifteen. Only about $2,100,000 of the capital had actually been paid up.

[148] *Laws of Michigan*, 1837, pp. 76–88. The act was modified somewhat in December, 1837. *Ibid.*, 1837–38, pp. 24–37.

[149] Listed in Utley, 214–15. *Detroit Daily Advertiser*, March 5, 1838, lists forty-two as having gone into operation.

a paper base of $11,000,000 banking capital. As the good Whig *Detroit Daily Advertiser* said before the new swarm was created: "There is a point beyond which the increase of banks is undoubtedly an evil."[150] And Governor Mason, in his message to the special session of the legislature on June 12, 1837, laid the cause of the country's troubles to over banking.[151] Yet this session authorized the banks to suspend specie payment until May 16, 1838, without forfeit. It also laid down certain rules for the banks to follow.[152]

Some of the "banking associations" set up under the law of 1837 were bona fide banks, but many were pure note manufactories, located at points difficult of access and used to promote speculation, frauds, and swindles. Note restrictions and specie provisions of the law were evaded; bonds and mortgages on "city lots" in the wilderness constituted collateral; wildcat banks held the notes of other wildcat banks as capital.[153]

The traveler in the woods of Shiawassee County, about to despair of finding inhabitants or shelter before nightfall, followed a timber trail to a clearing and ran smack into the "Bank of Shiawassee." At the mouth of Swan Creek near Monroe was Brest whose chief asset as a city was a colored map and prospectus of itself, which showed broad avenues lined with palatial homes, busy docks and warehouses, and noble vessels bearing the commerce of all lands. Almost fifty years later the local historian wrote: "The ruins of Nineveh or Baalbec are not more desolate now than are the ruins of Brest. The contemplative traveler standing there would never dream how great possibilities had been unrealized on that spot. That the wolves do not howl there to-day, is because they have been circumvented by the civilization which drove them to the wilds of the north, and not because of any development on the part of Brest itself. . . ."[154]

[150] January 27, 1837.
[151] *Ibid.,* June 14, 1837.
[152] Sale of specie by the banks to officers or agents was prohibited; dividends were prohibited during suspension; banks were not to purchase their own bills or bills of other banks at a discount; banks taking advantage of the law were to subscribe to the "safety-fund" law and submit to supervision of the bank commissioner. *Laws of Michigan,* 1837, pp. 311–14.
[153] Bank officers, business firms, and individuals often issued "specie certificates" —mere acknowledgments of specie received or held on deposit or sometimes only borrowed for a few hours or days.
[154] Utley, "The Wild Cat Banking System of Michigan," in *Michigan Pioneer and Historical Collections,* V, 216.

Brest, of course, had a bank, capital $100,000. When investigated by the bank commissioners it was found to have $16,000 in loans on bonds, $10,000 of bank stock, $12,900 in specie, and $84,241 of notes in circulation. On an unexpected return a week later the examiners found $138.89 in specie. The borrowed collateral (bonds and lot mortgages) had been returned to the owners, as had the specie; the bank still had the $84,241 of notes in circulation.

The Bank of Singapore "enjoyed an extensive circulation . . . from the fact that most people supposed it to be in Asia. . . . [It] would not, by any means, have smelled so sweet by any other name." This Asiatic wildcat busted while the noteholder was trying to find Singapore. A keg of borrowed specie was rushed madly through the woods ahead of the bank examiners. When the latter became personally acquainted with each coin and doubled back, no kegs of precious metal other than nails were to be found.

The Bank of Sandstone (Barry) was accused of redeeming its $5.00 notes in whetstones, $10 notes in grindstones, $20 notes in millstones, and larger notes in checks on any quarry in the state.[155] Somewhat less heavily secured were the notes of the Lenawee County Bank at Palmyra, which "made good fiat money, for it had only faith to sustain it. All the stockholders together could hardly have raised specie enough to pay a week's board for a pauper."[156]

Shortly Michigan was plastered with bank notes which found some sort of circulation from sheer necessity. Outside the state, however, they were hard to dispose of. Before the end of 1837 most of them were quoted at a discount of 12½ per cent, six months later at 25. New York and Ohio papers warned against them,[157] Buffalo merchants resolved not to accept them,[158] the *Indiana Journal* refused them in payment for subscriptions. "Doubtless some of them are good, but all are undercurrent in

---

[155] *Cleveland Herald and Gazette* (weekly) April 5, 1838. "We learn that the Sand-Stone Bank has failed, the 'hard currency' having been used up in Michigan by the Van Buren party in grinding the faces of the dear people."

[156] C. B. Stebbins, "Story of Another Pioneer," in *Michigan Pioneer and Historical Collections*, V (1882), 130.

[157] *Daily Cleveland Herald*, November 20; *Buffalo Commercial* in *Cincinnati Daily Gazette*, November 25; *Detroit Daily Advertiser*, December 6, 1837.

[158] The *Detroit Daily Advertiser*, January 11, 1838, printed a demand from "Equal" that Detroit merchants resolve not to buy any Buffalo goods.

this part of the State."[159] A settler near Lake Michigan (Indiana) who said he had come west to raise corn, not cities, found speculators and paper trash too much for him. He intended to settle in northern Indiana or Illinois "to rot." Most of all he blamed the free banking law of Michigan; aside from the notes of four Michigan banks, all the rest should be listed "expunged."[160] The *Detroit Advertiser* and the *Cleveland Intelligencer* waged verbal war over whether Michigan notes were more worthless than Ohio notes.[161] Northwestern Illinois could not decide whether Michigan money—about all they had—was better or worse than no money at all.[162] The money was variously described—"wild cat," "catamount," "yaller dog," "red dog," "blue pup," "paper trash," and "rags." "Of the best quality (red dog) it is said that it takes five pecks to make a bushel."[163]

Detroit banks had suspended on May 17, 1837, when news of suspension in the East arrived. Representatives of 31 of the Michigan banks (11 chartered and 20 general-law banks) met at Ann Arbor, May 1, 1838. It was decided that Detroit banks would resume specie payment May 10 and that the country banks should follow within sixty days. Banks, in receiving and paying, were not to discriminate between notes of the chartered banks and others.[164] But the idea did not work out very well. Not only were some of the chartered banks reluctant to accept the notes of the general-law banks, but there was bad blood between the Michigan State Bank, the pet of the "officeholders" or "junto," and the Bank of Michigan, which the Whigs favored. The *Detroit Free Press* claimed that the Bank of Michigan, by

[159] Indianapolis *Indiana Journal*, February 2, 1838.

[160] Letter in *Cincinnati Daily Gazette*, February 13, 1838.

[161] The *Advertiser*, May 30, 1838, accused Ohio citizens of demanding specie at Detroit and refusing Ohio bank notes. See also *Cincinnati Daily Gazette*, June 16, 1838.

[162] *Northwestern Gazette and Galena Advertiser*, March 31, 1838.

[163] *Niles' National Register*, LIV, 224 (June 2, 1838). "Trade in Detroit," said the *Maumee Express*, "goes on something after the following fashion: I'll give you seventy-five dollars for that pony. Done—but stop! What kind of funds? Black Cat—Can't take. Green cat—'Twon't do! Blue cat—No! Gray cat—Don't like it! Yellow cat—Won't have it; then give me White cat, and you shall have him. Then we won't trade." Quoted in Indianapolis *Indiana Journal*, June 23 [22], 1839.

[164] It was also resolved that the Detroit banks borrow a million dollars, more or less, "to sustain the interest of all sound banking institutions in the State." *Detroit Daily Advertiser*, May 4, 1838. "Wolverine" in a letter in *ibid.*, May 7, advocated that the Detroit banks borrow from the $800,000 or so of the state loan for internal improvements, use the loan to put Michigan bank notes to par, and use the notes to continue the improvements.

refusing to accept notes of the general-law banks was trying to ruin them.[165] The *Advertiser* inquired why, since in the eyes of the "Locos" all chartered banks were wrong, they did not "hurl into" the Michigan State Bank, through which the state transacted its business.

Michigan business felt encouraged with resumption by the Detroit banks in May. So limited was their note circulation, however, that they paid out relatively little specie; they sold drafts on New York for their own bills at 2 per cent. Business interests were claiming that Michigan currency was as good as that of any of the western states and as good as the notes of the country banks in New York. Hotels were full of people, commodity prices were good.[166] The Central Railroad was grossing $400 per day, the Detroit and Pontiac would soon be completed. But this was largely whistling in the dark. By midsummer conditions were obviously bad. The citizens of Pontiac met to consider suspension of debt collecting until the pressure of the times was alleviated, and fourteen news columns were required to advertise the mortgage sales of property in Monroe County.

The annual report of the banking commissioners, dated January 18, 1839, is a classic document, another proof of the futility of trying to create something out of nothing. "The feature of the act which authorized banking under the suspension law, that is to say, giving the sanction of law to the issue of promises to pay, not liable to redemption in gold and silver on demand, gave an irresistible impulse to their career, by opening the door for the debtor to liquidate his liabilities by transferring to the public at large his indebtedness to individuals." Followed the listing of every species of subterfuge, trickery, fraud, and financial hocus pocus known to the time.[167]

The singular spectacle was presented of the officers of the State seeking for banks in situations the most inaccessible and remote from trade, and

[165] July 21, 1838. The *Advertiser*, August 7, while admitting that the Bank of Michigan, after issuing notice, refused some such notes, said the Michigan State Bank refused the same without issuing notice. See also *Advertiser*, July 25, 26, 1838.
[166] Flour $8.50, mess pork $22, butter 16 cents, hams 12 to 14 cents, eggs 15 cents. *Detroit Daily Advertiser*, May 22, 1838.
[167] Quoted in Utley, "Wild Cat Banking System of Michigan," in *Michigan Pioneer and Historical Collections*, V, 219–20. Stock notes were given in subscription to bank stock, then counted as specie; specie was borrowed from established corporations and "specie certificates" verified by oath were exhibited, though canceled at the moment of their creation by a draft of like amount; entries were made in pencil so as to be easily changed; the notes, known by the "utterers" to be valueless, were converted into produce, land, and stock.

finding at every step an increase of labor by the discovery of new and unknown organizations. . . . Gold and silver flew about the country with the celerity of magic; its sound was heard in the depths of the forest; yet, like the wind, one knew not whence it came or whither it was going. . . . The vigilance of a regiment . . . would have been scarcely adequate against the host of bank emissaries who scoured the country . . . and the indefatigable spies . . . to which may be added perjuries, familiar as dicers' oaths, to baffle investigation.

Naturally the report blamed "the base dishonesty and gross cupidity of a few" rather than the law which was "established upon principles well digested and approved, and hedged round with so much care."

Viewing the effects of about $1,000,000 of worthless bank notes, the report continued:

It has been said, with some appearance of plausibility, that these banks have at least had the good effect of liquidating a large amount of debt. This may be true; but whose debts have they liquidated? Those of the crafty and the speculative—and by whom? Let every poor man from his little clearing and log hut in the woods make the emphatic response by holding up to view as the rewards of his labor a handful of promises to pay, which, for his purpose, are as valueless as a handful of dry leaves at his feet.

But the "poor man" was the one to whom the free-banking idea had made the greatest appeal; as usual, his self-appointed best friends and promisers had turned out to be his enemies. As the *Advertiser* said, the report merely recorded the failure

of this new fangled scheme of banking—conceived by half-witted politicians and cunning demagogs, in the spirit and practice of genuine *locofocoism*— in the same spirit and practice which is preached by Fanny Wright—and adopted by Van Buren, Benton and others, as the only radical cure for the evils and anti-republican tendencies of "associated wealth," "monopolies," and ruffled shirts. This new school of banking was got up by the new light financiers of Michigan, in opposition to "chartered privileges" and the "autocracy of wealth," and all that in order to make the rich poor and the poor rich. Well they have tried it. We hope they will now be satisfied.[168]

Interesting was the added comment that the report was worth preserving, for it would afford in the future a "very rare and curious illustration" of the early political and financial history of the country.

The regular or chartered banks which had been doing an honest and legitimate business were dragged down with the others. On

[168] *Cincinnati Daily Gazette*, February 9, 1839, quoting *Detroit Gazette and Advertiser*.

February 25, 1839, the Michigan State Bank suspended.[169] By December only three chartered banks (with one branch bank) and four general-law banks were still in operation;[170] according to the attorney general's report, forty-two banks were under injunction.[171] The general banking law of 1837 followed the banks; in 1844 the state supreme court declared it unconstitutional on the ground that it created corporations without the assent of two thirds of the members of the legislature. The causes of its failure were stated forty years later by one who remembered the wildcat system: ". . . the *theory* of that system was perfect. . . . But like some financial theories of the present day, it would not work in practice, for at least three good reasons. The banks did not keep the specie, and the real estate security was often worthless, and the whole machine was unconstitutional."[172]

When the failure of the general-law or "safety-fund" banking system became obvious, Michigan turned to the idea of a state bank. On April 2, 1839, the legislature had chartered the State Bank of Michigan, modeled on the second State Bank of Indiana.[173] But it was not the time for even a soundly planned bank

[169] *Detroit Daily Advertiser*, February 26, 1839. The *Advertiser* said the same causes could not affect the Bank of Michigan and the Farmers' and Mechanics' Bank. The Democrats said these two were in on the run on the Michigan State Bank, and the *Free Press*, March 7, said the *Advertiser* caused the run on the Michigan State Bank to compel it to suspend, with public money in its vaults. The State Bank was tied up with the Morris Canal and Banking Company loan, made advances to contractors, put out its own notes on ninety-day drafts, etc. See *Advertiser*, March 9, 13. As reported by a legislative committee in 1839 this bank had liabilities of $807,000 and assets of $352,000. *Ibid.*, April 25, 1839.

[170] The latter were the Bank of Marshall, the Detroit and St. Joseph Railroad Bank (Jackson), the Bank of Adrian, and the Merchants' Bank of Jackson County (Brooklyn). *Ibid.*, January 17; *Cincinnati Daily Gazette*, January 27, 1840. The "St. Joseph Bank" (Commercial Bank of Michigan ?) was said, in September, 1838, to be the only bank in Michigan which had never refused to pay specie; "its notes were hoarded like silver." *Chicago Democrat*, September 26, 1838.

[171] The bills of the general-law banks were well engraved on good paper. Possessed of not even souvenir value for some years, these notes were given to children to play with. It was said that during the Civil War some thousands of dollars worth were disposed of by Union soldiers in the South, where people valued them more than Confederate money.

[172] Stebbins, "Story of Another Pioneer," in *Michigan Pioneer and Historical Collections*, V, 130.

[173] While the bank was being discussed in the legislature the *Detroit Daily Advertiser*, January 8, opposed the plan as a Democratic political scheme. But April 25 it approved of the bank as created.

The State Bank, with 9 branches, was given a charter to run until January 1, 1860; capital was fixed at $2,000,000, one half to be subscribed to by the state; specie suspension on notes was forbidden; control of discounts and loans of the branches was placed in the hands of the directors of the bank who were to maintain their office or banking house at the state capital; directors might close a branch for insolvency, and the State Bank (and remaining branches) were to pay all

to get a start; by the end of the year it too was under injunction and winding up its affairs.

Wisconsin began its life as a separate territory with only the Bank of Wisconsin,[174] which had opened at Green Bay in 1835. The territorial legislature in 1836 chartered the Miners' Bank of Dubuque, the Bank of Mineral Point, and the Bank of Milwaukee.[175] Moses M. Strong, Solomon Juneau, Col. William S. Hamilton, Byron Kilbourn and other prominent early citizens were among the important organizers. Stock of the Bank of Milwaukee went on sale in June, 1837, at the time when all banks were suspending. The bank got off to a poor start and was in trouble from the beginning.[176] The *Milwaukee Advertiser* printed an "Exposition" of its affairs[177] which was answered by letters from the former president and cashier.[178] Its charter was repealed by the legislature early in 1839. The Bank of Mineral Point had similar difficulties.

The Bank of Wisconsin went off specie in June, 1837. The next legislature appointed a committee to investigate the banks of the Territory, which it did by way of a questionnaire. Although the committee reported the bank of Mineral Point to have violated several provisions of its charter, it reported the Bank of Wiscon-

---

debts of any closed branch. Stock subscriptions were to be paid in specie, 20 per cent down, 80 per cent in four semiannual installments. No notes of less than $1.00, nor any post notes of less than $50 were to be issued. Loans of branches were not to exceed two and one-half times the capital actually paid in. The president and directors were to constitute a board of fund commissioners for the management of the sinking fund, the internal improvements fund, the surplus revenue, the common school and university funds already created or to be created; they were authorized to borrow $1,800,000 to enable the state to pay for its share of the bank's stock and to enable the stockholders to pay for their shares. A sinking fund of various earnings (interest on state stock, etc.) was set aside to retire the state loan. The faith of the state was pledged for the redemption of all notes issued by the bank and for payment of all debts in case of its insolvency. By a supplementary act the branches were located at Detroit, Monroe, Adrian, Ann Arbor, Niles, Jackson, Pontiac, Mt. Clemens, and Marshall. *Laws of Michigan*, 1839, pp. 37–64, 107–8, 207.

[174] See Chapter VIII. For early Wisconsin banking, see Leonard Bayliss Krueger, *History of Commercial Banking in Wisconsin* (*University of Wisconsin Studies in Social Sciences and History*, No. 18, Madison, 1933).

[175] Congress approved with the condition that no notes be put into circulation until one half the capital had actually been paid in. The charters limited debts to outside parties, over and above specie on deposit, to three times the amount of capital actually paid in.

[176] Most of the stock subscriptions were not paid in to the full extent prescribed (40 per cent) and were declared forfeit in 1838. The affairs of this bank were involved in a factional struggle for control.

[177] February 24, 1838.

[178] *Milwaukee Sentinel*, February 27, 1838.

sin as sound and solvent.[179] But this bank's affairs were in a bad way. In a few months its notes were quoted at 50 per cent discount, lower even than the notes of the Michigan wildcats;[180] by late 1839 they were thirty cents on the dollar. Early in the year the cashier wrote to the chairman of the legislative investigating committee to explain that the Bank of Wisconsin had not resumed specie payments when the other banks did because of agricultural conditions in the northern parts of the Territory, the lack of exports, the inability of people to pay their debts, and stay laws of the legislature which made it unnecessary for them to do so.[181] In March, 1839, the legislature ordered the attorney general to start proceedings to close its affairs. It was said that the bank had $300,000 of notes in circulation and only $20,000 of "cash capital." Upon investigation it was found that $198,000 of unissued notes were on hand; outstanding liabilities were about $100,000 and assets were estimated at half this amount.[182]

By this time there was no good circulating medium in Wisconsin. Solomon Juneau wrote from Milwaukee in 1838 that there was very little money in the region and that most of that little was bad currency; two years later he was complaining of the competition of many peddlers, some of whom paid in silver or good eastern funds.[183] Milwaukee and Racine merchants discounted notes of the Bank of Mineral Point though they accepted those of the Illinois State Bank. Everyone tried to avoid the Michigan wildcat notes.[184] Various expedients had been resorted to. Mineral Point had issued $15,000 of 3 per cent certificates;[185] the "evidences of debt" of the Fox River Hydraulic Company at De Pere circulated as money, as did the notes of the Wisconsin Marine and Fire Insurance Company chartered in 1839. Governor Dodge in his message in December, 1839, emphasized the

[179] *Wisconsin Democrat*, February 3, 1838.

[180] For comparison, in April, 1839, notes of the Illinois State Bank, Missouri State Bank, and Indiana State Bank were quoted at par; the Bank of Michigan and the Farmers' and Mechanics' Bank of Detroit at 5 per cent discount; the Bank of Mineral Point and the Bank of Dubuque at 10 per cent; the State Bank of Michigan at 25 per cent. *Daily Chicago American*, April 23, 1839.

[181] Letter of cashier Henry Stringham, in *Wisconsin Enquirer*, February 2, 1839.

[182] *Milwaukee Advertiser*, July 13, 1839; Wisconsin *House Journal*, 1840–41, p. 135.

[183] Letters from Juneau, April 9, 1838, February 8, 1840, in *Calendar of American Fur Company Papers*, I, 448, 764.

[184] *Milwaukee Advertiser*, March 16, 1839; *Wisconsin Enquirer*, September 21, 1839.

[185] Mineral Point *Miners' Free Press*, November 3, 1837.

embarrassed state of the currency; with the Bank of Mineral Point the only bank operating, and it refusing to discount paper, debtors were in a bad way. He thought a twelve-month stay law would help. The legislature complied and the *Chicago American* said that Wisconsin had passed a " 'spunge law" which wiped out all debts. It appeared to be surprised at such an act of "bold, radical locofocoism" with its contempt for contracts and honor, and regarded it as just another evidence of the "demagoguism and popularity-seeking of the times."[186] The *Milwaukee Sentinel* defended the act for the relief of insolvent debtors and said they were as good as those of Illinois where they took "leg bail" and made sudden departures for Texas.

In 1839 the territorial legislature sought to create a "State Bank of Wisconsin," with five authorized branches, and capital of $1,000,000, one half the stock to be owned by the Territory. Col. William S. Hamilton was the chief sponsor. Congress did not give its approval so nothing came of the project.

§ § §

Railroads in the Northwest, though merely in the beginning stage, were giving indications of future importance.[187] Though relatively few people had seen a railroad, everyone was interested in them. Newspapers which had been full of canal items noticeably increased the news of railroads about 1835. Notices of meetings to organize railroads abounded on all sides; legislatures were granting charters by the dozen.[188] Plans for railroads to reach out from the East and from the South stimulated interest in connecting roads in the Northwest. As the Baltimore and Ohio crept slowly westward, representatives from Cincinnati and adjacent towns held a number of meetings in August, 1835, to help promote the idea of a Cincinnati and Charleston Railroad. Among the committee members appointed to engage in promotional work were Dr. Daniel Drake, Edward D. Mansfield, Judge

---

[186] Quoted in *Milwaukee Sentinel*, February 11, 1840.
[187] For discussion of canals versus railroads, see Chapter VII.
[188] "Zeno" in the *Cleveland Weekly Advertiser*, January 19, 1837, said the Ohio legislature had chartered twenty-eight or thirty in 1836 in addition to the twelve or fourteen previously chartered.

James Hall, William Henry Harrison, and George H. Dunn.[189] The Harrison-for-president movement was thus hooked up with the plans of South Carolina to reach the Northwest by rail.[190] The next year Ohio, Indiana, and Illinois sent delegates to the Knoxville Convention. Though the Louisville, Cincinnati and Charleston Railroad Company was chartered in 1837, the project ran into sectional, financial, and political obstacles, and did not come to fruition.[191]

While Cincinnati was flirting with the Southeast, Cleveland, desiring a choice of markets as well as cheap imports, put out a convincing sales talk to Pennsylvania in favor of building a railroad from Philadelphia, by way of Pittsburgh, to Lake Erie.[192] Predictions of future population growth and production were made which, though they looked big at the time, eventually proved to be quite modest. The "money tightness" and depression delayed these plans for some years.

Of the many railroads chartered by the four states in the 1830's only six or seven had any mileage in operation under steam power by 1840. The pioneer road was the Erie and Kalamazoo, chartered by Michigan Territory in 1833 when the country through which it was to run was assumed to lie in Michigan. In

[189] Mansfield published a pamphlet, "Railroad from the Banks of the Ohio River to the Tide Waters of the Carolinas and Georgia," with map, and an article, "Cincinnati and Charleston Rail-Road," in Hall's *Western Monthly Magazine*, V (1836), 538–48. Dunn and Hall were strong supporters of Harrison for president. Dunn later became president of the Lawrenceburg and Indianapolis Railroad.

Noah Noble, Whig governor of Indiana, in his message of 1835, urged co-operation with the Cincinnati and Charleston planners, and the legislature passed approving resolutions. Ohio, too, approved but like Indiana had put too much of the state's money in improvements within its borders to be able to purchase stock in trunk lines.

[190] The promoters emphasized commercial, social, and political advantages to both sections. Robert Y. Hayne pointed out that agricultural products from the Northwest could be exchanged for cotton from the South; that the South could export the former and the Northwest manufacture the latter successfully and without the need of a protective tariff. Thus the road would produce a "controlling and permanent influence on the peace and perpetuity of the Union, by practically increasing the reciprocal dependence of the North and South, by establishing prejudices, creating greater uniformity in political opinions and blending the feelings of distant portions into a union of hearts." *Proceedings of Knoxville Convention* . . . (Knoxville, 1836), 11.

[191] See Kohlmeier, *The Old Northwest as the Keystone of the Arch of the Federal Union*, Chapter II, for an excellent treatment of the northwestern and the southeastern trunk line.

[192] See *Daily Cleveland Herald*, January—February, 1837. The "Cleveland and Pittsburg" was "nearly located" to Warren by autumn; it was expected that the survey on to Pittsburgh would be completed the following spring. *Cleveland Herald and Gazette*, November 24, 1837.

November, 1836, when the oak rails connected Toledo and Adrian, a horse-drawn train was run over the road. Strap-iron rails about five-eighths inch thick were laid in the spring of 1837 and in July the *Adrian No. 1* (No. 80 of the Baldwin Locomotive Works), a twenty-mile-an-hour locomotive, went into action.[193] The same year the road inaugurated its "Pleasure Car" service—the first extra-fare train in the West.[194] In 1838 the Erie and Kalamazoo built the Palmyra and Jacksonburgh branch as far as Tecumseh; the road was also extended from Adrian to Clinton but horsepower only was used on this section.

Not far behind, chronologically, was the Mad River and Lake Erie, chartered by Ohio in 1832. This road, which benefited to the extent of $200,000 from state funds under the "plunder law" of 1837, as well as from county stock subscriptions, had completed some sixteen miles out of Sandusky by the end of that year. It seems that the company had a locomotive before it had any tracks; the *Sandusky* built at Paterson, New Jersey, for a New Jersey road was brought west by way of the Erie Canal. This locomotive (according to Dunbar the first west of the Allegheny Mountains) had an important influence; since its gauge was found to be 4 feet, 10 inches, the tracks were laid to conform. Ohio later made this the standard gauge by law, and it was adopted by roads in adjoining states. In December an experimental run was made near Sandusky; the locomotive was said to have drawn 4 cars and 150 "ladies and gentlemen" at speeds of from 20 to 50 miles per hour and stopped in 8 rods at high speed.[195] The next year the run through to Bellevue was made in 40 minutes, to the great alarm of the animals along the way.[196] It was hoped that fifty miles of the road would be completed in 1838 and that it would even be finished to Springfield by 1840.[197]

The "opening" of the Michigan Central early in February, 1838, has been described earlier in this chapter; one other important opening was to take place that year. When the Madi-

---

[193] Clarence Frost, "The Early Railroads of Southern Michigan," in *Michigan Pioneer and Historical Collections*, XXXVIII (1912), 500.

[194] This car had three compartments, eight passengers each, and a baggage compartment in the lower middle part. Fare in it was $2.25 for the thirty-three miles as compared to $1.50 in the horse-drawn car.

[195] *Ohio State Journal*, December 27, 1837.

[196] *Cleveland Herald and Gazette*, May 22, 1838.

[197] About thirty miles were completed by 1840; Springfield was reached in 1848.

son and Indianapolis Railroad was completed to Graham, seventeen miles out of Madison, in November, a grand "steam car ride" was announced and important state dignitaries were invited.[198] Since the Baldwin locomotive destined for the honor was thrown overboard from a boat which encountered a Gulf storm, the management borrowed the *Elkhorn* from Louisville for the occasion and brought it up by steamboat at a cost of $1,052. After being pulled up the hill over a dirt road to North Madison by five yoke of oxen, it performed creditably, took the visitors to Graham and back, then was returned home. A passenger train operated by horsepower over this route until March, 1839, when the replacement locomotive arrived safely; formal opening of the road to Graham took place April 1. The four-wheeled freight cars, about twenty-five-hog capacity, also came from the East, but the first passenger coach, used at the opening, was built in Madison. "It was very plain with small windows near the top of the car, lever brakes, and was about thirty feet long." The same month the road was leased to private owners.[199]

Work on the inclined plane between Madison and North Madison, about a mile and a third in length, with a rise of 413 feet and 2 cuts, continued from 1836 to 1841. On its completion in the latter year the cars were let down by gravity and pulled up by 8 horses driven tandem to each car.[200] The 30 odd miles of this road which were built by the state were railed with English iron T-rails, 45 pounds to the yard, delivered in lengths of 15 feet, 15 feet 9 inches, and 18 feet. They were laid on cedar crossties which were fastened to 10-by10-inch sills with locust pins.[201] The ties cost 25 cents each, the sills 8 cents per foot, and the rails $75 per ton delivered.

[198] This was not the first railroad operated in Indiana, however, since July 4, 1834, was celebrated by running a car, built at an expense of $222.12½, pulled by a "horse of unknown value," over a mile and a quarter of track then laid on the Lawrenceburg and Indianapolis Railroad.

[199] Robert Branham, Elias Stapp, D. C. Branham, and W. H. Branham until June, 1840, then to J. G. Sering and William Butt until June, 1841, when the state again took over. The lessees were to pay all operating expenses and turn over 40 per cent of the gross receipts to the state. In February, 1843, the state sold the road to the Madison and Indianapolis Railroad Company. C. G. Sappington, "The Madison and Indianapolis Railroad," in *Indiana Magazine of History*, XII (1916), 236-38.

[200] From 1848 to 1868 a two-cylinder engine and a pinion which worked in a rack in the center of the track pulled up the cars; in 1868 a cog engine did the work.

[201] When cedar proved too soft to hold the spikes, oak ties were substituted about five years later.

The Detroit and Pontiac Railroad charter of 1830—the first railroad charter in the Northwest—has been noted previously. Since its incorporators were unable to finish the road within the specified five years, the charter was abrogated in 1834. Another charter was granted to a group of Pontiac citizens under the name of Detroit and Pontiac Railroad Company, which was also authorized to establish the Bank of Pontiac. Sherman Stevens and Alfred ("Salt") Williams put up most of the original capital and Stevens, who was formerly in the fur trade, ran the bank, operated sawmills, and built the railroad. Contract for grubbing fifteen miles was let in the spring of 1836. Construction ran into a swamp as well as into opposition from some of the farmers who opposed the new road as threatening ruin to crops.[202] Instead of purchasing the road under the law of 1837 the state lent it $100,000; it also succeeded in borrowing a like sum from the state of Indiana.[203] In July, 1838, the road was opened to Royal Oak and in August, 1839, to Birmingham. On the horse-car service between Detroit and Royal Oak the passenger fare was $1.00, and freight 50 cents per hundred. From the profits a Baldwin locomotive, which was named *Sherman Stevens*, was purchased. The road was sold under an execution in 1840 to New York interests and was finally completed to Pontiac in 1843.

Two or three other short stretches of railroad were built in Michigan. The Detroit and Shelby Railroad completed twenty miles over which cars were operated by horsepower in 1838. It was soon abandoned. Some work was done on the River Raisin and Lake Erie road and on the Palmyra and Jacksonburg Railroad.

Illinois' pioneer railroad was the section of the Northern Cross from Meredosia on the Illinois River to Jacksonville. The first rail was laid in the spring of 1838, but the locomotive which had been ordered got "lost in passage"; however, a locomotive which had been ordered by the fund commissioners for the Bloomington and Mackinaw Railroad—at the time in no condition to support a locomotive—was delivered by boat to Mer-

---

[202] Sherman Stevens, "Early Days in Genesee County," in *Michigan Pioneer and Historical Collections*, VII (1884), 397.

[203] That is, it bought $100,000 of Indiana bonds for which it advanced $10,000.

edosia. In November it began operating on the road, which was not completed to Springfield until 1842.

Early railroad building is a fascinating subject, almost as insidious in its tendency to sidetrack the historian as is the fur trade. Many of the problems presented were new, different from those which arose in connection with either roads, canals, or steamboats. (The steamboat, for instance, showed no great inclination to leave its appointed path and start wandering overland.) And the lack of trained construction engineers—applied mathematics was not one of the colleges' fortes—made early building largely a matter of trial and error. But the American imagination was at work; already in mind were the coaches, sleeping cars, double-track railroads, and power units of the future. All that remained was to devise the mechanism and contrivances and to make them work.

Cuts, fills, and bridges were not so difficult; dirt, stone, and timber were familiar materials and workmen who could handle them were available. It was rather the apparently simple problem of laying a roadbed, of getting a rail to stay put, of getting cars and locomotives to stay on the rails, which caused the most trouble. Compared to the modern roadbed with its simple but substantial components of solid foundation, sound crossties laid in firm ballast, and steel rails spiked to the crossties, early railroads were complicated but flimsy affairs. Specifications and practices in roadbed construction varied but slightly. Usually mud- or ground-sills of rough-hewn (at least on the top side) timber were laid first. Locust or cedar was most lasting but cedar was too soft and locust was hard to work. On the sills were set and pinned the crossties, somewhat wider spaced than now. On the crossties were pinned the stringers of oak—4 by 6 inches or 4 by 8 inches—which were notched and pinned together at the ends. The rails of wrought iron, about 2½ inches wide and ⅝ inch in thickness, were nailed to the stringers with square wrought-iron nails or spikes whose heads were countersunk in holes in the rails. The ends of the rails were mitered or beveled to overlap. Sometimes the specifications called for stone posts or footings under the sills; other times the sills were dispensed with and the ties laid directly on the ground. There were also interesting combinations of stone sills, wood crossties, and stringers; of stone foundations, wooden sills, and stone ties; of crushed-stone foundations, timber crossties, and stone blocks to support the rails.

Ever present was the danger of loose-ended rails of the strap iron which, curving upward, had a tendency to catch over the carriage wheels, and crawl up through the floor. These "snake heads" might frighten a female passenger "half to death" by mussing up her skirts, or on occasion cause more lasting damage. Rigid was the rule that the engineer spot these loose ends, stop the train, and nail them down on the spot.

Railroad gauges varied in the United States. Some early roads in New York, Massachusetts, and Pennsylvania adopted the English practice of four feet, eight and a half inches. Others chose whatever width seemed suitable; many were under four feet, some were four feet ten inches, or even five feet. Though the T-rail, first whittled out in a pine model by Robert L. Stevens in 1830, was being rolled by English companies by the time western railroads were being built, few used them in the early years. After various experiments with rails and wheel rims, which included triangle rails in triangle-grooved rims, the tongue-and-groove system, double flanges, outside flanges, and inside flanges, it was finally determined that the last, in combination with the T-rail, was most effective in keeping the cars on the track. It required longer still to work out the beveled wheel rim to compensate for unequal-length paths followed on curves by wheels which were fixed to the axle. Also to determine the best way of fixing the rails to the ties.

By the time the railroad reached the West coach designers had abandoned the attempt to imitate the oval-shaped stagecoach and started over again with a rectangular boxlike carriage with cross seats or seats along the side. Couplings were link and pin, springs and brakes were crude or nonexistent. The woodburning locomotives emitted sparks in size and quantity; passengers suffered burned parasols and clothing. Since there was no way of preheating the water for the boiler and the capacity of the latter for generating steam was limited, it was not unusual to have to stop and let a new head of steam warm up. Hose connections between water tank and boiler were of leather and, being unprotected, in cold weather had to be thawed out carefully by open fires. Even rain could discourage the early locomotives. It was not without reason that early schedules advertised certain departures "weather permitting." There were critics cynical enough to pretend that, if the horse path were completely abandoned, the weeds between the rails would stop the locomotives in the summer.

Travel on the cars was informal. Passengers traveled by waybill, as would a barrel of salt. Trains often stopped, like stages, at the crossroads to pick up passengers, or to "make change" for the farmer's wife. The jokes circulated about the early locomotives and trains were about as numerous as those which attached to the Ford at a later date. One of the early locomotives[204] on the Meredosia and Jacksonville line, *The Betsey Baker,* was said to be so slow that the cowcatcher was put on the rear; when it finally ran off into a ditch, the costs of raising it being prohibitive, the operators just substituted mules.[205] All passenger trains were what George Ade later referred to as "lovers' accommodations" which would "wait at the station for the last farewell and long drawn out kiss of parting lovers, and would then move off slowly to make the separation more gradual." Like Irwin S. Cobb's "Lake-Gulf, Continental and Pacific Slope," many of these railroads had more name than mileage.[206] Many problems other than engineering were presented; boiler explosions were not as frequent as on steamboats but there were other types of accidents. As with the canal boats, some young blades were always seeking more action. The *Detroit Daily Advertiser* issued a warning: "It is not unfrequent that young men, and sometimes young women too, to whom travelling with the velocity of lightning is a novelty, will show their agility and lightness of foot by tripping from one car to another, and from the track to the car, while under full speed. And everyone can see that this must be attended with more or less danger."[207]

[204] A contemporary toast: "The locomotive, the only good motive for riding a man upon a rail." Though locomotives usually had male names, they were always referred to by those who built, repaired, and ran them as "she."

[205] The locomotive was later bought by "an enterprising individual" who equipped it with broad-rimmed wheels and ran it (with the assistance of a yoke of oxen) like a steam roller, on the dirt road from Alton to Springfield. The tracks of the strange contrivance intrigued travelers who traced the monster to its resting place. Dunbar, *History of Travel,* III, 1077.

[206] Cobb's road had a sign with the name of the railroad at each end of the line. One evening about dusk the engineer, mistaking the sign for track, ran off the end and seriously injured a traveling salesman from "Paduky."

[207] August 5, 1836.

§ § § §

While banks were "busting" and states were going bankrupt, people continued to live and to make a living. Settlements advanced, though not so rapidly, lands were cleared, trade was carried on, small industries were born and grew.

Though the Indian had largely gone, and cultivated fields and pastures occupied his former hunting ground; though the steamboat, canal, and railroad were displacing the canoe, batteau, and Conestoga wagon, the fur trade, the oldest of all, still occupied a position of importance; in fact, the region south of the Lakes was for a few years the center of interest of this great business.[208]

In its ramifications the trade was much more than the mere buying and selling of hides and furs: furs went to London, from London to Leipsig, from Leipsig to Greece and to China. Twine (nets), cloth, blankets, and guns came from England as well as the United States; blankets from France; beads, liquors, traps, hardware from various places; powder from the DuPonts. Fish, salt, pork, flour, lead, cooperage (for fish, spirits, etc.), lumber, boats, and the labor of trappers, farmers, boatmen and artisans all figured in.

After 1834, when John Jacob Astor sold his interest in the American Fur Company which he founded, its chief activities centered around Detroit.[209] Important changes were taking place in the fur trade. The advancing settlements were diminishing the furred animals in the Great Lakes region; beaver, the former backbone of the trade, was becoming less important as the result of competition of nutria and silk hats. At the same time muskrat was becoming a drug on the market. But raccoon, mink, and hides were rising in demand and price;[210] the best take in these products was in the area around the Lakes.

[208] For the fur trade prior to 1834, see Chapter VII.

[209] Offices of the company, now headed by Ramsay Crooks, were at New York; William Brewster held forth at Detroit, main office in the West; the "Western Outfit" was based at Prairie du Chien; the "Northern Department" at Mackinac; the "Northern Outfit" at La Pointe; Chapman's and Franchere's "Outfits" at St. Marys. Rix Robinson on the Grand River, Jean Beaubien at Chicago, Solomon Juneau at Milwaukee, and John Lawe at Green Bay ordinarily did business via Samuel Abbott, agent at Mackinac, but with Brewster at Detroit if communications were bad. Ramsay Crooks to William Brewster, November 4, 1834, *Calendar of American Fur Company Papers*, I, 8.

[210] Ramsay Crooks early in 1836 wrote to Pratte, Chouteau & Company of St. Louis that beaver could not possibly rise. "Game has disappeared like snow before a summer's sun," wrote Crooks to Wildes & Company of London. *Ibid.*, I, 149, 245–46.

At Milwaukee in 1835 Solomon Juneau, noting that the Indians hunted and trapped only enough to get liquor, was switching to trade with the speculators and farmers. He ordered wheat, corn, and flour for the Indian trade but also wanted pork, butter, cheese, lard, wine, whiskey, brandy, gin, tea, coffee, rice, raisins, lamp oil, white fish, pepper, nails, padlocks, lump sugar, putty, axes, scythes, white lead, figs, spices (all kinds), almonds, door latches, shovels, spades, hammers, needles, threads, linseed oil, rum, mackerel and codfish.[211] Clearly enough his fur trading post was converting into a general store.

In March, 1836, Lampson, the London agent for the American Fur Company, had written that the fur business had never been so profitable.[212] The company was paying $16 each for Northwest guns; dividends on capital stock out of profits through 1835 were 10 per cent, the next year 15 per cent.[213] But by June, 1836, the fur business was finding "money exceedingly scarce"; three months later the money market was worse instead of better; and by spring of 1837 the "state of things [was] truly alarming." Prices were falling rapidly; good English rifles could be had for $6.50. Leipsig-fair buyers (the European fur distributors) having heard of American conditions were waiting for lower fur prices. Rix Robinson, from the Grand River country of Michigan, wrote that "panic pervades even the wilderness."[214]

Determined competition added to the troubles of the depression. Not only was the German fur buyer Hötte in the Detroit area paying high prices for mink and raccoon, but the Ewings of Fort Wayne, aggressive, unscrupulous but capable operators, were proving a perpetual boil on the hide of the American Fur Company.[215] The Maumee-Wabash valleys were rich " 'coon"

[211] Juneau to Crooks, March 27, 1835. *Calendar of American Fur Company Papers*, I, 46. Already Gurdon S. Hubbard had converted his Danville Indian store to "white goods"; he himself moved to Chicago to become one of its leading citizens.

[212] C. L. Lampson to Ramsay Crooks, March 14, 15, 1836. *Ibid.*, I, 158, 159.

[213] Crooks to Wildes & Company, London, July 30, 1836; John B. Whetten to William Brewster, February 20, 1837. *Ibid.*, I, 211, 269.

[214] *Ibid.*, I, 194, 235, 283, 286, 291. "The present state of commercial distress exceeds anything of the kind ever experienced," wrote Crooks to Rix Robinson on Grand River, May 6, 1837; he asked Robinson not to draw on the company for funds due him and said the company would like to borrow from Robinson. *Ibid.*, I, 289.

[215] Alexander Ewing, Indian trader from Pennsylvania and Ohio, had settled at Fort Wayne in 1822. In 1825 he took his sons, William G. and George Washington Ewing, into partnership in the fur-buying business. After his death in 1826 the firm

country and the Ewings were strategically situated not only as to location but in personal connections. They had good men at work in the region and they induced others to come over from Crooks's company; through their contract with Suydam, Sage and Company of New York they had an excellent outlet and source of backing and supply. The Ewings, strongly entrenched at Vincennes and Evansville as well as in the Maumee region, even had the temerity to go after William Brewster of the American Fur Company in his own bailiwick of Detroit. Hötte was effectively "put down" and went home, but the Ewings did not suppress so easily.[216] Although early in 1839 Crooks had written Brewster, "kill them in your own way," two months later he suggested that it be done fairly and so as to stay within the bounds of reason.[217]

Both sides having lost heavily in the fur-buying war, 1838–39, in July, Crooks and the Ewings signed an agreement[218] which included the Ewing affiliates. There was to be no more competition. But W. G. Ewing soon found a flaw in the agreement and refused to be bound by it. The company decided to return to a belligerent position and carry on the war with vigor. When the Ewings spread rumors that their rivals were bankrupt, Crooks wrote that the company would be mortified if it did not gain a victory over the faithless Ewings, but that in killing them it would have to be careful not to kill itself.[219] Times were worse than in 1837; "the Company never was so poor." Nor were the Ewings grieving about it. W. G. petitioned the Ohio legislature (December, 1839) to destroy the company's competition in that state on the

---

of W. G. and G. W. Ewing continued until 1854. The Ewing Papers are in the Indiana State Library. The best account of the Ewing activities is in Paul C. Phillips, "The Fur Trade in the Maumee-Wabash Country," in *Studies in American History (Indiana University Studies,* Nos. 66–68, Bloomington, 1926).

[216] When George Hunt, American Fur Company agent, went over to the Ewings, the company brought in John Hollister, Captain John Furey, and others to replace him; Gabriel Franchere, one of the Astorians, was transferred from Sault Ste. Marie to Louisville, Evansville, and Vincennes to outbuy the Ewings. Furey wrote —probably January, 1839—that some of the persons under contract with the Ewings would sell to the company if the furs were taken out at night. *Calendar of American Fur Company Papers,* I, 560.

[217] February 9 and April 4, 1839, Crooks to Brewster. *Ibid.,* I, 577, 609.

[218] The Ewings were to be given $100,000 stock in the American Fur Company and have sole rights to the territory from Lake Erie to the Ohio. On August 18, G. W. Ewing wrote Brewster from Huntington, Indiana, to keep the agreement secret. Since the latter's writing was known locally, "let your clerk back your letters to me." *Ibid.,* I, 671, 681.

[219] Crooks to Brewster, December 31, 1839. *Ibid.,* I, 734.

ground that its charter gave it the right to trade only with the Indians and persons beyond the settlements. The next month G. W., who was a state senator, introduced a bill in the Indiana legislature to prohibit the company from exercising banking and other extraordinary privileges in that state. Crooks struck back and decided that either the Ewings or the company must be driven out of the Wabash country.

The warfare of 1839–40 had been as costly as that of the preceding season. Crooks and Brewster had held their own; G. W. Ewing was ready to call it quits. He was willing to share a portion of the business and engage in "mutual forbearance," at least for awhile. Crooks was inclined not to compromise, but when the Ewings declined to contest the field the following season the struggle eased off. A year later the last round in the big battle for furs in the Wabash country ended with the bankruptcy of what was left of the once powerful American Fur Company. W. G. Ewing wrote: "The Great American Fur Co. it seems has exploded! disappeared, overwhelmed with most miserable Bankruptcy! —they have met their just deserts;—they waged a Warfare against us, that cost us a loss of at least $60,000. But had we united with them in 1840 (when we were trying to buy our peace) we would have sustained double that loss, with a prostration of our Business."[220]

Compared with down-river pork shipments or grain exports shipped by the Ohio Canal, the dollar value of the fur business makes a small showing; yet the trade was relatively more important than the figures would indicate.[221] For the farmer, or his sons, the proceeds from trapping supplemented the income from crops and produce; further, it was mostly cash money. Local buyers, storekeepers, and artisans likewise received a share. The

[220] W. G. Ewing to J. W. Edmonds, March 23, 1843. Ewing Papers. The Ewings continued in the fur business a few years—in 1845 they made nearly $75,000—but after running into financial difficulties practically became the agents of Pierre Chouteau and Company of St. Louis for the Ohio-Michigan-Indiana country.

[221] The amount can only be estimated. Scattered through the papers of the American Fur Company and the Ewings are many entries which give clues. Brewster early in 1839 reported taking $40,000 of skins in Fort Wayne, Spafford and Hunt $25,000 at Madison, Wisconsin, Furey expected to get 40,000 skins at Indianapolis the following season, and Hollister reported $130,000 worth at Perrysburg, Ohio, for the season 1839–40. If the Ewings did as well, the totals were not inconsiderable. Fur exports from Michigan in 1837 were estimated at more than $400,000. *Hunt's Merchants' Magazine*, VI (1842), 341.

fur business largely sustained towns such as Fort Wayne, Noblesville, Logansport, Peru, Kokomo, Vincennes, and Evansville
until other mercantile interests and manufactories arose.[222]

Though the facilities of transportation within the region developed rapidly during the period 1835 to 1840, the over-all picture of agriculture, industry, and commerce did not change
greatly. The newer settlements in northern Illinois, Michigan,
and Wisconsin Territory at first produced no exportable agricultural surplus; rather they were dependent upon the older settlements of the region for flour, meat, and fruit. After a few years,
however, the newer areas began adding to the exportable total.
Some beef went out from Chicago in 1833, wheat began to be
shipped by 1838–39; Michigan exported a little wheat in 1835.[223]

From 1835 to 1839 while the total exports of the Old Northwest approximately doubled, the exports of wheat increased four-
teenfold, flour doubled, pork increased by 50 per cent and corn
(figuring in that used in whiskey and pork) did almost as well.
The gains in pork were about evenly divided between the Ohio-
Mississippi outlet and the northeastern outlet (canals and Great
Lakes). Most of the increase in wheat and flour went out the
northeast channel. Corn continued to go south.[224] This was the
natural result of the location of place of production and the relation of transportation charges to the bulk and value of the
export. The volume of agricultural stuff which went out by the
Great Lakes was the product largely of central and northern

[222] Phillips, "The Fur Trade in the Maumee-Wabash Country," 118. Milo M.
Quaife (ed.), *Growing Up With Southern Illinois 1820 to 1861 from the Memoirs
of Daniel Harmon Brush* (Chicago, 1944) contains data on the fur trade of the
period in southern Illinois.

[223] Using the Michigan Census of 1837 and United States Census for 1840 the
major grain products in Michigan were:

	1837	1840
Wheat	1,014,896 bu.	2,345,283 bu.
Corn	791,427	2,215,787
Oats	1,116,910	3,717,177

[224] Kohlmeier, *The Old Northwest as the Keystone of the Arch of the American
Federal Union*, 33. Of the 1839 exports of more than 800,000 barrels of flour 53
per cent went south, 40 per cent northeast, 7 per cent east; of more than 2,000,000
bushels of wheat nearly 97 per cent went northeast; of more than 1,000,000 bushels
of corn, 98 per cent went south; of some 300,000 barrels of pork and bacon, 69
per cent went south, 19 per cent east, 12 per cent northeast; of more than 30,000
hogsheads of tobacco 90 per cent went south, 9 per cent east; of 30,000 barrels
of whiskey 96 per cent went south, 3 per cent east; of 500 tons of wool practically
all went east. *Ibid.*, 33–34.

Ohio;[225] southern Ohio as well as most of Indiana and Illinois continued to ship the bulk of their produce down river.[226]

Imports into the region increased about one third between 1835 and 1839. The chief item was still salt (about one half the total tonnage), which came in about equal portions from New York and the Lakes, from the Kanawha Valley, and up river from New Orleans (Turks Island and Liverpool salt). Coffee and sugar came in mostly by way of New Orleans; merchandise —hardware, furniture, drugs, chinaware, and the like—arrived about equally by way of the northeastern and eastern (Pennsylvania-Ohio) routes. The newer settled regions of the Northwest took a larger portion of these imports than they furnished of exports, yet their exports were growing faster in relation to their imports than were those of the older areas along the Ohio. Despite the trend of increasing commerce by way of the canals and Great Lakes, however, a writer in 1838 predicted that "the time is not very distant when the trade between the northern and southern regions of the great North American Valley, will be-

---

[225] Of the wheat, Ohio furnished 82 per cent, Michigan 12 per cent, northern Indiana 6 per cent, and northern Illinois 1 per cent. *Ibid.*, 34. The following data in round numbers give an idea of the traffic through the Cleveland end of the Ohio Canal for three years.

Arrived [outbound]	1836	1837	1838
wheat (bu)	464,756	548,697	1,228,000
flaxseed	11,500	7,800	5,928
corn	392,000	280,000	105,000
mineral coal (bu)	84,900	184,600	71,000
flour (bbls)	167,000	207,000	282,000
pork	13,000	43,000	37,000
whiskey	7,000	12,000	10,000
butter (lbs)	900,000	773,000	585,000
lard	636,000	1,555,000	1,157,000
bacon			1,541,000
pig iron	1,031,000	1,017,000	1,006,000
tobacco (hgs)	3,851	1,445	
lumber (ft)	1,235,000	757,000	

Cleared [inbound]	1836	1837	1838
salt (bu)	22,334	63,255	63,000
lake fish (bbls)	4,000	6,200	7,284
merchandise (lbs)	1,314,000	1,994,000	17,018,000
gypsum	1,548,000	1,685,000	

Cleveland Herald and Gazette (weekly), January 5, 1838, January 9, 1839, and *The Hesperian*, III (1839), 118. The figures vary slightly in different reports.

[226] See "W.," "Northern Ohio," in *The Hesperian*, III, 115–19, for comparative figures on Cleveland, Portsmouth, and Cincinnati commerce. Cincinnati's exports in 1838 were estimated at $7,000,000, Cleveland's at $5,000,000; see also J. W. S., "Internal Trade," in *ibid.*, 355–61.

come more important than that of the whole valley with the eastern states."[227] He was still thinking in terms of canal-lake miles and costs of handling and loading; he did not foresee that in a few years the railroads would link the Old Northwest to the East in a way the canals could not.

In a lengthy appraisal of the progress of the Northwest James H. Lanman in 1840 noted that something of a feeling of distrust had been thrown around the western character as a result of the speculative tendencies of the middle 1830's. This spirit, however, had become discountenanced and the energies of the people had subsided into the accustomed channels of substantial industry. He ended his survey on a note of conservative optimism:

We see in its vast territory resources of unmeasured wealth. We perceive in the grand projects of its moral and intellectual improvement; in its gigantic systems of public instruction; in its projected lines of canals and railroads, designed to connect its remotest parts; in the sixty-one steamships which navigate the lakes, and the commerce which ploughs the waters of the Ohio; in the thriving villages that dot its surface; in the amount of agricultural and mechanical growth already attained; in the opulence of its "queen city" and state; and in the character of its sturdy and energetic population, working out with unexampled enterprise the first stern law of our human condition in earning their bread by the sweat of their brow— the framework of a mighty power. We know that the people are intelligent, that there are scattered through that section men who would be bright orna- ments to any nation, and who have contributed in no small degree to the advancement of the country. The northwest must necessarily, from its local circumstances, become in future time the great granary of the republic, because it possesses the largest amount of arable soil, capable of producing the most bountiful returns with the least labor; and these products may, under its projected means of inter-communication, be brought rapidly into a ready market. As "sculpture is to the block of marble, is education to the human soul"; and this remark will apply as well to states as to individuals. Under the guidance of moral and intellectual education, the territory will soon grow to ripeness. The only present drawback upon its prosperity are the crude and elemental character of its population, the hardships neces- sary to be encountered in the forest, and the unhealthy nature of its climate. When these obstacles are surmounted, and the means of general comfort are pressed into its service, we doubt not that it will become one of the most eligible places of settlement, and a most opulent portion of the republic, wielding, as it soon must, the balance of power in the country.[228]

[227] *The Hesperian*, III, 356.
[228] "The Progress of the Northwest," in *Hunt's Merchants' Magazine*, III (1840), 40.

XIII

Schools, Teachers, and Education

We must educate! we must educate! or we must perish by our
prosperity. If we do not, short from the cradle to the grave will be
our race. If in our haste to be rich and mighty, we outrun our literary
institutions, they will never overtake us; and only come up after the
battle of liberty is fought, and lost. . . .

Lyman Beecher, A Plea for the West

Education itself is but a means of achieving an end; and that end
is the moral and intellectual perfection of man.

Albert Picket, Address to the College
of Professional Teachers, 1837

RELIGION, morality and knowledge being necessary to
good government and the happiness of mankind, Schools
and the means of education shall forever be encouraged." Thus
spoke the framers of the Ordinance of 1787. But the Ordinance
did not, as sometimes stated, provide a school system for the
states of the Old Northwest. The words were merely an expression of sentiment, a gesture of approval of something which
seemed desirable; for fifty years they had, in general, no more
effective meaning than the words which followed them.[1] Washington in his parting advice said: "Promote then, as an object
of primary importance, institutions for the general diffusion of
knowledge"; and Jefferson made public education one of the two
hooks upon which representative government depended—a necessary prerequisite to the process of selecting the "good and the

---

[1] "The utmost good faith shall always be observed towards the Indians; . . .
and in their property, rights and liberty, they never shall be invaded or disturbed,
unless in just and lawful wars authorized by Congress. . . ."

The brief discussion of education in this chapter is not an attempt at a history
of the subject; rather it is an introductory outline supplemented by some background
material not easily available. A mere bibliography of the materials on education
would comprise more pages than the chapter. The published books and monographs—
histories of education in each state, of individual cities, of higher education, individual colleges, academies, and teachers—run into the hundreds; the published
articles, contemporary and recent, are more than ten times as numerous. In addition there are many unpublished monographs. The history of the school lands or the
legislative history of the common school systems alone would constitute bulky
volumes. Some essential material, source and secondary, on the different phases
of education is indicated in the notes which follow.

wise," or the natural aristocracy, into the offices of government.

The first states created from the Territory Northwest of the Ohio, entering as they did under the influence of Jeffersonian political philosophy, paid their respects to the idea. Ohio's constitutional provision was largely negative: "No law shall be passed to prevent the poor . . . from an equal participation in the schools, academies, colleges, and universities of this State, which are endowed, from the revenues arising from the donations made by the United States. . . ." Beyond permitting associations of persons to be incorporated for the purpose of holding estates for the support of schools, no mandate or provision for schools was included.

Indiana's constitutional fathers put on the legislature the duty "as soon as circumstances will permit, to provide, by law, for a general system of education, ascending in regular gradation from township schools to a state university, wherein tuition shall be gratis, and equally open to all." The constitution of Illinois did not even repeat the glittering generality of the Ordinance. Michigan, in 1835, assigned the legislature the task of providing for a system of common schools—one in each district for at least three months every year—and for a university.

In 1832, almost half a century after the Ordinance, two aspiring Illinois politicians expressed their honest thoughts on education. One, A. Lincoln said: "I can only say that I view it as the most important subject that we as a people can be engaged in. That every man may receive at least, a moderate education, and thereby be enabled to read the histories of his own and other countries, by which he may duly appreciate the value of our free institutions, appears to be an object of vital importance. . . ."[2] The other, George Forquer, noting that the durability of our republican institutions depended upon the virtue and intellectual energies of the people, said: "It is our duty therefore, to take every step in our power to dispense its [education's] benefits to the rising generation. But I must confess that, until our country becomes more densely populated, and less difference of opinion prevails on this subject, I doubt the practicability of preparing

[2] A. Lincoln in his communication to the voters, in Springfield *Sangamo Journal*, March 15, 1832.

any coercive system of common schools which would be sustained by the people."[3]

Much has been made, perhaps too much, of the illiteracy of the pioneer, of the lack of schools, and of the general backwardness of the southern emigrants in comparison with the eastern.[4] Schools do not necessarily produce literates; literacy—the mere ability to pronounce a few written words—has little to do with education; and there are other ways of getting an education than in schools. As James Hall said: "A human being may know how to read, and yet be a very stupid fellow. . . . Reading and writing are not magic arts; of themselves, they are of little value . . . and thousands of individuals with diplomas in their pockets, are far inferior, in point of common sense and information, to the common run of backwoodsmen."[5]

Certainly the pioneers' knowledge of geography, history, economics, and mathematics was no more hazy than that of the average citizen of today; and in that rather important matter of understanding and practice of government, as Robert Dale Owen said of the people of the cabins of the frontier West: "You feel that it is an equal [you meet there]. . . . The conversation, running over the great subjects of the day, branching off, perhaps, to questions of constitutional right or international law, assures you of it. I have heard in many a backwoods cabin, lighted but by the blazing log heap, arguments on government, views of national policy, judgments of men and things, that, for sound sense and practical wisdom, would not disgrace any legislative body upon earth."[6] The Andrew Jacksons, Abraham Lincolns, and Andrew Johnsons[7] were, to one way of looking, not unique, not even strikingly exceptional; like Daniel Boone they became known because they later got into conspicuous spots. In every western community of any size were other men just as able, men

[8] George Forquer to the voters, in *Sangamo Journal*, July 12, 1832. Forquer went on, however, to advocate immediate establishment of a university. See *post*, 397–98.
[4] Theodore Roosevelt, in writing *The Winning of the West*, said: "In examining original drafts of petitions and the like, signed by hundreds of original settlers of Tennessee and Kentucky, I have been struck by the small proportion—not much over three or four per cent at the outside—of men who made their mark instead of signing." The same holds for those of Indiana Territory.
[5] *Western Monthly Magazine*, I (1833), 51.
[6] Speech in U. S. House of Representatives, April 22, 1846.
[7] Johnson's opinions on constitutional issues as expressed in his vetoes were all later upheld by Supreme Courts not of his own choosing.

who in all probability would have accredited themselves just as well, had the accidents of history happened differently; Clio can only record as the Fates decree.

In the study of education, as in other things, one runs into paradoxes, contradictions. From the printed records—the messages of governors, speeches of legislators, proceedings of meetings, editorials, and letters in newspapers—it would appear that the pioneer's faith in schooling, in education, was deep, sincere, and general. At times it appears even awe-inspiring in its implicitness and naïveté. "If there be one feeling more powerful than another in the hearts of the millions of this land, even through its remotest forests, it is that the intellectual cultivation which circumstances may have denied them shall be secured to their children. They value, sometimes even beyond their worth, the literary advantages by aid of which the few commonly distance their competitors in the paths of emolument and honor."[8] If the people believed that "Knowledge is power"—"education is the foundation of our republican institutions"—"education is the basis of morality,"[9] and were accustomed to hearing themselves referred to by politicians as the "source of all wisdom," why then were both people and politicians so reluctant to provide schools, the means by which knowledge might be acquired?

One reason is obvious. There were so many matters more vital, more pressing than the luxury of schools;[10] making a living, living, came first; learning "how to live" could wait. Besides many people regarded their new homes in the West as temporary

[8] Robert Dale Owen, Speech in U. S. House of Representatives, April 22, 1846. As Tocqueville said: "The Anglo-Americans, already civilized, settled upon that territory which their descendants occupy; they had not to begin to learn, and it was sufficient for them not to forget. Now the children of these same Americans are the persons who, year by year, transport their dwellings into the wilds, and, with their dwellings, their acquired information and their esteem for knowledge. Education has taught them the utility of instruction, and has enabled them to transmit that instruction to their posterity. In the United States, society has no infancy, but it is born in man's estate."

[9] "Of all the traits which early western society cultivated, of all the ideals it sought to realize, this [moral education] seems most universally, most consistently, most earnestly and ardently desired." James M. Miller, *Genesis of Western Culture; The Upper Ohio Valley, 1800–1825* (*Ohio Historical Collections*, IX, Columbus, 1938), 93.

[10] Often demonstrated in the amount of space in governors' messages devoted to the topic. The ever present paragraphs on education are often perfunctory. In Governor Thomas Worthington's message to the Ohio legislature in 1817, schools received approximately one tenth as much space as the subject of internal improvements.

stops on the way to new pastures, and consequently cared little
about helping educate those whose want of education they might
never feel.

Another reason is somewhat more difficult to understand and
present; an attitude felt rather than clearly expressed. In addition to Pennsylvania Germans and Quakers, who opposed public
schools on principle and for financial reasons, there were many
among the substantial folks who were at best lukewarm towards
schools. Education had its satirists, cold indifferent friends, even
enemies. There were those who distrusted the pretensions of
the learned, who were jealous of the educated whom they believed
were, by custom and manner of thought, alienated from the
masses. Hence they treated the idea with coldness, suspicion,
and distrust.[11] Classic systems, certainly, struggled among the
pioneers with no noticeable result; the spirit of pioneer life was
not in them. "There were expressions in plenty of the appreciation of education by the pioneers, but no system attracted their
earnest support because none ever cherished their ideals or attempted to teach their science, philosophy or skill." None catered
to their needs as vocational education to the needs of industry
today. The pioneer aristocracy never supported the schools as
it supported its own religious or political institutions.[12] It was
strong for education—at least the three R's—as long as it
stopped short of "booklarnin'," for it "had a growing suspicion
that literary culture and craftiness went hand in hand and would
usually be found in company with some more objectionable form
of moral obliquity." A third reason, of course, was the ever
present factional, sectarian, selfish, and local jealousies and ma-
neuverings.

The first generation of settlers had educations such as were
available, and in such proportion as was the custom in the regions from which they emigrated. Settlers from Massachusetts
and Connecticut who came directly to the Northwest had one
advantage—they had not spent a generation or two on the frontier out of reach of the district school, academy, or college, as
had many of the emigrants from the South. The latter had been

[11] Well presented in an article in the *Cleaveland Herald*, January 16, 1823.
[12] Esarey, "The Pioneer Aristocracy," in *Indiana Magazine of History*, XIII,
273.

largely dependent upon private schools, usually few and far between. People from the Middle States occupied a status somewhere between, depending upon how long they had lingered in the western parts of New York, Pennsylvania, or Virginia.

Announcements of private schools in the Northwest appeared simultaneously with the first newspapers. Early issues of *The Centinel of the North-Western Territory* (Cincinnati) carry notices of "English schools" which offered the three R's and surveying.[13] In July, 1802, the following notice appeared in the Cincinnati *Western Spy and Hamilton Gazette*: "Mrs. Williams begs to inform the inhabitants of Cincinnati that she intends opening a school in the house of Mr. Newman, saddler, for young ladies on the following terms:—Reading, 250 cents; Reading and Sewing, $3.00; Reading, Sewing, and Writing 350 cents per quarter."[14]

In 1816 Mr. M'Kee advertised to open school in the Methodist meetinghouse at Columbus, and teach the several branches of English and classical learning. To encourage the pursuit of literature, Latin instruction, as a preliminary to the study of Greek, was to be free.[15]

In 1823 John Locke established the Cincinnati Female Academy; besides instruction in French, music, penmanship, and needlework, there was an assistant who had charge of the preparatory department. Apparatus was used for demonstrating chemistry, natural philosophy, astronomy, and the common branches—"the Principal had adopted the *demonstrative* method of teaching, by which a knowledge of *things* instead of *words* alone, is imparted."[16] About four years were required to complete the course of study. Public examinations were held in August. Even Mrs. Trollope was impressed by the progress of the young ladies in science: "one lovely girl of sixteen *took her degree* in mathematics . . . ," and another was examined in moral

[13] For instances, see issues of December 20, 1794, December 5, 1795.

The first schools in the Northwest were the French mission schools, such as those at Sault Ste. Marie and Mackinac between 1668 and 1671. Aside from the priests, La Mothe Cadillac, who recommended the establishment of a seminary for the common instruction of French and Indian children at Detroit in 1703, may be regarded as the pioneer advocate of education in the Northwest.

[14] For other announcements see Venable, *Beginnings of Literary Culture in the Ohio Valley*.

[15] Columbus *Ohio Monitor*, December 5, 1816.

[16] Drake and Mansfield, *Cincinnati in 1826*, 42.

philosophy. "They blushed so sweetly, and looked so beautifully puzzled and confounded, that it might have been difficult for an abler judge than I was to decide how far they merited the diploma they received." This outspoken English writer had her doubts, however, whether a quarter or two of political economy, moral philosophy, or quadratic equations would be such a career foundation "as would stand the wear and tear of half a score of children and one help." Six years later the first "infant school" was opened in Cincinnati; the object was considered a laudable one.[17]

The Cincinnati Female College or Institution conducted at the same time by Albert and John W. Picket in a suite of rooms in the Cincinnati College building emphasized the analytic or inductive method in the teaching of the usual subjects.[18]

At Detroit in 1801 the Reverend David Bacon and his wife instructed in reading, writing, and sewing, at approximately twelve shillings per month each, plus ink, and quills.[19] Two years later the Reverend Gabriel Richard, active Catholic leader, opened an academy for young ladies who, under four misses whom he had prepared for the work, received instruction in Latin, geography, ecclesiastical history, church music, and the practice of mental prayer. Other schools were soon started at Grand Marais, Springwells, and at the River Huron, under Indians and half-breeds prepared by Father Richard in the "first rudiments of the English and Latin languages, and some principles of algebra and geometry, so far as the measurement of the figures engraved on the tomb of the immortal Archimedes." At Detroit "better than thirty young girls . . . are taught reading, writing, arithmetic, knitting, serving, spinning, etc."[20]

Just after the war a Mr. Goff taught boys in one room of their log house in Detroit and Mrs. Goff instructed the girls in another. Although Mr. Goff, having exhausted his whiskey flask by mid-afternoon, was accustomed to chastise any boy who was too slow in getting the refill at the grocery, the girls learned, besides the rudiments, ladylike deportment and modesty. Boys' hands got

[17] *Cincinnati Daily Gazette,* March 22, 1830.
[18] *Cincinnati in 1826,* 43.
[19] A tuition bill is reproduced in *Michigan Pioneer and Historical Collections,* VII (1884), 42 n.
[20] Richard's memorial to the Michigan territorial legislature dated October 18, 1808.

feruled into puffiness on occasion; when they were to be roped,
the master threw the rope to the culprit and made him fetch it.[21]
A Mr. and Mrs. Kinney ran a successful school for both boys
and girls from 1823 to 1825, but Mr. Kinney's rounds with the
flask scared away the girls and broke up the school.[22] By 1835
the young ladies of Detroit, for $150 per annum, might receive
instruction at Mrs. Hector Scott's Young Ladies Institute, in
orthography, reading, writing, arithmetic, geography, history,
botany, astronomy, composition, and mythology; there were
extra charges for worsted fancy work, wax-fruit and flower making, theorem painting, and the use of pens, ink, globes, and
piano.[23] A number of Detroit families sent their children to
school in Montreal, New England, and New York.

Benjamin Sturgess advertised in the *Illinois Intelligencer*[24] in
1816 that he had opened a school at Prairie du Rocher, a healthy
place, and was instructing in "Writing, Reading, and Common
Arithmetic; also English Grammer [*sic*], Geography, Surveying,
Astronomy, Latin, and Greek languages."[25]

In Green Bay in 1817 Thomas S. Johnson signed to teach
reading, writing, and the English language "during the space of
nine months" at $6.00 per scholar per quarter.[26] Three years
later Matthew Irwin pledged $20 "and a quantity of vegetables"
for tuition for one child, and Louis Grignon pledged $100 "and
a proportionate quantity of vegetables" for tuition for five children, should a "Gentleman & Lady" teacher be found. Soon
J. Bte. S. Jacobs attempted to undertake the job, but there must
have been a slight misunderstanding between him and John Lawe,
another patron, for Jacobs wrote:

Your note in answer to mind of the 25th inst pleased me mush, as it
maid me cum to my right sencess; in one part of my leter to you I returnd

[21] B. O. Williams, "Recollections of Early Schools of Detroit," in *Michigan
Pioneer and Historical Collections*, V (1882), 547.
[22] William D. Wilkins, "Traditions and Reminiscences of the Public Schools of
Detroit," in *ibid.*, I (1877), 450.
[23] *Detroit Journal and Advertiser* (triweekly), October 3, 1835. Additional data
on the education of Detroit children may be found in the Askin, Malden, and
Mason papers in the Burton Historical Collection.
[24] Quoted in *Transactions of the Illinois State Historical Society*, 1903, p. 187.
[25] An editorial in the *Intelligencer*, November 27, trusted that the sons of Kaskaskia
would no longer be compelled to spend their days from morn till eve in "idleness
and debauchery," and predicted that Kaskaskia would some day be a towering city.
Quoted in *ibid.*, 188.
[26] "Early Schools in Green Bay," in *Wisconsin Historical Collections*, XII (1892),
453.

you thanks for your favour towards me, and in another part that you abused me. I did not mean to say so, it is a mistake on my part. I ment to say that you repremanded me several times in regard of the Blotter I kept last summer for you and my saying you was Jealous about my school I intended to mention that you gave me no answer to my note to you where I mentioned I would be quite happy if you would send you Children to school and I should charge you onley one Dollar per Child instead of two—and about minding receaiveing person with spirits and Whiskey, I was half drunk and I maid Ceremonies to get quite so.

in regard of making out my account against you, please to place to my Credit, your's and Mr. Frankes Children 7 Months schooling $84—as to my writing for you cupping [copying] invoices &c est les commission que je faiette—I did not inteand to ask you aney thing—but as I am a poor, reatch and Mr. Porlier has no Blanket of 2½ Pt. and my Girl as not aney I would which [wish] you to Let me have one & ½ the Coloured Thread and one dressed deer Skin

> To Forgive my errors
> Respectifully yours
> J. Bte. S. Jacobs.

Apparently Jacobs gave up, unable to "make a Livelyhood on one Gallon Pease 15 lbs. Pork per Month," got drunk, and dropped the school idea.[27] In 1823 Amos Holton was conducting a school, the contingent expenses of which were $133.88.

In the Illinois country one John Seeley is supposed to have taught a school in an abandoned squatter's cabin (in what became Monroe County) in 1783; it was conducted the following year by Francis Clark and an Irishman named Halfpenny. John Doyle, a soldier in George Rogers Clark's army, returned to teach in the American Bottom (Randolph County) in the 1790's. At Vincennes Abbé Benedict Joseph Flaget, shortly after 1792, had opened a school in which he taught the children the catechism, singing, and reading and writing. John Messinger, the surveyor, taught an evening school near Shiloh (St. Clair County, Illinois) in 1804; a schoolhouse was built in Shiloh in 1811. In 1818 the Reverend Jean Jean, recently from France where he had taught twenty years, said he would open a school at Vincennes in which he would teach Latin and French grammar, geography, and history, 9:00 to 12:00 A. M. and 2:00 to 5:00 P. M. at $8.00 per quarter.[28] The same year Mrs. Wood advertised a boarding school for young ladies. Spelling, reading, plain sewing, marking,

[27] *Wisconsin Historical Collections,* XII, 456–57.
[28] Vincennes *Western Sun,* August 1, 1818.

muslin work, writing, arithmetic, grammar, geography by use of the globe, history, and composition came at $15 per term; embroidery, print work, and filagree were $5.00 additional; dancing, painting, and French music "according to terms." Board, lodging, and washing were $60 for the term of twenty weeks.[29]

Mr. John Russell advertised his "High School" at Vandalia, Illinois, in 1830 as offering reading at $2.50 per quarter, writing and arithmetic for 50 cents extra, and grammar and geography for another 50 cents. Higher branches of mathematics, Latin, Greek, and French, "or either," were listed at $4.00. Boys under six were admitted; there was a "female department" under a woman teacher. Morals and good behavior were emphasized.[30] The Reverend J. M. Peck held a meeting at Rock Spring to organize a theological and high school; two professors would offer courses in Christian theology, mathematics and natural philosophy, and the languages. A building to accommodate thirty boarding students was contemplated.[31] In 1830, Peter Cartwright advertised a school at Pleasant Plains; elementary subjects, Latin, Greek, and moral philosophy were offered. Board was $1.00 per week in advance, otherwise $1.25. Edwardsville Female Academy announced its second term in the summer of 1831.[32] The next year the "Ladies Association for Educating Females" at Jacksonville was founded to aid young women to qualify for teaching. In 1835 the Jacksonville Female Academy was incorporated by the legislature. The Bloomington Academical Institution opened in May, 1834. The wife of the Reverend L. Foster offered instruction in spelling, reading, writing, geography, grammar, and "the ground rules of arithmetic"; natural philosophy, chemistry, and Latin were to be added later. Particular attention was given to "exterior accomplishments so important in a female," and to morals. It was hoped that a male department could be added by autumn.[33] Mr. Wolfe's advertisement announced courses in Greek, Latin, English, French, history, geography, elocution, arithmetic, algebra, and geometry at

[29] *Ibid.*, June 13, 1818.
[30] Vandalia *Illinois Intelligencer*, October 23, 1830.
[31] *Ibid.*, quoted in Indianapolis *Indiana Journal*, May 1, 1827; this school was moved to Alton in 1831–32 and later developed into Shurtleff College.
[32] Edwardsville *Illinois Advocate*, July 29, 1831.
[33] Springfield *Sangamo Journal*, May 24, 1834.

the Springfield Academy at $7.00 to $12.50 per session of five months.[34]

At Chicago, in 1830, Stephen Forbes, of Cleveland, took over the task of instructing the Beaubien children and any others he could sign up; compensation was $200 for a school year. A subscription school for thirty pupils was provided in the autumn of 1832 by John Watkins but only twelve pupils appeared, of whom only one third were white. The next year Miss Eliza Chappel started a semipublic "Infant School" for some twenty children, many of them from garrison families; tuition was $2.00 per quarter but parents who could not afford the price were urged to send their children anyway. Shortly the school promised "to become an institution of great usefulness."[35] Miss Frances L. Willard announced that her female school for the higher branches at Chicago would open in May, 1836. Music and daily religious instruction were emphasized.[36]

At Columbus, Ohio, Principal H. Wilcox advertised that his High School for Young Ladies would have an instructor with "gentleman like deportment and scholarly bearing" for French, Spanish, and Italian; also three women from Boston for the preparatory department. There would be daily "callisthenics" and due attention would be given to etiquette and female manners by "an accomplished lady."[37]

The Monticello Female Seminary, near Alton, was conducted in 1838 in a four-story stone building 44 by 110 feet; the principal, the Reverend Theron Baldwin, advertised that an attempt would be made to heat the dormitory room for forty pupils plus the classrooms by furnaces in the basement. The girls, whose minimum age was 14, were required to take care of their rooms and do their own ironing. "Some of the pupils *voluntarily* performed extra labor and a liberal compensation was allowed for their services. This will be continued hereafter and *encouraged* on the ground that it is truly noble in any young lady to make such exertions in order to obtain an education."[38]

From announcements such as these it is obvious that even the

---

[34] Springfield *Sangamo Journal,* May 24, 1834.
[35] *Chicago Democrat,* December 24, 1833.
[36] *Ibid.,* May 4, 1836.
[37] Columbus *Ohio State Journal,* April 20, 1833.
[38] *Alton Spectator,* December 13, 1838.

young ladies, whose education was sometimes a subject for hilarity, did not need to grow up entirely ignorant. Critics might make fun of the idea that delivering an oral essay at commencement time on some such subject as "The Hearthstone and the Universe" was considered so hazardous to the delicate female spirit and physique that it was necessary for a friend to stand by with a fan, but the fact probably was that the critics were slightly awed by the accomplishments of these young ladies.

At the Cincinnati Female Institution of the Messrs. Picket in 1830 the 150 "Misses" witnessed the presentation of gold medals for valor in the common branches, music, and painting. Parents and the "numerous and respectable board of visiters" had been highly pleased with the three-day public examination. Although the Reverend Timothy Flint, editor of *The Western Monthly Review*, addressed the young ladies as "My dear Children," his advice was both advanced and serious.

Assuming that the pupils had been trained not only to perform certain exercises "but to THINK and acquaint yourselves with history," they would realize that for centuries "the better half of the species was viewed, as a race holding to man the relation of butterflies to eagles." It had mattered not what was in women's heads so long as the heads were externally well turned. But a new era had arrived—and not that of Frances Wright, which separated one from both God and eternity—an era which admitted that women had minds and that it was permissible for them to use them. Beauty, splendor in dress, and charm were all very fine and not to be deprecated in the least, but considering that in the expected seventy years of life "the empire of beauty seldom lasts more than ten or fifteen, what is to sustain the beauty, who has no other possession, in the dreary interval when her roses have vanished, with her admirers, never to return? Knowledge, virtue, and truth are immortal." Further, knowledge was power, power over men as well as affairs; as the affairs which men managed became more complicated, more knowledge was required to manage men. But beware of the female pedant "who chatters deep things, like a parrot's lesson; and brings forth in show all her mental finery, every time you see her." School was only the beginning of education; life, which is "neither a gala, nor a festival, a dance, nor a hymn—but a scene of conflict, struggle, toil, and disappointment" would continue it. Take advantage of it and "like a generous wine . . . you will thus mellow with time. . . . If life were ten thousand years, instead of three score and ten, you would find enough, still remaining to learn."[39]

Competition among the private schools became keen and a certain amount of quackery crept in. Some teachers were quick to cash in on the new Hamiltonian system of foreign-language instruction by interlinear translations.[40] By it students learned to read first; grammar came later. It substituted "the cheerfulness and competition of the Lancasterian system for the dull solitude of the dictionary." Americans, with their flair for mechanical contrivances, were quick to improve upon this Scottish device. When one school advertised English grammar in thirty-four hours, and a complete knowledge of French in forty-eight lessons by use of a Grammar Machine, the *Liberty Hall and Cincinnati Gazette* said that it was possible to teach any language —Hebrew, Esquimaux, or Carraboo—in three hours; the secret was inoculation, as in smallpox, at 12½ cents per language. In event of war with China the army could be inoculated and be speaking Chinese instanter.[41]

Ohio enacted no general legislation on secondary schools prior to 1850, but between 1803 and 1840 well over a hundred academies, institutes, and high schools were incorporated.[42] Probably some of these never went into operation; on the other hand many were active which were never incorporated. The usual organization was a joint stock company, the shares of which were sold locally; the stockholders elected a board of trustees. The term "academy" predominated until after 1830, when "seminary," "institute," and "high school" came into more frequent

[39] *Western Monthly Review*, III (1829–30), 507 ff. A letter from a student at this school in 1837 is reproduced in the *Ohio Archaeological and Historical Society Publications*, XXV (1916), 10–11. The Reverend Joseph Doddridge, of Zanesville, Ohio, dilated on "The Necessity and Importance of Female Education," in the *Western Monthly Review*, I (1827–28), 296–300. He recommended Christianity, theology, languages, fine arts, geography, and history for the young ladies.

[40] See *Edinburgh Review*, XLIV (June–Sep., 1826), 47–69, and *Western Monthly Review*, III (1829–30), 67–76, 121–32, for a review of James Hamilton's books and discussions of his system. Students of Latin had probably been using Hamilton's system long before he gave it a name; it has remained popular to the present time.

[41] September 3, 1819. Which was about as well as some of the colleges claimed to have done in "area language" instruction during World War II.

[42] Edward A. Miller, in "The History of the Educational Legislation in Ohio from 1803 to 1850," in *Ohio Archaeological and Historical Society Publications*, XXVII (1918), 1–271, lists 112 through 1840.

use. These schools were more numerous in the Western Reserve than in other parts of the state. The manual labor–study type of school appeared in the middle 1830's and several such were chartered. One of them, Bishop's Fraternal Calvinistic Seminary, in Athens County (chartered in 1835), required manual labor for both males and females. During the same period some eighteen schools or educational societies were incorporated, the purpose of which was to found academies or otherwise aid in the advancement of education.[43] In spite of the western states' jealousy of corporations, even educational, these acts of incorporation in general merely limited the amount of stock issue or property which might be owned. Occasionally there were restrictions against engaging in banking or teaching peculiar religious tenets. The state, of course, reserved the right to alter the articles of incorporation at any time.

Indiana incorporated fewer than a dozen nonsectarian academies between 1818 and 1840, and of these several never developed beyond the act of incorporation. Among the more important were the Hanover Academy (later Hanover College, organized 1827, incorporated 1829), the Jennings Academy at Vernon (organized about 1828), the Richmond "Red Brick Academy" (organized about 1834), the Vincennes Academy (incorporated 1836), the Martinsville Female Academy (organized 1839), and the Crawfordsville Female Academy (incorporated 1840). Several of these schools were coeducational. The Quakers had the "Blue River Academy" near Salem (organized in 1831) and the Whitewater Academy at Richmond. The Disciples of Christ founded Haw Creek Academy near Ladoga in 1838.[44] The same year the Sisters of Charity opened St. Mary's Female Academy at Vincennes.[45] There were probably thirty-five or forty others.[46]

[43] Ibid., XXVII, 102.

[44] John Hardin Thomas, "The Academies of Indiana," in Indiana Magazine of History, X, No. 4 (Dec. 1914), 331 ff.; XI, 8–10, 25–26.

[45] The resident pastor, Father John Champomier, had opened this school first in 1823, with Sisters of Charity from Nazareth, Kentucky, serving as teachers, but support was lacking; Champomier returned to France and the sisters to Kentucky. Thomas T. McAvoy, "Catholic Education in Indiana," in Indiana History Bulletin, XXIII (1946), 58.

[46] Walter Jackson Wakefield, "County Seminaries in Indiana," in Indiana Magazine of History, XI (1915), 160–61, lists 38 schools up to 1840 besides the county seminaries doing seminary grade of work.

In addition to these schools Indiana had provided by law in 1818 for a trustee in each county to collect fines due the county for the public seminary therein.[47] The seminaries were to be maintained by fines and money payments by those who had conscientious scruples against going to war. Under a more ample statute of 1824 eleven county seminaries were incorporated. Provisions for management varied but in general a board, appointed or elected, was empowered to handle funds, make rules for governing the students, and establish rates of tuition. No standard course of study was set up, and not until 1832 did an incorporating act (to incorporate the Monroe County Female Seminary) specify subjects to be taught.[48] Twenty-eight county seminaries were organized between 1825 and 1840.[49] The county seminaries were, with the exception of a year or two, always outnumbered by the private schools; after 1830 the latter increased even more rapidly and the former faded out after 1843.

Illinois had nothing corresponding to the county-seminary system, but relied upon the private schools. The number incorporated increased noticeably in the middle 1830's; many of the new ones were of the study—manual labor type, which gave instruction from the common branches on up.

Michigan had a Classical Academy at Detroit, opened in 1818 under the auspices of the newly chartered university, and continued for nine years; in 1834 a private school took over the building. The Detroit High School, D. B. Crane principal, opened in August, 1833, for college preparatory and other scholars. The "common English branches," logic, rhetoric, history, double- and single-entry bookkeeping, practical arithmetic (by lectures) as applied in the mechanical, mercantile, and banking business, surveying, engineering, algebra, geometry, principles of navigation, Greek, Latin, declamation, and composition were all advertised. Also a full course in chemical and philosophical lectures was given each quarter to the whole school. Applicants might

[47] *Laws of Indiana*, 1817–18, pp. 355–57. The law was amended several times before being repealed by a general law in 1824; this was in turn amended then replaced by another general law in 1831.

[48] Languages, sciences, fine arts, ornamental branches, literature, and such other subjects as the trustees might specify. *Ibid.*, 1832–33, p. 31.

[49] Listed in Wakefield, "County Seminaries in Indiana," in *Indiana Magazine of History*, XI, 159.

commence their quarter at any time.[50] There were a number of private schools, some of them "female seminaries," but prior to statehood only about a dozen academies had been incorporated. After the general law of 1839 concerning the incorporation of academies, the number increased. Among the schools of the 1830's were: Spring Arbor Seminary (1835); Michigan and Huron Institute at Kalamazoo (1837); Kalamazoo Literary Institute (1838); Tecumseh Academy (1838); St. Philips College, Detroit (1839); Grass Lake Academy and Teachers' Seminary (1839); Marshall Female Seminary (1839); and Marshall College (1839).

The dividing line between the academies and common schools was naturally indistinct. Some schools which intended the "common branches" as a prerequisite for admission, hard put to make ends meet, opened their doors to beginners, and permitted students to enter at any time. Others merely advertised instruction in the common English branches "with no additional charge for teaching geography with the use of globes and maps." In small towns and outlying districts it was not unusual for the scholar to be requested to bring "one load of wood during the cold season."[51] Collecting tuition and board was a problem, hence, as in the elementary schools, payment was often accepted in kind. Three or four raccoon skins, a calf, a barrel of whiskey, or a half-dozen well-cured hams were, directly or indirectly, currency of the realm in the marts of Latin and moral philosophy as well as at the general store.

Some of the academies were without doubt pretty crude. Exceptional, however, rather than typical must have been the one described in 1827 by James Hall in the *Western Monthly Review*,[52] where

the neighboring youth acquired bad latin and worse manners; here they brandished their slate-pencils and *shinny sticks,* and exhibited their bloody noses and blotted exercises. Here were practised those athletic sports, and elegant devices, which invigorate the body, and amuse the mind. Wrestling, fighting, and stealing—gambling, swearing, and lying, furnished innocent

[50] *Detroit Journal and Advertiser,* October 4, 1833.
[51] *Detroit Gazette,* October 31, 1826.
[52] "Orlando" (James Hall), "The Academy," in *Western Monthly Review,* I (1827–28), 377–84. Though the school described was in Pennsylvania, the evils criticized were present, in some instances, in schools throughout the West.

enjoyment to those hours, which could be spared from severer studies. . . . Three pedagogues of great erudition and strict morality, to adopt their own account of themselves, wielded the destinies of this valuable institution. To one of them was committed the important charge of flogging the lisping infant through the spelling-book; the second scourged into larger lads a competent knowledge of arithmetic, English grammar, and geography, and the third enabled the happy pupil to relish the beauties of Horace and Homer, at the expense of a few fragments of skin, which might have been inadvertently left on his back by the other two. Aware of the difference of opinion, which has prevailed among the learned, as to the precise locality of the human soul, these zealous and humane gentlemen, left no part of the soil, committed to their care, unexplored; but planted syntax and prosody in every arable spot; that is in every spot, to which the lash could be conveniently applied. They considered ignorance, as a cutaneous disorder, and judiciously removed the offending part. Never was quack medicine of such universal application, as the schoolmaster's whip; if it cured dullness it could also cure its opposite, and the boy, who had more wit than the master, was sure to be scourged as much as he who had less.—The pugnacious lad was whipped for fighting, and the timid boy for cowardice. . . . Some were scourged for not learning so fast as the master's favorites, and others beaten for learning faster. In short the lash was never idle.

The master had "the sour, jealous, and revengeful glance of one, who feels his dignity in danger. . . . He wore a suit, of which the several component parts had once been gay and fashionable, but which was so soiled and worn, and withal so ill-sorted, that it seemed to be the cast-off finery of several owners. . . . His whole appearance was pedantic and foppish in the extreme. *Children are intuitively physiognomists;* they may not form nice estimates of character, but they readily distinguish the agreeable from the repulsive."

This sensitive lad had no doubt had bad luck and a justifiable complaint. Timothy Flint, the editor of the *Review*, made it clear that he did not agree wholly: While not desiring to see the rod used, "as quacks prescribe calomel in the regions of the west, by the ounce," still he surmised that there were, "in almost every school, some subjects upon whom no other application would be efficient."

The academies and seminaries were for the pioneer period what the colleges became at a later day—a means of carrying instruction somewhat beyond the elementary subjects—and were attended at some time or other by perhaps about the same proportion of the population as attends college in the twentieth century. Regardless of the lack of "grading," term units, credit units, teacher-training schools, uniformity of textbooks, libraries, and laboratories, some first-rate teaching was done in these schools. It would be difficult to assemble as much favorable testimony regarding lasting influences of teachers from the products of our modern educational factories as was left by the academy-educated pioneers of a century ago. The pace was not too fast, there were not too many distractions; the academic life offered leisure for physical, moral, and intellectual growth. Most of the painless short cuts and substitutes for geometry and logic had not yet been invented, adjusting to the "normal curve" had not been heard of, nor was it regarded as heresy or handicap to be "subject minded." Not that the personality, "the proper attitudes," were neglected; more or less successful attempts were made to teach something of "the true deportment of the lady and gentleman." That the academies were unusually successful in creating a liking for, a taste in, good literature, cannot be proved; many of their products claimed that they did. Sometimes, in later years, their "graduates" swore at them, but always swore by them; and in time complained generously of the shoddy education and pampered handling which their children received in improved schools.

Prior to the organization of district schools the rudiments of learning were supplied largely by select and subscription schools. Such a school might be organized by a number of parents and a teacher advertised for, or more often a teacher would settle upon a likely spot and start a school. Townsite promoters often advertised a blacksmith, a doctor, and a teacher as among the advantages of their particular metropolis; these key citizens probably ranked in importance in the order named. Among the many advertisements in the early newspapers for teachers it was often specified that the candidate, in addition to reading, writing, and arithmetic, be qualified to teach English grammar and geography. Probably these two subjects were more widely taught than is commonly believed. The private schools were by no means supplanted by tax-supported or public schools in the period prior to 1840. Cincinnati in 1833, several years after the establishment of public common schools, had twenty-four private schools with 1,230 pupils and twenty public schools with 2,000 pupils.[53] The subscription schools, with their flexible terms, often supplemented

[53] *The Writings of Caleb Atwater,* 182–83.

the short terms of tax-supported schools and made it possible for the large boys and girls, needed on the farms, to attend a few weeks in the "off season"; or for serious and ambitious teachers, after finishing their schools, to take additional courses.[54]

What was regarded by some as a cheap and efficient solution to the problem of education hit Cincinnati in 1815 in the form of a Lancasterian school.[55] Jacob Burnet, well-known politician, businessman, and historian, organized a stock company, got a building 96 by 88 feet, and opened a school on March 27 of that year. Teachers taught the rudiments to a few promising pupils for a few weeks then the latter became monitors, took charge of the instruction of blocks of pupils, and in turn produced more monitors or instructors.[56] Under this plan it was said that one master could teach five hundred pupils as effectively as ten. Besides the common branches, instruction was offered in history, geography, the classics, and "superior languages."[57] Detroit opened a Lancasterian school in 1818 under the auspices of the newly created University of Michigania; in time it had 180 pupils. Children of "the indigent" were charged $1.00 per quarter, others $2.50.[58] This school

had two distinct departments, one comprising the common English branches, on the ground floor, the room divided in the center, like church pews. The sexes sat on separate sides, and seated in classes of ten or twelve, facing

[54] The experience of A. D. P. Van Buren, later an important figure in the early educational history of Michigan, was typical. After teaching a school at Goguac prairie he "found that the test of proficiency was only obtained by a trial at the business," so he gathered up his books—the *Elementary Speller, The English Reader,* Olney's geography, Kirkham's grammar, Adams' arithmetic, and Comstock's philosophy—and in 1839 attended Mr. Smith Hawkins' select school in Battle Creek. "Mr. Hawkins was an excellent teacher; he was the Quintillian of all the grammarians that had ever instructed me. He governed his school by the power of kindness, supplemented by a love of study which he inspired in his pupils, and which made them studious and orderly." A. D. P. Van Buren, "The Log Schoolhouse Era," in *Michigan Pioneer and Historical Collections,* XIV (1889), 316.

[55] The Lancasterian system had reached the United States in 1805; Joseph Lancaster lectured on his system before Congress in 1819 and was admitted to a seat in the hall of the House. In contemporary references the spelling was frequently "Lancastrian."

[56] The first report or advertisement of this school, one and one-half columns in length, appeared in *Liberty Hall,* April 8, 1815, the second, April 15, 1816. Detailed accounts of the methods of teaching each subject, including sewing, appeared in *ibid.,* September, 1817, and in the *Western Herald and Steubenville Gazette,* September 19, 1817. The latter filled the entire editor's page.

[57] Fearon, *Sketches of America,* 227, listed the fees for common branches as £11 3d per quarter for stockholders, £13 6d for nonstockholders. Rates for the higher branches were double and treble these.

[58] *Detroit Gazette,* November 7, 1818. A parent who witnessed an examination was highly gratified with the progress made by the eight classes.

each other at a double desk. Beginning with the sand scratchers, each class presided over by a scholar taken from a higher class seated at the end of the desks to preserve order and give instruction for the day or week. There were broad aisles on the outsides, in which around half circles the classes recited their lessons to the instructor, standing within the circle with a pointer. The lessons for the juveniles, on placards upon the wall; all the classes reciting at the same time, it being a school graded into classes. At the entrance end, between the doors, upon a raised platform, were seated two monitors, a young gentleman and lady from the high school, with desks and chairs, overlooking the whole room, keeping order, giving instruction, and receiving reports from those presiding over classes, and probably receiving pay. The principal, Mr. Shattuck, over all; quietly entering the room, passing around, giving instructions, sometimes carrying a small rattan, or raw-hide, but seldom used, except to tap a pupil on the shoulder when found playing or dozing.[59]

The trustees of the Cleveland school district organized a school on the Bell and Lancasterian plan, "so deservedly popular" over the country, in 1828.[60]

There was quite a difference in opinion regarding the Lancasterian schools; advocates and critics were equally vociferous. The former seemed to regard it as a panacea extraordinary, the latter as a fraud and a sham. A defender said that this system came nearer the great desideratum of a free government than the old system; it was "the best plan of *public education,* by which the *rudiments* of learning may be *best* taught, to the *greatest* numbers, in the *shortest* time, at the *least* expense"; it resulted in permanent habits of activity of body and mind the most suitable to various avocations of later life.[61] On the other hand, it was described as a mere mechanical, parrotlike repetition

[59] Williams, "Early Schools of Detroit," in *Michigan Pioneer and Historical Collections,* V, 549–50.

Lemuel Shattuck spent most of his ready cash before leaving Albany, New York, purchasing for the "University" "certain books, lessons & slates"; he had been promised $800 per year as salary but had a difficult time collecting a little more than half of it. "It was not till recently that I have learned that a written communication, assuring me of having money refunded and a salery of 800 dollars from the Rev gentleman the President, was good for nothing." The Reverend Monteith was himself in debt. "It may be proper to remark that the University is merely a body of men who direct the concerns of education through the Territory, and that I have the only institution having their countenance. It is merely a name." "Lemuel Shattuck and The University of Michigania," edited by Milo M. Quaife and Florence Emery, in *Michigan History Magazine,* XVIII (1934), 238.

[60] *Cleaveland Herald,* May 9, 1828.

[61] A series of letters attacking and defending appeared in the *Detroit Gazette,* December, 1821—January, 1822. "Tully" ran a series of articles, many of which dealt with the Lancasterian System, in the *Cincinnati Daily Gazette,* 1828–30.

of facts; Pestalozzian rather than Baconian in concept. It was an imposition carried on "not by bare-faced and daring quackery, but by splendid exhibitions of *sing-song* questions and answers, and loud talk of superior attainments in the sciences, without a single benefit derived to scholars. . . ."[62] One could not be a blacksmith without training, but anyone, even children, could teach.

Sciolists and popularity seeking men are endeavoring to abolish all the old land marks in education, which time and experience have sanctioned, and rear up a system of mere show, calculated to make children prate like parrots. They would banish all deep study, and pupils, like passive vessels, must stand and receive knowledge, after the manner of pouring water into a vessel. . . . The best system by which in scholastic procedure, we can be guided, is a knowledge of mind, and a capability to turn that information to the same great ends, as an able commander turns the dispositions and energies of his troops in time of battle.[63]

More startling than the Lancasterian plan were the innovations attempted by Robert Owen and his imported intellectuals at New Harmony in 1825–26, but these were not so widely known or advocated, hence attracted less attention.[64] Of course, Frances Wright, who, though at large most of the time, spent some time in Indiana and Ohio, was too conspicuous to overlook. Aroused by the advanced educational ideas of this "mere petticoat slang-whanger" whose sentiments were so well suited "to bawds and debauchers," "Tully," who was still going strong in 1830, unburdened himself on the subject of innate depravity in youth, scholarship, discipline, and the duties of teachers and parents:

In the present state of society this imposed duty of instructors is often painful and laborious; but, as painful as the task is to the liberally educated mind, of contending against the immoralities and vicious dispositions of children, those who are independent in feeling and action, and firm to the purposes of their trust, will proceed fearlessly in discharging the task which is required of them by God and their country. The Utopian idea, that man can be governed *by* reason alone, has withered before every day facts.[65]

[62] "Tully" (No. 2), in *Cincinnati Daily Gazette,* May 1, 1829.
[63] "Tully," in *ibid.,* September 4, 1829, August 23, 1828. See also *Detroit Gazette,* November, 1821—February, 1822.
[64] See below, Chapter XV.
[65] "Tully," in *Cincinnati Daily Gazette,* July 29, 1830.

Supporting this argument against pleasant environment and delectable activity was a contribution and discussion on books and instruction in the teachers' column of the *Cincinnati Daily Gazette* which agreed that the popular ideas of the "hot-bed patent, steam teachers"[66] were detrimental. "So long as the scholar is permitted to trifle away his time over toys and pictures, he never will acquire the power of abstract thought—of clear and accurate investigation and analysis." Why waste four or five years over such, enfeeble the mind and corrupt the taste? Both better books and teachers were indicated.[67]

Almost as detrimental to serious efforts at public education were the contentions that Sunday schools provided effective schooling. Most prominently emphasized was the moral-training advantage, but the fact that they were "free" was not without its influence. "Where Sunday schools have been established, a great change in the habits and moral condition of children has been observed, and among the various charitable institutions now in existence, this has become decidedly the most popular."[68] The Indianapolis Sunday School Union said that "when we admit that it is very universally attested both in town and country, that the Sabbath scholar of a well conducted school who attends no other school, learns fully as fast as the one who constantly attends a day school and does not attend the Sabbath school, we have data from which to calculate its pecuniary advantages in the single article of intelligence."[69] A reader who did not like these "little pious frauds" remonstrated that if this idea was generally upheld, the people would become indifferent to development of a system of common schools.[70]

[66] Alluding to the Thomsonian steam-doctor system.
[67] February 9, 1837.
[68] Ravenna (Ohio) *Western Courier*, June 25, 1825.
[69] Seventh Annual Report, in Indianapolis *Indiana Journal*, July 7, 1830. See also article by "Benevolus," in *Edwardsville Spectator*, April 17, 1821. The Vandalia *Illinois Intelligencer*, February 11, 1825, copied more than three columns from the *Spectator* on the organization and work of Sunday schools in Sangamon, Morgan, Greene, Madison, and St. Clair counties, Illinois; the numbers of teachers, scholars and "verses recited" were tabulated. As in the other schools the problem of securing teachers presented itself. A communicated notice asking for assistance (teachers) in the Sunday schools, "now under the management of a precious few," appeared in the *Liberty Hall and Cincinnati Gazette*, June 2, 1821.
[70] Indianapolis *Indiana Journal*, July 14, 1830.

§

The movement for public schools in the Northwest naturally began in Ohio, and it was in that state that most was accomplished before 1840. During the decade between 1810 and 1820, while the population of the state was increasing from 230,760 to 580,434, first steps were made. Active advocates of public education were operating in Cincinnati and elsewhere in 1816 by way of corresponding committees which were instrumental in getting the newspapers to take up the cause. As was pointed out to the latter, they should have a direct interest in it: the more literates, the more subscribers.

Representative of this publicity were articles by "Lycurgus" published in the Cincinnati *Inquisitor* in 1818. The author stated that "in many places the robust native sons of Ohio . . . [were] growing up to manhood, with scarcely more intelligence than can be gleaned from the bare light of nature."[71] He advocated nine-months' schools taught by men competent in the English language, to be supported by an equal division of the proceeds from sections 16 plus a property tax. He said the only reason that the state did not have such schools was that half the people were not interested: those who had no children, those whose children were grown up, and those who had children but did not care whether they were educated or not. Other letters advocated taxation of nonresident property on the same basis as resident; "equal rights, equal taxes."[72] The *Western Herald and Steubenville Gazette* pointed out in 1819 that, though the two preceding governors' messages had advocated action, nothing had been done; it hoped some practicable system for education of all the youth of the state would soon be agreed upon, and that it would provide separate schools for the two sexes.[73]

[71] Copied in Chillicothe *Supporter*, October 28, November 4, 11, 1818. Governor Thomas Worthington in his message of December, 1817, had spoken of the great difficulty in getting teachers; all too often they were persons of profligate morals who took up teaching as a cover for idleness. He recommended establishment of a school at Columbus for teaching the common branches, at state expense, to boys whose parents could not afford subscription schools. These boys would be given preference for teaching jobs—to serve until twenty-one or longer if they wished. Hamilton *Miami Herald*, December 12, 1817.

[72] Columbus *Ohio Monitor*, December 22, 1821.

[73] February 20, 1819.

The first general law came in 1821.[74] Introduced by William Henry Harrison, this law merely made it permissory for townships to lay off districts and establish schools; neither a system nor taxes was provided for. Though this law accomplished little beyond recognition of a need, it started things. At the next session of the legislature, Caleb Atwater, lawyer, historian, prominent citizen of Marietta, and chairman of the House committee on schools, succeeded in getting Governor Trimble to appoint a commission to investigate schools and school lands.[75] The commission outlined a system of schools modeled upon that of New York, advised that the court of common pleas in each county be authorized to appoint five commissioners to lay off school districts and levy taxes, and that the legislature elect a superintendent of schools to manage all school funds.[76] Pamphlets were circulated and the newspapers renewed their efforts, but the legislature of 1822–23 "had a majority in both house, opposed to a school system and the sale of school lands, and all that was done by them, was to quarrel about these subjects. They finally broke up in a row and went home."[77]

But the discussion continued. Nathan Guilford, Massachusetts-born and Yale-educated Cincinnati lawyer and bookseller, used his *Freeman's Almanac* and the "Maxims and Advice of Solomon Thrifty" to further the cause.[78] Essays on common schools by "Old Citizen" and many others appeared regularly in the Cin-

[74] A law of 1806 had provided that in any township with a school section 16, twenty qualified voters might elect three trustees and a treasurer to handle the school section and to lay off school districts if thought advisable. A bill to tax banks for the support of schools passed the House but died in the Senate in 1812. It failed again in 1814. In 1816 a bill for the support and regulation of schools, the county court to appoint three examiners to license teachers and perform other duties, passed the Senate but failed in the House. In 1819 the House committee favored appointment by the Governor of a person in each judicial district to examine the status of the school lands and prepare a plan for schools; and Governor Trimble recommended discontinuance of long-term leases of the lands. The legislature failed to act.
[75] Atwater was chairman of the commission of seven; each member was assigned one of the seven different school-land grant districts: Atwater the "Congress Lands," John Collins the Virginia Military Lands, James Hoge the Refugee Lands, James Bell the U. S. Military Lands, Ephraim Cutler the Ohio Company Lands, Nathan Guilford the Symmes Purchase Lands, and Josiah Barber the Connecticut Western Reserve Lands. (See map, Chapter III, 117.) The commission was directed to report upon the condition of the school lands, upon the necessity of a school system, and a bill to establish the same. Atwater, *History of Ohio*, 259–60.
[76] *Liberty Hall and Cincinnati Gazette*, January 24, 1823.
[77] Atwater, *History of Ohio*, 262.
[78] The *Freeman's Almanac* was published at Cincinnati by Oliver Farnsworth, 1823–30, by Guilford and Farnsworth 1830–34.

cinnati *National Republican,* the Columbus *Ohio State Journal,* and elsewhere. The *Liberty Hall and Cincinnati Gazette* pointed out that though Ohio was nearly thirty years old, happily situated, and had a population of more than half a million, yet it was almost destitute of schools, had never endowed a college, built a bridge, dug a canal, nor made a decent road. The only "apology for her imbecility" was the newness of the country and the poverty of the people. It argued for a state ad valorem tax.[79] With the exception of the Mount Pleasant *Jefferson Gazette* and the *Western Star and Lebanon Gazette* the newspapers generally and generously backed the school-law idea. These two papers were published in Quaker communities where the people feared sectarianism and preferred "individually to have choice of their own teachers."[80]

In the state election of 1824 the three important issues of canals, schools, and taxes were widely discussed. Governor Morrow in his message recommended action; a joint committee of the legislature of which Guilford was chairman reported a bill; canal men supported the school bill, school men backed the canal bill, and both voted for the ad valorem tax.[81]

The law of 1825 created no school system; it did, however, recognize the principle of statewide taxation for schools. It made mandatory the laying off of school districts in each incorporated township, but no means of enforcement was provided.[82]

[79] July 25, 29, August 8, 1823.
[80] The opposition continued after passage of the law of 1825. The *Western Star and Lebanon Gazette,* September 20, 1825, criticized the law on the ground that different people, with different religions, preferred to choose their own teachers. The *Liberty Hall and Cincinnati Gazette,* September 23, said that the *Star's* argument was the best reason in the world for the law; the state should take schools out of the hands of sects and parties. The *Star* replied October 1. See also *Hamilton Advertiser,* October 4, 1825, *Ohio State Journal,* August 24, 1826, and the article copied therein from the *Jefferson Gazette.*
[81] For the canal bill, see Chapter VII; for the tax law, Chapter VIII. The report of the joint committee was published in the *Columbus Gazette,* January 22, 1825. It reviewed the history of education in other states, quoted the constitution of Ohio, and said: "A wise legislature will endeavor to prevent the commission of crimes—not by the number and rigor of her penal statutes—but by affording the whole rising generation, the means of moral and virtuous education; by extending its benign influence to all the paths of private life and social intercourse, and by strengthening the ties of moral duty."
[82] The county tax was fixed at one-half mill on the dollar (one twentieth of 1 per cent). If a township was not districted into school districts within five years, it was not to receive school moneys, either from the lands or tax. County officials were to collect and distribute the school tax and the court of common pleas was to appoint a board of examiners to license teachers. *Laws of Ohio,* 1824–25, pp. 26, 44, 56, etc.; *Liberty Hall and Cincinnati Gazette,* February 11, 1825. Later laws

As Governor Morrow said in his message of December, 1826: "It contains not sufficiently the principle of either compulsion or inducement to insure its general operation, and experience has shown that without one or the other of these the chances for its being carried into effect is in the reverse ratio to the necessity of its use." And "Citizen," arguing that if attention was concentrated on the elementary branches and both tax funds and school-land funds were used—say an average of $50 per district—it would be possible to have a badly needed free school for one quarter each year in the majority of districts. "Witness, fellow citizens, the throng of ragged, profane, vicious, whiskey drinking, noisy, mischief doing boys from five to twenty years old, who are rambling and prowling about on streets, two or three, or more nights every week, damaging property, disturbing the repose of the quiet, and worst of all ruining themselves, both for this world and for that which is to come."[83] Yet seven years after passage of the act, even though most voters agreed that there should be a three-months' school in each district, many districts were without schools; they did not receive $50, a teacher's hire for a quarter, in five years. Ardent school supporters blamed the neglect or indifference of the legislature.[84]

It was becoming obvious, that if Ohio was going to have public schools, the voters would have to levy and pay taxes. The school lands, instead of furnishing an endowment of easy revenues, had to a large degree proved a false prop. As Atwater had said in his report, more money was being spent in legislation regarding the school lands than was being received from them.[85] In fact it was stated that, had Ohio been given no school sections, the people would have got to work and probably had a school system by 1825.[86]

(1829, 1831, 1834, 1836, 1838) raised the county tax to two mills, made additional township taxes optional, and (1839) added a state tax. Other laws provided taxes for school buildings. For summary, see Miller, "Educational Legislation," in *Ohio Archaeological and Historical Society Publications*, XXVII, 44 ff.

[83] Columbus *Ohio State Journal*, April 26, 1827.

[84] *Hamilton Intelligencer*, December 10, 1831.

[85] Atwater's commission, 1822, had taken these words from the report of the House committee of 1819 (Jones of Wayne, chairman). The report appears in Atwater, *History of Ohio*, 254–59.

[86] *Liberty Hall and Cincinnati Gazette*, November 25, 1825; "Old Citizen" in the Columbus *Ohio State Journal*, December 8, 1825, said the school lands had been a great evil, since they had prevented Ohio having a system of education. He recommended that they be "abandoned."

Ohio, as the first state created out of the public domain, was the first to receive under the Ordinance of 1785 section 16 in each Congressional township "for the maintenance of public schools within the said township." When Manasseh Cutler made his bargain with Congress for the Ohio Company grant, he secured a grant of section 16 for schools, plus section 29 for the support of religion (the ministerial lands) ; John Cleves Symmes did equally well for his purchase between the Miami rivers. The Ohio enabling act granted section 16 to the inhabitants of each township and provided that where such section had been sold or disposed of, "equivalent . . . and most contiguous" land should be given the township. But it was not in the power of Congress to grant sections 16 in the Western Reserve, the Virginia Military Reserve, or the United States Military Lands, three areas which totaled more than ten and a half million acres. Hence adjustments had to be made which confused the situation appreciably.[87] It became difficult to follow the original idea that the school-land grant be used for schools in the township in which the land lay, or, where it was impossible to grant section 16, to use the lands for schools in the particular division or area for which the grant was made. In other words, the school-land grants were not made to the state at large. Consequently, in the tangled history of administration of the Ohio school lands local influences, as well as personal and political, played an important part. Squatters, lessees, and vested interests of sorts all had votes; there was no equally assiduous group to look after the interests of the schools.

In general, from 1803 to 1817 the Ohio legislature adopted the policy of temporary leasing of the school lands; from 1817 to 1823 that of permanent leasing; from 1823 to 1827 temporary leasing preparatory to sale; and from 1827 on the policy

[87] One thirty sixth of the Virginia Military Reserve (which did not have the rectangular township survey) was set aside for schools; in 1807 Congress appropriated eighteen quarter townships and three sections from the public domain to the northeast in lieu of the original grant. The quarter townships reserved for the United States Military Tract lay within the tract itself. Western Reserve school lands consisted of fourteen quarter townships, located in the U. S. Military Lands; in 1834 there was added 37,758 acres to be selected in the unlocated public domain.
  For land grants for schools, see George W. Knight, *History and Management of Land Grants for Education in the Northwest Territory* (*Papers of the American Historical Association,* I, No. 3, New York, 1884) ; and C. L. Martzolff, "Land Grants for Education in the Ohio Valley States," in *Ohio Archaeological and Historical Society Publications,* XXV (1916), 59–70. A convenient summary is in Miller, "History of Educational Legislation in Ohio," in *Ohio Archaeological and Historical Society Publications,* XXVII (1918), Chapter III.

of outright sale.[88] The policy of leasing proved unsatisfactory; unless there were special advantages, such as a damsite for a sawmill or gristmill, the settler saw no reason for leasing land when he could get it equally cheap in fee simple. As was later pointed out by the legislature, in general "only the lowest class of the community" took the leases; they did not improve the lands—in fact, they often stripped them—required constant supervision, and returned little revenue. Caleb Atwater, who followed school affairs closely, said: "Scarcely a dollar was ever paid over to the people for whose benefit the land had been given."[89]

In 1823 the legislature began a checkup of the school lands situation. The next year it admitted that the school-land revenues were "wholly unavailing" and asked Congress to confirm the right to sell the lands. When Congress complied, the legislature in 1827 and 1828 authorized the townships or districts to decide whether they wished to sell and fixed the terms of sale for those which did.[90] Many laws followed which made special provisions for sales, leases, revaluations, and extension of time for payment.

The state did not come out very well financially in liquidating the lands already leased and occupied. In some instances whole

[88] A law of 1803 provided for lease of sections 16 and of the United States Military Tract and Western Reserve lands for a period of seven and fifteen years; rent consisted of certain specified improvements to be made by the lessee. In 1805 township trustees were authorized to make leases for fifteen years to the best offers. In 1809 school lands of the Virginia Military Tract were offered for sale at a minimum price of $2.00 per acre, but instead of buying the land the purchaser received a ninety-nine-year lease, renewable forever, upon payment of survey charges and 6 per cent interest annually on the purchase price. In 1810 interest was postponed for five years after sale. Few lands were sold under these two laws. In 1810 township trustees were permitted to receive either money or produce as rent on section 16. Four years later lessees were forbidden to act as township trustees or treasurers. By a law of 1816 Virginia military lands were to be leased for ninety-nine years, renewable forever, at 6 per cent rental on appraised value, land to be revalued in 1835 and at twenty-year intervals. Essentially the same provisions were adopted for the remainder of the school lands, excepting those of the Western Reserve, in 1817. Township trustees administered the law in organized townships, county commissioners in unorganized townships, and the courts of common pleas in the U. S. Military Tract. Prior to 1816–17 some twenty-five special acts had granted leases of school lands in various localities on similar terms. During the next ten years thirty-two special, local, or modifying lease laws were passed. Miller, "History of Educational Legislation in Ohio," in *Ohio Archaeological and Historical Society Publications*, XXVII, 78–82.

[89] *History of Ohio*, 253. "The decade 1810 to 1820 was an orgy of robbing the schools." William McAlpin, "The Origin of Public Education in Ohio," in *Ohio Archaeological and Historical Society Publications*, XXXVIII (1929), 428. The *Hamilton Intelligencer and Advertiser*, February 18, 1822, had asked whether Ohio should proceed, session after session, to legislate for the sole benefit of the lessees of school land at the expense of the state.

[90] In reporting the act of 1827 the Columbus *Ohio State Journal*, February 22, favored sale of the lands and investment of the proceeds.

sections were sold for less than $100; some of the lands on the United States Military Tract were bid in by speculators as low as ten cents per acre.[91] Proceeds from the sale of the school lands, plus a small amount from the salt lands, were placed by the state treasury to the credit of the townships or regions (the military district, the Western Reserve, etc.). These funds were used for building canals and the state pledged its faith to pay annual interest. By 1836 they totaled nearly a million dollars. In 1837 Ohio's share of the United States surplus revenue was distributed among the counties, the net income to be used for the support of common schools, but this money was later (1850) pledged to the payments on the state internal improvements debt.

The school law of 1827 supplemented the law of 1825 in several provisions. It made it possible for the school directors, upon vote of the householders, to levy a tax for school buildings, appropriated all fines in justice of peace courts for immoral practices to the school fund, and authorized the court of common pleas to appoint a number of examiners equal to the number of townships. In 1831 teachers were required to get annual certificates of moral character and educational qualifications from two of the examiners. Negroes and mulattoes were barred from attending the schools.[92]

Although a majority of the townships of the state organized school districts under the law of 1825, schools were generally of poor quality and unevenly distributed. At best they ran but three months. Opposition to taxation for public schools came from politicians who had the school lands in hand, sometimes from the larger taxpayers, and from many of the poorer parents, the latter usually well supplied with offspring but reluctant to furnish the books and small equipment necessary for attending school.[93] In Cincinnati and elsewhere the proprietors of private schools were also opposed. The pro-school publicity continued unabated.

[91] Ohio *Executive Documents*, 1838, No. 69; Columbus *Ohio Monitor*, February 11, 1829.

[92] *Hamilton Intelligencer*, April 14–15. Directors (usually three) were officers of the school district and not to be confused with the township trustee. Laws of 1830, 1832, and 1834 provided a fine of $2.00 on any person who, having been elected director or treasurer, refused to serve.

[93] The politicians were particularly opposed in a belt of counties in the United States Military Tract. For abuses of school lands by lessees, see Columbus *Ohio State Journal*, October 12, 1826; *Cleaveland Herald*, March 4, 1830.

A series of unsigned articles, labeled "Thoughts on Education," or the like, was running more or less regularly in most of
the important Ohio newspapers. A writer in the Columbus *Ohio
State Journal* called attention to parents who refused "apparatus" (books, etc.) to their children, to factional and religious
squabbles in the townships, and to the distrust of the common
schools by the better-to-do families; also to the lack of school
buildings, of qualified teachers, and of serious effort to raise the
moral standards of the pupils. He insisted teachers should have
a thorough knowledge of the common branches, the first principles of science, and of the history of the United States. "The
civil and political history of the United States should be made a
branch of study in the common schools." Only thus could love of
country be inspired; history was the school of politics. Further,
history instruction should start with the existing life of the town
or neighborhood, then proceed to the "then" and the "there" by
way of books. In addition to individual treatment of the teaching
of each subject were discourses on ambition, emulation, the nature
of learning, of children, the importance of work, and discipline.
Discipline could best be had by a combination of dignity and kindness; "be not in haste to punish." The practice of certifying
teachers while the candidates were intoxicated was deprecated.
Special advice was given female instructors.[94]

At Cincinnati in 1831 was held a General Convention of the
Teachers of the Western Country, and from this meeting came
the Western Literary Institute and College of Professional
Teachers. Prominent promoters of this organization were the
Pickets of Cincinnati, who, though proprietors of the well-
known private school for females, were persistent and effective
workers for public schools.[95] At the annual meetings, which

[94] Columbus *Ohio State Journal*, June 15—August 3, 1833. A few weeks later
the *Journal* announced receipt of *Lectures on Education*, by George Brewster,
principal of the Cleveland Academy.

[95] Teachers' associations had been formed at Cincinnati in the early 1820's.
Albert Picket had been principal of Manhattan School, New York, and from
1818 to 1820 had edited *The Academician*, probably the first educational journal
in the country. In 1826 John W. Picket joined his father in Cincinnati where they
opened the Female Seminary. The Pickets were prolific writers of letters and
articles on education to the papers. For instance, the Columbus *Ohio State Journal*,
March 2, 1826, had six columns by John W. on education; three columns followed
on April 6, probably by the same author. In 1830 the Pickets' *Juvenile Expositor,
or Rational Reader, and Key to the Juvenile Spelling Book* (384 pages) was published at Cincinnati.

shortly were drawing visitors from the adjacent states and as far away as South Carolina, well-known teachers such as the Pickets, Milo Williams, Samuel Lewis, Elijah Slack, Frederick Eckstein, Alexander Kinmont, Thomas S. Grimke, and William Holmes McGuffey were hobnobbing with Daniel Drake, Lyman Beecher, Bishop John B. Purcell, Alexander Campbell, E. D. Mansfield, Calvin E. Stowe, and other prominent citizens. Early records of the meetings were published in *The Academic Pioneer, and Guardian of Education* (Cincinnati, 1831–32); starting in 1835 the *Transactions* of the society ran for six years. In 1833 a committee of the institute was seeking information regarding schools by way of newspaper questionnaires and preparing a manual of instruction for the Mississippi Valley.[96] In 1834 Miami College began publication of *The Schoolmaster, and Academic Journal*, a semimonthly periodical edited by B. F. Morris.[97] Three years later appeared in Cincinnati a small monthly called the *Universal Educator*, John W. Picket's *The Western Academician and Journal of Education and Science*,[98] and *The Common School Advocate*, edited by E. D. Mansfield, L. Harding, and Alexander McGuffey, which was distributed free to teachers.[99] *The Common School Advocate*, published at Madison, Indiana, also began early in 1837. These periodicals were

[96] Ravenna *Western Courier*, October 24, 1833. The next year a committee took up the problem of education as it related to the large influx of foreign immigrants. Edward D. Mansfield in his address of 1835 said, "Let us take their children then . . . and thus *amalgamate them* with our community." *Transactions*, 1835, pp. 78–79. In 1840 committees were appointed to make inquiry on the common schools, on high schools, on private schools, and other matters. Though the program of the organization was rather ambitious—to give the people "not a system, but . . . *the* system. . . . That excellent scheme of education which shall consist of the union of all truth,"—the addresses and papers were on the whole of high quality, the work of men who were scholars as well as educational promoters.

[97] *Western Monthly Magazine*, II (1834), 334.

[98] Prospectus in *Cincinnati Daily Gazette*, January 27, 1837. The first volume of this periodical (eight numbers) comprised 480 pages of articles, plus 224 pages of Proceedings of the College of Professional Teachers. The articles ranged from "Classical Literature" through Plato, Pestalozzi, and Philology, to the "Durability of Timber." The sources and uses of history were emphasized and the natural sciences recognized. John W. Picket was a heavy contributor.

[99] Called "Advocate" in *Cincinnati Daily Gazette*, January 24, 1837, but "Journal" in *Western Messenger* . . . (Cincinnati, 1835–41), VI, 212 (Jan., 1839).

The Columbus *Ohio State Journal*, July 20, 1838, wrote: "Among the signs of the times and as an evidence of the increase of the popular appetite for wholesome and invigorating food, we may mention the unprecedented circumstance of having received by one mail the present week, three periodicals, published in Ohio, and devoted to the subject of education." They were *The Common School Director* (State Superintendent's Office), the *Educational Disseminator* (about schools in general and Picket's books in particular), and *The Pestalozzian* (No. 4, published in Akron).

the teachers' colleges of the day; the editors directed the teachers; they and their friends wrote the textbooks which the periodicals advertised. Thus began, before a school system existed, the business of education in the West, a business frequently referred to by teachers of our day as a "racket."[100]

In 1836 the legislature asked Calvin E. Stowe, of the Lane Theological Seminary, to make a study of European school systems. After a trip to England and the continent, he made his *Report on Elementary Public Instruction in Europe . . . to the Thirty-Sixth General Assembly of the State of Ohio, December 19, 1837.*[101] Stowe was impressed with the Prussian system. The published *Report* was sent to each school district in the state and republished in Michigan and elsewhere.[102] The same year by a very close vote the legislature created the office of state superintendent of common schools; the annual salary was $500. Samuel Lewis, Massachusetts-born and self-educated Cincinnatian, was appointed to the job. Lewis performed prodigious labors—traveled 1,200 miles, mostly on horseback, visited hundreds of schools, interviewed people, wrote letters—and made his report the same year.[103] His work was partly responsible for the law which followed.

In the legislative session of 1837–38, William Johnston, representative for Carroll County, made what Judge Jacob Burnet, of Cincinnati, called the most powerful speech on education in Ohio history. Wishing the boys and girls of the state better

---

[100] A textbook war was on between eastern and Cincinnati publishers in the late 1830's. In 1839 Worcester and Company, publishers of Webster's readers, sued Truman and Smith, publishers of McGuffey's books, for plagiarism. Injunctions and accusations flew thick and fast. *Cincinnati Daily Gazette,* February 28, 1839.

[101] Published among other places, in *The Western Academician and Journal of Education and Science,* I (1837), 676–700, as "Report, On the Courses of Instruction in the Common Schools of Prussia and Wirtemberg."

[102] Stowe was on his own financially but the state later paid him $500. For Stowe's report, see Charles G. Miller, "The Background of Calvin E. Stowe's 'Report on Elementary Public Instruction in Europe' (1837)," in *Ohio Archaeological and Historical Society Publications,* XLIX (1940), 185–90.

[103] He recommended "school libraries; a state school fund of two hundred thousand dollars; township high schools; township Boards of Education; evening schools in towns and cities; county superintendents; a school journal to be distributed to school officers gratuitously; encouragement for the formation of Teachers' Institutes; authority for districts to borrow money to erect school-houses; the employment of women as teachers; and full reports from teachers and school officers." Quoted in Miller, "History of Educational Legislation in Ohio," in *Ohio Archaeological and Historical Society Publications,* XXVII, 33. Lewis' reports to the legislature are given in detail in William G. W. Lewis, *Biography of Samuel Lewis* . . . (Cincinnati, 1857).

opportunities than he had had in the "Yaller-Crick" settlements in the northern part of Jefferson County, he painted a sad picture of the schools:

The old Irish school master holds forth three months in the year in a poor cabin with greased-paper window panes. The children trudge three miles through winter's snow and mud to school. They begin at a-b, ab, and get over as far as b-oo-b-y, booby, when school gives out and they take up their spring work on the farm. The next winter, when school takes up, if it takes up so soon again, having forgotten all they had been taught previously in the speller, they begin again at a-b, ab, but year after year never get any further than b-oo-b-y, booby.

Samuel Medary of the Columbus *Ohio Statesman* pinned on Johnston the nickname "Booby"; it stuck and became one of which the orator and his friends were proud.

The act of 1838 for the support and better regulation of common schools pointed the way to a school system, headed by the state superintendent and stemming down through the county to the township and district officials.[104] It prescribed general rules within which the people might act and allowed much latitude in popular action. Upon its passage the Columbus *Daily Journal and Register* said that the responsibility for carrying its provisions into effect rested entirely upon the people.[105] Though he did not regard it as perfect, Superintendent Lewis thought it the best that could be passed, and "better adapted to our wants than any other school law that has come under our notice. . . . An arbitrary law . . . would do for despotic countries, but in a free country where the actors are a people whose action depends upon their own wills, there must be wide scope given. . . ."

The friends of schools were encouraged. "The common schools of Ohio are rapidly gaining popularity," said the *Cincinnati Daily Gazette*.[106] "We scarcely open an exchange paper, from

[104] The county auditor was made county school superintendent, the township clerk superintendent for the township. The latter took school enumeration, filled vacancies in directorships, and performed other assigned tasks. District meetings continued to elect three school directors as before. Miller, "History of Educational Legislation in Ohio," in *Ohio Archaeological and Historical Society Publications,* XXVII, 33–34.

[105] March 6, 1838.

[106] July 10, 1838.—Superintendent Lewis in his first report had listed 7,748 organized school districts in the state, or an average of about 7 per township. Lewis, *Biography of Samuel Lewis,* 149.

towns around us, that we do not see some article in praise of them." The legislation, however, was running ahead of public opinion. Since the legislature of 1839 made no provision for publication of the superintendent's bulletins, Lewis appealed to the press to print them.[107] Adverse petitions were presented and in March, 1840, the office of state superintendent was abolished; the duties attaching thereto were assigned to the secretary of state. Amendments further weakened the law, and for another decade Ohio struggled to reach the goal of a six-months school in each district.

Outside Cincinnati, few towns had better school facilities than were provided by the district schools. Marietta had by law in 1825 obtained the right to vote school funds in town meeting; Cincinnati established a tax-supported city system in 1829. In 1836, there were 5,500 of school age (six to sixteen) in a population of 29,000, of whom perhaps 2,000 attended school. The teacher salary outlay was $14,000 for forty-three teachers.[108] Two years later 2,900 scholars attended the city's common schools; fifty-five teachers drew $16,000 in salary. More teachers were needed, but the editor of the *Ohio State Journal* thought it would be better to raise qualifications and give more pay to those already employed, than to increase the numbers.[109] Graded schools were being advocated. In 1840 German-language schools were established. Toledo, Cleveland, and Portsmouth were given authority over their schools by law or charter between 1836 and 1838.[110] The law of 1838 made special school districts out of all incorporated but noncharter cities and towns.

Although the Ohio Asylum for Educating the Deaf and Dumb was incorporated in 1827, only limited state financial support was given for twenty years. State education for the blind began in 1837. Negroes and mulattoes were not enumerated or taxed for

[107] *Cincinnati Daily Gazette,* March 6, 1839. Lewis had been issuing *The Common School Director.*
[108] Fourteen male principals at $500 each, 10 males teachers at $300; 4 female principals at $250 each, 15 female teachers at $200. *Cincinnati Daily Gazette,* June 16, 1836.
[109] July 20, 1838.
[110] A committee of the Cleveland City Council in 1839 reported that the city had a school system to be proud of. The only trouble was a lack of accommodations. Some schools were held in lofts, others in cellars, and "scarcely one of our eleven schools has a commodious room." It recommended uniting four of the fifty-scholar schools into one central building. *Cleveland Weekly Advertiser,* April 25, 1839.

the public schools, although some did attend in Toledo and Cleveland. Schools for Negroes in Cincinnati and Columbus were supported as philanthropic projects or by the Negroes themselves.

In his first report Superintendent Lewis had listed 492,837 children of school age in the state; of this number 84,296 had attended school from two to four months, 62,144 had attended more than four months. "Teachers and legislators, vexed by the imperfections of our present schemes of education . . . are now eagerly waiting for that system of popular instruction which shall stand upon an infallible basis," said a speaker before the College of Professional Teachers.[111] It was to require many years to capture the other two thirds of the school-age population, to get better teachers and buildings, and to develop a more general interest in education. As for the system established upon an "infallible basis". . . .

Few have stated the case for public schools more soundly than Albert Picket:

We require, then, all that parents can do; all that schools and colleges can do, to train the young to the sternest principles of virtue; to the highest efforts of intellectual energy. But the majority, under any circumstances, must be limited in intelligence. The stronger, therefore, the reason, that profound knowledge should be extended to as many as possible, so that by intermixture in society with those of circumscribed acquisitions—their knowledge may become diffused—their habits of investigation, and their integrity by such intercourse, be worked into the minds of the mass, and become a part of their thoughts and mode of action. The attainments of well balanced minds exert great influence over those less fortunate, and the greater the number of the well-educated, the wider will be the reach of sound reasoning and correct principles of conduct.[112]

In the solid accomplishments up to 1840 no one group or element of Ohio's population did more valid work than another. Despite extravagant claims made for the Yankee influence,[113] the facts warrant no special credit for the worthy folks from

[111] Walter Scott, in *Transactions of the Western Literary Institute and College of Professional Teachers*, 1837, p. 229.
[112] *The Western Academician and Journal of Education and Science*, I, 499.
[113] "The great initial victory for public education had been won . . . primarily by New England ideas backed up by New England men" (Miller, "History of Educational Legislation in Ohio," in *Ohio Archaeological and Historical Society Publications*, XXVII, 18); "the ideas . . . were ideas of New England origin . . . the men who were chiefly responsible . . . were men of New England birth" (Miller, "New England Influences on Ohio's Public School System," in *Ohio Social Science Journal*, II [1930], 5); "Three men of Massachusetts birth were largely re-

the northeast sector. From the messages of the governors, the legislative votes on all educational bills (those that failed as well as those which became laws), the willingness to make financial sacrifices (taxes, salaries paid to teachers, etc.),[114] the administration of the land endowment, the nativity of scores of sincere and important leaders in the work, and above all from the hundreds of articles, letters, and editorials in the newspapers of the period, the evidence is clear.[115] If badges for merit in the uphill struggle were to be awarded, Cincinnati, with its almost 50 per cent foreign-born population by 1840, would have prior claims for locality, and the New York–Pennsylvania–Scotch-Irish–Presbyterian group on the basis of origins.

Indiana's public school annals in the first two decades of statehood are few; if anyone was happy as a result of their paucity, it must have been the children. The intent of the framers of the Constitution of 1816 for a "general system of education" was good, but the people and the General Assembly were slow to concede that "circumstances" permitted. A Senate committee on education in 1821 reported on the possibilities of a permanent income from the sale of the school lands[116] and cautiously

sponsible for the establishment of Ohio's public school system" (Utter, *The Frontier State*, 321); "These two classes of people [New Englanders and "the descendants of the 'poor whites'"] met and struggled for supremacy in Ohio, Indiana, and Illinois. . . . Where the New England people were in the ascendancy, as in Ohio, and also in Michigan and early Wisconsin . . . the zeal for education, religion, and local governmental control have been most marked. Where the southern element predominated, as for a time in Illinois, the result has been the opposite" (Ellwood P. Cubberley, *Public Education in the United States* . . . revised ed., Boston, 1934), 108–9.

Statements such as the last can only be accounted for on the basis of complete ignorance of the subject. In the Indiana Constitutional Convention of 1816, which wrote the first state constitution with a mandate for laws for a free general system of education from township schools to the university, there were two New Englanders out of forty-three members. The Illinois legislature which passed the law of 1825, certainly as advanced as Ohio's law of the same year, had fewer than a dozen New England-born members.

[114] Highest tax ratio on the valuation in 1829, for instance, was in the counties of Butler, Ross, Franklin, Montgomery, Highland, Preble and Clermont.

[115] The anti-New England argument is soundly if somewhat aggressively sketched in McAlpin, "The Origin of Public Education in Ohio," in *Ohio Archaeological and Historical Society Publications,* XXVIII, 409–47. The documents themselves are even more convincing.

[116] By territorial act of 1808 county courts were authorized to lease school lands for not to exceed five years; two years later to appoint a school-land trustee for each township. Philbrick (ed.), *Laws of Indiana Territory, 1801–9,* 667–68. In 1816 the law permitted the voters of a Congressional township to elect three school trustees to administer the funds. *Laws of Indiana,* 1816–17, pp. 106–7. The committee of 1821 calculated that if the school lands were sold at $3.50 per acre, the purchaser paying annually the interest on the sale price, and the proceeds funded for six years, the income for schools would be $181,177 per year.

recommended supplementary taxation by vote of the electors in the townships.[117] The legislature instructed a committee to prepare a bill for a general state system of education and "to guard especially against any distinction between the rich and the poor." No law was prepared until three years had elapsed. The law of 1824 made it permissible for the citizens of a Congressional township to levy school taxes "to be raised in money," but few did;[118] in 1828 sale of the sections 16 was authorized by a majority vote of the citizens of the townships.

The long law of 1833 incorporated the inhabitants of the Congressional townships, provided for election of a school commissioner in each county to handle the land-sale proceeds,[119] for election of three township trustees, for lease or sale of the school lands (one fourth down, balance in ten years, nontaxable until paid for), for creation of school districts, and for election of three district trustees. The district trustees, after affirmative vote of the freeholders for a school, were authorized to levy taxes, either in work, materials, or money, to build and maintain the school, to employ a teacher for at least three months, and to examine teachers. But after the schoolhouse was paid for, if any person, not intending to share in the school fund, wished to send his children to school, he could not be taxed for any purpose except maintenance of the schoolhouse—"he fulfilling his own contract with the teacher for tuition, fuel and contingencies, as in other cases."[120] The spirit of localism was carried to its ultimate in 1836 when it was made possible for any individual citizen to hire a teacher and draw his share of the school funds for his own children.

By this time Hoosier schools, as a system, were in a sorry

[117] "Your committee are aware, that to compel the people of a district to support a school against their will, might be considered an infringement of their natural rights. . . ."

[118] The law of 1824 assessed one day of work each week against able-bodied males of the district for the building of schoolhouses. Failure to contribute was subject to a fine of 37½ cents per day. This law did not make the establishment of schools mandatory; schools established were maintained by "rate bills" or graduated tuition. The three township trustees were given the management of the schools, including the power to examine teachers.

[119] If one was not already appointed under existing law. By vote in each township the funds might either be turned over to the state loan office or lent by the school commissioner.

[120] *Laws of Indiana*, 1832–33, p. 97 (Section 158 of the law approved February 2, 1833).

mess: the school law was "a mass of statutory provisions" difficult enough for the legally disciplined mind, "insuperable to the
ordinary citizen";[121] there was lax or no enforcement of the
laws; neighborhood squabbles over districting and schoolhouses
were common; dishonest trustees were not unheard of; school
terms were of various lengths; textbooks were of many kinds or
else lacking entirely. It is not hard to understand why the
teaching profession reached its lowest status in this period. As
the House Committee on Education summed up the situation
in 1840: "We present almost the only example of a State professing to have in force a system of common school education,
which does not know the amount, or condition of its school
funds, the number of schools and scholars to be taught, and to
receive the distribution of those funds."

By a provision in the Illinois enabling act, not given to any of
the other states created from the Northwest Territory, that
state received, in addition to the sections 16, 3 per cent of the
proceeds of sale of public lands within the state, not for roads,
but "for the encouragement of learning, of which one-sixth
part shall be exclusively bestowed on a college or university."
The Illinois legislature in 1819 provided for leasing the school
lands;[122] four years later it declared that there should be established "a common school or schools in each of the counties . . .
which shall be open and free to every class of white citizens
between the age of five and twenty-one." District trustees were
to examine and employ teachers; the voters might levy taxes
(up to ½ of 1 per cent) for teachers and buildings; 2 per
cent of the net taxes of the state, and five sixths of the interest
due from the state on the school funds which it had borrowed
were set aside for schools.

On paper this law appeared to put Illinois far in advance of
the other states, but the law of 1827 specified that no person be
taxed for schools without his consent, which left the schools in

[121] Message of Governor Samuel Bigger, 1842.
[122] "Old Rustic" wrote about two columns in the *Edwardsville Spectator*, December 26, 1820, advocating that the legislature take steps for expending the Illinois
school funds. He believed the whole should be used for the support of "good English schools"; spelling, reading, writing, and arithmetic were a base without which
one could not go higher. Such a school should be opened at each courthouse in the
state. Two hundred and fifty dollars (equivalent to $500 two years earlier) would
get a competent teacher; allowing $50 for board, the teacher would net $200 per
year.

about the same place that they had been—on a subscription basis;
two years later the 2 per cent appropriation was repealed, and
the law otherwise modified to make the organization of schools
more completely a voluntary act. In 1831, assuming permission
from Congress, the legislature provided for the sale of the
school sections on petition of three fourths of the citizens of the
township. Relatively little was realized from the sale; in some
townships the 640 acres were worth several thousand dollars,
but in others were hardly worth taxes. In December, 1832,
Governor Reynolds reported that the common school fund was
$29,514, most of which had been invested in "state paper"; ac-
cumulated interest was $9,983. Adding the returns from the
United States Three Per Cent Fund (from the sale of public
lands within the state) to date, a total of $108,842 (of which
the state had borrowed $60,605) was listed as available for
the support of schools.[123]

The Jacksonville *Illinois Patriot* maintained that, since the
state had two million dollars in lands and funds, plans for a
state system of common schools should be under way.[124] One
solution suggested for the problem of shortage of funds and
teachers was to have circuit-riding teachers: while one school
was reciting the others could be preparing their lessons. This
system was said to have been tried successfully in Bond County.[125]

The legislature of 1836–37 sought to put together the various
pieces of educational legislation into a coherent whole, but no
important changes resulted. Interest on the accruing school
funds was to be distributed to the counties; townships were to
elect trustees to handle school funds, lay off school districts,
examine and employ teachers, and pay out funds on the basis
of school attendance. Again in 1840–41 the legislature made
another attempt at simplification of the law; fifteen preceding
laws were repealed and a twenty-eight-page new law enacted.
The township trustees were empowered to examine teachers, or
to appoint a board to do so; teachers were required to have a

---

[123] Springfield *Sangamo Journal*, December 22, 1832. In 1835 Representative
William J. Gatewood reported to the legislature that the common school fund was
$97,741. Vandalia *Illinois Advocate and State Register*, February 14, 1835.

[124] February 15, 1834, quoted in *Sangamo Journal*, February 22. The editor of
the *Vandalia Whig and Illinois Intelligencer*, May 8, 1834, said it made no difference whether the people paid interest or taxes for schools.

[125] *Sangamo Journal*, June 14, 1834.

trustees' certificate; voters of the school district were authorized to elect school directors who were to fix school sites, build buildings, employ and pay teachers; local enumerations were to be taken and school funds were to be prorated to the townships on the basis of their school populations (all persons under twenty-one years). A general free public school system was not to be attained, however, until 1855.

The first educational convention in the state met at Vandalia early in 1833. James Hall, editor of the *Illinois Monthly Magazine*, made an address. At a second meeting late the following year sixty delegates, mostly members of the legislature, represented thirty counties. Efforts were made to disseminate publicity and gather information regarding schools. The Illinois conference of the Methodist Episcopal Church instructed its ministers to encourage the people to action in establishing public schools, and Professor Jonathan Baldwin Turner, of the recently established Illinois College, worked among the farmers to the same end. In his endeavor to lighten their labors in order that they would have more time to think of education, he introduced the Osage orange hedge as a substitute for rail fences.[126] The Reverend Theron Baldwin, principal of Monticello Female Academy and one of the founders of Illinois College, started publication of the *Common School Advocate* in 1837.[127] The *Alton Telegraph* published the Ohio school law of 1838 in the hope that it would be of some use in Illinois.[128] The Illinois State Educational Association was chartered by the legislature of 1840–41 "to promote by all laudable means the diffusion of knowledge in regard to education; and especially to render the system of common schools throughout the State as perfect as

---

[126] Samuel Willard, "Brief History of Early Education in Illinois," in *Fifteenth Biennial Report of the Superintendent of Public Instruction* (Springfield, 1884), cxiv.

[127] This periodical was short-lived. In 1841 E. R. Wiley, of Springfield, published *The Illinois Common School Advocate*, May to September. Baldwin had written from Vandalia in 1830: "Every step that I take here causes me to feel more and more the importance and necessity of education. I visited 27 families not long since in a section of this county in which there was not an individual who could read! . . . *Perhaps* there is no other section as destitute as that—(for it is somewhat celebrated) . . . principally, I believe, emigrants from Tennessee—*There is yet everything to be done here on the subject of education*. There is at present as a matter of course much apathy—and to some extent too it is deathlike in its character." Baldwin to Absalom Peters, May 21, 1830. Papers of the American Home Missionary Society.

[128] March 21, 1838.

possible." It would seem that this organization accomplished little. Newspapers, politicians, and ministers talked a lot about schools, but no one did much about them; it would seem that the people preferred that their children, as well as their cattle, run at large.[129]

In 1817 the *Detroit Gazette*, deploring the lack of schools in Michigan Territory, said that the obstacles in the way of them were not sufficient to account for their absence.[130] On the same day in 1817 that the Governor and Judges were promulgating grandiose plans for the "Catholepistemiad, or University of Michigania," they created a primary school. This was the Lancasterian school conducted at first by Lemuel Shattuck, who in his report at the end of the first year complained of the crowded quarters, lack of assistants, and expenses.[131] It was not a free school, since the parents of the 183 pupils had promised to pay an average of $2.60 per quarter. The defects of the school led to an airing of the merits and demerits of the Lancasterian method, which was soon abandoned.[132] Aside from a free school conducted by the nuns near St. Anne's Church in the middle 1820's there were no free schools in Detroit.

The territorial legislature in 1827 stipulated that each township with fifty inhabitants provide itself with a schoolteacher of good morals to teach reading, writing, arithmetic, spelling, the English and French languages, and good behavior, "for such term of time as shall be equivalent to six months for one school in each year."[133] Penalties of $50 to $150 were fixed on the town-

[129] See Chapter IV, 190. Long "Lectures" on "Education" and "Common Schools," frequently by ministers, appeared in the newspapers. Sometimes (see Springfield *Sangamo Journal*, April 14, 1838) they ran ten columns in length. They were usually stilted, pompous, and moral. More pointed were letters written by "citizens" or teachers. One of the latter (in *Alton Spectator*, January 11, 1838) called attention to the fact that Alton, population 3,000, supported four churches and five ministers, but only one schoolmaster, and he but poorly (seven scholars); could it be that only seven children in such a city needed instruction?

[130] August 8, 1817. The article, in French, warned the French to attend to the matter; there would soon be more "Yankees" in the Territory than French.

[131] *Detroit Gazette*, April 30, 1819.

[132] *Ibid.*, December, 1821, January—February, 1822.

[133] *Laws of the Territory of Michigan* (3 volumes. Lansing, 1871, 1874), II, 472–77. Townships containing 100 families or householders were to provide a schoolmaster for the equivalent of 12 months for one school in each year; those containing 150 families, a schoolmaster for the equivalent of 6 months plus an instructor in the English language for the equivalent of 12 months; those containing 200 families "a grammar schoolmaster of good morals, well instructed in the Latin, French, and English languages," and in addition provide a schoolmaster or teacher "as above described, to instruct children in the English language, for such term of time as shall be equivalent to 12 months for each of said schools in each year."

ships for failure to employ teachers. Inspectors, not exceeding five per township, were to be chosen to examine and certify teachers, and three trustees for each school district to manage the schools. The electors in the townships were authorized to vote poll and property taxes for school purposes, and to apportion them to the school districts. No children were to be denied the privilege of attending school because their parents were unable to furnish their share of the wood. The joker in this elaborate and confusing law was its last section: nothing in the act was to be obligatory on any township if two thirds of the voters at the township meeting voted not to comply with its provisions. It does not appear that any six-months, tax-supported schools were established as a result of this law.

In Detroit in April, 1830, a meeting was held to ascertain how many pupils could be counted upon if a common school was opened.[134] It was pointed out that the common branches were more necessary than a smattering of Greek and Latin.[135] Because of the unpardonable neglect of parents hundreds of children were not even receiving instruction in the rudiments. Whether Michigan remained a territory or became a state, something ought to be done about the matter. "It is a fact not to be disguised, that education among us is at a very low ebb." Sale of the school townships might help.[136] In 1834 the city census showed 1,496 persons of school age (between five and twenty years), of whom only 801 had received instruction. If this fact did not concern parents, no argument could do anything about it; it was a self-evident proposition.[137] The 1836 census listed almost three thousand of school age, of whom six hundred were attending the fourteen schools of the city.[138]

In 1833 the act to regulate common schools repealed all former school laws;[139] it authorized the election of three commissioners in each township, the division of the township into school dis-

[134] Detroit *North-Western Journal*, April 28, 1830. There were between 60 and 75 in the two schools under the "University" (classical and primary), 20 to 30 in other schools, and about 150 in no schools. *Ibid.*, May 5, 1830. The last figure seems low.

[135] *Ibid.*, May 12, 1830.

[136] *Detroit Journal and Michigan Advertiser*, September 14, 1831. By law in 1828 Congress had authorized the territorial legislature to take charge of school lands.

[137] *Ibid.*, April 8, 1834.

[138] *Detroit Free Press*, March 11, 1836.

[139] *Detroit Daily Advertiser*, June 23, 1836.

tricts, the lease of the school lands for three years, and the use of the proceeds for employment of a teacher for at least three months. Five inspectors were to be selected to examine and certify teachers.

As a result of the foresight of the Reverend John D. Pierce the problem of administering school lands was made much simpler in Michigan than in the other states of the Northwest. Pierce had discussed the importance of education with Gen. Isaac E. Crary.[140] Crary, as chairman of the committee on education in the constitutional convention, helped frame the constitutional provision for the first state superintendency of public instruction, then as "representative" went to Congress and helped phrase the supplementary act for the admission of Michigan.[141] This act did not grant the sections 16 to the townships (as in Ohio and Indiana) or to the state "for the use of the inhabitants of such townships" (as in Illinois), but simply to the state of Michigan "for the use of schools." "Thus, much was gained; we had secured a foundation on which to rear a superstructure, and materials with which to build."[142] On Crary's recommendation Governor Mason appointed Pierce, then working for the American Home Missionary Society, state superintendent of public instruction in 1836. The legislature requested a report and the next year he submitted his plan for the organization and support of primary schools, for a university with branches, and for disposing of the university and common school lands. Pierce went East, visited governors and college presidents, an educational institute in Massachusetts, and the meeting of the College of Professional Teachers at Cincinnati. His ensuing report was adopted, but, as Pierce said, it was "one thing to adopt a system, and quite another and very different thing to carry it into execution."[143] Schools, like the villages and "cities," for many years

[140] Pierce had read a copy of M. Cousin's report to the French minister of public instruction on the Prussian system.

[141] John D. Pierce, "Origin and Progress of the Michigan School System," in *Michigan Pioneer and Historical Collections*, I (1877), 40. Crary, pending the admission of Michigan, had been admitted to the House as a "spectator."

[142] *Ibid.*

[143] "It is conceded, as well by the friends as the enemies of our constitution, that it cannot exist and be maintained in its purity, simplicity, and power, in the midst of a people generally unenlightened and vicious. . . . Without education the fairest fabric ever reared in the long march of time must tumble unto ruin; and its name and memorial become and remain a by-word, a hissing and an astonishment to the nations of the earth. Let ignorance prevail and superstition

existed only on paper. Twenty years were to elapse before free schools for three months a year were an actuality in the townships of Michigan.[144]

The laws of Michigan Territory extended to Wisconsin at the time of the latter's separation; no special action was taken by the Wisconsin territorial legislature regarding common schools prior to 1840. A school district was organized in Milwaukee and a public school was taught there by Edward West in the winter of 1836–37; although it had about seventy pupils, it was not a free school. In 1845 a law was passed which permitted the village of Southport (Kenosha) to vote to tax itself for a free public school, but the school was not established until 1849, one year after Wisconsin became a state.[145]

§ §

So much has been written of early schools that other than general description is needless.[146] In the country they were held in vacant cabins, old barns, abandoned mills or forts, and in schoolhouses; in the villages and towns private homes, upstairs quarters over places of business, basements, and churches all served at one time or another. Schoolhouses were of the simplest architecture, usually rectangular in shape, though now and then a house with five corners was built. Some of the earliest buildings had no windows but only the door or an overhead opening for light. The greased-paper window marked an improvement and served until glass was more commonly available. Ventilation was no problem in these buildings—a fortunate thing in the asafetida

---

and bigotry will soon become lords of the ascendant, and crime of every species and of the darkest shades will increase and multiply, and security of property, of liberty and life, is at an end; and intemperance, injustice, and oppression, unterrified and unrestrained, will rival and triumph at noon-day."

[144] Pierce, "The Michigan School System," in *Michigan Pioneer and Historical Collections,* I, 41. The "rate bill," that is taxation on the basis of numbers of children sent to school, lingered in attenuated form in Michigan until 1869. Joseph Schafer, "Origin of Wisconsin's Free School System," in *Wisconsin Magazine of History,* IX (1925–26), 31.

[145] Schafer, "Origin of Wisconsin's Free School System," in *Wisconsin Magazine of History,* IX, 37.

[146] Three of the better articles on early schools are D. C. Shilling, "Pioneer Schools and School Masters," in *Ohio Archaeological and Historical Society Publications,* XXV (1916), 36–51; Van Buren, "The Log Schoolhouse Era in Michigan," in *Michigan Pioneer and Historical Collections,* XIV, 283–402; and David D. Banta, "The Early Schools of Indiana," in *Indiana Magazine of History,* II (1906), 41–48, 81–88, 131–38, 191–94.

season—but it is doubtful whether the sniffles were any more prevalent than in the steam-heated schoolrooms of today. Equipment was simple: some benches, a writing table or bench, a table or teacher's desk, a fireplace or stove, a water pail, later perhaps a hand bell, blackboard, and in the exceptional school a globe.

Country schools could not be conveniently located for all the families. A two- or three-mile trip to school had its compensations in autumn or summer, but in winter and spring it was another story. Though it was not, as some local historians have stated, "the custom to go to school, winter and summer, barefoot," nevertheless, the practice was not unheard of. Not even weather-hardened feet were immune to frostbite or the painful cramp from icy water; a heated stone carried along as a foot warmer helped on occasion.

No generalizations can safely be made regarding teachers: like politicians, preachers, or speculators, they were "critters" of various stripes. It might well be argued that, though education in the abstract received the deference of people in general, the vocation of teaching was not held in very high esteem. For one thing, the teacher did not work with his hands; consequently, his work was worth little. "The man who was disabled to such an extent that he could not engage in manual labor—who was lame, too fat, too feeble, had the phthisic or had fits or was too lazy to work—well, they usually made schoolmasters out of these, and thus got what work they could out of them." Furthermore, not all the teachers were worth respecting. Many were rolling stones, drifters from New England, Scotland, Ireland, or the East, who had less of either craftsmanship or ability to stay put than the journeymen printers, and who could even match the latter in their ability to consume hard liquor. There must have been just ordinary teachers; no doubt they constituted the great majority, but they seldom made the record. The sterling personalities, the natural teachers, those persons who would have been teaching whatever their vocations, many of these we have data on; also "the one-eyed teacher," "the one-legged teacher," the teacher who was educated for the ministry but who, owing to the habit of hard drink, took up pedagogy, "the lame teacher," the teacher who took to the fiddle, "the teacher who had fits," and "the teacher who got drunk on Saturday and whipped the entire school on Monday." (Some did not wait until Saturday, but did whatever effective teaching was done before noon, and snoozed the afternoon away.) [147]

On the other hand, it could be well maintained that teachers as a class were more highly regarded than today. The company of the unmarried teachers was enjoyed as they "boarded round"; they told tales, sometimes read to the family, lent a helping hand, minded the baby. Jealousies were aroused by a longer stay with one family than with another. If he was approved as a spelling-match conductor, the teacher would be regarded as outstanding in his profession. Certainly the teacher whose book learning was real and who knew how to handle young folks was a respected person in his community; often his renown—like that of a successful athletic coach in a later day—was statewide.

[147] "It is a well known fact, that in small towns school-masters for the most part are men of little or no acquirements or address, but are professedly men who never thought of becoming instructors of youth . . . until necessity compelled them, or ambition urged them to make the occupation subservient to some other object. To teach for a season or two, seldom longer, is the utmost of their intention. Their object gained, they absent themselves, leaving behind them nothing worth commemorating, but much that needs censure and condemnation. That there should be men of this description, charlatans in every sense of the word, whose sole object is to enrich themselves by imposing upon the credulity, and I may say apathy of the public, is not surprising;—knaves have abounded in every age,—but it is to me perfectly unaccountable, that a community should willingly suffer themselves to be hoodwinked by such persons, and cajoled by their flattering promises and monstrous pretensions." Henry Moore, "Education," in *Western Monthly Magazine*, V (1836), 414–15.

Thomas Peirce, Cincinnati poet, described a Yankee schoolmaster in his "Billy Moody" epic, in *National Republican and Ohio Political Register,* May 27, 1823:

"Notice being giv'n in every city print
    (And there were four, five, six—God knows how many)
In which he gave the public many a hint
    Of vast attainments—far surpassing any
Before possest: and, confident by dint
    Of puffing he could make a handsome penny,
He opened a school; and, proud am I to tell,
    For the first quarter he succeeded well.

"But ere the next was out, his school had dwindled.
    To half the number which it first contained;
For his kind patrons, finding he had swindled
    Them out of cash for which they nothing gained.
Their dormant fires of indignation kindled,
    Of his base impositions loud complained,
And felt no hesitation to declare
    A Yankee's word was spurious as his ware."

Or as some waggish scholar wrote on the wall at the end of the term:

"Lord of love, look down from above
    And pity the poor scholars
They hired a fool to teach this school
    And paid him fifty dollars."

Many teachers were ignorant, others merely queer. Good teachers were hard to get, nor were the low pay and lack of training facilities entirely accountable; it would seem that teaching has always attracted (or else protected and retained) more than its share of the constitutionally inept and impractical. Early subscription schools paid 75 cents to $1.50 per scholar per quarter, which might gross the teacher $6.00 to $10 per month, but part of the pay was likely to be taken in board or produce.[148] At a time when common labor was paid 62½ cents to $1.25 per day ($3.00 with a team), the teachers did well to average 50 cents. As late as 1842 an Indiana teacher contracted for a three-months school for $36.50 to be paid $25 in state scrip, $2.00 in "Illinois money," and $9.50 in currency. Baynard Rush Hall with a master's degree came from the East to head the newly created State Seminary at Bloomington in 1824 for $250 per annum. Cincinnati public schoolteachers by 1840 received about the same. The subject of teachers' pay was often discussed in the newspapers.[149] Teaching, of course, was but a part-time job for most country and village teachers; farming, horse trading, clerking in stores, working as "mechanics," buying and selling land were intermittent or continuous activities which teaching did not stop. Some teachers even accumulated property. Teaching was often a temporary occupation, a means of accumulating enough cash to embark upon medicine, law, or business.

Aside from the academies and a few colleges there were no formal facilities by which the teacher might improve his knowledge and practice; like the early printers and editors, many were practically self-educated. Governor Worthington's suggestion

---

[148] Arrangements varied. The teacher usually settled for a lower tuition rate if he got to board with the patrons. "Board" was about the same per week as tuition for a scholar for a quarter.

[149] The *Ohio Farmer and Western Horticulturist* (Columbus), December 15, 1838, sought to convince farmers that children were as important as horses. A farmer did not send a valuable horse to a dumb blacksmith. When a farmhand applied, he was asked, "Can you cradle? Can you drive a team?" etc. When a teacher applied, he was asked, "How much do you want?" If the choice lay between a $10 teacher and a $30 teacher, the former got the job. The Springfield *Sangamo Journal,* August 26, 1837, said that it was glad to note that people were waking up to the importance of this matter. The *Detroit Daily Advertiser,* October 3, 1836, asked why the legislature did not do something toward raising the character of "this useful profession." "There is a deep seated error in relation to this subject." Teaching was not held in the same esteem as stitching leather or welding iron. Why? When asked, "How can you afford to pay a teacher $30 per month?" the answer should be, "How can you afford to pay a tailor $8 for making a coat?" *Ibid.,* October 17, 1836.

made in 1817, previously mentioned, of training boys of indigent parents at state expense in return for their services as teachers, did not solve the problem. Almost twenty years later Governor Noble, of Indiana, regretted the low repute of the profession and the general reliance upon transient teachers with neither qualifications nor moral character. He thought that permanent settlers acquainted with the customs and manners of the people and interested in the development of the community would be a much better group upon whom to rely; he proposed a state seminary for special training of native teachers. With ignorant trustees and district examiners, who themselves may have had only a few terms of country school, examining teachers of similar attainments, the results can be imagined. Grammar, arithmetic, orthography, and geography became matters of individual preference. Even so, some of the examiners' devices for testing the intelligence of the candidate were no less amazing than similar devices concocted by the professional educationist of today. If they did not measure the teacher's qualifications in the common branches, they did measure his common sense. Not as dumb as it might appear on first glance was the answer of a hopeful candidate when asked whether the world was round or flat: "I can teach her either way." Obviously, that teacher had adjusted himself to his environment.[150] Favoritism in the employment of teachers, since the power lay entirely in local hands, was an evil. The relative, friend, or person who owed the trustee or director money had the advantage over persons whose qualifications were better.[151]

"An Examiner" in Ohio, speaking of the qualifications of teachers, pointed out that though the examiners by implication had the right to demand more, the law merely required that the teacher be acquainted with reading, writing, and arithmetic. As a consequence, "not *one-fourth* part of the common school teachers can pass an analytical examination upon the *principles* of arithmetic; not one-sixth know any thing of geography; and not one in *ten* ever heard of philosophical grammar." A teacher had

---

[150] An example of an examination by comparatively ignorant examiners is in *Cincinnati Daily Gazette,* May 11, 1839.

[151] Samuel Lewis, Ohio state superintendent, called attention to this fact in a letter published in the *Ohio Farmer and Western Horticulturist* (Columbus), July 1, 1839.

informed him that out of forty scholars in his school, but one
had ever reached the rule of three. This case may not have been
typical, but there were places where conditions were even worse.
Before the situation could be improved there would have to be
better standards set for teachers, reduction of the number of
scholars per teacher, higher salaries, and academies for better
instruction of teachers.[152]

Attention was also called to the fact that the personal appearance of teachers, as well as their manners and morals, were items
of consequence. "His very appearance speaks to them, and is sufficient to rule the school—*tenere scholam*. . . . All *peculiarities*, and
eccentricities, especially when affected, should be guarded against,
inasmuch as they are points very quickly caught and ridiculed
by the mimic desposition of youth. . . . He who undertakes to discipline the moral feelings of a youthful multitude, must be one
well versed in the subtleties of the human heart."[153]

Almost as diverse and numerous as teachers' personalities
and qualifications were the textbooks and methods of instruction.
Though children in country districts might start to school with a
Holy Bible or a copy of Foxe's *Book of Martyrs*—or no books
at all—the chances were that a few spellers, readers, and arithmetics of various authors and editions were available.[154] Uniform
textbooks for the whole class or school were practically an im-
possibility; especially was this true of the arithmetics, a half
dozen of which often constituted a neighborhood heritage.

Beginners usually started with the speller. Noah Webster's
Elementary Spelling Book, an all-time best seller in our history,
was the best known.[155] The proverbs, aphorisms, fables, and

---

[152] "Condition of Common Schools," in *Western Monthly Magazine*, III (1835),
165–67.

That good teachers did not result automatically from a certain amount of "cer-
tification" was recognized. Not even "an A. M., however well obtained" was evidence of an individual's qualifications to instruct: (1) The course of training in
most colleges was deficient; (2) not every A. M. stood high in his class or, if he
had knowledge, was able to impart it. T. S. Reeve, "Education, and the Best Means
of Acquiring It," in *Transactions of the Western Literary Institute and College
of Professional Teachers*, 1838, pp. 190–91.

[153] Henry Moore, "On the Qualifications of Teachers," in *Western Monthly
Magazine*, V (1836), 211–12.

[154] "I think it not too much to say that in my own 'Shiloh neighborhood,' all the
books, excluding Bibles, hymn-books and spelling-books, owned by the neighborhood, could have been packed in a bushel basket." Banta, "Early Schools of Indiana," in *Indiana Magazine of History*, II, 131.

[155] Approximately 77,500,000 copies in its first hundred years (1783–1883). There
was a Lexington, Kentucky, edition of Webster's *American Speller* in 1823.

moral "lessons" which have long been associated in the American mind with the McGuffey readers, were all herein set forth fifty years before McGuffey got under way. Some of the classic chunks of wisdom are still good even in the age of electronics: "A good boy will try to spell and read well"; "A duck has a wide flat bill"; "The moon is smaller than the Sun"; "The man who drinks rum may soon want a loaf of bread." And the moral of Fable I, "Of the Boy that Stole Apples" is still worth pondering. When the old man threw persuasive words and wads of grass at the boy in the tree without result, he used stones and found them more effective. So: "If good words and gentle means will not reclaim the wicked, they must be dealt with in a more severe manner."

Spellers were readers, "philosophies," and etiquette manuals. Among the competitors of Webster's *American Spelling Book* was Dillworth's. One of the early western spellers was Elisha Bates's *The Western Preceptor*, published at Mount Pleasant, Ohio, in 1821; this Quaker editor also issued a *Juvenile Expositor or Child's Dictionary* the same year.

Of the readers Lindley Murray's *English Reader* was a favorite.[156] A typical edition included prose chapters on "Select Sentences," "Narrative Pieces," "Didactic Pieces," "Argumentative Pieces," "Descriptive Pieces," "Pathetic Pieces," "Public Speeches," "Promiscuous Pieces"; Part II duplicated these headings in poetry. The first lesson endeavored to prepare the scholar for reading, for life, and for the hereafter:

[156] The first American edition was published in Boston in 1823. The title in the New London and New York 1829 edition was: *The English Reader, or Pieces in Prose and Verse from the Best Writers, Designed to Assist Young Persons to Read with Propriety and Effect; Improve their Language and Sentiments; and to Inculcate the Most Important Principles of Piety and Virtue, with a Few Preliminary Observations on the Principles of Good Reading.* E. H. Flint published a Cincinnati edition in 1833.

Lindley Murray was born in Pennsylvania, attended boarding school in New Jersey, became a lawyer, and after the American Revolution moved to England. He was interested in theology, philosophy, and botany. As a result of a lack of suitable lesson books in a near-by girls' school, he prepared his *English Grammar* in 1795. This book in time went through almost fifty editions. The *English Reader* (1799) was in its thirty-first edition in 1836. He also published an *English Spelling Book* (1804) which in time reached the forty-fourth edition, and many other text-books. Murray has been known as the father of English grammar. His friend John Dalton, the chemist, jokingly said, "that of all the contrivances invented by human ingenuity for puzzling the brains of the young, Lindley Murray's grammar was the worst."

Diligence, industry, and proper improvement of time, are material duties of the young. . . . The acquisition of knowledge is one of the most honourable occupations of youth. . . . Virtuous youth gradually brings forward accomplished and flourishing manhood. . . . Change and alteration form the very essence of the world. . . . Whatever purifies, fortifies also the heart. . . . To maintain a steady and unbroken mind, amidst all the shocks of the world, marks a great and noble spirit. . . . The veil which covers from our sight the events of succeeding years, is a veil woven by the hand of mercy. . . . The best preparation for all the uncertainties of futurity, consists in a well-ordered mind, a good conscience, and a cheerful submission to the will of Heaven.

The Goodrich readers, modeled on Murray's, were popular in the East but never had general use in the West. The B. T. Emerson readers became fairly well known by the 1830's; there were also distributed copies of Rufus W. Adam's *Young Gentlemen and Lady's Explanatory Monitor* . . . (5th ed., Columbus, 1818), the readers by the Pickets, first published in the East, then at Cincinnati, and many others.[157] James Hall, ever looking after the interests of the West, published his *Western Reader* (Cincinnati, 1833); the selections were limited to American writers and emphasized western topics. Timothy Flint, Otway Curry, Benjamin Drake, Mrs. Sigourney, Henry Clay, and George D. Prentice were among the authors included.[158]

Textbook history was made in 1836 when William Holmes McGuffey signed a contract with Truman and Smith, a small Cincinnati publishing house. This company was in 1834 publishing, among other items, Ray's *Little Arithmetic*, Smith's *Practical and Mental Arithmetic*, Smith's *Productive Grammar*, the *Picture Primer*, and the *Picture Reader*. Winthrop B. Smith had sought to get Miss Catherine Beecher to undertake the editing of his proposed *Eclectic Readers*, but she declined. Calvin E. Stowe, however, had married Harriet Beecher just before he went to Europe to study the Prussian educational system. Stowe was associated with McGuffey in the Western Literary Institute

[157] B. Bridge followed his *New American Speaker* (1837) with the *New American Reader,* No. 3 (1839); Henry Houseworth, Hoosier Schoolmaster, published his *Federurbian, or United States Lessons* . . . the same year. In 1833 Truman, Smith and Company of Cincinnati published *The Picture Reader,* exceptional for its illustrations.

[158] This reader was designed to follow its publishers' (Corey and Fairbank) *Elementary Reader.* Judging from its present scarcity *The Western Reader* must not have been widely used; it is almost as difficult to find as Harriet Beecher's *Primary Geography for Children,* published at the same time.

and College of Teachers and it was probably through this connection that McGuffey was brought to Smith's attention. McGuffey had previously published a treatise on *Methods of Reading* and had ready his *First Reader*. The *Eclectic* series which was intended primarily for the common schools planned to include a primer, a spelling book, and four readers. Within a year more than 20,000 copies had been sold; within six years some 700,000.[159] Despite charges of plagiarism from eastern publishers, the McGuffey readers soon established the standard for sense, simplicity, and morality. Most country schools got along with the *First* and *Second Readers*. Catherine Beecher's *The Moral Instructor* (1838) was published in the same series but did not prove so popular. In 1843 Smith took over control of the publishing house, which, after changing ownership several times, in 1890 became the American Book Company.

Spellers were readers, readers were in part spellers; grammars, speakers, preceptors, and geographies were also used for readers. A number of these were written by western teachers.[160] Murray's grammar was standard in its field; Samuel Kirkham abbreviated and simplified this book. Jedediah Morse had started writing geographies about the same time that Webster produced his first speller. His *A New System of Geography*, published in 1826, was announced as the twenty-fifth edition. John Kilbourn, compiler of *The Ohio Gazetteer*, published the *Columbian Geography* in 1815; his *Introduction to Geography and Astronomy* was in its sixth edition in 1826. Other geographies were Olney's, Moore's, Adam's, Woodbridge's and Smith's. Geographies of this period were not large books behind which the student might do his extracurricular reading, but were usually published in the regular reader or speller size (12 mo or 16 mo); they were the

---

[159] Henry H. Vail, *A History of the McGuffey Readers* (Cleveland, 1911), 47. See also Harvey C. Minnich, *William Holmes McGuffey and His Readers* (Cincinnati, 1936).

[160] H. T. M. Benedict, of Kentucky, revised and adapted the well-known *Murray's English Grammar* in 1833; Samuel Wilson of the same state was the author of *The Kentucky English Grammar* (1802) which was in its fifth edition by 1812; Joseph Buchanan (father of the famous Joseph Rodes Buchanan of therapeutic sarcognomy fame) published *A Practical Grammar of the English Language;* Leonard Bliss, of Louisville, received the approval of eastern critics with his *A Comprehensive Grammar of the English Language* (1839); Robert S. Holloway was the author of *An Easy and Lucid Guide to a Knowledge of English Grammar* (St. Clairsville, Ohio, 1833); and B. F. Ells put out his *The Dialogue of Grammar* in 1834.

only other books besides the spellers which ordinarily carried illustrations. Histories were solidly written books compiled by writers who were equally proficient in summarizing the history of Greece, England, or the United States. The history of Greece, Rome, and England was more frequently taught than that of our own country. Of the histories of the United States those by S. G. Goodrich and William Grimshaw were well known. They were essentially narrative and political; little or no attempt was made to write down to the young reader. The War for Independence naturally received the longest treatment and greatest emphasis, usually about one third of the entire text.[161]

Geographies and histories were not as well done as spellers, arithmetics, and readers. "The most amusing writers of the present day are the geographers," said a contemporary critic, who proceeded to demonstrate.[162] Pictures represented bear, buffalo, and elk riding down the Ohio to market on an ark; buffalo were described as "very domestic and harmless"; walnut wood as being used for ax handles and bows; among the United States territories listed (in 1834) were the Northwest, Missouri, and Oregon.[163]

Midwest Young America learned to cipher by way of Nathan

---

[161] "We know of no good school histories, especially American. Those in common use are very deficient. Some are too barren of incidents, others too diffuse. . . . The style of some is harsh and rugged, of others, weak and dull. It is not everyone who can write a good school history. It requires a man of genius; some one like Washington Irving, who can throw a charm about every subject he touches. The work of such a writer would very soon take the place of the histories by Goodrich, Hale, Webster, and others, whose compilations are very imperfect. . . ." Editor's note in *The Western Academician and Journal of Education and Science,* I, 90 n.

[162] "Geographies for the Use of Schools," probably by James Hall, *Western Monthly Magazine,* II (1834), 159–63.

[163] As valid today as a century ago is the criticism of a serious scholar and teacher: "The writing of elementary books for the young has, for the most part, fallen into the hands of . . . [those who] have not penetrated beyond the surface, and have considered *words only,* without seizing *principles,* and do not discover the inferior character of their attainments, until put upon inquiries which demand original thought, or . . . until they are called to communicate instructions to others. . . . The greater part of school books in present use, has, in consequence of erroneous views of the object of education, been written to render literary acquisitions easy to learners, or, in other words, to save them the labor of thinking. Committing to memory whatever is put before them, is found to be far less laborious than forming one idea out of others, or reasoning upon facts. . . . They [the books] favor not only the inability of those who assume to teach, but they foster in scholars, habits of mind at variance with all mental exertion and sound knowledge." "Elementary Books," probably by J. W. Picket, in *The Western Academician and Journal of Education and Science,* I, 359–60. Some liberty has been taken with the original in the arrangement of the quotation.

Daboll's arithmetic, or Smiley's, or Bennett's, or Pike's, or Jess's, or Dillworth's, or the *Western Calculator*. Compilers of these early arithmetics have been accused of being afraid of letting too much out in their instructions. The abstract rule would be laid down, then followed the problem. Explanations and examples were few; the scholar had to do his sums the hard way. Ray's arithmetic appeared shortly before 1840 and during the next generation became almost as well known as the McGuffey readers.

The other of the "three R's" was without textbooks. Having made a start in reading, the scholars were introduced to the art of "pot-hooks and hangers." A copybook of unruled foolscap sewn together at home might be lined by the teacher who carried a sharpened piece of lead for this purpose. The country teacher also was supposed to be an expert penmaker; sometimes he performed this job for the whole community. Goose quills were preferred, but turkey or even buzzard quills might do in a pinch. Later the imported Dutch quills were sold at the drugstore or general store bound in small bundles with the familiar red cord. Maple bark or sumac and oak balls and vinegar made an acceptable homemade ink; a sawed-off cow horn or a lead or pewter inkstand served as container. In his best fair hand the teacher set a copy of some moral or patriotic precept, which the scholar copied until he had mastered it. The whole school wrote at the same time, once or twice a day.

In the ungraded schools of the day classroom procedure was whatever the teacher chose to make it. Many of the early schools were loud schools. This system had its points: the teacher could hear the scholars study—sometimes the school could be heard "studying" a half mile away—and it was supposed to train the youngsters to think and figure in the busy noisy marts of trade. The Scot, Alexander Kinmont, eminent teacher of Cincinnati, conducted his school in the loud way. Spelling and reading lessons were heard in small groups; arithmetic was likely to be handled on an individual basis, each scholar forging ahead doing his sums with whatever help the teacher could give when he got stuck. Reading was something more than mere pronunciation and inflection (the latter clearly marked in the reader). A good teacher such as Mentor Graham, who taught Lincoln, might warm up the reader with a good tongue twister and make him bring out each long vowel and final consonant. "Read for sense. . . . Read aloud when you are alone. Put the book away. Write out . . . what you have read. Did you get all of it? Look and see."[164] Though Graham might correct the Dillworth speller, which pronounced "point" as "pint" and "are" as "air," it is doubtful whether his meticulous correctness materially changed the nasal twang of voice or eliminated all the "airs" and "gits" from his scholars' delivery. He used the rod sparingly, nor did he spoil the child. If the scholar was a little slow on the uptake, he might be confined to the top of a stump in the schoolyard until he mastered the assigned task. Learning was serious business; some things had to be done to make men and women out of boys and girls, to make a country out of men and women.

Teachers not as well qualified as Graham were more inclined to spread the word with the bark on. The switch, like the spring dosage of molasses and sulphur, was insisted upon by parents; a master who could not or would not use it might well be regarded as a failure. There were tough schools in which the scholars' ability to run out the teacher was rated above the ability to spell and cipher; there still are such schools. This practice must not be confused with the custom of "barring out the teacher" (or ducking him in the creek) to get a treat or a vacation, usually tried during the Christmas holidays.[165] The smart teacher stopped

[164] Kunigunde Duncan and D. F. Nickols, *Mentor Graham* (Chicago 1945), 135. This book, despite its many factual errors and divine-pattern theme, is an excellent portrayal of a sterling pioneer teacher. Teachers of this type refused to be bound by any mechanical "methodology." It was Kinmont, one of the best, who, when offered a $2,000 professorship at Cincinnati College, said: "Think of my being told how to teach school by a set of professional donkeys."

[165] Ebenezer Chamberlain, in a school near Connersville, Indiana, in 1832 was waited upon by a messenger who "axed me if I allowed to treat . . . He reckoned I a heap sight better treat, for he allowed I would stand a right smart chance to have a heap of fuss if I didn't." Teacher won out by way of a window and that evening at spelling school, in lieu of a treat, "gave a very serious and Yankee-like lecture" on the subject. "Chamberlain's Journal," in *Indiana Magazine of History*, XV, 241–42.

In Champaign, Illinois, in 1837, a teacher was forced to treat to black strap (whiskey and molasses) and everybody got drunk. His successor, refusing to treat, tried to ride away on his horse but was captured and forced to treat. Another teacher came forth with two gallons of whiskey after being tied out in the snow. Willard, "Early Education in Illinois," in *Fifteenth Biennial Report of Superintendent of Public Instruction*, cvii.

In 1835 a resolution was introduced in the Ohio legislature for an inquiry into the practicability of adopting some measure to prevent children barring out the teacher during Christmas holidays. *Cincinnati Daily Gazette*, January 28, 1835.

much trouble before it happened; for minor offenses the dunce block, foolscap, leather spectacles, or being made to sit on the girls' side (or vice versa) usually sufficed.

In regard to the "objectives," methods of instruction, and curriculum of the schools there was no more agreement than on what constituted the true religion. The West accepted much of what was, but modified, gave its own emphasis, sought ever after the system which would overcome class distinctions, establish "*New* facts, *New* principles," and adapt common school education "to the entire wants of the community."[166] Edward D. Mansfield said the objects of education were first, "discipline [of] the mind, moral and intellectual," and second, "attainment of such knowledge as may be of practical use in later life."[167] Alexander Campbell held that "excellence in education [would] consist in . . . teaching and training man to *think*, to *feel*, and to *act* in perfect harmony with his own constitution and with the constitution of nature and society around him." And Albert Picket agreed that "there is something to be taught in the schools besides the mere mechanical round of book lessons. There, the mind is to be developed, and the heart corrected; the disposition modified, and the principles fixed; the feelings trained, and the bias given for the residue of existence."[168] There was to be no gap between abstract learning and life: "Men are not educated to be mere walking *intellectual abstractions*, but *bona fide*, active, useful men."[169] It was up to the West to "improve the organization of human Society."

In the curriculum not even the three "R's" were safe from attack. It was argued that one month a year was sufficient for them; the rest of the time was wasted. As a result the children acquired a disgust for study and lost their habits of industry. Children should learn by doing; instead of studying formal

[166] The Western Literary Institute and College of Professional Teachers maintained practically a standing committee upon "The Expediency of Adapting Common School Education to the Entire Wants of the Community." The objective, curriculum, and methods are summarized in Allen Oscar Hansen, *Early Educational Leadership in the Ohio Valley* . . . (Bloomington, Illinois, 1923).

[167] *Transactions of the Western Literary Institute and College of Professional Teachers*, 1834, p. 140.

[168] Only occasionally did someone point out the contradiction between the idea of "giving a bias" in imparting knowledge, and republican institutions. Few of the professional educators seemed to be aware of it.

[169] *Ibid.*, 1835, pp. 88–90.

grammar, "Ohio and Pennsylvania grammar at that—I seen, I have saw, I done, I have did," they should be writing correct sentences.[170] Why learn the rules of grammar, if the scholar could not thereafter speak or write correctly? Geography and history were equally dry and futile when not understood. There was too much emphasis upon mere memory. And why so much attention in the academies to dead and foreign languages to the neglect of our own? The youth were not all designed for the same vocations, so why the same studies?[171] Thomas Smith Grimké, classical scholar, lawyer, and teacher, firmly contended that neither the classics nor "the mathematics" should form a part of the scheme for a general education. Other men trained in these fields such as Alexander Kinmont and Albert Picket agreed. Grimké emphasized the scientific attitude, "absolutely impersonal and experimental," and the mind ready to receive the product; at the same time he wanted "the truly Christian" education. Like many of the educators and ministers of the period he identified morality with the Christian religion. He was also an advocate of revised (phonetic) spelling.

The limitations of the scientific and vocational curriculum were pointed out, however:

The business of the workshop has a natural tendency to make machines of men, or but the wheels of a machine—artificial society—but the kind and beneficent intention of the school is, as far as possible, foreseeing this evil to guard against it, and to strengthen while it unfolds the whole man . . . provide such knowledge as shall connect him, not merely with the narrow circle of minds in which he moves but with all minds, living or departed that think or have thought nobly, generously, beneficently, grandly.

Even though the curriculum provide a grounding for teacher and pupil in the common branches and natural sciences, it might still be lacking. "Does it contain one particle of the constitution, and radical laws, under which he lives. . . . Does it contain a line of that long history of nations, the embodied *experience* of mankind, from which he may judge the future by the past?"[172] History had not only "the interest of drama, of which the world is the stage, and men and women its players," but just as the experience of the individual is the basis of his knowledge, "surely

---

[170] Letter in *Cleveland Herald and Gazette* (weekly), April 24, 1839.
[171] "Philo Tully" (No. 7), in *Cincinnati Daily Gazette*, June 5, 1829.
[172] "Condition of Common Schools" by "An Examiner," in *Western Monthly Magazine*, III (1835), 166.

the experience of the human race as a social mass, furnishes the true means of deducting the laws of social conduct in that mass."[173]

The people of the present day boast of the general intelligence of our country; and yet, forsooth, can this intelligence, as it is called, ferret out political corruptions? How few of the mass discriminate efficiently, or think correctly about passing events. We apprehend that the intelligence spoken of is not the right kind. But this knowledge, whatever it may be, is the product of the systems of education in vogue, both at *home* and in the *school-room*.[174]

The common schools, "the nurseries of universities and private schools," would, if properly managed, also be "a powerful engine in pouring forth the streams of knowledge among those who need it most"; an enduring support of our government and union. Children would become something more than passive instruments, "mere hewers of wood and drawers of water"; vague notions would give way to knowledge; liberality of sentiment and elevation of the individual would follow. Legislatures might pass laws, people cheerfully pay their taxes, but unless everyone worked seriously and constantly at the job of education, desirable results would not come. Good teachers would help, "teachers who, by patience, observation, and philosophic study of the workings of the human mind, have acquired a knowledge of what is elementary in thoughts . . . who know the *art* of going backwards with what they know, or with their knowledge, in order to make their scholars comprehend them."[175] But even good teachers would be of no avail if the foundations were sapped by injudicious or no education whatever at home.[176]

[173] E. D. Mansfield, "Uses of History," in *Transactions of the Western Literary Institute and College of Professional Teachers,* 1838, pp. 165–73.
The committee of the Western Teachers College appointed to study the Grimké plan found, besides the recommendation for excluding the classics and mathematics, a strong recommendation for "a thorough knowledge of our country—of its discovery and settlement—of its geography—of its customs, manners, and government—of its first settlers—of its eminent men, as theologians, statesmen and scholars. It also recommends a full acquaintance with all our best writers, and an accurate and extensive knowledge of the English language, together with the ready use of it, in composition and conversation. But above all, the strong and repeated recommendation of morality, piety, and a strictly religious life, founded on the practice of the Christian virtues and a close adherence to the doctrines of the Sacred Scriptures."
[174] John W. Picket, "Teachers, Parents and Common Schools," in *The Western Academician and Journal of Education and Science,* I, 32.
[175] *Ibid.,* I, 32, 33.
[176] Albert Picket in Address to College of Professional Teachers, 1837, in *ibid.,* I, 502.

Matters such as these were not settled in the pioneer period; they remain unsettled today. Little that is new has been added to the discussion in the interim.

§ § §

Colleges antedated a public school system by many years.[177] Through the efforts of Manasseh Cutler and his associates two townships in the Ohio Company Purchase were reserved by act of 1792 for the erection of a college or university; the same law set aside one township in the Symmes Purchase for an academy and other seminaries of learning.[178] The legislature of the Northwest Territory chartered the American Western University in 1802 (with Rufus Putnam as president of the board of trustees), but no school was established; two years later the Ohio legislature incorporated Ohio University.[179] Not until 1808 was an academic department organized under Jacob Lindley, a Presbyterian minister and Princeton graduate. In 1810 the college was organized under Princeton rules, an arts curriculum outlined, and Lindley made president. Two students were graduated in 1815. Despite reports of a "flourishing condition,"[180] the college was poor; in 1826 its revenues were only about $2,300 per year.[181] At the September, 1828, commencement

---

[177] Among the older studies of the colleges are George W. Knight and John R. Commons, *The History of Higher Education in Ohio*, Andrew C. McLaughlin, *History of Higher Education in Michigan*, and James A. Woodburn, *Higher Education in Indiana*, all published as numbers in *Contributions to American Educational History* (U. S. Bureau of Education, Washington, D. C., 1891). D. G. Tewksbury, *The Founding of American Colleges and Universities before the Civil War* (New York, 1932) serves as an introduction to the topic.

[178] By resolution of the territorial legislature in 1799 Rufus Putnam, B. I. Gilman, and Jonathan Stone were selected to lay off a townsite with a square for the colleges and lots for the professors, "bordering on or encircled by spacious commons." Athens, in Washington County (later Athens County), was the result.

[179] The board of trustees (twelve members plus the governor and president of the university), appointed by the legislature, was to administer the land grant. The original ninety-year leases were changed to ninety-nine years in 1805; in 1807 a law provided that the land was to be leased at $1.75 per acre or at its valuation if less than that amount. The faculty was ordered to report to the trustees "from time to time."

[180] *Niles' Weekly Register*, X, 414 (Aug. 17, 1816) reported that "a large stone college is now erecting" at Athens, and that its revenues were $30,000 per year. An announcement in the *Hamilton Intelligencer and Advertiser*, May 13, 1822, spoke of flourishing finances and a choice library. In 1817 the legislature authorized a lottery to raise $20,000 "to defray the expenses of completing the college edifice . . . and to purchase a library and suitable mathematical and philosophical apparatus"; in 1825 it appropriated $1,000 for debts and apparatus.

[181] Columbus *Ohio State Journal*, October 19, 1826.

"Athens College" conferred A. B. degrees upon ten graduates, one a colored man.[182] Robert G. Wilson, another Presbyterian minister, served as president from 1824 to 1839, when William Holmes McGuffey succeeded him. In the middle 1830's the legislature twice demanded reports on finances, number of professors and students, and instruction program. In 1838 the commissioners of the canal fund were authorized to lend $5,000 to the school, but in 1845 after financial and political troubles, it temporarily closed its doors.[183]

Miami University, chartered in 1809, was originally to have been at Lebanon, but in 1810 was established at the town of Oxford in Butler County. This town was laid out in an unsettled area, where a large part of the lands were disposed of "on terms which [it was said would] . . . not yield a revenue adequate to the support of a grammar school! . . . That it will attain to the rank of a second rate college, in the course of the present century, where it is now fixed, no well informed person has the courage to predict."[184] In 1818 shortly after the arrival of the Reverend James Hughes, "a man of learning, science, and piety," a grammar school was opened with six students. "Bording" was advertised at $1.50 the week.[185]

When the "teacher of the grammar school died in 1821" and the school closed, Cincinnati made a lively fight to have the school moved to that city.[186] The management of the school was accused of "stupidity and profligacy." Of $22,000 of land revenues only $1,600 had gone for teachers. "The balance has been expended principally for the service of secretaries, treasurers and surveyors, and for erecting buildings." Twenty thousand dollars

[182] *Ibid.*, September 25, 1828.
[183] The main facts in the history of Ohio University are presented in C. L. Martzolff, "Ohio University—The Historic College of the Old Northwest," in *Ohio Archaeological and Historical Society Publications,* XIX (1910), 411–45. Some interesting data on the early years of the college may be found in the William Woodbridge papers, Burton Historical Collection, Detroit Public Library.
[184] Daniel Drake, *Natural and Statistical View, or Picture of Cincinnati,* 158–59.
[185] Hamilton *Miami Herald,* November 9, 1818.
[186] In a bill providing for removal to Cincinnati it was argued that the school was no good where it was and could never be. Defenders argued that Oxford residents had bought their lands on promise of a college; besides, Cincinnati, full of paper-money maneuvering and houses of ill fame, was no fit place. *Hamilton Intelligencer and Advertiser,* February 25 1822. Many columns on the subject appeared in succeeding issues. In 1820, however, a dozen citizens of Oxford admitted, by petition, that the college had almost played out and recommended a vacation until it could get a suitable teacher. *Hamilton Gazette and Miami Register,* July 10, 1820.

would have supported two professorships and a tutor seven or eight years. The school had a bad location, was seldom heard of, and no one knew or cared anything about it.[187]

In 1824 it was announced that Miami University would open on November 1 with a president (who would teach moral philosophy and belles-lettres); a professor of mathematics, natural philosophy, and astronomy; and a teacher of languages. A large three-story brick building 60 by 85 feet, plus a 40- by 60-foot wing for study and lodging, was ready, and the trustees, acting under the eye of heaven, would administer piety, virtue, and science.[188] The school opened with the first three classes and three grammar-school classes. Its annual income at this time was about $4,000.[189]

The next year Robert Hamilton Bishop, a Presbyterian minister from the faculty of Transylvania University, became Miami's first president, and it was announced that, "God willing, the second year of Miami University will commence."[190]

At the time of its first commencement in September, 1826, the school reported 111 students;[191] at the second commencement nine A. B. degrees and three honorary A. M. degrees were conferred.[192] The faculty increased to thirteen members in 1829.

[187] *Liberty Hall and Cincinnati Gazette,* January 1, 1823.

[188] The Freshman class program: Horace, Collectanea Greca Majora, Euclid, Ancient and Modern Geography, Morrel's Rome, and Bible recitations once per week. Sophomore: Horace finished, Excerpta Latina begun, Greca Majora continued, Day's mathematical course begun, Euclid finished, Aam's Roman Antiquities, Morrel's Greece, Declamation, Bible once per week. Junior: Excerpta Latina finished, Greca Majora finished, English Composition, Day's mathematics continued, Natural philosophy and Astronomy, Tytter's Elements of Ancient and Modern History, Bible, and Declamation. Senior: Recite once a week to the Professor of Languages, Experimental Philosophy and Chemistry, Ramsey's America, Hedges' Logic, Lay's Political Economy, a course of lectures on Moral Philosophy, Themes and Forensics, and Declamation. Tuition was $10 per session, total expenses were $80 to $100 per year. *Hamilton Intelligencer and Advertiser,* September 20, 1824. The daily schedule was 5–7 A. M., 2–5 P. M. study; 7–8, 9–12 A. M. recitations; 8–9, 12–2, 5–8, meals and exercise; 9 A. M. and 8 P. M. prayers; 10 P. M.–5 A. M. sleep. There were two terms of five months each. *Hamilton Advertiser,* July 16, 1825.

[189] *Liberty Hall and Cincinnati Gazette,* January 1, 1823; Columbus *Ohio State Journal,* October 19, 1826.

[190] *Liberty Hall and Cincinnati Gazette,* September 30, 1825. The *Liberty Hall* was still critical; it noted a lack of literary excellence in the announcement that for a freshman there "will be as much Greek as may be necessary to get a moderate lesson in the Greek testament with tolerable ease."

Much of the early history of Miami is covered in James H. Rodabaugh, *Robert Hamilton Bishop* (*Ohio Historical Collections,* IV, Columbus, 1935).

[191] *Hamilton Advertiser,* September 27, 1826.

[192] One of the honorary degrees was granted "J. Hall of the Indiana State University" [Baynard Rush Hall of the Indiana State Seminary]. *Cincinnati Daily Gazette,* July 23, 1827, citing the *Hamilton Advertiser.*

At the time of the 1837 commencement, when twenty-five A. B. degrees were conferred, the school had an enrollment of 152 in which 14 states were represented.[193] By 1840 Miami had graduated more than two hundred and fifty students; during the period it was second in importance in the West only to Transylvania. In 1840 it was the largest college west of Pennsylvania. The school received no financial aid from the state nor did the state exercise any control over its policies.

In 1804 Congress granted Indiana Territory a township of land for a seminary of learning.[194] The second session of the territorial legislature "held at the Borough of Vincennes" resolved that "for as much as literature, and philosophy, furnish the most useful and pleasing occupations, improving and varying the enjoyments of prosperity, affording relief under the pressure of misfortune, and hope and consolation in the hours of death" (they would also be of great value to the Indians),[195] and incorporated Vincennes University. The Latin, Greek, French, and English languages, mathematics, natural philosophy, logic, rhetoric, and the law of nature and of nations were specified as proper studies. The trustees were required, as soon as funds permitted, to establish an institution for the education of females. A $20,000 lottery was authorized for equipment and support of the institution; professors and students were exempt from military duty. The Reverend Samuel Scott, Presbyterian minister who operated a private school at Vincennes, began instruction in 1810 (including the elementary branches), but the Indians were more interested in Tecumseh's plans than in the higher learning, and no funds were available for a female institution.[196] Although the school operated after a fashion from 1810 to 1825 when it became Knox County Seminary, the corporate organization was allowed to lapse. No state funds were appropriated for the school. In

[193] Ohio 92, Mississippi 17, Alabama 13, Kentucky 11, Indiana 7, Georgia 3, Tennessee 2, North Carolina, South Carolina, Illinois, Louisiana, Virginia, Pennsylvania, and Texas one each. *Ohio State Journal*, August 21, 1837.

[194] The law of March 4, 1804, reserved a township in each of the three districts of the Territory in which there were land offices; thus the later Michigan and Illinois territories received a township each.

[195] The trustees were "enjoined . . . to use their utmost endeavours" to get the Indians to send their children to the university; also to maintain, clothe, and educate them at its expense. Philbrick (ed.), *Laws of Indiana Territory, 1801-9*, 178-84. See also Curtis G. Shake, *A History of Vincennes University* (1928).

[196] Not added until 1856.

1822 the Indiana legislature took over the lands of this school for the new state seminary at Bloomington; two years later it declared Vincennes University no longer in existence.[197]

The enabling act for Indiana granted an additional township for a "Seminary of learning"; the legislature, January 20, 1820, chartered the "State Seminary" to be located at Bloomington, Monroe County, where President Monroe had selected the land grant. The village of about three hundred inhabitants was on the edge of settlements. After three years a two-story building 60 by 31 feet was completed at a cost of $2,400; a professor's house was also built for $891. Baynard Rush Hall, recently out of Union College and Princeton Theological Seminary, who had been visiting relatives in the New Purchase (probably with an eye out for the possible job), was elected teacher late in 1823 (or 1824).[198] When he opened school, probably May 1, 1825,[199] it was Latin and Greek rather than bookkeeping and surveying

[197] Acts of 1825 and 1827 provided for the sale of the Gibson and Monroe county lands. The old corporation was revived by an act of 1838 which contained a clause intended to prevent renewal of claim to the lands taken. Almost a century of litigation followed. In 1846 the trustees of Vincennes University were authorized to bring suit. The $30,099.66 award by a county circuit court was reversed by the Indiana Supreme Court, but the latter's decision was reversed by the United States Supreme Court in 1852. However, the only effect of the decision of the Supreme Court of the United States was to establish the justice of the claim of the university, settlement being left to the state legislature. In 1855 Vincennes recovered $66,585 (minus $16,625 for attorney fees to Samuel Judah, secretary to the trustees). The school reopened in 1853. In 1907 the General Assembly by special act awarded compensation to Vincennes University. The act was sustained by the Supreme Court of Indiana—*Hanley* v. *Sims et al.* (175 *Indiana,* 345)—in 1910, and Vincennes University was paid $120,548.

[198] According to Hall's somewhat confusing and often facetious account (*The New Purchase,* 265 ff.), among his competitors was a local citizen who could teach "sifring, reading, writing, jogger-free, surveying, grammur, spelling, definitions, parsin—," but who seemed more familiar with rendering lard than Latin. Hall's work, *The New Purchase or Seven and a Half Years in the Far West* was published in two volumes at New York and Philadelphia in 1843 under the pen name "Robert Carlton, Esq." A one-volume edition (somewhat modified from the original) was published at New Albany in 1855. The best edition is edited by James A. Woodburn (Princeton, N. J., 1916). This work, properly used, is an interesting source for the early years of the state seminary and pioneer life.

[199] For a discussion of the confusing evidence on this point, see James A. Woodburn, *History of Indiana University* (Bloomington, 1940), 16, note 10. (This work contains as the first six chapters the lectures of David D. Banta on the history of the seminary and the college from 1820 to 1850.) Main support for 1824 as the date is the report of Dr. David H. Maxwell, original sponsor of the school and president of the board, rendered to the legislature on January 2, 1828 (Indiana *House Journal,* 1827–28, p. 284), in which he mentioned May 1, 1828, as ending the first four years of the school. Newspaper accounts of the first term, second term, etc., on the other hand, point to May 1, 1825. Vincennes *Western Sun,* February 19, Indianapolis *Indiana Journal,* October 4, 1825. It does not seem probable that, as has been suggested, the trustees had held a term or two with only local notices.

which the "ten boys and young gentlemen," sometimes barefoot, received at his hands. Tuition was $5.00 per term; Hall's salary was $250 but he preached in addition. During the second year the trustees resolved that Hall also teach "English grammar, Logic, Rhetoric, Geography, Moral and Natural Philosophy, and Euclid's Elements of Geometry," but the capacity of both teacher and students had already been reached. Only the two ancient languages were taught the first three years.[200]

Early in 1827 the legislature created a Board of Visitors to visit, quiz, listen to, examine, and recommend to the trustees and General Assembly.[201] Governor James B. Ray in his December message reported that the board was well pleased with the proficiency of the scholars in science, literature, Latin, and Greek. Considering that the first two subjects had not been taught (or only for a term at most), the scholars were doing well.

Thirteen students attended the seminary the first year, fifteen the second, twenty-one the third. In May, 1827, John Hopkins Harney, of Kentucky, was elected "professor of mathematics and natural and mechanical philosophy and chemistry." A mass meeting of citizens had sought to influence the election in favor of a native or one who was possibly less of an "aristocrat and presbyterian." Harney walked from Miami, where he had recently graduated, to his new job.[202] Meanwhile, $30,000 worth of seminary lands had been sold, which, with moneys due from the state, gave the school an income of $2,000 per annum. The Governor recommended that it be made a college[203] and on January 24, 1828, Indiana College came into being.[204]

In view of the fact that democratic politicians were warning the people against the encroaching powers of the aristocracy by way of "rich men's larnin'," and that other Protestant sects were riled by the incumbency of two Presbyterians (with a possible

[200] Maxwell's report.

[201] It consisted of the governor, lieutenant governor, judges of the Supreme Court, the United States district judge, the United States district attorney, and seventeen named members.

[202] Or perhaps went to Paris, Kentucky, to pick up his bride. J. Stoddard Johnston, *Memorial History of Louisville from Its First Settlement to the Year 1896* (2 volumes. Chicago, 1896), I, 66 ff.

[203] Indianapolis *Indiana Journal*, April 3, December 11, 1827.

[204] As an intermediate step towards the creation of "the University of Indiana" contemplated in the report of the special committee of the legislature to that body in December 1821.

chair of theology in the offing), the act of 1828 was diplomatically phrased. It provided for the "education of youth in the American . . . languages" and prohibited the requirement of any particular religious opinions from professors or students, or the teaching of any sectarian tenets.[205] The religious situation was not helped, however, by the appointment in May, 1828, of Andrew Wylie, D. D., president of Washington College, Pennsylvania, to the presidency of the new college.[206] After a preaching and book-begging trip of some months, the new president was inaugurated in the autumn of 1829 and soon thereafter embarked upon the "New Departure."[207]

In his inaugural address, "Of What Advantage Is a College to the Community," President Wylie paid his respects to the professions of medicine, law, theology, and pedagogy, but did not forget to enlarge upon the advantages to that "most respectful class in society, the farmer." For the benefit of all twenty-five or thirty students he decided upon one principal study at a time, until it was completed.[208] The first catalogue (1830–31) contained two other statements of interest:

[205] The issue of sectarian lectures at the college was up for discussion in the legislature in the 1829–30 session. It appears that there had been quite a bit of trouble before Wylie's arrival and several students had seceded. Indianapolis *Indiana Journal*, January 16, 1830.

[206] The Presbyterian influence on higher education in the Northwest stemmed from Princeton and the "log colleges" of western Pennsylvania. The Reverend Thaddeus Dod had established an academy in Washington County, Pennsylvania, in the 1770's; it was incorporated in 1787 and in 1806 it became Washington College. When the Synod of Virginia in 1791 established an academy at Canonsburg, seven miles distant, the Reverend John McMillan gave up the little "Log College" which he had founded in 1773, and became its head. In 1802 Canonsburg Academy became Jefferson College, modeled upon Princeton's charter and laws.

Andrew Wylie, a farm boy of Irish descent, graduated from Jefferson College with honors in 1807, shortly became a tutor, then president in 1812. In 1817 he became president of the rival Washington College. Efforts to merge the two colleges failed, and Wylie was in a ticklish position when the offer of the Indiana College presidency came. Hall and Harney probably had suggested his name; also possibly Senator William Hendricks, who was a sophomore at Jefferson when Wylie was a senior. Wylie came to Indiana on horseback in the autumn of 1828 to make a survey of the situation, and finally gave his requested "speedy answer" of acceptance March 20, 1829.

For summary of the Western Pennsylvania influence, see Miller, *Genesis of Western Culture*, Chapter III; more detailed are the early accounts by Joseph Smith, *Old Redstone; or Historical Sketches of Western Presbyterianism* (Philadelphia, 1854), and *History of Jefferson College: Including an Account of the Early "Log-Cabin" Schools, and the Canonsburg Academy; with Biographical Sketches . . .* (Pittsburgh, 1857).

[207] Wylie had also been seeking funds "to procure an apparatus" for the college. He collected 235 assorted volumes on history, geography, belles-lettres, and moral philosophy "all new . . . and estimated to be very low at $600."

[208] In the catalogue for 1830–31 (Bloomington, Indiana, August, 1831) the curriculum for the Preparatory Department was given: English Grammar, Arithmetic, Geography, Ross' Latin Grammar, Viri Romae, Caesar, Mairs' Introduction. Com-

1. The students are required to assemble every morning shortly after day-break for prayers, and to receive such intimations concerning their duty as the president may from time to time, deem necessary.

2. It cannot be concealed that in some of the older states, where colleges have been multiplied to an injurious degree, the desire to attract numbers has operated to depress the standard of education; and the emulation, in too many cases, seems to have been which institution should surpass the rest in shortening the way to a Diploma. It is the ambition and will be the aim of those intrusted with the affairs of this Institution, to pursue an opposite course, one, which, should it meet with encouragement from the community, will render their Diploma, in every case, *a true document.*

The "day-break" requirement was soon abandoned; the "true-document" aspiration has never met overwhelming support from the people of any state.

At the first commencement of the college in the autumn of 1830 four students rendered their compositions and got their degrees. While they were speaking the comment was heard, ". . . he has been only one year from the stump." An outsider reported that "the rubbish had in a great measure been removed by the residence of a single year at a literary institution, and the latent fire of genius which hitherto had been smothered, now began to burst forth in all its native brilliancy, to the astonishment of those who knew the rustic before he exchanged the farm and the shop for the halls of science." All this was the more remarkable in that it existed in a country so new.[209]

Next to a mean church fight a college faculty fight has its points; combine the two with political, personal, and local

---

positions in English. First Class: Sallust, Cicero de Officiis, Cicero's Select Orations, Ovid, Virgil, Horace, Juvenal, Cicero De Oratore, Valpy's Greek Grammar. Compositions, Latin Themes. Freshman Class: Greek Testament, Minora, Majora 1st vol. Majora 2d vol. commenced. Compositions in English and Latin. Greek Theses. Sophomore Class: Majora finished, The Illiad. Colburn's Algebra, Cambridge Mathematics. Compositions and Themes, as in the Freshman Class. Junior Class: Mathematics finished. Mechanics, Astronomy, Physics, Mathematical and Physical Geography. Dissertations, and Themes and compositions, as before. Senior Class: Moral and Mental Philosophy, Evidences of Christianity in connexion with Natural Religion, Rhetoric, with a review of select portions of the Greek, Latin and English Classics, Logic, Political Economy, Constitution of the United States. Dissertations, and composition, in English and Latin. To such as may wish it, and who have completed the Latin course, Hebrew and French will be taught and if any student shall desire to make himself acquainted with any one or more particular branches of study, without completing the entire course, he shall be at liberty so to do, attaching himself for that purpose to any class which he may find convenient.
Any student who could read or write was admitted to the preparatory department. Indianapolis *Indiana Journal,* June 2, 1830.
[209] From a description written by a citizen of Illinois who was present. Vandalia *Illinois Intelligencer,* November 13, 1830.

jealousies, and the result is a scrap calculated to satisfy the pugnacious, partisan, and sensitive natives in high degree. Into such a fight the masterful and uncompromising Wylie plunged a few months after his arrival. The community split, faculty appealed to students, the student body took sides, numerous petitions were sent to the legislature.[210] Since the genial Professor Hall had already resigned and was on a temporary continuation of tenure, the quasi tragic but entirely comic fracas finally precipitated in a struggle between the dictatorial president and the silent, patient, and equally combative Harney.[211] Wylie was full of Latin, dignity, and Calvinism; Harney, was fortified with mathematics, a very formidable mien, and—a pocket knife. In chapel one celebrated Saturday, the president insinuated that Harney, who was sitting on the platform whittling on a stick, as was his custom, was preparing to stab him in the back. Confusion followed, "College was dismissed," and things developed apace. Some time later the calculating man of science and the determined man of moral philosophy and polite literature arranged to meet on a foot log across the little branch which flowed through the village,[212] and the president, relying more upon his early training than the classics, pushed Harney off into the water and mud. Professors being easier to replace than presidents the board soon dismissed Harney, who later became professor of mathematics at Hanover College, president of Louisville College, and the distinguished editor of the *Louisville Democrat*, one of the ancestors of the *Courier Journal*.

Repercussions from the battle lasted in local society and state educational circles for some years,[213] but though it lost a number of students, the college survived; it even survived the cholera

[210] A number of students had followed Wylie to Indiana from Washington College. It was said that these "foreigners" were better dressed than the natives, had more money, and were withal perhaps a little wickeder; that the "girls of the village, attracted by these glittering parts, gave their smiles more freely to the former than to the latter."

[211] Wylie apparently did not entirely follow his own precepts: ". . . enactments are never readily submitted to, which have no other foundation than the arbitrary will—the 'Sic volo, sic jubeo, stet pro ratione voluntas,' of the tyrant ruler. The yoke of authority is doubly galling when it is imposed by folly: and I have never yet known a fool, who was not also, to the extent of his power, a tyrant. In proof of this take the fact, that every stupid booby in the country, plays the despot in his family." "Lecture on College Government," in *Transactions of the Western Literary Institute and College of Professional Teachers*, 1838, p. 146.

[212] Now the Jordan River and mostly encased in concrete.

[213] See, for instance, letter by "Aliquis" in the Indianapolis *Indiana Journal*, February 3, 1835.

epidemic of 1833, and an attempt to make it into a manual labor institution. Since the school had income from a fund of some $60,000, a state appropriation was considered unnecessary. Besides, charges of sectarianism still circulated.[214] Nevertheless, upon recommendation of Governor Noah Noble in 1837, the legislature, on February 13, 1838, changed the title of the college to Indiana University. The act specified the education of youth in the "American, learned, and foreign languages, the useful arts, sciences (including law and medicine), and literature."

Whereas the Indians of Indiana Territory were expected to benefit from the blessings of literature and philosophy as dispensed by an institution of higher learning, the Indians of Michigan Territory were expected to furnish the means for establishing such an institution. By the treaty at Fort Meigs in 1817, Lewis Cass representing the General Government, the Ottawa, Potawatomi, and Chippewa tribes granted six sections of lands for education, half to go to the college at Detroit and half to St. Anne's Church, which was interested in education. Since selection of lands under the Congressional grant of 1804 ran into difficulties because of confusion of Indian titles, Congress in 1826 gave Michigan Territory two townships in replacement of the one granted earlier. A committee located the lands on the Maumee River at a point which later became the city of Toledo. In his first report the superintendent of public instruction estimated that the two townships of land would bring an endowment of $921,000 which would yield $64,912 per year for the support of a university. Pierce's estimate was not realized.[215]

In 1817 the versatile, stubborn Judge Augustus B. Woodward's brilliant mind gave birth to an idea even more intricate than his plans for the streets of Detroit. His plan for a Catholepistemiad or University of Michigania, though somewhat fanciful, was more than a historical curiosity.[216] Whether with

[214] In 1834 the Methodist Conference memorialized the legislature and stated that "one common hue, one common religious creed, characterized every member" of the faculty. The sectarian complexion of the school as well as the spirit of localism was to affect the general support of the school by the people of the state for many years.

[215] By 1843 the total proceeds were $137,000.

[216] Elias Augustus Brevoort Woodward was a graduate of Kings College, 1793, and a friend of Thomas Jefferson. In 1816 he published a book entitled *System of Universal Science. Consideration of the Differences of Human Knowledge and on the Classification and Nomenclature of the Sciences.* The spine bore the title *Encatholepistemia.* Gabriel Richard, graduate of Saintone College, France, and the University of Angers (philosophy and theology), had come to the United States

tongues in cheeks we do not know but the Governor and Judges "in the plenitude of their wisdom, arose to the following pitch of legislation."

Be it enacted by the Governor and the Judges of the Territory of Michigan, That there shall be in the said Territory a catholepistemiad, or university, denominated the catholepistemiad, or university of Michigania. The catholepistemiad, or university of Michigania, shall be composed of thirteen Didaxiim, or professorships: First, a Didaxia, or professorship, of Catholepistemia, or Universal Science, the Didactor, or professor, of which shall be President of the Institution; second, a Didaxia, or professorship, of anthropoglossica, or Literature, embracing all the Epistemiim, or Sciences relative to Language; third, a Didaxia, or professorship, of Mathematica, or Mathematics; fourth, a Didaxia, or professorship, of physiognostica, or Natural History; fifth, a Didaxia, or professorship, of physiophia, or natural Philosophy; sixth, a Didaxia, or professorship, of Astronomia, or Astronomy; seventh, a Didaxia, or professorship, of Chymia, or Chemistry; eighth, a Didaxia, or professorship, of Iatrica, or Medical Sciences; ninth, a Didaxia, or professorship, of Aeconomica, or Economical Sciences; tenth, a Didaxia, or professorship, of Ethica, or Ethical Sciences; eleventh, a Didaxia, or professorship, of Polemitactica, or Military Sciences; twelfth, a Didaxia, or professorship, of diegetica, or Historical Sciences; and thirteenth, a Didaxia, or professorship, of Ennaica, or Intellectual Sciences embracing all the Epistemiim, or Sciences relative to the minds of animals, to the human mind, to spiritual existences, to the Deity, and to Religion, the didactor or professors of which shall be Vice-President of the Institution.[217]

in 1792 and to Detroit in 1798. Soon after the creation of Michigan Territory he began urging the Governor and Judges to create a "College of Literature, Science and Arts . . . for the encouragement of literature, scientific knowledge and useful arts." In 1808 Woodward was ready to act, but nothing was done at the time. William Woodbridge, appointed secretary of the Territory in 1814, became a close friend of Father Richard.

John Monteith, A. B. Jefferson College 1813, attended Princeton Theological Seminary, then came to Detroit. (He returned East for ordination in 1817.) Father Richard took Monteith, a kindred spirit, under his wing; even furnished space for a Protestant meeting place in St. Anne's Church. These men were the principal individuals behind the idea of the University of Michigan.

Early history of the university is well outlined in William A. Spill, "The University of Michigan: Beginnings," in *Michigan History Magazine*, XII (1928), 635–61, XIII (1929), 41–54, 227–44; and in William L. Jenks, "The Real Origin of the University of Michigan," in *Michigan Alumnus*, XXIX (1923), 565–69, 597–601. See also the *Michigan Pioneer and Historical Collections*, index, for various accounts. The older histories, Andrew C. McLaughlin, *History of Higher Education in Michigan* (1891), and Burke A. Hinsdale, *A History of the University of Michigan* (Ann Arbor, 1906), have been largely supplanted by Wilfred Byron Shaw's *The University of Michigan . . .* (New York, 1920), and *The University of Michigan, an Encyclopedic Survey, Part One* (Ann Arbor, 1941).

[217] Quoted in Spill, "The University of Michigan: Beginnings," in *Michigan History Magazine*, XII, 652–54. The *Detroit Gazette*, January 15, 1819, published the charter without the technical names. The next issue contained a table of professorships and an elaborate explanation of the epistemic system, probably submitted by Judge Woodward.

The didactors were to be appointed by the Governor and receive salaries fixed by law. Public taxes were increased 15 per cent, and that portion of all future taxes was set aside for the maintenance of the university, which was further authorized to conduct four successive lotteries "deducting from the prizes in the same fifteen per centum." The new institution had neither students nor endowment. John Monteith, the Presbyterian minister, was made president with seven professorships, and Father Gabriel Richard held the remaining six; the salary for each professorship was $12.50 per year. A building was erected, the common school and a classical school were opened, and the "First College of Michigania" was established at Detroit.[218]

In 1821 the act of 1817 was repealed and the Catholepistemiad became the University of Michigan, under a board of twenty-one trustees. Three years later an advertisement in the *Detroit Gazette* stated that A. S. Wells had been engaged to teach Greek, Latin, mathematics, geography, and grammar. The editor said that "another attempt is about to be made to render this institution useful to the community."[219] Although the Michigan Supreme Court later ruled that the university had maintained a continuous corporate existence,[220] the first University of Michigan failed to get started.

Superintendent Pierce's report on a state system of education recommended a university to head it. By law of March 18, 1837, was created the modern University of Michigan at Ann Arbor, to consist of the three departments, one of literature, science and the arts, one of law, and one of medicine.[221] The regents, in co-

---

[218] Private donations and unused fire-relief funds were used. *Detroit Gazette,* October 10, 1817 and succeeding issues.

[219] October 8, 1824.

[220] *Regents of the University of Michigan* v. *Board of Education,* 4 *Michigan,* 213 (1856). Not until the 1920's, however, did the University of Michigan take advantage of this decision and change the date of its founding from 1837 to 1817.

[221] Professorships in the department of literature were: ancient languages; rhetoric and oratory; philosophy, history and logic; moral philosophy and natural theology, including the history of all religions; political economy; mathematics; natural philosophy; chemistry and pharmacy; geology and mineralogy; botany and zoology; fine arts; and civil engineering and architecture.

The bill originally contained provision for a professorship of theology, but when this was protested on the grounds of unconstitutionality, it was changed to "natural theology" as above. The *Detroit Daily Advertiser,* February 24, 1837, held that the Michigan constitution did not apply, since the institution was to be maintained by United States land grants. "No man can be liberally educated, who has not acquainted himself in some degree with the manifold proofs of the Divine wisdom and benevolence. . . ."

operation with the state superintendent, were authorized to establish branches in the different counties; these schools were supposed to serve as preparatory and teacher-training schools. In June the regents resolved to establish a branch in each senatorial district and to provide $500 toward compensation for a teacher in each.[222] The Pontiac branch was opened the same year; in 1838 branches were opened at Monroe, Kalamazoo, Detroit, and Niles. White Pigeon and Tecumseh followed in 1839, Romeo in 1842. There was a department for female education at all the branches except Niles, Pontiac, and Detroit. There was also a preparatory department at Ann Arbor, opened by two of the professors in 1840, which was sometimes called a branch.[223]

The maximum number of branches in operation at any one time was seven. The branches, with their emphasis upon the higher courses of English education and the classics, were, like the university itself, regarded by many as aristocratic schools. The university was criticized for not entitling students of modern languages and science to the highest honors, the same as those who pursued the classics. "What is most useful? Give the student ideas, learn him to think correctly, and he will express his thoughts with accuracy."[224] Since the first board of regents was not controlled by members of the clergy, the criticism was made that the institution was an infidel affair. To obviate this, ministers of various denominations were appointed to professorships of several of the branches, and four of the important professorships at the university were filled with ministers. When the branches proved a heavy drain upon the university's funds, the regents wisely decided not to dissipate its income and jeopardize its own existence.[225] Support was withdrawn a few years later (1846), and the constitution of 1850 freed the university of its branches.

Though the members of the board of regents were novices at the education business, they started out like veterans; at their first meeting they planned a building of "truly magnificent design"

[222] *Detroit Daily Advertiser,* June 26, 1837.

[223] By the original plan, probably Isaac Crary's idea, any county with sufficient population, which provided a suitable building, was to be eligible for a branch. "Branches" were also located at Grand Rapids, Parma, Jackson, Ypsilanti, Utica, Coldwater, and Mackinaw, but these received no support from the state.

[224] *Ibid.,* March 3, 8, 1837.

[225] On the branches see A. D. P. Van Buren, "History of the Old Branches of the Michigan University," in *Michigan Pioneer and Historical Collections,* V (1882), 43–46; routine in the Kalamazoo branch is described in *ibid.,* 418–22.

which would have used all the funds realized from previous land sales, or half the amount expected. Superintendent Pierce thought that qualified teachers, scientific apparatus, and libraries were also essential, and put a damper on the idea. In 1838 the legislature granted the university a loan of $100,000. The same year Asa Gray was appointed professor of botany and zoology; with $5,000 allotted for the purpose by the regents, he collected a library of some 3,700 items. The board also bought the mineral collections of Baron Lederer for $4,000, and a set of Audubon's *Birds of North America* for $970. A professorship of languages was added, and the university advertised as open for business in the summer of 1841. Candidates for admission were required to "adduce satisfactory evidence of good moral character and sustain an examination in geography, arithmetic, the elements of algebra, the grammar of the English, Latin, and Greek languages, the exercise and readers of Andrews, Cornelius Nepos, Vita Washingtonii, Sallust, Cicero's Orations, Jacob's Greek Reader, and the evangelists." Six students must have proved their cases, for in September they met with the faculty of two to begin pursuit of their studies.

Despite the special encouragement given Illinois for a seminary of learning by its enabling act,[226] it was the last state of the Old Northwest to establish one. Governor Bond in 1820 had recommended caution: "Whilst, however, we indulge the pleasing expectation of establishing a college within the state, let us not be hurried to so premature a commencement of the undertaking as to jeopardize the means provided for the purpose." A dozen years later the same George Forquer who doubted whether the people would support a coercive system of common schools, did believe that the time had come to utilize the means granted by the General Government for a "State University or Seminary of Learning." From the sales (past and future) of the two townships of land, the Three Per Cent Fund, and accumulated interest, he estimated a fund of $112,523—ample to build and endow a school which would promote the cause of learning, give the state

[226] That one sixth of the 3 per cent from sales of public lands within the state be set aside for this purpose. The enabling act granted an entire township in addition to the one previously granted the Territory by Congress by the law of 1804. The Illinois Agricultural and Mechanical College was created by law in 1866; the Illinois Industrial University was created by law in 1867. The latter school opened in 1868, the former in 1873.

prestige abroad, and also be the means of "converting some one of our villages into a populous and wealthy city."[227] Governor Joseph Duncan in 1834 urged the legislature to establish a state university, but legislative support was not forthcoming at this time; it was to require another quarter of a century. One of the reasons for the delay was the number of denominational colleges founded in the state in the 1830's.

By law of December 8, 1836, the first Wisconsin territorial legislature created a body politic and corporate, "The Wisconsin University." The board of twenty-one trustees, to which members of all religious denominations might be elected, was empowered to establish such colleges, academies, and schools as they thought proper.[228] Congress granted two townships in 1838 and the legislature selected a committee to locate the lands.[229] In July when Bishop Jackson Kemper of the Episcopal Church came through Madison, he said, relative to a late act of the legislature to establish "an university here": "Some of the Episcopalians are trustees —and we must look into this subject as it is decidedly important."[230] The citizens of Green Bay were also eager to get the land grant proceeds and the same year secured a charter for the "Wisconsin University of Green Bay"; the Protestant Episcopal Church was willing to turn over its mission-school buildings for the purpose.[231] No state college was opened in the territorial period; only Indiana and Michigan, of the states of the Northwest, had, before 1840, taken steps to realize the Jeffersonian idea of a state university as the capstone of an educational structure.[232]

[227] Details of Forquer's proposal may be found in the Springfield *Sangamo Journal*, July 12, 1832.

[228] *Milwaukee Advertiser*, March 25, 1837. See also Merle Curti and Vernon Carstensen, *The University of Wisconsin* . . . (Madison, 1949), Chapter II.

[229] When the committee did not act promptly the *Wisconsin Enquirer*, May 11, 1839, said that in justice to the interests of the Territory and the settlers it should get busy.

[230] "A Trip through Wisconsin in 1838," in *Wisconsin Magazine of History*, VIII (1924–25), 432.

[231] Green Bay *Wisconsin Democrat*, February 3, 1838.

[232] Ohio University was not a state university in the sense of being controlled by state-initiated policies and supported by the state or lands granted to the state. In 1829 the Ohio legislature in a memorial to Congress for two townships admitted that Ohio "has no adequate means of creating and fostering scientific institutions, without resorting to the odious measure of direct taxation." "Ohio has received no grant of this character, unless the land included in the Ohio Company's Purchase and Symmes' Purchase should be so considered, but neither the state nor the inhabitants of those districts have ever thus regarded them." Quoted in Miller, "History of Educational Legislation in Ohio," in *Ohio Archaeological and Historical Society Publications*, XXVII, 110–11.

More important in influence and numbers than the state colleges were the sectarian schools. In fact many people could not disassociate education from religion; most of the churchmen thought that higher education without religion was another idea of the devil's.

Best prepared, organized, and most aggressive in the college field were the Presbyterians; they either founded or controlled the majority of the schools, including the state colleges.

The College of Alma (New Athens) was chartered by Ohio in 1825; the next year its name was changed to Franklin College. The Reverend John Walker, associate Presbyterian minister of Cadiz, cultivated a strong abolition attitude in the college, but when as a result of debt it was sold at auction, it fell into the hands of an antiabolition group who ran it for a time under the name of Providence College.

Western Reserve College at Hudson (later moved to Cleveland), chartered in 1826 and opened the following year, was controlled largely by Presbyterian and Congregational ministers.[233] Charles B. Storrs, Andover graduate, became one of the first professors and later president. Storrs was of the "new-measure" or Finney-revivalist complexion. The college lacked both funds and students; three years after founding it had only six of the latter in its college department; after eight years only eighty-seven including the preparatory department.

In 1826 the Salem (Indiana) Presbytery arranged with John Finley Crowe, of South Hanover, to enlarge his boarding school into a classical preparatory school. The log-cabin school which became Hanover College opened its doors on January 1, 1827.[234]

The Lane Seminary at Walnut Hills (Cincinnati) was started

---

[233] "The Western Reserve College has not yet, we believe, went into operation." Columbus *Ohio State Journal*, October 19, 1826.

At the time of the commencement of 1833, "an unfortunate state of things" existed; the faculty had split over abolition, Professor Wright had resigned, all harmony in the social circle had been destroyed. The institution had become a seat of party feuds. Ravenna *Western Courier*, September 12, 1833.

Elizur Wright, Jr., who became professor of mathematics and natural philosophy in 1828, resigned in 1833 to undertake work in connection with abolition and in time came to be known as the "father of life insurance" in the United States. Life at Western Reserve is described in *Elizur Wright*, by Philip Green Wright and Elizabeth Q. Wright (Chicago, 1937), Chapter V. See also Helen H. Kitzmiller, *One Hundred Years of Western Reserve . . .* (Hudson, Ohio, 1926).

[234] "Like its predecessor at Bloomington, about all that can be said of it during the next quarter of a century is that it survived." Esarey, *History of Indiana*, I, 332. By 1840 Hanover had about forty students of college status.

by individual enterprise—the Rev. James Kemper, Ebenezer and
William A. Lane, New Orleans merchants, and others—and
chartered in 1829. It combined manual labor, literary, and theological exercises. Arthur Tappan, New York merchant and abolitionist, was one of its supporters. Lyman Beecher, then preaching
in a Congregational church in Boston, was "Presbyterianized"
and made president in 1832. A leading editorial in the *Cincinnati
Daily Gazette* expressed confidence that, though Presbyterian, the
school would not be

dwarfed and crippled by a narrow spirit of bigotry and exclusiveness. . . .
We hope the day is past never to return, when reference to *any sect* or
denomination, prejudice or self righteousness can put the question whether
any good thing can come out of Nazareth? . . . Although we of the West
are not so skeptical or destitute of high toned moral and religious character
as a learned and distinguished jurist and his friends at Boston would have
us believe, yet we present a wide field for earnest and affectionate labors
of sincere, intelligent, honest, and devoted Christian teachers.[235]

Many students came from New England and New York; the
enrollment reached ninety in 1832. Some of the Easterners petitioned against the serving of coffee, a harmful and expensive
drink, at the boardinghouse. Beecher had his church troubles and
Lane Seminary got into difficulties as a result of antislavery activities on the part of its students. When restraining measures
against antislavery agitation were taken in 1834, forty or fifty
students left school; about thirty of them later joined up with
Oberlin.[236]

The Reverend John M. Ellis, missionary in the western country since 1826, bought eighty acres at Jacksonville, Illinois, in

[235] December 28, 1832.
[236] Theodore Weld and other zealous antislavery students had debated immediate emancipation both at school and at large. Beecher had hoped that the excitement
would die down and that Cincinnati citizens would have no serious cause for complaint. Even James Hall, tolerant as regards Catholicism, Beecher's *bete noir,*
thought matters had gone too far. "We have seen boys at school wearing paper
caps, flourishing wooden swords, and fancying themselves for the moment, endued
with the prowess of Hector and Achilles . . . but this is the first instance, that we
have ever known, of a set of young gentlemen at school, dreaming themselves
into full-grown patriots, and setting seriously to work, to organize a wide-spread
political revolution. . . . Colleges are public property. . . . It is . . . *unfair.*
We object to the precedent." "Education and Slavery," in *Western Monthly Magazine,* II (1834), 268–73. The crisis broke when Beecher and Calvin Stowe were
away and only the Reverend J. Biggs, professor of church history and an anti-
abolitionist, was left. He, the citizens, and trustees acted. One professor, John
Morgan, was dismissed and the expulsion of Weld considered; the antislavery
society was ordered disbanded. Almost to a man the student body arose and left
the seminary. Ministers, newspapers, and citizens divided on the fight.

1828, and proceeded to erect a seminary of learning. His worries regarding the uneducated ministry of the West reached listening ears in the East and inspired seven young Yale theological men, Congregationalists and Presbyterians, to come to Macedonia. In 1829 they collected several thousand dollars from local residents and eastern nonresident landowners.[237] When early the next year it was announced that a building was almost ready for the "pupils," the *Illinois Intelligencer* wrote:

What an enlivening prospect dawns upon Illinois. In a part of our country, where the first cabin was erected but nine years ago, and among the prairies and groves which at that time were tenanted only by the wild deer and the wolf, a College has sprung into existence, as if by enchantment, which promises to be an honor to science and to our State. We hail it to be an omen of brighter days, and look forward with hope and pride to the time when the genial light of education shall be brought to every door in Illinois. . . . Our children will be educated; and the moral character of our State will rise with the increase of its physical strength.[238]

Julian Sturtevant opened the little preparatory school to about a dozen students in 1830; later in the year the Reverend Edward Beecher came as president. Without waiting for a charter (the Illinois Jacksonians had not yet overcome their fear of corporations in 1830), the Illinois group organized a college class in 1830; in 1835 Illinois College received a charter and graduated its first class.[239] These were the first degrees given in the state. The following term forty students were enrolled in the college,[240] probably twice as many in the preparatory department. The latter was abandoned in 1839, at which time the *Daily Chicago American* referred to the school as the only college in Illinois.[241]

[237] The *Quarterly Register of the American Educational Society* (November, 1830) said $13,000, and reported (May, 1833) $46,000 raised in the East by 1833. The *Illinois Intelligencer,* January 2, 1830, listed the original endowment at $16,000. The "Yale Band" were Theron Baldwin, John F. Brooks, Mason Grosvenor, Elisha Jenner, William Kirby, J. M. Sturtevant, and Asa Turner.

[238] January 2, 1830.

[239] Richard Yates, Civil War governor of Illinois, and Jonathan Edwards Spillman, author of the popular music of "Sweet Afton."

[240] *Alton Spectator,* February 12, 1836.

[241] *Peoria Register,* October 6, 1839; *Daily Chicago Democrat,* August 12, 1839. Although there were twelve "colleges" in Illinois by 1840, Illinois College was the only one granting degrees. The early history of Illinois College is sketched in James G. K. McClure, "Some Pastors and Pastorates during the Century of Presbyterianism in Illinois," in *Journal of the Illinois State Historical Society,* XIII (1920–21), 5–6. See also Theron Baldwin, *Historical Sketch of the Origin, Progress, and Wants, of Illinois College* (New York, 1832). The best history is Charles Henry Rammelkamp, *Illinois College; a Centennial History* (New Haven, 1928).

Illinois College ran into religious and anti-Yankee jealousies: strict Presbyterians distrusted the Yale–N. W. Taylor brand of theology; Beecher, Sturtevant, and William Kirby were accused of heresy in the Jacksonville Presbytery; and Peter Cartwright made fun of learned Presbyterian ministers who could not preach. Of the men connected with the early history of the college, Jonathan Baldwin Turner, brother of Asa, was the most remarkable intellectually. Doomed to be remembered best for his promotion of the Osage orange for hedges, he was in his day a keen analyst of men and affairs, broad-minded in religion and politics, and generally a distinct cut above most.

Two other Illinois colleges were conceived by the Presbyterian-Congregationalist influence in the 1830's. The Reverend Gideon Blackburn planned to enter lands for eastern investors at $2.00, take a commission for himself, and use the balance above minimum price to endow a theological seminary at Carlinville. The 17,000 acres accumulated for the purpose proved inadequate when the depression hit, so the project was delayed about twenty years. The other, the plan of the Reverend George W. Gale, a new-school Presbyterian of New York, was for a manual labor–study combination, to be financed through purchase of a township, laying off a townsite, and sale of lots.[242] The result was Knox College, incorporated in 1837. Within a year some forty students were enrolled in the academy; the collegiate department opened in 1843.

In November, 1832, the Reverend James Thomson, of Crawfordsville, Indiana, called together nine young men who decided to found a college some place in the Wabash country. Thomson and his brother were Miami graduates. Among the three other ministers present were John M. Ellis, Dartmouth 1822, Andover Theological Seminary 1825, formerly of Jacksonville, Illinois, and Edmund O. Hovey, Dartmouth 1828, Andover 1831.[243] The Presbyterianism of Wabash was tinged with Congregational-

---

[242] The Reverend George W. Gale, of New York, who founded the Oneida Academy in 1827, thought himself the originator of the system of "manual labor with study," of having the same hands become equally expert in handling the plow, hoe, ax, scythe, Virgil, Cicero, Euclid, and Paley. In 1830 he wrote to Charles Grandison Finney that the system would "be to the moral world what the lever of Archimedes, could he have found a fulcrum, would have been to the natural." Robert Samuel Fletcher, *A History of Oberlin College from its Foundation through the Civil War* (2 volumes. Oberlin, 1943), I, 42.

[243] Six of the Andover class of 1831 were ordained together and charged by the president to "build a college in the Mississippi Valley." They joined a dozen others, "The Band of Western Men," sent out by the American Home Missionary Society.

ism. The enthusiastic young missionaries believed that only a college could save the West from freethinkers, Catholics, Methodists, and the conservatism and ignorance of the Old Lights. A public meeting was held, some subscriptions pledged, but application for a charter ran into opposition in the legislature of 1833–34. As a result the charter specified nonsectarian teaching and that donors be permitted to vote for trustees. A building was completed and in December, 1833, Caleb Mills, also of Andover, taught the first class. The following spring the announcement of the summer term of "Wabash Manual Labor College and Teachers Seminary" stated that the trustees had arranged for students to labor one to three hours daily and "thus preserve their muscular energy and contribute very essentially to lessen the expense of their education."[244]

The plan to have the students work did not work out very well. "Making rails, cutting wood, clearing ground, providing copper stuff," and the like, at five cents an hour led to no overproduction. In 1839 the trustees dropped the "Manual Labor" designation, and adopted "Wabash College" as the name of the school. Professors of science and mathematics were appointed in 1834; the next year Elihu W. Baldwin, also of Andover Theological Seminary, accepted the presidency. The first college class began in 1835. Early the next year President Baldwin wrote: "The prospects of Wabash College do not fall short of my most sanguine calculations. We have five young men, all of good talents and decided piety, in our Freshman class, who are looking forward to the ministry. I find the ministers in this neighborhood an excellent class of brethren. The churches are small, the country is mostly covered with a thick forest; but a spirit of enterprise is abroad, which will ultimately realize the best hopes of our Eastern benefactor."[245] In 1840 the scientific and preparatory departments had 76 students, the classical, 24; there were 6 in the graduating class.[246]

[244] Board was $1.00 per week not including washing; room $1.00 per session; tuition $7.50. Indianapolis *Indiana Journal,* May 10, 1834.

[245] Baldwin to Absalom Peters, January 19, 1836. Papers of the American Home Missionary Society.

[246] In 1840, the year of President Baldwin's death, the assets of the college were: 70 acres of campus, 169 acres of Illinois land, 240 of Indiana land, two buildings listed at $15,000, apparatus and library $1,500, permanent fund $4,500, subscriptions due $5,000 to $6,000.

Many of the documents on the early history of Wabash are reproduced in James I. Osborne and Theodore G. Gronert, *Wabash College, the First Hundred Years, 1832–1932* (Crawfordsville, 1932).

One of the noted, and probably most notorious of the colleges of the West, was Oberlin, conceived by John Jay Shipherd, a Finneyite Presbyterian revivalist from New York, and his apprentice minister-student Philo Penfield Stewart, as part of the Oberlin Colony plan on the Western Reserve.[247] "God greatly prospered" Shipherd on an eastern trip and a gift of land and some cash was acquired. To facilitate the work-study idea the school was located in the woods nine miles out of Elyria, Ohio, in 1833. The first class met in December in the boardinghouse, the only building in the colony aside from a number of cabins. Among the small herd of work- and milk-producing cattle acquired were "Scrawney," "Scrawney's Mate," "Fire Brains," and "Hollow Horn." In 1834 the legislature incorporated the "Oberlin Presbyterian Society of Russia" (township) and the Oberlin Collegiate Institute, which planned for an academy, with male and female departments, a college, and a theological seminary.[248] James Dascomb, M. D., arrived as professor of chemistry and botany, and his wife became principal of the female department. Within a year the school claimed fifty of its thousand acres cleared, one building finished, another under construction, and one hundred students—all in the preparatory department.[249] Nevertheless, the school was in financial distress; Shipherd solved the problem by going to Cincinnati and getting the "glorious good fellows" who had seceded from Lane Seminary. Among the conditions which the seceders stipulated for joining up were that the Reverend Asa Mahan be secured as president, Charles Grandison Finney, key spark to the millennial revivalist group, as professor of theology, and John Morgan, their friend at Lane,

[247] Named after a French pastor whose life was published by the American Sunday School Union in 1830.

The *History of Oberlin College* by Robert Samuel Fletcher, previously cited, is perhaps the most thorough, complete, and best documented of any of the histories of the colleges of the Northwest.

[248] Shipherd had conferred with the Reverend George W. Gale regarding the latter's Oneida Institute manual-labor experiment; also with William Woodbridge, of Boston, an advocate of Fellenberg's Swiss experiments.

"The grand (but not exclusive) objects of the Oberlin Institute, are the education of gospel ministers and pious school teachers." Announcement in *Ohio Atlas and Elyria Advertiser,* October 17, 1833, and elsewhere.

[249] *Christian Advocate* in *Piqua Western Courier,* March 21, 1835. For $150 churches or individuals might establish "permanent scholarships"; "indigents" were expected to be taken care of by donors. This plan was soon abandoned. Stewart hoped to aid financially by his inventions which students would manufacture. Best known of these was the Oberlin Cooking Stove, a few of which were sold.

as a member of the faculty; also that they have freedom of speech and the promise of admission of Negroes to the school.

Shipherd again went East, got the men and the money, too, but from that time on Oberlin was in hot water up to its eyebrows—and loved it. Even the community was shocked. Besides abolition the school went in for "sanctification," "physiological reform," female reformers, coeducation, and general propaganda. The original rules had prohibited traveling on the Sabbath (penalty expulsion), using tobacco, and "tight dressing"; now were added attempts to repress the horrors of meat eating and tea drinking. (Those students who insisted on meat finally got some after almost a year of waiting.) Even the use of butter was questionable. The idea in the mid 1830's, as later expressed by one of Oberlin's critics, was to see "*who can live the longest* and eat the *least amount of wholesome* food."

Oberlin was criticized as unorthodox, as neglecting the classics, as a source of Whiggery, as a sink of iniquity, and seat of moral corruption. The more orthodox Western Reserve College at Hudson was jealous of Oberlin's success and took regular pot shots at her weaknesses.[250] The curriculum was suspected of inadequacy; as a result, in 1838, the American Education Society withdrew financial aid from Oberlin students. Lyman Beecher, of Lane Seminary, in an address delivered at Miami, called Oberlin an "extensive, wholesale, intellectual manufactory" which had "all the departments of instruction; male and female, from the infant school till the topstone is laid of the university." Discussing the dangers of confusing church and state the *Cleveland Advertiser* used Oberlin as a horrible example: ". . . a theological institution; and we defy a contradiction of the assertion, when we declare that if the members of that seminary had served their God with half the zeal they have served the cause of Whiggery, they might have saved a hundred souls a piece, by this time," and perhaps themselves as well.[251]

In 1837 a dismissed freethinking student, Delazon Smith, published at Cleveland a pamphlet under the cover title of *Oberlin*

---

[250] By 1841 Oberlin had more than five hundred students, Western Reserve only 140.

[251] October 20, 1836. The Hudson *Ohio Observer* (published as the *Cleveland Observer*, 1837–40) contained many articles and editorials on the Oberlin heresy.

Unmasked.[252] This was too choice to pass unnoticed. Faculty and students were accused of Negro worship, advocating miscegenation, being ranters, desperadoes, and bloodsuckers; the men and women students were charged with other practices more erotic than matriculating in the same classes.

Less spectacular but more serious were the attacks of Professor John P. Cowles, defender of the classics and opponent of diet reform and coeducation, who had been dismissed after a clash with Mahan. He published a series of sixteen letters in the *Cleveland Observer* in 1839–40. The peculiar Oberlin doctrines were taken to pieces, the lack of free discussion emphasized. He pointed out that the tyrannic Mahan and Finney had become slightly confused as to who was what: were they Oberlin, Oberlin God, and God they? It was small wonder that the Ohio legislature in 1839–40 was considering the recall of the Oberlin Institute charter. As Finney wrote in later life: "The history of Oberlin has been very romantic. If it were written it would prove that facts are sometimes stranger than fiction! . . . it reminds me of the saying 'a little one shall chase a thousand'. . . ."

The financial foundations of these Presbyterian colleges were not as strong as the religious and educational zeal of their founders. In 1843 the Society for Promoting Collegiate and Theological Education in the West, of which Theron Baldwin, formerly principal of the Monticello Female Seminary and editor of the *Common School Advocate*, was financial secretary, took Marietta (chartered in 1832 as the Marietta Collegiate Institute and Western Teachers Seminary), Illinois, Western Reserve, Wabash, and Lane Seminary under its wing. In fact, this society was organized to get good Yankee-"Presbygationalist" money for the sound colleges and see that none of it went to ultraist experimental stations such as Oberlin.

Baptists and Methodists, though full of the evangelical spirit, were not so long on colleges. Many of them agreed with Alexander Campbell that an educated minister was simply the assumption of "a sanctimonious air, a holy gloom . . . a pious sedateness . . . a kind of angelic demeanor in his gait, and a seraphic

---

[252] Full title was *History of Oberlin, or New Lights of the West.* Smith later edited the *New York Watchman*, papers at Rochester and Dayton, went to Iowa, got converted to Methodism, moved to Oregon, and became one of Oregon's first Senators.

sweetness in his movements."[253] Missionary programs, benevolent works, and education were opposed stubbornly by "Anti-Means" or Primitive Baptists as well as others; churches split over these questions.[254] In general, Baptist colleges, when established, were the result of the work of forward-looking individuals and groups rather than of the associations.

Ohio Baptists secured a charter for "The Trustees of the Granville Religious and Literary Society" in 1832; one teacher and a few students opened school in the Baptist meetinghouse.[255]

The Reverend John M. Peck's Rock Spring (Illinois) Seminary of 1827 was merged with Alton Academy five years later, and by the omnibus charter bill of 1835 received incorporation.[256] The next year, after a donation from Dr. Benjamin Shurtleff, the name was changed to Shurtleff College.

Judge Jesse L. Holman, of Aurora, Indiana, and a group of Baptist ministers finally succeeded in organizing an educational society in 1835 and "appointed a committee to endeavor to procure at the next session of the Legislature" a charter for the "Indiana Manual Labor Institute." It would appear that no charter was secured at this time.[257] The manual labor idea here, as elsewhere, was partly for pecuniary reasons and partly to disarm prejudices against students who might get "uppity" ideas regarding work. The founders were warned, however, not to be too dogmatic on the subject. "A host of moving arguments are to be brought forward in favor of allowing every one to do as he pleases, and above all we are not to be so harsh and bigoted and blind to our interest as to reject the son of a wealthy brother merely because he is not disposed to labor."[258] The Reverend A. R. Hinkley, of Franklin, opened a class there in 1837; soon thereafter the Reverend A. F. Tilton took over the instruction.

---

[253] *Christian Baptist* (Buffalo Creek and Bethany, Va., 1823–30), I, No. 6 (Jan., 1824).

[254] See Chapter XIV.

[255] In 1854 this school became Denison University.

[256] Alton, Illinois, McKendreean and Jonesboro, a Christian college which never organized. Alton had rejected a charter in 1833 which forbade the teaching of theology.

[257] No mention of a charter having been secured appears in the minutes of the trustees during the next four years, nor is the charter recorded in the card index in the office of secretary of state.

[258] M. Fairfield, general agent of the Home Mission Society for Indiana, to Holman, December 20, 1833, April 8, 1834, cited in John F. Cady, *Centennial History of Franklin College* (1934), 25.

Although the General Association of Indiana Baptists was won over to the idea of the college, its financial support was weak. About forty students were in attendance in the early years. In 1843 the name was changed to Franklin College.

In the Illinois Conference of the Methodist Episcopal Church in 1827 Peter Cartwright offered a resolution for establishing a college. The citizens of the village of Lebanon raised $1,385 for the school which began instruction as Lebanon Academy in 1828. Manual labor was emphasized; there was also a female department. Sponsored by the Missouri and Illinois conferences, and aided by a gift of land from Bishop William McKendree in 1830, the school was renamed McKendreean College (chartered 1835), then McKendree College. Classes began in 1836; two years later the catalogue announced 4 professors and 116 students in college and preparatory classes. At three "recitations" per day, four years would ordinarily be required, but industrious young men could finish in less.[259] The first class graduated in 1841.

In 1832 a committee reported to the Indiana Conference that since "next to religion . . . the lights of science [are] best calculated to lessen human woe and to increase the sum of human happiness . . . a seminary or college under good literary and moral regulations, would be of incalculable benefit to our people. . . ." Five years later the legislature gave a charter for establishing a school "forever to be conducted on the most liberal principles, accessible to all religious denominations." Bishop Robert R. Roberts threw himself into the work; Greencastle was selected as the site; in 1837 a building was begun and first instruction was undertaken by the Reverend Cyrus Nutt. The college was named Indiana Asbury University in honor of Bishop Francis Asbury.[260]

Kenyon College, of Gambier, Ohio, was founded by Bishop Philander Chase of the Protestant Episcopal Church; the funds were raised largely in England. Chartered in 1824 it undertook collegiate instruction in 1826. According to the Bishop's address to the convention of the Ohio Diocese, the primary purpose of the

---

[259] *Quincy Whig*, December 1, 1838.
[260] In 1883 the name was changed to De Pauw University. William Warren Sweet, *Indiana Asbury—De Pauw University 1837-1937* (New York, 1937) is the best history of this school.

school was to train poor children to be schoolmasters.[261] A four-story 110-by-44-foot building was completed in 1829;[262] about a decade later was erected Bexley Hall, one of the early Midwest examples of romantic and medieval architecture. In its early days Kenyon drew many of its students from the South.

The only nonsectarian nonstate college of importance was at Cincinnati. Cincinnati, the leading city and cultural center of the West, had never reconciled itself to the location of Miami University elsewhere. In 1806 a school association had been formed with a college in view. As Daniel Drake later wrote, "Its endowments were not exactly correspondent to its elevated title, consisting of only modest contributions; and an application was made to the legislature for permission to raise money by a lottery, which was granted. A scheme was formed, and a great part of the tickets sold: they have, however, not been drawn, and but little of the money which they brought, refunded. On Sunday, the 28th of May, 1809, the schoolhouse erected by the corporation was blown down; since which it has become extinct."[263] The institution was revived ten years later and a faculty, headed by the Reverend Elijah Slack, procured; also some property was acquired. Jacob Burnet, one of the trustees, announced the opening for May, 1819.[264] A building to house classes, a museum, and a chapel was about ready; the city library of two thousand volumes was also to be housed in it. This school was said to be the first privately endowed college north of the Ohio. In September, 1821, amidst a "solemn address and prayer," A. B. degrees were conferred on three, and an M. A. on a minister.[265] The depression of 1819–20 was too much for the college to sustain. In 1826 Cincinnati's historians wrote: "A large portion of the property . . . having been appropriated to the payment of debts . . . the trustees

[261] Columbus *Ohio State Journal*, November 19, 1829. It was emphasized that this was a poor man's college; total expenses for two terms of twenty weeks each amounted to $70. *Mount Vernon Aurora* in *Ohio State Journal*, August 20, 1827. See also Philander Chase, *A Plea for the West* (Philadelphia, 1826), an appeal on behalf of religion and learning for Ohio, especially for Kenyon College.
[262] *Ohio State Journal*, November 19, 1829.
[263] *Natural and Statistical View, or Picture of Cincinnati*, 157.
[264] Chillicothe *Supporter*, April 28, 1819. Judge Burnet subscribed $5,000 in cash, General Lytle, Arthur St. Clair, William Henry Harrison, and others additional cash and property—all told about $30,000—for the rebuilding of the Lancasterian school, in which the college was housed. "Historical Sketches—No. 1," by a "Septuagenarian," in *Genius of the West*, IV (1855), 35.
[265] *Liberty Hall and Cincinnati Gazette*, September 29, 1821.

have deemed it expedient to suspend the college exercises for the present."[266] The building was leased for other classes, among them the Lancasterian Department. The school came to life again in 1833. One of its faculty, Timothy Walker, wrote a law textbook, *Introduction to American Law* (1837) which, during the next two generations, went through eleven editions.

These then, omitting the medical schools,[267] were the more important colleges prior to 1840. Certainly it would not be for lack of choices that western sons would have to go East, spend their money, be subject to temptations, and possibly acquire profligate habits together with a gloss of eastern polish.[268] Quality was another thing. In fact it would have been next to impossible to distinguish between the better academies and the colleges. Outsiders thought little of them. Karl Postel, German writer and traveler, spoke of them as nothing but names;[269] Henry Caswall wrote of "the infant college, just rising in the backwoods, with its two or three teachers, themselves perhaps but lately released from school; its twenty or thirty students sustaining themselves by mechanical or agricultural labour, its log buildings, its scanty salaries, and its library barely supplied with the ordinary text books."[270] The London *Quarterly Review* in 1829 said:

Almost every city has a college, as it is called; though, in fact, they are little better, than our day schools. Yet degrees of bachelor of arts, and master of arts, are bestowed by them on boys of twelve and fifteen years of age; and announced with more form and pomp in their public papers, than those conferred at Oxford and Cambridge on competent scholars, at from twenty to twenty-five years of age. The whole construction of society seems opposed to any other system of education, than that of the most superficial kind.[271]

Aside from the age figure, this estimate did not miss it far.

Baynard Rush Hall who had had experience at the Indiana Seminary and Indiana College thought that the tendency of the

---

[266] Drake and Mansfield, *Cincinnati in 1826*, 41.
[267] See Chapter V.
[268] Allen Trimble, in Ohio Senate in 1824 (*Columbus Gazette,* January 22, 1824) and in his message as governor, December 19, 1826.
[269] *The United States of North America as They Are* (London, 1828), 105.
[270] *America and the American Church* (London, 1839), 199–200.
[271] In a review of Basil Hall's *Travels* (London *Quarterly Review*), XLI, 424 (Nov., 1829). Hall had made no such statement. The age named was too low even for the preparatory departments. Oberlin graduates in the first third of a century of the college's history averaged about twenty-five years of age. Fletcher, *Oberlin College,* II, 507.

colleges to trespass on the proper functions of the academies was detrimental to the development of the educational facilities in many communities:

An adequate cause of these evils may be found in the departure of colleges from the sole and legitimate end of their corporations, that of completing an education begun in academies and primary schools. It seems to be forgotten that the primary school, the academy and the college are each intended to occupy an appropriate and separate part in juvenile education; and that any encroachment of one upon the province of the other, must sooner or later be mischievous to both. Academies do occasionally aim at too extended a course of studies: but not until the colleges, stooping from their loftiness, have by their preparatory schools, enticed *children* and *boys* prematurely from the domestic schools, and with all their endowments and apparatus and libraries and corporations and facilities, *descended* to fit for their four regular classes, pupils that ought to have been fitted at home. Robbed, therefore, of pupils naturally belonging to their province, and threatened thus with destruction from the very quarter for which they were preparing scholars the academies are forced in self-defence to prolong their existence, by trenching upon the limits of the colleges.[272]

James Hall agreed that "we are by no means certain that the rapid multiplication of colleges in our country, will tend to promote the diffusion of knowledge, or to advance the cause of education." Colleges had to have means to provide the equipment, libraries, and division of labor among their faculties. If the patronage of the state legislatures and persons of wealth were confined to one college in each state, noble institutions might arise. "This however cannot be accomplished, because there are too many petty influences and prejudices, too much selfishness and narrow calculation, at work in our country, to admit of liberal and dispassionate action on such a subject." One good college, thought Hall, would be able to raise the standard and "control the lesser institutions around it by creating a sound literary currency, just as a mammoth bank may be made the balance wheel of a system of numerous monied institutions, inferior to herself."[273]

As regards libraries and apparatus, but few of the colleges of the period were as well fixed as a second-rate high school a cen-

[272] "Academies and Colleges," in *The Western Academician and Journal of Education and Science,* I, 371-72.
[273] "Colleges," in *Western Monthly Magazine,* V (1836), 220, 222.

tury later.[274] But since the bulk of the instruction was in Latin, Greek, moral philosophy, mathematics, composition, and oratory, it made little difference. Textbooks and a few volumes of literature were about all that were needed. The opinion prevailed that instructors of suitable attainments, mental and moral, could only be found among the ministry. Among these instructors were scholars of merit in the classics, religion, and literature; they were not prepared, either in training or inclination, to teach science, history, or political economy. Students, after struggling for four years to squeeze some meaning and knowledge out of Virgil and Valpy, were no doubt better prepared to read a newspaper, or write a good English sentence. Most of them learned to read, some of them to think, an accomplishment not surpassed by our multimillion-dollar college plants of today.

In the small towns in which the colleges were located the students were in close touch with the life of the community about them. Living largely in private homes, helping about the premises, loafing in stores and shops, borrowing a horse for a trip home (and bringing back some feed for their mount), borrowing books from the faculty—there was little cause for separation of town and gown. At first glance college expenses appear ridiculously low.[275] Board could be "hired" at a dollar per week, rooms were as low as a dollar per term, and "washing" seldom exceeded 12½ cents per week. Books were more expensive—75 cents to $1.50. Although most college students tried to dress better, rather than worse, than the farm and village lads, clothes were either homemade or of the equally durable store or tailor-made variety. Cleaning and pressing were nonexistent problems. Tuition seldom exceeded $7.50 per term and colleges advertised that $85 to $125 would cover all normal expenses for two terms of nine or ten months.

All things considered, however, going to college called for about the same financial outlay as a century later. At the manual-

[274] *The American Almanac* (New York, 1830–61) for 1840 listed the largest library, Kenyon, at 4,600 items, Granville and Marietta at 3,000, Illinois College 1,500, Indiana University 600, Wabash, University of Michigan, and others, none. These figures are probably mere guesses (Michigan for instance had one of the best libraries in the region) and practically meaningless. Eliminating the textbooks, none of them compared to the better private libraries.

[275] Eight students at Illinois College in 1830 banded together and contracted with a family to feed, house, and do the laundry for 83 cents per week each. *Illinois Intelligencer,* August 14, 1830.

labor schools (working at five cents an hour in credit), twenty hours labor would pay for a week's board; it still does. "Odd jobs" in town or on neighboring farms might bring from 37½ cents to 50 cents per day, as contrasted to $4.00 or $5.00 today. Teaching school for three months during the winter between college terms would probably net $50, or the major portion of a term's expenses; teaching today if permissible, would pay about the same in proportion. In other words, a dollar was about as hard for students or parents to get hold of in the 1830's as ten dollars a century later.

College life had its compensating features regardless of the formidable rules which confronted the students. To certain types of persons, wrestling with books is always preferable to pushing a plow, swinging an ax, or working at the counter.

Since the colleges of the period offered training which led largely to the ministry or teaching, and since the instruction was largely by ministers, much emphasis was placed upon the regulation of the morals and habits of the students. Early rising, prayers, church attendance, decorous conduct on all occasions, were either required or expected. Gambling, swearing, use of intoxicants, were generally prohibited; restriction of the use of firearms or burning of gunpowder in any way without permission was not unusual. Carrying dangerous weapons, "impure conversation," lewdness, breaking into rooms, destruction of property, nonpayment of bills, assaulting of fellow students, and riotous or uproarious conduct were covered in the college codes of the day. The more minute the regulations the more frequent their violation; few presidents or boards were willing to rely upon the rules of "common law, common decency, and common sense" for maintenance of standards of conduct and of judgment. Although Oberlin was the only college to admit female students in the collegiate department, girls were present in the female departments of a number of schools to complicate the problem; young men and women not infrequently roomed in the same homes, sometimes in the same college buildings. Ladies naturally were forbidden to receive gentlemen in their rooms. Oberlin made marriage of students a cause for expulsion.

In the absence of organized sport students let off energy in many ways. Debating or literary societies were absorbing activities, as were hunting, fishing, pranks, entertainments, parties, visiting, "shivarees," political rallies, loafing, and "chewing the rag." The heavy reverential atmosphere was broken now and then by holding a mock revival meeting, starting a fracas, or staging a revolt.

Whether the students were less easily regimented, the rules more strictly enforced, or whatever the cause, college "revolts" were more common than in recent times. The immediate cause usually had something to do with freedom of speech rather than dismissal of a popular athletic coach; although mere whirlwinds in a teapot, these disturbances did not pass unnoticed. In 1826 several trustees of Ohio University admonished parents and public of the dangers presenting. Why were there such frequent disorders? Were "children," as soon as weaned, capable of thinking and acting for themselves? The answer was "No!"

Yet the opinion is becoming very prevalent, and is producing the most disastrous effects on our youth, that it is improper to restrain, very improper to coerce children in the course, they pursue; and that it is enough to instruct, to reason with them, and to set before them motives to act right, and dissuasives from disorder and vice. Should such sentiments become prevalent, and form the general mode of education, our seminaries of learning must soon become schools of ignorance, folly and vice; and indeed our civil institutions cannot last more than a generation or two longer.[276]

Colleges were expected to do something more than disseminate knowledge; they were supposed to produce leaders of high character and sound judgment, to bolster the republic against the practices of preferment in use in the political world. Unless the people wanted to "plant our public places with ignorance and manure them with corruption," seminaries of learning would have to be encouraged.[277] Though the people might be suspicious of the efficacy of Greek, Latin, and logic, nevertheless, they had faith that colleges, somehow or other, made better men out of their sons.[278] Not all trusted their own colleges as being entirely

[276] Columbus *Ohio State Journal,* January 1, 1826.
[277] *Northwestern Gazette and Galena Advertiser,* January 17, 1835.
[278] Arguments pro and con on the classics are briefly summarized in contributions by Lyman Beecher and others to *Cincinnati Daily Gazette,* January 11, 1836. Capt. Basil Hall, noting that it was much more difficult to keep young men in school in the United States than in England, said: "What answer . . . can be made to a lad of sixteen, who sees before him so wide and tempting an area for his immediate exertions to expand themselves in? Who is certain that if he marries to-morrow, with scarcely a dollar in his pocket, he may rear up half-a-dozen children in as

up to the task; for sentimental reasons, purpose of prestige, and because of the established quality and reputations of the older colleges, many sons of the West went to eastern schools.

§ § § §

National character was being formed in many ways; also the character of the West:

Education is the corner-stone of the social edifice. It is the rock on whose firm foundation is erected that glorious fabric of liberty and law, which is our best inheritance, and proudest boast. It is that which distinguishes civilized from savage man; which draws the broad line of separation between the free, the intelligent, the useful citizen of our country, and
"—the poor Indian, whose untutor'd mind
Sees God in Clouds, or hears him in the wind."
It is that which elevates the child of poverty and labor, to usefulness and honor; which cultivates his talents, developes the resources of his mind, awakens the latent fire of his ambition, and enables him to start in the race of life on equal terms with the more favored sons of affluence. . . . It has not been by the instrumentality of the sword . . . that peace, order, and religion, are in our country; security and abundance in our dwellings. We owe all this prosperity, under Providence . . . to education.[279]

The status of education in the West at the end of the decade 1830 to 1840 might well be summarized by briefing a series of articles from the *Western Farmer: Journal of Agriculture and Rural Economy*:[280] It was axiomatic that public education should include instruction in language, numbers, and morals—the personal, social, civil, and political duties of the individual. General utility would require in addition, schooling in geography, travel, and observation of nature; history and biography; drawing; music; gymnastics; and the elements of the sciences. Thinking people believed that the farmer no less than the minister, teacher, lawyer, and doctor should be educated, females as well as males. Our system of government required it.

---

many years, and maintain them in abundance, till they are in a state to shift for themselves? Or who begs you to tell him in what respect Greek and Latin, or the differential calculus, will advance his project of demolishing the wilderness, and peopling the ground where it stood? . . . You can really say nothing in reply." *Travels in North America*, II, 172.

[279] James Hall, "The Formation of National Character," in *Western Monthly Magazine*, I (1833), 348, 349–50.

[280] April 8, May 6, 13, 1840 (Springfield, Ill.) and credited to J. W. Jenks and the Jacksonville *Illinois Sentinel*.

The West is a vast field, that is endowed by nature with almost all that [the] heart could wish as to natural advantages for cultivation and most internal improvement; and it is but for those now officiating on the stage to adopt proper measures for education, and the mind of the West will grow and strengthen with its natural growth until we shall present one of the greatest examples of human enterprize and intellectual greatness, that has ever graced the page of history.[281]

More eloquent if possible in the expression of faith in education was the following product of the pen of Editor John B. Dillon of the Logansport *Canal Telegraph*:

If the time shall ever come when this mighty fabric shall totter; when the beacon of joy that now rises in pillar of fire, a sign and wonder of the world, shall wax dim, the cause will be found in the ignorance of the people. If our union is still to continue, to cheer the hopes and animate the efforts of the oppressed of every nation; if your fields are to be untrod by the hirelings of despotism; if long days of blessedness are to attend our country in her career of glory; if you would have the sun continue to shed his unclouded rays upon the face of freemen, then EDUCATE ALL THE CHILDREN OF THE LAND. This alone startles the tyrant in his dreams of power, and rouses the slumbering energies of an oppressed people. It was intelligence that reared up the majestic columns of national glory; and this and sound morality alone can prevent their crumbling to ashes.[282]

[281] *Western Farmer: Journal of Agriculture and Rural Economy*, December 9, 1839.
[282] November 19, 1836.

XIV

Religion

The more we converse with men, whose general walk and character
evince real wisdom, worth and independent sincerity, the more we
find, that, like our own, their minds, in viewing this subject of all
absorbing interest, have wandered through all degrees of speculation,
confidence, distrust, doubting and anxiety; until finally they have
settled to rest, not in a creed of numerous articles—but of a few
simple truths, to which the mind clings more closely, the more they
are examined; which fluctuate not with our temperament, hopes and
fears; but which claim, like the great principles of morals, the steady
assent, under all changes and circumstances, which the mind gives to
the law of nature.

Timothy Flint, *Western Monthly Review*, May, 1830

NO CHAPTER in the history of religion in our country
offers more complexities or more interest than that which
deals with the Middle West in the first half of the nineteenth
century. The Westerner was ready to carry his Protestantism
through to its logical end, hence the West was the fertile
propagating bed for new divisions and sects. Separatists and
Puritans had come to the New World where they upheld the
standards of Congregationalism; as time passed, Congregationalists formed into orthodox and liberal, Old Calvinist, and New
Divinity parties. Other Puritans, Presbyterians, already divided,
further split into "Old Side" and "New Side," and, in the West,
suffered both the Cumberland Schism and the "New Light" or
"Christian" defection. Later they divided into Old School and
New School blocs. There were also Associate, Associate Reformed, Reformed, and Welsh Calvinists. Many of the Congregationalists became presbyterianized, while others became either
Baptists or Unitarians. Baptists split into Separates and Regulars,
rejoined and became United, but still there were General
(Regular), Particular (Separate), Primitive (Hard-shell or
"Whiskey"), and Free Will groups of Baptists. Tens of thou-
sands of Baptists became Disciples, Disciples became Christians,
Christians became Disciples. Besides there were Lutherans, Episcopalians, Catholics, Friends (who also split), Methodists, Re-

formed (Dutch, Swiss-French, German, for example), Shakers, Brethren, "Millerites," Jews, Mormons, Universalists, various types of Pietists, and many other religious groups.

Although revivalism and the question of freedom of the will precipitated sectarian difference, there were really dozens of matters of dogma and church organization and government which caused fission. Denominations split along one line on one issue, along another line on another. So numerous and complex were the schisms and crossings over and so illogical were many of them, that groups and sects not infrequently found themselves back in the fold whence they had started. So confusing did the history of the Protestant sects become that no historian, church or lay, has been able to make a clear and organized presentation of its course.

Religion is largely an abstract, a subjective thing. It is not capable of measurement as is railroad mileage, agricultural production, or the incidence of taxes; it is not, in the popular mind, so easily subjected to analysis as is a political platform, or to the empiric tests of a doctor's prescription. It is possible to chronicle the organizing of churches, list creeds, describe revivals, outline government and organization, portray individual churchmen, and estimate the relative numerical strength of denominations; but only in exceptional cases is it possible even approximately to calculate the relative importance of religion as a cultural force or to determine the exact part it has played in the lives and thoughts of the people.

To take the churchman's word on the relative importance of religion at face value might lead as wide of the mark as to accept his estimate of the morality of the pioneer, whom he often criticized as an ignorant, anti-Christian, Sabbath-violating, whiskey-drinking, depraved, gambling set of heathen hell bent on greased wheels, and destined to burn in the next world while making the most of the present. Or, to believe that pioneer society agreed when a churchman said that wine-, beer-, and cider-drinking persons were its deadliest foes, and that the sin most to be feared was that of wealth and luxury[1] might be as erroneous as to accept a

---

[1] As phrased by a Presbyterian missionary in Illinois: "I have no fear from anything but Sin—and the sins to which the people in this fertile valley are exposed will, as I apprehend, be wealth & luxury & pride. . . . the danger will be, not from *want*, but from abundance." Lucien Farnam, Princeton, Putnam County, Illinois, April 1, 1836, to Absalom Peters. Papers of American Home Missionary Society.

rationalist's evaluation of some of the strange goings on at a revival.

On the one hand, the historian might assume that religion was the most important social and cultural force in pioneer life; on the other, he might reason that the men of religious calling, like the abolitionists, troubled the world all out of proportion to their real importance, and dismiss them with a nod. Between these extremes there is no specific point of certain validity. To many people religious conviction was the most powerful force in life and it ruled their lives; to others it was acknowledged as a vital thing theoretically, but was not permitted seriously to interfere with other aspects of life. To many others it was of no direct concern whatever. It is futile to try to estimate the relative number of sincere believers in the pioneer period as compared with our times; it is impossible to prove or to disprove that it differed materially. Nor is it possible statistically to separate, in either period, those primarily interested in salvation by a certain formula from those interested in religion as a moral force, in church as a means of social control.

The story of religion in the Old Northwest is at times a story of high purpose, wisdom, heroic personalities, sacrifice, and service; it is also the story of ignorance, selfishness, bigotry, sectarian ambition, vested interests, conflicting personalities, and mean and petty politics. In other words, religion, despite its lofty aims and purposes, presented the same features as did the politics, business, and other human activities of the time.[2]

[2] An introduction to the bulky literature and source material on religion in the Old Northwest may best be had from the introductions and documents written and edited by William Warren Sweet in *Religion on the American Frontier: The Baptists* (New York, 1931); *The Presbyterians* (New York, 1936); *The Congregationalists* (Chicago, 1939); and *The Methodists* (Chicago, 1946). The bibliographies contained in these volumes are indispensable for the student of religion in the West. By the same author are *Circuit-Rider Days in Indiana* (Indianapolis, 1916); *Circuit-Rider Days Along the Ohio* (New York and Cincinnati, 1923); *The Story of Religions in America* (New York and London, 1930, 1939, and 1946); and *Revivalism in America* (New York, 1944). Useful also are Peter G. Mode, *The Frontier Spirit in American Christianity* . . . (New York, 1923); Colin B. Goodykoontz, *Home Missions on the American Frontier; with particular reference to the American Home Missionary Society* (Caldwell, Idaho, 1939); and Ray A. Billington, *The Protestant Crusade 1800–1860* . . . (New York, 1938). One of the early general works was Robert Baird, *Religion in America* . . . (New York, 1844). There are a number of unpublished monographs in the form of graduate dissertations, mostly at the University of Chicago, which deal with special phases of religion in the Northwest. The Papers of the American Home Missionary Society, important source materials, are in the Charles G. Hammond Library of the Chicago Theological Seminary. Specific references to works which deal with the various denominations are included in footnotes which follow.

§

Interest in religion, which climbed to a high pitch in the American colonies at the time of the Great Awakening after 1734, had declined by the time of the War for Independence. The war, politics, the establishing of the nation all served to distract interest from religion; further, the rationalistic philosophy of eighteenth-century Europe was taking firm root in the American mind. Many people became indifferent to religion or scoffed at it; fewer outstanding men, in comparison to the earlier period, were attracted to the ministry. Historians of religion described the succeeding period as "a very wintry season" or as one characterized by suspended animation in religious affairs. Conditions in the East were reported as bad;[3] in the West they were said to be even worse. Whole communities were characterized by early ministers as assemblages of rogues, robbers, counterfeiters, ganging outlaws, and intemperate reprobates.

The quiet revival movement which stirred in the East in the 1790's spread to the West where it became somewhat less quiet. Of the various denominations the Presbyterians were in the most strategic position to minister to and take advantage of the westward population movements. Already by the end of the French and Indian War they had begun to place missionaries west of the mountains in Pennsylvania, and by the end of the Revolution several ministers were settled there. In 1781 the Redstone Presbytery was established. Similarly, Presbyterianism spread across the mountains from Virginia and the Carolinas. Many of the prominent early settlers of the Kentucky country were of that faith. By 1785 there were enough congregations in this region to warrant the organization of the Presbytery of Transylvania, and the several churches established north of the

[3] In 1798 the General Assembly of the Presbyterian Church was "filled with concern and awful dread": "We perceive with pain and fearful apprehension a general dereliction of religious principles and practice among our fellow-citizens, a visible and prevailing impiety and contempt for the laws and institutions of religion, and an abounding infidelity, which in many instances tends to atheism itself. The profligacy and corruption of the public morals have advanced with a progress proportionate to our declension in religion. Profaneness, pride, luxury, injustice, intemperance, lewdness, and every species of debauchery and loose indulgence greatly abound." It appeared "that the eternal God has a controversy with this nation." *Minutes of the General Assembly . . . 1789 to A.D. 1820 Inclusive* (Philadelphia, 1847), 152–53.

Ohio River were, until 1799, under its jurisdiction. James Mc-
Gready, a Scotch-Irish Pennsylvanian, attended the Log College
of John McMillan in the Redstone country[4] and was licensed
by and preached in the Redstone Presbytery. This homely, uncouth minister discovered his real powers of persuasion, however, in the Carolinas, but his habit of distracting the people
from their work seems not to have been appreciated. By 1797
he was ministering to three churches in Logan County, Kentucky, and filling the members with the revival spirit. Soon Methodist preachers joined in the movement; people came from other
communities to witness the exhortations and conversions. Scores
of camp meetings were held, many of them interdenominational,
in the Cumberland and Green River settlements. Barton W.
Stone carried the spirit to his two little Presbyterian churches
in Bourbon County where shortly, in August, 1801, took place
the great Cane Ridge revival.

This, the most famous revival ever held in the West, has been
so frequently described that elaboration is unnecessary.[5] Following a period in which "a deep solemnity pervaded the entire community," individuals, listening to routine sermons, began to get
the trembles and feel "the mighty power of God." As the interest
developed, "bold, brazen-fronted blasphemers were literally cut
down by the 'sword of the spirit.' " Hardened frontiersmen, Indian fighters, cold-blooded politicians, notorious profligates, even
avowed infidels, affected by the preaching, began to fall. Meetings were rated by the "fallings"; at one meeting "50 fell," at
another "120," or "300 fell."[6]

[4] The original "Log College" was founded by William Tennant, Presbyterian
minister at Neshaminy, Bucks County, Pennsylvania, in the 1720's; in it he trained
his younger sons for the ministry. Several other "log colleges" followed.

[5] The standard work is Catherine C. Cleveland, *The Great Revival in the West
1797–1805* (Chicago, 1916). An older account is William Speer, *The Great Revival of 1800* (Philadelphia, 1872). See also James Gallaher, *The Western Sketch
Book* (Boston, 1850), Chapter III, and Richard McNemar, *The Kentucky Revival;
or, a Short History of the Late Extraordinary Out-pouring of the Spirit of God in
the Western States of America, Agreeably to Scripture Prophesies Concerning the
Latter Day. With a Brief Account of the Entrance and Progress of what the World
Calls Shakerism* . . . (Cincinnati, 1807).

[6] It was reported that those in a "fallen" state remained conscious of what
passed around them but meantime "their minds were directed to the holiness and
grandeur of God; the purity and sacredness of his law; the guilt and hatefulness
of sin; the great love of God in giving his Son to redeem lost man; the beauty
and glory of Christ as Mediator; the worth of the Soul; the preciousness of the
gospel; the value of time, the brevity of life; the solemnity of death, of judgment,
and of eternity." Gallaher, *The Western Sketch Book* (1852 ed.), 34.

Stone and others made elaborate preparations for the Cane Ridge meeting. A large tent was erected in a clearing; around it were laid off streets for tents and vehicles. Between ten and twenty thousand expectant visitors assembled for the sacramental service which opened on Friday, but the crowd stayed until the following Wednesday evening, by which time the preachers were exhausted. Present were dozens of preachers, Presbyterian, Baptist, and Methodist; a half dozen preached simultaneously from platforms, wagons, stumps, logs, and other vantage points. A young man who later became one of Ohio's famous Methodist preachers approached the meeting without great faith in these falling manifestations. Proud of his manhood and courage, he had said that if he were to fall "it must be by physical power and not by singing and praying." But when he witnessed the "vast sea of human beings . . . agitated as if by a storm," the mass mind permeated by "a strange supernatural power," his knees trembled, his lips quivered, and he had to sit down. He retired to the woods to think things over, then returned to the scene of excitement where the pitch had risen even higher. The scene was indescribable. The spirit swept over the sea of humanity, shrieks and shouts rent the very heavens—"five hundred were swept down in a moment, as if a battery of a thousand guns had been opened upon them"—the young man's hair rose on end, the blood ran cold in his veins, and a sense of suffocation and blindness overwhelmed him. Again he retired to the woods, and finally to a tavern, where he took a dram and left, feeling, as he described the experience, "that I was as near hell as I wished to be, either in this or the world to come. The brandy had no effect in allaying my feelings, but, if any thing, made me worse."[7]

All told it was said that between one and three thousand were "brought to the ground" at the Cane Ridge meeting, which served as a grand-scale model or goal for all later revivals. This particular phase of revivalism lasted four or five years longer; Kentucky ministers carried the idea across the Ohio, and by 1803 it had spread north to the Western Reserve. The Baptists and the Methodists rather than the Presbyterians, however, gained more numbers as a result.

[7] *Autobiography of Rev. James B. Finley . . .* , edited by W. P. Strickland (Cincinnati, 1853), 166–68. Finley underwent conversion, backslid into his worldly ways, but was reconverted several years later, at which time he became a Methodist.

The manifestations of extreme emotionalism, particularly the "bodily exercises"—the screaming, yapping, barking, flopping, head twisting, and jerking,[8] as well as the freer sexual relations which often accompanied them—naturally led to severe criticism. Some sober-minded and judicious men of religion attacked the revivals as extravagances put on by imposters incapable of spreading the word of God through better means; as performances designed to attract the giddier and rowdier elements of the population; as having no lasting effects; as breeders of alarming errors in doctrine; in fact as artful devices of the devil, who could convert from an old serpent to a turkey buzzard and "flutter and flop his foul wings over a fragment of his favorite carrion, and . . . raise dust enough to prevent you from discerning all the beauty that is visible among 'the cattle upon a thousand hills.' "

Defenders of the revivals, though often admitting that their meetings attracted the ignorant and profane elements of the population, used this very fact as an argument: Strong diseases required strong remedies; men of learning, books, and logic alone could not be relied upon to reach the roarers, snorters, and hardened blasphemers of the frontier. While the bodily exercises might not be conducive to religion, they were nevertheless a "very solemn, external call, well calculated to impress the mind, and ought to be improved." Even persons who were not convinced that revivals were affected by the immediate finger of God were silenced. Ballrooms and tippling shops were thrown open to the pious; people in the most profane settlements "where religion was not known and the name of God mentioned

[8] As Peter Cartwright said, the more people tried to resist the tendency "the more they jerked." Persons of all ranks and degrees were subject—"the person of eighty and the child of four; the master in affluence, and the slave in bondage; . . . the man of long religious standing, those of a recent date, and many who have no religion at all." Gallaher, *The Western Sketch Book,* 54. At later revivals, where certain classes of people thought it beneath their dignity to perform with the common run, the bodily exercises sometimes proved catching. "To see those proud young gentlemen and young ladies, dressed in their silks, jewelry, and prunella, from top to toe, take the *jerks* would often excite my risibilities. The first jerk or so, you would see their fine bonnets, caps, and combs fly; and so sudden would be the jerking of the head that their long loose hair would crack almost as loud as a wagoner's whip." *Autobiography of Peter Cartwright, the Backwoods Preacher,* edited by W. P. Strickland (Cincinnati and New York, 1856, and London, 1859), 17. As the paroxysms wore off, the subject frequently went into prayer. Children of five or six, ignorant persons even, prayed eloquently and introduced scripture so particularly as to put to shame doctors of divinity. Gallaher, *The Western Sketch Book,* 54.

only in blasphemy," where infidelity was triumphant, Christianity was considered a fable and futurity but a dream, began to form into societies and to meet weekly for social prayer. The revival confounded infidelity, "awed vice into silence, and brought numbers beyond calculation under serious impression." As for the argument that revivals led to Arianism, Socinianism, Shakerism, and other doctrinal errors, it was pointed out that these various "isms" had originated in Europe, had contaminated the East, and had but slightly penetrated the West where the revivals were most prevalent.[9]

Nevertheless, revivalism led to schism. Staunch Calvinists feared as much as anything that revivals would open the minds of Presbyterians to the doctrine of grace as held by the Methodists. When the Transylvania Presbytery was divided in 1802, the new Cumberland Presbytery was in the control of revivalist ministers who, eight years later, after failing to be upheld by the General Assembly, set up an independent presbytery and created the Cumberland Presbyterian Church. This group was more lenient also than were Presbyterians generally regarding the educational qualifications of their ministers. Converts were won, and in 1829, by which time they had eighteen presbyteries, the Cumberland Presbyterians formed a General Assembly of their own.

Two other offshoots of the Presbyterians may here be noted. Barton W. Stone and several other Kentucky ministers,[10] who had been ringleaders in the revival movement, began to have qualms regarding the orthodox tenets on election and predestination. These "New Lights" preached God's love for the whole world and believed that sinners could accept the newer means

[9] Arianism was named after Arius, a fourth-century Alexandrian theologian, who "maintained that Christ was of different substance from God" in opposition to Bishop Alexander. Socinianism (after a sixteenth-century Italian theologian Faustus Socinus) rejected the Trinity, the deity of Christ, the innate and total depravity of man, the vicarious atonement, etc.

When the Presbyterian Isaac Reed began his "nine years and 18,000 miles" of missionary service in the West in Kentucky in 1817, he first learned about the jerks and the fallings. "You will think, surely, these things were not among Presbyterians; but, my dear sir, they were. But many, who were then thought to have set out in religion, and to have begun in the spirit, seem like to end in the flesh, or like the washed sow, who returns to her wallowing in the mire. Ah, me! how many of them are now Arians, Socinians, and Shakers. . . . But some have stood . . . and seem like precious metal tried by fire. The blast was great, the chaff abundant, but there is some pure grain." *The Christian Traveller*, 56.

[10] Richard McNemar, John Thompson, John Dunlavy, and John Marshall.

of salvation. But the holding of such erroneous doctrines led to the suspension of the five ministers by the Synod of Kentucky. The suspended ministers then joined with others of like mind and organized a separate presbytery, but when it became apparent that they were really starting a new sect, something they had not intended to do, they dissolved their presbytery. Since it seemed impossible, however, to effect the unity of Christians under the existing organizations of the various denominations, they took the name "The Christian Church." The new sect was opposed to all forms of superior church organization and government—presbyteries, synods, conferences, and the like—not mentioned in the New Testament. Though two of the original five founders returned to the Presbyterian fold, and two went over to the Shakers, Stone traveled, preached, and organized new churches. From Kentucky the movement spread north of the Ohio where many new members were added. Later, the "Stoneites" or "Christians" were to be closely associated with other "New Lights"—the "Disciples"—who came to the West from Pennsylvania and Virginia.

Thomas Campbell was a Scotch-Irish Anti-Burgher,[11] who had been a minister and had conducted a school in County Armagh, Ireland. He came to Philadelphia in 1807, but when his views proved too liberal for the conservative Associate or Anti-Burgher Synod, he began preaching independently. Soon was organized "The Christian Association of Washington" which in 1809 adopted Campbell's "Declaration and Address" as its platform. "Where the Scriptures speak, we speak; where they are silent, we are silent," said Campbell.[12] When his organization was not embraced by the Presbyterian Synod of Pittsburgh, Campbell organized the Brush Run Church which licensed his son Alexander, recently arrived from Ireland. When this

[11] In 1644 the conservative Scottish Covenanters had split and an Associate Reformed Presbytery was organized; this latter group split about a century later—over the question of the oath exacted of burgesses—into Burghers and Anti-Burghers. Sweet, *Religions in America* (1939 ed.), 200.

[12] This address expressed a desire for unity—Christ alone was the head, His word was the rule; the terms were explicit belief in and conformity to that word. The church on earth was one, the New Testament was a perfect constitution for worship, discipline, and government. The "Declaration and Address" has been the *Magna Carta* of the great Restoration Movement. Morrison Meade Davis, *How the Disciples Began and Grew . . .* (Cincinnati, 1915), 53 ff. See also Winfred Ernest Garrison, *An American Religious Movement* (St. Louis, 1946).

church decided that the Scriptures called for immersion and ruled against infant baptism, the Redstone Baptist Association asked that it unite with them. Despite some minor differences in belief the union took place in 1813, and the "Campbellites" were nominally Baptists.

But Alexander Campbell's Calvinism was too flexible to permit of a real merger with the Baptists. Soon he established Buffalo Seminary at Bethany, Virginia, and began to preach and debate for the "ancient order of things." In 1823 he began publication of *The Christian Baptist,* which continued for seven years. The purpose of the journal was

the eviction of truth and exposure of error. . . . We know . . . that there is a goodly number of sensible and intelligent persons, at this day, entirely disgusted with many things called religion. . . . We have learned one lesson . . . never to hold any sentiment or proposition as more certain than the evidence on which it rests. . . . All beyond this we esteem enthusiasm—all short of it, incredulity. . . . Christianity is the perfection of that divine philanthropy which was gradually developing itself for four thousand years. It is the bright effulgence of every divine attribute, mingling and harmonizing, as the different colors in the rainbow, in the bright shining after rain, into one complete system of perfections—the perfection of GLORY to God in the highest heaven, the perfection of PEACE on earth, and the perfection of GOOD WILL among men.[13]

In his periodical Campbell attacked missions, Sunday schools, and sectarian societies. He disagreed with the Baptists on methods of preachings and opposed their emphasis on doctrine and the requirement of a particular religious experience. After being ousted from the Redstone Association, he was admitted to the Mahoning Association, but by 1826 the Baptists, from whom Campbell had drawn heavily for followers, began to cut out the Disciple churches. His next most fruitful sources of followers were the Republican Methodists[14] and the Presbyterians of the Barton W. Stone defection.

Campbell published *The Sacred Writings of the Apostles . . . ,* put out a hymnbook, and, in 1830, as a result of his interest in the second coming of Christ, began publication of his *Millennial Harbinger,* which continued for a generation. As Campbell's in-

[13] *The Christian Baptist,* I (1823), Preface and 1.
[14] A group which had opposed the newly constituted Methodist central authority and under the leadership of James O'Kelley had withdrawn in 1793.

fluence moved west, many Baptist congregations split, and the "Reformers" set up congregations of their own. Thousands of Kentuckians joined the Disciples, and the movement spread into Ohio, Indiana, and Illinois.[15] "Thus the movement which had begun as a protest against the numerous sects of Christians, instead of uniting them, had only succeeded in adding one more to the number."[16]

As the Disciples came into the home territory of the "Stoneite" Christians, there were those who, noting many similarities in belief, sought to effect a merger. Since both sects were established on a purely congregational basis, no obstacles prevented individual congregations from merging, and many did so in the early 1830's. Some of Stone's followers were opposed to this idea, however, and united with the Republican Methodists to form the "Christian Connection Church."[17] The two terms "Christians" and "Disciples" have been used more or less interchangeably down to the present time; since there is no central or higher governing body to determine officially the name of the sect, none has been designated.

§ §

Most important of the Protestant denominations in the Northwest were the Presbyterians, the Methodists, and the Baptists. Although the Methodists predominated numerically, the Presbyterians were more influential in education and more active in subsidizing missions.

Early steps in the westward advance of Presbyterianism have been noted. Churches were established at Cincinnati, Chillicothe, Dayton, Springfield, and Columbus in the 1790's and early 1800's.[18] In 1799 the Presbytery of Washington was set off from

[15] It was estimated that about ten thousand Kentucky Baptists joined the Disciples between 1829 and 1832. J. H. Spencer, *History of Kentucky Baptists from 1769 to 1885* . . . (2 volumes. Cincinnati, 1885), I, 642.

[16] Sweet, *Religions in America*, 344.

[17] This group, in 1926, voted for union with the Congregationalists. The union was effected in 1931, and, merging, the Christian General Convention and the Congregational National Council became simply the General Council of the Congregational and Christian Churches. Gaius Glenn Atkins and Frederick L. Fagley, *History of American Congregationalism* (Boston, 1942), 356–59.

[18] Several of Cincinnati's founders (or their wives) were Presbyterians; a church was organized in 1790–91 but a regular minister (Joshua L. Wilson) did not settle there until 1808.

that of Transylvania; three years later it contained five ministers and thirty-two congregations, some of which were in Kentucky. In 1814 the Synod of Ohio (Chillicothe region) was set
off from the Kentucky and Pittsburgh synods, and in 1829 the
Synod of Cincinnati was erected. Central Ohio felt the Pennsylvania influence; a number of the ministers came from Dickinson
College, then a Presbyterian institution. Northern Ohio, and
particularly the Connecticut Western Reserve, was influenced by
the combination of Congregationalists and Presbyterians sometimes referred to as "Presbygationalism."

In 1708 the Congregational churches of Connecticut accepted
the Saybrook Platform and in due course took a form of government which closely resembled that of the Presbyterians.[19]
From 1766 until the Revolution the General Association of the
Connecticut Congregational churches held joint conventions with
the Synod of New York and Philadelphia. The General Assembly of the Presbyterian Church (constituted in 1788 and holding
its first session in 1789) early took steps to strengthen the co-
operation between these two denominations, and in 1801 the
"Plan of Union" was adopted by the General Assembly and the
Connecticut General Association.[20] This plan, designed to "promote mutual forbearance, and a spirit of accommodation,"
afforded the adherents of both denominations in a newly settled
region the opportunity of forming a single congregation and of
calling a minister of either denomination. Church discipline
might be conducted according to the ideas of the majority of the
members, even though the minister were of the other denomination. Generous provisions were made for settling any disputes
between pastor and congregation, and for appeals.[21] From this

[19] See Sweet, *The Presbyterians*, 38; Williston Walker, *A History of the Congregational Churches in the United States* (New York, 1894), 200–13, 315–20.
[20] The plan probably was presented by Jonathan Edwards, the younger, president
of Union College, a delegate in the General Assembly. Union College, at Schenec-
tady, had been founded in 1795, largely through the joint efforts of Presbyterians
and Dutch Reformed. The "Plan of Union" was later approved "in spirit if not
in fact" by other New England Congregational state associations. Sweet, *The
Congregationalists*, 16.
[21] In a Congregational church with a Presbyterian minister difficulties could be
referred to the minister's presbytery or to a council of both denominations; in a
Presbyterian church with a Congregational minister, to the latter's association or
to a council. In a mixed congregation a "standing committee" was given super-
visory powers. Presbyterian ministers might appeal to their presbyteries, Congregational ministers to a decision of all male members of the church.

date the activities of Congregationalists and Presbyterians were voluntarily merged everywhere except in New England and in the South, and the Presbyterian influence came to dominate.

The Congregationalists, who had begun missionary operations in the Old Northwest through the agency of the Missionary Society of Connecticut (established in 1798), sought to exercise a proprietary interest in the region.[22] The Reverend David Bacon and his wife had made some missionary efforts among the Indians on the Maumee, at L'Arbre Croche, and on Mackinac Island in the early 1800's.[23] When, however, in 1803 the society cut its missionaries' pay from $7.00 to $6.00 a week, most of its appointees resigned.[24] As a consequence, the Presbyterians took over most of the churches in the Reserve. The first Congregational church on the Reserve was that at Austinburg (Richfield), founded in 1801. Others followed, and in 1805 a half dozen, organized under the Plan of Union, constituted the "Ecclesiastical Convention of New Connecticut," which, though it was voluntarily dissolved in 1808, reappeared as the Hartford Presbytery.[25] In the New England-settled areas where the Plan of Union was in operation, the Presbyterian form of government usually prevailed, even in churches preponderantly Congregationalist in membership. This fact was very largely the result of the sincere endeavor of the Congregationalists to co-operate with the Presbyterians,[26] although the ministers of the latter denomination clung more stubbornly to their form of government than those of the former. Many Congregationalists held

[22] The first Congregational church north of the Ohio was at Marietta (1796); there was also a Welsh Congregational church near Cincinnati (1803).

[23] The society found Bacon's plans too expensive and transferred him to "New Connecticut." In 1805 he contracted to buy almost a whole township of land on which he endeavored to found a model community (Tallmadge); he established the Congregational church at Tallmadge in 1809. For sketch of Bacon, see Milo M. Quaife, *David Bacon* (*Burton Historical Collection Leaflet*, IX, No. 3, Detroit, January, 1931).

[24] The Connecticut society asked the Pittsburgh Synod to employ men of its own choosing who would work in "New Connecticut" at the $6.00 wage.

[25] A similar number of small Congregational churches along the Muskingum had formed an association in 1809 which suspended operations about 1816 when the ministers and churches transferred to adjacent presbyteries.

[26] Yale and Andover presidents and professors advised their graduates to adhere closely to the Presbyterian standards. Cornelius E. Dickinson, "History of Congregationalism in Ohio before 1852," in *Papers of the Ohio Church History Society,* VII (1895), 40 ff.

the Presbyterian form of government to be superior for churches on the frontier.

Portage Presbytery was organized in 1818, Huron Presbytery in 1825. The Synod of the Western Reserve, erected in 1825, included Michigan Territory; most of the churches under its care, however, were either Plan-of-Union or Congregational churches. By 1837 there were three synods within the borders of Ohio, and the Pittsburgh Synod contained two Ohio presbyteries. At that time the state contained twenty-one presbyteries, 301 ministers, 448 churches, and 30,509 communicants.[27]

A group of enthusiastic graduates of Williams College, who became students at Andover Theological Seminary, had been instrumental in 1810 in the organization of the American Board of Commissioners for Foreign Missions. Among them was Samuel J. Mills, who, with John F. Schermerhorn and Daniel Smith, made western tours 1812–15 and reported upon the great need for religious facilities in the West.[28] In Illinois Territory, for instance, with more than 12,000 inhabitants, they found no Presbyterian or Congregational minister. Many persons who had been Presbyterians had gone over to the Baptists or the Methodists. As a result of these reports, the General Associations of Massachusetts and Connecticut gave the board their support and increased their subsidies for domestic missions. The Presbyterians likewise used the Board for missionary work among the western Indians.

The Board of Missions of the Presbyterian General Assembly and the Western Foreign Missionary Society of Pittsburgh also began to send workers into the West. John Monteith, sent out by the board, began work in and around Detroit in 1816. Samuel Graham and Benjamin Low were sent to Illinois, from which state the latter reported that of the several hundred inhabitants of Edwardsville not one made any pretension to religion; it was dangerous even to walk the street on the Sabbath. Isaac Reed

[27] Sweet, The Presbyterians, 47–48, citing "History of Presbyterians in Ohio to the Year 1870," by William E. Moore (MS.), who was the stated clerk of the Synod of Ohio in the 1880's.

[28] John F. Schermerhorn and Samuel J. Mills, A Correct View of that Part of the United States which lies west of the Allegany Mountains, with regard to religion and morals (Hartford, 1814); Mills and Smith, Report of a Missionary Tour through that part of the United States which lies west of the Allegany Mountains.

was deeply grieved when he saw boys playing ball in the seminary yard on the Sabbath in Kentucky: "Oh, how is my heart pained with the immoral and impious ways of people here."[29] According to Reed, when he settled as the minister at New Albany, Indiana, in 1818, there was not an installed Presbyterian minister in the whole of Indiana; his salary was $500.[30] Commissioned by the Missionary Society of Connecticut in 1819, he began to preach in the surrounding counties and in Kentucky. He organized a church at Bloomington and, later, churches at Indianapolis (1823), in Washington County, Johnson County, and Crawfordsville, Indiana, in Edgar County, Illinois, and elsewhere.

In 1821 in southeastern Indiana (included in the Synod of Ohio) there were a number of churches but only two Presbyterian ministers, neither of whom had a pastoral charge; in the rest of the state which lay in the Synod of Kentucky (Louisville Presbytery) there were six churches and five ministers, of whom only three of the latter were settled.[31] Some "infant" churches were without ministers. The whole region Reed regarded as a fertile missionary field; the people, he reported, were of "all kinds, regular and irregular, orthodox and heresy of the older States" and, though poor, were more inclined than most to be professors of some sort.[32] In 1823 the Salem Presbytery was erected, and two years later the Madison and Wabash presbyteries were set off. In 1825 there were forty-two churches of which eight only were supplied with pastors; there were ten ministers in the state and a number of missionaries.[33] The Indiana Missionary Society, at its third annual meeting at Vincennes in 1825, thanked the Connecticut and New York societies as well as the United Domestic Missionary Society for their interest and

[29] This incident occurred at Lancaster. Reed, *The Christian Traveller*, 58.

[30] *Ibid.*, 87. This rare book constitutes one of the best journals kept and published by any of the early western missionaries. Reed's wife and the wife of Baynard Rush Hall, first instructor at Indiana Seminary, were sisters. The Presbyterian influence at the state school began through Reed and Hall. See Chapter XIII, 388 ff.

Indiana's first Presbyterian church, established at Vincennes in 1806, had had a minister for a number of years after its founding.

[31] *Ibid.*, 131.

[32] *Ibid.*, 132.

[33] *Ibid.*, 195.

help in the western states.[34] The following year (1826) the Synod of Indiana was erected by the General Assembly.[35]

The United Domestic Missionary Society was formed at New York in 1822; reorganized four years later, it became the American Home Missionary Society. A dozen or more workers had been sent into the Old Northwest from 1822 to 1826.[36] A majority of the missionaries who served under these societies in the region north of the Ohio were—considering their training and previous affiliation in the East—Congregationalists; also working in the field were Presbyterian, Dutch Reformed, and Associate Reformed pastors. Most of the churches which they organized, however, were Presbyterian both in name and in government. This was particularly true in Indiana and Illinois, though a few Congregational churches were organized in Ohio and Michigan Territory. From 1826 to 1833 the bulk of the funds for the support of the Home Missionary Society came from Presbyterian sources, but after 1833 the New England Congregationalists contributed more noticeably. The voluminous correspondence of the agents and appointees of the society furnishes much information not only on the religious aspects of western life but on western life in general.[37]

Some of the missionaries conveyed the idea that the settlers were generally depraved and quite satisfied with their condition.

[34] The Indiana society had employed Reed, Hall, and four others on part time for missionary work in 1825. Reed, in a letter of 1824 to the United Domestic Missionary Society (*Christian Traveller*, 163 ff., and Society *Report*, 1825, 68 ff.), pointed out the backwardness of Presbyterian effort in the state as compared with that of Methodists and Baptists. There were more than thirty Methodist and more than twenty Baptist ministers in the state as compared with a dozen Presbyterians. *Christian Traveller*, 193.

In 1830 the Wabash Presbytery (covering fifteen or sixteen counties and some 60,000 people) had sixteen organized churches and but *"three* mere babes in the gospel ministry" to watch over them. Letter from the Presbytery, Princeton, Indiana, October 2, 1830, to Secretary of the American Home Missionary Society. Papers of the American Home Missionary Society.

[35] In addition to Reed's book other contemporary accounts of early Indiana Presbyterians are John M. Dickey, *A Brief History of the Presbyterian Church in the State of Indiana* (Madison, 1828), and James H. Johnston, *A Ministry of Forty Years in Indiana* (Indianapolis, 1865). See also Hanford A. Edson, *Contributions to the Early History of the Presbyterian Church in Indiana; together with biographical notices of the pioneer ministers* (Cincinnati, 1898).

[36] Including John McElroy Dickey, Isaac Reed, James H. Johnston, John M. Ellis, and Elbridge G. Howe.

[37] The activities of the society are well covered in Frederick Kuhns, "The American Home Missionary Society in the Old Northwest 1826–1861," MS. Ph.D. thesis, University of Chicago, 1947; see also Goodykoontz, *Home Missions on the Western Frontier*, and Sweet, *The Presbyterians* and *The Congregationalists*.

In the mining country around Galena a missionary reported that "the vices of Sabbath breaking, profane swearing, the free use of strong drink and the practice of gambling are very prevalent at least beyond any thing I ever saw. But I have not thought it my duty to make a *direct* attack upon them, from a persuasion that if they were not restrained from respect to the ministerial character nothing would be gained by incurring their displeasure. . . ."[38] "Brother we have no sabbath at the west. It is all lost in coming here. . . . If anything of it remains, it quickly falls off in the easy current of degeneracy—a wide and sweeping stream overflowing all its banks." The Catholics in the French settlements rode, fished, danced, played cards, and billiards and had parties on the Sabbath.[39] At Navarino (Green Bay) "Satan and sin [were] making fearful ravages all around with none to oppose,"[40] while at Milwaukee even professing Christians seemed "to forget that God's law extend[ed] over this wilderness. . . ."[41] Grand Rapids was credited with having two hundred barrels of whiskey but only one of flour.[42] It was hard to persuade people long unaccustomed to preaching to acquire the habit of listening to it again, and even those interested had a variety of notions and were hard to please. "One, as soon as any religious excitement exists, is for shouting, dancing, jerking, falling, etc. Another is a great stickler for 'the doctrine discipline and orders of the Presbyterian Church' and is for moving on in a calm even way, while nothing will suit a third, which does not tally with Dr. Hopkins. I find that it requires all my skill to keep them together, and I dare not leave them a week for fear something will go wrong."[43]

A few years later another missionary reported from Illinois:

[38] Aratus Kent, Galena, Illinois, June 4, 1829, to Corresponding Secretary Absalom Peters. Papers of the American Home Missionary Society. For additional material on Kent, see Gordon A. Riegler, "Aratus Kent, First Presbyterian Minister in Northern Illinois," in *Journal of the Presbyterian Historical Society*, XIII, 363–80 (Dec., 1929).

[39] J. M. Ellis, Kaskaskia, Illinois, August 7, 1827, to Absalom Peters. Papers of the American Home Missionary Society.

[40] Dr. R. S. Satterlee, Fort Howard, Michigan Territory, March 15, 1834, to Peters. *Ibid.*

[41] A. L. Barber (first agent to labor in Wisconsin), Milwaukee, M. T., October 2, 1835, to Peters. *Ibid.*

[42] William Page, Ann Arbor, M. T., March 2, 1836, to secretary of the society. *Ibid.*

[43] Solomon Hardy, Greenville, Bond County, Illinois, May 28, 1828, to Peters. *Ibid.*

"Among us, it is now what I should call a time of stupidity, in respect to religion. Not that we have any neglect of the means of grace. Meetings are well attended—on the Sabbath our house is generally filled—people listen with attention—but no sinners are converted. The word is heard but not obeyed. To human view the prospect is dark."[44]

Then there was the worrisome competition of the other sects. Enoch Kingsbury, writing from Danville, Illinois, in 1834, said:

The set time to favor Zion here does not appear to have come. Some sects have enjoyed a temporary prosperity. A few years since the Newlights or Christians possessed the field and produced a momentary flash which has since been succeeded by deeper darkness. Three years since the Baptists were the most numerous & influential. They mostly embraced the sentiments of Daniel Parker, opposed Sabbath Schools, Temperance Scs. &c—together with other denominations. For a year or two past they have been on the wane. Their peculiarities appear to operate against them. Two years ago the Mormonites in turning the world upside down came hither also. And many gave heed unto them. Now they are generally neglected. At present the Methodists are the most important sect in this region. I anticipate the time when presbyterianism will be more prosperous. . . . Around me is a very wide & desolate field. . . .[45]

Later, Canton was also reported as being in a bad way:

Of the Gospel the people here have been destitute. The Devil has had his emissaries there for years, but Christ *none*. I found Campbellites, Hixite Quakers, Universalists, Deists, &c, with *a very few professors* of the Religion of Jesus. . . . The better part of the community had become disgusted with the blackguard & slang which had been palmed off on them for preaching, and at first not knowing but this was a slice from the same loaf, did not generally come out—but they soon learned the difference, and the congregation increased in numbers, attention & solemnity.[46]

In Ohio the outlook was equally depressing:

I might state that the influence of our Church, is certainly felt to a considerable extent, & is undoubtedly the only instrumentality that prevents our Township from being overwhelmed with Universalism—that deadly poison to morality & vital godliness. I would not defame a denomination, which I hope are doing good in some places. I mean our Methodist Brethren—But O the dreadful influence *they*, or *their manner of doing*, their sentiments have had, in this region of country. It is an astounding

[44] Lucien Farnam, Princeton, Illinois, July 1, 1836, to Peters. Papers of the American Home Missionary Society.
[45] Enoch Kingsbury, Danville, Illinois, January 13, 1834, to Peters. *Ibid.*
[46] Levi Spencer, Canton, Illinois, January 2, 1843, to the secretaries. *Ibid.*

fact that most of the Universalists who have been bred here, or as such, have emigrated to this place, are apostates from that Church—and what seems to render their case hopeless is that whilst in connection with that Church, their whole religious instruction & training seems to have been to teach them to despise what we receive as the distinguishing doctrines of the Gospel. It places them out of our reach. The *sweet,* but *dubious* error they cleave unto, because they have been early & faithfully prejudiced against "the more excellent way". . . . This will in some measure account for the fact that the youth among us, who have heard much of this easy way, to heaven, cannot be made to feel the force of moral obligation & therefore remain strangers to vital piety. Our Sabbath breaking can be traced up partially to this source. . . . I have no quarrel with the Methodists—we have always lived in peace with them—some of them are our personal friends.[47]

Other Ohio missionaries reported in like vein. Richmond, a village of four hundred souls, was described as one fifth infidel.

We have Methodist and Baptist churches & a few Episcopal families & the dividend is necessarily small. . . . All at once & by surprise we were visited, by six Methodist ministers . . . from a neighboring Methodist ch. And more popular talent, for a long time, I have not seen displayed than was displayed by one of the ministers, & after all he was a mere bag of wind, but well calculated to produce popular effect. . . . They labored till everybody was tired out & it seemed to me that they would well nigh blow out all the religion in the place.[48]

Near by at Newburgh Methodists and Disciples withdrew from the Presbyterian meetings, and the Sabbath school which had been a union undertaking was taken over "clandestinely" by the Methodists. "It is grievous & to me heart rending, to be compelled to state such things of the professed followers of Christ —but truth requires it."[49] Huron on the lake "is a very wicked place, has three Nine Pin allies . . . but few attend church."[50] "Through all this region Universalism reigns almost triumphant & undisputed, & exerts its deadly influence on soul & body."[51] The "New Congregationalism," was doing "great mischief"; ministers were creating disaffection and multiplying evils. Some

[47] Jacob Tuttle, Jefferson, Franklin County, Ohio, April 4, 1838, to Milton Badger. *Ibid.*
[48] Ferris Fitch, Richmond, Cuyahoga County, Ohio, March 13 and October 31, 1837, to Absalom Peters. *Ibid.*
[49] John Keys, Newburgh, Cuyahoga County, Ohio, June 9, 1838, to Milton Badger. *Ibid.*
[50] Fitch to Peters, October 31, 1838. *Ibid.*
[51] S. I. Bradstreet, Perrysburg, Wood County, Ohio, October 1, 1838, to Peters. *Ibid.*

"Oberlin ministers," influenced by Charles Grandison Finney, who was "rotten in principle and far gone, if not irrecoverably, in the road of Arminianism and error,"[52] were taking a stand against Presbyterian efforts.[53]

Worse still was the general indifference or the lack of religious sentiment on the part of some people:

Worldly men of any considerable reflection through their natural aversion to religion associate the weakness of the advocates with the cause which they support and look upon religion almost of course as unworthy the regard of their grade of intellect. And it is here Dear Sir that we open our eyes to a dark feature in the prospects of the West. I mean the tendency of this state of things to the general prevalence of Anti-Christian principles and the worst forms of infidelity & Atheism. And unless the efforts of your Society & of the friends of religion and education in this region be increased many fold and followed by the marked blessings of heaven, I tremble for the principles which shall prevail and the scenes which shall be acted on this stage in future years. I ask you Sir can we ever expect that this torrent is to be stemmed by men of inferior talents and qualifications?[54]

Trouble with ardent spirits added to the spiritual troubles. At Richmond, Indiana (and probably elsewhere), was to be faced "the *dreadful fact,* that professors of religion from Orthodox Presbyterian, Congregational, and Baptist churches, and who in their native towns were members of temperance societies, come to this and, instead of aiding us to remove the evil, increase it an hundred fold; for they not only make use of ardent spirits; but intoxicate others with it."[55]

One expects complaints such as these, but it comes as somewhat of a shock to discover at least one minister who found a community which was too Presbyterian. Gull Prairie, Michigan

[52] Cutting Marsh, Stockbridge near Green Bay, Wisconsin Territory, May 8, 1837, to Absalom Peters. Papers of the American Home Missionary Society.

[53] Fitch to Peters, February 7, 1837. *Ibid.*

[54] This letter ended: *"Do not by any means give any part of my remarks on this subject to the public."* J. M. Sturtevant, Jacksonville, Illinois, September 5, 1830, to Absalom Peters. B. C. Cressy wrote from Salem, Indiana, November 8, 1830, to Peters: "Among others [here], there is an army of professed Deists. The spirited exertions of Christians . . . have around them sons of Belial to contend earnestly for the claims of their master the Devil." James B. Morrow wrote from Canton, Ohio, January 21, 1828: "The Deists at Canton . . . are taking a systematic & decided course of operations—their number is considerable, and many of them are men of influence in their sphere. . . . The introduction of a *preacher* of Deism here, will form an era in the religious history of Canton, ominous of fearful results. . . ." His letter of July 21, 1828, was even more pessimistic. *Ibid.*

[55] Peter Crocker, Richmond, Indiana, October 12, 1836, to Peters. *Ibid.*

Territory, was settled by about a hundred Presbyterians and Congregationalists,

who in the infancy of the settlement were going to have an Eden on the
foot stool, with nothing but angels, for neighbors—nine deacons and three
ministers. But so much salt of the earth, piled upon one place, lost its
savour—just as I believe it always will in similar cases. Sourness, and
discord has been the result. These Christian township colonies on prairie
lands however well intended, and fascinating in the prospect, we are afraid,
are a sort of religious selfishness—a holy worldly mindedness—a petty
joining of God & mammon—a smug way of laying up treasures on earth
under the show of benevolence and self denial, which sooner or later will
turn into a hornet's nest. (I write you perceive not for publication, but as
intellect fancies, and conscience approves) We hope however the pious
errors of Gull Prairie will not be punished everlastingly. There are some
signs of repentance. One deacon is about to leave, and two ministers told
me they also were going away & intended to be more useful men. When
the salt shall be . . . scattered we may expect more salvation. I preached
& preached again to them. . . . They can now support a pastor if
they will.[56]

Either way, whether trying to improve the widespread "moral
waste" or managing the "salt of the earth," the ministers had
a task which required as much hard labor and perseverance as
subduing the forests and prairies to cultivation; it was no job
for a boy. As James Hall, ever interested in the welfare of the
West, wrote in 1831: "Our cause of complaint, against several
of the Eastern Societies, has been, their sending out young, in-
efficient, inexperienced men, as agents—men just from their
books—or rather *boys* just from college—without any knowledge of human nature, deficient in common sense, and some of
them lamentably ignorant of everything but their Bibles. They
had better send none—for not only do these gentlemen do no
good, but they do great harm."[57] And an experienced minister
wrote that "we want a man that is not frightened at wickedness
in any shape but will be ready to meet it & put it down. . . . He
must be able to *talk* as well as *preach* & speak *extempore* as well
as *write*."[58]

Nevertheless, education could not be dispensed with. As J. M.

[56] William Page, Ann Arbor, Michigan Territory, March 2, 1836, to the secretary
of the society. *Ibid.*
[57] Hall, at Vandalia, Illinois, August 20, 1831, to Peters. *Ibid.*
[58] Stephen Peet, Euclid, Cuyahoga County, Ohio, October 1, 1828, to Peters. *Ibid.*

Sturtevant, of Illinois College, pointed out, the woods were full of farmers, carpenters, and shoemakers who added the secondary function of preaching—"men who possess no intellectual elevation above the great mass of the population whom they address." To compete with preachers of this type some educated ministers admitted that all that was necessary was to make a great noise, then mingle in a few ideas if possible.[59]

Though the agents of the American Home Missionary Society were more settled than were the Methodist circuit riders, still theirs could not be called a sedentary occupation. Excerpts from a few pages from the journal of Isaac Reed for May 1–15, 1826, give an idea of the activities of a missionary:

Re-crossed the Wabash, and rode 38 miles down the river. . . . Rode 32 miles without stopping . . . was thoroughly drenched. . . . [Next day] felt a little dull and sore . . . read some in Josephus; preached at 4 o'clock . . . visited two families . . . rode 32 miles back . . . rode five miles to Terre Haute . . . but no congregation assembled . . . preached at night [Saturday]. . . . preached at 11 o'clock [the Sabbath] in the court house. . . . Rode six miles in the morning. . . . rode to New-Hope meeting house . . . preached at 4 o'clock. . . . Retraced the way to Scaffold prairie, about 33 miles. . . . Weak from fatigue of yesterday . . . rode about 13 miles; visited three families. . . . Rode 12 miles today. . . . rode 10 miles today. . . . preached at night. . . . Started for home. Had to swim our horses across Fish creek . . . rode 34 miles. . . .

In thirty-four days Reed preached sixteen times, "had two seasons of asking the shorter catechism to families," baptized one child, constituted one church, administered the Lord's Supper, visited and prayed with one dying person, made twenty-eight visits with families, and traveled 394 miles.[60]

Pay was poor and when received from the local churches was usually in kind. The agents of the American Home Missionary Society referred constantly to the newness of the country, the scarcity of money, and the unwillingness of those who had any to part with it. "Provisions were scarce—commanding a high price & nothing in return would be received but money," wrote William Page from White Pigeon, Michigan Territory, in 1830. He had had to borrow $25 from a friend and had illness expense besides. He estimated his salary from the people of the several

[59] J. M. Sturtevant, Jacksonville, Illinois, September 5, 1830, to Absalom Peters. Papers of the American Home Missionary Society.
[60] The Christian Traveller, 181–84.

communities in which he worked at $100 "and not a dollar in money at all." Samuel Vance, "clark" of the Paris church, Edwards County, Illinois, explained to the society that the people were unable to support a minister—"the people generally poor and mony scarce the land office dreans all the money from this Contry." The Reverend E. G. Howe and wife "is both Sick at this time . . . we have Eighteen Subscribers in this Church the Subscrbtion . . . amounts to Something over one hundred dolers and about the same in New hope and the most of that in trade, we think that not Sifisiant to Support Mr. Howe and as he has no other means of support we Humbly Solicite your aid. . . . ."[61]

From such a well settled community as Richmond, Indiana, Peter Crocker received about $150, "seventeen only in money"; his ministerial labors cost him more than $100 a year beyond what he received. "Though the money pressure is a subject of general and bitter complaint, and some do suffer much on account of it, the haters of God and lovers of sin seem to find it easy to carry forward their worldly and wicked plans."[62] Another minister received but one five dollar bill in two and a half years. Food he could get, but clothing, postage, and other items required cash.[63]

Even the society was accused of niggardliness on occasion. Mrs. Amorett C. Adams, wife of the Reverend Charles Adams, had for nine years dedicated herself to the cause of missions, but, when the society withheld an expected grant to her husband, she unburdened herself in plain language:

Why this delay on your part is a mystery we cannot solve. We have managed to get along by disposing of some household articles necessary to be sure but which we could better do without than *bread*. We have also been compelled to dispose of our little home at a great sacrifice to meet the payments before referred to & some debts contracted while trying to get along without assistance before coming to this place. Our present wants are numerous. Our little ones need shoes & other suitable clothing for the season. We have no feather bed, designed to purchase one but have not the means. Husband needs an overcoat or wrapper—but enough of this—I will make no further inventory of our wants.

[61] Vance to Peters, July 14, 1827. Papers of the American Home Missionary Society.
[62] Crocker to Milton Badger, April 13, 1839. *Ibid.*
[63] Sylvester Cochran, Vermontville, Michigan, March 3, 1840, to the society secretaries. *Ibid.*

Are you parents? contrast your situation with that of the poor missionary in this western wild & enquire of the Lord the path of duty in reference to our case, & may you be directed so that you will not stand condemned when Christ shall say "Inasmuch as ye have done it unto one of these my brethren ye have done it unto me" is the prayer of your servant.

There followed a postscript in which this cultivated lady stated that her husband was moving to another church, and a post-postscript in which she informed the society that if the officers decided to do anything about it, the Adams' post office address was still the same.[64]

Then there was the problem of wives, which the society did not face as boldly as did the Methodist authorities. Many Westerners believed that a good preacher was more likely to remain among them if he married a western woman. As they said, "if an eastern minister comes here *with* a wife she will be discontented, and cause him to return. If he comes without a wife he will probably go to the east for one and we shall see no more of him before there is no chance of keeping him, unless he marry in this country." Ministers who were contemplating a western ministry were advised seriously "to weigh this subject."[65]

By 1831 the society had 463 missionaries laboring among 577 congregations and districts, most of them in the West.[66] By this time, however, the controversy between the "Old School" Presbyterians with their stricter scruples over the constitution of the church and the "New School" Presbyterians was approaching a showdown. The New School men had strayed somewhat from the old-line discipline and doctrine,[67] and were flirting with abolitionism.[68] Old School men grew restive under the yoke of the Plan of Union, and, since nearly all of the ministers who labored

[64] Adams' alleged "Oberlinism" was the root cause of the society's displeasure. A letter from Providence, Bureau County, Illinois, November 18, 1845, to the society. Papers of the American Home Missionary Society.

[65] Solomon Hardy, Greenville, Bond County, Illinois, May 28, 1828, to Absalom Peters. *Ibid.*

[66] Sweet, *The Presbyterians,* 105.

[67] The Samuel Hopkins—Timothy Dwight—New Divinity—New England influence. Between 1820 and 1833 the Plan-of-Union churches often sent standing committeemen instead of ruling elders to represent them in presbyterial and synodical meetings and to the General Assembly. This practice was not favored by Old School Presbyterians. In 1828 Nathaniel W. Taylor, of Yale, preached a sermon which went even further than the Hopkinsians. Albert Barnes, who accepted the advanced Taylor views, was for several years the storm center of heresy charges and trials.

[68] See Chapter XV, 617 ff.

for the society in the Old Northwest were either Congregationalists or New School Presbyterians, the society began to feel the
repercussions. In the General Assembly of 1835 the Old School
group succeeded in placing the burden of dissolving the Plan upon
the General Association of Connecticut which had sponsored it.
A schism in the General Assembly of 1836 was narrowly averted;
with New School forces in the majority and abolitionism to the
front, southern presbyteries and synods threatened secession.[69]
In 1837 the Old School group controlled the General Assembly's
proceedings, directed the western synods to "take order" regarding the doctrinal and constitutional soundness of their ministers
and churches, exscinded four synods,[70] and created the Board of
Foreign Missions of the Presbyterian Church as a rival to the
American Board of Commissioners for Foreign Missions (now
Congregationalist).

As a result of these actions 509 ministers, 599 churches, and
some 60,000 members were stricken from the roll of the Presbyterian Church and without an appeal. Some of them transferred to Congregational churches, but the majority organized
the New School General Assembly in 1838. Despite court action,
the Old School General Assembly retained the boards and other
properties of the Presbyterian Church.[71] A spirited struggle ensued between the two groups for adherents in the Old Northwest.[72] The Synod of Indiana was about equally divided in so
far as the ministerial members were concerned; an Old School

[69] This controversy is well covered in Frederick Kuhns, "Slavery and Missions in
the Old Northwest," in *Journal of the Presbyterian Historical Society*, XXIV,
205–22 (Dec., 1946).
[70] Exscinded were the Synods of Utica, Geneva, Genesee, and the Western
Reserve.
Troubles of an Old School Presbyterian were indicated by a letter in the Ravenna
Western Courier, March 27, 1834. At a "protracted meeting" the writer had heard
the preacher state that "conversion consists in *resolving* to serve God"—that "we
do not inherit our sin from Adam," etc., doctrines variant from the Presbyterian
articles of faith.
[71] The dispute was carried to the Supreme Court of the Commonwealth of
Pennsylvania in 1839. The court granted the New School following the right to
claim their General Assembly as the "constitutional" one. Old School men won a
retrial, but further action was not taken.
The Old School General Assembly continued to meet annually; the New School
met in 1838, 1839, and 1840, then triennially until 1849 when the annual sessions
were resumed.
[72] In the struggle for adherents the Old School Presbyterians were more successful in southern Ohio, Indiana, and Illinois. Relatively few Old School churches
were to be found on the Western Reserve, in northern Indiana, or in southern
Michigan between 1837 and 1840.

synod was constituted in 1838.[73] Similarly in Illinois the Old School presbyters seceded from the Synod of Illinois (formed in 1831) and set up their own synod.[74] The Synod of Michigan (formed in 1834) was preponderantly New School. The Old School elements succeeded only in organizing the Presbytery of Michigan (1840), with three ministers; it was attached to the Old School synod of Indiana.[75] In 1839 the Presbytery of Wisconsin (later, of Milwaukee) was formed by joint action of the Presbyterians and the Congregationalists; as earlier in New York and Ohio, Congregational churches were to be "accommodated." The next year (1840) the Presbyterian and Congregational Convention of Wisconsin was organized; churches of both denominations were admitted on an equal footing.[76]

During these internecine struggles among the Presbyterians the chief heresy hunter in the Old Northwest was Joshua L. Wilson, of Cincinnati, who in 1831 had started *The Standard* to defend the Old School doctrines. When Wilson went after the Reverend Asa Mahan of Cincinnati, friends of the latter brought charges against Wilson. The case was so confused that the synod, to which it was appealed, gave both sides "advice and injunction" and let it go at that. Wilson, a member of the committee which selected Lyman Beecher for the presidency of Lane Seminary, soon decided that Beecher's theological views were unsound. When the Cincinnati Presbytery refused to investigate Beecher, Wilson in 1834 made formal charges; when Beecher was acquitted, Wilson appealed to the Cincinnati Synod. When the synod merely cautioned Beecher "to be more guarded in the future," Wilson took the case to the General Assembly. But with this body in New School hands the chances for action were slight, and Wilson withdrew his appeal.[77]

[73] "Records of the Synod of Indiana (Old School) 1838–1848," pp. 17–18; "Records of the Synod of Indiana (New School) 1826–1847," pp. 256–57. Transcript copies in the library of the McCormick Theological Seminary, Chicago, Illinois.

[74] MS. Minutes, Synod of Illinois (New School), 1831–1855, pp. 117–19, 132–33, 137, 142; MS. Minutes, Synod of Illinois (Old School), I, 1–4. Illinois State Historical Library.

[75] John Comin, "History of the Presbyterian Church in Michigan," in *Minutes of the 100th Annual Meeting of the Synod of Michigan*, 1934, pp. 50–58.

[76] Charles J. Kennedy, "The Presbyterians on the Wisconsin Frontier," in *Journal of the Presbyterian Historical Society*, XVIII–XIX (Dec., 1938—Mar., 1940), *passim*.

[77] For a sketch of this controversial character, see R. L. Hightower, "Joshua L. Wilson, Frontier Controversialist," in *Church History*, III (1934), 300–16. The Wilson Papers are in the Durrett Collection, University of Chicago Libraries.

Edward Beecher, president of Illinois College, J. M. Sturtevant, and William Kirby, professors, were also charged with heresy for their New Haven doctrinal leanings. When they were acquitted by the Centre Presbytery, the case was appealed to the Illinois Synod; but, since their accuser's record was vulnerable, nothing further came of it.[78]

The Presbyterian schism strengthened Congregationalism in the region. Several churches in Illinois and Michigan set up independently from their former Presbyterian allies. Home missionaries Asa Turner and William Carter of the "Yale Band" helped form the Congregational Association of Illinois in 1835; others organized the Congregational Union of Fox River in the same year, and the Rock River Association in 1838; additional Congregational associations were formed in Michigan and Indiana in 1837 which, though short-lived, indicated a trend.[79] In 1838 the Central Ohio Association was organized; it contained several Congregational churches which had been either disowned by the Presbyterians or frowned upon by the agents of the American Home Missionary Society, or both, and there were several other Congregational associations in Ohio by 1840.

Nominally Congregationalists but almost a breed apart were the "Oberlinites." Though the Oberlin men usually received their licensure and ordination in the Lorain County Congregational Association, few "orthodox" churches, either Congregational or Presbyterian, were willing to run the theological risk of admitting to fellowship the men trained under Finney, Mahan, Henry Cowles, and John Morgan. The doctrine of Perfectionism to which they had been exposed made them suspects.

There were several other brands of Presbyterianism in the Old Northwest besides the main-line Old School and New School groups. The Cumberland Presbyterians, mentioned earlier in this chapter, had their greatest strength in Kentucky and Tennessee, but they had spread into the southern parts of Ohio, Indiana,

[78] Matthew Spinka (ed.), *A History of Illinois Congregational and Christian Churches* (Chicago, 1944), 44–45.

[79] The first Congregational Church in Indiana was probably the one formed in 1833 at Bath, Franklin County, just across the Ohio border. There were fewer than a dozen Congregational churches in the state preceding 1840. Frederick Kuhns, "A Sketch of Congregationalism in Indiana to 1858," in *Indiana Magazine of History,* XLII (1946), 346–50. See also Nathaniel A. Hyde, *Congregationalism in Indiana* (Indianapolis, 1895).

and Illinois and into the Military Tract in Illinois.[80] They seldom merged with New School congregations but did on occasion, particularly in southern Illinois, blend with Old School members.

Associate Presbyterians, Associate Reformed Presbyterians, and the Reformed or "Covenanter" Presbyterians[81] also had congregations in the Old Northwest. In 1844 the Associate Presbyterians were reported as having approximately 5,000 communicant members, 108 congregations, and 36 ministers in the Northwest.[82]

In the struggle for souls on the frontier the Presbyterians were at a certain disadvantage by reason of both doctrine and type of training of ministers required. The preacher who had prepared his sermons in a theological seminary and who delivered his polished discourse from a manuscript fired the hearts of only a small percentage of those who had been brought up on the eloquence of western stump oratory. The Presbyterians generally distrusted the emotionalists, though some of their agents were willing to adopt some of the methods of the latter. "The people expect the preacher or the office seeker will come to them. So it is by itinerating is the only way that your society [Home Missionary Society] can reach many and extensive sections of the country. . . . the people in the West must see & hear for themselves."[83]

The revivals and protracted meetings of the Presbyterians and the Congregationalists were usually more decorous than

[80] In 1833 the Cumberland Presbyterians had thirty-two presbyteries and six synods; in 1843 fifty-seven presbyteries and thirteen synods, one in the Republic of Texas.

[81] For the origin of the Associate Reformed Presbyterians see *ante*, note 11. They had formed the General Synod in 1803, but in 1820 the Synod of the West withdrew. The latter comprised two subsynods; most of the congregations were in western Pennsylvania, Ohio, Kentucky, Indiana, Illinois, and Michigan.

Following the Settlement of 1689 some Scottish Presbyterians renounced both church and state and in 1743 formed the Reformed Presbytery of Scotland. They set up their first presbytery in America in 1744 and a synod in 1808 which in 1825 took the name "General Synod."

In 1733 a formal separation from the Church of Scotland was made by a group which protested the growing centralization and strange new doctrines; they set up the Associate Synod. The first Associate Synod in America was formed in 1753. In 1858 the Associate Reformed and the Associate Presbyterians formed the United Presbyterian Church.

[82] Embraced in four presbyteries in Ohio, one in Indiana, and one in Illinois. W. I. Cleland and James P. Miller, "Associate Presbyterian Church in North America," in I. Daniel Rupp (ed.), *An Original History of the Religious Denominations at present existing in the United States* . . . (Philadelphia, 1844), 10.

[83] John M. Ellis, Kaskaskia, Illinois, May 23, 1827, to Absalom Peters. Papers of the American Home Missionary Society.

were those conducted by the more numerous Methodists and Baptists; the emphasis was different:

Our appointments for each day . . . were, a prayer meeting at 10 o'clock in the morning, preaching at 11,—a recess of a few minutes, then prayer till 2 P.M., when we had preaching again, and neighborhood meetings in the evenings. . . . The work has been attended with no noise, no extravagances—but marked by great solemnity, a deep sense of guilt, and of obligation to repentance—and clear views of Jesus Christ as the *only* hope of sinners. The doctrines preached, were the entire depravity of the sinner; the necessity of the Holy Spirit in regeneration; the rectitude of God's claims upon the sinner, and his obligations to an immediate and unconditional compliance with those claims; the justice of God in the sinner's condemnation, the nature and extent of the atonement; the fulness and freeness of the offers of mercy and the fearfully aggravated doom of gospel rejection.[84]

Such heavy going required a certain type of mind; it left little outlet for the exuberance of those who wished to engage the devil in a personal gouging match. As a consequence the Methodists and the Baptists frequently carried the offensive:

Calvinism is caricatured & a tirade of abuse poured upon its poor defenseless head;—some of the preachers commence, carry on, & finish revival meetings with such preaching. And, where they have the vantage ground, they wedge in, at every point their mechanical and distinctive peculiarities, compel us to, virtually, endorse them as the most scriptural & practical, or to withdraw, leaving the impression that we are sectarian, or don't believe in the life and power of religion (as they call it). "So they wrap it up."[85]

Though American Presbyterianism differed considerably from that of its Scottish and Irish ancestry, it still retained much of the rigid and serious character imparted to it by Bucer, Calvin, Knox, and others. Dr. John Witherspoon in the colonial period had done much to bring about American modifications. Nevertheless, American Presbyterians adhered to the three main principles of church government: (1) the Church is "one in the sense that a smaller part is subject to a larger, and a larger to the whole," and "the principles of government laid down in the Scriptures bind the whole Church"; (2) the officers of the Church are the presbyters, "who minister in word and doctrine," and all of whom belong to the same order; (3) the right of the

---

[84] Lucien Farnam, Princeton, Illinois, July 1, 1835, to Peters. *Ibid.*
[85] L. L. Radcliff, Prairie du Chien, Wisconsin, May 25, 1838, to the secretaries. *Ibid.*

members "to a substantive part of the government of the Church." "It is not holding one of these principles that makes a man a Presbyterian, but his holding them all."

Despite the rigidity of Calvinistic doctrine, Presbyterianism maintained one of the most democratic polities of any of the churches on the frontier. In theory, the members, when they united with the church, had conferred upon them by Christ, guided by the Holy Ghost, the right to elect and set apart for life or good behavior their ruling elders whom they declared to be their representatives. The elders and the ministers constituted the session, the representative body which carried on the government of the local church. When a number (four or more) of ministers and ruling elders in a given district desired to do so, they formed themselves into a presbytery which attached itself to the nearest synod. The minister was not a member of the church or churches he served but of the presbytery which contained the church or churches, and his choice, licensure, ordination, installation, transfer, and dismissal from a presbytery had to be in accordance with the constituted rules of the church. To the presbytery was given the general oversight of all the churches within its bounds and the inspection of church records; it had duties and responsibilities pertaining to the education, ordination, and service of ministers; it had judicial functions within the church government.

Next in order above the presbytery as a judicatory was the synod which embraced all the presbyteries within its geographical bounds. An elder, a minister, or a church might appeal a decision in a case of discipline to the synod. The synod, subject to the approval of the General Assembly, might "new-model" itself or regroup its presbyteries as the need arose. Appeals in case of discipline could be carried from the synod to the General Assembly.

The General Assembly was the highest governing body of the church. It created boards and commissions for the guidance and administration of the church, for education, home and foreign missions and the like. It was presided over by the moderator. The trustees handled fiscal affairs, and the stated clerk was responsible for keeping the records, making the annual reports of the boards, and taking care of official publications. Despite the fact that the General Assembly possessed great powers and was the highest judicial tribunal, even its general enactments, particularly those which involved constitutional changes, were subject to review and ratification by the presbyteries; only their approval or ratification could make these acts constitutional and binding on the whole church.

The revised Constitution of 1820 passed over in silence the close relationships which had obtained between the Presbyterians and the Congregationalists since 1801; the ensuing uncertainty as to its interpretation led the Old School Presbyterians in time to base their claim that the Plan of Union was unconstitutional on versions of the Constitution in force before 1801. The rigid character of Presbyterian polity was one of the important causes of the schism in 1837–38. In 1840, or two years after their own General Assembly had been constituted, the New School commissioners voted away the appellate jurisdiction which had formerly been exercised by that Assembly. The synods then became the final courts of appeal and, as "provincial assemblies," assumed more of the powers formerly delegated to the higher body, though they did not supplant the latter as a general coordinating and morale-stiffening factor in the life of the whole Church.[86]

§ § §

Methodism came to America in a more or less haphazard fashion about ten years before the War for Independence. Scattered ministers in the colonies sent a "call for help" to England in 1768, and a handful of missionaries came over; but for most of them it was a temporary mission. The first Methodist Conference, held at Philadelphia in 1773, assigned ten preachers to American circuits. Of these first missionaries all but Francis Asbury returned to England during the war. The followers of John Wesley, receiving but little co-operation from the colonial Anglican clergy, soon struck out on their own. Important early gains were made in Maryland and Virginia and to a lesser extent

[86] Edward D. Morris, *A Book of Remembrance: Presbyterian Church New School 1837–1869; an historical review* (Columbus, Ohio, 1905), 96–98. For Presbyterian organization see Charles Hodge, *What is Presbyterianism?* . . . (Philadelphia, Presbyterian Board of Publication, 1855).

in the Middle States,[87] where it was said that the Calvinists and the Universalists had "very much retard[ed] the work of God" by keeping "heart religion" from the people.[88] Likewise, some progress was made in lifting a few Presbyterians and Baptists "out of the Calvinian and Antinomian quicksands" in Virginia and the Carolinas.

From England in 1784 Wesley sent three men, among them Dr. Thomas Coke, to establish an ecclesiastical organization among the Methodists in America. Asbury and others were willing to co-operate but on condition that the project be carried out in the American way. After strenuous effort, scores of widely scattered preachers were rounded up for the famous "Christmas Conference" at Baltimore. This conference in ten days not only secured the independence of the Methodist Church in the United States but formulated the rules which, with amendment, have guided it since. By majority vote Coke and Asbury—both previously appointed by Wesley—were elected superintendents, and the conference adopted the Twenty-four Articles of Religion,[89] a discipline based upon Wesley's *Larger Minutes*, and the Wesleyan service and hymns. Several preachers were ordained as deacons, then as elders. Thus the young and numerically weak Methodists were the first of the denominations to secure an independent national organization. Circumstances and American leadership had created a wider gap between the Church of England and the American Methodists than Wesley had intended.

Following the Revolution Methodism spread west from North Carolina and Virginia into the Tennessee and Kentucky country, thence across the Ohio into the Northwest. By 1800 there were some fourteen circuits west of the Alleghenies; two of these—the Scioto and the Miami circuits—were in the Northwest Territory. Four years later the Ohio district, with five circuits, was organized. The Whitewater circuit in Indiana Territory was

[87] The conference in the spring of 1784 reported 42 circuits and 14,988 society members of whom only 2,589 resided north of Maryland. Sweet, *The Methodists,* 11. Wesley and Asbury had tried to keep Methodism as a movement in the Church of England, but the loyalty of the leaders to the English government during the Revolution had made this well-nigh impossible in America.

[88] *Ibid.,* 15, citing Asbury to Wesley, September 20, 1783.

[89] Adapted by Wesley from the Thirty-nine Articles of the Church of England.

formed in 1805.[90] When Benjamin Young was sent to the Illinois country in 1803, he found the "bulk of the people given up to wickedness of every kind . . . . stealing, fighting and lying."[91] In 1812 the Ohio and Tennessee conferences were set up; southeastern Indiana lay within the former, Illinois Territory in the latter. Methodism was introduced into Michigan Territory as early as 1804, but no important work was done until the 1820's; Methodists were in Wisconsin Territory by 1836.[92] By 1840 there were eight annual conferences which lay, either in whole or in part, within the Old Northwest.[93]

Of all the denominations the Methodists were the best equipped for success on the frontier: effective organization, self-sacrificing workers, and popular doctrines assured the wide and rapid spread of their church.

In England John Wesley had built up a more or less arbitrary system of government for his followers by the appointment of "helpers" and "assistants," or personal representatives, to supervise the helpers. When the system was extended to America, it was importantly modified. Prior to 1773 in the colonies the quarterly meeting conducted what little business there was, but starting in that year the annual conferences were only advisory to the "general assistant," Wesley's representative. With the separation of American Methodism in 1784, however, the conference assumed the power of electing deacons and elders and of admitting candidates into the ministry and into conference membership.[94] The "general conference," first held in 1792, in 1808

[90] Preachers from Kentucky had preached on Clark's Grant four years earlier. One of the earliest was Benjamin Lakin, whose Journal, 1794–1820, is published in Sweet, *The Methodists,* Chapter VII.

[91] Letter from Randolph County, Indiana Territory, June 1, 1804, quoted in James Leaton, *History of Methodism in Illinois, from 1793 to 1832* (Cincinnati, 1883), 34 ff.

[92] The Reverend William Case was appointed to Detroit by the New York Conference in 1809; he made one convert and quit. Shortly thereafter the Reverend William Mitchell organized a church with seven members. The present Central Methodist Episcopal Church was organized on March 21, 1822. For a historical sketch of early Detroit Methodism, see Louis Long, *A Century of Service, The History of Central Methodist Episcopal Church* (Detroit, 1922).

[93] The Ohio, which included a part of Virginia (1812); Pittsburgh (southeastern Ohio and parts of Virginia and Pennsylvania, 1824); Erie (northeastern Ohio and a corner of Pennsylvania); North Ohio; Illinois (1824); Indiana (1832); Michigan (1836); and Rock River (northern Illinois and Wisconsin Territory, 1840). Map in Sweet, *The Methodists,* 62.

[94] The yearly conference met in sections until 1796, when six separate conferences were formed. Asbury had proposed a council of bishops and presiding elders to run the affairs of the church, but this idea did not prove popular, and in

defined its powers, under certain restrictions, to govern; this action became in effect the constitution of the Methodist Episcopal Church.[95]

The basic unit in the Methodist organization was the local class or, if there was more than one class, the society. The class consisted of "believers," over whom was placed a leader. By Wesley's *General Rules* (1743) it was the class leader's business to visit each member weekly, "to enquire how his soul prosper," as well as "to advise, reprove, comfort, or exhort" the members, and to administer any donations for the poor. Above the class leader were the exhorter and the local preacher. Both were licensed although the latter was not necessarily ordained; if not ordained, the preacher could not administer the Lord's Supper, though he could baptize and perform the marriage ceremony. The Lord's Supper would be administered by the presiding elder on his quarterly rounds of the circuits. The local classes and societies made up the circuits. The leaders, exhorters, and local preachers (if any of the latter) were under the supervision of the circuit riders and the quarterly conference. The quarterly conference was composed of the class leaders, exhorters, stewards, and preachers of the circuit, both local and traveling—all in charge of the presiding elder. Circuits were united into districts, districts into conferences. The annual conference and the bishop controlled the appointments of the preachers to their circuits, matters of discipline and dress, and even the preachers' matrimonial ventures.

Despite its episcopal polity, the Methodist Church appeared to be democratic. This feature came about through the system of itineracy; for of all the religious workers on the frontier the circuit riders were the most picturesque, the best known, and among the best loved. Graduates of "Brush College" rather than of eastern colleges and theological seminaries, they supplemented the Bible, the *Discipline*, and Wesley's *Sermons* with a knowledge of forests and streams, of animals and men. Their

---

1792 the first general conference was called to be held thereafter every four years. In 1808, its size having become unwieldy, it was decided to make the body a representative one, with a delegate for every five members of each annual conference. Sweet, *The Methodists*, 38 ff.

[95] This subject is developed in detail in James M. Buckley, *Constitutional and Parliamentary History of the Methodist Episcopal Church* (New York, 1912), 121 ff.

"parchments of literary honors were the horse and the saddle-bags."[96] Though not uniformly dressed, the circuit riders were usually recognizable—perhaps by the straight-breasted coat, high collar, long waistcoat, sometimes short breeches and stockings, long hair, often a wide-brimmed fur hat of a light shade. It was said that even the chickens could recognize these harbingers of salvation, and that "as they approached the farm house these domestics would make for the barn or coop, and stand there with tears in their eyes until the honored divines departed."[97]

More distinctive than his dress, however, were the mien, the bearing, and the strength of purpose of the circuit rider; to many of these parsons were attributed "sparks of natural genius." Circuits were often large—a hundred miles and more around. Hardships were common and duties manifold. Though at times the itinerant might have to swim swollen streams several times in a day to reach his destination, no excuse was accepted for his failure to arrive on time, inasmuch as people who assembled from a distance for a "preaching," if disappointed, would like as not be missing the next time he came around.[98] The presiding elder kept track of punctuality. The itinerant preacher supervised, counseled with the class leaders and the local or lay preachers, ministered in matrimony and death, advised in family matters, kissed all the children, examined their heads, expressed an opinion as to their future usefulness, brought the news, and spread the Gospel. He preached every day in the week, except perhaps Monday, and at least twice at the Satur-

[96] John C. Smith, *Reminiscences of Early Methodism in Indiana.* . . . (Indianapolis, 1879), 39. On the circuit rider see also Sweet, *Circuit-Rider Days in Indiana,* and *Circuit-Rider Days along the Ohio* (New York, Cincinnati, 1923); Elizabeth K. Nottingham, *Methodism and the Frontier: Indiana Proving Ground* (New York, 1941); *Autobiography of Peter Cartwright; Autobiography of Rev. James B. Finley;* James B. Finley, *Sketches of Western Methodism* . . . (Cincinnati, 1854); Fernandez C. Holliday, *Life and Times of the Rev. Allen Wiley,* edited by D. W. Clark (Cincinnati, 1853); Elnathan C. Gavitt, *Crumbs from My Saddle Bags* (Toledo, 1884); Leonard B. Gurley, *Rev. William Gurley, Pioneer Ohio Methodist Preacher* (Cincinnati, 1851); Maxwell P. Gaddis, *Foot-Prints of an Itinerant* . . . (Cincinnati, 1855).

[97] Gavitt, *Crumbs from My Saddle Bags,* 69.

[98] For instance, Joseph Hickox in 1815 covered fifty-seven miles of wilderness around Detroit three times each fortnight, swimming his horse or ice jumping at five fordings each trip. Yet when he thought of the multitudes perishing for lack of knowledge and the privileges of free salvation, such hardships seemed insignificant. "Life and Times of Rev. Joseph Hickox," in *Michigan Pioneer and Historical Collections,* I (1877), 472. For experiences of sleeping with the children, dogs, chickens, and other varmints in the homes of adherents, all for $100 a year and boarding around, see Elijah H. Pilcher, "Forty Years Ago," in *ibid.,* V (1882), 82 ff.

day-Sunday "two-day" meeting. Monday was ordinarily the day of rest or "preacher's day"; then horse, clothes, and person received some attention, or the few books in the saddlebag library were read.

The annual conference, through the bishop, held a firm and at times a rigid control over the lives of the itinerants. Preferences for particular appointments on the part of the preachers were generally subordinated to larger ecclesiastical interests, and it seems that not even prayers availed much in obtaining the desired placements. As James B. Finley said, "Those who are the most in the habit of praying for appointments, are those who are generally most disappointed; for if their prayers were answered, it would be against the prayers of whole churches, who pray to be delivered from them."

In the matter of dress a general censorship was exercised; a tendency toward dandyism was held as bad as heresy. Even the junior preachers on the lookout for wives had to compromise judiciously between the dictates of fashion and "the good old way." Marriage was frowned upon during the four-year itineracy.[99] Unmarried ministers were required to consult with their brethren before mentioning matrimony to a young woman. (Just who the brethren were was not always clear, but the presiding elder often assumed the role of counselor.) Nevertheless, young preachers, if not in position to succumb themselves, sometimes generously turned over winsome young ladies whom they had discovered to fellow itinerants whose terms were nearly over.

There were some of the most refined and intelligent young ladies belonging to this charge, any one of whom would have been competent to have filled the place of a Methodist minister's wife. But knowing the law of the church and the penalty if a young minister married before he had served his full four years in conference, I dared not as much as squint at any one of them, much less to make any propositions. However, like the Quaker whose conscience would not permit him to fight in the defense of his country, but who could tell others where to shoot and not be likely to miss their man, I referred my successor to one of these young ladies, and Rev.

[99] One of the main considerations for admission of preachers to the conference was their marital status. Joseph Tarkington in his *Autobiography* . . . , edited by T. A. Goodwin (Cincinnati, 1899) said that it was a rule "as inexorable as death" that the itinerants not be married. This was not generally true (see Finley, *Sketches of Western Methodism*, 49–50), but it is true that many itinerants who did marry were forced to "locate," which in the early years meant loss of conference membership.

William Sprague took a prize in Miss Zeruba Hall; and soon after Miss Aremintha Stoddard followed her good example.[100]

The General Conference of 1784 had allowed single preachers $64 per year; traveling expenses were added eight years later. In 1816 the *Discipline* allowed the single preacher $100 and twice that amount to a married man. Moreover, some provision had already been made for the preacher's children. But collecting the allowances from the conferences was another matter, although the stewards labored diligently to provide against hardship in this respect. Payment was rarely all in currency, and payments in kind were not always so easily handled as were those, for example, of a tavernkeeper who told his preacher to settle with him at the end of the year. When accounts were balanced, the preacher was surprised to find that, credited with 50 cents for short sermons, 25 cents for long sermons, 12½ cents for family services, etc., the tavernkeeper was actually indebted to him.[101] As late as 1838 an Illinois preacher on the Wabash circuit received $100 and furnished his own horse; the next year, on the Urbana circuit, both horse and overcoat were donated. The latter lasted six years.[102]

As communities increased in population through the 1820's and 1830's, more preachers were stationed or "located" and more meetinghouses were erected. The itinerant had one advantage over the resident preacher: one rousing sermon would last at least once around the circuit and still be good after his transfer. Some thought that there was some connection between the long hours that a preacher spent in deep thought while traveling through the somber forests and the romantic and eloquent turn of his thought and expression.[103] At any rate, while ministers of most denominations waited for the people to call them, the Methodist circuit rider rode forth to call the people. Even after he had settled down, the circuit rider held a warm spot in his heart for the intimacy of the class meetings in the cabins; fine and commodious meetinghouses could not take their place.

[100] Gavitt, *Crumbs from My Saddle Bags,* 172–73.
[101] *Ibid.,* 153.
[102] "The Pioneer Preacher in Illinois," contributed by J. O. Cunningham, *Journal of the Illinois State Historical Society,* III, No. 2 (July, 1910), 61 ff.
[103] Timothy Flint, "Religious Character of the Western People," in *Western Monthly Review,* I (1827–28), 270.

As is apparent from earlier citations in this chapter, the Methodists were frequently criticized by their fellow Protestants both for their doctrine of salvation and for their manner of preaching. In fact, it has been stated that generally the Protestant sects prospered in the West in inverse ratio to their intellectual attainments.[104] True, many of the earlier Methodist preachers concentrated on doctrinal preaching: "Repentance, faith, justification, sanctification, the possibility of falling from grace, with the doctrine of atonement as contradistinguished from the Calvinian view, and occasional brushes at Church polity and ordinances as held by other denominations, formed the staples of the sermons. . . ."[105] In time the oratorical style overshadowed the polemic; beautiful expressions and rhetorical flourishes "were regarded as of more importance than orthodoxy itself." Then came the didactic style of sermonizing, illustrated with anecdotes and homely incidents.[106] But whichever fashion prevailed, rough and tumble preaching was always effective.

Like their Baptist brethren, many Methodist ministers entered upon their careers as a result of a "call" from on high. Unfortunately, there was nothing to prevent the call from descending upon the ignorant and the crude as well as upon erudite and qualified persons. As a consequence, some preachers of the former sort tried to compensate for their lack of understanding with bluster, brimstone, and the "holy whine"; some blubbered; others bellowed.[107]

Much has been written of the camp meetings; perhaps the revivalistic tactics and emotional excesses connected with them have been overemphasized.[108] Revivals were the spectacular

---

[104] Rusk, *Literature of the Middle Western Frontier*, I, 46.

[105] Finley, *Sketches of Western Methodism*, 216.

[106] *Ibid.*

[107] Kirkland, *A New Home*, 202.
A story of uncertain origin told of a farmer who had criticized the preacher and stated that he could do better. Soon afterward, while plowing, the "call" came from the bushes (where a neighbor was hidden) each time he passed. So he put away the team, put on his meeting clothes, and shortly faced the class: "Brethren and Sisters . . . Ah . . . Brethren . . . Ah . . . Ah . . . I guess I've shot my wad." Thus ended his preaching.

[108] "The camp meeting was never recognized as an official Methodist institution, and the name 'camp meeting' does not appear in the indexes of the General Conference *Journals* or in the Methodist discipline." Sweet, *The Methodists*, 69. On the subject see also the same author, *Revivalism in America: Its Origin, Growth and Decline*, 129 ff.; Nottingham, *Methodism and the Frontier*, 61 ff.; and Walter Brownlow Posey, *The Development of Methodism in the Old Southwest, 1783-1824* (Tuscaloosa, Ala., 1933), 17 ff.

manifestations which struck the eyes and caught the ears of travelers, and which called forth the barbs of critics. Though the Methodists had no monopoly of this method of disseminating the Gospel and of saving souls, the fact remains that revivals were more closely associated with them than with the other denominations. A camp meeting was customarily substituted for one of the quarterly meetings within each quarterly conference. Consequently, folks could attend several meetings within a radius of fifteen or twenty miles each summer.

Though it was claimed that the jerks and other physical manifestations of ecstasy attendant upon camp meetings disappeared soon after they came under Methodist management, it appears that this was not strictly true. Many instances are related of how the preachers re-enforced the Spirit's operations with their own good muscles, of bullies winning "wrastlin' contests" with the devil but never with the Spirit, of hardened sinners falling at two hundred yards after being hit by God.[109] In fact, the strong, passionate men of the fighting type were, next to young women, most susceptible to the revival technique.

Representative of the travelers' descriptions is that by Ferrall of a camp meeting held under the tall oaks and elms near Cincinnati:

Three sides were occupied by tents for the congregation, and the fourth by booths for the preachers. A little in advance before the booths was erected a platform for the performing preacher, and at the foot of this, inclosed by forms, was a species of sanctuary, called "the penitents' pen." People of every denomination might be seen here, allured by various motives. The girls, dressed in all colours of the rainbow, congregated to display their persons and costumes; the young men came to see the girls, and considered it a sort of "frolic"; and the old women, induced by fanaticism, and other motives, assembled in large numbers, and waited with patience for the proper season of repentance. At the intervals between the "preachments," the young married and unmarried women promenaded round the tents, and their smiling faces formed a striking contrast to the demure countenances of their more experienced sisters, who, according to

[109] See, for instance, *Frontier Sketches*, edited by D. P. Kidder for the Sunday School Union of the Methodist Episcopal Church (New York, 1851). When Rowdy Bill, a famous gouger got into it with the devil, while the antagonists flopped frantically about on the ground the preacher, who could see both contestants clearly, announced the battle round by round. When Bill finally got on top, his wife could contain herself no longer: "Gouge him, Billy!—gouge him *Billy! gouge* him." During the fracas, part of the audience very sportingly rooted for the underdog. Hall, *The New Purchase*, 388.

their age or temperament, descanted on the folly, or condemned the sinfulness of such conduct. Some of those old dames, I was informed, were decoy birds, who shared the profits with the preachers, and attended all the "camp-meetings" in the country.

The psalmodies were performed in the true Yankee style of nasal-melody, and at proper and seasonable intervals the preachings were delivered. The preachers managed their tones and discourses admirably, and certainly displayed a good deal of tact in their calling. They use the most extravagant gestures—astounding bellowings—a canting hypocritical whine—slow and solemn, although by no means *musical* intonations, and the *et ceteras* that complete the qualifications of a regular camp-meeting methodist parson. During the exhortations the brothers and sisters were calling out —Bless God! glory! glory! amen! God grant! Jesus! &c. . . .

After sunset the place was lighted up by beacon fires and candles, and the scene seemed to be changing to one of more deep and awful interest. About nine o'clock the preachers began to rally their forces—the candles were snuffed—fuel was added to the fires—clean straw was shook in the "penitents' pen"—and every movement "gave dreadful note of preparation." At length the hour was sounded, and the faithful forthwith assembled. A chosen leader commenced to harangue—he bellowed—he roared—he whined —he shouted until he became actually hoarse, and the perspiration rolled down his face. Now, the faithful seemed to take the infection, and as if overcome by their excited feelings, flung themselves headlong on the straw into the penitents' pen—the old dames leading the way. The preachers, to the number of a dozen, gave a loud shout and rushed into the thick of the penitents. A scene now ensued that beggars all description. About twenty women, young and old, were lying in every direction and position, with caps and without caps, screeching, bawling, and kicking in hysterics, and profaning the name of Jesus. The preachers, on their knees amongst them, were with Stentorian voices exhorting them to call louder and louder on the Lord, until he came upon them; whilst their *attachées,* with turned-up eyes and smiling countenances, were chanting hymns and shaking hands with the multitude. Some would now and then give a hearty laugh, which is an indication of superior grace, and is called "the holy laugh." The scene altogether was highly entertaining—penitents, parsons, caps, combs, and straw, jumbled in one heterogeneous mass, lay heaving on the ground, and formed at this juncture a grouping that might be done justice to by the pencil of Hogarth, or the pen of the author of Hudibras; but of which I fear an inferior pen or pencil must fail in conveying an adequate idea.

The women were at length carried off, fainting, by their friends and the preachers began to prepare for another scene. From the time of those faintings, the "newbirth" is dated, which means a spiritual resurrection or revival.[110]

[110] Simon Ansley Ferrall [O'Ferrall], *A Ramble of Six Thousand Miles Through the United States of America* (London, 1832), 71–76. Other contemporary descriptions may be found in Finley, *Autobiography,* 362 ff.; James Flint, *Letters from America,* 231 ff.; Timothy Flint, *History and Geography of the Mississippi Valley,*

There were solemn and serious revivals, too, in the temples
of the forest where

> On their rustic seats, fresh cleft, and hewn
> From the huge poplars, and in many a range
> Of circling rows dispos'd, in quiet sat
> The expectant multitude.
>
> . . . .
>
> A thousand tongues, in one proud anthem rose;
> And as it rose, far through its hoary depths,
> The forest shook; and from the distant hills,
> Like the far rush of many waters, deep,
> Long, and reverberating echoes came.
> Loud burst the song; now swelling to the sky—
> Now soft'ning down, and at each measur'd close,
> Along the woods expiring; till at length
> 'Twas hush'd into a stillness so intense,
> That the half sigh of penitence alone,
> Throughout that multitude, was audible.[111]

Even the confusion of the penitents' ring with its praying,
groaning, and shrieking had a certain impressive aspect. Persons

144 ff.; and L. Garrett, *Recollections of the West* (Nashville, 1834), 29. Hall, *The New Purchase,* Chapter XLVIII, gives a Presbyterian report of sermons and arguments of the peoples' preachers. Two articles of value are William Cooper Howell, "Camp Meetings in the West Fifty Years Ago," in *Lippincott's,* X (1872), 203–12, and Robert L. Shurter, "The Camp Meeting in the Early Life and Literature of the Mid-West," in *East Tennessee Historical Society's Publications,* No. 5 (1933), 142–49.

Mrs. Trollope's well known description of a camp meeting held on the borders of Indiana and Ohio, August 14, 1829, given in her *Domestic Manners of the Americans,* I, 139 ff., was modified somewhat from her original draft. Passages omitted are indicated in brackets: "His arm was [very cordially] encircling the neck of a beautiful girl who knelt beside him, with her hair hanging dishevelled upon her shoulders and her features convulsed with the most violent agitation. [I saw the youth press his cheek to hers;] Soon after they both fell forward on the straw as if unable to endure in any other attitude the burning eloquence of a tall grim figure in black. . . . accompanied with sobs, groans and a sort of low howling, [so closely resembling that of a distant wolf that they must have caught it thence,] inexpressibly painful to listen to. . . . The exhortation closely resembled that I had heard at the 'Revival,' [at the Presbyterian Church in Cincinnati,] but the result was different . . . [I wandered alone into the forest where I committed to paper a part of what I had witnessed—my memory therefore has not cheated me—and the above statement may be depended upon as strictly true, though by no means so full of circumstances as I would have made it, but common decency forbids my dwelling on much that I saw; and nothing can excuse the mention of it but the burning indignation which makes me feel exposure of such atrocity to be a duty.] I understand that a very *satisfactory* collection was made by the preachers [from their poor victims] for Bibles, Tracts, and *all other religious purposes.*" Trollope MS. in Indiana University Library. See also Donald A. Smalley's edition of *Domestic Manners of the Americans* (New York, 1949), 167–75.

[111] Micah P. Flint, "The Camp Meeting," in *Western Monthly Review,* I (1827–28), 35–36; reprinted in the *Methodist Magazine.* On the hymns and writers see *Methodist Quarterly Review* (New York, 1859), 401 ff.

sincerely seeking an experience of conversion exerted a psychological effect on those who had come to watch. "There was noise, confusion and disorder, but it was not raving. They knew what they did, though they did it extravagantly: they were rational and had a purpose, tempered with good desires and a loving spirit. Their judgments were doubtless in abeyance, but their affections were warmed with a love that made all around them happy in some degree, unless overwhelmed with the terror of evil."[112]

Rowdies were attracted by the goings on and excitement of the camp meetings but usually proved only a nuisance. The fact that the grounds were well lighted by beacon fires and guarded only increased the temptation to slip in and out. Mimicking the preaching and singing was a favorite trick. It was not impossible for young whippersnappers to be echoing the proceedings from the adjacent woods one hour and singing at the top of their voices or guarding the mourners the next.

Nor were these emotion-stirring tactics confined to big preachings and camp meetings; they appeared at class meetings in the homes as well.[113] Though the so-called "better classes" might scorn the revivals, a large element of the population enjoyed them. They served as picnics; they furnished excitement and of-

[112] Howell, "Camp Meetings in the West," in *Lippincott's,* X, 211.

[113] As described by an English settler: "I attended a class meeting held in a house about two miles from our residence; but the manner in which it was conducted was by no means congenial to my views and sentiments. The company being assembled and seated, the one acting as leader, rose from his seat, which was a signal for the others to do the same. A sort of circle or ring was then immediately formed, by the whole assembly taking hold of hands, and capering about the house surprisingly. Their gesture could not be called dancing, and yet no term that I can employ describes it better. This done, worship commenced with extempore prayer, not indeed in language or style the best selected, but with this I have nothing to do. I have no right to question the sincerity of the individual, and if his taste differed from mine, it is no proof that his was wrong. The following part of the service was exceedingly exceptionable. All the persons present being again seated, an individual started from his seat, exclaiming in a loud and frantic shriek, 'I feel it,' meaning what is commonly termed among them the power of God. His motions, which appeared half convulsive, were observed with animated joy by the rest, till he fell apparently stiff upon the floor, where he lay unmolested a short time, and then resumed his seat. Others were affected in a similar manner, only in some instances the power of speech was not suspended, as in this, by the vehemence of enthusiasm, for I cannot give it a more moderate name.

"Finding in this mode of worship little that I could really respect, I resolved not long afterwards to absent myself from them altogether. I found moreover that some of the most rapturous members were far from being exemplary in their conduct, practically considered." Rebecca Burlend, *A Tree Picture of Emigration: or Fourteen Years in the Interior of North America* . . . (London, 1848, reprinted, Chicago, 1936), 144–45.

fered emotional outlets. They filled a need supplied in part in our own times by organized sports, jazz, and movies. Baynard Rush Hall, though not disinclined to poke fun at the ranting type of preacher, admitted the social value of the camp meetings:

Indeed, a camp-meeting *out there* is the most mammoth picnic possible; and it is one's own fault, saint or sinner, if he gets not enough to eat, and that the best the land affords. It would be impossible even for churlish persons to be stingy in the open air; the ample sky above the boundless woods around; the wings of gay birds flashing in sunshine, and the squirrels racing up gigantic trunks and barking and squeaking amid the grand branches; and what then must be the effect of all on the proverbially open-hearted native born Westerns? Ay! the *native* Corn-Cracker, Hoosier, Buckeye and all men and women "born in a cane-brake and rocked in a sugar trough,"—all born to follow a trail and cock an old fashioned lock-rifle, —all such are open-hearted, fearless, generous, chivalric, even in spite of much filth and scum and base leaven from foreign places. And hence, although no *decided* friend to camp-meetings, spiritually and morally and theologically considered, we do say that at a *Western* camp-meeting as at a barbecue, the very heart and soul of hospitality and kindness is wide open and poured freely forth. We *can,* maybe, equal it in here; but we never try.[114]

He concluded that "under the direction of wise and talented *men*, a camp-meeting may possibly be a means of a *little* permanent good; but, with the *best* management, it is a doubtful means of much moral and spiritual good. . . ."

Timothy Flint, himself a preacher and thoroughly appreciative of western conditions, wrote of these "awakenings":

Living remote, and consigned the greater part of the time, to the musing loneliness of their condition in the forests, or the prairie; when they congregate on these exciting occasions, society itself is to them a novelty, and an excitement. The people are naturally more sensitive and enthusiastic, than in the older countries. A man of rude, boisterous, but native eloquence, rises among these children of the forest and simple nature, with his voice pitched upon the tones, and his utterance filled with that awful theme, to which every string of the human heart every where responds, and while the woods echo his vehement declamations, his audience is alternately dissolved in tears, awed to profound feeling, or falling in spasms. This country opens a boundless theatre for strong, earnest and unlettered eloquence, and the preacher seldom has extensive influence, or usefulness, who does not possess some touch of this character.[115]

[114] *The New Purchase,* 369.
[115] "Religious Character of the Western People," in *Western Monthly Review,* I (1827–28), 270.

In other words, the emotions were called upon to amplify and impress the thought or theme; the emotions of a simple folk were much less restrained and circumscribed than were their thoughts.

By midcentury the revivals were losing something of their earlier flavor and effectiveness. Allen Wiley, who preached in Indiana, wrote in 1846 that there had been two good camp meetings in that year. "When, however, we say they were good, I could not be understood to say they would compare with the former meetings. There was much more preaching talent at those meetings than the former; but there was not the same zeal in the preachers or people."[116]

Criticism of the more strenuous revivals even appeared in the newspapers. In 1831, apropos of the announcement of a four-day revival, editor John R. St. John of the *Cleaveland Herald* wrote: "We have only to remark that the mind is as susceptible of disease as the body." He agreed with an eastern paper that "an intellectual, or rather a religious *cholera morbus*" had broken out and was raging among the people. He spoke of religious demagogues who took their followers "to some wild woody place . . . and there, by platoons, pray and preach, and tear and astonish, and excite themselves and others into the wildest frenzies." He minced no words in analyzing the technique of revivalism, called it a system of chicanery, and said that preachers could be as ambitious, as fallible, and as dangerous as other men. [117] The Ravenna *Western Courier* reported the case of a man who "got delirium" at a protracted meeting and became a raving maniac; others had died of the same. "We forbear comment," said the editor.[118]

Not so spectacular as the revivals but of more fundamental importance were the publishing and book-distributing activities of the Methodists. Centralized in 1789, when the Methodist Book Concern was established, these publishing activities grew rapidly under the direction of Ezekiel Cooper in the early 1800's. In 1828 the Western Branch was established at Cincinnati (it

---

[116] "Methodism in Southeastern Indiana," in *Indiana Magazine of History,* XXIII (1927), 208. Wiley's article originally appeared in the *Western Christian Advocate* (Cincinnati).

[117] *Cleaveland Herald,* July 28, August 18, November 6, 1831. The *Advertiser* and other papers attacked St. John vigorously. He retired from the editorship early in 1832.

[118] March 27, 1834, February 12, 1835.

became independent in 1836), and soon the sales were running into thousands of dollars per year. Titles ranged in price from *Wesley on Original Sin* at $1.12½ to *Sabbath School Tracts* at three cents each.[119] An important part of the circuit rider's duties was to distribute and get the people to read these books and tracts; profits were distributed to the families of super-annuated preachers.

It was not long until the *Methodist Magazine*, begun at New York in 1818, was overshadowed by the *Christian Advocate and Journal* (1826). Within two years it was said that the latter's weekly circulation of 15,000 copies—a large part of it in the West—was the largest of any newspaper in the world. The first western Methodist periodical, the *Western Christian Monitor*, was published by William Beauchamp at Chillicothe in 1816. In 1834 Thomas A. Morris put out the first issue of the weekly *Western Christian Advocate* (Cincinnati). This periodical gained rapidly in circulation—5,700 subscribers were listed in 1837, 15,000 by 1840. The *Ladies' Repository and Gleanings of the West* was started in 1840 under the management of the Western Methodist Book Concern and had a general circulation.

§ § § §

The American Baptists stem from Roger Williams and the Providence Plantations where the first Baptist church in America was formed in 1639. Though the Baptists originally took no important part in the revivals of the Great Awakening in the 1730's, they registered important gains as a result of the divisions thereby created; whole congregations of New-Lights, or Separates (coming out of Congregationalism), often became Baptist. One result of the rapid increase in the number of New England Baptists was the chartering in 1764 of Rhode Island College (later Brown University) under the control of that denomination. By the 1750's the spirit of the Awakening had swept down from New England to Virginia,[120] where, as in North Carolina,

---

[119] For account lists see Sweet, *The Methodists,* 698 ff.

[120] Earlier New England Baptists had settled in Virginia in 1714, and Maryland Baptists had come in 1743. These groups were General Baptists (Arminian in doctrine), though they later accepted the Calvinistic views of the Regular Baptists. Sweet, *The Baptists,* 7.

the older groups of Baptists and other denominations looked with disfavor upon the whooping and whining Separate preachers.[121] Though the Separates had become popular among the poorer classes by the time of the Revolution, they had to fight hard for the religious liberty and the civil rights they eventually secured. Staunch supporters of Thomas Jefferson's bill for the separation of church and state in Virginia, they profited much from its passage in 1785; but not until after the war did any considerable number of people of the more prosperous classes join the Baptist ranks.

Following the Revolution, Virginia Separate Baptists spread into the Kentucky country, but many of the ministers there crossed over to the Regular Baptists, and the latter group had eleven of the eighteen Baptist churches in 1785.[122] Under the influence of the great western revival movement the two groups finally got together in 1801 on the basis of a compromise between the Arminian views of the Separates and the Calvinistic creed of the Regulars.[123] Kentucky Baptists participated with Presbyterians and Methodists in the western revivals of the early 1800's and added thousands of members to their churches. By 1820 they had 25 associations, 491 churches, and 31,689 members.[124] A decade later, however, the Baptists were losing their members by the thousands to the Campbellite movement.

Among the early comers to the Cincinnati settlement were numerous Baptists, most of whom had migrated from New York and New Jersey. The first Baptist association—the Miami— was organized in 1797; by 1812 there were four associations in Ohio with some 60 churches and 2,400 members. About the turn

[121] The "holy whine," a peculiar method of delivery which became a habit with many of the frontier Baptist preachers, was one of their objectionable practices.

[122] The first Baptist association west of the Alleghenies was the Elkhorn Association in Kentucky, formed by six of the Regular churches in 1785.

[123] Arminianism, after James Arminius, a sixteenth-century Dutch Protestant. Arminians did not accept the absolute predestination idea of Calvin but believed in conditional election and reprobation. They further held that none but believers might benefit from Christ's atonement, that man must be regenerated by the Holy Spirit to exercise true faith, that man might resist divine grace, and that he might relapse from a state of grace (whereas Calvin held for the perseverance of the saints).

In the union of 1801 both parties agreed that by nature man was a fallen and depraved creature; that "salvation, regeneration, sanctification, and justification are by the life, death, resurrection, and ascension of Jesus Christ"; that "the saints will finally persevere through grace to glory"; that believers in order to receive the Lord's Supper should be baptized by immersion; and that "each may keep up their associational and church government as to them may seem best."

[124] Sweet, The Baptists, 26.

of the century Kentucky Baptists formed several small churches across the Ohio from Louisville,[125] and churches appeared among the settlements on the lower Wabash a few years later. The Wabash Association was organized in 1808; the following year saw the formation of the Whitewater Association. Kentucky Baptists began preaching in the Kaskaskia region as early as the 1790's. The first churches formed there organized the Illinois Association in 1807.

Early Baptist ministers seldom received any training or assured pay. Most of them were simple farmers or mechanics (artisans) who, having received a call, were "raised up" by their churches and were permitted to exhibit their talents. If their "gifts" proved acceptable, they might be "licensed." Ordinarily the licensed preacher (who could preach but not administer the sacraments) had no congregation; there might be several of these "lay" preachers among the members of a single congregation. When the licensed preacher was called to minister to a congregation, he was usually examined by a council of brethren and ordained "by prayer and the laying on of the hands of the eldership." As the prospective preacher was expected to "show his gifts," so he was the most respected if self-supporting. Few Baptist churches made other than an occasional contribution to the preacher. The prejudice against an educated and salaried ministry was a matter of principle rather than of economics.

Though there were a number of Baptist divisions, all groups accepted the five essentials of separation of church and state, conversion as a condition of church membership, individual responsibility to God, congregational form of government, and immersion.[126] The terms General and Particular Baptists, better known in England, had little meaning in America.[127] After the

[125] Prominent among the early Kentucky ministers who worked in this region was William McCoy; his son Isaac became the first Baptist missionary to the Indians and the author of *History of the Baptist Indian Missions*. For his mission in Michigan Territory see Chapter X, 84–85. See also *John McCoy, His Life and Diaries,* by Elizabeth Hayward (New York, 1948). John McCoy was a brother of Isaac. The history of Indiana Baptists is covered in William T. Stott, *Indiana Baptist History 1798–1908* (Franklin, Ind., 1908).

[126] Sweet, *The Baptists,* 43. The argument regarding the "Imposition of Hands" as a symbol of receiving the Holy Spirit, which had caused some trouble in the colonial period, was not important in the West. Those who favored this ceremony were known as "Six Principle Baptists."

[127] The General Baptists were Arminian, that is, they believed in a general atonement and free grace; the Particular Baptists were Calvinistic.

Separates and the Regulars got together in the agreement of 1801 they were known as United Baptists. There was considerable doctrinal independence among the Baptist churches in the West. On one thing, however, they generally agreed: the full acceptance of Arminian doctrines was held under suspicion.

Early Baptist churches, like the Methodist, were the cabins of the settlers. Meetinghouses, which followed in time, very frequently were on or near the creeks after which the church was named. Though it was fundamental in Baptist belief that each church was independent, nevertheless, when a half-dozen churches were established in a community an association was formed. Individual churches sent "messengers" rather than delegates to the association, which often met quarterly; "messengers" elected the moderator and the clerk, the only officers of the association. The association adopted constitutions, set forth professions of faith, received inquiries from the churches on matters of faith and discipline, and sent circular letters of advice and warning to the member churches. In theory, the powers of the association were merely advisory, but on occasion churches were expelled for not taking advice. Associations corresponded with other associations. The association meetings were sometimes held in the woods, hundreds of church members attended, and the three or four Sunday sermons gave them the appearance of camp meetings.

Members entered the church "by experience, letter, or information, or recantation." Original entry, that is, "by experience," was passed upon by the church after the experience had been related; baptism by immersion followed. Baptizings, usually in the "crick," were events witnessed by all and sundry.

Baptist churches were among the most assiduous in policing the morals of members. Perusal of the minutes, record books, or "judicial records" of the churches reveals the handling of hundreds of cases, many of them amusing, of various forms of moral turpitude: fighting, drunkenness, malicious gossip, gambling, irregular sexual conduct. Extreme penalty was to "church" the offender, that is, put him out. The following extracts from the records of the Silver Creek Church are from a transcript in the Indiana University Library:

Abbott, James. Ordained minister, 2–12–'02. On 8–7–'02, church declares itself aggrieved with him for "disorderly life" (no details). Continued, and aid asked from other churches. 8–12–'02, call meeting held. Abbott confesses fault. Reconciled with church as whole. 9–11–'02, Wm. Harrod still at odds with Abbott. Personal conference with committee of four failed to mend quarrel. New committee chosen to effect reconciliation. 10–9–'02, report trouble settled. Disagreements involving Abbott, his wife, and the Harrods, Huffs, etc. continue during October, November, and December of 1802. 12–11–'02, Abbott silenced and excommunicated. 1–8–'03, Abbott publicly excluded from church for falsehood, and declared "a heathen and a publican."

On December 27, 1823, the following query was put:

"Whether is it consistent with gospel order for any member of a church in common cases to sue at law a brother or sister of his own church or of a sister church previous to bringing the same before the church?" The church thinks not.

Cleveland, Sally. Accused, 3–25–37, by Sr. Everett, of "immoral and unchristian conduct." Convicted and excluded. (No details of charge.)

Worrall, Claiborne G. Accused, 9–12–40, of fighting. Confessed and restored, 10–10–40.

Worrall, Claiborne G. Accused of fighting, 8–14–41. Continued at various times to 1–8–42. (Charge of instigating fight added.) Confessed, and restored with reproof.

Worrall, Alfred. Accused, 1–3–42, of fighting. Self accusation, hence restored with reproof. R. Smith dissatisfied, but reconciled after personal conference with Worrall.

Rogers, Philip. Accused self, 1–8–42, of advising Smith to strike Worrall with stick. Forgiven.

McCoy, James. Accused, July, 1858, of shooting Bro. Perry. Excluded. Restored, October, 1858.

Judicial business of the Providence Primitive Baptist Church, Gibson County, Indiana, was much the same:

Barrett, Lucinda and William, in cross suit against Breedlove, Wm., Margaret, and Nancy. Neighborhood quarrel. Opened, 11–22–28. Charges preferred, 12–27–28, in writing. Mrs. Barrett charged Nancy Breedlove with talking about her and saying "Durn." The Breedloves charged her with claiming more cotton from them than they owed, and with lying. Charge against Mrs. Barrett voted on, same date. Convicted. Whole case continued. 1–24–29, Mrs. Barrett asked for new trial claiming new evidence. Granted, and a second conviction reached, followed by exclusion.

Vickers, Nancy. Striking a woman in anger. Bad language. Accused, 3–27–30. Committee of two to labor with accused. Cited to attend next meeting. 4–24–30, sister confessed, admonished and restored.

Woods, John L. Accused self, 12–21–33, of dancing. Restored.

Reavis, Elias. Accused, 12–21–33, of drinking whiskey and dancing. Continued and accused cited to attend. 3–22–34, church informed of death of accused.

Strickland, Elisha. Accused self, 10–24–35, of angry and abrupt language. Restored.

Martin, Eleanor M. Accused, 5–23–40, of having illegitimate child. Excluded at same meeting.

Manning, Ede, and Strickland, James. Accused, 2–27–41, of being parents of illegitimate child. Strickland confessed. Both excluded. Strickland restored, 11–27–41.[128]

Which brings up the subject of that frontier phenomenon, the Primitive, "Hardshell," or Antimission Baptists.

After the second meeting of the General Missionary Convention of the Baptists in 1817, plans were undertaken for home missions in the West. Luther Rice, former missionary to India, was a leader in the movement; John Mason Peck, later prominent in early journalistic and antislavery history in Illinois, was sent to Missouri Territory in 1817, the first Baptist missionary in the West. Isaac McCoy established his Fort Wayne Indian mission in 1820 and the Carey Mission in Michigan Territory two years later.[129] At first the western Baptist churches seemed favorable, but suddenly churches and associations began to question, then to oppose missions. Churches split wide open on the question as to whether the idea of missions was agreeable to gospel order. Somehow the idea got into the minds of many persons that if one went to hear a missionary preach, he would be taxed so much for each sermon or each baptism, and for an annual amount besides. Shortly, the spirit of "unfellowship" spread to include Bible societies, Sunday schools, tract societies, and colleges; it deplored their zeal, strivings for power, and the ensuing "vast loss of money."

Causes for this movement are not too clear. The antimission crusades of John Taylor, Kentucky pioneer preacher, and Daniel Parker, of Tennessee, were influential; but so were the contentions of Alexander Campbell, publicized through his *Christian Baptist* and the *Millennial Harbinger*. The various societies were accused of greed, dishonesty, embezzlement, lacking in scriptural authority, and endeavoring to run the church. The societies with their organizations were regarded as a danger to the complete

[128] Extracts from transcript in Indiana University Library.
[129] See Chapter X, 84–85.

autonomy of the congregation; antimissionary Baptists viewed them in the same way the pioneer regarded corporations. Then jealousy on the part of frontier preachers of an educated ministry was a factor. As Peck said, "They 'knew their own deficiencies but they felt the irritability of wounded pride, common to narrow and weak minds.' "[130] The reluctance to part with the money was no doubt also an important factor.

With these attitudes the "anti-means" Baptists developed a scriptural or doctrinal argument against missions. It was, in substance, that a sovereign God did not need the help of human means to bring the elect into the fold; in fact, preaching did no good, for the nonelect could not be saved, and the elect were already saved. Missionary societies and the like were nonscriptural; they were Arminian contrivances. One group of the Primitive Baptists, known as the "Two-Seed" Baptists, accepted Daniel Parker's Two-Seed-in-the-Spirit doctrine: Adam and Eve were created originally from the good seed, the divine spirit. But after the serpent brought about the fall of man, there was also incorporated in all the daughters of Eve the seed of the serpent. Children born of the first seed were children of God; those born of the second seed were children of the devil. For the first mansions would be prepared in bliss; as for the latter they should go to the devil to whom they belonged. Preaching and missions had nothing to do with it.

The opposition of these Baptists to missions, colleges, and an educated ministry brought no credit to the sect. The bitter controversies consumed energy which might better have been used in other ways. The narrow Calvinism "led to bigotry and intolerance, and its absurdities brought the churches and ministers into disrepute among those who most needed their ministrations and their restraints."[131]

Like the Presbyterians, the Baptists of the Northwest had trouble with the slavery question. Kentucky churches had been arguing over slavery since early statehood days. In 1807 several Kentucky associations formed the Friends of Humanity Association; in general, it was ruled that slave-owning was incompatible with church membership. The movement made little headway in

[130] Rufus Babcock (ed.), *Forty Years of Pioneer Life. Memoir of John Mason Peck* (Philadelphia, 1864), 111.
[131] Sweet, *The Baptists,* 76.

Kentucky, but in 1809 James Lemen brought the issue to the meeting of the Illinois Baptist Association. When no antislavery stand was taken, he withdrew and formed an antislavery Baptist church at Cantine Creek (Bethel Church). Still the Friends of Humanity movement made little progress; in 1825 there were only eleven churches with some four hundred members. Lemen, a delegate to the Illinois Constitutional Convention in 1818, voted for immediate emancipation. In the exciting convention struggle of 1823,[132] Governor Edward Coles, himself a Baptist, Peck, and others fought vigorously against the convention, and antislavery Baptists put out the *Illinois Friends of Humanity Circular Letter*. Since the proslavery forces lost, the Friends of Humanity turned their attention to temperance, missions, and education. They played but little part in the abolition movement as later pushed by Garrison, Weld, Lovejoy, and other "Yankees."

Methodists, Baptists, and Presbyterians, then, were the big three in the period 1815 to 1840. Accurate statistics on membership are lacking, but it appears that, generally speaking, by 1840 the Methodists were numerically equal to the two other denominations combined; adding the Congregationalists to the Presbyterians' total does not materially change the picture.[133]

[132] See Chapter IX, 20–22.

[133] The seventh-census (1850) figures probably give as good a relative estimate as any (except for the Lutherans who increased rapidly with the German and Scandinavian emigration of the 1840's). The number of churches for each denomination for each state was:

	Methodist	Baptist	Presbyterian	Congregationalist	Lutheran	Catholic	Episcopalian	Christian	Friends
Ohio	1,531	551	663	100	260	130	79	90	94
Indiana	779	430	282	2	63	63	24	187	89
Illinois	405	282	206	46	42	59	27	69	6
Michigan	119	66	72	29	12	44	25	2	7
Wisconsin	110	49	40	37	20	64	19	4	

Minor groups for the region were listed as follows: Moravian churches, 220 (practically all in Ohio and Indiana); "Union," 87; German Reformed, 79 (71 in Ohio); "Free," 28; Dutch Reformed, 24; Mennonite, 10 (all in Ohio); Jewish, 3 (all in Ohio). In value of church property the rank was: Methodists, Roman Catholics, Baptists, and Episcopalians. U. S. Census. *Statistical View of the United States . . . Being a Compendium of the Seventh Census . . .* (Washington, D. C., 1854), 133–35.

§ § § § §

The minority religious groups can be treated only in brief. The oldest of all the Christian groups in the West was, of course, the Roman Catholic church. Catholic missions, largely Jesuit, dotted the map in all parts of the Northwest except the Ohio Valley by 1754. The *habitants* of Detroit, the American Bottom, Vincennes, and other French settlements had been Catholic from the beginning. Generally illiterate and to many English and American settlers a carefree and careless if not a "shiftless lot," they gave the appearance, as Charlevoix had noted in Quebec, of "a poverty hid by an air of being in easy circumstances, which seems not at all studied."

The Recollect Father de L'Halle, chaplain at Cadillac's Fort Pontchartrain, built St. Anne's Chapel, the mother church in the Northwest, in 1701. Other Recollect and Jesuit missionaries ministered to the important Detroit post during the French period. Shortly after the fire of 1805, Governor William Hull secured from Congress a donation of land for a church site, but when Fathers Gabriel Richard and Jean Dilhet were unable to accept the responsibility, the latter wrote: "Upon our refusal a similar offer was made to the Presbyterians, the Methodists and others, who gladly accepted it and introduced their false teaching into a Catholic section. What a sad outlook for the future."[134] In 1804 the parishioners incorporated the church "usually denominated Catholic Apostolic and Roman," by act of the territorial legislature. At the time the Detroit parish was estimated to have some three thousand parishioners.[135]

Father Sebastian Meurin, a Jesuit, who had perhaps previously ministered to the Kaskaskia settlement, was at Vincennes by 1749 and the parish records begin at that date.[136] In 1763 when the

[134] Jean Dilhet, *État de L'Église Catholique ou Diocèse des États-Unis ...,* edited and translated by Patrick W. Browne (The Catholic University of America, *Studies in American Church History,* Washington, D. C., 1922), 114.

[135] *Ibid.,* 118.

[136] The Mission of the Holy Family under Father Jean François Buisson de St. Cosme had been established at Cahokia in 1679 and a chapel built. After its destruction by fire a new church was built. There were other early missions in the Northwest between 1670 and 1700.

François de Montmorency Laval had been made Vicar Apostolic of New France in 1658 and had arrived at Quebec the next year. He became bishop of the newly created See of Quebec in 1674.

order against the Jesuits was executed,[137] Father Julian Duvernay (Devernai) left Vincennes, and that village was without a priest until Father Gibault of Cahokia and some Detroit priests gave the people part-time service; from 1785 to 1789 Gibault was located at Vincennes.

The French-Canadian phase of Catholicism in the Northwest ended in 1789 when the Holy See put the region under the control of Bishop John Carroll of the Baltimore diocese. When three years later Father Benedict Joseph Flaget was sent to the Old Post, he found religion practically nonexistent. With the declining importance of the French settlements in the Northwest, Catholicism waned for a period.

The first western see was established in 1808 at Bardstown, Kentucky, a center of settlement for Catholics from Virginia, Maryland, and the Carolinas; Flaget was made bishop. When Flaget began inspection of his diocese in 1813–14, he found Catholic activity north of the Ohio at low ebb. Besides neglected Vincennes—where "twenty years more without priests and they will have forgotten even the sign of the cross"—and the Illinois settlements, he visited Cincinnati and Chillicothe. Father Edward Fenwick was sent to Ohio on missionary work. In 1817 Flaget had to intervene in the affairs of the St. Anne's congregation at Detroit; to settle local troubles, he placed the church under interdict.[138] The next year he visited Detroit, reconciled the dissensions, and started the building of a new church. He found the church at the River Raisin in poor condition. In 1819 he encouraged the half-dozen Catholic families in Cincinnati to build a church.

As the population of the Bardstown diocese increased, Flaget suggested a separate see for Detroit and that Illinois be included in a bishopric at St. Louis. Rome created the new diocese of Cin-

---

An introduction to the history of Catholicism in the West may be had from John Gilmary Shea, *History of the Catholic Church in the United States* (4 volumes. New York, 1886–92), II, III. Martin J. Spalding, *Sketches of the Life, Times and Character of the Rt. Rev. Benedict Joseph Flaget . . .* (Louisville, 1852) is the standard work on Bishop Flaget. Thomas T. McAvoy, *The Catholic Church in Indiana 1789–1834* (New York, 1940) is an excellent recent study.

[137] Jesuits were banished from the missions of the Northwest by the Superior Council of New Orleans a decade before the suppression of the Society by Pope Clement XIV.

[138] On rebuilding of Detroit after the fire one matter of dispute was the removal of a cemetery. Father Gabriel Richard had been unable to restore harmony.

cinnati (which included Michigan Territory) in 1821 and made
Edward Fenwick bishop. Indiana and Illinois were left under the
jurisdiction of Bardstown. Father John Leo Champomier at
Vincennes was the only resident priest in Indiana at the time;
with the aid of the Sisters of Charity of Nazareth (Bardstown),
he started an academy and by combing the settlements, Catholic
and non-Catholic for aid, began construction of the pretentious
St. Xavier Cathedral.[139]

The small scattered Ohio congregations around Zanesville,
Lancaster, Cincinnati, and elsewhere had been augmented by
German settlers and Irish canal workers. Bishop John B. Purcell, Fenwick's successor, in 1834 found many Catholic groups
unprovided with priests. Though he estimated thirty thousand
Catholics in the state, there were only nine brick and eight wooden
churches.[140]

The diocese of Detroit was founded in 1833; Father Gabriel
Richard would have been the logical choice for bishop, but he
had been sued and prosecuted as a result of his stand regarding
the bigamous conduct of a parishioner. Instead the Reverend
Frederic Résé was appointed and St. Anne's Church became his
cathedral. The oldest Catholic missions and churches in the
Northwest lay within his diocese.

Indiana had perhaps twenty thousand Catholics in 1830.[141]
In 1834 the new see of Vincennes was established to include
Indiana and eastern Illinois: Father Simon Bruté de Rémur
became the first bishop.[142] He found the new church unplastered
and cold, many of the French Catholics indifferent. Inspection
of his see revealed congregations at Chicago (Father Ignatius
St. Cyr), and Fort Wayne (Father Stephen Theodore Badin);
scattered Catholic families were located in eastern Indiana and
along the line of the Wabash and Erie Canal.

The development of Catholicism in the Northwest by the middle 1830's was not of such proportions as would explain the out-
burst of violent anti-Catholic attacks. It is highly probable that

[139] The main part of the structure, of brick, was to be 60 by 115 feet; a 135
by 15 foot transept was to be built later.
[140] Shea, *History of the Catholic Church in the United States*, III, 620.
[141] McAvoy, *The Catholic Church in Indiana*, 169.
[142] For Bruté's work see Sister Mary Salesia Godecker, *Simon Bruté de Rémur,
First Bishop of Vincennes* (St. Meinrad, Ind., 1931).

the East was more worried about the Pope's conquest of the Mississippi Valley than were the citizens thereof.[143] Eastern religious and other publications as well as such prominent citizens as Samuel F. B. Morse[144] led in the attack. Catholic missions and schools were viewed as particularly obnoxious. The editor of one eastern paper wrote: "It is an ascertained fact that Jesuits are prowling about all parts of the United States in every possible disguise, expressly to ascertain the advantageous situations and modes to disseminate Popery. A minister of the Gospel from Ohio has informed us, that he discovered one carrying on his devices in his congregation; and he says the western country swarms with them under the names of puppet show men, dancing masters, music teachers, peddlers of images and ornaments, barrel organ players, and similar practitioners."[145] The *Home Missionary* (New York) spoke of the Catholic influence which would co-operate with infidelity and native depravity to make voters and legislators.

Lyman Beecher in his *Plea for the West* accused the Catholics of taxing themselves and getting gifts from Europe in order to give free education to Protestant children even to the neglect of their own. The *Cincinnati Journal,* which professed to be a liberal publication for orthodox Christians of all denominations, published a strong anti-Catholic article, which the *Liberty Hall and Cincinnati Gazette* characterized as a discredit to the publishers.[146] The *Cleveland Whig* published an account of "Another Nunnery Blown Up" (in Pittsburgh)—girls found in delicate conditions, dead infants in the subterranean recesses of the priests' seraglios, etc.—"When will the people open their eyes to the abominations and dangers of popery? How long will protestant parents suffer their innocent, amiable and virtuous daughters to become the victims to the lusts of incarnate devils?"[147]

James Hall, then editing the *Western Monthly Magazine*, and

[143] See Billington, *The Protestant Crusade,* Chapter V, *passim.*

[144] Morse's "A Foreign Conspiracy against the Liberties of the United States" was published originally as twelve letters in the *New York Observer* (a Presbyterian weekly), in the autumn of 1834, under the pen name of "Brutus."

[145] *American Protestant Vindicator . . . ,* December 24, 1835. This semimonthly, published in New York 1834–45 under various titles, was the official organ of the American Protestant Reformation Society.

[146] March 5, 1833.

[147] Copied in Piqua *Western Courier,* August 15, 1835. See also issue of October 10.

Charles Hammond of the *Gazette* tried to stem the tide of intolerance. Hall wrote: "Why is it that the catholics are pursued with
such pertinacity, such vindictiveness, with such ruthless malev-
olence? Why cannot their peculiar opinions be opposed by argument, by persuasion, by remonstrance, as one christian sect should
oppose each other. We speak kindly of the Jew, and even of the
heathen; there are those who love a negro or a Cherokee even
better than their own flesh and blood; but a catholic is an abom-
ination, for whom there is no law. . . ."[148] Hammond spoke
well of the goodly number of Catholics in the city—respectful,
orderly, industrious citizens. The *Catholic Telegraph* was published at Cincinnati, 1831–36; in 1837 the Reverend John Martin
Henni began publication of *Der Wahrheits Freund*, a German-
Catholic paper.

In 1836 the Young Men's Bible Society of Cincinnati accused
the Catholic church of withholding the Scriptures from the
people. When at about the same time the College of Teachers[149]
manifested uneasiness regarding the Catholic influence in education, Bishop Purcell replied to the statements in a lecture delivered in a Protestant church. Alexander Campbell, having, at
least to his own satisfaction, annihilated atheism and Robert
Owen in the great debate of 1829, now challenged all comers to a
debate on Catholicism. Bishop Purcell took him up and the controversialists met in a Baptist church. The debate lasted a week.
Campbell failed to demolish the Catholic religion and the bishop
made but few converts; Protestantism gained nothing and
Catholicism lost nothing. Dissatisfied with the way the *Gazette*
had reported the debate, Campbell wrote that he had not had a
fair deal; that Editor Hammond had said he (Campbell) would
"have a damned hard time of it," and called him a "heresiarch";
that Catholics had boasted that, with the Virgin Mary in heaven
and Charles Hammond on earth to defend them, they could not
lose.[150] For a time religious bickerings rivaled politics in the newspapers as a subject of controversial matter.

[148] "The Catholic Question," in *Western Monthly Magazine*, III (1835), 375–90.
The quotation is from page 377. For Hall's argument with Eli Taylor, who in
1836 published both the *Cincinnati Journal* and the *Western Monthly Magazine*,
and Hall's loss of the editorship of the *Magazine*, see Chapter XV.
[149] See Chapter XIII, 355.
[150] *Cincinnati Daily Gazette*, January 16, 18, February 4, 7 ff., 1837.

The followers of George Fox, the Friends or Quakers,[151] came to the Northwest chiefly from the South. From the 1720's northern Quakers had been moving south. The Indian wars, the decline of whaling, and the abundance of land in the large southern colonies all contributed to the drift; Virginia, the Carolinas, and northern Georgia became centers of Quaker groups. But the Society of Friends early took a stand against slavery which not only put them at a disadvantage in competition with slaveholders but marked them as being in opposition to the beliefs prevailing in the South. It appears, however, that the slavery explanation for the movement to the Northwest has been overemphasized, especially as concerns the earlier migration. The areas in which the Quakers prevailed were not strongly proslavery in sentiment. Dissatisfaction with the soil and crop possibilities may have been a more important factor than was slavery. Then there were the dire prophecies of Zachariah Dicks, who in the early 1800's was proclaiming in Georgia and South Carolina that there would be "an internecine war within the lives of children then living. . . . O Bush River! O Bush River! how hath thy beauty faded away and gloomy darkness eclipsed thy day!"

The exodus to the Northwest began in 1799–1800 when some North Carolina families gathered their possessions, slowly found their way north, rested awhile with other Friends in western Pennsylvania, and crossed the Ohio. Within a year an estimated eight hundred Quakers had settled on the north or west side of the Upper Ohio.[152] Other movers came west from New Jersey and Pennsylvania; by 1826 more than eight thousand Quakers centered in and around Belmont, Jefferson, Harrison, and Colum-

[151] Originally called "Children of the Light," then "Friends of Truth," and finally the "Religious Society of Friends." Fox said: "In 1650 we were first called Quakers by Justice Bennett, because I bid them tremble at the word of the Lord."

[152] H. E. Smith, "The Quakers, Their Migration to the Upper Ohio, Their Customs and Discipline," in *Ohio Archaeological and Historical Society Publications,* XXXVIII (1929), 45. For map of settlements in Ohio, see *ibid.,* 66.

Main routes of travel, then and later, were: (1) by the Kanawha Road by way of Patrick Court House, Virginia, Marberry's Gap in the Blue Ridge, across Clinch Mountain, by way of Pack's Ferry on New River to the falls of the Kanawha and to the Ohio; (2) by the Kentucky Road across the Blue Ridge at Ward's Gap, across the New River by way of Wythe Court House, thence by Abingdon to Cumberland and across Kentucky to Cincinnati; (3) by Poplar Camp and Flour Gap through Brownsville and Lexington, Virginia, to the Ohio; (4) by the Magadee route over the Virginia Road from Richmond to the mouth of the Kanawha; Carolinians would join this road at Lynchburg or Fincastle. The last was the most used route after 1810. Stephen B. Weeks, *Southern Quakers and Slavery* (Baltimore, 1896), 246–47.

biana counties in Ohio. A decade later, attracted by better and cheaper land, many moved west to Morgan and Washington counties. Families from Guilford County, North Carolina, who early settled in Miami County, Ohio, were joined by hundreds of others from the South. They spread up along the Whitewater Valley in eastern Indiana, where there were perhaps ten thousand Quakers by the time of statehood (1816).

The basic doctrine of the Friends was that of the Universal Inner Light—the Spirit of Christ in every man—which was sufficient guide to worldly conduct and salvation. As Fox said, "It is not the Scripture, but the Holy Spirit who gave the Scripture, who leads unto all truth." No middlemen were needed; though there were Quaker preachers, they were neither employed nor paid.

The organization of the Society of Friends was simple: membership came by birth or application and acceptance. The Yearly Meeting—of which there eventually came to be twelve in the United States—was the head body. (The Ohio Yearly Meeting was established in 1813, the Indiana in 1821.) All other meetings—Preparative, Monthly, Quarterly—reported to the Yearly Meeting.[153] When a number of Friends in a community received consent of the nearest Monthly and Quarterly Meeting, they might set up a Preparative Meeting and construct a meetinghouse. The Monthly Meeting was the executive body of the district; it appointed overseers from and for each Preparative Meeting, officiated at weddings, and kept records of membership, births, deaths, and removals. Quarterly Meeting represented a larger district and usually rotated its place of sitting. There were in 1826 five "Quarters" in the Ohio Yearly Meeting. The Yearly Meeting stood in the same relation to the Quarterly Meeting as Monthly to Preparative.

Meetinghouses, whether for the local meeting or the Yearly Meeting, were similar: there was a "gallery" or raised platform at one end separated by an aisle from the rest of the room, and a folding partition down the middle to divide the men from the women. The partition was open for public meeting, closed for

---

[153] There was also the Meeting for Sufferings, originally held weekly to help suffering or persecuted Friends. Later, held two or more times yearly, it became a charity-business meeting.

business meeting. Worship might be silent, meditative, or there might be preaching.

Despite their pacific tendencies, the Quakers fought some strenuous battles. One was the Hicksite "heresy." Elias Hicks, a prominent minister and member of the New York Yearly Meeting, advanced rather modern ideas. He denied the fall of man and the existence of a personal devil. Heaven and hell were states of mind, Christ was divine in so far as he "had of the divine nature in him . . . and so far every other man." The Scriptures he held in light esteem and the first chapters of Matthew and Luke he believed were fabulous. "We have only the woman's account of this [the miraculous conception], whose interest it was to make it so." Since the Friends had no Sabbath schools or a teaching ministry, it was not always easy to hold their members to the fold. Hicks split the Society wide open in 1827–28; it was estimated that approximately one third of the members in the Yearly Meetings of New York, Philadelphia, Baltimore, Ohio, and Indiana became disaffected.[154] Thereafter the Friends were either Orthodox or Hicksite,[155] and the two groups maintained parallel and duplicate organizations. Both maintained the same distinguishing views on oaths, peace, intemperance, and the ministry of women.

The Friends in general opposed tax-supported schools, military service, and slavery; though agreed on the last subject, they disagreed on the method of abolition. As a consequence, by the early 1840's, a division developed among Quakers of the Northwest between the gradual and immediate emancipationists. Charles Osborn's (and Elisha Bates's) *Philanthropist*, published at Mount Pleasant, Ohio, 1817–22, and Benjamin Lundy's *Genius of Universal Emancipation* were the first abolition journals of importance in the West.[156]

Not to be confused with the Quakers were the Shakers, followers of "Mother Ann" Lee, who came to New York on the eve of the Revolution. From the eastern communities three missionaries came to Kentucky at the time of the Great Revival. Some of the Barton W. Stone following went over to Shakerism.

---

[154] Luke Woodard, *A Historical Sketch of the Schism in the Friends Church in the Years 1827–1828* . . . (Plainfield, Ind., 1912), 2.
[155] The seceding group disclaimed the "Hicksite" designation; they adhered to the original name, "The Religious Society of Friends."
[156] See Chapter XV.

Richard McNemar became an active leader and pamphleteer. At Union Village, near Lebanon, Ohio, developed the main Shaker settlement; there were other groups at Shaker Heights, Ohio, and on Busseron Creek, a few miles above Vincennes.[157]

Calling themselves the United Society of Believers, the Shakers attracted the attention of travelers and controversialists far out of proportion to their importance. They repudiated marriage, the root of all evil, and were famous for the peculiar jitters and hand clapping in which they indulged while at worship; also they uttered a gibberish known as "the gift of tongues," totally incomprehensible to themselves or anyone else. The tales of obscene practices and debauchery which had been circulated regarding the Shakers in New York pursued them to Ohio. Mrs. Trollope considered the Shakers the "most amusing" of all the sects. The following, in general, was recruited from the less intelligent people. They rejected literature, learning, amusements, arts. On the other hand, they were clean, hard working, and temperate. Their success at farming[158] and accumulation of property aroused some jealousy, while their early practice of celibacy created as much interest as the later Mormon practice of plural marriages. They were accused of breaking up families and attacking and beating children because the devil was in them; one girl was said to have been locked in a barrel and rolled around for two hours.[159] Never very populous—perhaps eight or nine hundred at the most[160]—the Shaker communities, as the pioneer said, tended to peter out.

Another group which attracted attention largely because of

[157] On the Shakers see John Patterson MacLean, *A Sketch of the Life and Labors of Richard McNemar* (Franklin, Ohio, 1905), *Shakers of Ohio* (Columbus, Ohio, 1907), and "The Society of Shakers . . . ," in *Ohio Archaeological and Historical Society Publications,* IX (1900–1), 32–116. McNemar's book, *The Kentucky Revival . . . with a Brief Account of . . . Shakerism,* was published at Cincinnati in 1807. *The Other Side of the Question* (Cincinnati, 1819), an answer to Abram Van Vleet's *An Account of the Conduct of the Shakers* (Lebanon, 1818), was probably by McNemar. *A Selection of Hymns and Poems; for the Use of Believers* (Watervliet, Ohio, 1833) under the pen name of "Philos Harmoniae" may have been McNemar's. John Dunlavy published his *The Manifesto, or a Declaration of the Doctrines and Practices of the Church of Christ,* at Pleasant Hill, Kentucky, in 1818. A manuscript account book of the Shaker settlement on Busseron Creek, 1815–22, is in the Indiana Division, Indiana State Library. The most recent work on the Shakers is Julia Neal, *By Their Fruits; the Story of Shakerism in South Union, Kentucky* (Chapel Hill, N. C., 1947), a story of the Kentucky Shakers.

[158] For development of the ancestor of the Poland China hog, see I, 188.

[159] Depositions in the Lebanon *Western Star,* copied in *Miami Herald,* September 12, 26, October 2, etc., 1817.

[160] Bernhard, Duke of Saxe-Weimar-Eisenach, said there were six hundred in Union Village. *Travels through North America,* II, 140.

industry and thrift was the German Separatists at Zoar in Tuscarawas County, Ohio.[161] Two years after their settlement in 1817, 157 of these pietistic pacifists from Württemberg organized the communal-religious Society of Zoar and incorporated it under the laws of Ohio.[162] Under the leadership of the former Württemberg school teacher, Joseph Michael Bimeler, the thrifty and industrious Germans farmed, made their own manufactured products, and prospered. Bimeler considered himself the mouthpiece of the Holy Ghost and sought to lead his people to happiness by preaching a religion of the heart rather than one of outward manifestations. Like George Rapp at Harmony, he built himself a fine house. In the 1820's the Society took in some $20,000 in cash for work on the Ohio Canal in addition to the receipts from supplies sold to contractors. In the early 1830's they admitted 170 new arrivals, mostly relatives and friends. At that time they had more than 10,000 acres of land and 60 good buildings, many of them with red-tile roofs. A number of inquiries and applications for membership came from Americans.[163]

Though Zoar was one of the longest-lived communistic settlements in the West, it in time came to the usual end. In 1895 Levi Bimeler, a descendant of Joseph, began to blast communism in his one-man monthly paper, *The Nugitna*. He issued a declaration of independence. "Communism—Humbugism! . . . Communism may be a good thing in the interior of Africa, but in the center of the highly civilized state of Ohio it is an outrage. . . . And as to the abolition of fortune's distinctions, Phew!—. . . . Only fools,

[161] This sect based its beliefs on the teachings of Johann Arndt (1555–1621), Johann Andreä (1586–1654), and Christoph Oetinger (1702–1782). They rejected baptism, confirmation, and other ordinances. Their beliefs are set forth in the three volumes of discourses in German by Joseph M. Bimeler titled *The True Separation or Second Birth . . . and Spiritual Crumbs from the Table of the Lord* (Zoar, 1856–61). The Zoar community is well covered in E. O. Randall, "The Separatist Society of Zoar . . . ," in *Ohio Archaeological and Historical Society Publications,* VIII (1900), 1–105; and *History of the Zoar Society* (Columbus, 1904). See also George B. Landis, "The Separatists of Zoar, Ohio," in *Annual Reports of the American Historical Association,* 1898, pp. 165–220; Edgar B. Nixon, "The Society of Separatists of Zoar," MS. Ph.D. thesis in Ohio State University Library.

[162] When one of the members later sued for partition of the property, the Seventh United States Circuit Court decided, 1851, in the case of *John G. Goesele et al v. Joseph M. Bimeler* that the lands were held in trust by Bimeler for the Society, and that the articles of association did not constitute a joint tenancy or perpetuity in property. The Supreme Court upheld the decision the following year: individual members could have no rights in the property except in use. 14 *Howard,* 589 ff.

[163] Edgar B. Nixon, "The Zoar Society: Applicants for Membership," in *Ohio Archaeological and Historical Society Publications,* XLV (1936), 341–50.

religious bigots or self-conceited ones are so blind as to believe
that there is no difference in rank and fortune" in the Society.
"What fools we are to labor for the benefit of a few favored
ones; to keep the Don Juans in their positions of ease, luxury
and revelry."[164] The common property was subsequently divided
(1898).

Moravians had come into the Ohio country prior to the Revolution. The missions at Gnadenhütten, Schönbrunn, Sandusky, and
on the White River in Indiana had declined in importance with
the passing of the Indian, but other Moravian settlers came and
clannishly located on good farm lands, mostly in Ohio and Indiana.[165] Also came groups of Mennonites, including the Swiss, a
number of whom settled in Holmes and Wayne counties, Ohio.[166]

As interesting as the Shakers and far more numerous were the
Mormons. Long before their ideas of plural marriages aroused
the ire of the pioneers, the Mormons were a notorious and much-
publicized sect.[167] Joseph Smith, the Prophet of Palmyra, had
established his Church of Christ, with six members, April 3,
1830. When he dispatched a mission of three to go west to
preach to the Indians, one of the preachers, Parley Pratt, a recent
convert, led the party to Mentor, Ohio. There Sidney Rigdon, an
emotional and humorless Campbellite preacher, who had
quarreled with Campbell over communitarianism, was converted;
he delivered his little flock at Kirtland over to the new faith.
Soon he persuaded Smith that Kirtland was the eastern border of
the Promised Land; a new revelation confirmed it.

In 1831 a few score followers from New York joined Smith
and the more numerous Kirtland group. Smith, with his miracles,

[164] *The Nugitna,* December 30, 1895, March 23, 1896.
[165] The census of 1850 listed 160 Moravian churches in Ohio, 57 in Indiana, 2
in Illinois, and 1 in Michigan.
[166] The census of 1850 listed ten Mennonite churches in the Northwest, all in
Ohio. For the Swiss settlements in Allen and Putnam counties see D. A. Gratz,
"Historical and Genealogical Sketch of the Swiss Mennonites . . . ," in *Ohio
Archaeological and Historical Society Publications,* XLIX (1940), 282–88.
[167] The literature on even the Middle West phase of Mormonism bulks large.
The best survey of it is in the bibliography and notes of Fawn M. Brodie, *No Man
Knows My History* (New York, 1946). Mormon newspapers published prior to
1840 were the *Evening and Morning Star* (Kirtland, Ohio, and Independence,
Missouri), June, 1832—September, 1834; *Latter-Day Saints' Messenger and Advo-
cate* (Kirtland, Ohio, 1834–37); and *Times and Seasons* (Nauvoo, Ill., 1839–46).
Of the non-Mormon papers the ones which carried most Mormon news were those
of the Western Reserve, particularly the Ravenna *Western Courier, Painesville
Telegraph, Painesville Republican,* and the Illinois papers, 1839–40.

prophecies, and revelations, soon attracted followers. The more enthusiastic among them began to see visions, mounted stumps to preach to imaginary congregations, chased balls of fire through the fields, and had bodily exercises. Far more amazing than these manifestations of zeal, however, was the success Smith had in attracting a number of people of ability and means and separating them from their property, a feat the secret of which the popular frontier sects never seemed to learn.

Influenced no doubt by Rigdon (who had heard Owen debate Campbell in 1829) and by the need for greater resources with which to carry out his plans, Smith by revelation set up the United Order, a semicommunistic organization, the detailed workings of which are not clear.

Smith's main interest was the building of the New Jerusalem. For a time it appeared that the site of Zion would be Independence, Missouri, to which a sizeable contingent of followers removed. Though the temple site for the new Zion was chosen, things did not work out well. The Missouri settlements ran into troubles, not the least of which was the direct opposition of Missourians. At Kirtland the prophet had his family troubles, legal troubles, and religious troubles. Not all of them could be resolved by revelation. (Debts, for instance: Though as early as 1831 Smith had resolved that any debts were to be paid by the Bishop of Zion "out of that which the Lord shall put into his hands," the Lord did not always co-operate.)

To take men's minds from such worldly problems, Smith built a temple in Kirtland and ordered the building of The Temple in Zion. But the problems remained, and the dissolution of the Kirtland Order and the abolition of communism did not help; the Church still kept its hold on private property. Inspiration from Egyptian relics—papyri and mummies—resulted in the production of the Book of Abraham; the dedication of the temple brought forth beautiful ritual and temporary ecstasy; the Book of Abraham and Joseph's marital troubles developed the practice, if not the official proclamation, of polygamy.

The Kirtland Mormons were deeply involved in the land speculation of the mid-1830's. The temple, steam mill, and other holdings were mortgaged to the limit. Joseph's credit was good and he made the most of it.[168] By another revelation he organized the Kirtland Safety Society Anti-Banking Company, capital stock "not less than four million dollars." Rigdon was made president. Though not recognized under the laws of Ohio, the bank succeeded in circulating some thousands of its notes locally. For a brief period everyone seemed rich. But the Mormon bank did not even wait for the crash of 1837; it staged its own collapse in March of that year. Smith owed thousands, the Mormon leaders perhaps $150,000, to outsiders.[169] The hands of the law were close upon him—thirteen suits and seven arrests in less than two years. Truly his kingdom was of this world. He went to Missouri and the Kirtland Church went to pieces. Dissensions, disaffections, and open fights abounded. Finally some six hundred of the faithful followed the discredited leader to Missouri.

At Far West (where Cain killed Abel) rather than at Independence (the site of the garden of Eden), Smith began anew. Recruits were coming in from England and elsewhere. Smith purged the saints of his most dangerous rivals,[170] revived the United Order into a sort of corporate state,[171] and indirectly at least sanctioned the organization of Sampson Avard's secret militia, the Danites. But all in vain. The inhabitants of northwestern Missouri not only did not like Mormons; they wanted their lands. After considerable violence on both sides Smith and other leaders spent a term in Liberty jail. It was Brigham Young, the energetic convert with the "gift of tongues" of 1832, who led the exodus of 1839 to Illinois.

Around Quincy and environs Democratic politicians and land speculators welcomed the saints with open arms. After his "escape" from jail, Smith was made treasurer of the church and "Trustee-in-Trust." He swapped the Missouri lands and the eastern lands of new recruits for some lands around Nauvoo ($18,000) and a large parcel ($80,000) of land in Iowa Terri-

[168] Smith estimated his own land in Kirtland at $300,000. *Painesville Telegraph,* January 27, 1837.
[169] Brodie, *No Man Knows My History,* 199–202.
[170] Particularly Oliver Cowdery and John and David Whitmer, his earliest associates.
[171] July 8, 1838. By revelation the saints were to deed all their property to the church but individuals were to be returned a parcel of land sufficient for their families. In addition each saint was to give one tenth of his income to the church. The plan was subsequently modified into a long-lease system; the four "corporations"—farmers, mechanics, shopkeepers, and laborers—were to run the economy.

tory (the Half-Breed tract) to which the agent had no title. Despite this fraud and the devastations of the ague, the Mormons did quite well. There was much Yankee shrewdness mixed with the orders which came from on high; though not the first to identify "the goodness of God with the making of money," Smith did it effectively. Mills, foundries, power and navigation dams, a community farm for those who had no money for land, lumbering, a hotel, and other projects kept all busy. The close political balance in Illinois enabled the Mormons to play both sides of the street; most of the newspapers had decided to live and let live as far as the newcomers were concerned.[172] The work of foreign missionaries, among them Brigham Young, brought hundreds of new members. Smith and other leaders took advantage of the United States bankruptcy law of 1841 to ease out from under their debts,[173] Young returned to lend his talents to establishing the new community, the Illinois legislature granted a charter which practically created a state within a state. Further troubles lay ahead, troubles which were to cost the prophet his life, but they run beyond the chronological limit of this work.

Perhaps no complete explanation of Mormonism is possible; several factors, however, can be indicated. One was the complex and resilient personality of Joseph Smith. Another was the spirit of the times, a spirit of flux and experimentation which welcomed new "isms" and sects. A third was the nature of the Mormon religion, which offered pleasure and power in this world as well as in the next. The words of Smith's latest biographer cannot be improved upon:

There was a fine robustness about it that smelled of the frontier and that rejected an asceticism that was never endemic to America. The poverty, sacrifice, and suffering that dogged the Saints resulted largely from clashes with their neighbors over social and economic issues. Though they may have glorified in their adversity, they certainly did not invite it. Wealth and power they considered basic among the blessings both of earth and of heaven, and if they were to be denied them in this life, then they must assuredly enjoy them in the next.[174]

[172] When Smith went to Washington in 1839 to try to get action from the General Government on the $2,000,000 damage suit of the church against Missouri, both Henry Clay and John T. Stuart, Whig representative from Illinois, sought to gain the Mormons a fair hearing.
[173] In 1841 Smith listed his debts at $73,066.38. There was also an item of $33,000 hanging over from Kirtland days.
[174] Brodie, *No Man Knows My History*, 187–88.

The very features which attracted followers from the poor in England and the poor and not so poor in America were, however, finally to bring down upon the Mormons the wrath and violence of the Middle West pioneers. The American recruits to Mormonism came from various sources, but the Baptists and the Disciples furnished the largest percentage. Rigdon, a former Campbellite, gloated over this fact; he said that Mormonism had "puked the Campbellites effectually, no emetic could do half so well."[175]

Although Millerism as an organized movement did not reach the West until after 1840, nevertheless, it was followed with interest in the newspapers for several years prior to that date.[176] William Miller was born in Massachusetts, fought in the War of 1812, and underwent conversion in 1816, at which time he began a serious study of the Bible. Concentrating his interest upon the prophecies, in 1818 he concluded that the world would come to an end in about twenty-five years, but not until 1831, when he was forty-nine years old, did Miller begin to preach and publish this prophecy. Many of his original converts were rural and small-town Baptists, but as camp meetings were held and the "Great Tent" raised in Concord, New Hampshire, the "Midnight Cry" spread to the cities.[177]

Overlooking the thirteenth verse of the parable,[178] Miller finally fixed the date of the Second Coming as between March

[175] *Latter-Day Saints' Messenger and Advocate*, January, 1837, p. 438, cited in *ibid.*, 206. In 1844 Smith spoke of 200,000 followers. Fewer than one tenth of this figure would probably have included all at the time.

In 1832 Alvan Stone, Baptist missionary in Illinois, noted that "a number of deluded fanatics" were joining the Mormons and preparing to set off for the New Jerusalem. One, a Methodist exhorter, had worn out his horse in the endeavor to overtake and join a Mormon band. He finally made it, was made a Mormon preacher, and on his way back tried to walk on the waters of Silver Creek. "His ability to swim, however, not his faith saved him." Shortly thereafter he began to destroy all his property. *Journal of the Illinois State Historical Society*, III, No. 4 (Jan., 1911), 92–93.

[176] The best of the older studies of Miller is Sylvester Bliss, *Memoirs of William Miller, Generally Known as a Lecturer, on the Prophecies, and the Second Coming of Christ* (Boston, 1853). A more recent study written from the Adventist viewpoint is that by Francis D. Nichol, *The Midnight Cry* . . . (Washington, D. C., 1944), which contains an excellent bibliography on the Millerite movement.

[177] This favorite watchword of the Millerites was based upon the parable of the wise and foolish virgins—the latter of whom were caught short of oil: "And at midnight there was a cry made, Behold, the bridegroom cometh; go ye out to meet him." Matthew 25:1–13.

[178] "Watch therefore, for ye know neither the day nor the hour wherein the Son of man cometh."

21, 1843 and March 21, 1844, and the flaming comet of that year, said to be visible in broad daylight, as well as other signs and wonders led many people to believe that the end was at hand. The Millerites were accused of various forms of fanaticism and of acquiring ascension robes and taking up their positions on the hills and housetops as the day of the Second Coming approached; numbers of them did close their businesses to await the event. Cartoons, caricatures, and broadsides heaped ridicule upon them. The date fixed, however, passed without anything unusual happening. Miller and his followers, though disappointed, merely figured that they had miscalculated; the leading Millerite newspapers—*Signs of the Times* (Boston) and *The Midnight Cry* (New York)—resumed publication, and a new date was fixed—October 22, 1844.[179]

At Cincinnati, which became the western center of Millerism shortly after 1840, Miller's followers had erected a large tabernacle which was said to seat fifteen hundred persons. In 1844 Miller lectured to a crowd reported to number four thousand people. Like many other groups in the country this congregation after holding a meeting on October 22 went home "filled with great spiritual elation" quietly to await the fulfillment of the revised schedule. Again, however, nothing happened and the Millerites suffered additional ridicule. But the faith of the leaders was not destroyed, and though they ceased fixing definite dates the belief that Christ would come "the second time without sin unto salvation" continued to be their central belief. Their following came to be known and survived as the Seventh-Day Adventists.

Of the religious groups not previously discussed the most important were the Episcopalians and the Lutherans. Their creeds and organization call for no special treatment. The Episcopalians, strongest in Ohio, comprised largely upper-middle-class people from the eastern states. Although Bishop Philander Chase established the diocese of Ohio in 1818, churches were not numerous.[180]

---

[179] *The Western Midnight Cry* was founded by Joshua V. Himes at Cincinnati late in 1843; in 1845 the name of this weekly was changed to *The Day Star*. In January, 1843, at Cleveland was started *The Second Advent of Christ*. Files of these papers are in the Western Reserve Historical Society Library.

[180] In 1841 the *American Almanac* listed 132 Episcopalian ministers in the whole Middle West of which 54 were in Ohio. Caswall, *America and the American Church,* 323–24, estimated some three thousand Episcopalians in Ohio. The *Church Standard* (later the *Western Episcopalian*) was published in Gambier, 1830–1836.

The diocese of Michigan was organized 1833–34 but remained attached to that of Ohio. The qualifications for ministers in the Protestant Episcopal Church were severe—about six years training—consequently there was a shortage of ministers of this faith on the frontier.

The Lutherans were most numerous among the German immigrants. Their churches centered largely around Cincinnati, Detroit, Fort Wayne, Sandusky, and the Belleville–St. Louis region. Reformed and Evangelical churches were also attached to the German settlements. The New School Presbyterians were friendly toward these German Protestants (and toward the Scandinavians and the Welsh), and after 1835 the American Home Missionary Society co-operated in subsidizing ministers.[181]

The colonial Pennsylvania Germans were largely German Reformed, Lutheran, and Mennonite. From the evangelical Philip William Otterbein, who came from Germany to serve as pastor of the Reformed Church at Lancaster in 1752, and the like-minded Mennonite Martin Boehm came the defection from the Reformed Church which led to the formation of the Church of the United Brethren in Christ.[182] The first formal conference, held in Otterbein's parsonage in Baltimore in 1789, drew up a confession of faith in five articles, and a set of disciplinary rules;[183] a conference in 1800 adopted the name United Brotherhood in Jesus Christ and made formal election of bishops. With the emigration of United Brethren families to Ohio, particularly to the Miami Valley, in the early 1800's came the organization of the Miami Annual Conference. The first General Conference, held in 1815, drew up the *Book of Discipline*, a more definitive Confession of Faith and set of rules for the church.

[181] The Evangelical Church was launched by Jacob Albright, a Lutheran convert to Methodism, among the Pennsylvania, Maryland, and Virginia Germans in the early 1800's.

In 1840 the German Evangelical churches in and around St. Louis organized the Evangelischer Kirchenverein des Westens, which organization in the 1840's aided a number of pastors in Indiana, Illinois, and Wisconsin Territory. Carl E. Schneider, *The German Church on the American Frontier* . . . (St. Louis, 1939), *passim.* In 1934 this Evangelical group merged with the Reformed Church to form the Evangelical and Reformed Church in America. For the other see note 184.

[182] Among the older histories of the United Brethren are Henry G. Spayth, *History of the Church of the United Brethren in Christ* (Circleville, Ohio, 1851), and Daniel Berger, *History of the Church of the United Brethren in Christ* (Dayton, Ohio, 1897).

[183] Weekly attendance at class or prayer meeting, abstention from "all backbiting and evil speaking," and "a quiet and godly life" were stipulated. The washing of feet as an outward sign or ordinance was made optional.

Though the United Brethren ministers preached almost exclusively in German in the early years, there was a close fellowship among them and the Methodist ministers; at times they used the same churches and held common revivals. The possibility of union of the two denominations was discussed in 1810, but a treaty of amity and friendship was about the only result. The union of the Evangelical Church and the Church of the United Brethren was also discussed.[184]

Early United Brethren churches were organized in southern Indiana between 1810 and 1815; the Indiana Conference was established in 1830.[185] The first class in Illinois was formed in 1830, and soon the group was active in McLean and adjoining counties. Itinerants were sent into the Embarrass, Kankakee, Sangamon, Spoon River, and Rock River valleys. The Wabash Conference was organized in 1835.

These "Dutch Methodists," as they were called in the West, advocated fervid evangelism, simple piety, and stern morals. Their Quarterly Conferences were as assiduous as the Methodists and Baptists in guarding the well-being and day-to-day conduct of the members. They ruled against profanity, gambling, dancing, slavery, horse racing (and later against county fairs and baseball). For years they even tried to get the ministers to forego the use of tobacco.[186]

Universalists and Unitarians were not numerous and were confined largely to Cincinnati and a few of the larger towns; they were usually classified as being practically nonreligious by the evangelical denominations. The First Congregational (Unitarian) Church of Cincinnati, organized in 1824, had among its distinguished pastors Adam Bancroft, father of George Bancroft, the historian, and William H. Channing, nephew of William Ellery Channing.

Persons of the Jewish faith were widely scattered and had no synagogues except in Cincinnati.

[184] In 1946 the Evangelical Church (Albright group) merged with the United Brethren in Christ to form the Evangelical United Brethren in Christ; the church is episcopally organized and akin to the Methodist.

[185] See Adam B. Condo, *History of the Indiana Conference of the Church of the United Brethren in Christ* (n.p. n.d.) for the Indiana church history.

[186] By 1871 the Illinois Conference was able to report that most ministers had given up the habit, "and to those brethren who are its slaves, we humbly beseech them, by the Grace of God, to leave off as a beverage; and if used at all, only as medicine. Show thyself pure in habit as well as in doctrine." Quoted in Lynn W. Turner, "The United Brethren Church in Illinois," in *Papers in Illinois History . . . 1939* (Springfield, 1940), 53.

The Negro population was not large. A few Negro churches, largely Methodist and Baptist, were organized in Ohio, Indiana, and Illinois. A few Negroes worshiped in the white churches; the First Baptist Church of Cleveland was organized by members of both races in 1833, as was the Union Church at New Buffalo, Michigan, a decade later.[187] The American Home Missionary Society did not subsidize any Negro churches in the Northwest.

In addition to the organized churches there were the various tract and Bible societies, some of which were ostensibly nonsectarian, which helped in the spread of religious influence. Then a lot of general religious-moral uplift was propagated in the newspapers. Hundreds of gems such as the following could be culled from the press of the period: "Women, who have fed their minds with the maxims of fashion, fall into a deplorable void as they advance to years. The world forsakes them and their reason likewise departs;—to what shall they betake themselves? The past furnishes regret; the present vexations; the future fears. Religion calms all: In uniting her votaries with their God, it reconciles them to the world and to themselves."[188]

It has been said that religion was "probably the most pervasive cultural influence" in the early West,[189] and that it was "the most universally pervasive intellectual force of the frontier."[190] Whether it was more important than schools, newspapers, and other cultural influences is beside the point; certainly it is not to be underestimated. Though the popular mind might not appear critically to distinguish between religion and goodness, irreligion and wickedness, there is much evidence that many people did make the distinction. A certain amount of conformity and respect was paid religion out of deference to social convention.

As in the colonial period, the churches offered much opportunity for training in self-government; particularly was this true of the Presbyterian, Baptist, and those churches organized on the congregational basis, such as the Disciples. Even the women participated, directly or indirectly, and voted long before they gave serious thought to the political ballot.

[187] On the Negro churches see Carter Woodson, *The History of the Negro Church* (2d ed. Washington, D. C., 1921), 121 ff.
[188] *Cleaveland Register,* September 21, 1819.
[189] Rusk, *The Literature of the Middle Western Frontier*, I, 38.
[190] Pease, *The Frontier State,* 23.

There is no doubt that the churches performed a definite function in the supervision of the private and public morals of their members, and exercised some sort of influence on non-members. In the struggle for decency and order, however, the religious-minded were not always willing to practice the principles of forbearance and democracy which they proclaimed; they often consigned to the devil those who did not agree with them, and the devil's cohorts fell outside the rules.[191] Though religious freedom was an accepted part of the constitutional foundation of the government of a free people, there were ways of applying pressure other than through government. Mrs. Trollope noted this and must have thought it was too delicate a subject even for a book not outstanding for its delicacy of treatment of Americans:

A three years' residence in America has shown me most clearly that a religious tyranny may be very effectually exerted without the aid of government. I shall not expect to escape the charge of impossible exaggeration if I describe the species of petty persecution that I have seen exercised on religious subjects in America. The whole people appear to be divided into an almost endless variety of religious factions. I was told in Cincinnati that to be well received in society, it was indispensably necessary to declare that you belonged to some one of these factions—it did not much matter which. As far as I could make out, the Methodists were considered as the most pious, the Presbyterians as the most powerful, the Episcopalians and the Catholics as the most stylish, the Universalists as the most liberal, the Swedenborgians as the most musical, the Unitarians as the most enlightened, the Quakers the most amiable, the Dancing Shakers the most amusing, and the Jews as the most interesting. Besides these there are dozens more of fancy religions whose designations I cannot remember, but declaring yourself to belong to any one of them, as far as I could learn, was sufficient to constitute you a respectable member of society.

Having thus declared yourself, your next submission must be that of unqualified obedience to the will and pleasure of your elected pastor, or you will run a great risk of being "passed out of the church." This was a phrase that I perpetually heard, and upon enquiry I found that it did not mean being passed neck and heels out of the building at the discretion of the sexton, but a sort of congregational excommunication which infallibly betides those who venture to do any thing that their pastor and master disapproves.[192]

[191] For instance, Judge Jacob Burnet of the Supreme Court of Ohio in 1828 ruled that an atheist or one who did not believe in God could not be a witness. *Hamilton Intelligencer,* November 11, 1828.

[192] Trollope MS. Note Book I (Cincinnati, 1830–31), in Indiana University Library.

XV

Literature—Science—Reform

The tide of emigration brings not, like an oriental river, golden sands upon its bosom; and those social comforts, and liberal arts, which flourish only in the sunshine of wealth, are seldom the companions of the hardy pioneer, in his lonesome journey, or the inmates of the cabin in the wilderness.— So far then from deserving any reproach, for having done so little for literature and science, I venture to assert that we deserve great credit for even that little; especially when it is recollected how much we have accomplished in other departments of improvement.

James Hall, *Western Monthly Magazine,* August, 1833

WHEN he wrote the above words James Hall was, no doubt, thinking of literature in the narrow sense, and not as the total of preserved writings of a language or a people. He would perhaps have been astonished, in his day, to be told that a century later historians would find in the newspapers of his favorite region a literature so voluminous and rich in content that it would be impossible for any one man or group of men to digest and exhaust it.

Travelers from abroad noted, along with the American's tendency to profanity, tobacco chewing, and leaning back on the hind legs of a chair, his devotion to newspapers. To some, this, too, seemed a bad habit, an evidence of a lack of culture. Wrote Mrs. Trollope:

In truth, there are many reasons which render a very general diffusion of literature impossible in America. I can scarcely class the universal reading of newspapers as an exception to this remark; if I could, my statement would be exactly the reverse, and I should say that Americans beat the world in letters. The fact is, that throughout all ranks of society, from the successful merchant, which is the highest, to the domestic serving man, which is the lowest, they are all too actively employed to read, except at such broken moments as may suffice for a peep at a newspaper. It is for this reason, I presume, that every American newspaper is more or less a magazine, wherein the merchant may scan while he holds out his hand for an invoice, "Stanzas by Mrs. Hemans," or a garbled extract from Moore's Life of Byron.[1]

[1] *Domestic Manners of the Americans,* I, 128.

Since 1690, when Benjamin Harris published at Boston the one and only issue of *Publick Occurrences Both Forreign and Domestick*—"to be furnished once a moneth (or if any Glut of Occurrences happen, oftener)," American Newspapers had come far. A century later Philadelphia and New York had daily newspapers, and two papers, *The Pittsburgh Gazette* (1786) and *The Kentucke Gazette* (1787), had been started west of the mountains. From the office of the latter William Maxwell went to Cincinnati, and in 1793 began *The Centinel of the North-Western Territory*, the first newspaper in the Northwest.[2] This pioneer paper was a little 8½-by-10½ inch, four-page, three-columns-to-the-page, weekly. Under the slogan "Open to all parties— but influenced by none," the editor, in addition to giving news on Indian threats and national and European affairs, issued an appeal for local contributions—poems, essays, and advertisements.[3] In 1799 appeared, also at Cincinnati, *The Western Spy, and Hamilton Gazette*, which under different titles maintained an existence throughout our period.[4] Late in 1804 came the

[2] The history of newspapers of the region remains to be written; beginnings only have been made. An introduction to the subject may be had from Rusk, *Literature of the Middle Western Frontier,* II, Chapter III. Osmon C. Hooper, *History of Ohio Journalism* (Columbus, 1933), is sketchy but very useful; the *Union List of Ohio Newspapers Available in Ohio,* compiled by Arthur D. Mink (Columbus, 1946), is an important aid for locating thousands of volumes. The comprehensive "History and Directory of Indiana Newspapers," compiled by Logan Esarey and Donald F. Carmony, unfortunately, is still in manuscript. Franklin William Scott, *Newspapers and Periodicals of Illinois 1814–1879 (Illinois Historical Collections,* VI, Springfield, 1910) outlines the history and lists the holdings of Illinois papers as of date of publication. Douglas C. McMurtrie, *Early Printing in Michigan . . .* (Chicago, 1931), and *Early Printing in Wisconsin* (Seattle, 1931), contain the newspaper record in these states to 1850. These works should be supplemented by the appropriate titles in the WPA American Imprints Inventory: *A Check List of Ohio Imprints 1796–1820* (Columbus, 1941); and *A Check List of Wisconsin Imprints, 1833–1849* (Madison, 1942). The "Bibliography of American Newspapers 1690–1820," by Clarence S. Brigham in *Proceedings of the American Antiquarian Society,* new series, XXIII-XXXVII, has been revised and published as the *History and Bibliography of American Newspapers, 1690–1820* (2 volumes. Worcester, Mass., 1947). Winifred Gregory (ed.), *American Newspapers 1821–1936—A Union List of Files Available in the United States and Canada* (New York, 1937), serves as a finding list. The best sources are the newspapers themselves, main collections of which are in the state libraries or state historical society libraries at Columbus, Indianapolis, Springfield, Lansing, and Madison, and in the libraries of the Historical and Philosophical Society of Ohio at Cincinnati, the Western Reserve Historical Society at Cleveland, the Chicago Historical Society, the leading university and public libraries of the five states, and in the county courthouses.

[3] In 1796 Maxwell sold the paper to Edmund Freeman who changed the name to *Freeman's Journal*; in 1800 the paper was moved to Chillicothe, the new territorial capital. Drake, *Natural and Statistical View, or Picture of Cincinnati,* 152.

[4] As *Western Spy,* etc., to 1822, as *National Republican, Cincinnati Republican,* etc., to 1842.

Liberty Hall and Cincinnati Mercury, to begin its life of a century and a decade; in December, 1815, the name was changed to *Liberty Hall and Cincinnati Gazette*.[5] As a weekly, semi-weekly and, after 1827 a daily, this paper was the most important single newspaper source for the history of the Old Northwest prior to the Civil War. Charles Hammond, editor from 1825 to 1840, was one of the outstanding editors of his day. Other important Ohio papers established before 1815 were *The Scioto Gazette* (1800), and *The Supporter* (1808), both at Chillicothe; the Steubenville *Western Herald* (1806); the Zanesville *Muskingum Messenger* (1809); the Worthington *Western Intelligencer* (1811); the *St. Clairsville Gazette* (1812); and *The Miami Intelligencer* (at Hamilton, 1814).

The *Western Intelligencer* became the *Columbus Gazette* in 1817, then in 1825 the *Ohio State Journal*, under which title, with slight changes, it has continued to date. In 1816 David Smith, of New Hampshire, earlier connected with the *Intelligencer*, helped found the *Ohio Monitor and Patron of Husbandry* at Columbus. In 1835 Jacob Medary consolidated the *Monitor* with his *Western Hemisphere* (1833), which two years later Samuel Medary and Brothers renamed the *Ohio Statesman*. Under slightly varying titles, the *Journal* and the *Statesman* confronted each other from the opposite sides of the political fence for three quarters of a century.

Indiana's first newspaper, the *Indiana Gazette,* appeared at Vincennes in the summer of 1804. Elihu Stout, the editor, had formerly worked on the *Kentucke Gazette* at Lexington. The earliest known issue of the *Gazette*, in the Indiana State Library, is dated August 7, 1804, and is numbered as volume I, number 2. A fire destroyed the *Gazette* press, probably some time in 1806. The paper was revived as the *Western Sun*, volume I, number 1 being dated July 11, 1807.[6] Other papers established before the end of the territorial period were the *Western Eagle* (1813–15 at Madison, 1815–16 at Lexington); the *Cornucopia of the*

---

[5] In 1883 it became the *Commercial Gazette*; in 1898 the *Cincinnati Commercial Tribune*. The *Daily Cincinnati Gazette* began in June, 1827, and continued under this title until 1883.

[6] In succession this paper became *The Western Sun and General Advertiser, Jones' Vincennes Sentinel, The Vincennes Indiana Patriot*, and then the *Western Sun* again.

West published at Lexington in 1816; the Corydon *Indiana Herald* (1816–18); the Corydon *Indiana Gazette* (1816–24); the Vevay *Indiana Register* (1816–19); and the Brookville *Plain Dealer* (1816–19).

Territorial Illinois had to depend largely upon outside papers since only one Illinois paper, the *Illinois Herald* (Kaskaskia, 1814), was published before 1818. Renamed the *Western Intelligencer* in 1816 and *Illinois Intelligencer* in 1818, the paper moved to Vandalia, the new capital, in 1820.[7]

Newspapers rapidly increased in numbers during the decade following the War of 1812; they marked the advance of settlements as certainly as did the organization of new counties or the laying out of roads. By 1826 there were at least sixty in Ohio.[8] Among the important newcomers were the *Cincinnati Gazette*, the *National Republican*, and Moses Dawson's *Cincinnati Advertiser*; the *Piqua Gazette*; the *Newark Advocate*; the *Zanesville Express*; the Ravenna *Western Courier*; and the *Cleaveland Herald*.[9] The last named appeared October 19, 1819; at the time it had not a single subscriber.

The Vincennes *Indiana Centinel* began publication on March 14, 1817. The following year appeared the Charlestown *Indiana Intelligencer* and the Jeffersonville *Indianian*. Three early Lawrenceburg papers were the *Dearborn Gazette* (1817), *Indiana Oracle* (1819), and *Indiana Spectator* (1824). The Richmond *Weekly Intelligencer* began in 1822 and the *Public Leger* in 1824.[10] Indianapolis' first newspaper, the *Indianapolis Gazette* (1822), anticipated the moving of the capital by three years. The *Western Censor and Emigrant's Guide* started early in 1823, but John Douglass, formerly of Madison and Corydon, bought

[7] The paper was started by Mathew Duncan who sold it to Daniel Pope Cook. The small four-column pages were printed in large type with the long S. Few copies of this paper have been preserved. The first bound volume, incomplete (Illinois State Historical Library), begins with *Western Intelligencer*, May 15, 1816. See *Transactions of the Illinois State Historical Society*, 1903, pp. 179 ff.

[8] See Hooper, *Ohio Journalism*, 68–69 for list.

[9] Cleveland's first paper was the short-lived *Cleaveland Gazette and Commercial Register* (1818) which, under the title of *Cleaveland Register*, survived until 1820.

It was the *Cleaveland Herald* (1819) which stubbornly held on to the old spelling some years after Cleveland dropped the extra "a." It noted, January 13, 1831, that its new neighbor the *Cleveland Advertiser* had adopted the new spelling (used in the act of incorporation of 1814), which was all right if the people wanted it that way. With the advent of a new editor the *Herald*, in April, 1832, fell in line.

[10] *Niles' Weekly Register*, XV, 294 (Dec. 19, 1818) said that there were nine papers in the state and another in prospect. There were possibly thirteen papers published during 1818–19.

it, and in January, 1825, changed the title to the *Indiana Journal*. It was Indiana's most important paper of pre-Civil War days.[11]

The *Indiana Democrat*, the *Journal's* political *vis-à-vis*, was started in 1830; in 1841 it became the *Indiana Sentinel*. The Terre Haute *Western Register and Advertiser* and the Bloomington *Indiana Gazette and Literary Advocate* were both publishing by 1826, as were the Centreville *Western Emporium*, the *New-Harmony Gazette*, and the Connersville *Fayette Observer*. The Richmond *Public Leger* named sixteen papers as being published in 1826, none of which was farther north than the National Road.[12] The first paper north of the Wabash was the Logansport *Pottawattomie and Miami Times* (1829–31); the *Cass County Times*, the *Republican and Indiana Herald*, and the *Canal Telegraph*, all of Logansport, followed. The Lafayette *Free Press* was founded in 1829. South Bend's first paper was the *North-Western Pioneer and St. Joseph Intelligencer* (1831). The *Richmond Palladium*, one of Indiana's most important pre-Civil War papers, was started in 1831. The directory of Indiana newspapers put out by Douglass and Maguire of the *Indiana Journal* in 1833 listed twenty-nine papers then publishing. In 1837 there were at least fifty papers in Indiana,[13] in 1840 there were sixty-nine weeklies and four semi- and triweeklies.[14]

The pioneer *Illinois Herald* was followed by the Shawneetown *Illinois Emigrant* (1818), which the next year was renamed the *Illinois Gazette*; in 1820 James Hall became editor.[15] The *Edwardsville Spectator* was begun in 1819, and the Kaskaskia *Republican Advocate* in 1823; the latter was renamed the *Kaskaskia Republican* the following year.

The four papers which survived the convention struggle of 1824[16] were augmented in the next ten years by additional

---

[11] To continue until 1904 when *The Indianapolis Star* took over the continuity.

[12] October 28, 1826. This list, like that of the *Indiana Palladium's* enumeration of July 22, 1825 (17), was probably incomplete.

[13] Fifty-two are listed in the *Indiana Journal*, June 3, and in the *Cincinnati Daily Gazette*, June 23, 1837.

[14] George S. Cottman "Early Newspapers of Indiana," in *Indiana Magazine of History*, II (1906), 110.

[15] Hall and Henry Eddy were the publishers. *Illinois Gazette*, May 27, 1820.

[16] The *Star of the West*, started at Edwardsville in 1822 and renamed the *Illinois Republican* in 1823, ceased publication after the election. Edward Coles, in a note penned in the front of the bound volume of the *Illinois Intelligencer*, 1822–25, in the Illinois State Historical Library, listed four papers in Illinois in 1825. He included the *Illinois Republican* but not the *Edwardsville Spectator*; samples of the four were bound in at the end of this volume.

papers in the older settlements in the south as well as by new ones in the northern settlements. The *Sangamo Spectator* had a brief life at Springfield 1827–29; in 1831 Simeon Francis began publication of the *Sangamon* (in 1832 changed to *Sangamo*) *Journal*.[17] The same year John York Sawyer started the *Illinois Advocate* at Edwardsville; the following year it was moved to Vandalia, the state capital. In 1836, after various alterations, the title became *Illinois State Register and People's Advocate*. In 1839 this paper was moved to Springfield where, as the *Illinois State Register*, it could engage in more intimate conflict with the Whig *Sangamo Journal*.[18] Two papers were printed at Alton in the early 1830's (the *Spectator* and the *American*), and the *Observer*, previously published in St. Louis, began to be issued from Alton in 1836. The Jacksonville *Western Observer* dated from 1830,[19] the *Illinois Patriot* from 1831,[20] and the *Illinois State Gazette* from 1834.[21] The *Danville Enquirer* and the *Beardstown Chronicle and Illinois Bounty Land Advertiser* appeared in 1833. The *Illinois Champion and Peoria Herald* was established in 1834, and the Quincy *Illinois Bounty Land Register* in 1835. Meanwhile, Galena, far to the north, had been publishing the *Miner's Journal* since 1826;[22] the *Northwestern Gazette and Galena Advertiser* began in 1834. John Calhoun's *Chicago Democrat*, Chicago's first paper, began in 1833. The *Chicago American*, published by T. O. Davis, put out its first issue in June, 1835. The *Commercial Advertiser* was published by Hooper Warren, 1836–37, then the press was moved to Lowell and used by Benjamin Lundy and Zebina Eastman to print the *Genius of Universal Emancipation*, 1838–39. The *Weekly Tribune*, published at Chicago, 1840–41, expired when it was sold to Elisha Starr who started the *Milwaukee Journal*. Early in 1838–39 the *Alton Telegraph*, in listing the newspapers'

---

[17] This paper, as the *Illinois State Journal*, continues to date.
[18] The *Illinois Republican* published at Springfield, 1835–39, merged with the *Register*. The *Register* continues to date.
[19] Philip D. Jordan, "Portrait of a Pioneer Printer," in *Journal of the Illinois State Historical Society*, XXIII (1930–31), 175–82, gives an interesting sketch of James G. Edwards and the paper which lasted less than two years.
[20] Continued from 1837 to 1844 as *The Illinoisan*.
[21] Stephen A. Douglas solicited subscriptions for this paper when he first came to Illinois. In 1835 it combined with the *News* (1834) under the title of *Illinois State Gazette and Jacksonville News*.
[22] From 1832 to 1836 the title was *The Galenian*; from 1836 to 1838 the *Democrat*.

political line-up, accounted for thirty-six papers in Illinois.[23] At least nineteen papers were started along the line of the Illinois River and the Illinois and Michigan Canal route between 1836 and 1840. Counting campaign sheets, there were about fifty-two Illinois papers in 1840.[24]

Michigan's first newspaper of importance was the *Detroit Gazette* which published its first issue July 25, 1817.[25] Early numbers contained sections in French as well as in English. The paper was not revived after the destruction of its office by fire in 1830. The *Michigan Herald*, "established by the Junto[26] to help them keep their offices and to get others, against the will of the people,"[27] was published from 1825 to 1829. The first paper outside Detroit was the *Michigan Sentinel*, started at Monroe in 1825.[28] The *North-Western Journal* began publication at Detroit in 1829 as an anti-Jackson paper; it changed its name a year later to *Detroit Journal and Michigan Advertiser*. In 1830 the *Detroit Courier*, an anti-Masonic paper, was started but it was absorbed in 1835 by the *Journal*. In 1833 the *Journal* became a semiweekly, then soon a triweekly under the title of *Detroit Journal and Advertiser*; on merging with the *Courier* in 1835 the title became the *Detroit Journal and Courier*. In June, 1836, publisher George L. Whitney and editor Franklin Sawyer, a Harvard graduate, published the first issue of the *Detroit Daily Advertiser*. The *Oakland Chronicle* at Pontiac was also started in 1830. On May 5, 1831, the Detroit *Democratic Free Press and Michigan Intelligencer* issued its first number. In 1835 the *Daily Free Press* began publication. This paper had the first power press used in the West.[29] The *Journal* and the *Free Press* were the leading Whig and Democratic antagonists in Michigan in the 1830's.

Wisconsin's first newspaper, the *Green-Bay Intelligencer*, was

[23] *Alton Telegraph*, February 28, August 1, 1838, June 2, December 21, 1839.

[24] Scott, *Newspapers of Illinois*, lii. Seventeen newspapers were started in 1839, several of them "campaign ephemera." About half of the thirty-odd papers started or revived in 1840 ceased shortly after the election. *Ibid.*, lv.

[25] In 1809 James M. Miller and Father Gabriel Richard had published at least one issue of the *Michigan Essay; or, the Impartial Observer*.

[26] See Chapter XI, 232–33.

[27] *Democratic Free Press and Michigan Intelligencer*, May 5, 1831.

[28] Announcement in *Michigan Herald*, May 17, and advertisement for advertisements in *ibid.*, November 22, 1825.

[29] Tom S. Appelgate (comp.), "A History of the Press of Michigan," in *Michigan Pioneer and Historical Collections*, VI (1883), 65.

started by Albert G. Ellis at Navarino in December, 1833;[30] in 1835 it added *Wisconsin Democrat* to its title. This paper expired the following year and its equipment, in the hands of the Sholes brothers, was used to put out the *Wisconsin Democrat* (1836–40). Though short-lived, the *Intelligencer* is an important historical source for these early years of the region. Byron Kilbourn and his associates founded the *Milwaukee Advertiser* in 1836 to promote the political and business interests of West Milwaukee, and Solomon Juneau set up the *Milwaukee Sentinel* to do the same for the East Side. The two papers took opposite sides on all important issues, including the proper way to spell Milwaukee. The *Belmont Gazette* was published by James Clarke for about six months, 1836–37; when the legislature moved to Burlington, Clarke went along and began the *Wisconsin Territorial Gazette and Burlington Advertiser*. The press of the Belmont paper was removed to Mineral Point where in September, 1837, it was used to print the *Miners' Free Press*, one of the important papers of the territorial period. William S. Hamilton was one of the sponsors of this paper. After his Jacksonville, Illinois, *Western Observer* failed, James G. Edwards moved across the Mississippi to Fort Madison, then in Wisconsin Territory, and in 1836, before the interested eyes of Black Hawk and other natives, ran off the first number of the *Fort Madison Patriot*. It lasted until the division of the Territory in 1838 when Edwards moved to Burlington, Iowa Territory. The *Racine Argus* began publication in 1838 but after a few months Josiah Noonan bought the equipment, took it to Madison, and put out the *Wisconsin Enquirer*, the first paper in the new capital. The *Madison Express* appeared late the following year.

The early papers usually started as single-sheet affairs; the sheet, once folded, gave four pages approximately 14 or 15 by 20 or 22 inches in size, which would accommodate four to six columns of type each. Make-ups varied, but typically the first page carried two or three columns of brief advertisements; the remainder of the page might be filled with laws of Congress or the state legislature, legislative debates, addresses, memorials,

[30] Facsimile of front page of first number in McMurtrie, *Early Printing in Wisconsin*, frontispiece.

a serial installment, articles on agriculture or temperance, Major Jack Downing's correspondence, Indian fights and other exchanges, and material extracted from English or eastern periodicals on events of the Napoleonic wars and South American revolutions. Biblical history and other historical items were always good filler. Now and then was inserted an *"Interesting Occurrence."* Page two (with some papers page three) was the important page. Here could be found one or more columns of editorials followed by from a half to two columns of unheaded paragraphs of comment, signed letters, and news. The remaining two pages were filled with "exchanges" extracted from other papers either with or without credit, poems, advertisements, and miscellany.

Conspicuously absent to the eye of the modern reader were noticeable headlines. Capitals or boldface type but slightly larger than the capitals for the regular body type usually sufficed for the job. In 1814 when news came by way of a letter and word-of-mouth account from the postrider, the *Miami Intelligencer* ran the line "Destruction of Washington" in one-eighth-inch capitals.[31] Rumors of Jackson's victory at New Orleans—"Great News—if true"—rated italic heads about a half inch high in the *Zanesville Express*. Definite news of the peace, however— "Peace Huzza Huzza"—was announced in small boldface italic.[32] This story received about six inches of type as compared to ten times as much space given the state legislative proceedings. As late as 1838 such an important paper as the *Ohio State Journal* was using one-eighth-inch capitals for headlines on its main paragraphs. This practice was not the result of a lack of larger type, for the advertisements were often set in letters one inch or larger in size;[33] it was merely the custom. Perhaps the editors were holding back for possible bigger events.[34] By the late 1830's, however, the inhibitions were breaking down; they were practically thrown overboard in the excitement of the election of 1840. "O K OLD KUYAHOGA," in capitals about

[31] September 12, 1814.
[32] February 2, 23, 1815.
[33] The first page of the *Cincinnati Daily Gazette*, March 3, 1831, was practically a handbill on "Spring goods" set in two-inch block capitals.
[34] Like the later St. Louis editor, who, finding that in his absence a cyclone had been headlined in the largest type, said that his plans were spoiled; he had been saving that type for the Second Coming.

an inch high confronted the eyes of the readers of the *Cleveland Herald and Gazette*;[35] "O K ILLINOIS TO THE RESCUE," was a four-column streamer head of the same size in the *Quincy Whig*; and the editor of the *Sangamo Journal* practically threw the case at his readers when he denied certain charges against Harrison in about thirty different faces and sizes of type.[36]

Though the brevier or minion body type was about the same size as that used by modern papers, in the older papers it gives the appearance of being much smaller. This effect is partly an illusion, the result of the solid, seldom broken and but slightly ventilated columns. But the smaller papers had only enough of this size to set four or five columns of type; many short pieces and parts of the longer ones would be set in type a size or two smaller. Not infrequently the President's message or other long pieces would run two columns in brevier, switch to nonpareil, and finish off in agate or even the microscopic pearl or diamond. Successful printers got rid of their second- or third-hand type which ran to the smaller sizes, and their papers came out in new dress. They sold their old type to someone starting a paper farther west. Many Ohio papers made this transition in the 1820's. Indiana and Illinois followed in the 1830's. It is interesting (but hard on the eyes) to follow the discarded small types across the map and the calendar. Contrasts were striking: while the *Chicago American* in the middle 1830's was putting out a six- or seven-column page in sizeable type, the *Democrat* was still being printed in the smallest type possible to read. Aside from small conventional woodcuts in the paragraph advertisements (stages, steamboats, beaver hats, saddles) the columns were seldom broken. Infrequently a small crude map would be reproduced, or a display advertisement with cuts.[37] Crude woodcut cartoons made their advent in a few papers during the campaign of 1840.

About the time the printer (publisher) got a set of new type,

[35] October 14, 1840.
[36] July 5, 1840.
[37] Maps were sometimes reproduced in negative, that is with black areas and white lines. See, for instance, the 4-by-5-inch map of Texas in *Cincinnati Daily Gazette*, May 13, 1836.
Unusual were advertisements such as the Menagerie or Circus display, two columns wide and half a page deep with cuts and big type, in the *Sangamo Journal*, June 10, 1837.

he aspired to a seven- or eight-column page in the superroyal size (20 by 25 inches or larger), but some even managed a double elephant (27 by 40), or even the imperial (30 by 44) size.[38] When the paper became a semiweekly or triweekly or a daily, it usually reverted to a smaller size, though the weekly issue would likely continue in the larger size. Cincinnati papers reached the semiweekly stage in the early 1820's. The first daily in the Northwest, the *Cincinnati Commercial Register*[39] (December, 1825), proved premature, and soon ceased publication, but in June, 1827, Messrs. Morgan, Lodge, and L'Hommedieu put out 125 copies of the *Daily Cincinnati Gazette*, the first permanent daily in the Northwest. Within ten years Cincinnati had seven daily papers.[40] The *Cleveland Herald* put out a daily in 1832, the *Advertiser* followed in 1836; the *Ohio State Journal* published its daily, the *Columbus Daily Journal*, in 1837. The *Detroit Journal and Advertiser* in 1835–36 issued successively a semiweekly, a triweekly, then the *Detroit Daily Advertiser*; the daily *Detroit Free Press* was begun in 1835. The *Chicago Democrat* and the *American* became dailies in 1839 as did the *Galena Democrat*, but the last did not survive long.[41] The *Indiana Journal* became a semiweekly in 1828, a triweekly in 1838, but Indiana had no daily until the legislative session of 1841.

Papers at the state capitals ordinarily put out semiweekly or triweekly issues during legislative sessions some years before such issues became regular. Most papers continued the weekly editions, and sometimes the others as well, after they became dailies.[42] With the different issues printed on different sizes, as

[38] The large-sheet fashion came into use in the East in the 1830's following the English practice started when papers were taxed by the page. The *New York Mirror*, May 23, 1835, spoke of plans of one of the papers to enlarge "so that it will require two boys, at least, to hold it for perusal." The *Journal of Commerce* in the 1850's reached a size approximately 3 by 5 feet. Frank L. Mott, *American Journalism* . . . (New York, 1941), 295. These blanket sizes did not reach the western papers until the cylinder presses came, usually in the middle 1840's or later.
[39] Published by S. S. Brooks, edited by Morgan Neville, and printed on a half-sheet royal.
[40] Listed in *Ohio State Journal*, November 7, 1837. Dawson's *Advertiser* and Benham's *Cincinnati Morning Journal* were the latest additions. In 1841 Charles Cist listed seven dailies, the *Advertiser and Journal* being one. *Cincinnati in 1841: Its Early Annals and Future Prospects* (Cincinnati, 1841), 93.
[41] *Quincy Whig*, October 12, 1839. The census of 1840 reported Ohio as having nine dailies, Michigan six, and Illinois three.
[42] It is this fact, among others, which makes it necessary to use the whole title carried by the paper in citations to newspapers; the weekly, semiweekly or triweekly and daily of the same paper often carried slightly different titles.

well as the same issue reverting to smaller size when paper shortages presented, these papers gave future binders and librarians something of a problem.

During election years, particularly 1836 and 1840, special campaign sheets were issued by many papers. These might take the form of a special three- or six-month subscription to the regular paper which, for the period, might become a semiweekly, or more likely be issued under a separate title such as *Old Hickory, The Log Cabin*, etc.[43] Aspiring editors and politicians took advantage of the stimulated news interest to start new papers; if they succeeded, if their party won, the paper survived. Most of the new ones, however, proved ephemeral.

Politics, laws and legislative debates and reports occupied relatively more space in the leading party organs, especially those published at the state capitals, though these subjects constituted an important part of the contents of all. But scissors and exchanges furnished in addition as great a variety of stuff—excepting only pictures and sports—as is offered by twentieth-century papers of similar size. In fact many of them had more solid material, not counting "personals," than most county-seat papers carry today. Contents can only be sketched in broad outline.

In foreign news, after Bonaparte was off the scene, South America and Greece were favored, then the French trouble and Texas, but at any time "Late and Interesting from Africa" might slip in. In 1825 the papers had in the visit of General Lafayette a windfall as fortuitous and fortunate newswise as the later visits of Kossuth and Jenny Lind. Indian wars, Santa Fé, the western fur trade, roads, canals, railroads, agriculture, money, prices, travel and description, accidents, crimes, and the like were always "Highly Important and Interesting News."

Feature articles abounded. A random selection of a handful of papers of the period will yield such items as "True Charity," "The Inebriate," "On the Shortness of Human Life," "The Widow and Her Infidel Son" (heart-rending), "Woman," "Storm at Sea," "Courtship," "Human Grandeur," "The Destiny of the American Republic," "The Seducer" (truly heart-rending), "A Tale of Honor," "To Parents," "The Sagacity of a Dog," "Perpetual Motion," "Mother at Home," "Education," "Buried

[43] See Chapter XI, 236, note 276.

Alive," and scores of others. Clichés relieved the printer of think-ing up heads: "Highly Important," "Startling Intelligence," "Dis-tressing Narrative," "Singular Adventure," "Melancholy Event," "Atrocious Outrage," "Horrid Murder," "Horrible Atrocity," "New York Erect" (voted the right way), were pat labels. Throughout this deluge of typographical outrages wound the inevitable and ubiquitous sea serpent, often carrying its own affidavits, battling with whales, sinking ships, sometimes getting killed, though ball and shot glanced from its form as from a rock, but ever returning to wend its immortal way.[44] Perhaps it was not mere chance that sometimes placed temperance articles in the wake of the serpent.

When the sea serpent hibernated and politics were dull, there always remained "The Female Heart" which, like a garden,

when well cultivated, presents, a continued succession of fruits and flowers to regale the soul, and delight the eye, but when neglected, producing a crop of the most noxious weeds, large and flourishing, because their growth is in proportion to the warmth and richness of the soil from which they spring. Then let this ground be faithfully cultivated—let the mind of the young and lovely female be stored with useful knowledge, and the influence of women, though undiminished in power, will be like the diamond of the desert, sparkling and pure, whether surrounded by the sands of desolation, forgotten and unknown, or pouring its refreshing streams through every avenue of the social and moral habit.[45]

Long letters on divers subjects also made good filler; signers ran from "Homer" to "Cornplanter." Politics or potatoes, it made no difference. Typical of the light approach was the serious appeal for the organization of an "Anti-Potato Eating Society." If one fed not the lion meat, he became gentle and playful; why did the Irish always fight?—they ate potatoes. The French

[44] There was even a sea serpent junior. "A young sea Serpent believed to be the progeny of the great Sea Serpent, has been killed on the sea shore of Gloucester. He is about three-and-a-half feet in length, and in the largest part perhaps three inches in circumference; and has thirty-two distinct hunches on his back." *Ohio Federalist* in the Hamilton (Ohio) *Philanthropist*, October 31, 1817.
One of the best of all was the great inland sea serpent, descended from the mammoth, which was propagated by the artist George Winter with the connivance of John B. Dillon of the *Logansport Telegraph* in 1838. The authors used both their poetic and editorial licenses on this one, which was discussed throughout the country. For the pertinent documents see Donald Smalley, "The *Logansport Telegraph* and the Monster of the Indiana Lakes," in *Indiana Magazine of History*, XLII (1946), 249–67, and *The Journals and Indian Paintings of George Winter* (Indiana Historical Society, 1948), 49–51.
[45] *Ohio State Journal*, April 3, 1828.

Revolution was started by the *Rooks* which, having eaten all above ground, ate potatoes. "In my opinion there is more to be dreaded from the effects of eating that vice-engendering root, than from all other causes of moral, and physical evil put together."[46] That the long Fourth of July orations were read with interest is indicated by follow-up comments. Also the "communications"; editors hesitated to cut and summarize; they reproduced in full.

Then there was the poetry, for which some editors had a weakness. Quite a list of papers could be compiled which carried, on the average, two columns of poetry; the output varied from possible verse to the nth degree of nonsense.

The newspaper advertisements presented a verbal and pictorial view of the social and economic life of the day. Early issues of the country press indicated clearly the simplicity and sparseness of commerce and business in the small towns.[47] Besides a few notices of "estrays taken up," studs at stand, nonresident tax sales, bank notes acceptable, "new goods" (dry and hard), "wool carding done," and "patent" medicine blurbs, there was little to sustain the news. As community and paper developed, the list lengthened: legal and land-office notices; stagecoach and steamboat advertisements; drugs; hat factories; brick presses; property and sheriff's sales; general merchandise; detailed listings of dry goods, ribbons, and trimmings; tailor shops; stoves; pumps; spelling books; umbrellas; musical instruments; taverns; saddles; schools; books; boats; trusses; vehicles; and pianos were added items. A representative weekly paper would thus fill five of its twenty columns. By the middle 1830's display advertisements were no longer confined largely to Cincinnati, Cleveland, and Detroit papers, nor to lotteries and "patent" medicines. Cuts were no longer limited to a few standardized coaches, boats, boots, and hats, but ranged from drums, pianofortes, furniture, and gigs, to teeth, stockings, clocks, silverware, vests, and lions. Subscrip-

---

[46] Ravenna (Ohio) *Western Courier*, July 17, 1829.

[47] "Look Here!" said Peter Kimmel, of Kaskaskia, in 1814, "The subscriber wishes to purchase a quantity of BEEF HIDES, AND PORK. ALSO ALL KINDS OF FURS." *Illinois Herald*, December 13, 1814. "Hoosiers and Wolverines, Behold Suckers!!!!!!," advertised the proprietor of the Man Trap in Chicago in 1833, when he announced a constant supply of bread, cakes, pastry, and liquors. He thanked the above-mentioned friends as well as his liberal patrons, the Potawatomi. *Chicago Democrat*, December 10, 1833.

tion notices for libraries, museums, and lecture courses increased; also advertisements for books, balloon ascensions, schools, and amusements.

Advertising grew even during the depression of the late 1830's. The mammoth-size seven-columns-to-a-page *Sangamo Journal*, for instance, usually covered all of page one, half of page three, and all of page four with advertisements; these included advertisements from Beardstown, Alton, St. Louis, and other towns. Notices such as the following were not infrequent: "We have no space for many articles of news—the great influx of advertising . . . prevents the insertion of many articles already in type."[48] The dailies had far less news per issue than the weekly issue of the same paper; they were three-fourths advertisements.

Getting the news in a period of uncertain roads and mails was a problem. Lack of news as well as lack of paper could result in delayed or missed publication. Failure of the mails to bring the exchanges was an accepted excuse for a half-sheet issue.[49] In addition to the general uncertainty and slowness of the mails, newspapers had two other hazards: the practice of carrying papers "outside the mails,"[50] and the "dirty work" done by postmasters and carriers of the opposite party who saw that their own editors got the scoops.[51] Papers could count on free exchanges with other papers of their region, but not always with the eastern papers—excepting of course the organs of their party at Washington from which they copied so much of the national political news. *Niles' Weekly Register* was an almost indispensa-

[48] Piqua *Courier and Enquirer*, November 2, 1839.

[49] Some early papers were started ahead of the mails. The *Indianapolis Gazette*, for instance, in its early months, made contact with the mails at Connersville, some sixty miles away.

[50] On slowness of the mails see Chapter VII. Carrying papers "outside the mails" meant paying the carrier a small fee on the side for carrying papers; when hard going was met he could dump the papers without very much risk of jeopardizing his mail contract. Even as mail, papers, being bulky, were the first articles to be laid aside. Subscribers usually paid postage on papers quarterly at their own office. Rates are illustrated by the charges at the Jacksonville, Illinois, office, 1831–32: Illinois weeklies, thirteen cents the quarter; *Niles' Weekly Register, National Intelligencer, New York Observer*, etc., 19½ cents; dailies such as *The New York Post, New York Journal of Commerce, United States Gazette*, etc., 39 cents; eastern monthlies such as *Godey's Lady's Book*, 31½ cents; *Illinois Monthly Magazine*, 15 cents, etc. Frank J. Heinl, "Newspapers and Periodicals in the Lincoln-Douglas Country 1831–1832," in *Journal of the Illinois State Historical Society*, XXIII (1930–31), 391–92.

[51] The *Indiana Journal*, December 19, 1837, accused the postmaster of holding out on the President's message, always an important piece of news, until after Terre Haute and St. Louis papers had received it. Such notices were common.

ble compendium of affairs, in itself a sort of national clipping service. In view of their dependence upon exchanges it is hard to understand why the papers in general printed so little local news; aware as many of them were of the importance of the newspaper for historical reference, at the same time they valued news in inverse ratio to the distance from which it came. Now and then a gossipy editor proved an exception and mixed in short paragraphs on local weather, crops, town affairs, and people.

Speed and quantity of news increased rapidly by the middle 1830's. The *Cleveland Herald* of December 23, 1837, contained Washington news under date of December 15; the *Sangamo Journal* had this issue of the *Herald* by January 6. Some papers, the *Herald* for instance, anticipated the mail by getting eastern papers from travelers. The editor of the Ravenna *Western Courier* said that, what with the Seminole War, Congress, Europe, Texas, the French trouble, abolition petitions, and legislative affairs, there was so much news he could not use it all.[52] A few papers, especially those published at the state capital or leading city, added a column or less of state news: marriages, deaths, and commercial items.

Few newspapers were founded as purely business enterprises. Although they might announce their nonpartisanship, they could not maintain it; the political stake and the desires of the readers were against it. Consequently, what had been merely a column of news items and "milk-and-cider" observations developed into the heart of the paper, the editorial column. The Midwesterner of a century ago liked his sermons and editorials full of fire.[53] Editors strove to please. Some were formally educated men, others had no schooling beyond the print shop or "poor man's college"; some were respected for their scholarship and ability,

[52] January 28, 1836. This paper had been filled with canal matters for several years.

[53] ". . . out of our twelve millions we may possibly have fifty thousand who care about some other reading, than the coarsest and grossest slang of politics. Strong palpable high seasoned political abuse, as warm as it can be swallowed, is all that is required for the rest." "Smelfungus," on "The Miseries of Authorship," in *Western Monthly Review,* I (1827–28), 525.

That subscribers took the papers largely for their political views, however, would be hard to prove. A check on the Jacksonville, Illinois, post office credit postage list of 1831–32 shows Illinois and Missouri papers being frequently subscribed to by men of the opposing political faith. Heinl, "Newspapers and Periodicals in the Lincoln-Douglas Country, 1831–1832," in *Journal of the Illinois State Historical Society,* XXIII, 413.

others were feared for their reckless and trenchant pens; some discussed measures, others attacked men; some used needles, others cleavers. But nearly all wrote vigorous and understandable English. Since the main purpose of the paper was to influence votes, the warfare among the editors knew few truces. In the very short intervals between political bouts editors continued the fighting on local and personal issues. At times the editorial warfare was merely tilting with windmills—slanging,[54] blackguarding horseplay for the practice, or for the edification of the readers—but often it was serious epistolic gouging, a smelly logomachy waged with malice and intent. Editorials ran the range from mere written stump speeches which depended upon their blatancy and emotional appeal for effect, to long, closely written, didactic, expository, logical essays from which it was possible to learn all the essentials of government and economics. In the hands of top-notch writers, contributions of the latter type compare favorably with either the state papers of high officials or the general literature of the day.

Samples of the former type are mildly stimulating; it was a weak half column which could not assemble a dozen pet names for the enemy such as "detestable caitiff," "notorious scoundrel," "craven wretch spotted with vices," "hireling slave," "felonious renegade," "spotted traitor," "craven braggart," "convicted felon," and "Judas Iscariot." When the *Illinois Advocate* and the *Alton Spectator* were engaged in a tiff over a local political affair, the former spoke of the editor of the latter as a "Blue Bellied" correspondent and asked "the little man in diapers" how many provisions his papa had sold to the enemy during the late war with Great Britain.[55] The same editor, perhaps jealous of the competition, wrote: "Some poor devil's gall bladder having burst, the youthful editor of the *Shawneetown Journal*, has suffered its contents to be put in that paper, and served for its subscribers. Alas for Shawnee!"[56] Delicate yet effective was the repartee between two Cleveland editors. Said the editor of the *Advertiser*: "For a booby will talk of what RUNS in his head."

[54] Commonly used as a verb—to abuse, insult, spread canards about. See for instance *Illinois State Register and Peoples' Advocate*, 1836–37, particularly December 1, 1837.

[55] *Illinois Advocate and State Register*, June 14, 1834.

[56] *Ibid.*, June 3, 1835.

Replied the editor of the *Herald*: "The application of a fine tooth comb, may present some of his most *sprightly* and *native* ideas in a *form* not to be mistaken."[57] More artistic in the way of name calling was the following: "The gentleman . . . is a raw, green ignorant, impudent, ill bred fellow . . . a false malicious slanderer; a scoundrel and puppy."[58] Despite the apparent anticlimax one has the feeling that the party of the first part finally got the party of the second part called.

Rarely did times become as dull as the editor of the *Quincy Whig* complained of, when he said there was little afloat out of which to manufacture an editorial: "Even the *Argus* was so stupid last week, as to be unworthy of a remark."[59] Nor seldom was it necessary to protest the light passes made between rival editors as the *Illinois State Register* did in April, 1840, when the *Chicago American* (Whig) and the new *Chicago Weekly Tribune* (Democrat) gently slapped each other: "They ought to take the gloves off, and not be afraid of hurting each other."

One would surmise that when bloodthirsty editors met, ears would fly, Adam's apples pop out; and sometimes efforts to these ends were made. Assaults, even challenges to duels, occurred now and then, but between temper outbursts editors often fraternized, sometimes arm in arm. When an old enemy whose strength and weakness had been tested departed from the scene, there was a sense of loss, even of regret. Parting shots were not always as bitter as that sent by the editors of the *Illinois State Register* after the editor of the Vandalia *Free Press and Illinois Whig*, when the latter suspended: "Good bye friend Hodge! We wish you better luck in some employment more suitable to your temper and abilities."[60]

Though some editors came into newspaper work from the outside, most of them came up from the printing shop.[61] Just as it was the destiny of the "devil" to become an editor, so the editor

---

[57] *Cleaveland Herald*, February 16, 1832.

[58] *Edwardsville Spectator*, August 8, 1820. This was almost as dirty a dig as a later editor took at his rival, against whom a bastardy suit had been brought: "He now writes Democratic editorials inside the county jail."

[59] April 6, 1839.

[60] November 30, 1839.

[61] For instance, thirteen of the proprietors of the *Cincinnati Gazette* up to 1839 had served as printers. In turn printers from the *Gazette* became publishers of the *Ohio State Journal*, the *Dayton Journal*, and the *Hamilton Intelligencer*. Hooper, *Ohio Journalism*, 83–84.

"was the embodiment of every requirement from the editor down and the devil up. He was typesetter, job printer, foreman, business manager and pressman, as well as editor, and did not shrink from the duties of roller boy upon occasion." As apprentice or "devil" he had done chores, carried papers, undergone discipline, and learned the trade. As printer he had set type, run the press, and shown an inclination to be a rolling stone. Printers were reputed to be heavy drinkers—whether more so than lawyers, keelboatmen, or canal workers would be hard to prove. One fact is striking, however; drunk or sober the printer-editor generally learned, somehow, not only to be a good compositor, but a grammarian and a writer of readable and forceful English. Though the style of the time called for long, even mellifluous sentences (with a comma every three words whether needed or not), as noticeable as a volcano in a prairie were slips such as the following which got by editors Noonan and Sholes of the *Wisconsin Enquirer*: "We are free to say, that we done what little we could. . . ."[62] Some editors stood out in contrast by reason of their short-sentence, direct-approach styles; while some were notorious sticklers, veritable martinets, regarding rules of composition, capitalization and grammar, others emphasized the use of judgment.[63]

That the press fared best in the hands of printers was a belief of editors who had long had the smell of printers' ink in their nostrils. Wrote Charles Hammond on the invasion of journalism by outsiders:

It is not the printers, but the half-starved adventurers and the avaricious capitalists, who have degraded the profession and injured the business by their ignorance and incompetency. . . . If a lawyer owns a printing office he can easily sell it and resume his own trade. If he cannot live at that, he is not fit to be an editor. Let the merchant go back to tape-selling; let the physician go back to making pills; let the shoemaker stick to his last—and then will the printers, having a clear field, exalt the character of their profession, and show themselves, as they generally are, worthy

[62] November 23, 1839.

[63] Stories such as told regarding Wilbur F. Storey, of the *Detroit Free Press* and later famous as the editor of the notorious *Chicago Times,* were told and retold around newspaper offices. When a young printer ran into trouble regarding capitalization, Storey is supposed to have yelled somewhat as follows: "Haven't I told you that there are only two words in the English language that *have* to be capitalized—Jesus Christ, and Wilbur F. Storey—and if you are short of capitals be sure to capitalize Wilbur F. Storey."

followers of such men as Franklin, and Niles, and Buckingham, and Gales, and the Bradfords.[64]

The editor's job was not an easy one; there were problems both material and otherwise which made it a hazardous occupation. As described by one of them:

The path of an editor is not over thickly planted with roses. In the silence of the night, when men forget that they live, or bathe their spirits in rosy dreams of bliss—when sorrow has forgotten to tug at the heart and ambition to fire the brain—he sleeps not. By the dim lamp he wanders through the fields of thought, or by the shore of the sea of knowledge, gathering pebbles wherewith to build his feeble fabric. Often he is misunderstood—taunted—mocked—disappointed. Often does icy neglect freeze his glowing thoughts and nip his young hopes.—The careless sneer—the crushing insinuation—the covert slander—the open denunciation—all wait to feast upon him.[65]

"The first problem of the printer was to get paper, the second to get news, the third to get paid."[66] Next to trouble with the mails, previously discussed, the most common difficulty was getting paper. Given a sufficient quantity of good rags, some water, fuel, and experience, papermaking is not a complicated process. Pennsylvania had led in papermaking in colonial times; later artisans from Bucks, Chester, Delaware, and Montgomery counties came west. In 1791 the Reverend Elijah Craig, Baptist minister of Georgetown, Kentucky, added to his industries—a fulling mill, tavern, general store, and distillery—a papermaking mill. This mill, Craig, Parkers, and Company at Royal Spring, was for several years the only one west of the mountains from which newsprint was obtainable.[67] Jackson and Sharpless in 1796 added to the supply when they opened their mill on Redstone Creek, near Brownsville, western Pennsylvania. A mill was opened by Coulter, Bowman, and Bever near the mouth of Little Beaver Creek, just across the line in Ohio, in 1807.[68] The prod-

[64] *Cincinnati Daily Gazette,* August 16, 1839.
[65] Quoted in *Logansport Canal Telegraph,* November 5, 1836.
[66] Mary Alden Walker, *The Beginnings of Printing in the State of Indiana* . . . (Crawfordsville, 1934), 15.
[67] This mill, forty by sixty feet, had a stone basement and was two and a half stories high. It burned in 1837. There is a tradition to the effect that Elihu Stout and George E. Smoot, of the Vincennes *Western Sun,* brought paper from this mill on horseback, on which they printed the 1807 revision of the Indiana territorial laws known as the John Rice Jones Code.
[68] Zadok Cramer, *Navigator* (Pittsburgh, 1808); John W. Browne (pub.), *Browne's Cincinnati Almanac* . . . (1810).

uct, a pure linen and cotton rag paper, bore the watermark C. B. & B. with a spread eagle sitting atop of OHIO.[69]

In 1810–11 Christian Waldschmidt, from Germany by way of Pennsylvania, set up a mill on the Little Miami; paper from this mill, which continued until 1850, was used by the Cincinnati *Western Spy* in January, 1811.[70] An advertisement for rags by R. and A. Pitcher, of Lancaster, Ohio, had appeared in the Chillicothe *Supporter* on March 24, 1810, but evidence of paper production is lacking. H. and I. Ingham, from Pennsylvania, leased a gristmill on Kinnikinnick Creek in Ross County in 1812, and for several years manufactured high-quality paper; the manufacture was continued by D. Crouse, builder and leaser of the mill after 1819. The Inghams later (1831) set up their "Machine Paper Mill," also in Ross County.[71] A mill had operated at Steubenville, probably prior to 1815; in that year a steam paper mill was erected. Other Ohio mills followed. In 1826 Isaac Mooney, who had worked in the mills on the Little Miami, erected a two-vat mill on Big Creek, about twelve miles north of Madison, Indiana. By 1840 three Indiana mills were listed.

Though these early western mills helped, the bulk of the newsprint came from Philadelphia by way of Cincinnati jobbers. In November, 1802, the *Scioto Gazette* apologized for issuing only a half sheet; the Monongahela had not been navigable.[72] The *Cleaveland Register*, out of paper for six weeks, published for three weeks in 1818 on a 10-by-16-inch sheet; then the editor himself had to go to the Ohio River for paper and no issues could be expected until he returned.[73] The *Indianapolis Gazette* in December, 1826, appeared with an 8-by-10-inch page, on paper borrowed from local merchants. And the legislature was in session! The *Illinois Gazette* in February, 1822, found boatmen and water unreliable and put out a half sheet.[74] The *Chicago Democrat* had paper trouble in 1834–35, put out some numbers on a 9-by-13-inch page, then skipped several weeks. Having failed to

---

[69] Facsimiles of watermarks of the early papers are reproduced in Dard Hunter, "Ohio's Pioneer Paper Mills," in *Antiques*, XLIX (1946), 36–39.

[70] *Western Spy*, January 26, 1811.

[71] Advertised in *Chillicothe Advertiser*, December 11, 1831. The first paper machine in America was set up by Thomas Gilpin on the Brandywine, near Wilmington, Delaware, in 1817.

[72] November 13, 1802.

[73] December 8, 1818.

[74] February 16, 1822.

get paper from Detroit, the editor purchased paper in St. Louis but it did not get through because of the roads.[75] Hundreds of such failures and explanations could be cited. Transportation—or lack of credit for building up a reserve of paper—was the chief difficulty, but not the only one.

The *Edwardsville Spectator* missed the issue of January 30, 1821, because it had lent ink to two neighbors who were slow in repayment. The editors of the *Illinois Intelligencer* in 1826 and of the *Illinois Patriot* in 1833 apologized for misses as a result of indispositions of families and staffs.[76] The *Illinois Advocate* missed two issues because its office was open and the weather cold.[77] Editor Sawyer of the *Western Ploughboy* explained that one of his journeymen, "member of the Temperance Society, has been so unwell as to be under the necessity of taking a certain kind of *medicine,* which has completely disqualified him from the duties of the office."[78] Another editor lost his journeyman because the latter got tired of setting up too many temperance articles. The editor of the Xenia *Ohio Gazette* on return from a two-day honeymoon found his shop closed and attached by holders of a mortgage not due for months. The Jackson wags had rumored that the "Clay printer had jumped town."[79] Then there was the Illinois editor who could not get out his paper because he had the shakes so bad that he had to use both hands to hold his breeches on.[80]

And the simple hand-powered equipment required both hands and legs. Early presses of the Franklin, Washington, and "Ramage" patterns had frames and platens of wood, bed pieces of marble. The hand-set type was inked with a ball of buckskin filled with wool, a sheet of paper laid on, the type bed cranked up under the platen, and the impression made with the pull of a lever. Since on the Ramage press the platen was but half the size of the bed, two pulls were necessary to print one side of a sheet. Some outfits were pretty crude. The publisher of the Rushville, Indiana, *Dog-Fennel Gazette* is said to have used a long pole

[75] March 4, 1834, January 21, March 25, etc., 1835.
[76] March 16, 1826; November 2, 1833.
[77] February 23, 1831.
[78] Quoted in *Illinois Advocate,* November 18, 1831.
[79] Ravenna *Western Courier,* December 11, 1829.
[80] *United States Gazette,* cited in *Logansport Canal Telegraph,* June 25, 1836.

attached to a tree for leverage; having printed one side he rested until the readers caught up with him, then printed the other side. Specimens of print from the more primitive presses have the appearance of having been "worked with swamp mud on a cider press." In 1830, the *Hamilton Intelligencer* paid $250 to the Cincinnati Type Foundry for an "Imperial Smith Press." The *Cincinnati Gazette* in 1836 installed an imperial press designed by Isaac Adams, of New York; it automatically inked the type, placed the sheet, removed and piled it, and could print 750 copies per hour. Josiah Warren, Cincinnati manufacturer who later became more famous for his social theories, invented and built a press which would print from a continuous roll of paper. He installed it in the office of the Evansville (Ind.) *Southwestern Sentinel,* February, 1840, but the printers sabotaged it and Warren removed and destroyed it.

Whether printed on the crudest or most improved presses of the day, the papers possessed the distinctive features of hand-set type; with good type and a firm impression on moistened rag paper the best of them are excellent samples of the printer's art —clear, clean, and free of "ETAOIN SHRDLU'S"—even after reposing for more than a century in the dust of archives.

The few papers which were lucky enough to contract for the printing of national and state laws had a financial prop to lean upon.[81] But before the editor or publisher could expect to get remunerative political preferment, he had to make his paper influential; to do that, he had to keep it going. Outside Cincinnati, Columbus, Cleveland, Detroit, Indianapolis, Springfield, and other important towns, advertising (except for patent medicines) was scarce and rates low; the amount of commercial printing was small.[82] Consequently, willy-nilly papers had to depend largely upon their subscribers, a rather uncertain source of income.

Subscription rates were not low—$2.50 to $4.00 per year with a discount for cash or advance payment. But most papers were

[81] A law of 1814 authorized the publication of United States laws in two papers in each territory; in 1818 the number was increased to three. Compensation was $1.00 for each pamphlet page.

[82] In the 1830's the *Cincinnati Gazette* charged about 75 cents for single insertions of one square (12 lines), $5.00 for a month, $15 for six months, $20 for a year without change. Its circulation at the time was probably the largest in the region.

willing to accept produce; grain, pork, flour, rags, wood, flax, wool, skins, salt, tallow, potatoes, and many other articles were regularly advertised for. The defunct *Miami Intelligencer* ran a request for "quoin" from its delinquent subscribers but stated it would accept produce; in its endeavors to liquidate its debts a little good whiskey would be acceptable.[83] The editor of the *Illinois Advocate* informed his subscribers that he belonged to "the eating class of politicians, and that bacon, hams, butter, eggs, flour, etc., etc., will, at any time, be gladly received" in payment for papers or job work.[84]

Editors regularly pleaded, begged, cajoled, threatened, and otherwise tried to get subscribers to pay. The *Hamilton Advertiser* under the head "Most Interesting" copied a solid square of type which, read vertically, horizontally, or diagonally, forwards, or backwards, still read, "Pay the Printer."[85] The proprietors of the *Detroit Courier, Democratic Free Press,* and *Detroit Journal* in 1833 published a joint notice to the effect that they were putting their delinquent accounts in the hands of a collector; subsequent subscriptions were to be on a cash basis.[86] The *Rising Sun* (Ind.) *Times* complained of people subscribing to foreign (eastern) papers to the neglect of their own.[87] When the *Edwardsville Spectator* passed out as a result of lack of "precious metals," the editor of the *Illinois Intelligencer* wrote: "We regret to say, . . . that there is a reprehensible negligence in our community to extend its fostering care and protection to public prints in general."[88] When the last issue of the *Kaskaskia Democrat*[89] came out endorsed *"sic transit gloria mundi,"* the *Illinois Advocate* explained that this was *rale Turk* and meant "gone to the Devil at last."[90] The editor of the Xenia *Ohio Free*

[83] On December 14, 1833, the Lawrenceburg *Indiana Palladium* ran the following: "*Cold Comfort*—A western editor complains that he has no wood,—that his chips are all gone—and that he has now to *warm* himself by a *cold* stove. The Baltimore visitor pities his disconsolate situation, and recommends that he do, as many worthies [have] done before him—cram the stove full of exchange papers, put a light to them—sit cross-legged upon the imposing stone, and meditate upon the mutability of human affairs."
[84] March 23, 1833.
[85] July 6, 1826.
[86] Ravenna *Western Courier,* January 2, 1834.
[87] Copied in *Indiana Journal,* October 17, 1834.
[88] October 28, 1826.
[89] January 7, 1832.
[90] January 27, 1832.

Press in the autumn of 1837 furnished his readers with a phren-
ological chart: "Think of it, some 500 subscribers fingering their
skulls to find the bump of *payativeness*."

Newspapers changed hands often; casualties were numerous.
Between 1820 and 1840 prices of goods, wages, and paper had
about doubled; newspapers had doubled in size yet their prices
were about the same.[91] County newspapers aspired to a subscription list of 350 to 400 but did not always make it. The *Detroit
Gazette,* after three years, had 118 subscribers; it had received
payment for only 96 since establishment. Advertisements were
adequate, but only half paid.[92] The *Cincinnati Gazette,* the leading paper in the region, by the late 1830's had a circulation of
about 1,000 for the daily, 400 for the semiweekly, and 2,800 for
the weekly edition.[93] In 1841 the circulation of the seven Cincinnati dailies was estimated at 5,612, or an average of 800; four
triweeklies were listed at 1,100 total, and the six weekly editions
at 8,050.[94]

Some of the editors of these western papers suffer in no wise
in comparison either with their contemporaries in the East or
with the editors of a later period. They were the journalistic
predecessors of the Murat Halsteads, the Joseph Medills, and
the Whitelaw Reids, of the Wilbur F. Storeys and the Edward
W. Scrippses.

There was James Wilson, from Londonderry, Ireland, by way
of the Philadelphia *Aurora* to the editorship of the *Western
Herald and Steubenville Gazette,* 1815–38.[95] Carrying at the
masthead of his paper the motto, "Principles, Not Men," this
staunch Jeffersonian Republican hewed to the line regardless of
the behavior of the chips. He upheld Ohio in its war against the
second Bank of the United States, favored a tariff, refused advertisements for runaway slaves, denounced the Anti-Masonic
movement, and almost alone, when Ohio got illusions of canal
grandeur, questioned the financial soundness of the schemes.[96]

---

[91] *Daily Chicago Democrat,* June 10, 1839.
[92] *Detroit Gazette,* July 14, 1820.
[93] Hooper, *Ohio Journalism,* 74.
[94] Cist, *Cincinnati in 1841,* 93–94.
[95] For brief sketch see Weisenburger, "The Middle Western Antecedents of
Woodrow Wilson," in *Mississippi Valley Historical Review,* XXIII, 375–90.
[96] See Chapter VIII, 592, 604–5.

Although he held firm in his belief in the right of instruction to representatives,[97] he reserved the right to instruct the instructors —so vigorously in the opposition to Benjamin Tappan's appointment to a Federal judgeship that Tappan sued him for $8,000. " 'Hear both sides' is a maxim which every honest man will bear us out in. Our own opinions we have never feared to express, but we hope we shall never fail to have due respect for the opinions of others."

Wilson did not approve of the confusion which he saw in the Jackson camp and made what to a number of Jeffersonians was the logical transition into the ranks of the Whigs. "Hold up your heads like corn—don't hang them down like taters."[98] After suffering seven years of Jackson he wrote to a friend: "The Goths & Vandals, now seated in high places, must be pulled down, and when down *kept down*."[99] When Harrison was elected, Wilson, after "laboring in a minority for 12 long years," acted on the assumption that "when a man has friends he ought to use them," and asked for jobs for two of his six sons of voting age.[100] Wilson served in the Ohio legislature, as examiner of land offices under Monroe and Adams, as director of the Farmers' and Mechanics' Bank, as associate justice on the Jefferson County Court, and as president of the Steubenville, Cadiz, and Cambridge Turnpike Company. In 1832 he established the Pittsburgh *Pennsylvania Advocate,* but retained editorship of the *Herald* until 1838 when he turned it over to his son Robert C. Wilson. He rejoined his son in 1840, however, long enough to put out *The Log Cabin,* a Harrison campaign paper. Wilson then re-

[97] He heartily approved of a fellow editor's words: "The fraudulent pretense that the . . . representative may . . . disobey the injunctions of his immediate constituents . . . is absurd and anti-republican, and politically blasphemous."

[98] Wilson to Elisha Whittlesey, October 10, 1828, October 19, 1829. Whittlesey MSS., cited in Weisenburger, "The Middle Western Antecedents of Woodrow Wilson," 380.

[99] Wilson to Whittlesey, March 26, 1836, December 15, 1838, cited in *ibid.,* 382.

[100] Wilson had ten children (one set of triplets), seven of them boys. "I have so many boys I do not know what to do with them. I cannot afford to set them up in any business and my friends must take care of them." Wilson to Whittlesey, January 23, March 30, 1841, cited in *ibid.* One son, named after Henry Clay, became a clerk under Whittlesey and auditor in the Treasury under Harrison, and another, William Duane, a clerk under Thomas Ewing, secretary of the treasury. The latter was later, 1852–53, an owner and editor of the *Chicago Tribune.* Henry Clay Wilson married a daughter of Samuel Medary, his father's bitter journalistic adversary; another son committed equal heresy by becoming a Methodist minister.

tired from business with enough property for a respectable living; he died of the cholera in 1852.[101]

Opposing Wilson in the early days but generally on the same side politically after 1828, was Charles Hammond, probably the best-known editor in the Northwest prior to 1840. Born in Baltimore, a student of law in Virginia, Hammond was admitted to the bar at Marietta in 1801. He wrote a defense of Arthur St. Clair, governor of the Northwest Territory in 1802, for the *Scioto Gazette,* and became publisher of the St. Clairsville *Ohio Federalist* in 1813. As a member of the legislature he led the fight against the Bank, as a result of which he became widely known. Some of his articles on constitutional subjects were published in the *National Intelligencer.* In 1822 he began the practice of law in Cincinnati but journalism was in his bones; in 1825 he became editor of the *Liberty Hall and Cincinnati Gazette.* Hammond's austere moral principles stood somewhat in contrast to some of his verbal viciousness. He opposed young ladies drinking toasts at a Fourth of July celebration, even among friends, and refused to believe that ladies of Cincinnati attended the races. "What is the position of ladies on a race course but objects of gloating lust for the host of loafer sensualists who there congregate?" He called John Bailhache, in 1814 editor of the Chillicothe *Fredonian,* a "vagrant foreigner" and his paper an "unprincipled vehicle of slander." Later the two became political friends. When accused of spreading a story of calumny against Jackson's mother, he denied it as an infamous canard. On the other hand he spared no feelings in 1828 in discussing the General's own marital affairs.[102] He denied being a political *friend* to any Jacksonian but admitted personal friendship.

Hammond opposed Birney's *Philanthropist*[103] and its methods but at the same time opposed those who threatened violence to them. "We are opposed to abolitionism and anti-slavery efforts. But we are not afraid to hear the advocates of these measures

---

[101] Charles Hammond wrote of Wilson and John Saxton, editor of the Canton *Ohio Repository,* 1815–71, as samples of successful editors. "If, of the many who have toiled as printers and spent their strength as editors, few have reaped any harvest better than poverty and discredit, here are examples to prove that a plain printer in a proper place can work out for himself a pecuniary independence, without any sacrifice of independent principles." Quoted in Hooper, *Ohio Journalism,* 45.

[102] When he published *Truth's Advocate* for the campaign.

[103] Moved from New Richmond to Cincinnati in 1836.

speak." He fought Moses Dawson of the *Cincinnati Advertiser* in print yet lunched with him and teased him about it.

Hammond deplored a subsidized press. "When the power and patronage of the government is lavished in support of a prostitute Press, the morals of the people become corrupted, their prejudices excited, and their ignorance wielded to the basest of purposes."[104] He realized that: "In all political contests there is a constant tendency on the part of the press to provoke by violence and indulge in licentiousness," but believed the press less responsible than the people.

Pray, what is the liberty of the Press? Is it to do and say anything that passion or malignity may dictate? And all without responsibility or reproof? Surely not. The Press is amenable to the laws of the country. It has no privileges beyond a private individual—and its abuses should be corrected, if necessary, by legal proceedings. . . . It has a right to speak freely, but candidly, of public men and public measures. It has a right to speak the truth, and the whole truth, when connected with the public interest. No one could wish it to proceed further; and none can think that is an attempt to gag the Press which is merely a legal effort to seek redress for a wanton and malicious libel.

He protested the idea that certain topics of public interest were taboo because dangerous.

No tyranny can be more unbearable, more untolerable, than that of the momentary impulses of the masses. We have stood up, and we shall continue to stand up against it. In short the MONSTER FEW, speaking to the passions and prejudices of the many, shall not control the *Cincinnati Gazette* upon the Catholic, the Abolitionist, the Texan, or any other question.[105]

On Hammond's death in April, 1840, his paper, of which he had been more than just a part for fifteen years, carried only an eight-line notice. A year earlier he had written:

> The world's a printing house. Our words and thoughts,
> And deeds are characters of various sizes,
> Each soul is a compositor, whose faults
> The Levites may correct, but Heaven revises.
> Death is the common press, from whence being driven,
> We're gathered, sheet by sheet, and bound for Heaven.

[104] *Cincinnati Daily Gazette,* August 15, 1837.
[105] *Ibid.,* December 1, 1835.

William Cooper Howells, editor of the *Hamilton Intelligencer,* wrote of Hammond: "He was not equalled in Ohio or surpassed in the Union, and our highest ambition would be gratified in occupying his exalted place."[106] Webster called him "the greatest genius that ever wielded the political pen."

In 1828 Hammond had recognized John Bailhache as an editor who "for many years has stood at the head of the editorial corps in Ohio." Bailhache, formerly of the *Fredonian* and the *Scioto Gazette* at Chillicothe, became editor of the *Ohio State Journal* about the same time Hammond joined the *Cincinnati Gazette.* Although one of the leading papers in the state the *Journal* did not prosper, and in 1835 Bailhache sold out. In his valedictory he wrote :

Much has recently been said, and not without some cause, respecting the present degradation of the periodical press, and the facility with which it lends itself to the evil purposes of even the worst of men. In my opinion the cause of the prostitution complained of lies not so much with the conductors of these mighty engines as with the people themselves. Editors and publishers are constituted like the rest of the human race. They cannot subsist on air, nor carry on an expensive business without money. After having been led, perhaps by false or greatly exaggerated representations, to embark their all in the establishment of a newspaper, it is quite natural that they should be unwilling to give it up, even when they have ascertained that success is now impossible. It, therefore, follows that, after a few unavailing struggles to preserve their independence, some of them finally submit to become the tools or instruments of designing individuals, or of a political party.[107]

The remedy was obvious; let subscribers pay honestly and promptly. The paper could then become a blessing rather than curse, by bending its energies in the right direction.

Bailhache moved to Illinois where, under the motto "United We Stand—Divided We Fall," he took over the recently founded *Alton Telegraph,* which under his editorship, 1837 to 1841, was one of the best-edited papers in the state.

Powerful pen wielder against Hammond, Bailhache, and all National Republican-Whigs, was Samuel Medary, one of the most noted and notorious editors of the Middle West's history. Reared in the Quaker faith and educated at Norristown Acad-

---

[106] *Hamilton Intelligencer,* April 9, 1840. Howells was the father of William Dean Howells.
[107] Hooper, *Ohio Journalism,* 80.

emy, Pennsylvania, Medary came to Clermont County, Ohio, in 1825. He started the *Ohio Sun* at Bethel in 1828 to help the Jackson cause. Later he published the *Ohio Farmer and Western Horticulturist* at Batavia and Columbus. In 1837 he became editor of the *Ohio Statesman,* to serve intermittently for twenty years.

There was no more bitter a partisan than Medary; under his editorship the *Statesman* became the leading Democratic organ of the Northwest. What Democrats were to Horace Greeley, all Whigs were to Medary. Regardless of Quaker background, he was said to be willing to back the pen with the fists. Whether, after "strutting and swaggering," he actually invited the editor of the *Ohio State Journal* to a fight is immaterial;[108] mutual invitations and acceptances would have been in order. In the campaign of 1840 a Whig blacksmith put on a street scene in Columbus. After flaying Medary he finished his "dirty job" by taking a copy of the *Statesman* in his tongs, burning it, then washing the tongs and his hands.

Medary was interested in agriculture, railroads, public health, and constitutional reform. He hated abolitionism and abolitionists. As state printer he and his paper fared well; later he was appointed governor of Minnesota Territory and of Kansas Territory. The Civil War proved too much for him. Early in 1861 he issued the first number of the *Crisis,* which, despite its appeal to the intellect rather than the emotions, was hailed as the organ of treason and the office was mobbed. Medary was arrested for conspiracy, but was never put on trial under indictment. On his death in 1864 the *Ohio Sun* which he had founded said that "his greatest anxiety seemed to arise from the fear that he would outlive constitutional liberty." And the *Cincinnati Commercial* wrote: "He gave up to party what was meant for mankind. That was the sum of his faults."[109]

George A. Chapman, of the Terre Haute *Wabash Enquirer* (1838–41), and later of the *Indiana Sentinel* was, if possible, an even more rabid partisan than Medary. To him not only were all Whigs liars and scoundrels, but even a Democrat, if remotely suspected of saying or thinking one good thing of a bank, was ditto. Chapman, already famous as the result of the rooster em-

---

[108] *Ohio State Journal,* August 13, 1839 so stated.
[109] Quoted in Osman C. Hooper, *The Crisis and the Man* (Columbus, 1929), 33.

blem and "Crow, Chapman, Crow" slogan, was welcomed into the field of Indianapolis journalism by S. V. B. Noel of the *Indiana Journal*:[110]

> The editor of the Dunghill Oracle has resorted to the contents of a whiskey bottle to drown the sorrow and trouble we have brought upon him. . . . When our informant last saw him he was in the same condition as the bird that defiles its own nest. . . . a meeting of the Dunghill Clique was called. . . . After a two hours' operation with soft soap and water, the committee reported that they had attended to the business referred to them, that the friends of the editor could again approach him without putting handkerchiefs to their olfactories, and asked to be discharged.[111]

Chapman threatened suit but thought better of it; he could out-word Noel. T. J. Barnett, Noel's successor, later drew a pistol on Chapman in the post office. Chapman's forte lay in punch-filled paragraphs which frequently were personal and sometimes bordered on the vulgar. For fifteen years he and his brother Jacob Page Chapman established the line of Jeffersonian principles for all Democratic papers and Democrats in Indiana. There is no better—or worse—example of editorial knock-down-and-drag-out bludgeonry in Midwest journalism than the *Sentinel-Journal* struggle of the early 1840's.

Of different type was Dr. E. W. H. Ellis of the *Goshen Democrat,* one of the most widely quoted Democratic editors in 1839–40. Ellis divided his time between the practice of medicine, editing, and politics. He was a man of wide culture; his editorials had the substance of statesmanship. Whereas Chapman was feared for his reckless pen, Ellis was respected for his scholarship and ability. He discussed acts and measures, Chapman individuals; Ellis respected most people, Chapman none. Chapman was an editor of the George D. Prentice type, without the literary ability or strong financial backing of the great Kentuckian; Ellis on the other hand was an editor of the Greeley type.

Not so well known before 1840 was John D. Defrees, Indiana's most distinguished antebellum journalist. Defrees was born in Tennessee, served his printer's apprenticeship in Piqua, Ohio, read law in Tom Corwin's office, and in 1831 moved to South Bend where with his brother he started the *North-Western Pioneer and St. Joseph Intelligencer*. Later he sold this paper to

---

[110] Noel had come from Fort Wayne in 1835; he had been co-founder of the *Fort Wayne Sentinel* in 1833.

[111] *Indiana Journal,* October 1; *Indiana Sentinel,* September 28, 1841.

Schuyler Colfax, one of his printers, and took over editorship of the *Indiana State Journal*. Endowed with abundant energy Defrees was nevertheless an assiduous student of books; he became well grounded in politics and government, and loved history. In politics a staunch Whig (later a Republican), he was ever a master, never a follower. He had courage, humor, and a temper which he kept under control. This fact, together with his known skill with a rifle, may explain a career singularly free from personal brawls. He added the latest mechanical improvements to the *Journal* and wrote with "a terse Saxon force and direct 'drive' at the purpose in hand, rare in these days." Defrees served as government printer, with brief intermissions, from his appointment by Lincoln in 1861 through the Hayes administration.

Illinois had no great editors during the period but there were a number who raised their papers well above the level of mediocrity. John York Sawyer of the *Illinois Advocate,* Samuel S. Brooks of the *Illinois Herald*, the *Illinois State Gazette and Jacksonville News,* and other papers, John Calhoun and John Wentworth of the *Chicago Democrat,* Hooper Warren of the *Edwardsville Spectator* and later of the abolitionist Chicago *Commercial Advertiser,* and John Bailhache of the *Alton Telegraph,* were men of influence in their day. Simeon Francis of the *Sangamo Journal* was alternately lyrical in spreading the advantages of the Sangamon country and vociferous and thorough in doing the same for Whig doctrines. Francis and Lincoln spent many hours together; Lincoln furnished ideas, Francis printed them.

John P. Sheldon and Ebenezer Reed of the *Detroit Gazette* were outstanding in early Michigan journalism. Reed joined Duff Green on the *United States Telegraph* in 1828, but Sheldon, after his press burned in 1830, for a while edited the *Democratic Free Press.* Sheldon, a fiery Jacksonian, had freely criticized Judge William Woodbridge of the territorial supreme court. The court struck back, made a rancorous attack on Sheldon, and declared him guilty of contempt. The editor refused to pay his $100 fine and went to jail where in April, 1829, three hundred of his friends assembled for a dinner.[112]

[112] This interesting and politically complicated case may be followed in the files of the *Gazette,* 1828–29. The court's opinion was published in the *Michigan Herald,* March 12, 1829; see also William W. Blume, *Transactions of the Supreme Court of the Territory of Michigan* (6 volumes. Ann Arbor, 1935–40), V, 107–8, 337–70.

Many other editors, important in their day, might be mentioned. Since a newspaper's domain does not conform to political boundaries, one is almost inclined to include George D. Prentice, founder of the *Louisville Journal*. His writings were "full of wit and fire and his paragraphs exploded like nitroglycerine; he fought out his quarrels with pen or pistol, as the case required." None was more widely quoted in the region—the Whig papers for doctrine, the Democratic papers in attempts at refutation.

Papers customarily carried banner heads which often had political significance. The *Western Sun* and others posted Paine: "Independence is my happiness, and I relate things as they are, without respect to place or persons." The *Chicago Democrat* and the *Indiana Republican* followed Franklin: "Where Liberty dwells, there is my country." "*Verite Sans Peur,*" boasted the *Detroit Gazette*, while the *Sangamon Journal* began its long life under the aegis of "Not the glory of Caesar, but the Welfare of Rome"; the *Ohio Argus and Franklin Gazette* carried the same. The slogans of Wilson and Bailhache have already been cited. The *Scioto Gazette* in the 1820's published under "The Time of Life is Short—to Spend that Shortness Basely, were too long," but by 1840 had switched to "Intelligence is not wisdom, but leads to wisdom." The *Western Intelligencer* began with, "Truth, Equality and Literary knowledge are the three Grand Pillars of Republican Liberty," while the Circleville *Olive Branch and Pickaway Herald* posted, "Our Country—our whole Country—and nothing but our Country." The St. Clairsville *National Historian's* heading was brief and to the point: "Daylight and Fair Play," while the *Ohio City Argus* emphasized "Federal Union and Republican Government." James Hall's *Illinois Gazette* held itself "Free to prove all things, and hold fast the best." The favorite of the Democratic-Republican (later Democratic) papers was "A Light and Simple Government."

An interesting custom maintained by many papers was the "carrier's address." At New Year's a literary piece, perhaps a poem or essay written for the occasion by the editor or some literary personage, would be run off separately and distributed by the paper boy. The carrier expected a gratuity in return for the greeting to the new year. John Finley's well-known verses "To

Indiana" and "The Hoosier's Nest" were part of the New Year's Address written for the *Indiana Journal* in 1833.[113]

The influence of the papers and editors is impossible of measurement; one can measure definitely advertising results, not educational or moral values. To those who believe that the best journalism is that which merely collects and publishes the news, who deny that the editor has any more right to inflict his personal views upon his reader than a teacher upon his pupils, journalism of the pioneer period would not appeal. But these editors did not do the thinking for their readers; they were not dictators talking down to the people; they talked with them and at them. They had convictions and expressed them; their writings were, in a period in which a premium was placed upon oratory, more influential than orations and more generally studied than school-books or sermons. To the people who read these papers modern editorializing would seem as anemic as cambric tea compared to their squirrel whiskey.[114] One thing is fairly certain: Beyond first-hand knowledge attained by actual practice, it was the newspapers that furnished the bulk of the knowledge of the essentials of representative government. Not every citizen read them it is true, but those who could not, got them secondhand. They were passed around, pored over, and discussed as are but few periodicals or books of our day. Educationally, beyond the three R's, they were far more important than schools.[115] Certainly it would be but a shell of a history of the period—of education, manners, literature, as well as politics and business—which did not reckon with the newspapers. Even the papers of the time were aware of this fact. Wrote the Detroit *North-Western Journal* in 1829: "It is a matter of general notoriety, that the history of the North Western Territory, of which this section of the country was once a part, is yet to be written"; it promised to

[113] For Finley see *post*, 561.

[114] There were exceptions of course. The *Daily Chicago American*, which devoted its interest chiefly to the commercial and business interests of Chicago, did little political ranting. When it criticized the Democrats it always spoke of the *ultra-Democrats*, out of deference to those merchants who were of that party.

[115] Newspapers were even used in schools. The *Illinois Intelligencer*, November 29, 1823, spoke of the editor of another paper having received an order for a supply of his papers for use in a public school. It commended the practice; if more widely followed there would not be so many listless and ignorant people and noisy politicians who knew nothing.

help by giving more time and space to education, history, religion, and affairs in general, as well as to politics. And Editor John B. Dillon, soon to become the first historian of Indiana, wrote:

The newspaper is the great instrument of civilization. All the books ever written are but a feather in the scale compared with newspapers, as a means of affecting the mass. What is the circulation even of a popular novel, to that of a paragraph which runs the round of the press? The one is read by thousands, the other by millions. It is almost entirely to the influence of newspapers that the superior intelligence of the middle classes is to be attributed. Contemptible as may be deemed the information derived from this source. . . . Yet we know that there are in the middle classes many men of high rank in intellect. What has chiefly furnished them with food for reflection, and given them a general, although perhaps superficial, knowledge of almost every subject? The newspaper; that despised and seemingly insignificant messenger, bringing every day some new fact or some new idea, and thus adding by little and little to their mental stores, until they have accumulated to an extent for which the cause would have appeared at first inadequate.[116]

Or as the rhymester phrased it:

When the newspaper came to Ohio
    It sounded the Indian Alarm;
It fostered the trade that the pioneers made,
    And brightened the woodland and farm;
It offered its trifle of culture,
    It offered a chance for debate,
And it sturdily wrought, bringing thought after thought,
    For the upbuilding here of a State.[117]

§

Second only in importance to the newspapers as sources for the study of social and cultural history are the periodicals or magazines.[118] The line between the newspaper and magazine is indistinct. Some might be classified in either category. There was the *Philanthropist*, for instance, started at Mount Pleasant, Ohio,

[116] *Logansport Canal Telegraph*, June 25, 1836.

[117] Hooper, *Ohio Journalism*, 185.

[118] The best guide is Rusk, *Literature of the Middle Western Frontier*, I, Chapter III. See also Bertha-Monica Stearns, "Early Western Magazines for Ladies," in *Mississippi Valley Historical Review*, XVIII (1931–32), 319–30; Venable, *Beginnings of Literary Culture in the Ohio Valley*, Chapter III; and William T. Coggeshall, "Literary Enterprises in Cincinnati," in *Genius of the West*, V (1856), 97–100, 130–33. The abolition periodicals are covered later in this chapter; for medical periodicals see Chapter V; for religious periodicals, Chapter XIV.

August 29, 1817, by Charles Osborn. This little three-column 9- by 11-inch Quaker weekly resembled a newspaper more than a magazine; among the poetry, allegories, temperance articles, moral and political observations, exchanges, essays on "Prejudice," and the like, foreign and domestic news and weather comments were interspersed. A motto from Dr. Johnson gave way to a scripture quotation. Osborn sold out to Elisha Bates in October, 1818.[119] Under Bates's editorship the idea of the Friends that man should be the friend of man was emphasized; also antislavery material. It appears that Bates discontinued the *Philanthropist* in 1822 after having started (1821) *The Moral Advocate, a Monthly Publication, on War, Duelling, Capital Punishment, and Prison Discipline*, which continued through at least three volumes.[120] Bates later (1828?–36) put out *The Miscellaneous Repository*, largely concerned with refuting the Hicksite heresy. Some numbers of the publication were issued in England, later ones in St. Clairsville.

In 1823 at Connersville, Indiana, appeared a "poor little fortnightly affair," the *Western Ladies Casket*, edited by a lady. It flourished a headpiece of "weary looking flowers" and a motto:

> Improve, excel, surmount, subdue your fate
> So shall at length enlightened man efface
> That slavish stigma seared on half the race.

Though a sister publication, the *Ladies Garland*, of Harpers Ferry, Virginia, hoped the "western lady might find her Casket starred with many a precious gem,"[121] the gems proved to be largely extracts from English magazines, the *Edinburgh Encyclopedia*, treatises on chemistry, and such.

In 1822–23 was published at Dayton *The Gridiron*, a literary journal which carried the motto,

> . . . burn, roast meat burn
> Boil o'er ye pots, ye spits forget to turn.

[119] Until recently the *Philanthropist* was listed as having been started by Elisha Bates. Whether Osborn is the same person who joined Elihu Stout on the Vincennes *Western Sun* in 1819 is not certain, but it appears probable, since he published several pieces on Indiana. A file of Osborn's volumes I and II of the *Philanthropist* (August 29, 1817—October 8, 1818), lacking a few pages, is in the Indiana University Library. Bates started the numbering again with volume I. An incomplete file of his two volumes is in the library of the Western Reserve Historical Society.
[120] Rusk, *Literature of the Middle Western Frontier*, I, 190.
[121] February 28, 1824, cited in Stearns, "Early Western Magazines for Ladies," 321. A one-column prospectus was published in various newspapers. See for instance *Hamilton Intelligencer and Advertiser*, August 11, 1823.

John Anderson, "sole proprietor," between reprints of hackneyed bits of humor, gave warnings to local gamblers and offered comments on things in general. This 8-page, 5-by-8-inch magazine was a sort of primitive.

The Microscope and General Advertiser, started in Louisville in 1824 by T. H. Roberts, was mobbed and moved across the river to New Albany. The editor promised "to lash the rascals naked through the world," filled his paper with fictitious characters such as Timothy Tightlace, Nelly Nettletongue, and Titus Tadpole, and added spicy verse.[122] The publication was short-lived, but the semiobscene wit and satire of its columns, though not unusual on the frontier, were more often spoken than printed.

In 1823–24 the versatile Horton J. Howard, editor, map maker, and publisher of botanic medical books, published at Mount Pleasant, Ohio, the *Juvenile Museum*, one of the first "juveniles" west of the Alleghenies. It was a semimonthly.

The first Cincinnati literary publication was the *Literary Cadet* (November, 1819), a 6-by-10-inch weekly edited by Dr. Joseph Buchanan, a versatile genius who besides writing textbooks and preparing medical lectures invented a tubular copper boiler intended to propel a flying machine. After twenty-three issues the *Cadet* was taken over by the *Western Spy*, which continued under the title of *Western Spy and Literary Cadet*.[123] The *Spy's* chief claim to literary remembrance was as the original publisher of Thomas Peirce's "Odes to Horace in Cincinnati." Competition for literary attention soon came from the *Olio* (John H. Wood and Samuel S. Brooks) which ran for about a year, 1821–22. On the demise of this periodical John P. Foote, Benjamin Drake, and others, still believing that Cincinnati would support a literary journal, planned the *Cincinnati Literary Gazette*. This weekly ran for a year, 1824. Although it had a number of western contributors—Benjamin Drake, Thomas Peirce, Mrs. Julia L. Dumont,

[122] That *The Microscope and General Advertiser* had been endeavoring to live up to its name may be inferred from the following letter in the issue of December 23, 1824:

"Dear Tim——The gang of modesties, who have hitherto found so much fault with your paper, are beginning to draw in their tail (as the saying is in the country) and look——cheap, (as the saying is in town). They have been frequently asked, why they dislik'd the Microscope? Finding themselves unable to support the charge of *immodesty,* they then declar'd that you were too personal in your remarks. That is, Tim, your pictures are too well drawn, and your characters too plainly delineated. For my own part, I took no interest in the exhibitions until I heard the general murmuring in the ranks of dissipation. . . .

Jehus' *doux yeux*"

[123] Until 1823 when it became the *National Republican and Ohio Political Register*.

Dr. J. Locke—attention was devoted largely to eastern and European subjects. On the demise of the *Gazette* Drake and Mansfield, of the *Cincinnati Chronicle*, issued the *Cincinnati Chronicle and Literary Gazette*, which, though resembling more a newspaper than a magazine, carried the bulk of the literary output from 1826 to 1831.

In 1831 John H. Wood, Cincinnati bookseller, began publication of the semimonthly *Cincinnati Mirror and Ladies Parterre*, "A voice in the Wilderness," with the intention of concentrating on the West.[124] He secured William D. Gallagher, recently married and ready for a career, to edit the magazine, which had eight hundred subscribers. Although original stories on western subjects and the editor's poetry furnished some of the contents, still many exchanges and copied tales were necessary to fill the eight pages of each issue. In 1833 when Thomas H. Shreve joined Gallagher in the project the title was changed to *The Cincinnati Mirror, and Western Gazette of Literature and Science*, a weekly. In April, 1835, the *Chronicle*, then edited by James H. Perkins, ceased publication; Drake, Mansfield, and Perkins merged themselves and their defunct paper into the *Mirror* as editors and proprietors. In October, 1835, James B. Marshall purchased the paper and the title was changed to *The Buckeye and Cincinnati Mirror*. Marshall's valedictory came in January, 1836, but the journal continued at least until September before expiring.

The first monthly magazine of importance in the Northwest, and second in the West, was Timothy Flint's *Western Monthly Review*[125] started at Cincinnati in May, 1827. Flint, who was already known as a preacher and author, aspired to foster a *western literature*; his magazine was to be a literary review and publishing medium for that literature.

---

[124] The first two volumes were put out in a three-column 9½-by-11½ page. Beginning with volume three the size was increased to a 10½-by-13 page. Subscription was $1.25 per year in advance, or $1.50 payable in six months. A charge of 12½ cents extra was made for city carrier delivery. The subscription price was later increased to $3.00.

[125] At first called the *Western Magazine and Review*. The first magazine of importance in the West was *The Western Review and Miscellaneous Magazine*, a monthly publication devoted to literature and science, Lexington, 1819–21. Caleb Atwater called this the "first attempt to publish a work of this kind in the West." See volume I, 177. For Flint as historian and novelist see below.

We see no possible harm, that can result from encouraging authorship, especially in a new country, to the utmost extent. . . . Instead of wishing there were fewer books published, than there are, we wish there were five times as many. It shows a mind above the common, even to have the ambition to make a book. More good than harm, we dare affirm, will ordinarily result from publishing even a dull book. . . . Dull books are necessary for dull readers.[126]

His intention was, where possible, to praise rather than to blame. Although Flint thought, "We are physically, and from our peculiar modes of existence, a scribbling and forth-putting people" and "beneath the shade of the huge sycamores of the Miami, or cooling the forehead in the breeze of the beautiful Ohio, and under the canopy of our Italian sky, other circumstances being equal, a man might write as well, as in the dark dens of a city," he found that he had to provide most of the contributions himself. Articles, reviews, essays, and poems flowed from his pen; at the same time Flint was finishing his voluminous *History and Geography of the Mississippi Valley* and writing three novels.[127] No doubt the editor began to feel some of the "Miseries of Authorship," as described by "Smelfungus."[128] As contributors became more numerous the quality of the *Review* declined; more nonwestern material was included. The fact that there was a lapse of two months between the volumes indicates that all was not smooth going. In June, 1830, the editor indicated his intention of carrying on as a quarterly, but this was his valedictory for the *Review*, a magazine historically second in importance only to its successor.

Hardly had the *Western Monthly Review* folded before James Hall, of Vandalia, started his *Illinois Monthly Magazine*, October, 1830. The editor's plan was to devote the magazine to criticisms and reviews of new books, descriptions, tales, essays on rural economy, scientific papers, literary intelligence, and fugitive poetry; also "Notices of the fine and useful arts." Like Flint, Hall found it necessary to be his own chief contributor. He wrote articles, travels, copied extracts from his own books, garnered

---

[126] *Western Monthly Review*, I (1827–28), 17.

[127] In the advertisement to the issue of the first volume he wrote: "The public has judged, and correctly, that most of the articles in this work, have been from one hand."

[128] *Ibid.*, I, 523–27.

statistics, conducted "Notes on Illinois," and wrote reviews.[129]
Hall's own writings, plus contributions from Morris Birkbeck,
John Mason Peck, Governor Edward Coles, Salmon P. Chase,
and other important western men constitute the valuable portion
of the contents, but it was impossible to publish on this material
alone. The editor drew upon *Blackwood's,* the *New England
Magazine,* newspapers, and other sources; selections on the
"Sources of Genius," "Civilization of the Ancient Mexicans,"
"The Culture of Silk" (from a government document), gunpowder, and children's books added filler. The editor apologized
for this sort of thing, but his calls for help went largely unheeded.
Vandalia offered limited facilities for both literary and financial
support. There was some truth to the statement that Hall was
trying to publish a literary magazine in a state that had more
Indians and horse thieves than interested readers.[130]

Desiring to give his magazine more general circulation and "to
identify its character with that of the western country at large,"
Hall moved to Cincinnati, the literary and publishing center of
the West.

In January, 1833, appeared the first number of the *Western
Monthly Magazine* "a continuation of the *Illinois Monthly
Magazine,* conducted by James Hall."[131] To promote the cause
of science and useful knowledge, to make it the medium "for
disseminating valuable information and pure moral principles,"
and to devote attention "chiefly to elegant literature" were the
endeavors of the editor.

The literature of the West is still in its infancy, and we trust that we are
not unconscious of the responsibility which rests on those who attempt to
direct it. . . . the literature of our country has never exerted the influence
to which it is entitled. A vast portion of our education and talent is possessed by those who are immersed in the cares of business; and those elegant
or solid acquirements which should enlighten the public mind, and give
dignity to the national character, lie buried like the ore in the mine, or are
only used to enliven the private circle, or the domestic fireside.[132]

[129] Hall stated that he wrote 350 of the 576 pages in volume I. *Illinois Monthly
Magazine,* II (1831–32), 105. This ratio also held for the second volume.
[130] Volume I was printed by Hall and Robert Blackwell at Vandalia; one issue
of volume II was printed in St. Louis, the other numbers by Corey and Fairbank,
of Cincinnati. Complete files of the two volumes are scarce. In the Huntington
Library copy the articles written by the editor are initialed "J. H."
[131] Published by Corey and Fairbank.
[132] *Western Monthly Magazine,* I (1833), 1–2.

Support for the new venture was encouraging, both from contributors and subscribers.[133] Since the best literary talent in the West was now at Hall's command, he confined his own writing largely to reviews and travel sketches. The small payment for contributions no doubt helped, but more important was the fact that here was a magazine by Westerners and for Westerners, for which no apology was necessary.[134] Featured were western travel sketches, biographies, narratives of early history of the West, interpretations of western character, and information on the resources and institutions of the western country. The frequency with which articles were immediately lifted by other publications (as well as quoted in this history) gives some indication of their quality and appeal. Above all Hall, conscious of the glory of the West and its traditions, and confident of its future, conducted the *Western Monthly Magazine* as a medium for integrating and disseminating propaganda—not for outsiders so much as in the endeavor to create in Westerners a belief and pride in their cultural institutions equal to what they already had in their military prowess and material resources.

As subscriptions grew to more than three thousand (at $3.50), the magazine was increased from forty-eight to seventy-two pages. Collections were difficult, however; cost of collections was larger than the printer's bill.[135] In 1835 when Lyman Beecher in his *A Plea for the West* made strong statements against the Catholics, Hall struck out vigorously at illiberal demagogues, defended Catholics as patriots and men, and made a strong plea for toleration. But many people in the West at this particular time were in no tolerant mood. When subscribers attacked the editor and canceled their subscriptions—even unpaid-for subscriptions—Hall replied stoutly, but the mischief had been done; he took a vacation. In his "Letter from the Editor De Jure to the Editor De Facto"[136] he sarcastically pointed out the dangers of an editor engaging in the absurd heresy of thinking, or even

---

[133] The magazine started with about five hundred subscribers and had nearly three thousand by the end of the year. Contributors were paid a dollar a page and prizes were awarded. In volume II, of thirty-seven signed articles, thirty were by western writers.

[134] *Ibid.*, III (1835), 94.

[135] Volume III (1835), 92. Unpaid subscriptions by 1836 apparently totaled between $7,000 and $10,000. Volume V (1836), 8. The publishers were in turn Corey and Fairbank, Eli Taylor, Taylor and Tracy, and Flash, Ryder and Company.

[136] *Ibid.*, IV (1835), 130–33. For the anti-Catholic agitation see Chapter XIV.

discussing public questions. To make matters worse, his publishers were also publishing the *Cincinnati Journal*, a religious weekly which upheld Beecher and the anti-Catholic crusade. Hall's policy of putting Americanism above sectarianism stood little chance against his hard-shelled opponents who believed in clerical domination.[137] His criticism of abolitionists also contributed to the trouble. In June, 1836, he turned over the editorship to Joseph R. Fry, who finished out the year. In 1837 the magazine was merged with Gallagher's *Western Literary Journal, and Monthly Review* (which started in June and ended in November, 1836) to become the *Western Monthly Magazine, and Literary Journal* (new series). Under the new title and the editorship of Gallagher and Marshall only five numbers (February to June) were published (at Louisville).

Hall, after leaving the magazine, turned his energies towards business, and though he tried no more journalistic ventures, he continued active with his pen. His six years as editor had made him known throughout the West and in the East as well. No magazine published in the region since Hall's has ever occupied a position of similar importance and influence in relation to the West.

Gallagher was not yet through, however; whereas Hall had many interests, Gallagher in this period had one—literature. In his *Western Literary Journal* he had sought "to represent to ourselves and our neighbors, correctly and thoroughly, the literary character of the Great West." During its brief career the *Journal* published largely original material—essays, tales, poems—consequently the editor drew upon his own talents for approximately half the contents. The *Journal* was never a financial success and the merger did not help; during the half year of its life the *Western Monthly Magazine, and Literary Journal* did not take in enough money to pay for its cover.[138] Well aware of the difficulties, but loving the pursuit and believing that it could be made to yield a *quid pro quo*,[139] Gallagher launched at Columbus in May, 1838, *The Hesperian: A Monthly Magazine of*

---

[137] The threatened prosecution of the editor for libel did not materialize. For Hall's summary of the status of the controversy in 1836 see his "Remarks," V (1836), 239 ff.

[138] See volume I, 362 (June, 1837).

[139] *The Hesperian*, I, 91.

General Literature, Original and Select.[140] Otway Curry was partner and co-editor for some months. The editors made no pretense to confine this publication to original and western writings; they expected to draw upon the best available. Approximately a third of each issue of some ninety pages was given over to "Select Miscellany," from European and American sources, nor were the reviews limited to western publications.

Although the *Hesperian* was moved to Cincinnati in April, 1839, its finances did not improve. The November issue was its last. Gallagher was beginning to realize that literature did not pay. The previous year he had written of the earlier editors, Flint, Hall, and Hunt, who

more ready to labor than able to labor for nothing, took down their sickles and went into the field . . . who first visited the literary springs of the Mississippi Valley, and irrigated the broad West with the bright and refreshing waters thereof. Notwithstanding the lightness of the harvests, the exertions of these gentlemen were arduous and long-continued; and each, when compelled by losses, disappointments and vexations, to quit the field and return his sickle to its peg, had bound up a goodly number of comely sheaves, the heads of whose stalks were filled with choice grain.[141]

Gallagher hung up his sickle temporarily; it was not to rust, merely rest.

Less important as a magazine on the West, but equally important as a western magazine, was the *Western Messenger; Devoted to Religion and Literature*, started at Cincinnati in June, 1835, by a group of friends of New England background and Unitarian belief. The idea was to promote Unitarianism and encourage western literature. Like other western literary periodicals the *Messenger* soon found that there was neither enough western literature nor demand for it, to maintain a magazine. "Our people, perhaps, have as yet no literature because they have nothing to say. They are busy living, doing, growing. The age of reflection and imaginative reproduction has not yet arrived."[142] Soon the editors turned their attention largely to eastern and English literature. The magazine attained a belated recognition

[140] The title pages of bound volume I read: *The Hesperian; or Western Monthly Magazine.*
[141] *Ibid.,* I, 91.
[142] *Western Messenger,* V (1837–38), 71.

for originally publishing some of the writings of George Keats, temporary resident of Louisville where the *Messenger* was published part of the time, and of his brother John Keats.[143] It also published some of Emerson's first poems. Ephraim Peabody, James Freeman Clarke, W. H. Channing, and James H. Perkins were editors at one time or another during the *Messenger's* existence until April, 1841.[144] Among the valuable western contributions were the sketches by Mann Butler, Kentucky historian, on "Manners and Habits of the Western Pioneers."

More extensive in appeal than the literary magazines was *The Family Magazine; or, Monthly Abstract of General Knowledge,* which was first published at Cincinnati in January, 1836. This accumulative popular encyclopedia made no pretense of being "a work replete with originality of ideas or style," but served as a vehicle for transmitting in "condensed but perspicuous form," history, geography, fine arts, natural history, agriculture and rural economy, useful arts, natural science, biography, travels, poetry, and miscellaneous reading. The numerous illustrations were an innovation in western magazine making. The subscription list was probably the largest of the monthlies of the region, but the magazine was discontinued in 1841.[145]

The *Monthly Chronicle of Interesting and Useful Knowledge,* edited by Edward D. Mansfield, was started in December, 1838. *The Rose of the Valley* began early the next year. This magazine has been characterized as "perhaps the lowest point in journalistic mediocrity."[146] Its contents matched its name. The *Evening Visitor,* a weekly "devoted to science and literature," was edited at Zanesville, Ohio, in 1837, by Mrs. P. W. Ball, who enriched its contents with "interesting articles from her pen." The *Mothers' and Young Ladies' Guide,* edited by Mrs. Maria Herrick, of Ohio City, survived for at least three volumes in the late 1830's.

There were a number of attempts at college literary magazines. The Miami *Literary Focus* ran for a spell in 1827–28; the *Literary Register* was published at Bloomington, Indiana, in 1832, the

---

[143] Rusk, *Literature of the Middle Western Frontier*, I, 180–81.

[144] The publication lapsed October, 1839—May, 1840. For an attempt to unravel the places of publication and editorships see *ibid.*, I, 183, note 162.

[145] The magazine claimed (volume I, preface) "an increase of five thousand" during the first year, but Cist, *Cincinnati in 1841*, 95, estimated its circulation in 1841 at three thousand.

[146] Rusk, *Literature of the Middle Western Frontier*, I, 186.

Budget of Fun in 1835 (?), and the *Equator of the Weekly Press and Gazette of Our Family, School and Church Interests* in 1840. The only issue of the latter that the author has seen is full of Plato, Andrew Wylie, and Sunday school notes. *The Yellow Jacket*, its contemporary, was so caustic as to have to be printed out of town. *The Madison Museum*, devoted to news, literature, and amusement, also ran briefly in 1832–33.

The total circulation of these western literary periodicals was not large; far more people subscribed to eastern periodicals. It was small in comparison even to the western religious publications. Nevertheless, the better of these publications were much more widely read than their circulation indicates. Newspapers copied and quoted extensively; the names of Hall, Flint, Gallagher, and of many of the contributors became generally known. As Flint said in 1828:

Albeit we live in the geographical center of the "celestial empire," most of the Atlantic people phrase our CITY a village, and our writers meet with unwonted indulgence of criticism, and no little marvel and astonishment at our writings, *considering the place. from which they come!!* Yet even in these our backwoods we weekly turn over the leaves of forty periodicals.—Still we only dip our foot in the ocean. Like Camilla we only skim over the leaves of the harvest.

§ §

The literature of a new world and a dawning age! The intellectual developments of a people, young but not barbarous—free but not lawless —possessing the experience and learning, yet untrammelled with the prejudices and superstitions of old, and though but a germ of the "millions yet to be," composing a nation which has, like Hercules, shown all the giant in the cradle! Their inward impulse, the freedom of unchained thought and the restless energies of a newness of life! Their sources of inspiration, the legends of three momentous epochs—the early settlements, the Indian wars, and the revolution—to which the human heart with its features and phenomena and the godlike work of its own improvement, adds a permanent field of study and research, to the philosophers of every age! Their community of letters wide and comprehensive, embracing in its fostering arms at once the child of the palace and the cot! What is there to prevent this most characteristic and peculiar portion of a growing nation from heaving up a pile of intellectual achievement, with which the moss-grown, mind-monuments of the "elder time" shall compare, as the gorgeous gloom of that *moral* sky with the rising sun light of the perfect day.[147]

[147] *Cincinnati Daily Gazette*, June 21, 1838.

These were not the words of Hall, Flint, or Gallagher, but of Charles Hammond, for the nonce as mellifluous as any of the men of letters. Jealous of the attention paid to European and eastern subjects in literature to the neglect of equally important American themes, men of the western band set a high goal for a western literature—one not yet achieved—but towards which they contributed the energies and enthusiasm which overcame the initial inertia.[148] Though Midwest writers of the pioneer period raised no colossal "mind-monuments" to overshadow even previous American literary art, produced no great or even first-class novels, dramas, or poetry, the importance of their efforts was greater than has been recognized by the general histories of American literature.[149] These works, as well as the anthologies, confining their attentions largely to the "belles-lettres" or so-called "creative writing," are inclined to overlook the other half—the harder-to-find fragments and miscellany, the editorials and letters, fugitive essays, orations, articles and sermons, almanacs and readers, tales and ballads—which constitute an equally important part of the literature. Only by one steeped in the totality of these writings, competent in history, government, geography, and science as well as literature in the narrower sense, would an estimate of these writings possess validity. The leading student of the subject has posed the question as to whether the leaders "and the great number of obscure authors who were their unconscious collaborators did not succeed in creating a body of literature invaluable for the record it contains of the growth of civilization during a unique epoch."[150] The answer should be in the affirmative.

Only in broadest outline can the literature of the Northwest be here treated. The subject is a special one, for which the general historian—notoriously nonliterary—is but ill-equipped.[151]

---

[148] Their attitude was that if it was necessary for western writers to have a seaboard endorsement, why was it not necessary to send to salt water for governors, senators, and representatives.

[149] William T. Coggeshall, in *The Protective Policy in American Literature* (Columbus, 1859), discussed the reasons for this lack of recognition: "Within a period of ten years, counting backward and forward from 1830, there existed a literary circle of which Cincinnati was the center, which, as a whole, has never had a superior in America." Somewhere between Coggeshall's estimate and that of the writers on the history of American literature, should be an acceptable mean.

[150] Rusk, *The Literature of the Middle Western Frontier*, I, vii.

[151] Basic to any study of the subject is the notable two volumes of text and bibliography by Rusk. Chapters V and VI of Dorothy Anne Dondore, *The Prairie and the Making of Middle America* . . . (Cedar Rapids, Ia., 1926), contain valuable ma-

No more than western institutions did western literature spring spontaneously into being. The satirical sketches of early frontier types in Hugh Henry Brackenridge's *Modern Chivalry* (1792–97), an "aboriginal classic," were well known in the West; also novels such as Gilbert Imlay's three-volume *Emigrants* (1793). Charles Brockden Brown in 1799 had said that "the incidents of Indian hostility, and the perils of the Western wilderness, are far more suitable" for arousing the sympathy and passions of the reader than "puerile superstition and exploded manners, Gothic castles and chimeras."[152] The tales of Byron and Scott were on sale in the bookstores and pirated in the magazines and newspapers; James Fenimore Cooper's influence was being felt.

In the literary and intellectual history of the Northwest in the first half of the nineteenth century four figures loom in high relief above the skyline like poplars in the forests of the Ohio Valley. They were James Hall, Timothy Flint, Daniel Drake, and William Davis Gallagher. One was a poet, one was a scientist, doctor and teacher, two were writers of fiction; all were editors, historians, writers of verse, men of affairs, publicists, and protagonists of the West.[153]

James Hall, born in Philadelphia in 1793, came from a literary family.[154] He did not attend school until twelve, had an unhappy experience in an academy[155]—but did learn some Latin and French—worked in a store, read law, fought in the War of 1812, and as an artillery lieutenant sailed on the Decatur expedition to Algiers. After a mix-up and army court martial while on duty at

---

terial. The work by Venable, *Beginnings of Literary Culture in the Ohio Valley*, though uncritical, is indispensable. The works of William T. Coggeshall—*The Poets and Poetry of the West . . .* (Columbus, 1860); *The Protective Policy in American Literature*; "Literary Enterprises in Cincinnati," in *Genius of the West*, V (1856), 97–100—are useful, as is the *Personal Memories . . . 1803–43*, of Edward D. Mansfield (Cincinnati, 1879). The writings of the Drakes, Gallagher, Flint, Hall, Curry, and others, and particularly the magazine articles, not only those published before 1840, but in the magazines of the 1840's and 1850's—the *Literary Review*, the *Western Literary Messenger*, the *Genius of the West*—are, of course, important sources.

[152] *Edgar Huntly*, preface, iv.

[153] On intellectual grounds Henry Rowe Schoolcraft would rate alongside these four, but the nature of his major writings (explorations and Indians) and the fact that he was not so widely known at the time might justify putting him in another category. See below.

[154] The best study of Hall is John T. Flanagan, *James Hall, Literary Pioneer of the Ohio Valley* (Minneapolis, 1941). A biographical sketch by J. F. Meline was published in the *Cincinnati Commercial*, October 16, 1868. The best brief sketch is in Venable, *Beginnings of Literary Culture*, Chapter XII.

[155] See *ante*, 341–42.

Pittsburgh in 1817 he resigned his commission and resumed the study of law.[156] Contact with Morgan Neville of the *Pittsburgh Gazette* and a series of articles which he wrote for that paper led Hall to embark upon his western ventures in 1820. It was the "legends of the West, scattered in fragments over the land" that were more alluring than imaginary clients or prospective fees.

As he traveled leisurely down the Ohio in a keelboat, he noted not only the "wild, solemn, silent sweetness" of the river scenery, but ranged ashore where he hunted, talked to the people, and heard their tales and their tunes. Arrived at Shawnee-town he wrote of his trip in a series of letters which were published first in the Philadelphia *Port Folio*, 1821–25, then as a book, *Letters from the West* (London, 1828).[157] Eight years in the office of the prosecuting attorney and as judge took the young lawyer on circuit of ten counties, where he learned the byways and lived among the settlers. During part of this time he edited the *Illinois Gazette*. While state treasurer he lived in Vandalia and edited the *Illinois Intelligencer*; he also contributed, under the name of "Orlando," tales, poems, and essays to Flint's *Western Monthly Review*.

In 1828 Hall edited at Cincinnati *The Western Souvenir, a Christmas and New Years Gift for 1829*.[158]

> Oh! a new Souvenir is come out of the West
> Through all the wide borders, it flies with a zest;
> For, save this fair volume, we souvenir had none—
> It comes unprecedented, it comes all alone;
> So glossy in silk, so neat in brevier
> There never was book like our new Souvenir!

Of the fifty-seven pieces, Hall wrote twenty or more; Timothy Flint, Otway Curry, John B. Dillon, and Benjamin Drake were among the other contributors. Best known of the selections was

---

[156] For one side of the case see Hall's *Trial and Defense* . . . (Pittsburgh, 1820).

[157] The letters were written to his friend Morgan Neville. A few were published in the *Illinois Gazette* in 1820. Hall's brother, John E. Hall, was editor of the *Port Folio*. The full title of the book was *Letters from the West; Containing Sketches of Scenery, Manners, and Customs: and Anecdotes Connected with the First Settlements of the Western Section of the United States* (London, 1828).

[158] Published by N. and G. Guilford, printed by W. M. Farnsworth. This little 3½-by-5½ book of 324 pages, embellished with seven steel engravings and bound in rose silk, has long been a collector's item.

Morgan Neville's "The Last of the Boatmen," a tale of Mike Fink.[159]

In 1829 Hall published *Winter Evenings. A Series of American Tales* (Philadelphia). While busy with the *Illinois Monthly Magazine* and various other activities he wrote *Legends of the West* (Philadelphia, 1832) and *The Harpe's Head; a Legend of Kentucky* (Philadelphia, 1833).[160] During the period in which he edited the *Western Monthly Magazine* he published *Sketches of History, Life and Manners in the West* (1834),[161] *Tales of the Border* (Philadelphia, 1834), and *Statistics of the West, at the Close of the Year 1836* (Cincinnati, 1836). Never one to confine his energies to one field, Hall had meanwhile become connected with the Commercial Bank of Cincinnati; he was cashier by 1840, president in 1843. Abandonment of editing did not stop the books. *Notes on the Western States . . .* (Philadelphia, 1838), *The Wilderness and the Warpath* (New York, 1846), *The West: Its Commerce and Navigation* (Cincinnati, 1848), *The West; Its Soil, Surface and Productions* (Cincinnati, 1848), and *The Romance of Western History* (Cincinnati, 1857) followed. From 1836 to 1844 he worked on the biographical sketches for the three folio volumes of *History of the Indian Tribes of North America*. This monumental work, partly the project of Thomas L. McKenney, formerly of the "Indian Department," included 120 color plates made from original paintings in the War Department; the subscription price was $120. It has been rated as Hall's most important historical accomplishment.[162]

[159] Neville was the son of Maj. Presby Neville, Lafayette's aide; his mother was a daughter of Gen. Daniel Morgan. He served as sheriff of Allegheny County, editor of the *Pittsburgh Gazette*, and moved to Cincinnati in 1824. The next year he became editor of the short-lived daily *Cincinnati Commercial Register*. He wrote widely for the western papers and was active in the educational and literary activities of Cincinnati. For a sketch of Neville see John T. Flanagan, "Morgan Neville, Early Western Chronicler," in *Western Pennsylvania Historical Magazine*, XXI (1938), 255–66.

[160] Published in London, 1834, as *Kentucky: A Tale*.

[161] One volume appeared at Cincinnati in 1834; the two-volume edition was published at Philadelphia and St. Louis in 1835.

[162] Hall had met George Catlin, painter of American Indians, at Cincinnati, 1835–36, and talked over the possibilities of such a publication, but Catlin was not interested. McKenney, who had served as superintendent of the Indian trade for six years, conceived the idea of such a publication even earlier than Hall. The plates were made from reproductions or copies of original paintings made by Charles Bird King, James Otto Lewis, A. Ford, Henry Inman, G. Cooke, and Peter Rindisbacher, in possession of the War Department. All but a dozen of the originals were destroyed in the Smithsonian Institution fire of January 15, 1865. A complete

Hall's literary activities may be briefly summarized under three heads: as critic, as romancer, and as publicist and historian.

As critic Hall had two basic criteria for judging novels—morality and patriotism. If a writer had these, and was enthusiastic about the West, many shortcomings could be overlooked. He saved his heavy guns for the foreigners who criticized his West, "depraved men. . . . poor touts of a craven ministry," and for those who believed that America, the West, had no literature of its own. His criticism is not important on aesthetic or literary grounds, but as the best contemporary expression of the voice of the West.

As romancer and tale teller—one novel and fifty tales—Hall's chief contribution was the portrayal of authentic characters and backgrounds—the country, the rivers, and the forests. "The sole intention of the tales . . . is to convey accurate descriptions of the scenery and population of the country. . . . The only merit he claims for them is fidelity."[163] As was said of Shakespeare: "Ben Jonson and he did gather humours of men dayly, where ever they came."[164] He knew the people, their speech, manners, attitudes, and life. Although himself a pioneer in the reporting of pioneer speech, he reproduced it but sparingly and not too well.[165] His tales have a certain grace and charm, but the structure is poor, dialogue frequently unreal, and the most convincing characters are usually the minor ones. Too often the style is stilted, expository, and rambling. The romances are valuable for their facts of background rather than for literary merit. Though not afraid to write of the crudeness and short-comings of western life, Hall never quite succeeded, in his fiction, in making the portrayal register; he held the position of an onlooker, rather than that of an actor in that life. His poetry, in which he dabbled, was mediocre.

The conflict between the early influence of the English essayists

---

set of the copies is in the Peabody Museum, Harvard. The three volumes were originally published by three different Philadelphia publishers, 1836–44, and a London edition was also issued. The Edinburgh edition of 1933–34 is in a much reduced size. The Hall-McKenney work in the original edition is rare; many sets were cut up and the plates sold separately.

For a fairly complete bibliography of Hall's works see Flanagan, *James Hall*, 207–8.

[163] Quoted in *Legends of the West*, preface.
[164] *Letters from the West*, 235.
[165] Hall seemed to have difficulty in co-ordinating his pen with his ear.

and romantic poets on the one hand and the western environment on the other may be the reason Hall has been called "a frustrated realist."[166] Or he may simply have lacked the ability to compose primarily literary pieces. The historian and publicist spoke more convincingly. Though connected with no school or college, Hall was essentially an educator. Through his books, reviews, essays, addresses, and compilations he was propagating ideas neither sectional nor class, but American. On education his views were broad and sound; neither a national literature nor a nation could exist without a liberal national education, which should be made available to men and women both by schools and other means. Though making no moral defense of slavery, he deprecated the abolition movement. He was one of the first to point out the errors and inconsistencies of the Indian policy of the United States and set forth a constructive program. His conscious plea for the West was on sentimental and cultural grounds, not economic or political. He fully realized the importance, dignity, and interdependence of all law-abiding classes and the need of co-operation of all sections in a harmonious nationalism. He was the advocate of no "ism" beyond that combination of individualism and nationalism necessary to effective representative government among an enlightened people. As was written at the time of his death, "Nobody who would understand how the people of the great Valley became what they are should neglect Judge Hall."[167]

Timothy Flint as a boy in Salem, Massachusetts, had watched his uncle depart with Rufus Putnam for Marietta in 1788.[168] After graduating from Harvard he served twelve years as a Congregational minister, but disliking theological controversies and seeking a change for his health, he embarked with his family for the West in 1815. At Cincinnati he was well received, but soon pressed on to the call of duty. Several months were spent in itinerant preaching in Indiana and Kentucky, and several years at St. Charles, Missouri, where he fought in vain against the sins

---

[166] Flanagan, *James Hall*, 149.

[167] *The Nation*, VII, 394 (Nov. 12, 1868). For Hall's ideas on the American way of life see quotation, *ante*, 105–6.

[168] W. D. Gallagher has a biographical sketch of Flint in the *Cincinnati Mirror*, III, 36–37. John Ervin Kirkpatrick, *Timothy Flint, Pioneer, Missionary, Author, Editor 1780–1840* . . . (Cleveland, 1911), is the most complete biography; for an estimate of Flint's work it should be supplemented by Venable, Dondore, and Rusk.

of the frontier French. Ever in ailing health, Flint sought relief at an outpost on the Arkansas where the whole family suffered the fever. On the way back to Missouri on a boat operated largely by the family and in the midst of a severe storm, Mrs. Flint gave birth to a baby which lived only a few days. It was buried on a high bank opposite a bluff. A year or two in southern Missouri followed, marked by illness and debts and hard work. The years 1822 to 1825 were spent preaching and teaching in Louisiana; at Alexandria on the Red River the family took root, though Flint himself did not. Illness returned, a trip to the Sabine boundary did not help, and Flint bade his family good-by, and returned to Salem "to die."[169]

Had Flint died at this point his name would not have figured in the history of the West. Health improved, however, and he wrote, largely from memory, *Recollections of the Last Ten Years . . . in the Valley of the Mississippi . . .* (Boston, 1826).[170] This firsthand account of the West, based upon ten years of experience and thousands of miles of travel, was an immediate success. Flint returned to Alexandria, finished his two-volume novel *Francis Berrian, or the Mexican Patriot* (Boston, 1826), and moved with his family to Cincinnati early in 1827. While editing and writing for the *Western Monthly Review* he wrote *A Condensed Geography and History of the Western States . . .* (2 volumes. Cincinnati, 1828),[171] *George Mason, the Young Backwoodsman . . .* (Boston, 1829), *The Life and Adventures of Arthur Clenning* (2 volumes. Philadelphia, 1828), and *The Shoshonee Valley; a Romance* (2 volumes. Cincinnati, 1830).[172] At the same time he was lecturing, writing encyclopedia articles, translating voluminously, planning an American bio-

---

[169] By steamboat to Wheeling, via the National Road to Baltimore.

[170] Venable says that there was a London reprint but no evidence of such has been found. See Kirkpatrick, *Timothy Flint*, 306–7.

[171] *The History and Geography of the Mississippi Valley. To Which Is Appended a Condensed Physical Geography of the Atlantic United States, and the Whole American Continent* (2 volumes. Cincinnati, 1832, Cincinnati and Boston, 1833), though labeled a "Second Edition" is in large part a separate work. Most of the *Condensed Geography*, partly rewritten, was incorporated in volume I, while volume II carries additional material.

[172] For an estimate of Flint's fiction see Dondore, *The Prairies and the Making of Middle America*, 218 ff. and index; Rusk, *The Literature of the Middle Western Frontier*, I, 288 ff. In *Shoshonee Valley* Flint put enough materials, plot, melodrama, and characters to have sufficed for a score of the later "westerns." At the time of writing this novel he promised "never again to perpetrate offences of romance on a large scale."

graphical dictionary, and traveling. *Indian Wars of the West: Containing Biographical. Sketches of Those Pioneers Who Headed the Western Settlers in Repelling the Attacks of the Savages together with a View of the Character, Manners, Monuments and Antiquities of the Western Indians,* his most popular work, appeared in 1833.[173]

For some months in 1833 Flint edited *The Knickerbocker*[174] in New York, but soon returned with his family to his Alexandria home, where he continued to write articles, planned a second part for his *Recollections,* and a revision of his principal works.[175] In 1840 while on one of his frequent trips to New England, he realized that his lifelong illness had won the battle. He wrote his family that he would be gone by the time the letter was received. The shock and a fever were too much for Mrs. Flint who preceded her husband in death by a month.

In a period of about eight years then, Flint had written more than a dozen volumes and scores of articles, short tales, reviews, and sketches. Of these works the *Recollections* and the *Geography* were the most important, but in the writings of a man "whose novels were histories and whose histories were novels," it is hard to choose.[176] Though full of obvious faults his writings contain descriptions excelled by few. As his friend Gallagher said, he wrote as he talked, "rapidly, eloquently, poetically, carelessly" and from the heart. "Blighted by the mildews of disease almost from his birth,"[177] Flint wrote not only to make a living, but from the deeper urge of contributing something with ennobling and civilizing qualities to the literature and history of the West. The charm, zest, and potential achievements of life in the West were captured and preserved by this middle-of-the-road, almost nonsectarian, Presbyterian who had experienced years of hardships living that life.

---

[173] At least fourteen editions of this work were published at Cincinnati between 1833 and 1868. Also in 1833 was published at Boston, *Lectures upon Natural History, Geology, Chemistry, the Application of Steam, and Interesting Discoveries in the Arts.* "This curious book [was] an *omnium gatherum* from many sources." For a bibliography of Flint's works, see Kirkpatrick, *James Flint,* 305–13.

[174] From the editorship of which Charles Fenno Hoffman had retired.

[175] None of which he ever published.

[176] For contemporary estimates of Flint see citations in Kirkpatrick, *James Flint,* 257 ff; also Dondore, Rusk, etc.

[177] As Flint wrote of Charles Brockton (Brockden) Brown in *Western Monthly Review,* I (1827–28), 484:

> There are, who will not see in earth, or sky,
> Nor find deep in the chambers of their heart
> The Great Invisible. . . . Nature's eloquence
> Pours in my ear a mystic strain from heav'n. . . .
> My senses caught the glorious argument.[178]

Flint well knew that his claim to remembrance would be based upon his work as historian rather than as litterateur. In a period when Bancroft, Parkman, and Motley were viewing history upside down from the seats of the mighty and interpreting with the aid of Providence, here was a man, a minister, anticipating by almost a century the "moderns" and "the New History":

History, to be of any value, must be sternly impartial, and strictly true; and all, that bears a different character, serves but to perpetuate error, and propagate distrust. The studied eulogium of our own country, its heroes, and its institutions, and the bitter sarcasm upon other nations, which is sometimes mistaken for history, has no claim to that sacred title, however exalted it may be in point of style, however powerful its argument, or copious in its details.[179]

And again:

A fair history of the society of a country village would be a thousand times more interesting than a novel; and besides the interest of the picture it would be one of the most useful views of society that can be presented. But taste has not yet matured sufficiently to relish such a picture, and, perhaps, the historian does not yet exist who has the requisite discrimination and felicity to draw it.[180]

He wrote largely of "the short and simple annals of the poor," because that class included the bulk of society.[181] Almost at the beginning of his writing years the historian had written regarding his labor:

We console ourselves with the confident persuasion, that it will one day be allowed us, that we have done something towards illustrating the country, over which we have so extensively travelled. The time is at hand, when the political and moral claims of this great region, will be as well understood, and as promptly admitted, as its physical extent and resources are at present. . . . We can easily enjoy, in anticipation, the eagerness, with which the future historian will repair to them [his collections] as a synopsis,

---

[178] Quoted from "The Being of A God," in *Western Monthly Review*, I (1827–28), 528.
[179] *Ibid.*, I, 543.
[180] *Arthur Clenning*, II, 148.
[181] *George Mason*, 3–4.

of most of what has been said, and written in the Western Country, touching its own natural, moral and civil history.[182]

The anticipation was prophetic: the historians have—and do.

On the tomb of Timothy Flint at Salem, Massachusetts, are the words written by his cousin and friend, Dr. James Flint:

> He painted on his glowing page
>   The peerless valleys of the West;
> That shall in every coming age,
>   His genius and his toils attest.

Daniel Drake grew up on a small Kentucky farm where he learned the tasks necessary to the days and seasons.[183] Spelling, arithmetic, some surveying, and a taste for natural sciences he acquired from various teachers and books. From the medical books of a cousin he got the beginnings of his main life interest. Apprenticed to Dr. William Goforth, versatile but eccentric Cincinnati physician, young Drake received his certificate, then attended, and finally got a degree from the University of Pennsylvania. From about 1815 to 1850 Daniel Drake came about as nearly dominating the profession of medicine in the Middle West as has ever been possible for one man.[184] Had Drake done nothing but practice and teach medicine, he would have been a busy man; had he only edited his medical journals, written his articles, and produced the *Diseases of the Interior Valley,* his accomplishments would have been notable;[185] but add to this the general literary, educational, and intellectual activities of this "galvanic battery of mental energy," and it is easy to understand why his contemporaries referred to this leonine personage as a "colossus."

[182] *Western Monthly Review,* I, iii, v. James K. Paulding drew heavily upon Flint for the setting and materials of his novel *Westward Ho!* In his copy of Flint's *Geography* (in the Hill Memorial Library, Louisiana State University) Paulding wrote: "The author of this work . . . was a Presbyterian Clergyman, but without the stiff and sour bigotry of the sect, and possessing the most warm and liberal feelings. He . . . had in him the elements of a great Poet. He wrote a description of the Mississippi Valley by far the best ever written, and many other articles of a miscellaneous character, all bearing the stamp of genius. He was an honest unsophisticated man, and I consider him among the very first American writers, for vigor of style and depth of thought and feeling. I always had a high respect and regard for him." Quoted in Arlin Turner, "James K. Paulding and Timothy Flint," in *Mississippi Valley Historical Review,* XXXIV (1947-48), 105.

[183] Daniel Drake, *Pioneer Life in Kentucky* (Cincinnati, 1870).

[184] For Drake's medical work, see Chapter V and references there listed.

[185] Drake's collected addresses and pamphlets constitute four bound volumes.

Drake's writings, other than medical, were not voluminous. In 1810 he wrote *Notices concerning Cincinnati*; five years later the *Natural and Statistical View, or Picture of Cincinnati and the Miami Country*. His "Remarks on the Importance of promoting Literary and Social Concert in the Valley of the Mississippi . . . ," published in 1820, and the oration or *Discourse on the History, Character and Prospects of the West* . . . in 1834, contain the essence of his ideas; but viewing medicine as he did as a broad field of social science and culture, many of Drake's contributions on geography, history, and education are to be found in his medical addresses and articles. Not even George D. Prentice wielded a more devastating pen than Drake when attacking quackery in any form, nor did he yield to James Hall in his general exuberance over the West. If much of his writing was didactic, fluid, and declamatory, he had a reason:

The literature of a young and free people will, of course, be declamatory. . . . Deeper learning will no doubt abate its verbosity and intumescence; but our natural scenery, and our liberal political and social institutions must long continue its character of floridness. . . . If cold, literal, and passionless, how could it act as the handmaid of improvement? In absolute government all the political, social, and literary institutions are supported by the monarch—here they are originated and sustained by public sentiment. In despotisms it is of little use to awaken the feelings or warm the imagination of the people—here an excited state of both is indispensable to those popular movements by which society is to be advanced. Would you arouse men to voluntary action on great public objects, you must make their fancy and feelings glow under your presentations; you must not merely forward their reason, but their desires and will; the utility and loveliness of every object must be displayed to their admiration; the temperature of the heart must be raised and its cold selfishness melted away, as the snows which buried up the fields when acted on by an April sun; then, like the budding herb which shoots up from the soil, good and great acts of patriotism will appear. Whenever the literature of a new country loses its metaphorical and declamatory character the institutions which depend upon public sentiment will languish and decline, as the struggling boat is carried back by the impetuous waves of the Mississippi as soon as the propelling power relaxes. In this region low-pressure engines are found not to answer—high steam succeeds much better; and although an orator may now and then explode and go off in vapor, the majority make more productive voyages than could be performed under the influence of a temperate heat.[186]

[186] From *History, Character, and Prospects of the West*. Drake was also on occasions, tedious. One hot afternoon while delivering an exhaustive and exhausting address on temperance, a listener interrupted, "Let's adjourn a while and take a drink!" An intermission followed in which some of the audience fortified themselves for the second half.

From the time that Drake became president of the "School of Literature and the Arts"—a Cincinnati literary club—in 1814, until his death in 1852, he was one of the leading generating forces and active workers in the promotion of schools, colleges, libraries, museums, and literature. At one time or another he was official or nonofficial president of almost every club or lyceum in the city. It was as "dean" of these forums whose membership contained the intellectual elite of the West in the 1830's, and as inspirator in general, that much of Drake's importance lay. When not presiding at the Lyceum, the "Inquisition," or the Semicolon Club, he was holding informal gatherings at his home.[187] To one or another of these meetings came sooner or later most of the distinguished visitors from outside as well as leading citizens of the Queen City. Young writers received stimulation and encouragement; they also made useful contacts. The interrelationships of members of the Cincinnati group, largely by marriage, were numerous; the business and professional interrelationships were diverse and broad. In this interesting circle, which had largely pre-empted the leadership held by the Lexington group of an earlier period, Daniel Drake, "the Franklin of Cincinnati," for two decades occupied a position second to none. The central theme of his larger aim was expressed in an address of 1833: "In short we should foster western genius, encourage western writers, patronize western publishers, and create a western heart."[188]

William Davis Gallagher, born in Philadelphia in 1808, came west with his widowed mother and three brothers in 1816. The log school and the Lancasterian Seminary in Cincinnati constituted his schooling. While a boy at the seminary he learned to set type and helped on a small newspaper; he could not understand why some stuff was set in short lines with rhymes at the end. He helped J. W. Gazlay on the *Western Tiller* a year or two, and Morgan Neville on the *Commercial Register*, the first

[187] The Semicolon Club's name was explained to Venable as follows: Christopher Colon discovered a new world; those who discovered new pleasures deserved half as much credit. Among its members were John P. Foote, Benjamin Drake, James Hall, E. D. Mansfield, Calvin Stowe, Harriet Beecher Stowe, Nathan Guilford, and Mrs. Caroline Lee Hentz. These literary coteries are described in Mansfield's *Personal Memories*, in Venable, *Beginnings of Literary Culture*, and in the writings of other participants.

[188] *Remarks . . . on the Importance of Promoting Literary and Social Concert in the Valley of the Mississippi* (Louisville, 1833).

daily. He published his first verses in John P. Foote's *Literary Gazette* in 1824. He also wrote for the *Saturday Evening Chronicle*, of which Benjamin Drake was editor. For a brief period, 1830 to 1832, Gallagher, a strong Clay admirer, published the *Backwoodsman and Greene County Courant* at Xenia. Followed the venture on the *Cincinnati Mirror* previously noted. By this time the poor young writer with the haughty carriage (William "Dignity" Gallagher) was a member of the Lyceum and Inquisition Club; he knew Hall, Drake, Prentice, Neville, and other writers and important persons. His first little volumes of poetry, *Erato No. I* and *Erato No. II*, were published in 1835; *No. III* followed in 1837. The short-term editorship of the *Western Literary Journal* in 1836 was followed by a period in Columbus where he worked on the *Ohio State Journal*, managed by his younger brother, and wrote for the *Cincinnati Gazette*. It was during this period that *The Hesperian* was started. When it expired Gallagher entered upon ten years of literary and political writing for the *Gazette*.

In 1840 he edited *Selections from the Poetical Literature of the West*.[189] Besides fourteen of his own poems there were selections from Prentice, John M. Harney, Otway Curry, Thomas H. Shreve, James H. Perkins, Micah P. Flint (son of Timothy Flint), Mrs. Amelia B. Welby, Mrs. Julia L. Dumont, Mrs. Caroline Lee Hentz, and twenty-eight other authors. Among his own poems were two of his best known—"Miami Woods" and "The Mothers of the West."[190]

Gallagher was poet, publicist, and promoter of the West. His interests were broad; agriculture, transportation, government, education, labor, all fell within the domain of his pen. A staunch Whig (later Republican), Gallagher believed in "the dignity of intrinsic manhood, the nobleness of honest labor, and the glory of human freedom." The idea of "progress" interested him much; he was a liberal in the true sense. Though some of his

[189] Cincinnati, 1841.

[190] This was the first part of "Miami Woods" which by 1856 developed six more parts. While Gallagher was connected with the editorship of the *Gazette*, he was appointed private secretary to Thomas Corwin when the latter became Secretary of the Treasury. He edited the *Louisville Daily Courier*, and in this capacity was challenged to a duel by Prentice, a fellow Whig. He later edited a farm journal, helped organize farmers' and mechanics' societies, served as customs collector, pension agent, etc. He wrote articles on many subjects. In 1881 he published at Cincinnati *Miami Woods and Other Poems*.

"reform" poems were flavored with the doctrine of Christian Socialism, there was no inconsistency between his poetry and politics.

Government, said Gallagher, was the means by which the rules of action of society made themselves felt; government had three elements—form, principles, men. Principles, to be put into form, require parties.

I regard PARTY, indeed, as the very essence of FREEDOM. . . . [But] with or without parties, there can be no real development or progress, while turbulence and dishonesty inflame men's minds and destroy their confidence.

Human ingenuity is fruitful in expedients to reform the world. One scheme seeks to do it by a sort of politico-physiological sliding scale, which shall prevent people from coming into the world faster than there is just so much food ready for them to eat, just so much clothing ready for them to wear, and just so much work ready for them to do—while another scheme expects to attain the same end, in part at least, by preventing people from going out of the world, when they have forfeited the right to curse society longer with their presence and their crimes, through an abolition of the death penalty. A third scheme seeks to cure the evils of the world, by a new order of society, laid off with the precision of a geometrical showplate, by the aid of the mental rule and compass, into orders, spheres, harmonies, sections, and other divisions and subdivisions almost numberless—while a fourth would destroy all society, by an abrogation of all government. A fifth scheme looks to an "organization of labor," in opposition to combinations of capital, as the grand moral and social panacea—while a sixth would cure all ills by a general division of property, brought about through the enactment into law of "a new and polite method of robbing one's neighbors."[191]

There was a humane spirit and sincere desire to do good behind most of these schemes. Too often, however, they reckoned not how much man had to unlearn from the past, and tried too much too fast. Having discredited themselves, fast-anchored conservatives hissed "infidels," "dupes," "madmen" at the reformers. The true progressive "must guard against what is manifestly one of the weaknesses, and I fear one of the sins, of our day: the pride of being ranked a *Reformer*. Names make not things, though things will make themselves names." Man must possess "that bold, distinct, individual character" before he could

---

[191] *Facts and Conditions of Progress in the North-West* . . . (Cincinnati, 1850), 52–53. One organization, the "Organization of Labor," Gallagher thought the first practical idea among all these panaceas, clothed in the muscles and sinews of healthy action. "I bid it Godspeed." *Ibid.*, 57.

be true either to others or to himself. History showed not that governments had been too little respected by the people, but too much respected; men in their servility suffered their minds to be shackled and bodies to be yoked by church and party. Christianity and the "Representative Principle" went hand in hand to make possible the "Experiment in Humanity," an experiment which had its greatest chance of success in "the north-eastern most part of this Inland Valley." Chance would never operate the engine, only man, governed by the laws of truth, justice, mercy, love, and duty. "Material Progress can be nothing but the outward manifestation of an inward truth—the visible correspondence of Spiritual Progress." Literature—the "Literature of Humanity" —would help achieve this experiment. This literature, pervaded by the beautiful and true, speaking to and from the common heart, would abandon fabled gods, let them wage their wars of lust, rapine, and revenge; leave adventurous bards and lecherous princes to shift for themselves, and seek its themes in the world about us, where was to be found much of good and hope.

Serious thoughts such as these paralleled beautiful lyrics on "May," "August," "The Cardinal Bird," "The Brown Thrush," and the mysticism of the poet as expressed in the finished "Miami Woods,"—

> A solitary sorrow atheming
> A lonely grief.

Few have loved nature as manifested in the Ohio Valley as well as Gallagher; none has expressed that love any better:

> Land of the West!—green Forest Land!
>   Clime of the fair, and the immense!
> Favorite of Nature's liberal hand—
>   And child of her munificence!
>   Filled with a rapture warm, intense,
> High on a cloud-girt hill I stand;
>   And with clear vision, gazing thence,
> Thy glories round me far expand:
>   Rivers, whose likeness earth has not,
> And lakes, that elsewhere seas would be,—
>   Whose shores the countless wild herds dot,
> Fleet as the winds, and all as free;
>   Mountains that pierce the bending sky,
> And with the storm-cloud warfare wage,—

Shooting their glittering peaks on high,
To mock the fierce red lightning's rage;
Acadian vales, with vine-hung bow'rs
And grassy nooks, 'neath beechen shade,
Where dance the never resting Hours,
To music of the bright cascade;
Skies softly beautiful, and blue
As Italy's, with stars as bright;
Flow'rs rich as morning's sun rise hue,
And gorgeous as the gemm'd midnight.
Land of the West! green Forest-Land!
Thus hath Creation's bounteous hand,
Upon thine ample bosom flung
Charms such as were her gift when the
Grey world was young.[192]

These four men were but the leaders in literary and historical activities in the Northwest. Many others are deserving of more than mere mention. Young Edward Deering Mansfield, Princeton graduate, arrived in Cincinnati in 1825, where he was welcomed at the home of Daniel Drake.[193] There he became imbued with literary ambitions. With Benjamin Drake, Daniel's brother, he compiled and wrote *Cincinnati in 1826*, and both were connected with the *Cincinnati Chronicle*. In 1834 he published his *Political Grammar*, as a result of which he became a professor in Cincinnati College. All told he wrote ten books, most important for historical purposes being his *Daniel Drake* (1855), and *Personal Memories* (1879). Journalism and education were his leading activities. Benjamin Drake went on to write *Tales and Sketches, from the Queen City* (1839), his biographical sketch of William Henry Harrison, and later his lives of Black Hawk and Tecumseh. Some of Drake's stories on western life are as good as any produced by Hall.

Other Cincinnati novelists were Frederick William Thomas, Mrs. Caroline Lee Hentz, and Thomas H. Shreve, the last two better known for their poetry. Though Thomas made Cincinnati his headquarters between 1831 and 1840 and traveled in the Mississippi Valley, the settings for his novels are mostly eastern.[194] Whether Shreve's novel *Betterton*, announced in 1837,

---

[192] As published in the Piqua *Courier and Enquirer,* July 8, 1837.
[193] Mrs. Drake was Mansfield's cousin and adopted sister.
[194] *Clinton Bradshaw; or, the Adventures of a Lawyer* (1835); *East and West* (1836); and *Howard Pinckney* (1840).

was published is uncertain.[195] Mrs. Hentz's melodrama *Lovell's Folly* (1833) also had an eastern setting.

Through the periodicals and newspapers with which they were connected, through the Philosophical Society of Ohio, the Western Literary Institute and College of Professional Teachers, and other channels, the activities and influences of the Cincinnati group reached out in various ramifications; in a way they headed up the historical-literary activities of the region. Before leaving the proximity of Hall, Flint and Company, a further word about the status of history and historical literature of the period seems in order.

Long before Lyman Copeland Draper, Reuben Gold Thwaites, Frederick Jackson Turner, Theodore Roosevelt, Milo M. Quaife, Clarence W. Alvord, and others of recent times rediscovered the history of the West, there was a group of regional historians whose interest and enthusiasm led to the first systematic study of the history of the region. Though lacking the means and training available to modern scholarship, the work of these writers was on the whole good; often it possessed charm and literary qualities which entitle it to wider acquaintance and appreciation than it has received.

The first historical literature of the Northwest was that produced by the French explorers and writers—Hennepin, Lahontan, Charlevoix, the Jesuit Fathers, and many others. With the English advance came the writings of Christopher Gist and George Croghan, of Major Robert Rogers, Jonathan Carver, and Alexander Henry. The French and Indian War had its chroniclers and journalists, as did the Revolution. The American settlements in the Ohio Valley were followed by the works of John Filson, Gilbert Imlay, and the first of the travel writers. The War of 1812 brought forth more journals, histories, memoirs, and controversial pamphlets, to be followed by a crop of gazetteers and a larger contingent of travel writers.[196]

A writer in the *Western Academician* in 1837 pointed out

---

[195] *Western Monthly Magazine, and Literary Journal,* I (1837), 214. This may have been the book published in 1851 as *Drayton, an American Tale.*

[196] Prominent among the histories of the "Late War" were those by Robert B. McAfee (Lexington, 1816), and Henry Marie Brackenridge (Baltimore, 1817). For an introduction to some of these writers, see William H. Venable, "Some Early Travelers and Annalists of the Ohio Valley," in *Ohio Archaeological and Historical Society Publications,* I (1887–88), 230–42.

that the individual enters upon his inquiries regarding history at an early stage in life; that in the process he would "find it expedient to trace back the course which has been delineated. . . . In this course *general histories* and *compendiums*, are the last in order."[197] Many Westerners, conscious of the two centuries of local history already behind them, agreed; the romance and adventure, the wars, the settlements, the development of governments, improvements and schools, were worth recording and study. And beyond this history lay the evidences of prehistoric life even more intriguing:

> Then turn thee to the past—
> Sublime, immortal, vast!
> Lone garner of the wrecks that evermore
> Forth from the windings of the shadowy shore
> Of present life are cast.[198]

At Vincennes in 1808 was organized the Vincennes Historical and Antiquarian Society; for many years it held regular meetings at which addresses were delivered.[199] About the time that Caleb Atwater published the prospectus for his "Notes on the State of Ohio,"[200] the *Ohio Monitor* printed a long editorial on the importance of collecting and saving data on the antiquities of Ohio, in which there was a growing interest.[201] Hall, Birkbeck, and others organized, somewhat prematurely perhaps, a state Antiquarian and Historical Society for Illinois in 1827; addresses and proceedings were published but the society soon lapsed. The next year Governor Lewis Cass and friends incorporated the Michigan Historical Society to procure and preserve the objects and information concerning the natural, civil, literary, ecclesiastical, and aboriginal history of the country.[202]

---

[197] "W. S." in the *Western Academician and Journal of Education and Science,* I (1837–38), 177.

[198] Otway Curry, "The Lore of the Past," delivered at Hanover College Union Literary Society, 1837.

[199] Usually published in the *Western Sun.*

[200] Chillicothe *Supporter,* February 10, 1819.

[201] November 9, 1822.

[202] *Detroit Daily Advertiser,* May 15, 1838. At a later meeting the society resolved to ask the legislature for aid in gathering information concerning the first settlers and settlements. *Ibid.,* March 3, 1837. In 1834 was published at Detroit *Historical and Scientific Sketches of Michigan.* Most of the papers contained therein had been delivered to the society. Cass, Schoolcraft, Henry Whiting, and John Biddle were the contributors. Schoolcraft dealt with the origin of the Indians, the others with early history and natural resources of the state.

Historics, too, we now may claim,
Which gathering up the scraps of fame,
In archives soon will pickle down,
A future treasure of renown.[203]

The Historical Society of Indiana was organized in 1830; among the active organizers were Jesse L. Holman, Jeremiah Sullivan, Isaac Blackford, James Whitcomb, David Wallace, and William Graham. It was incorporated the following year in the name of Benjamin Parke, John H. Farnham, Bethuel F. Morris, and James Blake. The Indiana society has had the longest continuous existence of any state historical society west of the mountains. The Historical and Philosophical Society of Ohio was started in 1831. At the meeting in 1832 Benjamin Tappan, in a presidential address, outlined plans for study of antiquities and early history, botany, and geology. In its first *Transactions* were papers by Dr. Samuel P. Hildreth, James H. Perkins, Jacob Burnet, and William Henry Harrison.[204]

The *Detroit Journal*, on receipt of the fifth number of Hall's *Western Monthly Magazine*, observed that the publication would become an important auxiliary to the study of literature and history: "Many a veteran pioneer of the West is still living on the very theatre of his early adventures; and the individual history of each would of itself be rich in materials which . . . would not fail to be highly amusing and instructive; and not a moment should be lost in rescuing such materials from the mouldering relics of time 'mid which they have been partially hidden, before they are lost to us forever."[205] And in 1836 when the *Milwaukee Advertiser* published a piece on Indian mounds, it said that the readers might smile over the idea of a state "just born," contemplating its antiquities.[206] Nevertheless, it spoke of a projected "Milwaukee Academy of Science and Literature," to preserve such facts as would illustrate the history of Wisconsin and promote the general diffusion of knowledge.[207]

One of the first local historians of importance was Caleb At-

---

[203] Whiting, *The Age of Steam.*
[204] Volume I of the *Transactions* was published in two parts in 1838 and 1839.
[205] May 7, 1833.
[206] *Milwaukee Advertiser*, November 24, 1836.
[207] *Ibid.*, September 8, 1836. The next issue mentioned the work done by James Hall in Illinois, and the work of the Michigan Historical Society.

water, of Ohio. Of Massachusetts birth, with an M. A. degree
from Williams College, he came to Circleville in 1815. In turn
teacher, minister, legislator, editor, and commissioner to treat
with the Indians, Atwater was ever the historian and antiquarian.[208] At the time of the announcement of his "Notes on the
State of Ohio" in 1819 Atwater was a member of the Lyceum
of Natural History of New York and of the American Antiquarian Society of Massachusetts. This work was not published
at the time. In 1826 he published an address on *The General
Character, Present and Future Prospects of the People of Ohio.*
After the negotiations at Prairie du Chien in 1829 and a trip to
Washington, Atwater published his *Remarks Made on a Tour
. . .* (Columbus, 1831). Here not only the Indians of the Upper
Mississippi were discussed thoroughly, but also the country and
the white inhabitants. In 1833 (Columbus) he published his
Writings, which contained *A Description of the Antiquities Discovered in the Western Country,* and the *Remarks.* The long-
planned *History of the State of Ohio,* the first history of any of
the states of the Northwest, was published at Cincinnati in
1838.[209] The author discussed the geography, economic geology,
and flora and fauna of the state, as well as its people and political
history. Narrative history from the coming of the French through
the War of 1812 was full; the author wrote from firsthand
knowledge on internal improvements and education.

Michigan achieved a state history almost as soon as statehood.
Charles H. Lanman in the *History of Michigan, Civil and Topographical* (New York, 1839), concentrated largely on political
history but gave some attention to settlements and pioneer life.

Illinois had in 1837 sought to get a state history written. The
specifications laid down by a committee of interested persons
called for a complete work, embracing all stages of progress—
political, military, commercial, literary, moral, and religious—
complete in its parts, methodical in arrangement, accurate and

[208] For Atwater and his work, see Clement L. Martzolff, "Caleb Atwater," in
Ohio Archaeological and Historical Society Publications, XIV (1905), 247–71, and
Henry C. Shetrone, "Caleb Atwater: Versatile Pioneer," in *ibid.,* XIV (1905),
79–88.
[209] Salmon P. Chase had published a forty-eight-page *Preliminary Sketch of the
History of Ohio* (Cincinnati, 1833) for his *Statutes of Ohio and of the Northwestern
Territory,* which was issued separately. Atwater's last important work, *An Essay on
Education,* was published in 1841.

discriminating in details, impartial and divested of all political, religious, and local prepossessions. A committee of correspondence was appointed to gather materials and to help the Reverend John M. Peck who was requested to undertake the job.[210] The work was not written; it was to be fifteen years before Illinois had a history.[211]

As interested in the Indians and "antiquities" as Atwater were Lewis Cass and Henry R. Schoolcraft, the latter for a number of years Indian agent and superintendent in the Upper Lakes region. Schoolcraft's works of travel and description were written largely from personal observations; they contained, however, long passages on the Indians of an earlier day.[212] His essay on the "Origin and Character of the North American Indians" was followed in 1839 by two volumes of *Algic Researches*, a collection of Indian folk tales, and a presentation of the author's ideas and theories regarding the Indians.[213] In 1844–45 his *Onéota, or The Red Race of America* was issued in eight numbers, and this work was revised and appeared (Buffalo, 1851) as *The American Indians. Their History, Conditions, and Prospects*. Schoolcraft's writings on Indians were finally gathered together in his most pretentious work, *Information respecting the History, Conditions, and Prospects of the Indian Tribes of the United States* (5 volumes. Philadelphia, 1853). Others interested in the Indian lore were John Delafield, Jr.,[214] and William Henry Harrison,[215] both members of the Historical and Philosophical Society of Ohio.

The Kentucky historians[216] had no monopoly on the subject of

[210] *Sangamo Journal*, April 29, 1837. See also series of articles copied from the Alton *Western Pioneer* (probably by Peck, the "senior editor"), in *ibid.*, February—April, 1838.

[211] John Reynolds, *Pioneer History of Illinois* (Belleville, 1852).

[212] *A View of the Lead Mines of Missouri* (New York, 1819); *Narrative Journal of Travels . . . to the Sources of the Mississippi River . . .* (Albany, 1821); *Travels in the Central Portion of the Mississippi Valley . . .* (New York, 1825); and *Narrative of an Expedition through the Upper Mississippi to Itaska Lake . . . in 1832* (New York, 1834).

[213] From which Longfellow got much of the material for Hiawatha.

[214] *An Inquiry into the Origin of the Antiquities of America* (New York, 1839).

[215] *A Discourse on the Aborigines of the Valley of the Ohio . . .* (Cincinnati, 1838).

[216] For example, Robert B. McAfee, *History of the Late War in the Western Country* (Lexington, 1816); Samuel L. Metcalf[e], *A Collection of Some of the Most Interesting Narratives of Indian Warfare in the West* (Lexington, 1821); John A. M'Clung, *Sketches of Western Adventure . . .* (Maysville, 1832); Humphrey Marshall, *History of Kentucky . . .* (Frankfort, 1812; 2 volumes. 1824); Mann Butler, *A History of the Commonwealth of Kentucky* (Louisville, 1834).

the Indian wars. The Black Hawk War resulted in the publication by J. B. Patterson, Rock Island printer, of the *Life of Black Hawk* (Cincinnati, 1833) ;[217] in John A. Wakefield's *History of the War* . . . (Jacksonville, 1834) ;[218] and in Benjamin Drake's *The Life and Adventures of Black Hawk* . . . (Cincinnati, 1838), which, though sympathetic in treatment of the Indian cause, proved to be a very popular work.

Biographical writing was confined largely to campaign biographies of candidates for public office. Moses Dawson of the *Cincinnati Advertiser* published his *A Historical Narrative of the civil and military services of Major-General William H. Harrison* . . . in 1824. Although a pro-Harrison publication, the work contained useful documentary material. James Hall's *A Memoir of the Public Services of William Henry Harrison* appeared in 1836. Both Dawson and Hall knew Harrison well and probably had his assistance on these biographies. Charles S. Todd and Benjamin Drake also did *Sketches of the Civil and Military Services of William Henry Harrison* in 1840, which brought the story of the General's life practically down to date. For the record rather than for an election campaign John McDonald wrote *Biographical Sketches of General Nathaniel Massie, General Duncan McArthur, Captain William Wells, and General Simon Kenton* . . . (Cincinnati, 1838).

Of the numerous gazetteers on the states of the Northwest, those by John Kilbourn on Ohio (originally published in 1816 but which went through many editions), and John M. Peck on Illinois (1834), were by residents. John T. Blois, author of the *Gazetteer of the State of Michigan* (1st ed. Detroit, 1838) had resided in the territory and state for several years. Although largely descriptive, these publications contained some history.

These men, together with Hall and Flint, were the more important of the historians of the Northwest prior to 1840. Jacob Burnet, Dr. Samuel P. Hildreth, James H. Perkins, and John B. Dillon, later to write books of some importance on the history of the region, were, during this period, writing only articles or

[217] See Chapter X, note 66 for comment.
[218] Wakefield served as a scout in 1813, studied medicine and law, and later settled in St. Paul, Minnesota. For full title of his work see Chapter X, note 60. A second edition appeared at Cincinnati in 1836, all but three hundred copies of which were lost by fire.

addresses. By midcentury their books were supplying a more connected history.[219] This group overlapped with writers such as Consul Butterfield, William H. English, B. A. Hinsdale, William H. Venable, and Lyman Copeland Draper who in turn maintained the continuity to Justin Winsor, Theodore Roosevelt, Frederick Jackson Turner, Reuben Gold Thwaites, Louise P. Kellogg, Clarence W. Alvord, Joseph Schafer, and the numerous living historians who have written on the history of the Old Northwest.

Though the Cincinnati group dominated the literary scene, there were other writers of significance. Mrs. Caroline M. Kirkland (pen name Mrs. Mary Clavers) who experienced the crudities of pioneer life in Michigan in the 1830's, wrote *A New Home—Who'll Follow? or Glimpses of Western Life* (New York, 1840). For a woman of delicate education and feelings she did well in this semifictional book of observations and descriptions. Though inclined to "cuteness" and a somewhat artificial and stilted style, Mrs. Kirkland had eyes to see, ears to hear, and a mind which functioned. The rival villagers of "Montacute" and "Tinkerville" are the principal characters of

[219] Burnet published his *Notes on the Early Settlement of the North-Western Territory* at Cincinnati in 1847; Hildreth, *Pioneer History . . . of the Ohio Valley, and Early Settlement of the Northwest Territory,* at Cincinnati in 1848; Perkins the *Annals of the West . . . from the Discovery of the Mississippi Valley to the year 1845,* at Cincinnati in 1846; Dillon, *The History of Indiana . . . to the Close of the Territorial Government in 1816 . . . ,* at Indianapolis in 1843. John W. Monette, though not a resident of the Northwest, should also be mentioned, for his *History of the Discovery and Settlement of the Valley of the Mississippi . . .* (New York, 1846), the most pretentious of all.

Of these writers, Perkins was the most interesting character. Disgusted with the requirements and standards of mercantile life he came to Cincinnati in 1832, where he became lawyer, writer, editor (of the *Chronicle*), minister, and minister to the poor. Broken in health and low in spirit he is supposed to have committed suicide in 1849. "James H. Perkins—A Sketch" (anonymous), in *Genius of the West,* V (1856), 14–16.

Dillon in the *Logansport Telegraph* in an advance notice of his work wrote: "The nature of the task demands much time and untiring research; and when completed, it will not form, of itself, a complete history, but it will furnish to the future historian, the materials upon which he may work, and without which (or a similar collection) all his efforts and his talents will be spent in vain. . . . If our history is to be regarded with feelings of interest, by those who are to come after us, shall we not value the history of those who have gone before us? The manners and customs, and the toils and dangers that marked the character, and attended the pursuits of the pioneers of Indiana, are passing away, if they have not already vanished, and those who now wish to share in the excitement and danger of a frontier life, must travel far towards the setting sun. . . .

"Many interesting facts, connected with the early settlement of Indiana, have been perverted, or lost forever, because they were never recorded, and the stream of tradition seldom bears to the present, faithfully, the history of the past."

the tale, but Mrs. Campaspe Nippers, "the village information bureau," is a character limited to no locality or time. The description of life, manners, and frontier characteristics are realistic and valid, the understanding sympathetic, and the observations sound. The author's success led to a follow up, *Western Clearings* (1845), a collection of sketches on aspects of frontier life.

Baynard Rush Hall, first instructor in the Indiana Seminary and Indiana College, though publishing after Mrs. Kirkland, dealt with the southern Indiana folk of a decade earlier. In 1843 under the pen name of "Robert Carlton" he presented *The New Purchase, or Seven and a Half Years in the West*, a unique study of pioneer life in and around a college town.[220] Hall has been criticized for his condescending and supercilious attitude and, at times, biting pen, but considering that this Easterner with a classical-theological education was dumped into the middle of the backwoods to teach Latin and Greek, that he found himself more or less accidentally embroiled in an academic-theological embroglio, it is rather to be wondered at that his treatment of persons and life was as sympathetic as it was. It is not necessary to read between the lines to detect that Hall came to like the surroundings and people more than he, himself, may have realized; at any rate he delivered himself of a "right smart" amount of firsthand material. His book, along with Mrs. Kirkland's, would be on any list of a half dozen necessary for a picture of the life of the period.

Of an entirely different type from the fiction of Hall and Flint was the work of William Joseph Snelling, who at Boston in 1830 published anonymously *Tales of the Northwest*, "one of the earliest calls for realism ever made in America."[221] Between 1820 and 1828 young Snelling made his headquarters at Fort Snelling at the mouth of the Minnesota River where his father was commandant. He spent much time with the Indians, both on the plains and in the Wisconsin country. Feeling that neither the romanticists nor the agent-and-travel observers such as School-craft had truly handled the task, Snelling sought to portray in fiction the traditions, character, and psychology of the Indian.

[220] See Chapter XIII, note 198.
[221] Fred Lewis Pattee, *The Development of the American Short Story* (New York, 1923), 64. Snelling's *Tales of the Northwest*, with an introduction by John T. Flanagan, was reprinted at Minneapolis, 1936.

At his best he might be compared to Cooper as a narrative writer; on the other hand he was guilty of moralizing, artificial dialogue, and tediousness, some of the weaknesses he deprecated in others. Nevertheless, writing at a time when the American short story was in its embryonic stage, Snelling's work, though hardly known at the time, left us an antidote for the writings of both the romanticists and Indian haters.

The earliest poets of the Northwest—not counting Indians— were the *voyageurs*, whose chants and doggerel helped pass the time spent en route; most of them remained nameless. Arent Schuyler de Peyster, British officer at Mackinac and Detroit at the time of the War for Independence, though best known for his letters, also rendered rhymes in meter, some of which he later published. Keelboatmen and other men of the western waters also had their songs, a few of which were preserved by Morgan Neville, James Hall, and other contemporary editors. Frontier bards added to the ballads inherited from Scotland and England their own contributions in celebration of epochal events and heroes of the West; inspired improvisers converted the airs of old ballads into stirring revival hymns,[222] and during election years, particularly 1840, rhymesters and doggerel scribblers cut loose on all sides. Village poetasters and sweet singers contributed their masterpieces to the newspapers and literary journals for purposes of local prestige or to help out the printer, while now and then an unsung Homer started an epic which fortunately perished long before completed.[223]

[222] For a partial list of these songsters, see Rusk, *Literature of Middle Western Frontier,* I, 312 ff. *The Colombian Harmonist* (Cincinnati, 1816), was compiled by Timothy Flint.

[223] None comparable, however, to Richard Emmons, of Kentucky, who finally delivered himself of a 1,200-page, four-volume epic, *The Fredoniad,* in 1827. Timothy Flint called this "the most monstrous collection of maudlin, silly and incongruous verses, that ever were, or, we hope, ever will be put together." *Western Monthly Review,* II (1828–29), 181.
Representative of the original newspaper poetry, of which hundreds of columns were printed annually, were the twelve stanzas on "The Western Wilds" *a la* Mrs. Sigourney, published in the *Sangamo Journal,* March 22, 1832. Stanzas 1, 4, 6, 7, and 12 follow:

> "Who says our Western wilds are sad?
>   Who sings so faint a lay?
> What scene can make that spirit glad,
>   Which here cannot be gay?
>
> "How fresh, careering o'er the wild,
>   Our western breezes play!
> The heavy heart of care's beguil'd,
>   And leaping, hails the day!

The poetic output of the period was extensive; the number of poets of importance was small. Obviously lacking in technical skill, and generally classified as "imitative and conventional," none of these poets, judged on any large portion of his work, would deserve first-class rank; still a surprising number, perhaps in a poem or two, and particularly when writing on western subjects, hit melodious notes of simplicity and sincerity, which, if not art, is something just as good. Discovery of these gems is ample reward for perusal of much that is mediocre and trivial.

Of the Cincinnati group there were Gallagher's friends, Otway Curry and Thomas H. Shreve. Curry, "a child of the wilderness," was carpenter, journalist, editor, lawyer, state legislator, and something of a recluse. "The Lore of the Past" was published separately at Cincinnati in 1838, but most of his poems appeared in the newspapers and literary journals. Shreve, though of a mathematical and legal turn, gave most of his life to journalism. He was essentially an essayist but was known in his day also as a poet. In "Reflections of an Aged Pioneer" he caught something of the nostalgia of the old settler for the woods and waters before they were defiled by art and progress. Charles A. Jones, also of Cincinnati, was not so well known. In 1835 he published a little volume at Cincinnati, *The Out-Law and Other Poems*, which was highly praised locally.[224] Jones loved the Cincinnati area and the Ohio; he wrote hastily and for fun. After contributing frequently to the *Mirror* and other publications for several years he gave his attention to law.

Frederick W. Thomas, who was associated one time or another with the *Commercial Advertiser*, the *Democratic Intelligencer*, and the *Daily Evening Post*, dedicated *The Emigrant*,

---

"The deer is seen at peep of morn:
    The wolf at close of day;
And merry sounds the hunter's horn,
    When he brings home his prey.

"And see! our rugged prairie men;
    O, who more free than they;—
They're tall, they're stout—they ne'er give out;
    Who dares them to the fray?

"But free as the wild winds that sweep
    Along our boundless plains,
Are we, and still the boon we'll keep,
    While earth—while heav'n remains."

[224] By Josiah Drake, in *Western Monthly Magazine*, IV (1835), 273-75.

or Reflections while Descending the Ohio, to Charles Hammond
in 1833:

> Those western pioneers an impulse feel
> Which their less hardy sons scarce comprehend;
>
> . . . .
>
> There is a welcome in this western land
> Like the old welcomes which were said to give
> The friendly heart where'er they gave the hand;
> Within this soil the social virtues live,
> Like its own forest trees, unprun'd and free—

Thomas was better known for his novels.

Verses appeared from unexpected places. Editors, lawyers, merchants, ministers, politicians, explorers, generals, even farmers tried their hands—and made not only the newspapers but the anthologies. Charles Hammond, Salmon P. Chase, John B. Dillon, Thomas Peirce, and John H. Bryant, farmer brother of William Cullen Bryant, appear in the leading collections of western poetry, along with Hall, Gallagher, Micah P. Flint, and James H. Perkins.[225] Schoolcraft published at least two poems in independent form;[226] Henry Whiting, army officer at Detroit, published *The Emigrant* in 1819;[227] Joseph S. Welsh, of Indiana, propagated morality and patriotism in the *Harp of the West*.[228]

A few poets were what might be called "one-poem" poets. William O. Butler, though he spent most of his life in Kentucky, fought in the Harrison campaigns of 1812–13. From that experience and from his feeling for the Ohio River he got his chief

[225] Coggeshall, *Poets and Poetry of the West*. John H. Bryant, a squatter in Bureau County, Illinois in 1831, later became a successful farmer, legislator, and businessman.

[226] *Transallegania, or the Groans of Missouri* (New York 1821), and *The Rise of the West, or a Prospect of the Mississippi Valley* (Detroit, 1830). In this thirty-six-page work was included a poem by Henry Whiting.

[227] Also *Ontwa, the Son of the Forest* (136 pp. New York, 1822), *The Age of Steam* (Detroit, 1830), *Sanillac, a Poem* (155 pp. Boston, 1831). *The Emigrant,* which has been quoted in various places in this history, was a description of the year-round work and pleasures of the pioneer farmer. Whiting, born in Massachusetts in 1788, entered the army as a cornet in 1808 and served until his death in 1851, by which time he had achieved the rank of brevet brigadier general. From 1816 to 1845 Detroit was his home. He was a man of intellect and a poet of some ability. A number of his contributions appeared in the *North American Review.* For sketch of Whiting see William L. Jenks, "Henry Whiting," in *Michigan History Magazine,* XVI (1932), 174–82. An obituary notice is in the *Detroit Daily Advertiser,* September 19, 1851.

[228] A volume of more than two hundred pages published at Cincinnati in 1839.

poetic inspiration. A major general in the Mexican War and candidate for the vice-presidency in 1848, Butler is probably best known for his poem "The Boatman's Horn."[229] Likewise John Finley, editor of the *Richmond Palladium*, whose "Hoosier's Nest" was probably the most widely quoted western poem of the period. More indicative of his tolerant assurance however were the lines of "To Indiana":

> Blest Indiana! in thy soil
> Are found the sure rewards of toil,
> Where harvest, purity and worth
> May make a paradise on earth.
> With feelings proud we contemplate
> The rising glory of our State;
> Nor take offense by application
> Of its good-natured appelation.
> Our hardy yeomanry can smile
> At tourists of "the sea-girt Isle,"
> Or wits who traveled at the gallop,
> Like Basil Hall, or Mrs. Trollope.
> 'Tis true among the crowds that roam,
> To seek for fortune or a home,
> It happens that we often find
> Empiricism of every kind.
>
> A strutting fop, who boasts of knowledge,
> Acquired at some far eastern college,
> Expects to take us by surprise,
> And dazzle our astonished eyes.
> He boasts of learning, skill and talents,
> Which in the scale, would Andes balance,
> Cuts widening swaths from day to day,
> And in a month he runs away.

Of the female poets, one of the earliest was a Mrs. Lard, of somewhere in Indiana, who in a twelve-page poem, *The Banks of the Ohio* (1823), attempted a retrospect of the history of the Ohio Valley from earliest times. Mrs. Julia L. Dumont, of Vevay, contributed numerous virtuous verses to the *Literary Gazette*, the *Mirror*, and other publications. Mrs. Amelia B. Welby, protégé of George B. Prentice in Louisville, began publishing innocent and graceful verse in the late 1830's; Poe rated her high among our "poetesses." Though a resident of Louisville, she

[229] See *ante*, I, 441, for the poem.

was closely associated with the Cincinnati group. Her larger success came in the 1840's. So with Alice Carey, whose first verses were published by the Cincinnati papers in 1838; encouraged by Otway Curry, later by Poe and Rufus W. Griswold, she went on to even greater national fame.

Not all the amateur poetry was confined to sweetness and light, sentimental drivel, or eulogizing the West in "abortive epics" or imitative heroic couplets. There was a streak of satire which outcropped intermittently in unsigned verses as well as in the writings of Thomas Peirce of Cincinnati. Peirce interrupted a career as hardware merchant to take a medical degree, but returned to business. His *Odes of Horace in Cincinnati* were first published in the *Western Spy and Literary Cadet* in 1821–22, then as a collected volume in 1822.[230] Unlike those of his contemporary, Thomas Johnson of Kentucky,[231] Peirce's barbs were not fabricated for shock power, but flung forth for fun; if slight irritation resulted, that would be part of the fun. The Byron influence is indicated. In the thirty-one odes Peirce poked fun at politicians, poets, hotel characters, pedants, and dandies. The verses "Billy Moody," published in the *National Republican and Ohio Political Register* in 1823, dealt with the life of a Yankee schoolteacher in the West. His third work, *The Muse of Hesperia, a Poetic Reverie* (1823), revealed the themes of western history which should be given attention by the poets.

William Ross Wallace, who was educated at Indiana College and Hanover, published *The Battle of Tippecanoe, Triumphs of Science, And Other Poems* at Cincinnati in 1837 when he was seventeen. "Daniel Boone" and "An American Mound" were also on western subjects. Both Poe and Bryant were later enthusiastic in praise of his work; in his day he was regarded by some critics as the leading western poet. He spent most of his life in Kentucky.

The argumentative and controversial literature, largely political and religious, has been sampled elsewhere; in total amount it exceeded all other. In it, as much as in tale and poetry, the spirit

---

[230] This volume is scarce. There are a few extracts in Coggeshall, *Poets and Poetry of the West*.

[231] *The Kentucky Miscellany* was advertised for sale in Lexington and Danville in 1789. Rusk, *Literature of the Middle Western Frontier*, I, 319 ff. A fourth edition was published in Lexington in 1821.

of the West expressed itself, but as a writer in the *Western Monthly Magazine* said, it was in a way an impediment to literature. Such writing kept the mind in an unhealthy state either of excitement or depression, and developed cunning and hypocrisy rather than the calm serenity necessary to the best work of the poet, historian, and philosopher.[232]

Westerners were proud of their accomplishments in the literary field no less than on the field of battle, nor were they unappreciative of outside approbation. In 1833 when New York's leading newspaper, the *Courier and Enquirer*,[233] printed an encomium on western literature, newspapers were glad to note that the East was learning that the West was something more than a "valley of the shadow of darkness and moral death [filled with] heathens, bears, and buffaloes."[234] The *Courier and Enquirer* called the prospects of the Great Valley the most gratifying ever opened to the contemplation of man; the fruits of mind were keeping pace with material advancement; "and before we can say such a thing is wanting in that wonderful region, it is already there." It continued:

Literature too begins to spring up among the trees not yet decayed, and displays an originality and strength corresponding with the richness of the soil whence it derived its nourishment. Removed, in a very considerable degree beyond the influence of fashion and the incitements of imitation, it exhibits traces of a distinctive character that give it a fresh and wholesome individuality, extremely agreeable to our taste. We confess we are heartily tired of the endless imitations of Scott, Byron, and Moore, and the rest of them, and stand ready to welcome something new, even though it should smack a little of the "Horse," contain a touch of the "Alligator," and betray a small sprinkling of the "Steamboat." Any thing is better than eternal sing-song imitation.

We like the writings of James Hall, of Mrs. Dumont, and above all of Timothy Flint. . . . There is a wholesome vigour and purity about these writers, far different, and let us say far superior, to the false, exaggerated, and sickly productions of a worn out school, which exhibits little else than extravagant adventure, destitute of probability, and extravagant sentiment scorning all the restraints of morals and religion, and rushing headlong in violation of the law of God and man, under the mask of exquisite sensibility. . . . We see nothing of this in our honest homebred writers, except

[232] H. J. G., "American Literature—Its Impediments," in *Western Monthly Magazine*, III (1835), 21–29.
[233] Edited by the picturesque, bombastic, and duel-fighting Col. James Watson Webb.
[234] Elyria *Ohio Atlas* copied in *Cleveland Herald*, May 8, 1833.

where they are seduced into it by a bad habit of imitation. What they give us is wholesome food at least, though it may not be served upon plate.[235]

And the *Edinburgh Review*, basing its comments on Mrs. Trollope's report which certainly did not give too good a character to the West, became worried lest the people who were busy displacing the forests and doing "battle with the rattle snake," become overcivilized. Surprised at the intellectual advantages of Cincinnati ("Our astonishment has been speechless. . . ."), it asked what town in England, Scotland, or even Ireland could turn up its nose at this frontier outpost. "The manners can in general only be coarse. The men can have little or no leisure. But what must be the spirit of the place!"[236] Even Cleveland admitted that Cincinnati was becoming the "Athens of the West."[237]

Next to Cincinnati, Detroit stood second in the Northwest as a cultural-literary center between 1815 and 1840. Considering that most of these years were spent in territorial status, its record was all the more remarkable. The intellectual group which included Cass, Schoolcraft, Father Gabriel Richard, the Reverend John Monteith, Henry Whiting, Charles C. Trowbridge, William Woodbridge, Douglass Houghton, and others, has received less notice than deserved. Detroit was not a publishing center comparable to Cincinnati; it lacked literary periodicals to attract and advertise its writers and scholars.

At any rate, the West was trying to leaven its crudeness with products of the pen as well as the forest. For as Flint had said: "The ornament, the grace, the humanity and even the lesser morals of society . . . essentially depend upon the cultivation of literature. A community without it is like a rude family without politeness, amenity and gentleness."[238]

§ § §

Excepting newspapers, western writings comprised but a small portion of the reading of the people. Though proud and sec-

---

[235] Elyria *Ohio Atlas* copied in *Cleveland Herald,* May 8, 1833.

[236] "The Americans and Their Detractors," in *Edinburgh Review*, LV, 482–83 (July, 1832).

[237] *Cleveland Herald and Gazette* of August 25, quoted in *Cincinnati Daily Gazette,* September 1, 1837.

[238] *Western Monthly Review*, I (1827–28), 9.

tional-minded on matters of soil, history, and trade, this attitude did not hold with reference to literature; otherwise western writers and magazines would have had less cause for complaint.

There were relatively few books among the early settlers. The first white settlers, the French, were simple folk, largely illiterate; the first American settlers were squatters, ex-soldiers, half-farmer half-hunter types from Virginia and the Middle States who had neither the time nor inclination for reading.[239] True, some of the Western Reserve settlers brought books with them; so did William Henry Harrison and a number of the "pioneer aristocracy" from the South. And in Detroit John Askwith (in the 1790's), the merchant John Askin, various British army officers, and many of the priests had collections of books. The first nonprivate library in the Territory was the Putnam Family Library or Belpre Library, a joint stock enterprise organized in the Marietta neighborhood in 1796, which operated for some twenty years. Locke's *Essays*, Samuel Johnson's *Poets*, Gibbon's *Decline and Fall*, Hume's *History of England, The Practical Farmer*, and other titles were available, perhaps as many as a hundred or more. A subscription library ($10 per share) was started at Cincinnati in 1802 with $340. The "Coonskin Library" in Athens County was started in 1803 with a $73.50 investment in books.[240] Goldsmith, Josephus, Smith's *Wealth of Nations, Don Quixote, Scottish Chiefs, Plutarch's Lives, Arabian Nights*, and Morse's *Geography* were among its holdings.

Daniel Drake and friends had planned a subscription library in 1808 or earlier, but not until 1814 was the Circulating Library of Cincinnati opened with three hundred volumes.[241] Several hundred volumes were purchased, some from Miami University, in 1815; soon the holdings totaled 1,400 items. The library was well supplied with books in law, history, and theology; modern classics and fiction were also represented. The library was open Saturday afternoons. Among the directors in 1816 were Daniel

[239] Venable and other writers have forgotten this fact. "The first settlers of the North-western Territory, coming chiefly from the most cultured New England stock, considered books a necessary part of their household goods." *Beginnings of Literary Culture*, 135.

[240] Initial funds were the proceeds from the sale of furs.

[241] The *Liberty Hall*, August 21, 1815, said "not yet 1000 volumes" and gave the opening date as September, 1814. Many subscribers were delinquent in paying up. The 1816 catalogue gave the opening as April 14, 1814. For a list of library catalogues see Rusk, *Literature of Middle Western Frontier*, II, 85–88.

Drake and Thomas Peirce. The Young Men's Mercantile Library was organized in 1835; from some fifty members and seven hundred volumes it grew to several hundred members and 1,400 volumes by 1840. The Apprentice's Library was even larger.

Dayton citizens secured the incorporation of a public library in 1805. Books were to be drawn by lot; "proprietors" were to be fined three cents for each tallow drip or turned-down page suffered by books while in their hands. The library was never large; it was sold at auction in 1835. The Delaware Public Library Company sold shares at $1.00 and accepted gifts of books in 1825.[242] There were about 160 such libraries incorporated in Ohio by the end of 1840. Some never went into operation, most of them were small.

The Vincennes Library was founded in 1806 and incorporated that same year by the legislature of Indiana Territory; from donations and contributions it soon acquired between three and four thousand volumes, which made it one of the largest libraries north of the Ohio. The Detroit Library was incorporated in 1818, although it had organized and received books the preceding year.[243] The investment of ninety shares at $5.00 each was entrusted to the Reverend John Monteith. A new constitution was made as well as an appeal for new funds in 1830.[244] The Indianapolis Town Library was being reorganized in 1835. The *Indiana Journal* thought it a good thing because the reading of useful books helped prevent crime and vice; "a reading and industrious community is very apt to be a moral and religious community."[245] The Galena, Illinois, Library Association collected about $300 and sent East for books in 1836.[246] Practically every town of 1,000 to 1,500 population either had or had tried to have a subscription library by 1840. The colleges and academies collected libraries of varying sizes,[247] while at the state capitals were collections of books for use of legislators and judges. Wisconsin Territory, for instance, in 1837 spent the $5,000 Con-

---

[242] *Delaware Patron*, October 27, 1825.
[243] *Detroit Gazette*, July 25, 1817.
[244] *North-Western Journal*, March 3, 1830.
[245] April 24, May 15, 1835.
[246] *Northwestern Gazette and Galena Advertiser*, March 5, 1836.
[247] See Chapter XIII, 411–12.

gressional appropriation for a library of eight hundred law books and four hundred standard books in history, philosophy, English essays, and the like.[248] Michigan's first constitution provided that court fines go to the support of libraries.

Bookstores were to be found in most towns. Putnam and Clark advertised about three hundred titles at Zanesville in 1815.[249] Among them were Bolingbroke's works, *Don Quixote,* travels, books on chemistry, geography, and religion. Byron, Goldsmith, Cervantes, Cowper, and other authors were on sale in Detroit in 1817. Cleveland booksellers listed some scores of titles in the 1820's; in addition to English authors were histories, grammars, and "grammars" of chemistry. Thomas Johnson's shop in Columbus carried a long list of theological books; also travels, Scott's novels, Gibbon, Josephus, Plutarch, Tacitus, Milton, Cowper, and others.[250] P. C. Canedy and Company, of Springfield, Illinois, in 1832 advertised Watson's *Theological Institutes, Faber on Infidelity,* Dick's *Philosophy of a Future State, The Holy Land, Memoirs of the Empress Josephine, The Court and Camp of Bonaparte,* Day's *Consolations,* Bigland's *History of Birds, Fishes, etc.*[251] Cincinnati and Louisville dealers advertised widely in the papers of Ohio, Indiana, and Illinois. The Western Education Book Store of Louisville, for instance, offered school, classical, law, medical, theological, and miscellaneous books; also mathematical instruments, maps, globes, astronomical and chemical-physical apparatus, and geological specimens.[252]

For those interested in short cuts to the literary heritage there were "libraries" of select literature—the "digests" and "omnibuses" of a century later. An advertisement for Woodworth's *Literary Casket and Ladies and Gentleman's Pocket Magazine* of New York promised sections on American biography, original essays, reviews, original moral tales, desultory selections, drama, a forum, female character, and "acedemical register."[253] Woodworth also published the *Authors Literary Index and the Poet's Prompter. Carey's Library of Choice Literature* (Philadelphia, 1835–36) appeared weekly at $5.00 the year. *Waldie's Select*

[248] Burlington *Wisconsin Territorial Gazette,* July 10, 1837.
[249] *Zanesville Express,* October 19, 1815.
[250] *Columbus Gazette,* March 3, 1825.
[251] Springfield *Sangamo Journal,* June 28, 1832.
[252] *Vandalia Whig and Illinois Intelligencer,* October 23, 1834.
[253] *Edwardsville Spectator,* May 1, 1821.

Circulating Library (Philadelphia, 1832–42) was another publication of the same sort.[254] David Christy, of Cadiz, Ohio, started the sixteen-page quarto semimonthly *Historical Family Library* in 1835. The idea was to reprint valuable histories, starting with Hallam's *Middle Ages*.[255] From Boston came the *Euterpeiad: or, Musical Intelligencer* (1820–23), containing musical information and belles-lettres. The *Museum of Foreign Literature, Science, and Art* was also advertised in the newspapers.[256]

Farm manuals, almanacs, home-remedy books,[257] home legal advisers, and "letter-writers" were sold at bookstores, by mail, and by agent. One of the "self-educators" guaranteed "a choice selection of the most elegant, significant, and approved forms of commending, dispraising, protesting, conjuring or beseeching, expressing gratitude, benediction, malediction, blessing times and days, cursing ditto, breaking off a subject, introducing of similitudes, invoking muses, concluding letters &c, &c."[258]

This was the period in which the vogue of English and eastern writers was flourishing. American publishers were putting out the books of English authors at less cost than those of American authors. Mrs. Hemans, Thomas Moore, Byron, Scott, Burns, Cowper, and many lesser lights were known almost as well in the West as at home.[259] The work of the older writers—Chaucer, Shakespeare, Jonson—were commonly available in various editions. *The Edinburgh Review* and *The Quarterly Review* (current numbers of which were reissued from American presses) were among the magazine accessions of leading libraries; college professors, ministers, and other professional men were subscribers. Foster's reprint of *Blackwood's* was for sale in western bookstores.

No eastern writer occupied a position in the West in any way comparable to that of Scott or Byron. Cooper, Irving, and Bryant were known and read; Holmes, Whittier, Longfellow were becoming known. Poe and Emerson were practically unknown.[260]

[254] Advertisements in *Illinois Advocate* and elsewhere, 1835.
[255] *Cincinnati Daily Gazette*, January 13, 1836.
[256] *Brookville Enquirer*, etc., 1825 *passim*.
[257] See Chapter V.
[258] *Edwardsville Spectator*, December 5, 1820.
[259] *Ivanhoe, The Lady of the Lake*, etc., were reported in Michigan backwoods homes in the early 1840's. *Michigan Pioneer and Historical Collections*, XXXI (1901), 222.
[260] Rusk, *Literature of the Middle Western Frontier*, II, 31–32.

Eastern periodicals of the more substantial type were received by a few families in most western towns, although their circulation was small in comparison to that of the religious periodicals. By the 1830's weekly editions of New. York, Philadelphia, and Washington papers were received by thousands of western subscribers and were available in the local newspaper offices, larger hotels, and public reading rooms.[261] Toward the end of the period the *Saturday Evening Post* and *Godey's Lady's Book* were probably the most popular of the magazines.[262]

Personal libraries of significance were not numerous, though here and there, even in the small towns, were exceptional individuals with libraries of several hundred volumes; a few—lawyers, editors, or historians perhaps—had libraries comparable to the better college libraries. But books were to be found in unexpected places. The traveler in southwestern Wisconsin Territory in 1838 found them in town dwellings, neat farmhouses, in log cabins. "I have *always* found books and newspapers—of books many standard and historical works, together with the new novels—of newspapers, those of New York, Baltimore, Washington, and Philadelphia were common, and generally the State papers of the *former home* of the Wisconsin emigrant."[263]

Books were made as well as read in the West. By the 1820's Cincinnati had taken the lead as publishing center from Lexington, but book publishing was by no means confined to the Queen City. Wherever there was a printing press there was a potential or actual publishing office. The bulk of the books made by local presses were legislative journals, laws, household-remedy books, political and religious tracts, almanacs, proceedings of religious and fraternal organizations, and the like, but perusal of early imprints inventories reveals occasional publication of literary works at obscure and unusual places. At Salem, Indiana, in 1818,

---

[261] The reading room conducted by Kingsbury and Burnham in Detroit offered current periodicals and pleasant surroundings in 1837, presumably for a small fee. *Detroit Daily Advertiser*, January 16, 1837.

[262] Godey's announcements in western newspapers in 1837 of the coming of Mrs. Sarah Josepha Hale to his *Lady's Book* usually were about three fourths of a column in length.

[263] W. R. Smith, *Observations on the Wisconsin Territory*, 99–100.

Gideon W. Hart, a Franklin County (Ohio) farmer and miller, had in 1825, 142 books in his library which he valued at $514.75. Although a number of them were medical items, there were philosophies, histories, chemistries, military manuals, and a "cyclopedia." He kept a record of lendings. List furnished the author by Professor Robert Irrmann, of Beloit College.

for instance, was published *The Life of Bonaparte, Late Emperor of the French* . . . , "By a citizen of the United States," while at New Harmony were printed Thomas Say's *American Conchology* and Michaux's *Sylva* with their many color plates. These interesting frontier print jobs were hand-stitched and often bound in sheep or calf by local craftsmen, creditable jobs even by modern standards.

Town forums, lyceums, and literary societies furnished outlets for papers and oratorical offerings, some of which made the magazines. The young men of Vincennes had a "Thespian Society" as early as 1806. Chemical societies which had quite a vogue in the 1820's indicated the rising interest in science. By 1840 practically every town had or had had a "lyceum." Piqua, Ohio, in 1837 was claiming that almost every village half its size had a lyceum to beguile the winter evenings and disseminate knowledge of chemistry, natural history, astronomy, and philosophy.[264] When Douglass Houghton announced a series of twenty-six lectures on chemistry at Detroit in 1830 ($2.00 for the series, $4.00 for a family of three), the *North-Western Journal* offered a prize of $25 in books to the apprentice who would submit the best summary in writing.[265] In these clubs and societies aspiring young people learned the rudiments of parliamentary law, rules of debate, got acquainted with periodicals and books, and, though never in sight of a college, were privileged to deliver the equivalent of a commencement oration ever so often. Here the editors and orators could really get pointers on the art of grandiloquence. For instance, Thomas Lippincott, addressing the Edwardsville Forum in 1821, delivered himself in part as follows:

At the bar, I see some of our associates who already fill conspicuous places there, or who hope, ere long, to fill them, contending perhaps against the proud aggressor on the poor man's rights—or defending the character of the innocent from the rude, assassin-like assault of defamation; or, it may be, pleading the cause of the widow and the fatherless. O who would grudge the toil of years, if necessary, to give efficacy here! Methinks I hear the lucid argument, demonstrating the truth; the impassioned tone, denoting noble earnestness and zeal, and all the artillery of eloquence brought to bear, for the protection of the distressed. And when the orator has finished his

[264] Piqua *Courier and Enquirer,* July 22, 1837.
[265] November 3, 17, 1830.

harangue, and gained his cause, and the astonished hearers wondering where such eloquence could be acquired, how would we exult, could we answer—in the Forum! . . .

But hark! Methinks I hear a WHITEFIELD or a CHALMERS—ascended from the forum to the sacred desk—urging on the fallen human race, the wisdom and the necessity of seeking restoration to the favor of an offended Deity. . . .

Led by the word of truth, he pierces the abodes of bliss. The music of the spheres seems to accompany him with symphonious harmony, when the song of angels, and alleluias of ransomed mortals, dwell on his descriptive tongue! But Oh! what glory breaks on the raptured hearers, when the Son of God is drawn by the vivid orator, seated on his refulgent throne, and smiling with love ineffable, on the happy spirits whom he has redeemed! . . .

Hail to the school where such powers may be acquired! Happy the hour when, led by a laudable desire to enjoy an intellectual feast, this little band associated! Again I say, all hail!

And when the tongues that now feebly attempt to wield the weapons of argument, are silent in the dust—and when the pens that will now bring from the resources of mental wealth, and from the stores of learning, the varied sweets, of science, of philosophy, and of poetry, to instruct and to delight us, shall have mouldered with the hands that guide them, may our sons, and our sons' sons still cherish, and still draw instruction, virtue, and delight, from THE EDWARDSVILLE FORUM![266]

At the lyceums and public lectures the amateur could compare his speeches and papers with those of the professionals, with Robert Owen, Emerson, Alexander Campbell, Henry Clay, and many others of national fame.

Oratory had a wider appeal than the theater. Public assemblies, whether stump speakings, Fourth of July celebrations, camp meetings, or court trials brought forth the stentorian voice, flowery periodic sentences, and classical allusions. Elocution teachers set up "new branches of education" in towns and competed with the dancing masters. Public speeches were talked over and analyzed in post-mortem examinations as were the sermons of Puritan ministers in an earlier day. Unfortunately many of the noblest efforts were extemporaneous and unrecorded; like the speeches of William Pitt, they can only be judged by the awe which they inspired.

Certainly not to be overlooked as an educational factor was the influence of bench and bar; it was probably second in importance only to that of the newspaper. Law, oratory, politics, and

---

[266] *Edwardsville Spectator*, December 4, 1821.

knowledge were somehow associated in the popular mind. True, there were no legal requirements for admission to the bar, and court was not always conducted by the rules sanctioned by the House of Lords or the Supreme Court; but the profession attracted many men of outstanding ability. Though many lawyers covered their ignorance of the law with verbiage and judges substituted common sense for "basic principles," it is probable that they arrived at fewer ludicrous decisions than their learned successors of a later century. It was no accident that men such as Thomas Corwin, Thomas Ewing, John McLean, Joshua Giddings, Benjamin F. Wade, Salmon P. Chase, James B. Ray, O. H. Smith, Richard W. Thompson, Henry S. Lane, Tilghman Howard, Edward A. Hannegan, Stephen A. Douglas, Abraham Lincoln, and many others, were orators as well as lawyers. On the other hand, a number of the profounder students of the law have been largely lost to history because they held no conspicuous public office; what is more remarkable, some of the most eloquent trial lawyers and orators have also been lost to fame. People enjoyed the joust of wits in court; they liked to see the wheels of the law go round. Court days brought in the people; the arguments were rehashed, criticized, and mulled over by the hitching rack.

Every man is a politician, and becomes, to some extent, acquainted with public affairs. In some of the other states, few persons go into a court of law, unless they have business. It is not so here. Court week is a general holiday. Not only suitors, jurors, and witnesses, but all who can spare the time, brush up their coats, and brush down their horses and go to court. A stranger is struck with the silence, the eagerness, and deep attention, with which these rough sons of the forest listen to the arguments of the lawyers, evincing a lively interest in these proceedings, and thorough understanding of the questions discussed. Besides those alluded to, there are a variety of other public meetings. Every thing is done in this country in popular assemblies, all questions are debated in popular speeches, and decided by popular vote. These facts speak for themselves. Not only must a vast deal of information be disseminated throughout a society thus organized, but the taste for popular assemblies and public harangues, which forms so striking a trait in the western character, is, in itself, a conclusive proof of a high degree of intelligence. Ignorant people would neither relish nor understand the oratory, which our people receive with enthusiastic applause. Ignorant people would not attend such meetings, week after week, and day after day, with unabated interest; nor could they thus go, and *remain* ignorant.[267]

[267] James Hall, "On Western Character," in *Western Monthly Magazine*, I (1833), 52–53.

The satiric poet, Thomas Peirce, saw the lighter side of the fierce forensic battles:

> With person of gigantic size,
> With thund'ring voice, and piercing eyes,
> When great *Stentorius* deigns to rise,
>   Adjacent crowds assemble,
> To hear a sage the laws expound,
> In language strong, by reasoning sound.
> Till, though yet not guilty found
>   The culprits fear and tremble.[268]

Judges and lawyers on circuit carried their libraries in their saddlebags, plenty of anecdotes and jokes in their heads. Jogging along in the mud they practiced stump speeches on each other, held moot courts, imitated preachers, and at least once rested their horses while they tried a 'possum for trespass on a public highway. Lawyers in general had a reputation of being heavy drinkers, but since this was true of other vocational groups also, the charge may be dismissed.

Amateur theatricals were performed in Cincinnati in 1801–2 and again a few years later. The Vincennes "Thespian Association" staged performances as early as 1814. Garrison officers improvised a theater in a storehouse at Detroit and put on invitational performances in 1817; other performances were probably held, for a town ordinance regarding theatrical and other exhibitions was passed in 1825. During the next fifteen years amateur plays were staged in one way or another in Indianapolis, Lafayette, New Harmony, Dayton, Springfield, Illinois, and other towns.

Professional players under the direction of William Turner appeared in Cincinnati in 1811; in 1815 and 1816 Turner and his "Pittsburgh Company of Comedians" returned to contest the field with Samuel Drake who had monopolized the Kentucky Theatre for several years. In 1819 a group of stockholders erected a building in Columbia Street which had a pit, two rows of boxes, a large gallery, and a "punch room." When this building (the Cincinnati Theatre or the Citizen's Theatre) was opened in March of the following year, Cincinnati witnessed plays by Drake's company, Collins and Jones, and others. In 1827 Junius Booth, supported by Mrs. Alexander Drake, played "Othello,"

[268] *Horace in Cincinnati.*

"Richard III," and other roles. Two years later Edwin Forrest played in "The Virginian," "Hamlet," and "William Tell"; and Louisa Lane (later Mrs. John Drew) played several roles in "Actress of All Work" and "12 Precisely."

N. M. Ludlow, who had come west with Drake in 1815 and later brought his own company to St. Louis, joined up with a circus manager, rehabilitated a former bathhouse on Sycamore Street in Cincinnati, and in the summer of 1829 opened the "Dramatic-Equestrian Theatre."[269] The combined circus-theater arrangement gave the Drakes keen competition. James Caldwell, proprietor of the American Theatre in New Orleans, also invaded the Ohio River towns; in 1832 he occupied the Citizen's Theatre but soon was completed the Globe and Caldwell's New Cincinnati Theatre with Grecian columns, elegant furnishings, and a seating capacity of perhaps 1,500. The old theater burned in 1834 and the new one in 1836, but in 1837 Scott and Thorne opened the $40,000 National Theatre; it had a stage larger than that of London's Drury Lane and was richly furnished. Prices were from 25 cents to $1.00. The depression put a damper on expensive amusements, but various companies offered programs to the larger towns accessible from the Ohio River in the late 1830's.

Detroit, being off this circuit, was dependent upon eastern companies. A company of players under H. H. Fuller arrived from Buffalo in 1827 and was granted a license to perform. After a season the troupe moved on to Cleveland. In 1833 another company came for a summer season, and the next year two more, but Detroit did not have as numerous opportunities to see professionals perform as did Cincinnati, Louisville, or St. Louis.[270] Nevertheless, the *Free Press* in 1837 spoke of a rapid succession of "sterling comedy, showy melo-drama, gorgeous spectacle, broad farce, and delightful vaudeville and drama."[271] In 1838 two theaters, the City and the National, were opened.

Vincennes, Columbus, Springfield, Indianapolis, and other

[269] Ludlow's *Dramatic Life as I Found It. A Record of Personal Experience; with an Account of the Rise and Progress of Drama in the West and South . . .* (St. Louis, 1880) is an encyclopedic work which contains much of value on other subjects besides the theater and actors.

[270] Of the more than seven thousand performances advertised in the Middle West down to 1840 Rusk (I, 412) estimated that Cincinnati had more than one third, Louisville less than one third, St. Louis about one fifth, Detroit less than one eighth.

[271] August 9, 1837.

towns were favored with a visit from professional companies now and then. Alexander McKenzie in Chicago was granted a theater license (for $75) by the common council in 1839.[272] The same year Joseph Jefferson's traveling troupe opened in the Mac-Kenzie theater in Quincy, Illinois, with "The Poor Gentleman" and Bulwer's new play "The Lady of Lyons." "The beauty and fashion of the town" attended. The editor of the *Quincy Whig* said there was no reason why the people of Quincy should not enjoy a good play as well as those of Philadelphia or New York. The company moved on to Alton, then played the main towns along the Illinois River on its way to Chicago. The company returned the following May.[273]

Few actors of prominence were Westerners. Alexander Drake, who came west with his father in 1815, came to be well known as did his sister Julia (later Mrs. Fosdick and still later Mrs. Dean), and his wife, the former Miss Denny, who went on to eastern and European successes. The *Theatrical Apprenticeship of Sol. Smith*, the autobiography of a traveling actor in the West in this period, is unique.[274]

Shakespeare led in choice of selections, but Sheridan, Goldsmith, George Colman, and many lesser playwrights were represented. It was the general practice to put on two plays during the performance, the second being a farce, extravaganza, or musical-comedy piece. Scenery and trappings were ordinarily of the simplest, yet there were times when staging for extravagant spectacles ran to between $1,000 and $1,200. Audiences were not infrequently disturbed by outside ruffians or inside drunks; galleries constituted an uncertain overhead.

Plays based on western life were seldom offered, and when they were, did not prove popular. Mrs. Hentz in 1832 wrote "Lamorah, or the Western Wild," the scene of which was laid on the banks of the Ohio.[275] It was presented by Caldwell's com-

---

[272] *Daily Chicago American*, April 17, 1839: "We are aware that theatres are obnoxious to a respectable and intelligent portion of *every community*; but they are permitted, on the ground of general expediency, if for no other reason."

[273] *Quincy Whig*, May 18, 1839, May 2, 1840. See also *Autobiography of Joseph Jefferson* (New York, 1889), Chapter II. Young Jefferson—the third Joseph and destined to be the most famous of the family—was with the troupe.

Edwardsville had had a three-days' performance by the Ludlow and King troupe out of St. Louis in 1820. They performed in a private home. *Edwardsville Spectator*, May 2, 1820.

[274] Published in Philadelphia by Carey & Hart, 1846.

[275] Reviewed in *Western Monthly Magazine*, I (1833), 59–66.

pany in the New Theatre in Cincinnati for several performances, but the play was apparently not as good as her "De Lara, or the Moorish Bride," for which she won a $500 prize from a Boston theater manager. Other western writers to try their hands at the drama were Lewis F. Thomas, of Cincinnati, brother of the novelist, whose "Osceola" was produced at New Orleans, Louisville, and Cincinnati; Robert Dale Owen who wrote "Pocahontas; a Historical Drama" (1837), which was performed by amateurs in the West and later produced in New York; Mrs. Alexander Drake whose "Leona of Athens" had a four-night run in Cincinnati in 1834; and William Ross Wallace who made an adaptation from Bulwer of "Leila, or the Siege of Granada," 1838. There were various anonymous "originals" and adaptations announced, and sometimes performed.

Art and music were relatively unimportant activities in the period; what little there was centered largely around Cincinnati. In 1826 Drake and Mansfield noted that "Mr. F. Eckstein, an intelligent and highly ingenious artist of this city, is about to commence the formation of an Academy of Fine Arts. . . ." Apparently the venture failed but Eckstein became the teacher of Hiram Powers and was referred to as the "Father of Cincinnati Art."[276] James H. Beard, from New York by way of Painesville, Ohio, settled at Cincinnati in 1834 where he became known as a portrait painter. Though he painted portraits of Henry Clay, John Quincy Adams, and William Henry Harrison, he was best known for his animal pictures, especially those of dogs. His portraits of children pleased Miss Harriet Martineau.

Sometime in 1831 arrived at Cincinnati the eccentric and interesting Frankenstein family.[277] John, the oldest child, modeled in clay and painted portraits at an early age. While on an eastern trip he made a portrait of William H. Seward and later became known for two religious pictures, "Isaiah and the Infant Savior" and "Christ Mocked in the Praetorium." Godfrey N., as a boy, using coffee, hog's blood, and diluted ink as colors, painted a whole village. He became a sign painter and later opened a studio

[276] For Ohio art see Edna Maria Clark, *Ohio Art and Artists* (Richmond, Va., 1932).
[277] The parents, John A. and Anna C., had just brought their family from Germany. The father was a "professor of languages" and a musician, but became a cabinetmaker. The children were John, Godfrey N., Marie M. C., George L., Gustavus, and Eliza. The family later moved to Springfield, Ohio.

in Cincinnati. When the Academy of Fine Arts was organized in 1838 Godfrey Frankenstein became president. The next year an exhibit of about a hundred and fifty items was held, the first of importance in the West.

William H. Powell began his career as an artist in 1833 and four years later painted a series of allegorical pictures for a Cincinnati theater. After studying in Europe he returned to win the commission to paint "De Soto Discovering The Mississippi" for the rotunda of the Capitol in Washington. Later he received $10,000 from the Ohio legislature for "The Battle of Lake Erie."[278]

Vermont-born Hiram Powers grew up in Cincinnati doing odd jobs. He early showed skill for fine mechanical work which was developed while he worked in a clock and organ factory from 1822 to 1829. It was Powers' skill and the imagination of a Swabian and a Frenchman which led to the development of a work of museum art worthy of a distorted genius.

The Western Museum Society of Cincinnati, established by Daniel Drake and others as a stock company in 1818, was originally intended as a collecting and exhibiting institution for the natural history and antiquities of the West. Audubon was curator of its exhibits for a while in 1820, but the museum was a losing proposition until the advent of M. Joseph Dorfeuille.[279] This enthusiastic Louisiana naturalist discovered that the truths of science were not as salable as the atrocities of nature and creations of the imagination. Soon were exhibited "specimens of animals that did not exist [and] deformities that ought not to exist." When a mermaid and some wax-figure caricatures of the human race were added, customers began to pour in. Murderers (and their victims) always proved more popular than the figures of Tecumseh or Napoleon. So Dorfeuille applied to Powers to make him some more wax figures. So faithful were the Powers models that on occasion the subjects took the places of the figures. Once when a critic made unflattering remarks regarding the lack

---

[278] Other paintings of Powell's were "The Burial of De Soto" and "Washington Taking Leave of His Mother."

[279] Dorfeuille (Dorfel) was a Swabian by birth, who had traveled widely. The French version of his name has been explained on the basis of Lafayette's visit and the popularization of things French.

On the museum see Walter B. Hendrickson, "The Western Museum Society of Cincinnati," in *The Scientific Monthly*, LXIII, 66–72 (July, 1946).

of resemblance of the wax figure to the original, the statue got down from its pedestal and argued with him.

While engaged upon this work Powers met Auguste Hervieu, the French painter who had come to Cincinnati with Mrs. Trollope. Hervieu had done a mammoth painting of the "Landing of Lafayette at Cincinnati," which, though it contained portraits of all important personages present and some who were not, had failed to make him any money. The two artists combined their talents and, with Mrs. Trollope furnishing ideas, "The Infernal Regions" was the result. Here against realistic backgrounds mechanized figures carried on their work with diabolic energy; later a little railroad was added to facilitate the hellish transportation job involved in getting the sinners to the pits. Electrified railings and other objects gave out a galvanic shock when touched by unsuspecting visitors. The result was sufficiently horrible and frightful as to be irresistibly attractive. Young girls came for a taste of the excitement "which," said a contemporary commentator, "a comfortable and peaceful, but cold and monotonous manner of life denies them. This strange spectacle seems to afford a delicate agitation to their nerves, and is the principle source of revenue to the museum." Churches advertised the Inferno, excursion parties came to Cincinnati to get a foretaste of doom eternal; when the exhibition was closed temporarily, newspapers announced that fact.

Dorfeuille removed his show to New York in 1840. Powers, financed by Nicholas Longworth (as were others), went to Italy in 1834 to study and in time became one of the most influential American sculptors of his day.[280]

There were dozens of other painters, sculptors, and miniature carvers in and out of Cincinnati in the 1830's. Henry Kirke Brown, a portrait painter from the East, came to Cincinnati in 1836 where he turned to sculpture; equestrian statues in bronze became his specialty. Miner K. Kellogg, native Cincinnatian, after study in Europe became an expert in the old masters and a specialist in Oriental life.

[280] One of his early works was a marble bust of Judge Jacob Burnet, of Cincinnati. He later made busts of Jackson, Webster, Calhoun, and other national figures.

It has been stated that Frederick Franks, who had studied in Munich and had an art gallery in Cincinnati, made the pictures for the chamber of horrors. *History of Cincinnati* . . . , compiled by Henry A. and Mrs. Kate B. Ford (Cincinnati, 1881), 237–38.

There were other Ohio artists. Thomas Cole, whose family had settled in Steubenville in 1819, came into painting by helping his father design and color wallpaper blocks. After tramping the southern part of the state in an endeavor to find patrons he returned to Steubenville and began to sketch from nature. He received his greatest inspiration from the Ohio River, its hills and valleys. Later as a landscape painter in Philadelphia and New York he became generally credited as being the originator of the American school of landscape painting. Sala Bosworth, of Marietta, painted portraits in numerous Ohio towns and, following descriptions given by the pioneers, made pictures of early scenes around his home town. Charles Sullivan also produced historic views of the Marietta region, the best known of which was "The Mound Builder's Earthworks in 1788."

In Indiana Christopher Harrison, first lieutenant governor of the state, was also one of its first artists.[281] He had migrated from Maryland about 1808 and settled in the wilderness near the sight of Madison. After 1815 a merchant and farmer in and near Salem, he sketched in water color and painted in oil. None of Harrison's work has survived. The earliest Indiana portrait known—that of Gen. Hyacinth Lasselle—was painted presumably at Vincennes by one Lewis Peckham, late army officer from Rhode Island, sometime between 1815 and 1820. Chester Harding was a painter of portraits and art teacher in Vincennes and did a portrait of Daniel Boone when the old pioneer was about ninety.[282] Charles Alexandre Lesueur, Lucy Sistaire, David Dale Owen, and other artists and engravers whose activities centered around New Harmony are treated later in this chapter. Among the most famous of the paintings of the region were those produced by Charles Bodmer, the Swiss artist employed by Maximilian, Prince of Wied-Neuwied, who worked out of New Harmony in the winter of 1832–33. These paintings and drawings of western scenes were reproduced in the atlas which accompanied Maximilian's *Travels in North America*.[283]

George Winter, English-born artist who settled at Logansport,

---

[281] For political controversy with Governor Jennings, see Chapter IX, 13–14.
[282] Mary Q. Burnet, *Art and Artists of Indiana* (New York, 1921), 10.
[283] *Reise in das Innere Nord-America in den Jahren 1832 bis 1834 . . .* (2 volumes and atlas. Coblenz, 1839–41; English edition, London, 1843). Bodmer made most of the paintings.

Indiana, in 1837, painted portraits, landscapes, and miniatures. What George Catlin was for the western Indians Winter was for the Miami and Potawatomi. For a number of years the artist seems to have made a living by having a one-man raffle or lottery every so often, at which time he would "sell" a whole group of paintings. Some of his oil canvases of battle scenes were in the heroic size; most of his Indian portraits were small water colors.[284]

Better known than Winter was James Otto Lewis who left a better record of his painting than of his life. It appears that Lewis was a member of Ludlow's theatrical troupe which was stranded at St. Louis in 1820. At any rate he engraved the Chester Harding portrait of Daniel Boone while in Missouri that year. He accompanied Thomas McKenney, the Indian superintendent, on his tour of inspection in 1826–27, engraved a portrait of Lewis Cass in 1831, and painted some eighty-five Indian portraits and treaty scenes. In 1835 he published the *North American Aboriginal Portfolio* at Philadelphia; the seventy-two plates "painted from life by J. O. Lewis at Detroit in 1833" were poorly engraved and did not do the artist justice. Charles Bird King, student of Benjamin West, copied some of the Lewis portraits for the War Department, and some of these appear to much better advantage in McKenney and Hall's *Indian Tribes of North America* than in the Lewis *Portfolio*.

The most famous of all early western artists was John James Audubon, whose original works would today probably bring more money at auction than those of all others combined. He is sketched in the section which follows.

§ § § §

The casual student of the history of the Middle West, even the student who "had a course" in the subject, might justifiably be nonplused by the mention of science in the pioneer period. It is doubtful whether he could name two scientists in the fields of botany, geology, and zoology, and identify their work. Yet

[284] For sketch see *The Journals and Indian Paintings of George Winter,* in which volume many of the artist's best extant paintings of Indians are reproduced. The original paintings are in the possession of the Tippecanoe County Historical Association, Lafayette, Indiana.

before there was a single university in the region, and a half century before there was a graduate school in science in the country, men, whose names will be remembered long after those of eminent successors have been generally forgotten, were pioneering in these fields.

It is impossible to separate the science of the West from science on the West. Likewise, since the natural scientists did not confine their activities to the site of their residence, it is impossible to confine the subject strictly to the boundaries of the Old Northwest. The West opened new fields to the soldier and the settler, to the politician and the merchant, and also to the scientist. Quite logically it was the natural sciences which first developed.[285]

A decade before Louisiana was acquired or a single state had been created in the Northwest, Thomas Jefferson was discussing with André Michaux, the French botanist, the possibility of an exploratory expedition, to be accompanied by scientists, into the Far West. Nothing came of this project at the time, and Michaux spent the years 1794 and 1795 largely in the Ohio Valley. He was an indefatigable traveler and collector, and, though in the pay of the French government, made valuable contributions to American botany.[286] His son, François André Michaux, traveled some two thousand miles on a trip through the Ohio Valley in 1802. Observations on plants and agriculture were recorded briefly in his *Travels*.[287] But his major work, completed after further travels, was *North American Sylva*. This work, of which three volumes with 155 colored plates were published at Paris 1810–13 (supplemented by the volumes later added by Thomas Nuttall), constitutes one of the important botanic contributions of our history.[288]

[285] The best survey of the subject is Arthur Deen, "Frontier Science in Kentucky and the Old Northwest, 1790–1860," MS. Ph.D. thesis, Indiana University, 1938.

[286] Portions of the journal of the elder Michaux were published in *Proceedings of the American Philosophical Society*, XXVI (1889), and in Thwaites (ed.), *Early Western Travels*, III. On his return to France Michaux published his work on North American oaks.

[287] *Travels to the Westward of the Allegany Mountains . . . in the year 1802* (London, 1805). The first edition, in French, was published in Paris, 1804.

[288] The first English edition of *Sylva* was issued at Paris in 1819; the second English edition, using the original copper plates imported by William Maclure, was printed at New Harmony in 1841. Nuttall worked on out to the Pacific coast in the 1830's, then published a three-volume supplement to Michaux's *Sylva* (New Harmony, 1841, and Philadelphia, 1849). The *Sylva* was republished at Philadelphia in 1857 in three volumes, and Nuttall's work was added in two more volumes in 1859.

John Bradbury, the English botanist, spent three years in the western country; his book, *Travels in the Interior of America, in the years 1809, 1810, and 1811* (London, 1817), contained, besides "Remarks . . . Useful to persons emigrating," observations on the natural history of the region north of the Ohio.

David B. Thomas, of New York, who was essentially a pomologist, spent the summer of 1816 in the region north of the Ohio. Near Circleville on the prairie he observed many herbaceous plants which were new to him, among them the wild indigo and a red rose (*Rosa caroliensis*). In Indiana he was surprised to find the black locust growing as large as the beech and walnut; here he first saw the hackberry. Between Vincennes and Fort Harrison (Terre Haute) he counted eighty species of trees and plants; he estimated that three fourths of the plants of this region were not found in the eastern states.[289]

Botany and a host of other sciences received inspiration with the arrival in the West of Constantine Samuel Rafinesque in 1818.[290] After visiting friends in Louisville the singular-appearing scientist journeyed down the Ohio to Henderson, where he met Audubon. Whether exploring the canebrakes, killing bats with Audubon's Cremona violin (and "discovering" a number of new fish which he accepted on faith from Audubon's description), or gathering plants and herbs, this "odd fish" was as exultantly enthusiastic as a child.[291] At Rappite Harmony he "went to

---

[289] *Travels through the Western Country in the summer of 1816, passim.*

[290] Rafinesque, the son of a French father and a Grecian-born German mother, was born in Constantinople in 1783. He grew up in Marseilles, Leghorn, and Palermo, largely self-taught. From 1802 until 1805 he worked in Philadelphia where he met and was befriended by Dr. Benjamin Rush and the merchant, John D. Clifford. He left a wife, who later remarried, and a four-year-old daughter in Europe when he returned to the United States in 1815. He came west to Kentucky where he again met Clifford. The latter, who was interested in natural history, had become a Lexington merchant and member of the Board of Trustees of Transylvania University. He and Rafinesque made several trips before Clifford's death in 1820.

The most complete life of Rafinesque is Call, *The Life and Writings of Rafinesque*. A useful sketch of his western period is Huntley Dupre, *Rafinesque in Lexington, 1819–1826* (Lexington, 1945). Rafinesque's works are listed in T. J. Fitzpatrick, *Rafinesque; A Sketch of His Life with Bibliography* (Des Moines, 1911).

[291] Rafinesque had been so introduced by letter to Audubon. One of the "odd fish" which Audubon described was the Devil-Jack Diamond fish, which was four to ten feet long and covered with bullet-proof scales which would strike fire when hit with steel. This species (number 91), as well as others, troubled scientists until David Starr Jordan in 1877 straightened out the classification of Ohio River fishes: Rafinesque was credited with 45 of the 111 species listed. Review of Rafinesque's *Memoirs of North American Fishes*, in *Bulletin of the United States National Museum*, No. 9 (1877), 1–50.

herbonize in the meadows" with Dr. Christoph Miller, the botanist, then visited Shawneetown, Louisville, Lexington, and walked across Ohio on his way back to Philadelphia, where he spent the winter of 1818–19.[292]

From 1819 to 1826 Rafinesque was professor of botany and natural history at Transylvania. The energies and accomplishments of the man were extraordinary. Beside teaching medical botany, medical mineralogy, and medical zoology, he gave outside lectures on botany, lessons in French, Spanish, and Italian, made many visits and field trips, wrote about two hundred articles, and started the *Western Minerva, or American Annals of Knowledge and Literature.* In the first (and only) number of this "quarterly" the editor had several poems and articles on legislation, ethics, metaphysics, astronomy, meteorology, physics, botany, and archaeology.[293] In 1822 he sought an appointment as professor of public economy in the law school; of his ability to handle that subject he had the greatest confidence, since it was one of his favorites. Two years later he succeeded in getting a charter for a company to establish a botanic garden, of which he became superintendent; at the same time he was gathering material for his *Tellus or History of Mankind,* which in ten years grew to one hundred books of five thousand pages. Though the broad-minded Horace Holley, president of Transylvania, was not in favor of science, he tolerated and in a way protected the sensitive but erratic professor. But Rafinesque was not happy. He felt unappreciated and did not believe that the West was "yet mature for Sciences." Some years earlier he had sounded out Jefferson regarding a professorship at the contemplated University of Virginia; he renewed his quest in 1824, listed his publications, and set forth his qualifications in comparative philology. "I have studied it deeply, comparing 400 Eastern languages with about 85 American languages of which I have vocabularies." The next

---

[292] Here he completed his large map of the Ohio River, recorded his "travels and discoveries," published a review of Thomas Nuttall's *Genera,* sent many fishes and fossils to his friend Swainson in England, exchanged shells and fossils with Lesueur, and sent to Curvier and Blainville seventy new genera of animals which were published in the *Journal de Physique* in 1819.

[293] Dupre, *Rafinesque in Lexington,* 17. After being printed this first number was suppressed and never distributed. It was reprinted in 1949 from a set of the original page proofs preserved in the Academy of Natural Sciences of Philadelphia. In William Gibbes Hunt's *Western Review and Miscellaneous Magazine* in 1819 Rafinesque had written articles on lightning, botany, pumpkin-seed oil, foxes, and salivation of horses. *Ibid.,* 24.

year he sought a patent for his "Divitial Invention," a scheme for issuing divisible certificates for bank stocks and deposits (the coupon system), as currency, which would cause a "revolution in Money Matters."[294] In 1826 Rafinesque, having turned against President Holley even, left Lexington for Philadelphia, where he spent the remaining fourteen years of his life.

Ichthyologia Ohiensis, or Natural History of the Fishes Inhabiting the River Ohio, a ninety-page booklet, had been published at Lexington in 1820. The *Ancient History, or Annals of Kentucky,* which contained a survey of the ancient monuments of North America and a "Tabular View of the Principal Languages and Primitive Nations of the Whole Earth" (39 pages), was published at Frankfort in 1824. In 1828 came the first volume of *Medical Flora, or Manual of the Medical Botany of the United States* (Philadelphia) ; the second followed in 1830. Between these two volumes appeared the *Pulmest, or the Art to Cure the Consumption.*[295] Followed books on the Bible, banking, antiquities of the Western Hemisphere, colleges, celestial wonders, and the pleasure and duties of wealth. All told more than nine hundred articles and books, written in English, French, and Italian, were published by Rafinesque in Europe and the United States.

If Rafinesque was an interesting character, he was also a controversial one. He has been called a liar and a fraud, a "fish-taker" who had located all the Indian tribes of the past three thousand years: "Strange metamorphosis of genius! that can make an apothecary's muller of such a learned head."[296] Thomas Peirce referred to him as "Professor Muscleshellorum," a

> Bolanus, happy in a skull
> Of proof unpenetrably dull,

whose real name, on the title page of his books, bore "the proportion to his scientific titles, as a paper-kite to the length of its tail."[297] He was called the best field botanist of his time, the greatest naturalist in America; he was credited with most impor-

[294] He apparently received the patent. In his article, "Patent Divitial Invention," in the *Saturday Evening Post,* VI, No. 290 (Feb. 17, 1827), he gave the date of patent as August 23, 1825. See also Fitzpatrick, *Rafinesque,* 32n.
[295] For Rafinesque's panacea see Chapter V, 304.
[296] See Daniel Drake in *Western Journal of the Medical and Physical Sciences,* III (1830), 459, apropos Rafinesque's pulmel panacea.
[297] *The Odes of Horace in Cincinnati,* 22–24, 102.

tant contributions towards a more natural classification of plants, and recognition of the part played by deviations and mutations over periods of time.[298] Agassiz said that "he was better than he appeared." All could agree with David Starr Jordan when he stated that, "No more remarkable figure has appeared . . . in the annals of science."

Caleb Atwater was interested in trees and shrubs as well as history and antiquities; in his *History of the State of Ohio* he listed many of the some four thousand native plants of the state. John L. Riddell, who lectured on botany and chemistry at the Cincinnati Medical College, published *A Synopsis of the Flora of the Western States* (Cincinnati, 1835), and a catalogue of Ohio plants the following year.

For the northern parts, early botanic collecting was done by Thomas Nuttall, who visited the region west of Lake Michigan in 1813.[299] Accompanying the Cass-Schoolcraft expedition of 1820 was Professor D. B. Douglass, of West Point, who enumerated 110 plants of which 3 were new species.[300]

Thomas Say, an entomologist rather than a botanist, who accompanied Major Stephen H. Long on the expedition to the source of the St. Peter's River in 1823, listed some of the plants of the Wisconsin country,[301] as did Douglass Houghton (later state geologist of Michigan), who accompanied Schoolcraft's expedition of 1832 to the sources of the Mississippi.[302] From these sources and from his own work, Increase Allen Lapham, Milwaukee botanist and geologist, compiled a list of more than eight hundred species of Wisconsin plants.[303] Lapham became a field man for Louis Agassiz, Asa Gray, and the science depart-

---

[298] Clearly stated in a letter of December 1, 1832, published in *Herbarium Rafinesquianum* (Philadelphia, 1833), 11–12. See E. D. Merrill, "A Generally Overlooked Rafinesque Paper," in *Proceedings of the American Philosophical Association, LXXXVI* (1942), 74.

[299] In his *Genera of North American Plants* . . . (2 volumes. Philadelphia, 1818), he described thirteen new species.

[300] D. B. Douglass and Dr. John Torrey, "Plants of the Northwest," in *American Journal of Science and Arts, IV* (1822), 56–69.

[301] William H. Keating, *Narrative of an Expedition to the Sources of St. Peter's River* . . . (2 volumes. Philadelphia, 1824).

[302] Schoolcraft, *Narrative of an Expedition through the Upper Mississippi to Itasca Lake.*

[303] Lecture of March 10, 1842, in Lapham Papers, Wisconsin State Historical Society Library. Lapham issued brief catalogues at Milwaukee in 1836 and 1838. In 1839 Dr. John Torrey, one of Asa Gray's collaborators, gave Lapham credit for discovering that *Anemone patens* was indigenous to the United States. Torrey to Lapham, September 4, 1839.

ment of Harvard College. In 1840 Josiah Quincy thanked him for the gift to the Harvard Library of the catalogue of Wisconsin plants.[304] Lapham later did work in meteorology and geology.

John James Audubon was primarily an artist who portrayed birds, yet in his two most important works Charles Darwin cited him more often than any other scientist excepting only Augustus Gould and Alfred Wallace. He was, and probably will remain, the best known of the scientists of the West.[305] While nominally keeping store at Louisville (his friend Ferdinand Rosier kept store while Audubon hunted birds), Audubon met Alexander Wilson, the ornithologist; the latter's plan for publishing his drawings may have given Audubon the idea of publishing his own.[306] In 1810 the partners moved their store to Henderson, then to Ste. Genevieve, Missouri. Soon Audubon returned to Henderson without his partner; his wife, Lucy Bakewell Audubon, now kept store. Ever seeking to make a success of her husband, Mrs. Audubon encouraged a venture in the commission business at New Orleans with her brother Thomas Bakewell. When the business was ruined by the War of 1812, Audubon went to jail in Louisville for debt but was released through bankruptcy proceedings. At this time even the birds looked like enemies.

During the brief period in 1819–20 when he was curator at the Cincinnati Museum, Audubon met Daniel Drake, Elijah Slack, William Henry Harrison, and other prominent persons.

[304] The friendship and correspondence between Gray and Lapham was sincere and mutually beneficial; it continued for many years.

[305] The best life of Audubon is Francis Hobart Herrick, *Audubon the Naturalist* (2 volumes. New York, 1917). A more popular account is Constance M. Rourke, *Audubon* (New York, 1936). Also useful are [Lucy Audubon], *John James Audubon* . . . (New York, 1869), and Maria R. Audubon, *Audubon and His Journals* . . . (2 volumes. New York, 1897). Besides his *Birds of North America*, Audubon's chief works were *Ornithological Biography* (5 volumes. Edinburgh, 1831–39)—the text which accompanied the *Birds*, and *The Viviparous Quadrupeds of North America* (New York, 1845–46). The sixty "Episodes" of the *Ornithological Biography* were collected by Professor Herrick and published as *Delineations of American Scenery and Character* (New York, 1926).

Audubon was probably the natural son of Lt. Jean Audubon of the French Navy and a Creole girl named Rabin. He was born in San Domingo in 1785, adopted by his father and Mme. Audubon in 1794, and spent his boyhood in Nantes. He studied drawing at Paris 1802–3. In 1803 the young man came to his father's farm near Valley Forge, Pennsylvania, where he studied birds and became engaged to Lucy Bakewell. In 1804 Audubon became a partner in a general store at Louisville.

[306] The accounts of Wilson and Audubon of this meeting are at great variance. Wilson claimed he received neither a single bird nor act of civility; Audubon said they hunted together and that Wilson found new species. What might have grown into a mere friendly rivalry developed into quite a struggle as a result of the provocations of George Ord and others interested in Wilson's work. Each later accused the other of copying certain of his drawings of birds.

It was about this time that he definitely decided to publish his ornithology. While he wandered up and down the great valley, occasionally painting portraits but ever hunting and painting birds, Lucy taught or acted as governess in Kentucky and Louisiana, earning at times as much as $3,000 a year.[307]

Fortified with a new suit of clothes and Lucy's encouragement, Audubon went to Philadelphia in 1824. Though he met the leading artists[308] and was introduced to the Academy of Natural Sciences, where his drawings were exhibited, he received no encouragement for publication from George Ord and the Wilson backers. Two years later, carrying letters of introduction from Henry Clay, De Witt Clinton, and others, Audubon went to England. At Liverpool, Manchester, Edinburgh, and finally London he was received and promoted by newly acquired friends. Between being entertained nightly and painting portraits in the daytime to meet expenses, writing papers, joining scientific societies, and receiving honors, he was a busy man. Throughout it all he never deviated from his main purpose—to get his drawings published, life-size. Successful exhibitions, the friendship of Professor Robert Jameson of the University of Edinburgh, and the admiration of W. Home Lizars, the engraver, for the drawings, led to Lizars undertaking publication of the first number of *The Birds of America*. But after Audubon had gone on to London he received word that Lizars could not go through with the job. This proved fortunate, however, for Robert Havell, Jr., one of the leading engravers of the British Isles, undertook to finish the colossal work.[309] Audubon worked assiduously; the latent man-

[307] At Natchez in 1822 Audubon received some lessons in oils from a traveling portrait painter; the lessons were continued at Philadelphia in 1824 under Thomas Sully.

[308] Including Thomas Sully, Robert and Rembrandt Peale. He also met Charles Lucien Bonaparte and Charles Alexandre Lesueur.

[309] By the prospectus of 1827 it was planned to publish in parts, five plates to a part, at two guineas per part. In 1829 when ten parts had been published it was announced that there were four hundred drawings. Later the plates were extended to 435.

The copper plates were double elephant size (29½ by 39½ inches); approximately a hundred thousand prints had to be colored by hand. Getting uniform colors and coloring was only one of the many problems confronted. *The Birds of America* "in point of size is perhaps to this day the largest extended publication in existence." Herrick, *Audubon*, I, 358. The work was in press twelve years and cost more than $100,000 to produce. Individual prints have since sold for several times the original subscription price ($1,000 in the United States) for the entire set. All told about 175 or, counting those who later completed sets, possibly 190 or 200 sets of the original edition were sold.

agerial ability which failed to show in the store business was put
to the test and proved; the seemingly shy artist-scientist promoted, financed, and sold his work. In time he went to Paris
where he received the patronage of the French government.

In 1829 Audubon returned to collect and paint from Pennsylvania to Louisiana. Returning to Europe in 1830 with Mrs.
Audubon, he began the text for his drawings, the *Ornithological
Biography,* which eventually became five volumes of some three
thousand pages. Audubon had to publish the first volume at his
own expense. In 1836–37 he made another American tour; more
birds, more paintings. *The Birds* finally grew to 435 plates (1,065
life-size birds) which portrayed 489 supposedly distinct species
of American birds. Back in England in 1838 he witnessed the completion of the plates; two volumes of the *Biography* remained to
be completed, however. When Audubon left England in 1839,
he was probably the best-known American who had sojourned
there since Benjamin Franklin.

The Birds of America later went through various editions.
The Viviparous Quadrupeds of North America with 150 colossal
imperial folio plates was published at New York, 1845–46.

Audubon had his detractors, some of whom compared him to
Baron Munchausen. His *Journals* were debated for reliability;
he was accused of inaccuracy and worse. Most of his derelictions
can be explained by the fact that he was not a trained scientist;
he was inaccurate on minor points, and perhaps forgetful. The
fact detracts but little from his accomplishments in three fields:
as naturalist, as artist and publisher, and as good-will ambas-
sador to England and Europe.

Not so well known as Audubon or Rafinesque was Charles
Alexandre Lesueur. While in his early twenties he and François
Peron had accompanied the Napoleonic scientific expedition to
Australia; on their return they were credited with having discovered more new zoological species than all the naturalists of
modern times before them.[310] Lesueur came to the United States
with the geologist William Maclure in 1816 and for seven years
was curator of the Academy of Natural Sciences at Philadelphia.
In 1826 they both moved to New Harmony, where for the next

---

[310] Adrien Loir, *Charles Alexandre Le Sueur* . . . (Le Havre, 1920), 9. Lesueur
signed his name both with the capital S and without.

twelve years Lesueur taught, drew portraits and scenes, studied, traveled, and collected. Lesueur's first interest was ichthyology; he was the first to study the fishes of the Great Lakes, and his monograph on suckers was an important contribution in its day. He planned an American ichthyology for which he made several plates, but the project was abandoned. The tall, bearded man who liked to go bareheaded and sometimes barefoot in summer, was rated by Agassiz as the second-best ichthyologist in America.[311] His collections and his drawings, however, were more famous than his scientific writing. These consisted of sketches and water colors of American scenery to the number of about 1,200 which he left to the Museum of Natural History at Le Havre, France.[312] Lesueur returned to France in 1837; Maclure had gone to Mexico, Thomas Say had died, and Lesueur had lost his pocketbook which contained his savings. The last years of his life were spent near the Museum in Paris and in directing the new Museum of Natural History at his native city of Le Havre.

Unlike Rafinesque, Audubon, and Lesueur, Thomas Say (1789–1834) was of American birth. Of Philadelphia Quaker ancestry—his father, however, had fought in the Revolution—his formal education was brief. Say joined the band of distinguished scientists at New Harmony in 1826; two years later he married Lucy Way Sistaire. Self-taught, modest, industrious, and careful, he became the first efficient describer of North American insects and one of the outstanding entomologists of his day.[313]

In 1816 Say had planned a work on American entomology, but only the first part was published the following year at

[311] Charles Bodmer, the artist with Maximilian of Wied, portrayed Lesueur with his gun and dogs.

[312] Fewer than a hundred of these sketches have been reproduced. Photographic copies of 803 of them are in the possession of the American Antiquarian Society at Worcester, Massachusetts. For a listing and brief sketch of Lesueur's American drawings, see R. W. G. Vail, "The American Sketchbooks of a French Naturalist, 1816–1837," in *Proceedings of the American Antiquarian Society*, new series, XLVIII (1938), 49–155. See also André Maury, *Charles-Alexandre Lesueur, Voyageur et Peintre—Naturaliste Havrais (1778–1846)* (reprinted from the *French-American Review*, July–September, 1948). Microfilm copies of Lesueur's drawings in the Havre Museum are now in the library of the American Philosophical Society in Philadelphia. A few original sketches are in the possession of the Purdue University Library. Lesueur also made two of the drawings for Say's *American Conchology* and 9 of the 54 plates of Say's *American Entomology*. Mrs. Say, who made most of the beautiful drawings, studied art with Lesueur.

[313] The best biography is Harry B. Weiss and Grace M. Ziegler, *Thomas Say . . .* (Springfield, Ill., 1931).

Philadelphia. He had published articles in national scientific journals as early as 1819. As one of the journalists on Stephen Long's expedition of 1823 he saw much of the Northwest; he reported on zoology, botany, and Indian customs of the region. The *American Entomology* was published at Philadelphia 1824–27; the fifty-four plates of this beautiful work were made by several different engravers. After a trip with Maclure to Mexico, Say announced publication, by subscription, of his *American Conchology*.[314] This unfinished work, plates and all, was executed at the school press in New Harmony in 1830.[315] Say's complete writings on conchology were not edited and published until almost a quarter century after his death.[316]

Say's work was largely taxonomic. His descriptions were brief but clear. Quantitatively he was one of our leading entomologists, having been credited with identifying a total of 1,575 species. He received many scientific honors and corresponded with many scientists in both hemispheres. He was entirely indifferent to money and business yet was vastly acquisitive regarding books and other necessary tools which money would buy. Though Lesueur had contributed to Say's *Conchology* by his drawings, the latter could not find time to translate Lesueur's ichthyology. His health possibly impaired by irregular work habits, Say died at Maclure's house in 1834.

Geology received its first notice of importance in the West by way of the Cass-Schoolcraft expedition of 1820. Chalcedony, jasper, agate, and sardonyx were located, but the big interest was in the native copper resources.[317] The beds of iron sand along Lake Superior were reported to exceed anything of the kind in

[314] *New-Harmony Gazette,* October 17, 24, 1827.
[315] *American Conchology, or Descriptions of the Shells of North America. Illustrated by Coloured Figures from Original Drawings Executed from Nature.* Only six numbers or parts had appeared when Say died. Mrs. Say made sixty-six of the sixty-eight drawings (Lesueur made two); the plates were engraved by Cornelius Tiebout, L. Lyon, and I. Walker; the prints were colored by Mrs. Say and the pupils. For brief description of this work see Richard E. Banta, "The American Conchology: A Venture in Backwoods Book Printing," in *The Colophon,* new series, III (1938–39), 24–40.
[316] W. G. Binney (ed.), *The Complete Writings of Thomas Say on the Conchology of the United States* (New York, 1858).
[317] The famous nugget of pure copper on the Ontonagon River, estimated by Alexander Henry in 1776 as weighing five tons, was estimated at one ton by Schoolcraft. Its weight was later determined to be about two tons. For the later interesting history of this boulder, see Angus Murdoch, *Boom Copper* (New York, 1943), Chapter VIII.

the United States; the coal beds along the Fox of Illinois were also noted. William Keating, of the University of Pennsylvania, the mineralogist on the Long expedition of 1823, recognized the comparatively recent existence of a vast extinct lake in the Minnesota region (Lake Agassiz).

In 1809 William Maclure, after working in each state and territory of the Union, published his "Observations on the Geology of the United States,"[318] and thereby won for himself the title "Father of American Geology." Though Robert Owen took him for a financial fall, and his dreams of a new education and scientific center at New Harmony went askew, Maclure did not stop work. In 1832 he published the *Essay on the Formation of Rocks* at New Harmony. Following neither the Neptunists (the earth originally all water), nor the Volcanists (all liquid fire), he went after the truth firsthand. He divided rocks into aqueous, volcanic, and doubtful, studied stratification, and attempted to classify the rocks. When the facts did not clearly indicate the classification, he presented the evidence with his conclusions.

George W. Featherstonhaugh, the Englishman, turned to geology after the death of his American wife. His work on the expedition to survey the St. Peter's ("Minnay Sotor") was both topographical and geological. The lead, copper, and coal areas of northern Illinois and the Wisconsin country were studied for their economic importance.

By the 1830's the states were becoming interested in their mineral resources. Ohio authorized a survey by law in 1837; the next year W. W. Mather reported to Governor Vance that 12,000 square miles of the state were underlaid with coal. Iron, salt wells, clays, marls, and soils were reported on and some of the geological formations classified.[319] Michigan began geological surveys with the first year of statehood; Douglass Houghton

[318] *Transactions of the American Philosophical Society*, VI (1809), 411–28. The work was revised and republished in the *Transactions* in 1818.

Maclure, born in Ayre, Scotland, in 1763, first came to the United States in 1782 as representative of a commercial firm. By 1796, when he was independently well-to-do, he had made the United States his home. Soon he turned his attention to science and education. He was founder and for seventeen years president of the Philadelphia Academy of Natural Sciences. For his educational interests and relations with Owen see below.

[319] W. W. Mather, *First Annual Report on the Geological Survey of the State of Ohio* (Columbus, 1838), 5.

was put in charge; his assistants were Bela Hubbard and C. C. Douglas. Before the original appropriation expired in 1841 material was gathered for five annual reports.[320] Many salt springs were discovered; the copper resources of the Upper Peninsula were compared in value with those of Cornwall. Houghton, who was also interested in chemistry and botany, was well liked for his personal qualities and respected for his scientific accomplishments. On his suggestion the geological survey was combined with the land survey, but he had hardly begun on the new work when he was drowned on the coast of Lake Superior in 1845.[321]

The Indiana survey, also authorized in 1837, was turned over to David Dale Owen. As a boy Owen had studied under Fellenberg in Switzerland; later he studied chemistry, natural philosophy, mathematics, and drawing at Glasgow. After the failure of his father's utopia at New Harmony he loafed with his brothers for a while, then took up in turn printing, chemistry, manufacture of castor oil, medicine, and geology.[322]

As Indiana's first state geologist Owen worked along utilitarian lines. To gain an over-all view he worked the Ohio and Wabash banks, sampled the interior of the state by zigzag lines, outlined the coal areas and the depth of the deposits, investigated the possibilities of iron, called attention to the oölitic limestone, and observed the soil. He was careful and a stickler for the precise use of terms. His brief report was written for the layman as well as the specialist.[323] His work served as a basis for further geological research. Although much was later added, few of his conclusions were discredited.

In 1839 Owen resigned his position as state geologist to accept the position of United States geologist. His later surveys of

[320] *Geological Reports* (Michigan Historical Commission, 1928).

[321] For a brief survey of Houghton's work, see George P. Merrill, *The First One Hundred Years of American Geology* (New Haven, 1924).

[322] David Dale Owen returned to London in 1831 where he enrolled in London University; his interest in chemistry and geology were stimulated here. He returned to New Harmony in 1832, set up a museum and laboratory, and then, 1835–37, spent two terms of five months each at the Medical College of Ohio at Cincinnati. In 1837 he married Caroline Neef; they took a "geological wedding tour" to Mammoth Cave.
The career of this member of the Owen family is well covered in Walter Brookfield Hendrickson, *David Dale Owen, Pioneer Geologist of the Middle West* (*Indiana Historical Collections*, XXVII, Indianapolis, 1943).

[323] *Report of a Geological Reconnoisance of the State of Indiana;* . . . (Indianapolis, 1838). Printed also in Indiana *Senate Journal*, 1837–38, pp. 126–57.

Illinois, Wisconsin, Minnesota, Iowa, and Arkansas areas were models of their kind; his drawings and sketches were not the least interesting part of these reports. He delivered many lectures and wrote many articles, in one of which he explained the famous footprints of the Angel Gabriel on the stone at New Harmony as a piece of primitive handiwork.[324] By the age of forty-five David Dale Owen had risen to a position of national and international prominence in geology.

Increase Allen Lapham had given his attention to geology before his botanic work became known. In Ohio in the early 1830's he worked on the problem of the granite and greenstone boulders—foreign rocks—and concluded they had been brought down by a great flood from the north. He did not think it mattered much whether the earth came from the tail of a comet, was hollow as Captain Symmes claimed, or was filled with matter a thousand times hotter than red-hot iron; he did believe that study of the rock formations and fossils was basic. Geology was not a speculative science, but based on observations, facts, and deductions from facts. He even had the courage to question the theories of Sir Charles Lyell as laid down in *Principles of Geology*.[325] The first important geological investigation of Wisconsin was reported in Lapham's *Topographical and Geological Description of Wisconsin* (1844). Like Owen, Lapham was a fieldworker rather than a theorist, but the theorists valued his observations.

Geology seems to have been taught by Rafinesque at Transylvania as early as 1821; it was taught at Hanover in 1837; possibly Samuel P. Hildreth taught the subject at Marietta in the late 1830's. Douglass Houghton, while state geologist, was professor of geology and mineralogy at the University of Michigan, but he met no classes; the subject was not definitely taught there until 1845–46.

But little work was done in paleontology in the period; Owen had given fossils some attention on his first Wisconsin expedition

[324] Schoolcraft had held that they were footprints. Owen wrote: "It appears to me much less improbable that some aboriginal artist should have exhibited unlooked-for skill in intagliating a rock, than that man should have been coëval with the crustacea." "Regarding Human Foot-prints in Solid Limestone," in *American Journal of Science and Arts*, XLIII (1842), 15.

[325] He said that Lyell seemed to think the world never had a beginning; that all changes which had ever taken place were produced by causes now in operation. Lapham to Darius Lapham, January 3, 1835. Lapham Papers.

of 1839, but not until his expeditions of 1847–50 were important beginnings made in this field. Lapham was also one of the pioneer paleontologists of the West.

Western science had its fantastic periphery. Besides Rafinesque's fictitious fish and geology according to Genesis, the journalistic contributions on the sea serpent, and wild ideas in the field of medicine, there were other manifestations of the West's individualism and self-sufficiency. Most noted of these was John Cleves Symmes's theory of concentric spheres.

Symmes, a nephew of the founder of Cincinnati, had been a captain in the War of 1812. From observing the rings of Saturn he decided that all globes are hollow. In April, 1818, he proclaimed "the earth to be hollow and inhabitable within; the poles of which are open twelve or sixteen degrees," pledged his life in support of this truth, and declared himself ready to explore this "concave," to "find a warmer country and rich land stocked with thrifty vegetables and animals if not men. . . ."[326] The following year he laid down his twenty-two points in which he located the opening as several hundred miles from the north pole on the American side, explained how the moon forced in and expelled air through the opening, and explained the dark complexions of Eskimos as the result of the hot climate.

The French Academy refused to consider Symmes's theory but the author of it was not discouraged. Comparing himself to Columbus and reflecting that "the schools of Europe were not so profound and daring in their conceptions," he went to work lecturing and petitioning for help. The secretary of the American Philosophical Society wrote him that madness had always been imputed to the first philosophers and that he was a "jealous but feeble advocate" of the theory.[327] Symmes threw down his glove to the geologists; if they did not reply "within a reasonable time," the world would proceed to give judgment. He then requested all learned societies to go on record for or against, and showered Congress with petitions for aid for a polar expedi-

---

[326] Circular letter of April 10, 1818, Symmes Papers, Wisconsin State Historical Society Library; *Inquisitor Cincinnati Advertiser,* November 2, 1819.

[327] Eber J. Bell to Symmes, May 22, 1821. Symmes Papers, II, 19. In a letter to the society, July 19, 1821, Symmes explained that he had not paid postage, as formerly, because of lack of funds. He referred them to the *National Intelligencer* of November 7, 8, and December 11, 1821, for his publications. Symmes Papers, II, 25.

tion.[328] Even the legislature of Pennsylvania memorialized Congress in Symmes's behalf. Though some members of Congress thought the theory as plausible as that of Copernicus in his day, most of the petitions were laid on the table; they continued to arrive, however, for several years.

Symmes lectured widely; Charleston, Trenton, Boston, and other points listened, even contributed some money. A benefit performance of "Revenge" by an amateur company, was given at the Cincinnati Theater in March, 1824. Not desiring to put all his eggs in one basket, Symmes sent letters to the "magistrates of Copenhagen," to various cities of Germany, and to the British government. To the last he wrote: "Can it for a moment be supposed that an Omniscient Being, having in view animation and diversity as two of the leading features of creation—would confine these features to the mere shell or surface of this immense and immeasurable orb and leave all within an inert and useless mass of matter?"[329] Playing no favorites, Symmes approached the Russian government.[330] In 1825 *Niles' Weekly Register* wrote: "John C. Symmes, our countryman who has resolved that the earth is hollow and populated, has accepted an offer of the emperor of Russia, through count Romanzoff, to make a polar expedition under the patronage of the 'deliverer'—who has not *land* enough above ground to satisfy his ambition."[331]

Unfortunately Symmes did not get to lead the expedition. Exhausted by his eastern tour of 1826 he became ill; he was jailed for three days in New York for a small debt to a landlord. He returned to Cincinnati in 1829 and died a few months later on a farm near Hamilton—land left him by his uncle Judge John Cleves Symmes. His son, Americus, crowned his monument with a hollow globe, open at both ends, and appropriate inscriptions. The son sought to convince the world of his father's theory; fifty years later he was still a firm believer in it.[332]

Needless to say the newspapers had a lot of fun with the hole

[328] Symmes's memorial for two vessels, which he asked the people of the United States to sign, was published in *Niles' Weekly Register*, XXII, 401 (Aug. 24, 1822).

[329] Symmes Papers, II, 13 (April 8, 1821).

[330] G. Poletica, Russian minister, wrote Symmes, August 7, 1820, to make application through the minister at St. Petersburg, whose recommendation "will be . . . no doubt better attended to than mine."

[331] *Niles' Weekly Register*, XXVIII, 212 (June 4, 1825).

[332] Letter from Americus Symmes quoted in Ford and Ford (comps.), *History of Cincinnati*, 74.

in the earth from which came a haze often thickened by the winds "heaping it upon itself," and which made it difficult to see things clearly. The idea was always apropos to the fuzzy concepts of political opponents. Possibly only phrenology and homeopathy offered more possibilities for smart observations. Regardless of the ridicule many simple minds believed in Symmes's theory; some preachers found Biblical support, though disagreeing slightly with the "scientist" as to the temperature of the nether world.

Though not published until later, Richard Owen, brother of David Dale Owen, was no doubt conceiving his theory that the geological formations of the earth were bounded by equilateral spherical triangles. Within these large triangles were smaller ones. The appearance of Owen's globular map was that of a conglomeration of problems in spherical trigonometry. He conceived "an analogy between the formation of the earth and of its inhabitants. . . . Our planet typifies an ovule from the Solar Matrix: in its earlier igneous chaotic state it bore analogy to the yet undeveloped amorphous structure of the vegetable ovules and the animal ovum."[333]

Also during the period Joseph Rodes Buchanan was thinking out his system of neurology or therapeutic sarcognomy, first presented in his book *Sketches of Buchanan's Discoveries in Neurology*, published the year he graduated from Louisville Medical Institute (1842).[334] Buchanan combined animal magnetism, phrenology, and medicine—each of which had fantastic possibilities—into a wonderfully incoherent system which enabled him to control any part of the brain and hence any part of the body. The "bumps" on body and brain being connected, it remained merely to transfer the influence from one brain (and body) to another. This he accomplished by the nervauric and psychic power of certain "sensitives," who could transfer health from an area in one person to a spot which needed it in another. These gifted operators could go further; they could act as psychometers—on perfect strangers even—measure their talents

---

[333] Richard Owen, *Key to the Geology of the Globe* (New York, 1857), 36.

[334] Buchanan's father was professor of medicine at Transylvania; from 1846 to 1856 Buchanan was professor of medicine and medical jurisprudence at the Cincinnati Eclectic Institute; from 1849 to 1856 he was editor of *Buchanan's Journal of Man*.

and analyze their thoughts, characters, and propensities. The possibilities of the technique were limitless. Buchanan anticipated lie detectors, aptitude tests, psychiatrists, and historians who could write books by way of psychic impulses rather than use of documents. His system would provide health, regulate insanity and crime, make education easy, and "promote the general social happiness."[335] Carried through to its logical possibilities it would provide peace, not only on earth but among the planets.

As with literature, the work of the scientists, both serious and fantastic, became known to the people largely through the newspapers and periodicals; relatively few read their books.

§ § § § §

One aspect of the great reform movement, the temperance movement, has been noticed in another chapter;[336] prison reform, care of the lame, halt, and blind, and general humanitarian uplift were only in their incipiency by the end of the 1830's. Two movements, however, deserve comment: nonreligious socialistic experiments and abolition.

The Rappite community at Harmony on the Wabash, the Shaker communities in Ohio, and the Mormon communities in Ohio and Illinois were primarily religious enterprises.[337] George Rapp was a leader of one of the numerous pietistic sects which sprang up in the wake of the Protestant revolt; a Württemberg vinedresser, full of strong convictions and Biblical quotations, he built up a small peasant following. He emphasized that in Adam's original state, in Jesus Christ, and in the ideal resurrection, the male and female elements were combined in the same individual; he also emphasized the imminence of the Second Coming.

In 1803 Rapp and his son came to the United States; his adopted son Frederick came soon thereafter. The Rapps bought land near Zelienople, Pennsylvania, and by 1805 had some six

---

[335] For the development of Buchanan's psychometry, anthropology, and "the law of linear direction *which governs all life in all worlds,*" see Pickard and Buley, *The Midwest Pioneer: His Ills, Cures, and Doctors,* 228–38. The most complete study of Buchanan is Hugh M. Ayer, "Joseph Rodes Buchanan." MS. M.A. thesis, Indiana University, 1949.

[336] Chapter VI, 371–72.

[337] For Shakers and Mormons, see Chapter XIV.

hundred persons busy at work.[338] The settlers signed an agreement to turn over all cash, land, and chattels to the superintendents "as if the members had never possessed them." A part of the agreement, soon canceled, provided for a refund if the member withdrew. Rapp and his associates promised to supply the necessities of life and religious and secular education. By 1811 the property of the community was estimated to be worth $220,000.[339]

Desiring better transportation, a warmer climate, and probably to get away from the settlements, Rapp in 1813 sent Frederick to scout for a new location. On the east side of the Wabash about fifty miles above its mouth (by water) he found a flat well-drained meadow of fertile land. Rapp purchased about 15,000 acres from the government, another 10,000 from settlers—some of it in adjacent counties—sold his Pennsylvania property for $100,000, and moved his colony bag and baggage to Harmony in the spring of 1815.[340]

[338] Of the first contingent of 125 families, about one third split off and settled in another county; some fifty others arrived, however.

[339] Bradbury, *Travels in the Interior of America in the Years 1809, 1810, and 1811,* 334. Biggest item was nine thousand acres of land, with improvements, $90,000. Stock, goods, and inventories, etc., were listed at $75,000.

Other travelers who gave firsthand reports on the Rappites were Melish, *Travels in the United States . . .* ; Woods, *Two Years' Residence . . . on the English Prairie*; Schoolcraft, *Narrative Journal* (1821); [William N. Blaney], *An Excursion through the United States and Canada during the Years 1822–23* (London, 1824); and William Hebert, *A Visit to the Colony of Harmony, in Indiana . . .* (London, 1825). The Pennsylvania and Indiana Harmonies are sketched in John S. Duss, *The Harmonists* (Harrisburg, 1943), Chapters I–III.

[340] This was not "a great sacrifice" since, by Woods's inventory of assets, only $129,000 was represented by nonmovable property. Frederick Rapp referred to a profit of about $8,000 on the transaction. It appears, however, that the purchasers did not pay out the full purchase price.

A pioneer party was sent ahead to Indiana in the summer of 1814. George Rapp wrote from "Harmoni," Pennsylvania, to John L. Baker via "Vincennes India Territory," July 2, 1814; September 14 and 17 Romelius L. Baker took advantage of a "transport" to write his brothers John and Jacob at "New Harmonie, Indiana Territory" that a "considerable contingent" would leave Pennsylvania yet that autumn. On October 31 Frederick Rapp sent to George Rapp at "Harmonie, Indiana Territory," an inventory of goods sent, together with a notice of an unfilled order for some merchandise received from a merchant of Corydon, Indiana Territory. From this George Rapp must have been in Indiana by early autumn. On December 13 and 14 Frederick and others left for Indiana. Christoph Miller to George Rapp, December 17, 1814. The letter was directed to "Emmersonville Postoffice, Gibson County, Harmonie Indiana Territory." In it Miller sent greetings to his mother and to Frederick, and asked why they had not heard from Rapp for so long a time. Manuscript letters in Indiana University Library. See John C. Andressohn (tr. and ed.), "The Arrival of the Rappites at New Harmony," in *Indiana Magazine of History,* XLII (1946), 395–409.

The exact amount of land purchased by George Rapp and associates is difficult to ascertain. The government original entry book and the deed record books in the

Despite the ravages of malaria log buildings were erected, fields put under cultivation, orchards and vineyards planted. Though the book which recorded the members' original investments was destroyed in 1818, the colonists did not stop work; a stone-and-brick blockhouse-granary was completed, a cutoff of the Wabash was dammed, a gristmill built. Soon the Harmonists were producing exportable foodstuffs, hats, cloth, boots, wagons, harness, and whiskey. They established branch stores at Vincennes and Shawneetown. Since their own wants were simple and they worked under rigid discipline, they got ahead; they accepted only specie and notes of the Bank of the United States. In time a fine church, with black walnut, cherry, and sassafras columns, a house for Rapp, a tavern, spacious community houses, and other improvements were added.

The Harmonists attracted quite a lot of attention on the frontier, not all favorable. The natives were jealous of their success and tendency to keep money in one-way circulation; they did not pretend to understand the religion and way of life of these outsiders. The practice of celibacy was even less understandable, and since the Harmonists spoke only German and made no effort to explain these matters, even in that language, rumors arose.

That Rapp's regime was a religious and economic dictatorship seems clear; his vassals were well fed with both material and spiritual food. For simple, ignorant and hard-working peasants this sufficed. Now and then possibly some ultra-individualistic young man or maid escaped into the outer world, wore whatever clothes he or she chose, set up noncommunal, noncelibate establishments, and took their chances on punishment in the next world. There was, however, no outward manifestation of general discontent. Though George Rapp did have a printing press,[341] and Frederick was a very capable businessman—he was also a member of the Indiana Constitutional Convention in 1816

Posey County Court House, Mount Vernon, record approximately 15,000 acres as purchased between 1814 and 1817. See Elfrieda Lang, "The Inhabitants of New Harmony According to the Federal Census of 1850," in *Indiana Magazine of History,* XLII (1946), 361.

[341] Several pamphlets or small books edited or written by George Rapp were printed.

—the society, except for its trade, remained a world within a world.

In the midst of this prosperity and seeming contentment Rapp decided upon another move. The practice of celibacy was general enough to prevent a natural increase in members; attempts to gain new recruits from Germany had failed.[342] Whether Frederick, who was by now probably as powerful a voice in the society as his father, decided it would be good business to sell, whether Rapp thought his colony could best be controlled under the pressure of pioneer work, or for whatever reason, the decision to sell had been made.[343] It was at this time that Richard Flower, of the English settlement of Albion in Illinois, to which the Harmonists had sold much goods, offered to sell Harmony on commission.[344] The Rapps agreed.

In the summer of 1824 Flower called upon Robert Owen, whom he may have had in mind as a purchaser, at New Lanark, Scotland, gave him a glowing description of the Wabash country, and sold him a bill of goods.

Robert Owen, the seventh son of a saddler, was born at Newton, Montgomeryshire, Wales, in 1771. At a tender age his eagerness to get back to school after breakfast resulted in his burning his stomach on a spoonful of hot flummery. This allegedly made him reflective and he said, was "a great influence in forming my character." At eight or so he wrote three sermons, but later finding that Sterne had done the same, destroyed them. At

[342] The evidence of celibacy is conflicting. Even the rumor later spread to the effect that Rapp murdered his son John and later Frederick for not putting away their wives presumes that they had wives. Frederick in a business letter of June 27, 1823, spoke of "my little girl." When Donald Macdonald visited Harmony with Owen in 1824 he reported meeting Frederick, "Mrs. Rapp and her grand daughter." *Diaries of Donald Macdonald,* 268. Earlier, at Economy, Rapp's new settlement, Macdonald had spoken of meeting George Rapp and being "introduced to his daughter." *Ibid.,* 228. Rosina sent greetings to her "father" in a letter December 17, 1814. In this same letter (Christoph Miller and Romelius [Baker] to George Rapp, then at Harmony) Dr. Miller, later the herb-hunting companion of Rafinesque and head of Rapp's press, wrote: "On the 13th and 14th I and many others felt great concern for Frederick and those who accompanied him. The Wagner woman especially caused me some tribulation (or temptation?) [Anfechtung]. On Christmas I am resolved to speak on the salvation of sinners, a subject on which I possess a great deal of material. I shall be obliged to alternate now and then [in preaching] and at such times when I feel that you are not opposed to me and since it is demanded by many. Father, I am walking in the paths of lust, but I shall still render sufficient service to the Lord Jesus, to you and the community. . . ." Andressohn (tr. and ed.), "Arrival of the Rappites at New Harmony," 407.

[343] In fact the site of a new settlement, near Pittsburgh, had already been purchased.

[344] Richard Flower and his son were going to England in 1824 partly on business and partly to avoid the heated convention-slavery struggle of that year in Illinois.

ten he became a draper's assistant in Stamford; eight years later
he began to manufacture yarn with three employees in Manchester. Further experience was gained as superintendent of the
Drinkwater mill. Owen had read a lot; he was thinking, too.
Perhaps it was some childhood grief or frustration of his own
which aroused his interest in the lives of the mill children. While
helping organize a new firm Owen visited Glasgow where he
met Caroline Dale, daughter of David Dale, wealthy Scotsman
and owner of cotton mills at New Lanark. Owen's firm bought
the mills, Owen married Caroline Dale, and his firm made him
manager of the new purchase.

Owen's work in the New Lanark mills is too well known to
dwell upon. He improved working conditions, provided schools,
bettered home life and living conditions of his employees—often
to their own resentment—manipulated his partners, who at first
had controlling ownership, to his ends, and all the while made
more money. In 1812 he published a brochure on the New
Lanark establishment; the next year came *A New View of
Society: or, Essays on the Principle of the Formation of Human
Character*. The Owen boys, Robert Dale, William, David Dale,
and Richard were educated according to the advanced ideas of
their father—private tutors, Fellenberg's work-study school at
Hofwyl, Switzerland (all but William), the Andersonian Institute at Glasgow, travel, and experience.[345] By the 1820's Robert
Owen, then in his early fifties, felt the urge to reform society in
a large way; he became an excellent example of the not uncommon type which operates one set of activities with facts, figures,
and actualities, another set with fancies, emotions, and words.
When Flower presented his proposition, Owen turned to his
son Robert Dale—who, though lacking the business acumen, most
resembled his father—and said ". . . what say you, New Lanark
or Harmony?" The answer, which came without hesitation, was
"Harmony."[346] In October, 1824, Robert Owen, accompanied

[345] The Owen daughters were Anne Caroline, Jane Dale, and Mary.

[346] In March—April, 1824, Robert Dale had accompanied his father on a trip
from Edinburgh to Newcastle, Leeds, Manchester, Leicester, and London. They
looked into everything, talked to many people. Robert Dale took notes, made drawings, gathered material for his *Outline of the System of Education at New Lanark*
(Glasgow, 1824); his father prospected for a loan for a community experiment.
Of Rothschild Robert said: ". . . never saw a man so tormented with too much
money as he seemed, in my life." Entry of April 2, 1824, Robert Dale Owen's notebooks. (It was a torment which the Owens' would soon not have to worry about).
Robert Owen either failed to get the loan or abandoned the idea when he decided
to plant his community in America.

by his son William, Capt. Donald Macdonald,[347] and Richard Flower, and armed with letters of introduction, came to the United States. His purpose was twofold: first, to inspect the Harmony site; and second, to discuss his plans for a new moral world with statesmen, capitalists, editors, intellectuals, and other persons of influence.

Few communal enterprises in our history have attracted the interest of Owen's short-lived experiment. The reasons are first, the importance of the persons who sponsored it; second, the location on the borders of the frontier; third, its influence on later communal attempts; and last, the importance of New Harmony as a cultural and scientific center for years after the utopian scheme collapsed.[348] At Philadelphia the party met Thomas Say,

[347] Captain Macdonald, retired on half pay from the Royal Engineers, had become interested in Owen's theories about three years earlier. His diaries, which differ in details from later Owen accounts, are the best contemporary, firsthand account of the first two trips to the United States, 1824-25 and 1825-26. The *Diary of William Owen* begins on November 10, 1824, following the arrival of the party in New York, and runs through April 10, 1825.

[348] Many volumes have been written on New Harmony and its people, but no good history of it yet exists. Although much material has become available since the publication of George B. Lockwood's *The New Harmony Movement* (New York, 1905), it remains the best introduction to the subject. Frank Podmore, *Robert Owen. A Biography* (2 volumes. New York, 1907); Richard W. Leopold, *Robert Dale Owen. A Biography* (Harvard Historical Studies, XLV, Cambridge, 1940); *The Life of Robert Owen by Himself* (New York, 1920); Robert Dale Owen, *Twenty-Seven Years of Autobiography. Threading My Way* (London, 1874); and the biographies of David Dale Owen and Thomas Say, cited previously in this chapter, cover the leading persons concerned. Various Owen manuscript collections are widely scattered. The three notebooks kept by Robert Dale Owen, 1822-24, are in the Purdue University Library. Maclure papers and other manuscripts are in the Library of the Workingmen's Institute at New Harmony. Selections from the correspondence of William Maclure and Marie Duclos Fretageot, edited by Arthur E. Bestor, Jr., are published in *Education and Reform at New Harmony . . . (Indiana Historical Society Publications,* XV, No. 3, Indianapolis, 1948). Representative contemporary accounts are available in Thomas C. Pears, Jr. (ed.), *New Harmony, An Adventure in Happiness. Papers of Thomas and Sarah Pears (Indiana Historical Society Publications,* XI, No. 1, Indianapolis, 1933); and *The Diaries of Donald Macdonald 1824-1826 (ibid.,* XIV, No. 2, Indianapolis, 1942). Some of the William Pelham letters, still in private hands, were published in Harlow Lindley (ed.), *Indiana as Seen by Early Travelers (Indiana Historical Collections* [III], Indianapolis, 1916). The manuscripts of Miner Kilbourne Kellogg are in the Indiana Historical Society Library. Of the various travelers' accounts those of William Hebert, *A Visit to the Colony of Harmony in Indiana . . .* (London, 1825); Bernhard, Duke of Saxe-Weimar-Eisenach, *Travels through North America;* Simon Ansley Ferrall, *A Ramble of Six Thousand Miles through the United States of America* (London, 1832); and Maximilian, Prince of Wied, *Reise Durch Nord Amerika* (Coblentz, 1838-43) with its pictures and maps, are most useful. Paul Brown, *Twelve Months in New-Harmony . . .* (Cincinnati, 1827), presents a partial and angry description. Mrs. Caroline Dale Snedeker in *The Town of the Fearless* (New York, 1931) gives a romanticized account; Marguerite Young's *Angel in the Forest* (New York, 1945), despite its subtitle of "A Fairy Tale of Two Utopias," contains a good impressionistic estimate of Owenism. The author is

librarian of the Academy of Natural Sciences, Charles Alexandre Lesueur, the naturalist and artist, and Madame Marie Duclos Fretageot, who had a school for young ladies. In Washington they met President Adams, Secretary of War Calhoun, and some Chocktaw and Chickasaw chiefs. Flower told Owen that Rapp had had other offers for Harmony and urged him to move on. From Pittsburgh in December George Rapp took Owen out to Economy, his new settlement, which an advance party was building. Some days later the Owen party arrived at Mount Vernon, Indiana, from whence they drove to Harmony. While William Owen and Macdonald visited Albion, Robert Owen and Frederick Rapp talked business. By January 3, 1825, they had come to terms; it appears that Owen promised to pay $100,000 in cash and to give two notes of $20,000 each, payable in one and two years.[349]

While the young men continued their visits over the surrounding country and drew up notices of the proposed association, Owen hastened back East to spread the news.[350] Twice he addressed the House of Representatives; the President, most of the cabinet, senators, and Supreme Court justices were present.[351] At Philadelphia William Maclure showed a warmer interest than had Congress. It was probably his influence that led Owen to broaden his plan to include artists and scientists as well as producers of more material things; supposedly even they could work the few hours per day necessary to support themselves under the new order. Besides Maclure had money.[352]

---

much indebted to Richard E. Banta for use of his manuscript "Documentary Source Book" of New Harmony which made available much material not otherwise accessible.

[349] The deed, dated December 10, 1825, records $125,000 for about 19,250 acres plus improvements. Deed Record D, Posey County, Indiana.

[350] William and Macdonald visited Albion, Princeton, Vincennes, etc. Dr. Miller ran off one hundred copies of one of the prospectuses on the Rappite press at Harmony. On January 22 William wrote William Pelham of Zanesville, Ohio, apparently in answer to an enquiry, that his father proposed to form a society "on the Principle of united production and consumption, to be composed of persons practicing all the most useful occupations necessary to the well being of a complete establishment. . . . a new Community on the Principle of complete equality. . . ." Quoted in Lindley (ed.), *Indiana as Seen by Early Travelers*, 416.

[351] February 25 and March 7, 1825. A number of these men had earlier received copies of the *New View of Society*. Owen showed them a model of his proposed community edifice, designed by Stedman Whitwell, for the housing of a community of two to five thousand persons.

[352] He had been a partner in the firm of Miller, Hart and Company of London prior to moving to Philadelphia; whether he continued to represent his old firm

Owen, well experienced in publicity, had no difficulty getting recruits; it was said that nine hundred in Philadelphia alone desired to join up. Recent immigrants who had found the land of promise more promising and less rewarding than they had anticipated, people who had a little property and did not know what to do with it, people for whom the problem of making decisions in life was too great, a few who were genuinely attracted by the new life as by a new religion, these and the usual percentage of cranks, misfits, and "advanced thinkers" composed the following.

The last of the Rappites pulled out from Harmony by boat in May, 1825. Some eight hundred pious, industrious, phlegmatic producers had gone;[353] a similar number of simple, well-meaning, individualistic incompetents, joined a number of temperamental, artistic visionaries, and a few substantial citizens in another attempt at a socialistic communitarian experiment.[354] On April 20 and May 1 Owen explained his purpose "to introduce an entire new state of society; to change it from an ignorant selfish system to an enlightened social system which shall gradually unite all interests into one. . . ." The change could not be made all at once; New Harmony was to be the "half-way house between the old and the new." For a while there would be pecuniary inequality; scientists and educators would be brought in under inducements. A constitution for the "Preliminary Society"

---

during Philadelphia days is not clear. At any rate he had made a fair fortune. His will at the time of his death in 1840 listed a million reals in Spanish securities, convents and estates in Spain, property or mortgages on property in England, France, Virginia, 10,000 acres and 30 buildings at New Harmony, books, collections of minerals, prints, copper plates of engravings, etc. No adequate study of Maclure has as yet been published. A contemporary sketch, "A Memoir of William Maclure, Esq.," by Samuel George Morton, read before the Academy of Natural Sciences of Philadelphia, 1841, gives the main facts of his life. The Maclure papers at New Harmony throw some additional light on Maclure's work.

[353] George Rapp had taken about one hundred persons to Economy for pioneer work a year previous. Years later, under the stairs in Community House No. 2, was found the following inscription:
"In the twenty-fourth of May, 1824,
We have departed. Lord, with
thy great help and goodness,
In body and soul, protect us."

[354] As Miner Kilbourne Kellogg said of his father, ". . . he had no love of money, his heart was in some way inclined another way. . . . This wavering between the choice of a line of personal benefit or a line of general good of humanity kept his mind in just that unsettled condition as prepared it for the reception of any plausible doctrine that promised a revolution in the accepted order of things. . . ." Kellogg MSS. Indiana Historical Society Library.

was drawn up. All persons except persons of color might become members; the latter might be "helpers." Owen as proprietor and founder was to appoint the management committee. In a year or two the members were expected to take over and form "a community of equality and independence."[355] A credit system was arranged at the store upon which each family (or individual) might draw in proportion to the number of useful members. Education of children, medical services, and old-age benefits were mentioned. The Preliminary Society established, Owen shook hands all around, left his son William on the spot—and returned to England.[356]

The next two years at New Harmony presented almost everything but harmony. It was a story of babes lost in the woods of ideas, everybody talking, few working.

Within a few months after Owen's departure dissatisfaction was expressed over the allowances of the "Good Folks"; those who raised food "became of such importance as to seem to think none of any account but themselves." The management committee gave up all idea of farming until Owen should come again; "the hogs have been our Lords and Masters this year in field and garden."[357] Sincere believers noted that "men generally do not work as well as they would for themselves." When production failed, meetings were held, resolutions passed. Much planning resulted, little work; it was a system under which the dissatisfied farmer might become a printer, bookkeeper, or teacher, the dissatisfied writer a farmer. It did not work.[358] The spirit of general tolerance, religious and otherwise, did not compensate for this

---

[355] Members were to provide their own household furniture, small tools, etc. The society was not to be answerable for any individual debts of its members.

[356] William, now about twenty, was characterized by his brother, Robert Dale, as ". . . scarcely decisive enough . . . too easily imposed upon, & too inactive. . . ."

[357] Thomas Pears to Benjamin Bakewell, September 2, 1825. (Pears had been Audubon's business partner at Henderson, Kentucky.) Bakewell, wealthy glass manufacturer in Pittsburgh, was Lucy Audubon's uncle. He was trying to found a co-operative society at Pittsburgh and wrote Pears on September 10 that Owen was "sadly mistaken in representing money as nearly useless even at commencement." *Pears Papers,* 26, 35.

[358] A worker on a building showed jealousy towards the teacher who could quit at four o'clock, but got the same pay. When the teacher asked him if he would like to change places, he refused but still felt a grievance.

Some Rappites had been left in charge of various properties—manufactories, livestock, etc.—until Owen could take over; also a large supply of necessaries had been left for temporary subsistence of the Owen followers. Kellogg MSS. The new settlers should have had time to get in ample crops on fields already under cultivation.

fact; tolerance could not hold a community together as religion held the Mormons, Shakers, and Rappites.[359] There were weekly concerts, music and dancing at the Hall (which scandalized some); the boys over twelve in the half-day Pestalozzian school became such a nuisance that it was resolved that "they be employed during the regular hours for business."[360] On October 1, 1825, appeared the first issue of the *New-Harmony Gazette*; its motto was: "If we can not reconcile all opinions, let us endeavor to unite all hearts."[361] Though it gave a rosy account of the progress of manufactures, it admitted that "an accession of skilful hands . . . is still desirable." There was a housing problem: "Without actual experience, one cannot realize the difficulty of getting house-room in this place."[362]

Rule by the committee was peculiarly arbitrary for the free new world. "Thus you see we are living under an aristocracy, and must continue to do so until Mr. Owen returns," said Thomas Pears. Mrs. Pears added her word: "He ought to have called it despotism. . . . It makes my blood boil within me to think that the citizens of a free and independent nation should be collected here to be made slaves of."[363]

Anyway the young people of both sexes found the labor moderate, their recreations "frequent and innocent"; they pleased themselves if not each other. William Pelham, too, seemed happy, with $7.00 cash on hand and a presumable allowance of $1.54 per week from the committee. All were looking forward to Robert Owen's second coming—except possibly some of the women who

[359] Owen did not believe in the inspiration of the Scriptures, but Baptist, Methodist, and other ministers were free to preach at New Harmony; several did.

[360] When an Irish schoolmaster, having difficulty in keeping his boys in a drill line in formation, finally used a fishing pole on their rears, they yelled, "Old School! Old School!" and scattered. Later, however, Miner Kellogg and some of his fellow pupils were marched about without shoes in cold weather to harden their systems. Also they were worked. Kellogg MSS.

[361] The *Gazette* ran through three volumes. Some news was taken from exchanges, but the bulk of its contents were essays on socialism, moral subjects, Owen tracts, and scientific articles.

[362] William Pelham, formerly of Boston, England, Philadelphia, and Zanesville, to his son William Creese Pelham, Zanesville editor, October 25, 1825. Quoted in Lindley (ed.), *Indiana as Seen by Early Travelers*, 389. Twenty additional recruits from Pittsburgh "will have to retrace their steps." Letter of November 27. *Ibid.*, 393. Pelham had become editor or printer of the *Gazette*. On December 16 he wrote: "We have no lumber . . . no means of cooking whatever . . . no bedding for anybody . . . the sugar is gone, quite gone . . . we are all in good spirits. . . ."

[363] *Pears Papers*, 40. Sarah Palmer Pears was the daughter of the Reverend John Palmer, of Birmingham, England, who was associated with Joseph Priestley in his revolt against intolerance.

viewed with horror the community costume (for women a knee-length petticoat and pantaloons) which Robert Dale Owen had planned. Perhaps it was thought of this which threw Mrs. Pears into a spell of hypo: ". . . it is almost too much for me. I feel so forlorn that I could say with Cowper, 'I am out of Humanity's reach.' But . . . my lot is fixed. I feel like a bird in a cage shut up for ever." Meanwhile the "Revd. Mr. Jennings . . . preached in the forenoon in the Church, and this afternoon appeared on horseback in his military dress to exercise the troops";[364] the *Gazette* delivered 123 copies in town and sent 175 to mail subscribers and exchanges; some members, having failed to withdraw more by way of debts at the store than they had produced, and others who found their sectarian religious views in disfavor, withdrew, and William got worried about his father's energetic recruiting, the housing shortage, and the lack of mechanics and domestic laborers, especially cooks and laundresses. But such prosaic matters, plus food shortage and malaria, or "Pone Bread and Musquetoes," were not to stand in the way of the "most feasible plan for improving the position of mankind . . . ever devised."[365]

Robert Owen and party[366] landed at New York on October 1, 1825. Here he learned of the unfavorable publicity, especially from the religious press, that New Harmony had been receiving. Owen released more publicity and got a model of his proposed community through the customs; he then addressed a public meeting, and called on the governor and the Bonapartes.[367] Later he went to Philadelphia, where possibly he helped organize Maclure's group of scientists and teachers who were to join the colony; meanwhile Macdonald and Whitwell went to Washington, presented "the Model" to President Adams, then called upon Jefferson at Charlottesville. When Macdonald and Whitwell got

---

[364] William Pelham to his son, November 27, 1825, in Lindley (ed.), *Indiana as Seen by Early Travelers*, 395.

[365] William Pelham to son, January 8, 1826. *Ibid.*, 403.

[366] Robert Dale Owen, Capt. Donald Macdonald, and the architect-planner, Stedman Whitwell.

[367] Among those who expressed interest in Owen's plan was a Mr. Page, who dressed in a green gown. "He said he understood the magical art, and had for some years been recommending communities on Mr. Owen's plan, in which he would establish theatrical religion. He called himself 'The Page of Nature; the Page of History; King David's Page, and Hisom Hieroglyphicus.'" Macdonald asked himself whether he, too, might not be going insane. *Macdonald Diaries*, 310–11 (Nov. 11, 1825).

to Pittsburgh, they found that Owen had purchased a keelboat and started West with his party. The boat was icebound twenty miles downstream. Owen went on by stage to Wheeling and thence to Cincinnati where he took a steamboat and the two young men boarded the keelboat.[368] When the boat (the *Philanthropist*) was freed of the ice, it proceeded down river. Among the passengers were Robert Dale Owen, the Sistaire sisters, Lesueur, Say, William Phiquepal d'Arusmont, Dr. Gerard Troost, chemist and geologist, and (after Wheeling), Maclure and Madame Fretageot. At Louisville they met Joseph Neef, former Maclure protégé, who promised to sell his farm and join them in the spring.[369] Wagons met the party at Mount Vernon on January 23–24; scholars, books, and scientific paraphernalia made the remaining few miles in safety.[370] These were the people who were to make New Harmony famous for many years after the community broke up.

Owen had arrived eleven days earlier. Already he had proposed that the people form a permanent "community of equality, based on the principle of common property."[371] A committee was selected. Mrs. Pears viewed it all with forebodings: "I feel more distressed . . . than I can express. . . . All the troubles I have formerly experienced . . . never affected my heart with so deep a gloom, so hopeless a sense of absolute despondency. . . . I am confident I shall never be able to perform what he appears to expect from the women. . . . Oh, if you could see some of the rough uncouth creatures here, I think you would find it rather hard to look upon them exactly in the light of brothers and sisters."[372] But Robert Dale Owen found the good fellowship and

[368] Maclure and Madame Fretageot had gone on to Steubenville, then to Wheeling, where they were picked up by the boat.

[369] Maclure had been impressed with Pestalozzi's school in Switzerland in 1805; Pestalozzi recommended Joseph Neef, the former Napoleonic soldier who carried a musket ball in his head, to open such a school in the United States. Maclure supported him for two years while he learned English; Neef then opened a school near Philadelphia, moved it, and then abandoned it for a farm near Louisville.

[370] About 100,000 francs (50 tons) of French books and philosophical apparatus came by way of New Orleans.

[371] Pears said Owen had at first praised everyone, and said that they had not suffered as he had anticipated; that they had reached the "half-way house"; then three days later that they had "only got 'one third of . . . [the] way.'" Letter of March 21, 1826. *Pears Papers*, 76.

[372] Mrs. Pears to her uncle, Benjamin Bakewell, January 28, 1826. *Ibid.*, 60.

"absolute freedom from all trammels" wonderfully pleasant; he helped pull cabins for a spell, broadcast grain for one day—until his arm got sore—then helped "certain of the young girls" bake bread. He was not "haunted by doubts" as to the success of the social experiment. And Pears expected "that in six months the New Harmony machine will go like a piece of clock work."

The constitution and declaration of principles were adopted February 5, 1826. Equality of rights, duties, and property were specified. Man's entire character was said to be the result of his formation, his location, and the circumstances under which he existed. Six departments of the community were established: agriculture; manufactures; literature, science, and education; domestic economy; general economy; and commerce. All accounts, individual and departmental, were to be balanced and results announced weekly. As Robert Dale Owen said later: "It found favor with that heterogenous collection of radicals, enthusiastic devotees to principle, honest latitudinarians, and lazy theorists, with a sprinkling of unprincipled sharpers thrown in. . . ."

A group of "American Backwoodsmen" (according to Macdonald), or some respectable families who had conscientious scruples against signing the constitution (according to the *Gazette*), withdrew to some near-by land which they got from Owen and set up Macluria. Also a group of English families leased some other land from Owen and started Community No. 3—Feiba-Peveli. This group had the best farmers and the best land.[373] By mid-February Thomas Pears, who still liked the system, was "completely out of humor with the practice here." Like many a state, the society was floundering in the morass of accounts (finances).[374] So the committee finally asked Owen to take over the management for the rest of the year. Owen agreed to do so if 5 per cent on a fair appraisal be paid him by the

[373] Stedman Whitwell, wishing to improve upon the lack of system in American place names, had devised a scheme of lettering the degrees of longitude and latitude, then spelling the location. By this arrangement some interesting names resulted: New Harmony became Ipba Veinul; Yellow Springs, Ohio—Irap Evifle; Pittsburgh—Otful Veitoup; London—Lafa Vovutu.

The seceders got no bargain since they had to pay $83.60 and $85 per acre, got seven years credit, "and five years afterwards to pay for it."

[374] Pears (who had gone from bookkeeping to wool picking) and his children had not been allowed enough by the committee of the Preliminary Society to pay board. Pears to Bakewell, February 16, 1826. *Ibid.*, 65.

society.[375] The question for debate then was, was each signer of the constitution liable to the limit of his assets, or only his own pro rata? which, considering the assets, was a somewhat scholastic matter at best. On March 4 the members signed; a new committee of administrators was set up. A few weeks later the constitution was "now as nothing." "I am heartily tired of it; and if I knew how, I would get out of it quickly," wrote Pears. The *Gazette,* however, was still optimistic, though a more threatening split was at hand—the Maclure following of intellectuals plus William Owen, Robert Dale Owen, Whitwell, *et al.,* were going exclusive; they were about to establish Community No. 4.[376] Owen offered them the woods, but the idea of chopping their own trees did not appeal; they reconsidered. Since many members had come to New Harmony for their children's education, this threatened schism was a serious danger.

The new rules added not to the general happiness. Children of fourteen were taken away from their families and put in boardinghouses, both sexes together. (Mr. Owen said they would soon get used to the system.) Room having thus been made, each housekeeper had to take in two other families, at least one of which was to have a child under the age of two. Some of the women did not like the arrangement. Other members, finding the labor stepped up to eleven hours a day, contemplated with longing the four-hour day they had understood would be sufficient. The original community, now short of cleared land and good workers, was hard pressed. The people criticized the officers, as Pears said, on the theory that "the blacker others are, the whiter they become themselves." Factions and parties arose sufficient to overthrow any system, "much more one in which the most powerful bond of union, that of individual interest is unknown."[377]

Persons who still believed in the "system" thought perhaps Mr. Owen was of too sanguine a temperament to make it work;

[375] Both Owen and Maclure thought the appraisal of $126,520 too low by $20,000 but accepted. The arrangements between Owen and Maclure were not clear, even to themselves. (Owen later stated that though Maclure put $150,000 into the New Harmony venture, his liability was limited to $10,000.) Owen was to put up $20,-000 additional for operating expenses. For a discussion of Owen and Maclure's investment in New Harmony and their financial relations, see Bestor (ed.), *Education and Reform at New Harmony, passim.*

[376] Pears said that they intended to make those who could not leave into "hewers of wood and drawers of water for them."

[377] Bakewell to Pears, March 23, 1826, in *Pears Papers,* 79.

that in his bigotry against bigotry he had cast out an important factor, religion. Also it seemed to some that Mr. Owen in New Harmony, trying to enforce the redesigned community garb as well as work rules, was a very different man from Mr. Owen speaking in New York, Pittsburgh, and Washington. It appeared to some persons both inside and out that he had "conceived the rough features of his general system from considering forced services or statutory labor." Between doing the laundry for a few dozen field workers during the day and attending the endless business meetings and discussions during the evening, more than one good housewife who thought she had enough on her hands in her own household, became both confused and exhausted. Thomas Say, tied up in the double-bloomer neckless ensemble of the male costume, found the handling of insects had not sufficiently calloused his hands for gardening. Virginia du Palais, young and pretty (who had probably joined up "on account of an unhappy attachment"), found her singing and piano playing interrupted by the necessity of milking the cows. Concerts, dances, and an occasional wedding kept the young folks happy; the school children found their chores not too difficult. Rapp's still was no longer in use, but drinking members (the Duke of Saxe-Weimar mentioned only Irishmen) found opportunities "of getting whiskey and fuddling themselves from the flat boats that stop here."

Ignoring the disintegration which was going on about him, Owen lashed out in a Fourth of July manifesto against the "trinity of most monstrous evils"—private property, religion, and marriage based upon these two. This "Declaration of Mental Independence" did not disturb the members, who were accustomed to "old Bob's" ideas, as much as it did outsiders.

Those who had come to get something for nothing and the chronic discontents were departing; so were some of the sincere theoretical communists. The 5 per cent was too much for them. A few—Miner Kellogg's father for one—thought the idea could still be accomplished, but Owen could only advance him $20 (plus his blessing) for a new community. "A very warm advocate of socialism . . . who possessed a good farm and some means near Jeffersonville," took them in.[378]

---

[378] The usual disagreements—results of financial malnutrition—followed this community; the sheriff's visit closed its history.

On July 30 a fourth society, the New Harmony Agricultural and Pastoral Society, was organized. Then a group of mechanics and artisans undertook to purchase $23,000 worth of land and buildings.

The one bright spot in New Harmony was the schools. After the dictatorial Robert L. Jennings was relieved of pedagogical duties, Neef and Robert Dale Owen were put in charge; a more "benevolent superintendence" prevailed.[379] From the infant school where the main idea was to surround the children with conditions favorable to their development, through mechanics, mathematics, science, drawing, music, languages, and gymnastics, the Owen-Maclure-Pestalozzian system prevailed. Maclure outlined the main idea:

The great or fundamental principle is, never to attempt to teach children what they can not comprehend, and to teach them in the exact ratio of their understanding without omitting one line in the chain of ratiocination, proceeding always from the known to the unknown, from the most easy to the most difficult; practising the most extensive and accurate use of all the senses; exercising, improving, and perfecting all the mental and corporal faculties by quickening combination; accelerating and carefully arranging comparison; judiciously and impartially making deductions; summing up the results free from prejudice, and cautiously avoiding the delusions of the imagination, a constant source of ignorance and error.[380]

Mesdames Neef and Fretageot handled the infants, Neef assisted by four daughters and one son had charge of pupils age five to twelve. In the "School for Adults" (over twelve) the pupils had the advantage of lectures on chemistry by Dr. Gerard Troost, the Dutch naturalist and geologist, on natural history by Say, and on experimental farming by M. Phiquepal d'Arusmont. The industrial school, Maclure's own pet, was an innovation; not even Owen's New Lanark schools had anything comparable. Few pupils anywhere were so fortunate as to receive instruction in science at the hands of scholars such as Say, or in printing and engraving from an artist-scientist such as Lesueur. Miner Kellogg was probably not the only boy who became an enthusiastic collector of specimens or an artist as the result of

[379] Jennings was born in England, brought up to a military life, and later became a Universalist preacher.
[380] William Maclure, "Pestalozzian System of Education. . . ," in The American Journal of Science and Arts, X (1826), 145–51. For a fuller presentation of the educational system, see Bestor (ed.), Education and Reform at New Harmony.

interesting teaching. Even military drill seems to have been made interesting, as it should be. Fortunately the Owen report-card system seems not to have been generally employed. This machine consisted of a plate with ten subjects and scales: self-attachment, affections, judgment, imagination, memory, reflection, perception, excitability, courage, and strength. Each scale was divided into hundredths; a sliding indicator was to show the exact status of progress.

Yet the educational system, too, failed. Teachers did not accept the equality idea; instead of pooling their talents in order that all pupils could receive instruction from each, they divided the pupils into groups, one teacher to each group. Teachers and artists were temperamental. As the Duke of Saxe-Weimar said, "In spite of the principles of equality which they recognize, it shocks the feelings of people of education, to live on the same footing with everyone indiscriminately, and eat with them at the same table." Finally the Education Society was organized. Maclure's followers contracted for $49,000 of buildings and land (nine hundred acres) on a thousand-year lease. They endeavored to incorporate, but the Indiana legislature, doubtful of their Christianity, refused to co-operate. Owen, in his farewell address, blamed the schools for failing to amalgamate the whole into a community.

The various societies fought with each other and with the original society; they squabbled with Owen and Maclure over boundaries and rights. In September Owen sought to get all the communities to unite in "The New Harmony Community Number 1," government to be vested in himself and four directors for five years, at the end of which period they might decide on the future government. Macluria, having split over a religious issue, lost ninety-six members. These accepted Owen's latest plan but the Education Society refused flatly. By this time New Harmony was not a "community" but a place, "a central village out of and around which communities have formed"; each occupation regulated its own affairs, distributed its produce, and paid a small percentage towards general town expenses. Things were about back to the place where they had started. Paul Brown reported that "the individual sufferings from the privations and embarrassments arising out of the continual shifting of arrangements, as well as the circumscription of subsistence, deadened the wonted sympathy of many ingenuous souls. Money was in higher repute than in any other town, and became almost an object of worship . . . there was no politeness between the single persons of the two sexes, but a dark, sullen, cold suspicious temper, and a most intollerable miserly allusion to individual property as the standard of worth. . . ."

By April, 1827, Owen and Maclure were at outs over the educational program. Maclure was not so much interested in communalism as in strengthening the lower classes by education; Owen's chief objection to Maclure's schools was that they did not teach the community spirit.[381] They also had financial differences. Maclure posted a notice "not to trust Robert Owen on my account, as I am determined not to pay any debts of his," and Owen reciprocated. According to Paul Brown, Maclure prosecuted Owen for recovery of $40,000 and Owen got a writ on Maclure for $90,000. A compromise was finally effected and Maclure got a deed for his share of the property.[382] Thus two hard-headed businessmen, the one interested in a new moral world, the other primarily in science and education, had apparently let their obsessions interfere with the ordinary requirements of business memoranda and contracts.

On May 26 Owen delivered his farewell address and followed it the next day with counsel to the "ten social colonies of equality and common property on the New Harmony estate." Almost a year later, on his return to New Harmony, he was partially convinced that the new social order had failed. He could not understand why, with himself furnishing the money and the ideas, it had not worked. "I had hoped that fifty years of political liberty had prepared the American people to govern themselves advantageously." Perhaps that was the answer.

The various communities, as well as the scattering of settlements which were offshoots of New Harmony, all eventually passed into individual hands. A visitor almost twenty years later found the subject of socialism unpopular. In later years Owen generally laid the cause of failure to the fact that the people did

---

[381] See Bestor (ed.), *Education and Reform at New Harmony*, index.

[382] Maclure also bought some 7,430 acres (including some land in Pike County, Indiana, and White County, Illinois) from Frederick Rapp by deed dated March 1, 1830; the price was $11,000. Posey County Deed Record G.

not understand the principles. The people were too weak to stand the attractions of the outside world. Perhaps Josiah Warren, another socialist who seemed unable to keep from making money, had the right answer when he said that everything at New Harmony "went on delightfully except pecuniary affairs." Utopia as usual had been wrecked upon the twin rocks of human nature and arithmetic.

Owen returned to England and projected new communal societies in Mexico but abandoned the idea. He revisited New Harmony in 1829. In April of that year he and Alexander Campbell held their great debate at Cincinnati on the evidences of Christianity. Though the issue was never really joined—there was no common denominator, the two men merely ran on in parallels—like the battle of Blenheim, 'twas a famous one, but no victory. Newspapers in the West reported it in detail. Nothing done by Owen up to that time had attracted so much attention. His twelve "fundamental laws" and detachment of man from a Supreme Being aroused wrath among those who had paid little attention to his social experiments.[383] But possibly as Emerson said of him in 1845: "He was the better Christian in his controversies with Christians."

Owen took renewed hope with the quickening interest in Fourierism in the 1840's, returned to the United States, and proclaimed that he had come to "effect in peace the greatest revolution yet made in human society." Later he drew up a plan for a federation between Great Britain and the United States by which both would declare their interests to be the same, admit it their duty to terminate war, and "live in peaceful industry and friendly exchange." At the age of seventy when asked how many disciples he had who would carry on after his death, he said, "Not one."[384]

[383] *Debate on the Evidences of Christianity; Containing an Examination of the "Social System"* . . . *between Robert Owen* . . . *and Alexander Campbell* . . . , as reported by Charles H. Sims, was published, two volumes in one, 251 pp., 301 pp., Bethany, Va., 1829. A second edition was published in Cincinnati that same year. Timothy Flint's review is in *Western Monthly Review,* III (1829–30), 427–39. At the time of the debate Flint had treated it somewhat humorously. Owen answered by posting his twelve Fundamental Laws which he said the editor of the *Review* had dared not publish because they were true. *Ohio State Journal,* May 28, 1829.

[384] The Reverend Adin Ballou, later founder of the Hopedale Community in Massachusetts which Owen visited in 1845, wrote of Owen: "Robert Owen is a remarkable character. In years nearly seventy-five: in knowledge and experience superabundant; in benevolence of heart transcendental; in honesty without dis-

The years following the breakup of the Owen-Maclure social experiment, the golden years, had no relation to Owenism other than the personnel involved and the stimulus provided by it. The Owen sons, Frances Wright, Josiah Warren, and others furnished ideas and excitement for years to come. In science, art, education, and politics New Harmony furnished more leaders than any other community of its size in the West. No other town was quite like it.

§ § § § §

Few topics in American history have received as much attention as slavery and the antislavery movement; on none has there been less agreement. Evidence, specific facts, are subject to check; interpretation is subject largely to the interpreter. One of the leading historians of the abolition movement in the region says: "The Old Northwest began the organized crusade against slavery, carried it through to a successful conclusion, and saved the Union in the process."[385] Individually the three parts of this statement appear to be facts, yet the question remains, would the third have been necessary except for the first? Or would the Civil War have come regardless of whether there had been an antislavery crusade? Would slavery have continued to exist for another generation had there been no Civil War? If not, did the game justify the candle? These are questions which no historian can answer.

That the Old Northwest figured more prominently in the antislavery movement than was formerly recognized by historians is now obvious.[386] However, at no time in the history of the Northwest was abolition the major interest of any but a small portion of the population; at no time did it determine the

---

guise; in philanthropy unlimited; in religion a skeptic; in theology a Pantheist; in metaphysics a necessarian circumstantialist; in morals a universal excusionist; in general conduct a philosophic non-resistant; in socialism a Communist; in hope a terrestrial elysianist; in practical business a methodist; in deportment an unequivocal gentleman." Quoted in John Humphrey Noyes, *History of American Socialisms* (Philadelphia, 1870), 88.

[385] Dwight Lowell Dumond, *Antislavery Origins of the Civil War in the United States* (Ann Arbor, Mich., London, 1939), 98.

[386] See particularly Gilbert Hobbs Barnes, *The Antislavery Impulse 1830–1844* (New York, London, 1933); Dumond, *Antislavery Origins of the Civil War;* and Barnes and Dumond (eds.), *Letters of Theodore Dwight Weld, Angelina Grimké Weld and Sarah Grimké* (2 volumes. New York, London, 1934), Introduction.

economic destinies of the region or ever, save perhaps in Ohio, seriously affect the political balance.

The abolition movement in the West stemmed largely from the great revival movement started in western New York in the mid 1820's by the Reverend Charles Grandison Finney. The iron front of Calvinistic predestination had already been penetrated at its weakest point—infant damnation. Individuals wavered, even college bulwarks tottered. Few could execute the straddle as well as Lyman Beecher, who, with the assistance of Dr. Nathaniel W. Taylor of Yale, learned to preach original sin with his mind and a liberal gospel of individual responsibility and revivalism with his heart. But Finney with his "new measures"—long protracted meetings, the "holy band" of newly converted helpers, the "anxious seat," and public prayer by women—was too much for even Beecher. Appealing to reason as well as to emotions, Finney hit straight at the heart of Calvinism: original sin or innate depravity was merely a deepseated selfishness; it required not the miracle of the Holy Ghost to cast it out; the sinner could do it himself. The opposite of sin was "disinterested benevolence"; converts "should set out with a determination to aim at being useful in the highest degree possible" to the interests of God's kingdom. Finney's gospel, which encouraged men to work as well as to believe, found its outlet in the realm of social reform—temperance, benevolent works, education, abolition. It appealed to the youthful, the ardent, the people with a mission.

Theodore Dwight Weld, a student at Hamilton College, had deprecated the Finney movement, but when the revivalist concentrated upon him, he succumbed. Weld, with his personality, energy, and pride became a host unto himself.[387] Soon his services were in demand at widely scattered points. The Tappan brothers (Arthur and Lewis) and other New York reformers with means were promoting nonsectarian benevolent associations.

[387] Weld already had the reform impulse, having been influenced profoundly by the ex-English army officer, Charles Stuart, principal of the Utica High School. Weld's further education at George W. Gale's Oneida Institute was financed by Stuart. Oneida was financed in part by Arthur Tappan, wealthy New York merchant and reformer. Weld and Stuart both became members of Finney's "holy band." It was said Weld's eloquence was so great as to determine a number of liquor dealers at Rochester to abandon business. Barnes, *Antislavery Impulse*, 206, note 28.

The rather conspicuous failure of "The Asylum for Females who have Deviated from the Paths of Virtue" did not stop activities; temperance, Sabbath observance (including no mails), the free-church movement, observance of the Seventh Commandment, manual labor colleges, college training for Negroes, all were overshadowed by the interest in slavery. The "sword of the spirit" was centered in this subject; the result was the American Anti-Slavery Society, founded in 1833.

It was as agent for Tappan's Society for Promoting Manual Labor in Literary Institutions that Weld came west in 1831. He spoke widely, made many antislavery converts. At Huntsville, Alabama, he met and won James G. Birney, son of a wealthy Louisville trader and manufacturer, himself a slaveholding planter and prominent attorney. On the Western Reserve he won recruits; at Western Reserve College at Hudson he made a disciple of Professor Elizur Wright and split the faculty. All the while he was looking for a location for a western manual labor theological seminary. Friends had pointed out the importance of the West.[388] At Cleveland he had said: "The Great Valley of the Mississippi is a cradle in which a giant in his swaddling clothes is sleeping. These swaddling clothes he will soon burst. And the time is not distant when he will sway the world! It lies with the present generation to decide whether he shall tread down the nations in blood or whether his march shall be the march of resurrection over the graves of ignorance and sin."[389] The site which Weld finally selected was Lane Seminary in Cincinnati. Here then came Lyman Beecher as president, and Weld and a group of his young disciples who were to follow Tappan's plan of making Lane Seminary the headquarters of western abolitionism. Beecher was an abolitionist, but not an ultra; he was not willing to die, or even lose his job, for the cause. When Garrisonians fell out with the advocates of colonization, he sought to reconcile the conflicting parties even as he had sought to reconcile Calvinism and the New Theology. When the Weld band came to Lane, Beecher boasted of "the most talented, spirited, heroic phalanx I ever met." When their antislavery

---

[388] Letter to Weld cited in Barnes, *Antislavery Impulse*, 40. The Birney and Weld papers are in the William L. Clements Library, University of Michigan.
[389] From Hudson *Ohio Observer*, October 1, 1832, cited in *ibid.*, 215.

crusade ran afoul of local sentiment, the trustees (in Beecher's absence) put a curb to their activities and most of the students left.[390]

The immediate abolitionists were too much for Beecher and Cincinnati.[391] Beecher now called his "heroic phalanx" a bunch of "He-goat men, who think they do God a service by butting everything in the line of their march which does not fall or get out of the way." But before Weld and his followers left Lane for the more congenial atmosphere of Oberlin College, he had again met Birney, now back in Kentucky, and the two men joined forces. The Lane rebels moved to Oberlin in the spring of 1835; by summer a group of them were in the field working assiduously to convert Ohio to the doctrine of "immediate abolition, gradually accomplished." The attack was on moral grounds; the economics of slavery did not interest Weld missionaries. Violence was not infrequent; it was present when one hundred delegates— Birney, Oberlin students, Quakers, Weld converts—met at Zanesville to organize the Ohio State Abolition Society.

On the first of January, 1836, Birney began publishing his *Philanthropist*.[392] Meanwhile, Garrison had denounced the churches and the "black hearted clergy." When abolition threatened to divide the General Assembly of the Presbyterians, Beecher turned against both revivalists and abolitionists. But the Lane rebels triumphed in the West; by the end of 1836 their stand that slavery was a *sin* as well as an evil became the main plank of the abolition platform.[393] Revivalism became more of a weapon than pamphleteering. With the backing of the American Anti-Slavery Society Weld's band was increased to seventy; they were assembled for intensive training in New

[390] The great Lane "debate" ran for eighteen nights; it was really an antislavery revival meeting. It opened on the question, "Ought the people of the slaveholding states to abolish slavery immediately?" and then turned to consideration of whether or not the movement for colonization of freed Negroes was entitled "to the patronage of the Christian community." The decision was for "immediate abolition gradually accomplished" and opposition to colonization. The faculty refused to go along, and the *Cincinnati Daily Gazette,* October 22, 1834, contained an announcement, signed by Beecher, Biggs, and Stowe, to the effect that the school's antislavery society and colonization society had been abolished by decree of the faculty. Although student organizations and activities were to be encouraged, these matters bore on a subject of highly political interest and were "too absorbing for healthful study." For the Lane controversy see Chapter XIII.
[391] There had been some ugly anti-Negro riots in Cincinnati in 1830.
[392] At New Richmond, January 1—April 8, 1836, thereafter at Cincinnati.
[393] Barnes, *The Antislavery Impulse,* 103.

York, then turned loose to win the West, especially Ohio, Indiana, and Illinois, to the cause. "The Seventy" fanned out into the country—the cities were to "be burned down by back-fires." Within a year the abolitionists were claiming two hundred societies with nearly fifteen thousand members in Ohio, the bulk of whom were in Quaker- and New England-settled counties.[394] Their numerical strength in Indiana, Illinois, and Michigan was not large.

The abolitionists as an organized and evangelical minority made a noise in the West entirely out of proportion to their numbers. Though the majority of the citizens might have admitted, had they given the subject serious consideration, that slavery was an evil, perhaps even a sin, there was nothing either immediate or direct in their minds which they intended to do about it.

After the discussion over the Missouri question died down,[395] the newspapers contained scattered articles on colonization,[396] with now and then an account of slight trouble or threatened trouble over the return of a fugitive slave.[397] The colonization societies were organized without arousing much discussion; even a certain amount of sympathy, or at least indifference, existed as to underground railroad activities. But the abolitionists were a different thing.

By 1835 the evangelical abolitionists were so active that opposition and bitterness were expressed even in the Western Reserve. A Cleveland meeting resolved that the abolitionists were "unwise, dangerous, and deserving the emphatic reprehension and zealous opposition of every friend of peace and

---

[394] Caleb Atwater, in his *History of Ohio* published in 1838, said that there were seventeen thousand abolitionists in the state. Trumbull County (on the Reserve) claimed 2,249 abolition society members. *Ohio Statesman,* January 7, 1839.

[395] See Chapter IX, 17–18.

[396] The *Hamilton Intelligencer* in the early 1830's was particularly prolific on colonization articles and addresses.

[397] For instance, the "impartial account" by a witness, copied from the New Albany *Chronicle* in *Liberty Hall and Cincinnati Gazette,* March 10, 1821, of the appearance on February 8 of forty-three armed Kentuckians to recover one Moses after the court had given him his freedom. The sheriff had assembled the militia and some persons were wounded, but order was restored.

In 1819 when it was rumored that five hundred freed slaves from Virginia were to be settled in Brown County, Ohio, the editor of the Chillicothe *Supporter* (June 16) wrote: "Much as we commiserate with their situation we trust our Constitution and laws are not so utterly defective as to suffer us to be overrun by such a wretched population."

of the country." The tendency of their actions was "towards anarchy, disunion, civil war, bloodshed and murder."[398] Similar meetings were held at other Ohio towns;[399] some of them prohibited the use of any building for abolition assemblies. Even the Ohio Methodists in General Conference in 1835 unanimously denounced abolition agitation. The *Daily Post*, the *Cincinnati Whig*, and the *Cincinnati Republican* all denounced Birney. The *Republican* even sought to get the people to oppose the organization of an abolition society. In July, 1836, a mob attacked the *Philanthropist* and damaged the press; a public meeting selected a committee of which Jacob Burnet and Nicholas Longworth were members to warn Birney not to resume publication. Charles Hammond of the *Gazette*, however, though not favoring the abolitionists, stood firm on their right to be heard. Abolition activity, bad as it was, was insignificant in comparison to the mob spirit as applied against freedom of the press. "Freedom of the press and constitutional Liberty must live or perish together."[400] Birney was soon again publishing his paper. When Matilda, a mulatto girl on the way to Missouri with her master and father, escaped from a steamboat when it stopped at Cincinnati, Birney employed and protected her. When discovered he was indicted under Ohio law, defended by Salmon P. Chase, and finally saved by a technicality before the Ohio Supreme Court.[401]

In the big fight in Congress over the "gag rule" regarding the presentation of petitions against slavery, John Quincy Adams was supported by three Ohioans—Charles Hammond, Joshua Reed Giddings, who was elected to the House from Jefferson County in 1838, and Senator Thomas Morris who presented numerous petitions from his state. Though a supporter of the Van Buren administration, Morris was so decided in his anti-slavery stand that his party in Ohio abandoned him in favor of Benjamin Tappan, who, though a brother of Arthur and Lewis, was not then an abolitionist. Benjamin Wade, then serving his

---

[398] *Cleveland Herald,* August 11, 1835.
[399] Circleville, Granville, Zanesville, Painesville, Marietta, Willoughby, St. Albans, Brimfield, New Lisbon, Mt. Vernon, Middlebury, Grafton, and Mount Pleasant. Weisenburger, *The Passing of the Frontier,* 372.
[400] *Cincinnati Daily Gazette,* August 4, 1836.
[401] *Ibid.,* March 21, 25, April 6, 7, 10, 1837.

first term in the Ohio Senate, represented the abolitionist Whigs of the Western Reserve.

The Mahan affair gave Ohio abolitionists additional material. John B. Mahan, Brown County minister, was surrendered to the governor of Kentucky when the latter requisitioned him under the fugitive slave law for harboring and aiding runaway slaves. Though Mahan was acquitted by a Kentucky court, Kentucky sent commissioners to Columbus to get better co-operation from Ohio.[402] As a result the legislature passed a law for the more effective and speedy recovery of fugitives.

The indenture of Negroes in Indiana ceased to be of importance after the repeal of the law in 1810, though a number of indentures were held for many years thereafter. In Illinois there were some 746 indentures still in force in 1830.[403] Transfers and advertisements for runaway servants were common until the later 1820's. Kidnaping of free Negroes appeared at times a better organized activity than the underground railroad. The latter had its lines in Illinois as in Ohio and Indiana.[404]

Jacksonville was "thrown into a state of great excitement" in the autumn of 1833 by a summons signed by Lewis Tappan and others for a meeting to organize for immediate emancipation. Forced from one hall by an opposing crowd the abolitionists went to another and organized their society.[405] Professor James Buchanan (one of Birney's Lexington friends) of Carlinville, the Reverend Robert Holman (a Birney friend of Huntsville days), and Edward Beecher of Illinois College joined the movement.

The increasing abolitionist activities and gag-rule discussions resulted in more frequent newspaper mention of slavery. In general the *Alton Spectator*, the *Chicago American*, and the

[402] In his message to the legislature the Governor of Kentucky had spoken of Ohio abolitionists conniving with Kentucky slaves; the spirit of abolition abroad in the land was threatening the overthrow of all social intercourse between the states. *Cincinnati Daily Gazette,* December 14, 1838. The *Gazette* had previously (November 8) referred to the law of 1834 as a humiliating offering to the demands of the slave states and advocated its repeal.

[403] Newton D. Harris, "Negro Servitude in Illinois," in *Transactions of the Illinois State Historical Society,* 1906, p. 51.

[404] The three main lines in Illinois were (1) by way of Chester, Eden, Coulterville, and Nashville to the Illinois River; (2) Alton, Jacksonville, the Illinois River, Ottawa and to Chicago; (3) Quincy, Galesburg, Princeton, and La Salle to Chicago. *Ibid.,* 52.

[405] Jacksonville *Illinois Patriot,* November 2, 1833.

Sangamo Journal were antiabolition in attitude; the *Alton Telegraph*, however, took a decided stand against the gag rule. The legislature of 1837 passed strong antiabolition resolutions, though Lincoln and a few other senators voted against them. The same year the Lovejoy affair attracted nationwide attention.

Elisha P. Lovejoy, son of a Presbyterian minister, graduate of Princeton Theological Seminary, had been editing the *St. Louis Observer*, a religious paper. Straight talk against injustice to a Negro led to attacks on his paper. In 1836 Lovejoy moved his press to Alton, but the friendship of substantial businessmen of New England ancestry did not prevent its being destroyed, supposedly by a St. Louis mob. With the backing of Alton citizens he set up anew; his *Alton Observer* pulled no punches in its attacks against vice of all kinds and mob violence. By 1837 the crusading Puritan who coolly and constantly preached obedience to God's law had come over to abolition. His stand was too vigorous even for John Mason Peck, Baptist leader of New England ancestry who used a critical pen against Lovejoy in his *Western Pioneer*. It was charged that Lovejoy had promised not to publish an antislavery paper; two more presses were destroyed. At a public meeting Lovejoy defended his stand, then prepared to carry on. When a third press was landed and stored in the warehouse of Godfrey, Gilman, and Company in November, an armed mob attacked, overpowered the few guards, killed Lovejoy, and destroyed the press.[406]

The violence and threat to freedom of the press brought many antiabolition papers to the defense of Lovejoy. The untoward event did much to forward the organization of antislavery societies in Illinois. The next year citizens of Hennepin backed Benjamin Lundy in publishing his *Genius of Universal Emancipation* at that place.[407]

Ohio abolitionists had discussed the question of a political

[406] The mayor's account of the affair was widely published in the papers in December. Edward Beecher's *Narrative of Riots at Alton* . . . was published at Alton in 1838.

[407] Actually published at Lowell, November 8, 1838—September 8, 1839. Lundy was assisted by Zebina Eastman. The *Genius of Liberty,* established by the La Salle County Anti-Slavery Society, was edited by Eastman and Hooper Warren, formerly of the *Edwardsville Spectator* and the *Chicago Commercial Advertiser,* December 19, 1840—April, 1842.

organization at the meeting of the Ohio Anti-Slavery Society as early as 1837, but the *Philanthropist* opposed the idea of "an ordinary political party." Two years later the *Painesville Republican* promoted the idea, but the Ohio Anti-Slavery Convention at Massillon in May took no action. The Xenia *Ohio Free Press* called for another convention which when it met in September disclaimed support for Democrats or Whigs and endorsed the Liberty party. A number of the important antislavery leaders, however, remained Whigs. Regarding the attempt to make abolition a political issue the *Detroit Daily Advertiser* said: "Should they do so, the sun, ten years hence, will not shine upon these *United States*."[408]

Outside Ohio the abolition movement was of relative unimportance. In the election of 1840 Birney and Earle, the Liberty party candidates, polled 892 votes in Ohio (out of a total of 273,831), 294 in Michigan, 160 in Illinois, and 30 in Indiana. Something of more general concern than the issue of slaveholding as a sin would be required to get the people of the Northwest to vote and to act on slavery.

§ § § § § §

By the beginning of the fourth decade of the century the Northwest was contemplating its past and foreviewing its future. Ahead were Manifest Destiny, a war on foreign soil, and a great sectional conflict; also economic advances which would make it aware of its "growing, increasing, swelling power," as well as of the humanitarian responsibilities of "the Young Democracy." The realist appraised the future in terms of the past; one year was like another. Interesting were an editor's predictions for 1839:

The present session of Congress will be of uncommon interest and importance—(it always has been)—There will be a great noise about the country—whenever it thunders; and a great dust will be kicked up—by coaches and horses—unless the roads are McAdamized.

There will be more books published this year than will find purchasers; more rhymes written than will find readers, and more bills made out than will find payers—

[408] April 15, 1837.

Those who have debts to pay and no cash will lose their credit—

Many an old sinner will resolve to turn over a new leaf this year, but the new leaf will turn out to be blank—

Many things will be wondered at this year and turn out to be miracles—

Many a man will grow richer this year, in a dream—

Whoever is in love this year will think his mistress an angel. Whoever gets married will find out whether it be true—

Whoever hires money out of the banks will be in no hurry to see the last day of grace—

Whoever runs in debt this year will be dunned—

Finally; we are of the opinion that this will be a wonderful year, just like all that have gone before it. Politicians will make fools of themselves, pettifoggers will make fools of others, and women with pretty faces will make fools of both themselves and others. The world will go round and come back to the place from which it set out, and this will be the course of many a man who should be up and doing. There will be a great cry and little wool, as at a shearing of pigs or a session of Congress.[409]

The romanticist, however, was more moved by the prospects. He saw an age which "inculcates the Humanities of Life, and prosecutes inquiries touching the condition and prospects of man." Changes in institutions were demanded and would be had, but since they would come from the spoken and recorded will of the people there was nothing to fear. Man would hardly dare abuse the "Representative Principle" with its guaranty of civil liberty.

Let us hope he will not abuse it, and bring himself to shame. And here, in this beautiful land of the North-West, which has been given him for his inheritance while that great principle was establishing itself in our political institutions and making itself plain to his moral perceptions, let us *work* that he may not abuse it. Let us labor to lay the foundations of institutions for the future, under which no man, of all over whom they may extend, shall suffer wrong at the hand of his brother.[410]

The great experiment of the power of peace and freedom upon man was to have its most favorable chance in the West. In anticipation of its success it is useless to try to improve upon the words of James Hall:

No imperial wealth has been poured into this country; no vain monarch has erected here his pyramids, his palaces, his walls, his military roads, to perpetuate his own name. This has not been the theatre whereon some forced and struggling commercial colony, flying from persecution, has

[409] *Quincy Whig*, May 4, 1839—probably copied but no credit given.
[410] Gallagher, *Progress in the North-West*, 60.

obtained a precarious foot-hold among savage fortresses—to perish with cold, hunger, disease and war—but the spirit of liberty alighted here, and invited her willing children, and gave to each the power to pursue happiness in his own way, beneath the shelter of laws which operate equally upon all. She nerved them with manly strength, assured them of a happy independence, and guarding to them the fruits of labor, she now hovers over their increasing numbers like an angel of peace and plenty.

This is civilization; the bridal of nature and art; the beautiful consummation of that promise, "Thou shalt have dominion over all the earth." It is the bloodless triumph of mind over matter; its gentle progress, as it melts away obstacle after obstacle, and proceeds to beautify and ennoble its transient residence on the earth, before it re-ascends to the bosom of its Maker. There are feelings of exalted joy in the contemplation of this peaceful union of men for worthy objects, which seem prophetic of that millennium, where "the lion and the lamb shall lie down together, and a little child shall lead them"; when the universal mind of the human family shall be in unison with the perfect beauty of nature; when the immortal intellect shall rise above the narrow confines of the body, and expand into fuller sympathy with the grandeur of its eternal destiny.[411]

[411] In review of Chase's *Statutes of Ohio,* in *Western Monthly Magazine,* V (1836), 631–32.

BIBLIOGRAPHICAL ESSAY

BIBLIOGRAPHICAL ESSAY

This brief essay is intended merely as a general introduction to the historical materials on the Old Northwest, 1815–40. For obvious reasons no attempt is made to list all items referred to nor to make a clear-cut distinction between source and secondary material. More particular bibliographical information may be obtained from the bibliographical footnotes which accompany the text at the appropriate places. Full citations are given in the first reference to individual items in the footnotes.

GUIDES AND BIBLIOGRAPHIES. There are no comprehensive bibliographical guides to the history of the region. The most generally useful single bibliography is Ralph Leslie Rusk, *The Literature of the Middle Western Frontier* (2 volumes. New York, 1925). Solon J. Buck, *Travel and Description 1765–1865 . . . (Illinois Historical Collections,* IX, Springfield, 1914), lists the works of travel and description for a part of the region. The bibliographies in Clarence W. Alvord, *The Illinois Country, 1673–1818* (Springfield, 1920), and Theodore C. Pease, *The Frontier State, 1818–1848* (Chicago, 1918), furnish a base of departure for Illinois, while Peter G. Thomson, *A Bibliography of the State of Ohio . . .* (Cincinnati, 1880), is a guide to the historical and other literature relating to that state.

Early imprints for the five states may be checked as follows: Eleanor R. Kyle, "Early Ohio Imprints" (MS. M.A. thesis, University of Illinois, 1932), which does not incude public documents and periodicals; *A Check List of Ohio Imprints 1796–1820* (Ohio Historical Records Survey, Columbus, 1941); Mary A. Walker, *The Beginnings of Printing in the State of Indiana . . . to 1850* (Crawfordsville, Ind., 1934), and the supplement 1804–1849 by Douglas C. McMurtrie *(Indiana Historical Society Publications,* XI, Indianapolis, 1937); Harriet P. Wyrick, "A Check List and Study of Illinois Imprints through 1850" (MS. M.A. thesis, University of Illinois, 1932); Douglas C. McMurtrie: *Early Printing in Michigan, with a Bibliography of the Issues of the Michigan Press, 1796–1850* (Chicago, 1931); *Preliminary Check List of Michigan Imprints 1796–1850* (Michigan Historical Records Survey, Detroit, 1942); *Early Printing in Wisconsin, with a Bibliography of the Issues of the Press, 1833–1850* (Seattle, 1931); and *A Check List of Wisconsin Imprints, 1833–1849* (Wisconsin Historical Records Survey, Madison, 1942).

Winifred Gregory (ed.), *American Newspapers 1821–1936, A Union List of Files Available in the United States and Canada* (New York, 1937), serves as a finding list. Arthur D. Mink (comp.), *Union List of Ohio Newspapers Available in Ohio* (Ohio State Archaeological and Historical Society, Columbus, 1946), and Franklin W. Scott, *Newspapers and*

Periodicals of Illinois 1814–1879 (*Illinois Historical Collections,* VI, Springfield, 1910), are the standard guides for newspapers of the two states. The comprehensive history and directory of the newspapers of Indiana compiled by Logan Esarey and Donald F. Carmony, though still in manuscript form, is available for use at Indiana University.

The two books by Louis C. Karpinski, although they treat particularly of the maps of Michigan and the Great Lakes region, serve as an excellent introduction to the maps of the Old Northwest. They are: *Bibliography of the Printed Maps of Michigan, 1804–1880, with a series of over one hundred reproductions of maps constituting an historical atlas of the Great Lakes and Michigan* ... and *Historical Atlas of the Great Lakes and Michigan* (Lansing, 1931). Karpinski has also collected photographic facsimiles, available in several libraries, of manuscript maps relating to America prior to 1800.

Since the materials for the history of the Old Northwest are located largely in the historical libraries of the region—particularly in the Library of the Historical and Philosophical Society of Ohio (Cincinnati), the Ohio Archaeological and Historical Society Library (Columbus), the Western Reserve Historical Society Library (Cleveland), the Detroit City Library —Burton Collection, the Indiana State Library and the William Henry Smith Memorial Library (Indianapolis), the Indiana University Library (Bloomington), the Illinois State Historical Library (Springfield), the Library of the Chicago Historical Society, the Newberry Library (Chicago), and the Wisconsin State Historical Library (Madison)—the catalogues and special lists of the holdings of these libraries are important. The author has also found very useful the bibliographical knowledge and detailed lists of R. E. Banta and Ernest J. Wessen, Middle West Americana specialists.

MANUSCRIPT COLLECTIONS. Most of the important manuscript collections pertaining to the history of the Old Northwest have been published, at least in part, in the publications of the various state historical societies. There are a number, however, which the student of the region cannot afford to overlook.

The Library of the Western Reserve Historical Society has among other holdings the Connecticut Land Company papers; the Virginia Military Land surveys; and the most extensive manuscript collection in the Old Northwest on the Shakers of Ohio and adjoining states. Besides these larger collections it possesses many journals, record books, and miscellaneous manuscripts, most of them pertaining to the history of the Western Reserve.

In the Burton Historical Collection of the Detroit Public Library are the William Woodbridge papers. Woodbridge was secretary of Michigan Territory, collector of customs at Detroit, one of the territorial judges, a delegate to Congress, a member of the Michigan constitutional convention, and governor of Michigan. His papers reflect the varied interests and activities of his long public career. They are particularly valuable for a study of shipping and commerce in the period from 1815 to 1825. The papers of Judge Augustus B. Woodward, though fewer in number, throw light not only upon public affairs in the territorial period but upon one of the most interesting intellectual characters of the Old Northwest. The Solomon Sibley papers pertain largely to legal matters. The several thousand items in the Joseph Campau collections consist largely of merchandising and real estate records, legal and business correspondence. The Eurotas P. Hastings papers comprise business and family correspondence on the period between 1808 and 1840. Hastings was president of the Bank of Michigan, a leader in Presbyterian and civic activities. His papers and correspondence reflect his interest in the work of the American Board of Home Missions, as well as in business and other enterprises.

The Historical and Philosophical Society of Ohio has the following collections and papers: the Torrence collection, including papers of Judge George P. Torrence, Gen. James Findlay, Gorham Worth, Thomas Sloo, Jr., and many others; the John Stites Gano papers, generally earlier than 1815, but containing a few items 1815–17; the King papers, relating primarily to Rufus King, Edward King, and Sarah Worthington King; the Lytle papers, containing letters to and from Gen. William Lytle and various persons in the Cincinnati area; the Walker papers, primarily letters to Timothy Walker from persons in various parts of the United States; the Clarke papers, the bulk prior to 1815, but containing a few items between 1815 and 1840; the Bates papers (Isaac Bates, Clark Bates, and others), relating to business transactions in the Cincinnati area.

In the Ohio State Archaeological and Historical Society Library are the papers of Joshua Reed Giddings, congressman and abolitionist, which bear on the period after 1821. The Charles Hammond papers cover the whole period, 1815–40. As editor of Ohio's leading newspaper, 1825–40, Hammond's interests touched upon all phases of Ohio history. In the Charles E. Rice collection are letters of Ohio governors, judges, various other state officials, and pioneers, 1815–40. The papers of Thomas Worthington, Ohio governor and United States senator, an extensive collection, also cover the whole period. In the Darius Tallmadge collection are many records of the stagecoach business and related businesses from 1817 to 1836. The collection of the papers of Samuel Williams and Samuel Wesley Williams constitutes a large and comparatively unexploited source for the study of the history of the Old Northwest. Samuel Williams (1786–1859) was chief clerk in the office of the surveyor general of the Northwest Territory, was prominent in the affairs of the Methodist Episcopal Church, and was connected with the founding of the *Ladies' Repository,* of which his son, Samuel Wesley Williams, became editor. These papers cover a multitude of subjects, including land-office business, pioneer life, Ohio schools, and Methodist affairs.

The Indiana University Library holds other Williams papers, a collection of some three thousand items. In the same library are the papers of David H. Maxwell (1786–1854). Maxwell was one of the founders of Indiana

University and president of the Indiana State Board of Improvements from 1836 to 1838. This library also has a number of Henry Clay manuscripts, largely political letters on the period; the Judah papers: the papers of Samuel and Samuel B. Judah which include letters relating to politics, roads, canals, and railroads; the John B. Niles papers: politics, law, banking, railroads; the William Polke papers: largely concerning the removal of the Potawatomi Indians; and the correspondence of Charles H. Test, 1824–45, state senator and secretary of state.

In the Indiana Historical Society Library is the William H. English collection, which includes papers of prominent Indianans gathered by English and the proceedings of the Masonic Lodge of Lexington, Indiana. New Harmony material is included in the Miner K. Kellogg recollections and the William A. Twigg papers. The Kellogg papers also contain good Cincinnati material. In this library also are papers of Samuel C. Vance, Lawrenceburg, and Lawrence M. Vance, his son, of Indianapolis. The Samuel Williams papers in this library include surveys and land office sales in Indiana and letters of Samuel Widney of De Kalb County, Indiana, to Williams. The Calvin Fletcher material includes a lengthy diary (1818–64, detailed after 1830), and letters of Fletcher who came to Indianapolis in 1821 and of members of his family. Fletcher was a lawyer, farmer, banker, civic and church leader. Other papers pertaining to the period 1815–40 are those of Jeremiah Sullivan, Tilghman A. Howard, John K. Graham, John Caldwell, and William M. Pratt. In the field of business are the account book (1827–49) of Nicholas McCarty, Indianapolis merchant, who had branch stores in other Indiana towns, and papers of M. C. Van Pelt, Shelbyville merchant. Also of interest are the registers and day books of the Union Inn at Indianapolis in the 1830's.

The Indiana State Library has the Ewing papers (Indian affairs), the Tipton papers (Indian affairs, politics), the Noah Noble papers (politics), the Allen Hamilton papers (Indian affairs and business), the Elisha Embree papers (business and politics), and the Lasselle papers (early Vincennes business).

In the Illinois State Historical Library are the papers of Pierre Menard, politician and merchant; the Pascal P. Enos papers (Enos was an early Springfield merchant and Federal land agent, who was interested in agricultural societies); the John F. Brooks papers, which deal with the early days of Illinois College, Illinois life, and Presbyterianism; the Black Hawk War papers, which contain official correspondence, letter books of Gen. Henry Atkinson, Governor John Reynolds, etc.; and the records of the Connecticut Association, which founded the Wethersfield Settlement in Henry County.

In the Library of the Chicago Historical Society are the journals of Jeremiah Porter, Presbyterian missionary, which contain descriptive material on Michigan, Wisconsin, and Illinois in the period after 1831. The papers of John J. Hardin, Illinois lawyer and politician, are also available in this library.

The extensive collection of Grignon, Lawe, and Porlier papers are in the Library of the State Historical Society of Wisconsin. These deal with the fur trade and the development of settlements along the line of the Fox-Wisconsin rivers. Some of the letters have been published in the Society's *Collections*. The papers of Morgan L. Martin, prominent Green Bay attorney, land speculator, and Democratic politician, relate to the period after 1827. The papers of George Boyd, Indian agent at Mackinac and Green Bay, 1819–41, deal with problems in general as well as those of the Indian agent. The papers of Increase A. Lapham contain material on land surveys in Ohio, but are more valuable for a study of the scientific work of one of the leading scientists of the area.

The papers of the American Home Missionary Society in the Charles G. Hammond Library of the Chicago Theological Seminary at Chicago constitute a voluminous and important source not only for the study of the activities of the Presbyterian and Congregationalist agents and missionaries in the West but for the description of the land and the people.

PUBLIC DOCUMENTS. The *Statutes at Large of the United States*, the *Annals of Congress* and the *Congressional Globe*, and the various Congressional documents, census reports, etc., are obvious sources which need no comment. The *American State Papers* . . . (38 volumes. Washington, D. C., 1832–61), particularly the volumes on *Indian Affairs, Public Lands,* and *Finance*, are basic for the study of the public lands and Indian cessions, as are Charles J. Kappler (ed.), *Indian Affairs. Laws and Treaties* (2 volumes. Washington, D. C., 1904); Charles C. Royce (comp.), *Indian Land Cessions in the United States* (U. S. Bureau of American Ethnology, *Annual Report*, 1896–97, pt. 2, pp. 521–997, Washington, D. C., 1899); and Thomas Donaldson, *The Public Domain* . . . (Washington, D. C., 1884). Clarence E. Carter (ed.), *Territorial Papers of the United States* (Washington, D. C., 1934–   ): *The Territory Northwest of the River Ohio, 1787–1803* (volumes II, III, 1934); *The Territory of Indiana, 1800–1816* (volumes VII, VIII, 1939); *The Territory of Illinois, 1809–1814* (volume XVI, 1948); *The Territory of Michigan, 1805–1837* (volumes X, XI, XIII, 1942, 1943, 1945); Theodore C. Pease (ed.), *The Laws of the Northwest Territory, 1788–1800* (*Illinois Historical Collections*, XVII, Springfield, 1925); Francis S. Philbrick (ed.), *Laws of Indiana Territory, 1801–1809* (*Illinois Historical Collections*, XXI, Springfield, 1930, and reprinted with supplementary Indiana material in *Indiana Historical Collections*, Indianapolis, 1931); Louis B. Ewbank and Dorothy L. Riker (eds.), *The Laws of Indiana Territory, 1809–1816* (*Indiana Historical Collections*, XX, Indianapolis, 1934); the statutes, House and Senate journals, Supreme Court reports, and legislative and executive documents of the four states of the Old Northwest, 1815–40, constitute a body of material pertinent to various topics. Francis Newton Thorpe (ed.), *Constitutions, Colonial Charters, and Other Organic Laws*

(7 volumes. Washington, 1909), contains the enabling acts and state constitutions.

STATE HISTORICAL PUBLICATIONS, HISTORICAL SOCIETY PUBLICATIONS, AND HISTORICAL PERIODICALS. Second only in importance to the contemporary newspapers and periodicals for a study of the history of the period are the publications of the historical societies, both state and private, and of the historical commissions and bureaus of the five states of the Old Northwest. Included in these publications are hundreds of articles as well as a large amount of source material. Oldest of the state society publications are the *Wisconsin Historical Collections* (Volume I- , Madison, 1854-   ). The Society began to publish its *Proceedings* separately in 1887. In 1905 it began issuing its *Publications*—Draper series, Calendar series, Wisconsin History series, and Biography series. In 1922 it began publishing Joseph Schafer's *Wisconsin Domesday Book* of which the following volumes have appeared: *General Studies—A History of Agriculture in Wisconsin* (Madison, 1922); *Four Wisconsin Counties; Prairie and Forest* (1927); *The Wisconsin Lead Region* (1932); and *Town Studies* (1924).

The 39 volumes of the *Michigan Pioneer and Historical Collections* (Lansing, 1874–1915) are particularly rich in pioneer reminiscences; these publications were succeeded by the *Michigan Historical Publications* (6 volumes. Lansing, 1916–1920). The *Illinois Historical Collections* date from 1903; 32 volumes have been issued to date. The *Publications of the Illinois State Historical Library* began in 1899 and starting with *Publication* No. 4 (1900) include the *Transactions of the Illinois State Historical Society*; in 1937 the title was changed to *Papers in Illinois History and Transactions*. The *Indiana Historical Society Publications* date from 1886; volume XV appeared in 1949. The *Indiana Historical Collections* comprise 31 volumes (1916-   ). The *Ohio Historical Collections* began in 1931; 11 volumes have been published to date.

The *Chicago Historical Society's Collection* began in 1882 and ran to 1928—12 volumes. The *Bulletin* of the Chicago Historical Society was issued from 1922 until 1926, revived in 1934 and continues to date. The 35 volumes of *Fergus' Historical Series* (Chicago, 1876–1914) pertain largely to the Chicago area.

Oldest of the state historical periodicals is the *Ohio Archaeological and Historical Society Publications* (Columbus), which began in 1887, and in 1898 became a quarterly. In 1928 the Society began issuing *Museum Echoes*, a monthly bulletin. The *Indiana Magazine of History* (Indianapolis and Bloomington) began in 1905, the *Journal of the Illinois State Historical Society* (Springfield) in 1908; the *Michigan History Magazine* (Lansing) and the *Wisconsin Magazine of History* (Menasha and Madison) began publication in 1917. All are quarterlies. Besides articles and reviews of books on the region these periodicals also contain some documentary material.

The Ohio Valley Historical Association published annual *Reports* or *Proceedings* (mostly Columbus, Ohio, 1907–19). The *Firelands Pioneer*, a quarterly magazine, was published by the Firelands Historical Society (Sandusky and Norwalk, Ohio, 1858–78, 1882–1937). The Western Reserve and Northern Ohio Historical Society issued its *Tracts*, 1-110 (Cleveland, 1870–1929), and then its *Publications* (1943–   ). The Historical Society of Northwestern Ohio in 1928 began issuing its *Quarterly Bulletin* (Toledo), which in 1944 became the *Northwest Ohio Quarterly*. The Historical and Philosophical Society of Ohio (Cincinnati) issued one volume of *Transactions*—edited by Jacob Burnet—in 1838–39. It issued two volumes of *Publications*, 1848–52, three volumes, 1873–85, from 1906 to 1923 put out 18 volumes of the *Quarterly Publications of the Historical and Philosophical Society of Ohio*, and 1924-34 issued 6 volumes of *Publications*. The *Bulletin of the Historical and Philosophical Society of Ohio* was started in 1943 and continues to date.

The *Mississippi Valley Historical Review* (1914–   ) is today the leading historical periodical for the whole region. Its past volumes contain many articles on the Old Northwest as well as documents and other source material. The Mississippi Valley Historical Association issued 11 volumes of *Proceedings* 1907/1908–1921/23 (1909–26); the proceedings are now published in the *Review*.

NEWSPAPERS. For the history of the early newspapers and discussion of the value of the newspapers as sources of history see Chapter XV. The newspapers listed below are important either because of content and length of life or because they represent an area or period not otherwise covered.

Outstanding throughout the period 1815–40 was the *Cincinnati Gazette* (*Liberty Hall, Liberty Hall and Cincinnati Gazette, Cincinnati Daily Gazette*). Under the editorship of Charles Hammond, 1825–40, this paper had no peer in the Northwest; its cover of politics, agriculture, education, and general affairs was excellent, its editorials were widely copied. Practically complete files may be found in the libraries of the Ohio State Archaeological and Historical Society at Columbus, the Historical and Philosophical Society at Cincinnati, and Indiana University.

Other Cincinnati papers used were the *Advertiser* (*Inquisitor Advertiser, Cincinnati Advertiser and Ohio Phoenix, Daily Advertiser and Journal*), 1818–40; the *Cincinnati Chronicle and Literary Gazette*, 1826–35; the *Cincinnati Chronicle,* 1836–40; the *Cincinnati Commercial Register*, 1825–28; the *Cincinnati Weekly Herald and Philanthropist*, 1836–40; the *Cincinnati Journal and Western Luminary*, 1831–37; the *Daily Evening Post*, 1835–39; the *National Republican and Ohio Political Register* (*National Republican and Cincinnati Mercantile Advertiser, Daily Cincinnati Republican and Commercial Register, Cincinnati Daily Republican*), 1823–40; the *Western Spy*, 1815–18; and the *Western Tiller*, 1826–31.

The *Steubenville Herald* (*Western Herald and Steubenville Gazette*), 1815–40, though preserved in interrupted files, is particularly useful for the earlier part of the period, as is the Chillicothe *Supporter*, 1815–21. The Chillicothe *Scioto Gazette* (*Scioto Gazette and Fredonian Chronicle, Sup-*

porter and Scioto Gazette), 1815–40, was one of Ohio's better papers; also very useful were the files of the Hamilton *Miami Intelligencer* (*Philanthropist, Miami Herald, Hamilton Gazette and Miami Register, Hamilton Intelligencer and Advertiser, Hamilton Advertiser, Hamilton Intelligencer,* etc.), 1815–40; the *Piqua Gazette* (broken files), 1819–34; the *Western Courier and Piqua Enquirer,* 1835–40; the *Delaware Patron and Franklin Chronicle* (scattered files), 1821–40; the *St. Clairsville Gazette* (scattered files), 1825–40; and the *Portsmouth Gazette* (etc.), 1818–25.

Next to the *Cincinnati Gazette* the practically continuous files of the Columbus *Ohio State Journal* (*Western Intelligencer, Western Intelligencer and Columbus Gazette, Columbus Gazette, Ohio State Journal and Columbus Gazette, State Journal and Political Register, Ohio State Journal and Register*), 1815–40, give the best National Republican–Whig presentation of politics. The *Ohio Monitor,* the *Columbus Press,* the *Western Hemisphere,* and after 1837 the *Ohio Statesman* were other Columbus papers, the last named being the outstanding Democratic paper of the region until the Civil War.

The *Cleveland (Cleaveland) Herald,* 1819–40, the *Cleaveland Gazette,* which became the *Cleaveland Register,* 1818–20, and the *Cleveland Advertiser,* 1832–41, together with the Ravenna *Western Courier,* 1825–38, were the principal papers of the Western Reserve.

The Vincennes *Western Sun,* 1815–40, the Madison *Indiana Republican,* 1816–33, the Madison *Republican and Banner,* 1833–40, the Indianapolis *Indiana Journal,* 1825–40, the *Indiana Democrat,* 1830–40, the *Richmond Palladium,* 1831–40, and the Richmond *Public Leger,* 1824–28, were among the more important Indiana newspapers. Scattered files of numerous others were used.

For the early years of Illinois history the more valuable newspapers are the *Western Intelligencer* (*Illinois Intelligencer,* etc., Kaskaskia and Vandalia), 1815–32, and the *Edwardsville Spectator,* 1819–26. The *Illinois State Register* under its varying titles (Edwardsville, Vandalia, and Springfield), 1831–40, was one of the two outstanding Illinois papers of the period of the 1830's; the other was the *Sangamo Journal* (Springfield), 1831–40. Other Illinois papers, whose scattered files supplement those of the state's two leading papers, were the *Alton Spectator,* the *Alton Telegraph,* the *Quincy Whig,* the *Chicago Democrat,* the *Chicago American,* the *Galenian,* the Galena *Miner's Journal,* the *Northwestern Gazette and Galena Advertiser,* and the Jacksonville *Illinois Patriot.*

The *Detroit Gazette,* 1817–30, was the principal Michigan newspaper for that period. The *Detroit Journal and Michigan Advertiser* (later the *Detroit Daily Advertiser*) was one of the two leading Michigan papers for the period 1829–40. The other was the *Democratic Free Press and Michigan Intelligencer* (*Detroit Free Press*), 1831–40. Available also are intermittent files of other Michigan papers.

For the period prior to the separation of Wisconsin Territory the *Green-Bay Intelligencer* (*and Wisconsin Democrat*), 1833–36, is indispensable for the history of the region west of Lake Michigan. For the later 1830's the Green Bay *Wisconsin Democrat*, 1836–40, the *Milwaukee Advertiser*, the *Milwaukee Sentinel*, the Mineral Point *Miners' Free Press*, the Madison *Wisconsin Enquirer*, and the *Madison Express* were the leading papers.

Other newspapers used may be identified by way of the footnote references to them.

PERIODICALS. Of the eastern periodicals the most valuable for the earlier part of the period is *Niles' Weekly Register* (Baltimore and Philadelphia, 1811–49), which includes many extracts from western newspapers no longer available. Freeman Hunt's *Merchants' Magazine and Commercial Review* (New York, 1839–70), *Hazard's United States Commercial and Statistical Register* (Philadelphia, 1839–42), and *De Bow's Review* (various titles, various series, New Orleans, 1846–80) contain numerous articles on the economic history of the Old Northwest. The *American Farmer* (Baltimore), 1st series, 1819–33, the *New England Farmer* (Boston), 1822–40, the *New York Farmer*, 1828–37, the *Genesee Farmer* (Rochester), 1831–39, and *The Cultivator* (Albany), 1834–40, are eastern agricultural periodicals of aid to a study of western agriculture. (The agricultural periodicals are listed in Albert Lowther Demaree, *The American Agricultural Press 1819–1860* [Columbia University Press, 1941]; the Illinois agricultural periodicals are listed in Richard Bardolph, *Agricultural Literature and the Early Illinois Farmer* [*Illinois Studies in the Social Sciences*, XXIX, Nos. 1–2, Urbana, 1948]).

Of the periodicals of the Old Northwest the most valuable for general history are Timothy Flint's *Western Monthly Review* (Cincinnati), 1827–30; James Hall's *Illinois Monthly Magazine* (Vandalia), 1830–32; Hall's *The Western Monthly Magazine* (Cincinnati), 1833–37; and *The Hesperian* (Columbus and Cincinnati), 1838–39. Of the western literary periodicals of the period prior to 1840 *The Western Literary Journal, and Monthly Review; The Cincinnati Mirror and Ladies' Parterre*, later *The Cincinnati Mirror, and Western Gazette of Literature and Science*, 1831–36 (for change of titles, etc., see Chapter XV); *The Western Messenger; Devoted to Religion and Literature* (Cincinnati and Louisville), 1835–41; and *The Family Magazine; or, Monthly Abstract of General Knowledge* (Cincinnati), 1833–41, were the most important. The literary periodicals published after 1840 contain articles on the earlier period, particularly *The Ladies' Repository and Gatherings of the West* (Cincinnati), 1841–76; *The Western Literary Emporium* (Cincinnati and St. Louis), 1848; and *Genius of the West* (Cincinnati), 1853–56. *The Western Journal of Agriculture . . . and Commerce* (St. Louis), 1848–56, is most useful for its articles on economic history. *The Magazine of Western History* (Cleveland), 1884–91, contains many articles of general interest on the Old Northwest. In 1891 the title was changed to *The National Magazine; A Monthly Journal of American History*, under which title it continued to publish until 1894.

For the western periodicals on medicine see Chapter V and bibliography in Pickard and Buley, *The Midwest Pioneer: His Ills, Cures, and Doctors* (Crawfordsville, 1945; New York, 1946); on agriculture see Chapter IV; on banking and finance see Chapters VIII and XII; on education see Chapter XIII; on religion see Chapter XIV.

BOOKS OF TRAVEL AND DESCRIPTION. The following are the chief travels of general interest on the period. John J. Audubon, *Delineations of American Scenery and Character,* edited by Francis Hobart Herrick (New York, 1926); this volume makes available Audubon's observations on men and manners in the West which appeared originally in his *Ornithological Biography* ... (5 volumes. Edinburgh, 1831–39). Karl Bernhard, Duke of Saxe-Weimar-Eisenach, *Travels through North America, during the years 1825 and 1826* (2 volumes. Philadelphia, 1828). J. Richard Beste, *The Wabash* ... (2 volumes. London, 1855). Morris Birkbeck, *Notes on a Journey in America* ... (Philadelphia, 1817; London, 1818); and *Letters from Illinois* (Philadelphia and London, 1818). Birkbeck was a capable observer and a good writer; he was one of the leading advertisers of the West in the 1820's. William N. Blaney, *An Excursion through the United States and Canada* ... (London, 1824). James Silk Buckingham, *The Eastern and Western States of America* (3 volumes. London, 1842). Rebecca Burlend, *A True Picture of Emigration* ... (London, 1848, reprinted Chicago, 1936). Michael Chevalier, *Society, Manners and Politics in the United States: being a Series of Letters on North America* ... (Boston, 1839). Ferdinand Ernst, *Travels in Illinois in 1819,* in *Transactions of the Illinois State Historical Society,* 1903. Estwick Evans, *A Pedestrious Tour of Four Thousand Miles, through the Western States and Territories* ... (Concord, N. H., 1819). William Faux, *Memorable Days in America* ... (London, 1823). Though a somewhat disgruntled Englishman, Faux frequently saw beneath the surface and was withal a shrewd observer. Henry Bradshaw Fearon, *Sketches of America* ... (London, 1818). Like Faux, Fearon was critical. Simon A. Ferrall [O'Ferrall], *A Ramble of Six Thousand Miles through the United States of America* (London, 1832). Gershom Flagg, "Pioneer Letters ... ," edited by Solon J. Buck, in *Transactions of the Illinois State Historical Society,* 1910, pp. 139–83. James Flint, *Letters from America* ... (Edinburgh, 1822). George Flower, *The Errors of Emigrants* ... (London, 1841). This work gave practical and sound advice based upon twenty years' residence in the Illinois country to emigrants and prospective emigrants, particularly from the British Isles. Flower also wrote *History of the English Settlement in Edwards County, Illinois* ... (*Chicago Historical Society's Collection,* I, Chicago, 1882). Richard Flower, *Letters from Lexington and the Illinois* ... (London, 1819), and *Letters from the Illinois* ... (London, 1822). The author was the father of George Flower and wrote his *Letters* to encourage emigration to the English Settlement. Elias Pym Fordham, *Personal Narrative of Travels* ... *1817–1818,* edited by Frederic A. Ogg (Cleveland, 1906). Charles F.

Grece, *Facts and Observations respecting Canada, and the United States of America* . . . (London, 1819). Basil Hall, *Travels in North America in the Years 1827 and 1828* (3 volumes. Edinburgh, 1829). Despite criticism by the more ardent protagonists of the West, the widely traveled English captain was a good reporter and critic; in addition to his estimates and analyses of the American way of life he is to be thanked for the almost two hundred sketches made with his camera lucida which constitute one of the best series of precamera pictorial views of our country. Mrs. Basil (Margaret Hunter) Hall, *The Aristocratic Journey* . . . (New York, 1931), thought less of the American West than almost any other travel writer. William Tell Harris, *Remarks Made During a Tour through the United States of America* . . . (Liverpool, 1819; London 1821), is more favorable to the Americans. Nicholas Hesse, *Das Westliche Nord-Amerika* . . . (Paderborn, 1838). In this little known book Hesse, himself a recent emigrant, gave good advice to prospective emigrants. Charles Fenno Hoffman, *A Winter in the West* (2 volumes. New York, 1835). This is one of the better accounts of the Old Northwest in the early 1830's. Thomas Hulme, *Journal of a Tour in the Western Countries of America,—September 30, 1818—August 8, 1819,* is reprinted in Thwaites (ed.), *Early Western Travels,* X, 17–84. Abner Dumont Jones, *Illinois and the West* . . . (Boston and Philadelphia, 1838). Jones is particularly good for his description of the prairie regions and of the people therein. Charles J. Latrobe, *The Rambler in North America* (2 volumes. New York, 1835). Thomas L. McKenney, *Sketches of a Tour to the Lakes* . . . (Baltimore, 1827), and *Memoirs, Official and Personal* . . . (New York, 1846). McKenney was superintendent of Indian affairs and was intimately acquainted with life at the western outposts. Frederick Marryat, *A Diary in America* (3 volumes. London, 1839). Harriet Martineau, *Society in America* (3 volumes. London, 1837), and *Retrospect of Western Travel* (3 volumes. London, 1838). Richard Lee Mason, *A Narrative of Richard Lee Mason in the Pioneer West, 1819* (New York, 1819). Maximilian, Prince of Wied-Neuwied, *Reise in das Innere Nord-America in den Jahren 1832 bis 1834* . . . (2 volumes and atlas. Coblenz, 1839–41). This work is particularly valuable for the paintings of Charles Bodmer, the Swiss artist, who accompanied Maximilian on his travels. John Melish, *Travels in the United States of America* . . . (2 volumes. Philadelphia, 1812). Samuel J. Mills and Daniel Smith, *Report of a Missionary Tour* . . . (Andover, Mass., 1815). Édouard de Montulé, *A Voyage to North America, and the West Indies, in 1817* (London, 1821). This edition does not include all of Montulé's North American travels as published in two volumes, *Voyage en Amérique, en Italie, en Sicilie et en Égypte, pendant les années 1816, 1817, 1818 et 1819* (Paris 1821). A complete translation of Montulé's North American travels with introduction by Edward D. Seeber is scheduled for publication in *Indiana University Publications, Social Science Series,* 1950, under the title *Travels in America 1816–1817.* This edition contains the author's illustrations. Dr.

Thomas L. Nichols, *Forty Years of American Life* (2 volumes. London, 1864). Thomas Nuttall, *A Journey of Travel into the Arkansa Territory during the Year 1819* . . . (Philadelphia, 1821). William Oliver, *Eight Months in Illinois* . . . (Newcastle upon Tyne, 1843, and reprinted, Chicago, 1924). Oliver's observations are particularly good on agriculture. Karl Postel (Charles Sealsfield), *Die Vereinigten Staaten von Nordamerika* . . . (2 volumes. Stuttgart and Tübingen, 1827). The English edition of volume I is entitled *The United States of North America as They Are* (London, 1827), and of volume II, *The Americans as They Are* . . . (London, 1828). John F. Schermerhorn and Samuel J. Mills, *A Correct View of That Part of the United States which Lies West of the Allegany Mountains* . . . (Hartford, 1814). Patrick Shirreff, *A Tour through North America; together with a Comprehensive View of the Canadas and United States. As Adapted for Agricultural Emigration* (Edinburgh, 1835). Shirreff was a level-headed British farmer who was both a good judge of people and of land. Thomas Scattergood Teas, "Journal of a Tour to Fort Wayne and the Adjacent Country, in the Year 1821," in Harlow Lindley (ed.), *Indiana as Seen by Early Travelers* (Indianapolis, 1916). David Thomas, *Travels through the Western Country in the Summer of 1816* (Auburn, N. Y., 1819). An excellent description of the Wabash country; Thomas was interested in trees and plants. Frances Trollope, *Domestic Manners of the Americans* (2 volumes. London, 1832). This work probably attracted more attention than any written on the West during the period; despite the bitter criticisms which it received, it was on the whole a not unfair treatment of western life. For background and criticism see Donald Smalley's edition (New York, 1949), introduction. Adlard Welby, *A Visit to North America and the English Settlements* . . . (London, 1821). Like Faux and Fearon, Welby was not too pleased with the American West. John Woods, *Two Years' Residence in the Settlement on the English Prairie, in the Illinois Country* . . . (London, 1822). John S. Wright, *Letters from the West; or a Caution to Emigrants* . . . (Salem, N. Y., 1819).

JOURNALS, MEMOIRS, AND DESCRIPTIONS. Hundreds of reminiscences and journals on the period, some of considerable length, are to be found in the volumes of historical collections and the historical periodicals of the five states. Many of them are referred to in the footnotes of this history; a complete listing can be had only by consulting the tables of contents of the publications. Of the separately published items the following are the more important. Some of them might be classified under several headings.

Daniel Harmon Brush, *Growing up with Southern Illinois* . . . , edited by Milo M. Quaife (Chicago, 1944), is one of the best pioneer reminiscences for Illinois on the period 1820–60. Jeremiah Church, *Journal of Travel, Adventures, and Remarks, of Jerry Church* (Harrisburg, Penna., 1845), is one of the lesser known journals; Church wrote firsthand of his experiences in Indiana and Illinois in the 1830's. Sanford C. Cox, *Recollections of the Early Settlement of the Wabash Valley* (Lafayette, Ind., 1860), is one of the better memoirs of the Wabash country. Henry W. Ellsworth, *Valley of the Upper Wabash* ... (New York, 1838). Henry L. Ellsworth, heavy investor in Upper Wabash land, who was commissioner of patents at the time, issued this book under his son's name; it contains valuable information on agriculture. Eliza W. Farnham, *Life in Prairie Land* (New York, 1846). Josiah B. Grinnell, *Sketches of the West, or The Home of the Badgers* ... (Milwaukee, 1845 and 1847). The first edition of this work, which consists of letters describing the author's travels through Wisconsin Territory, was a mere pamphlet of which only one or two copies are preserved. The second edition contains eleven additional letters and map. Robert Carlton [Baynard Rush Hall], *The New Purchase, or Seven and a Half Years in the West* (2 volumes. New York and Philadelphia, 1843; 1 volume. New Albany, Ind., 1855; 1 volume. Princeton, New Jersey, 1916). This work by the first instructor at the Indiana Seminary is the outstanding description of pioneer life in Indiana, and one of the best for the region. For Hall see Chapters IV, XIII and XV. *Incidents and Events in the Life of Gurdon Saltonstall Hubbard* ..., edited by Henry E. Hamilton (Chicago, 1888), throws much light on the early history of Chicago and the commerce of the region. *Wau-bun; the "Early Day" in the North-West*, by Mrs. John H. Kinzie (New York, 1856). This well known work, illustrated by the author, is one of the stand-bys for the early history of the region west of Lake Michigan. Mrs. Caroline Mathilda Kirkland ("Mrs. Mary Clavers"), *A New Home, Who'll Follow? or, Glimpses of Western Life* (New York, 1840), and *Western Clearings* (New York, 1845). For comment on Mrs. Kirkland's writings see Chapter XV. Increase A. Lapham, *Wisconsin; Its Geography and Topography, History, Geology and Mineralogy; Together with Brief Sketches of Its Antiquities, Natural History, Soil, Productions, Population and Government* (Milwaukee, 1844 and 1846). This work by Wisconsin's most famous scientist of the period is one of the rare items on the Northwest. John Ludlum McConnel in *Western Characters; or Types of Border Life in the Western States* (New York, 1853) attempted one of the most comprehensive books on the subject and produced one of the best. John Mason Peck, prominent Illinois missionary and publisher of gazetteers, in his memoir, *Forty Years of Pioneer Life* ... (edited by Rufus Babcock, Philadelphia, 1864), left us one of the better individual reminiscences on early Illinois. Isaac Reed's *The Christian Traveller ... including Nine Years, and Eighteen Thousand Miles* (New York, 1828) is one of the rarer items; it deals largely with the early years of Presbyterianism in Indiana. William Rudolph Smith, *Observations on the Wisconsin Territory* ... (Philadelphia, 1838). Edward Thomson, D.D., LL.D., *Sketches, Biographical and Incidental* (Cincinnati, 1857). This little known work, published by L. Swormstedt and A. Poe, for the Methodist Episcopal Church, at the Western Book Concern, contains biographical sketches of Otway Curry, Daniel Drake, Douglass Houghton, and others, and also essays on western character, religion, phrenology, medicine, and other subjects. Christiana H. Tillson, *Reminiscences of Early Life in Illi-*

nois, by our Mother (Amherst, Mass., 1873). This privately printed memoir is excellent for certain phases of pioneer life in southern Illinois.

GAZETTEERS AND GUIDE BOOKS. Publications of this type varied from full-sized books written by residents from firsthand material to small pocket manuals and compilations made by publishers for the market. A fairly complete list may be found in Rusk, *The Literature of the Middle Western Frontier,* II, 136–44, and in scattered entries in Buck. Useful for one purpose or another are the following:

William Amphlett, *The Emigrant's Directory to the Western States of North America* . . . (London, 1819). Lewis C. Beck, *A Gazetteer of the States of Illinois and Missouri; Containing a General View of Each State . . . and a Particular Description of their Towns, Villages, Rivers, . . . With a Map, and Other Engravings* (Albany, 1823). John T. Blois, *Gazetteer of the State of Michigan, in Three Parts, Containing a General View of the State, a Description of the Face of the Country, Soil, Productions, Public Lands, Internal Improvements, Commerce, Government, Climate, Education, Religious Denominations, Population, Antiquities, . . . With a Succinct History of the State, . . .* (Detroit, 1838). This was one of the more comprehensive of the gazetteers; its author was for some years a resident of Michigan. Edmund M. Blunt, *Traveller's Guide to and through the State of Ohio, with Sailing Directions for Lake Erie* (New York, 1833). Samuel R. Brown, *The Western Gazetteer; or Emigrant's Directory, Containing a Geographical Description of the Western States and Territories* . . . (Auburn, N. Y., 1817). This was one of the better known gazetteers for the earlier part of the period. Zadok Cramer, *The Navigator. . . .* Cramer began issuing this work in 1801. Under various titles it went through at least twelve editions by 1824 by which time it had become a book of almost three hundred pages. It included strip maps for the Ohio and Mississippi which showed rocks, ripples, channels, islands, creeks, bayous, sandbars, etc. Few emigrants started down the Ohio in their own boats without a copy of Cramer or Cumings. Samuel Cumings, *The Western Navigator; Containing Directions for the Navigation of the Ohio and Mississippi, and Such Information concerning the Towns, &c. on their Banks . . . Accompanied by charts of the Ohio River. . . .* (2 volumes. Philadelphia, 1822). This work was reissued as *The Western Pilot . . .* (Cincinnati, 1825, 1828, 1829, 1832, 1834, 1838, 1839, 1840, etc.) and, without the compiler's name, as *A Book for all Travelers: A New River Guide, . . .* (Cincinnati, various dates). Cumings apparently drew heavily upon Cramer's work. Jervis Cutler, *A Topographical Description of the State of Ohio, Indiana Territory, and Louisiana* . . . (Boston, 1812). Edmund Dana, *A Description of the Bounty Lands in the State of Illinois: also, the Principal Roads and Routes, by Land and Water, through the Territory of the United States* . . . (Cincinnati, 1819); and *Geographical Sketches on the Western Country: Designed for Emigrants and Settlers* . . . (Cincinnati, 1819). William Darby, *The Emigrant's Guide to the Western and Southwestern States and Territories* . . . (New York, 1818). *The Emigrant's Guide, or Pocket Geography of the Western States and Territories* . . . published by Phillips & Speer (Cincinnati, 1818). *Illinois in 1837.* . . . This work, published by Samuel A. Mitchell and probably compiled by him (Philadelphia, 1837), contained a letter by H. L. Ellsworth on the cultivation of the prairie and the letters from a rambler in the West. John Kilbourn, *The Ohio Gazetteer: or Topographical Dictionary* . . . (Columbus, 1816, etc.). Albert M. Lea, *Notes on Wisconsin Territory, with a Map* (Philadelphia, 1836). Samuel A. Mitchell, *The Principal Stage, Steam-boat, and Canal Routes in the United States* . . . (Philadelphia, 1834) and reissued under title of *Mitchell's Traveller's Guide* . . . (Philadelphia, 1836, 1837, 1838, etc.). This work is particularly valuable for its maps. John Mason Peck, *A Guide for Emigrants, Containing Sketches of Illinois, Missouri, and the Adjacent Parts* (Boston, 1831), reissued with additions as *A New Guide for Emigrants to the West, Containing Sketches of Ohio, Indiana, Illinois, Missouri, and Michigan, with the Territories of Wisconsin, Arkansas, and the Adjacent Parts* (Boston, 1836) ; *A Gazetteer of Illinois, in Three Parts* . . . (Jacksonville, Illinois, 1834; revised ed., Philadelphia, 1837) ; and *The Traveller's Directory for Illinois* . . . (New York, 1839). Peck's works on Illinois are of particular value since as missionary and prominent citizen he had firsthand facilities for knowing the state. R. B., *View of the Valley of the Mississippi: or the Emigrant's and Traveller's Guide to the West* . . . (Philadelphia, 1832). The author of this work was probably Robert Bache; besides the usual descriptive material it contains historical chapters and chapters on schools, churches, etc. John Scott, *The Indiana Gazetteer, or Topographical Dictionary* . . . (Centreville, Indiana, 1826, Indianapolis, 1833). John C. Smith, *The Western Tourist and Emigrant's Guide, with a Compendious Gazetteer of the States of Ohio, Michigan, Indiana, Illinois, and Missouri* . . . (New York, 1839). Oliver G. Steele, *Steele's Western Guide Book, and Emigrants' Directory, Containing Different Routes through the States of New-York, Ohio, Indiana, Illinois and Michigan* . . . (Buffalo, 1835). Henry S. Tanner, *Memoir on the Recent Surveys, Observations, and Internal Improvements, in the United States* . . . (Philadelphia, 1829, 1830) ; *A Brief Description of the Canals and Railroads of the United States* . . . (Philadelphia, 1834 and 1840) ; and *The American Traveller; or, Guide through the United States* . . . *with Tables of Distances, by Stage, Canal and Steam-Boat Routes* . . . (Philadelphia, 1834, 1836, 1839, etc.). Tanner was one of the most persistent map makers of the period.

THE EARLY HISTORIANS. The historical writings of Caleb Atwater, Daniel Drake, Benjamin Drake, Timothy Flint, James Hall, Edward D. Mansfield, and Henry Rowe Schoolcraft are listed and discussed in Chapter XV. Of these the most important for the period 1815–40 are: Caleb Atwater, *A History of the State of Ohio, Natural and Civil* (Cincinnati, 1838) ; *Remarks Made on a Tour to Prairie du Chien* . . . (Columbus, 1831) ;

and *Writings* (Columbus, 1833). Daniel Drake, *A Systematic . . . Treatise, on the Principal Diseases of the Interior Valley of North America . . .* (volume I, Cincinnati, 1850; volume II, Philadelphia, 1854); *Discourse on the History, Character, and Prospects of the West . . .* (Cincinnati, 1834). For Drake's medical writings see Chapter V. Benjamin Drake, *Tales and Sketches from the Queen City* (Cincinnati, 1839); *The Life and Adventures of Black Hawk . . .* (Cincinnati, 1838); with Charles S. Todd, *Sketches of the Civil and Military Services of William Henry Harrison* (Cincinnati, 1840); and with E. D. Mansfield, *Cincinnati in 1826* (Cincinnati, 1827). Timothy Flint, *Recollections of the Last Ten Years . . . in the Valley of the Mississippi* (Boston, 1826); *A Condensed Geography and History of the Western States, or the Mississippi Valley* (2 volumes. Cincinnati, 1828). James Hall, *Letters from the West; Containing Sketches of Scenery, Manners, and Customs . . .* (London, 1828); *Sketches of History, Life, and Manners in the West* (1 volume, Cincinnati, 1834; and 2 volumes, Philadelphia and St. Louis, 1835); *A Memoir of the Public Services of William Henry Harrison of Ohio* (Philadelphia, 1836); *Statistics of the West, At the Close of the Year 1836* (Cincinnati, 1836); *Notes on the Western States* (Philadelphia, 1838); with Thomas L. McKenney, *History of the Indian Tribes of North America* (3 volumes. Philadelphia, 1836–44); *The West: Its Commerce and Navigation* (Cincinnati, 1848); *The West: Its Soil, Surface, and Productions* (Cincinnati, 1848); and *The Romance of Western History: or, Sketches of History, Life and Manners in the West* (Cincinnati, 1857). These works together with Hall's numerous tales, articles, reviews and editorials constitute the most valuable one-man historical output on the region. "Nobody who would understand how the people of the Great Valley became what they are should neglect Judge Hall." Mansfield, *Cincinnati in 1826* (with Benjamin Drake); *Memoirs of the Life and Services of Daniel Drake, M.D. . . .* (Cincinnati, 1855); and *Personal Memories . . . 1803–43* (Cincinnati, 1879). Henry Rowe Schoolcraft, *Narrative Journal of Travels through the Northwestern Regions of the United States . . .* (Albany, 1821); *Travels in the Central Portions of the Mississippi Valley . . .* (New York, 1825); and *Western Scenes and Reminiscences . . .* (Auburn, Buffalo, 1853).

Other early historians whose works cannot be overlooked are: Moses Dawson, *Historical Narrative of the Civil and Military Services of William Henry Harrison . . .* (Cincinnati, 1824). James H. Perkins, *Annals of the West: Embracing a Concise Account of Principal Events, which have occurred in the Western States and Territories, from the Discovery of the Mississippi Valley to the Year Eighteen Hundred and Fifty* (Cincinnati, 1847, St. Louis, 1850). Thomas Ford, *A History of Illinois, from its Commencement as a State in 1818 to 1847* (New York and Chicago, 1854). Ford was legislator, judge of the supreme court, and governor of Illinois all during the period on which he wrote. It is the best of the early state histories by a participant; Ford's opinions of men and measures were freely and unreservedly expressed. John Reynolds (another Illinois governor), *Pioneer History of Illinois, the discovery in 1673 and the history of the country to 1818* (Belleville, 1852), and *My Own Times* (Belleville, 1855). James Henry Lanman, *History of Michigan, Civil and Topographical* . . . (New York, 1839). John W. Monette, *History of the Discovery and Settlement of the Valley of the Mississippi, by* . . . *Spain, France, and Great Britain, and the Subsequent Occupation* . . . *by the United States* . . . (New York, 1846). John A. Wakefield, *History of the War between the United States and the Sac and Fox Nations of Indians* (Jacksonville, Ill., 1834).

SECONDARY WORKS. Of the numerous state histories of the five states of the Old Northwest only two are comprehensive, scholarly works. They are: *The Centennial History of Illinois,* edited by Clarence W. Alvord (5 volumes, Springfield, 1918–1920), and *The History of the State of Ohio,* edited by Carl F. Wittke (6 volumes, Columbus, 1941–1944). Of the Illinois history, volume I, Clarence W. Alvord, *The Illinois Country, 1673–1818,* and volume II, Theodore C. Pease, *The Frontier State, 1818–1848* pertain to the period prior to 1840. Solon J. Buck's *Illinois in 1818* (Springfield, 1917) though not actually a volume of this history may for all practical purposes be so considered. The corresponding volumes in the Ohio history are II and III, William T. Utter, *The Frontier State 1803–1825,* and Francis P. Weisenburger, *The Passing of the Frontier, 1825–1850.* Logan Esarey, *A History of Indiana* (2 volumes. Fort Wayne, 1924) is the best of the single-author state histories. George Newman Fuller, *Economic and Social Beginnings of Michigan* (Lansing, 1916), is a sound study of the nonpolitical history of Michigan in the early period. A brief survey of Michigan may be had in Milo M. Quaife and Sidney Glazer, *Michigan: From Primitive Wilderness to Industrial Commonwealth* (New York, 1948); of Wisconsin in William Francis Raney, *Wisconsin; A Story of Progress* (New York, 1940). Frederick Jackson Turner's *The United States 1830–1850* (New York, 1935) contains a hundred-page chapter on "The North Central States" which is useful not only for its content but also for its references. Of the one-volume introductions to the history of the West, Frederic Logan Paxson's *History of the American Frontier, 1763–1893* (Boston, 1924) remains the best for the presentation of fundamentals. A more recent and extensive survey is Ray Allen Billington, *Westward Expansion, a History of the American Frontier* (New York, 1949); this work contains numerous maps and references. Beverley W. Bond, Jr., *The Civilization of the Old Northwest* . . . (New York, 1934), presents the background for the period before 1815. William Vernon Kinietz, *The Indians of the Western Great Lakes, 1615–1760* (Ann Arbor, 1940), though not dealing with the period under consideration in this history, is nevertheless useful for an understanding of the Indian problem of the period after 1815. George Dewey Harmon, *Sixty Years of Indian Affairs* (Chapel Hill, N. C., 1941), serves as an introduction to the Indian problem. Two standard treatises on the public domain are Payson J. Treat, *The National Land System, 1785–1820* (New York, 1910); and B. H. Hibbard, *A History of the Public Land Policies* (New York, 1924). Roy M. Robbins, *Our Landed Heritage. The Public Domain 1776–1936* (Princeton, N. J., 1942) contains chapters on public lands of the Old Northwest and also a good bibliography on the subject. Milo M. Quaife, *Chicago and the Old Northwest, 1673–1835* . . . (Chicago, 1913), is a study of the evolution of the northwestern frontier together with the history of Fort Dearborn and the beginnings of Chicago. Of the histories of Chicago the most scholarly is Bessie Louise Pierce, *A History of Chicago*. Volume I, *The Beginning of a City, 1673–1848* (New York, 1937) covers the period prior to 1840. Charles H. Ambler, *A History of Transportation in the Ohio Valley* (Glendale, Calif., 1932); Seymour Dunbar, *A History of Travel in America* . . . (4 volumes. Indianapolis, 1915); and William F. Gephart, *Transportation and Industrial Development in the Middle West* (Columbia University *Studies in History, Economics and Public Law*, New York, 1909), serve as a basis for the study of transportation. Albert L. Kohlmeier, *The Old Northwest, as the Keystone of the Arch of the American Federal Union* (Bloomington, Ind., 1938), is a careful study of the commerce of the Old Northwest in its relation to sectionalism and politics. Ralph Leslie Rusk, *The Literature of the Middle Western Frontier* (2 volumes. New York, 1925), is the outstanding work on the cultural history of the Old Northwest. Volume II of this work is a comprehensive bibliography of the works of travel and description, newspapers, periodicals, controversial writings, schoolbooks, drama, and poetry. James M. Miller, *The Genesis of Western Culture, the Upper Ohio Valley, 1800–1825* (*Ohio Historical Collections*, IX, Columbus, 1938) is a first-class study. The excellent book by Henry Clyde Hubbart, *The Older Middle West, 1840–1880* . . . (New York and London, 1936), though principally on the period after 1840, overlaps with the earlier period. William H. Venable, *Beginnings of Literary Culture in the Ohio Valley* (Cincinnati, 1891), though uncritical, is useful for the study of western literature, as is William T. Coggeshall, *Poets and Poetry of the West* (Columbus, 1860), and *The Protective Policy in Literature* (Columbus, 1859).

For special secondary works, monographs, articles, and collections of source material on the various topics covered in this history, see the appropriate chapters and the bibliographical notes contained therein. For agriculture Chapter IV, text, note 59 and subsequent notes; for banking and state finance Chapter VIII, note 1 and following notes, Chapter XII, notes; on commerce and industry Chapter VII, footnote references, particularly notes 3, 11, etc., and Chapter XII; on health and medicine Chapter V, text and notes; on pioneer life Chapter IV, note 10 and notes following; on education Chapter XIII, text and notes; on religion Chapter XIV, note 2 and scattered references throughout the chapter; and on transportation Chapter VII, text and footnote references.

Index

[No volume number is used for references to Volume I.]